THE HARDY FAMILY OF ARTISTS

Frederick Daniel, George, Heywood,
James and their descendants

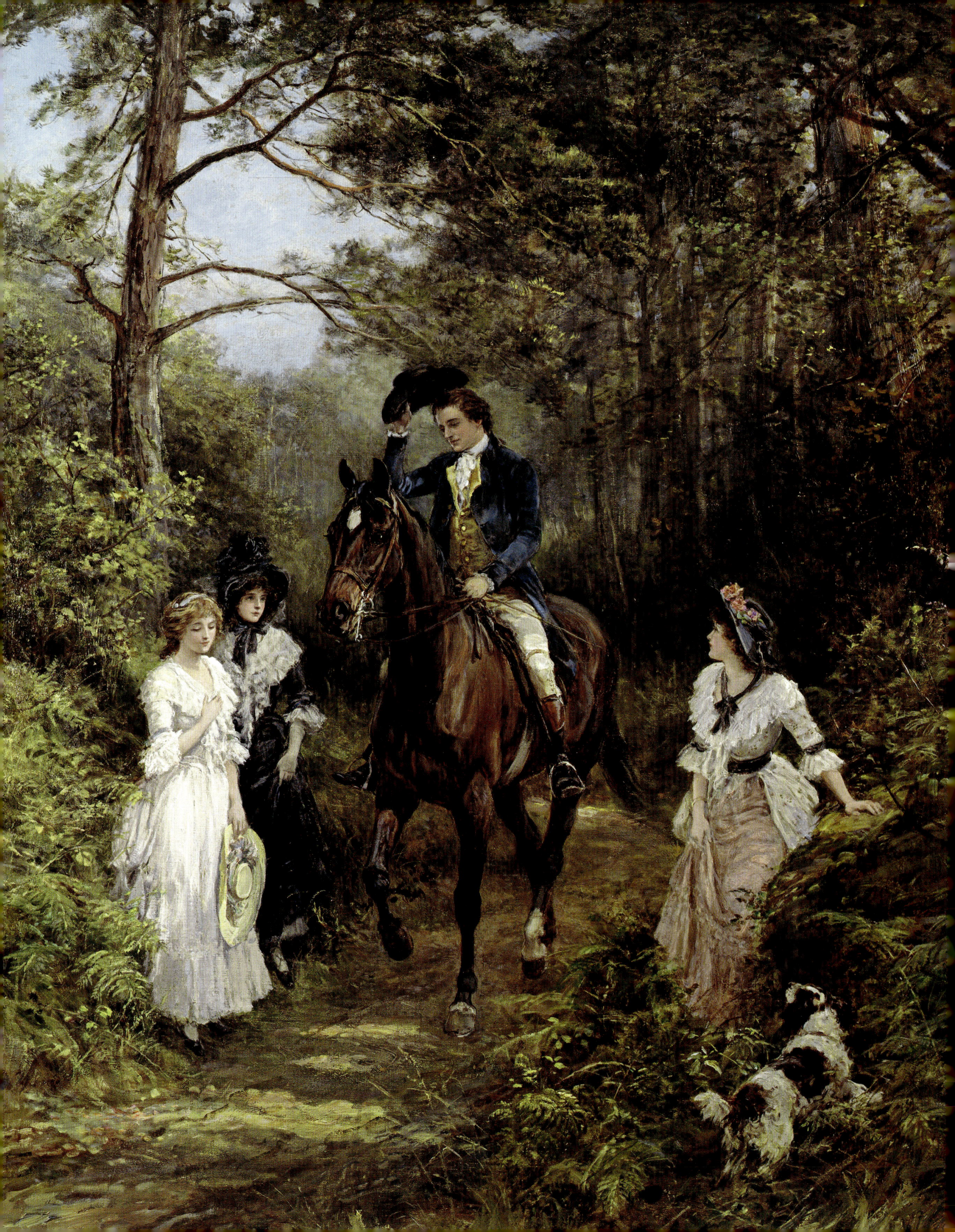

THE HARDY FAMILY OF ARTISTS

Frederick Daniel, George, Heywood, James and their descendants

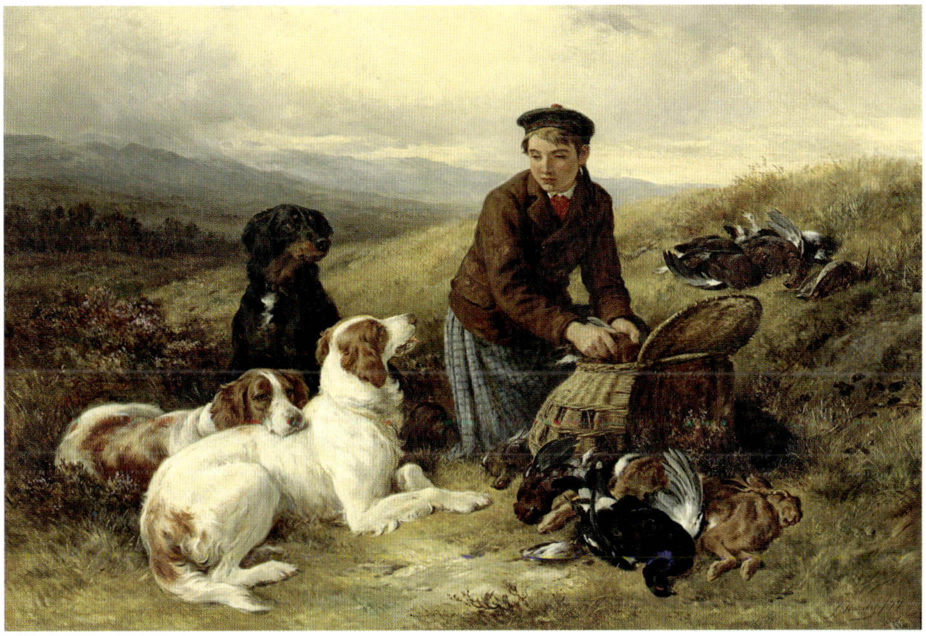

Kimber G. Hardy

ACC ART BOOKS

For Deborah and William

ISBN 978 185149 826 0

British Library CIP Data
A catalogue record for this book
is available from the British Library

Frontispiece: **The Meeting in the Forest, 1903**
Heywood Hardy. Oil on canvas.
104 x 84cm. PRIVATE COLLECTION

Title page: **A Young Gillie, with Setters and Dead Game, 1877**
James Hardy junior. Oil on canvas. 71 x 99cm. ROYAL HOLLOWAY, UNIVERSITY OF LONDON

MIX
Paper from responsible sources
FSC® C104723
www.fsc.org

Printed in China
for ACC Art Books Ltd.,
Woodbridge, Suffolk, IP12 4SD, UK

www.antiquecollectorsclub.com

CONTENTS

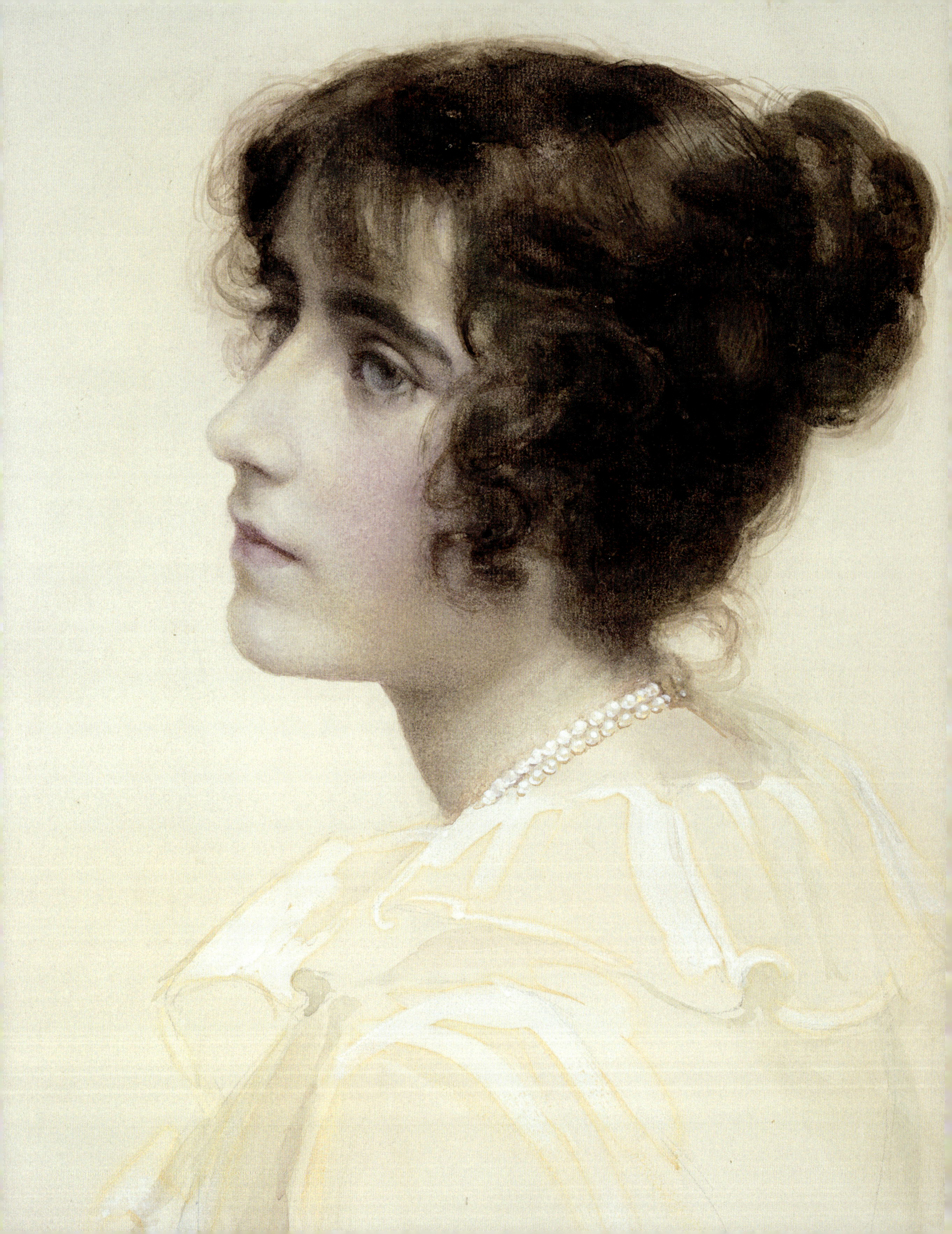

ACKNOWLEDGEMENTS

I am most grateful to the following galleries and organisations for supplying images of paintings in their collections, for answering enquiries and for allowing access to paintings and archives: Archives des Musées nationaux (Palais du Louvre, Paris), Ashmolean Museum of Art and Archaeology, Bromley Museum, Bury Art Museum and Sculpture Centre, Canterbury City Council Museums and Galleries, l'Agence photo de la Réunion des Musées nationaux et du Grand Palais (Paris), Leicester Arts and Museums Service, Museums Sheffield, National Library of Australia, Royal Holloway College, Smith Art Gallery and Museum, The Atkinson Art Gallery and Museum, The British Library, The British Museum, The National Catalogue Foundation, The National Gallery, The National Trust, The Powerhouse Museum (Sydney), the Royal Academy Archives (Antwerp), The Royal & Ancient Golf Club of St Andrews Trust, The Royal Collection, The Royal Society of Miniature Painters Sculptors and Gravers, The Russell-Cotes Art Gallery and Museum, Tunbridge Wells Museum and Art Gallery, Victoria and Albert Museum, Victoria Art Gallery (Bath), Wisbech and Fenland Museum and Wolverhampton Art Gallery.

My grateful thanks are due to HM Queen Elizabeth II for permission to reproduce images of several paintings in the Royal Collection that have not been published before. Many owners of paintings kindly provided images of their pictures. Pictures of two portraits of Lady Ida Sitwell painted by Heywood Hardy are included with very kind permission of Mrs Alexandra Hayward. I am most grateful to Lord Ronaldshay who arranged for photography of the picture of the Zetland Hunt painted by Heywood Hardy. Alexander A. Bove Jr. kindly gave permission to include an image of "Reading a Will" painted by Frederick Daniel Hardy. David Hardy Ivens very kindly provided information and photographs of his ancestors in the Hardy family. I am grateful to the following for information and for allowing access to paintings: Paul Donovan, who has been associated with the Cranbrook Museum for many years and established a study centre for the Cranbrook Colony, Eric Birbeck of The Haslar Heritage Group, Major Piers Rogers of the 1st Battalion Irish Guards, Renishaw Hall's archivist Christine Beevers, Dr Max Quanchi of the University of the South Pacific, the Churchwardens of Clymping Church, Horsforth Village Museum, the Bodleian Library, the Sussex Records Office and the West Yorkshire Archive. I am very grateful to Diana Steel, Andrew Whittaker and Lynn Taylor of ACC Art Books for their excellent advice, editing and design.

Alfred Lloyd Hardy, brother of the artist Frederick Daniel Hardy, carefully researched and documented the lives of artists in the Hardy family in the early years of the twentieth century. He contacted many members of the Hardy family. Fortunately I inherited from Capt. A. Hardy (a distant cousin of A.L. Hardy) his correspondence with A.L. Hardy and a copy of his research. Basil Long, Keeper of the Department of Paintings at the Victoria and Albert Museum, contacted A.L. Hardy for details about the artists in the family; Basil Long's notes of the conversations are in the archives of the Victoria and Albert Museum.

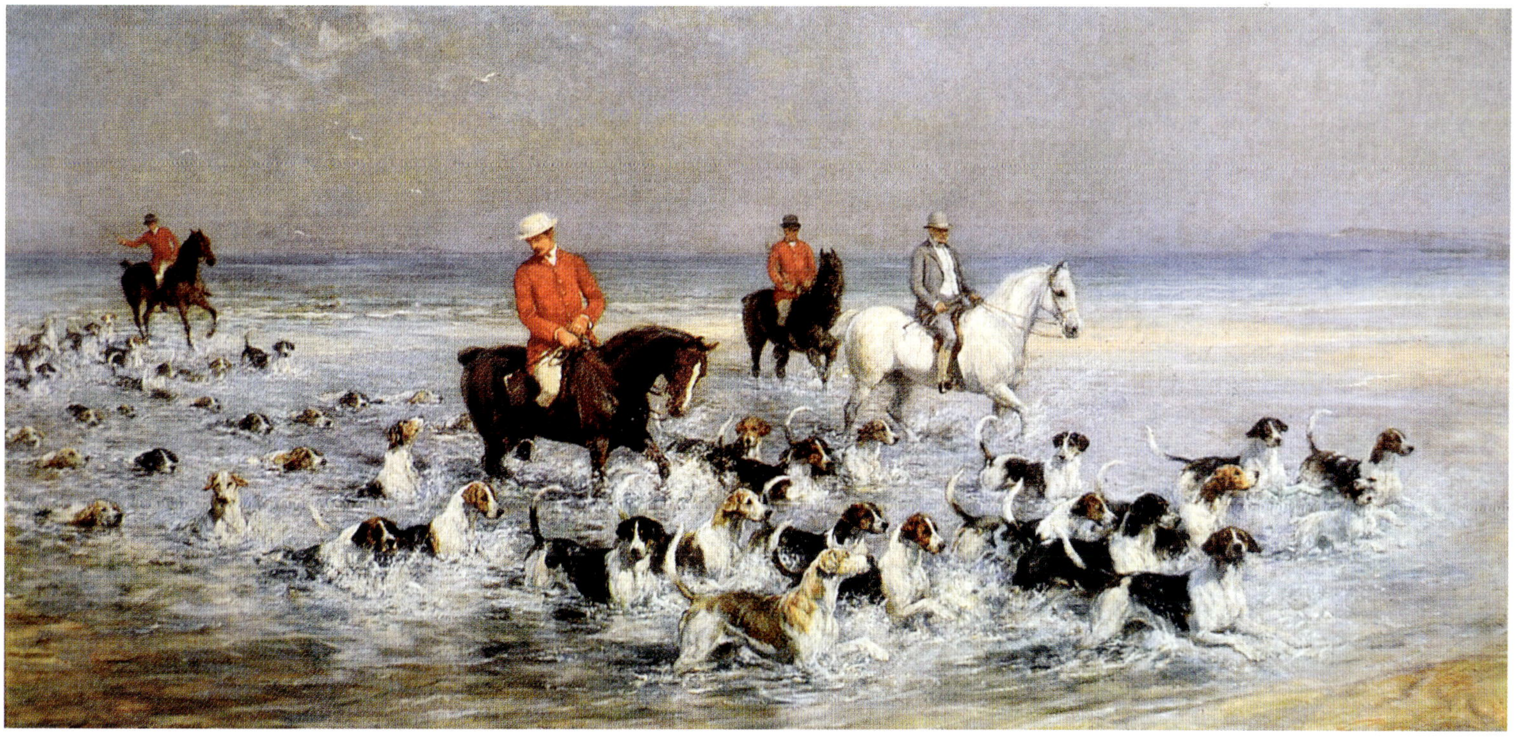

Above: A Summer's Day in Cleveland, 1889
Heywood Hardy. Oil on canvas. 54.5 x 104.6cm. Private collection

Opposite page: Lady Elizabeth Bowes-Lyon, aged nineteen, 1919
Mabel Emily Lee-Hankey. Watercolour. Royal Collection Trust/© Her Majesty Queen Elizabeth II 2015

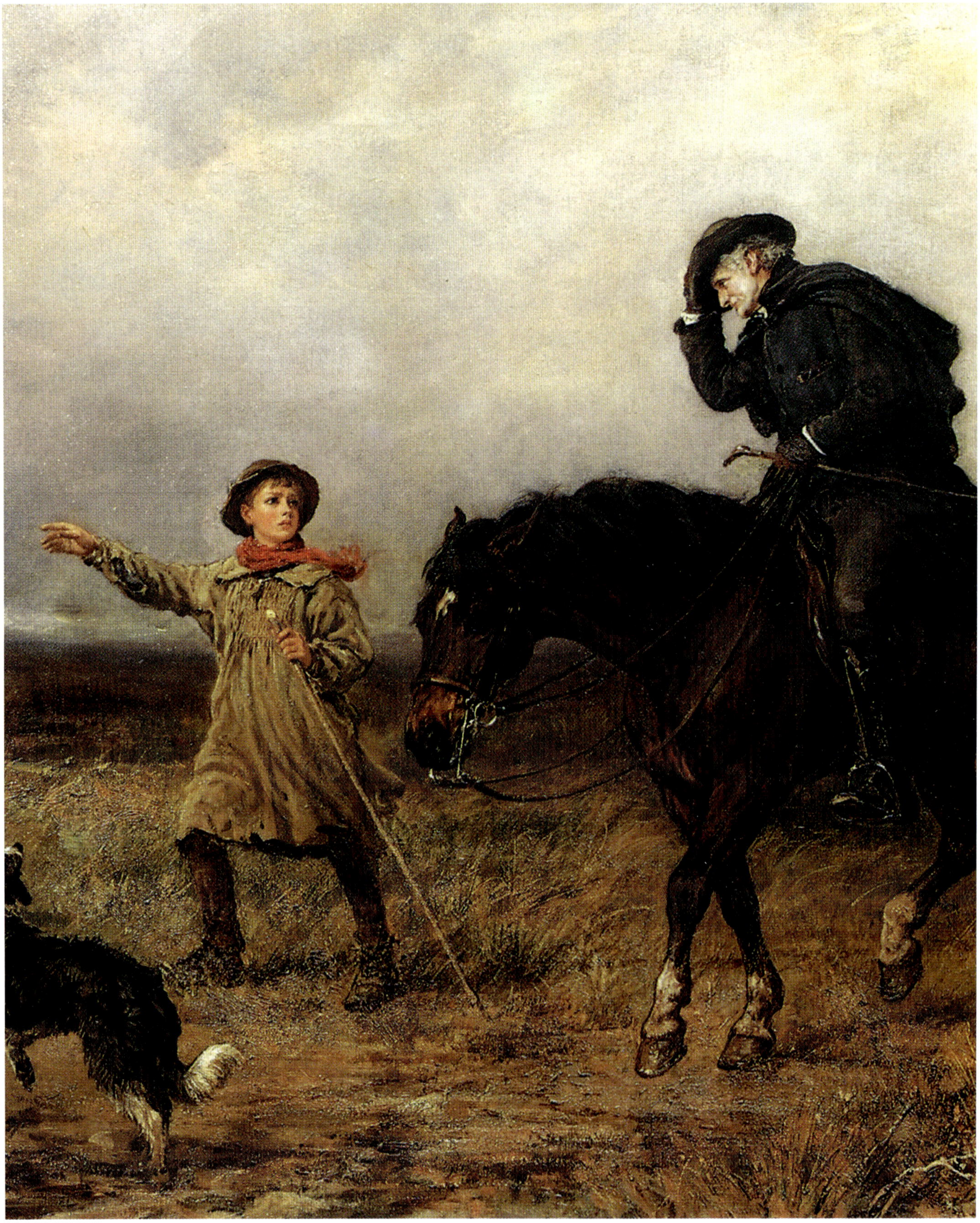

INTRODUCTION

Artists in the second half of the nineteenth century produced a remarkable record of life in Victorian Britain; for a few decades many painters carefully portrayed the family lives, work and sports of their times. Several artists in the Hardy family contributed to this fascinating pictorial record. They produced much of their best work just as the narrative tradition of British art reached its high point, between 1850 and 1875. And they helped to develop a new approach to animal and sporting art, leaving behind the romantic traditions of Sir Edwin Landseer.

Frederick Daniel Hardy spent his entire working life portraying the lives of families living in the cottages and houses of a small town in Kent, Cranbrook. His paintings were popular with a wide audience, but especially with industrialists who collected "modern" British art. F.D. Hardy also had a high reputation amongst writers and art critics who stimulated the revival of interest in Victorian art in the second half of the twentieth century. Christopher Wood, author of *Victorian Painting in Oils and Watercolour* (1996), thought that: "His early interiors have an extraordinary clarity and precision of observation comparable only to the Dutch masters of the seventeenth century." And Graham Reynolds said of one of his later paintings: "It has the charm of a slice of life arrested for all time, and we feel convinced when we see it that many late Victorian drawing-rooms looked just like this. " [1]

Though they documented many aspects of society, Victorian artists like F.D. Hardy were selective in what they portrayed; their paintings inevitably mirrored the aspirations, values and prejudices of their society. Important patrons of Victorian art, industrialists and landowners mainly in the north of England, had strong views about the paintings they wanted in their houses and there was little room for pictures showing the harsh realities of nineteenth-century life.

Most pictures by F.D. Hardy of cottage interiors and children's games represent an idyllic portrait of country life in Victorian England. Hardships were not completely ignored however; he painted pictures of exhausted and exploited domestic servants and seamstresses, a barefoot girl trying to find her drunken father in a tavern and a family coping with a leaky roof. Few collectors wanted to buy such paintings in the 1850s and 1860s, but for a few years in the 1870s there was a larger market for paintings that made critical social comments.

Narrative painting, storytelling in a frame, was very popular with the Victorians; they enjoyed interpreting the clues and signs, the objects and the facial expressions, attitudes and relationships of the people depicted. Included in this book are many contemporary comments about the paintings to illustrate how the Victorians themselves interpreted such pictures.

Frederick Daniel, George and James Hardy junior largely avoided painting the sentimental pictures that were some of the Victorians' favourites. Heywood Hardy painted a few sentimental pictures early in his career. But they all preferred a more unpretentious approach, with subtle narrative and humour.

Heywood Hardy, F.D. Hardy's cousin, was a versatile artist like his father, James Hardy senior. Heywood's long career began in the late 1850s and ended in 1928. The youngest of ten children, he was taught painting by other artists in his family who lived at Bath. He then studied in Paris and painted in Egypt, France and many parts of Britain and Ireland.

Heywood painted landscapes, portraits, animals and scenes of country life. But he was at his best when painting pictures of Victorian and Edwardian sports: horse-riding, hunting, horseracing, sporting dogs, shooting, fishing and golf. He painted portraits of several of the pre-eminent sportsmen of his day. Like John Ferneley, the great equestrian artist of the previous generation, Heywood moved between country houses to paint many of the famous Hunts. Riders, horses and sporting dogs were painted with a faithfulness that made him the favourite painter amongst wealthy country families in the north of England. Heywood Hardy became close friends with several of his patrons, sharing their interests in field sports and music. He painted some potboilers too; George Bernard Shaw, who worked as an art critic for several years, called them Hardy's "romance and horseflesh" pictures. But Shaw thought his paintings of horses were "capital".

Not all Heywood Hardy's paintings were idyllic country scenes. He was one of the first Victorian painters to illustrate the responsibilities of a country doctor in *The Village Doctor* (1872) and *Duty* (1880). (Vincent van Gogh asked a friend to find him an engraving of *Duty*.[2]) He painted a picture showing how horses were used in the construction of railways, a common sight in Victorian England but not one that any other artist ever recorded. And the response to his picture of a London cab horse, waiting at night in the cold rain, foreshadowed the public's response to Anna Sewell's "Black Beauty", published a few years later. A picture of golfing in 1900 includes barefoot caddies who are contrasted with golfers wearing boots and gaiters.

Heywood's elder brother James Hardy junior painted his best pictures late in his career; he became one of the best painters of sporting dogs set in Scottish landscapes. Heywood and James Hardy junior portrayed animals in a more realistic way than their predecessors; they avoided the more anthropomorphic approach of Sir Edwin Landseer.

Painting pictures was often a family business in the nineteenth century. The sons and daughters of artists in the Hardy family were usually taught painting by their parents or elder brothers and sisters, though several then attended the Royal Academy Schools. Traditions and skills were sometimes maintained for several generations. James Hardy senior began painting portrait miniatures in Brighton in the 1820s (after he had resigned, in a fit of temper, as Principal Trumpet in the Royal Private Band of George IV). He taught his daughter Ada Hardy how to paint miniatures. And Ada taught her daughter Mabel; Mabel Emily Lee-Hankey painted several portraits of Lady Elizabeth Bowes-Lyon, the future Queen Elizabeth the Queen Mother. The last commission that Mabel Lee-Hankey completed, when she was 75, was for Queen Elizabeth in 1943.

Opposite page: Duty (detail), 1880
Heywood Hardy. Oil on canvas. 83 x 118cm. Guildhall Art Gallery, City of London Corporation

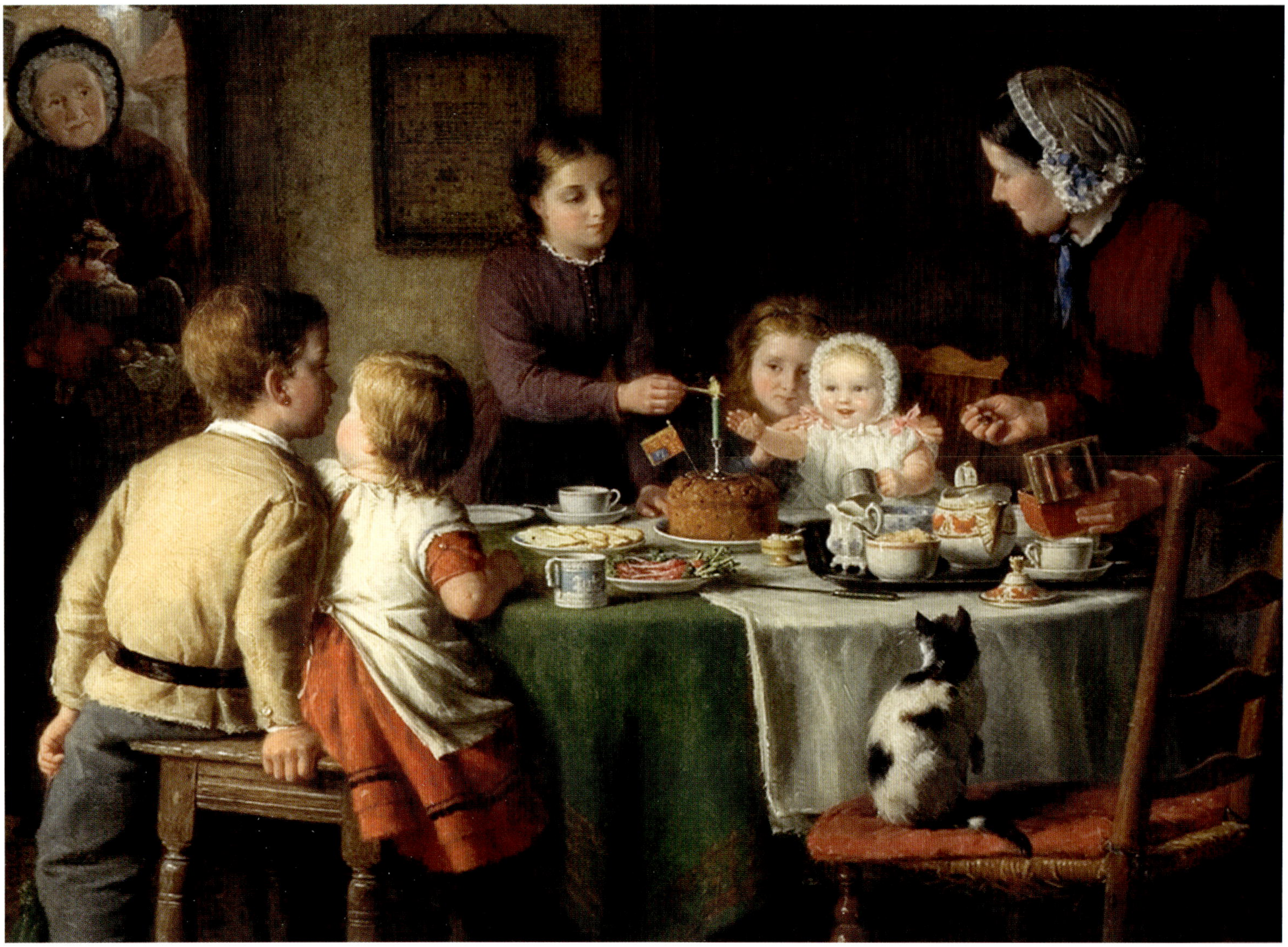

Baby's Birthday, 1867
Frederick Daniel Hardy. Oil on canvas. Detail. 66 x 91.5cm. © Wolverhampton Art Gallery

Heywood Hardy taught his daughters painting and music. Two of his daughters, a granddaughter and a great grandson became professional artists. Emily Hardy, the widow of painter David Hardy who died at a young age, was an artist and art teacher who taught drawing and painting to her four children. They all became professional artists and illustrators; her daughters took advantage of the increasing opportunities for woman artists to illustrate books and magazines. Artists in the Hardy family often married other artists, which no doubt increased the likelihood that their children would follow in their parents' profession.

The best works by Heywood, James and F.D. Hardy were popular with Victorian collectors and continue to enjoy a high reputation today. But little has been written about the artists and there are more than a few errors in the little that has been published. This book includes images of almost all their major works, together with contemporary critical comment whenever available.

The Hardy family of artists discussed here were descended from William Hardy (1715-1762), who was Land Steward to the Stanhope Family of Horsforth in Yorkshire and who also owned Low Fold Farm at Horsforth. William's father, John Hardy, had been Clerk and Steward to John Stanhope, Justice of the Peace and Lord of the Manor of Horsforth.

William Hardy's second son, also called William (1748-1824), was involved in a fight close to Low Fold Farm and, believing that he may have killed his opponent (he later learnt that his opponent had survived), fled Horsforth and eventually became Master of the Officers' Mess of the 10th Hussars. Four of his sons became musicians in the Royal Private Band of the Prince Regent (the Prince Regent, who became George IV, was Colonel of the 10th Hussars). The Hardy family of artists were descended from two of the musicians, George and James Hardy senior. Details of the genealogy of the artists can be seen in the family tree on page 11 and are described in Appendix A.

There were artists in other branches of the Hardy family descended from William Hardy senior who are not discussed in this book. John Hardy (1773-1855), father of Gathorne Gathorne-Hardy the first Earl of Cranbrook, was an amateur artist who drew portraits and caricatures. And there have been several exhibitions of the work of Jason Gathorne-Hardy, Lord Medway, eldest son of the fifth Earl. By coincidence, the first Earl lived near Cranbrook in Kent where two second cousins, Frederick and George, worked as artists for over 50 years.

The Hardy Family of Artists: Abridged Family Tree

See Appendix B for a more detailed family tree

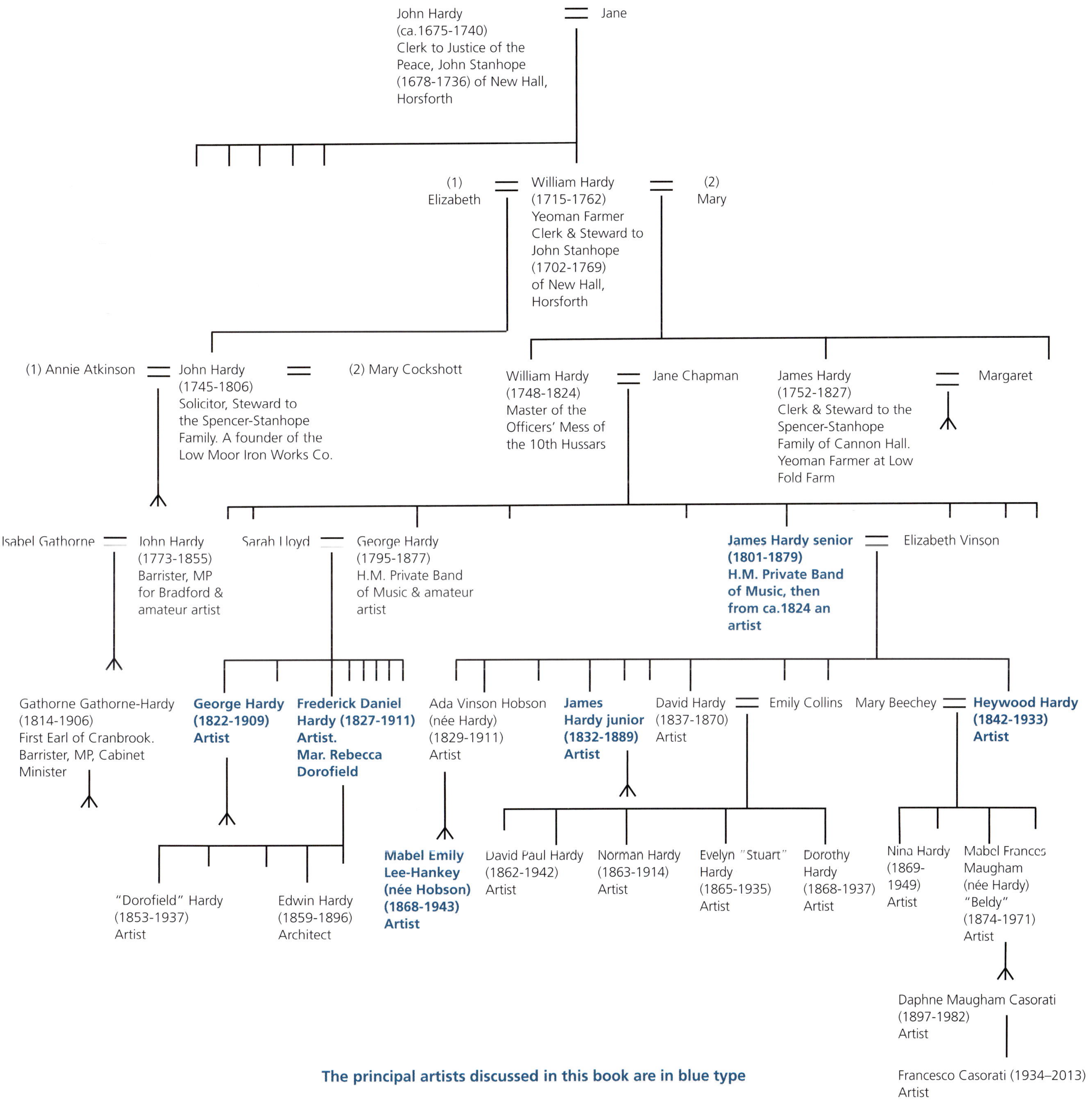

The principal artists discussed in this book are in blue type

CHAPTER ONE

Frederick Daniel Hardy: the 1850s

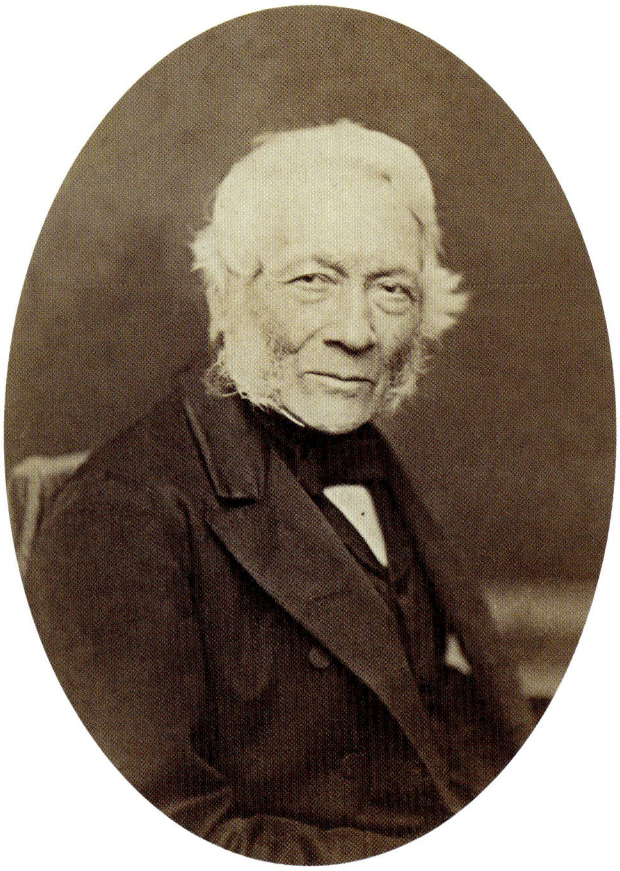

Plate 1: George Hardy senior
From the Photograph Album of George and Sarah Hardy and their children. George Hardy senior, a musician in the Royal Private Band of Music and amateur artist, was father of Frederick Daniel and George Hardy.

F.D. Hardy was born at 2 Brunswick Cottages in Windsor on 13 February 1827, the son of George and Sarah Hardy. George (1795-1877) (Plate 1) was born in London in 1795; at the age of 16, when at Brighton, he joined the Boy's Band of Music that was attached to the 10th Hussars (George's father was Master of the Officers' Mess of the 10th Hussars). George then became a horn player in the Private Band of Music of the Royal Households of George IV, Queen Adelaide and Queen Victoria. He was also a member of the State Band of Music from 1842 until his retirement in 1869.[3]

Besides being a musician (playing the horn, violin and piano), F.D. Hardy's father, referred to here as George Hardy senior to distinguish him from his son, the artist George Hardy, became an enthusiastic amateur artist. At Windsor, where he lived from about 1825 to 1867, he took lessons from James Duffield Harding, a well-known teacher of landscape painting who taught John Ruskin, and from his artist friend Edmund Bristow, who lived at Windsor all his life and had several royal patrons.[4] *View of Windsor* (Plate 2) shows the influence of Harding, who painted similar pictures of Windsor.

Two paintings of Windsor Park by George Hardy senior, one painted in 1836 and another in 1862 (Plate 3) showing the artist leaning against a tree near his stool, are in the Royal Collection at Windsor.

Thomas Webster RA, who had no children, took a great interest in the education and early careers of the Hardy brothers. George and F.D. Hardy were distantly related to Webster, whose family formerly lived at Henley, through their maternal grandmother's family (the Curtis family) who had long been residents at Henley.[5] Webster and the Hardy family at Windsor had a common interest in music and had connections with the Royal Household; Thomas Webster's father had been a member of the Royal Household and Webster had trained as a chorister at St George's School, Windsor, before he attended the Royal Academy Schools from 1821, where he was awarded the Silver Medal in 1825.

The style of painting that was initially adopted by both George and F.D. Hardy, which emphasized an accurate portrayal of detail, was no doubt influenced by Webster's work. In common with the Pre-Raphaelites, Webster was greatly concerned with the accurate and detailed depiction of nature. Webster once exacerbated his gout by standing for hours "to study the effect of reflection in the ice", but he nevertheless insisted that he be taken back to a frozen pond by being wheeled in a bath chair to continue his studies.[6]

From the age of 17, F.D. Hardy studied for three years (1843 to 1846) at the Royal Academy of Music in Hanover Square with a view to following his father's profession. He played the violin in an orchestra for a while, but when he was about 20 years old he stopped his music studies (though he remained a keen amateur pianist and violinist) and began to study painting. His brother George, who was four years older and had attended the Royal Academy Schools, helped him. George had just had his first painting accepted at the annual Royal Academy exhibition.

Plate 2 (opposite page top): View of Windsor
George Hardy senior. Oil on canvas. 33 x 44.5cm [7] PRIVATE COLLECTION

Plate 3 (opposite page below): Windsor Castle from the Great Park, dated 26 June 1862
George Hardy senior. Watercolour on paper. 13.8 x 22.3cm. ROYAL COLLECTION TRUST/© HER MAJESTY QUEEN ELIZABETH II 2015 [8]

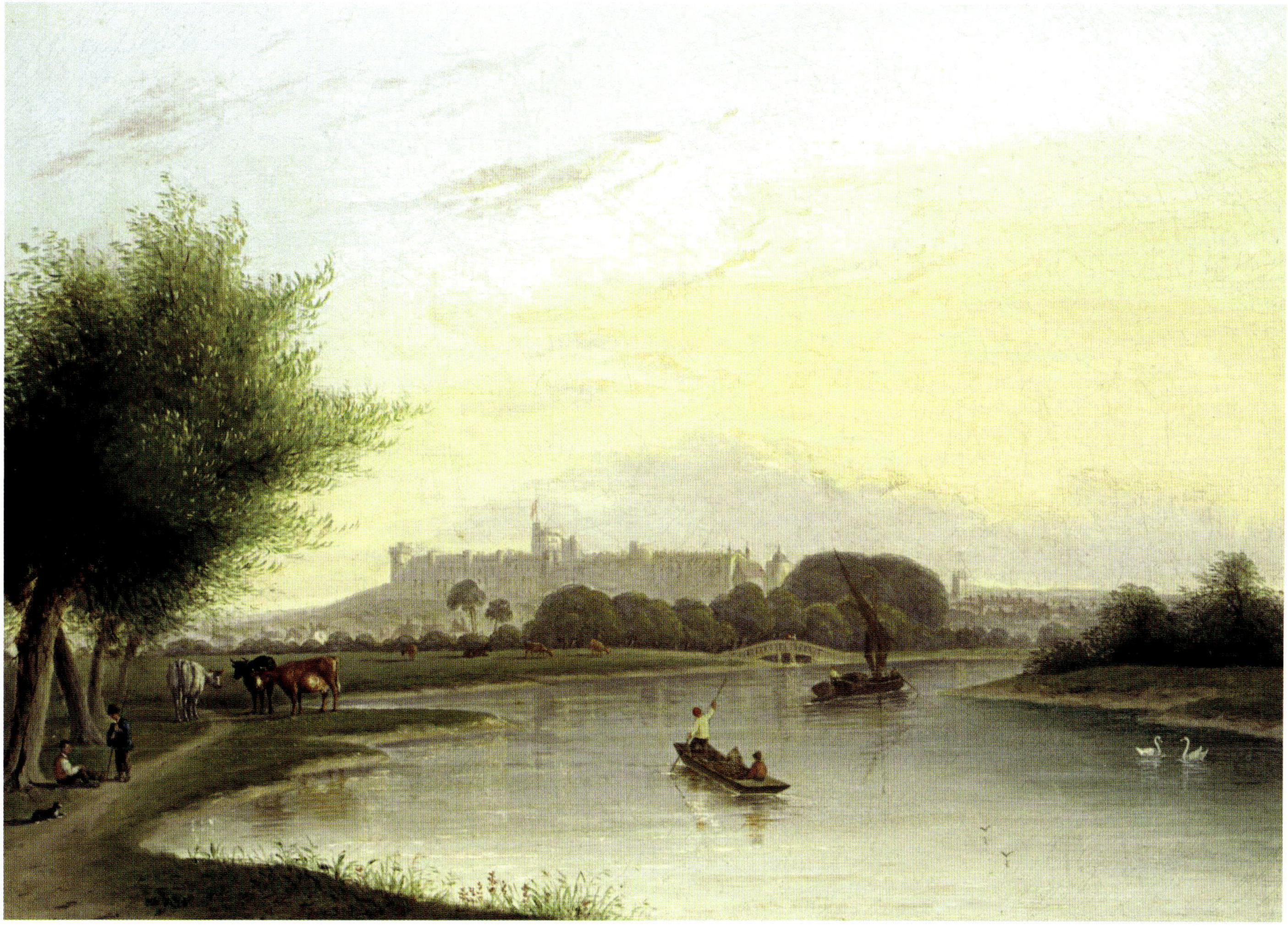

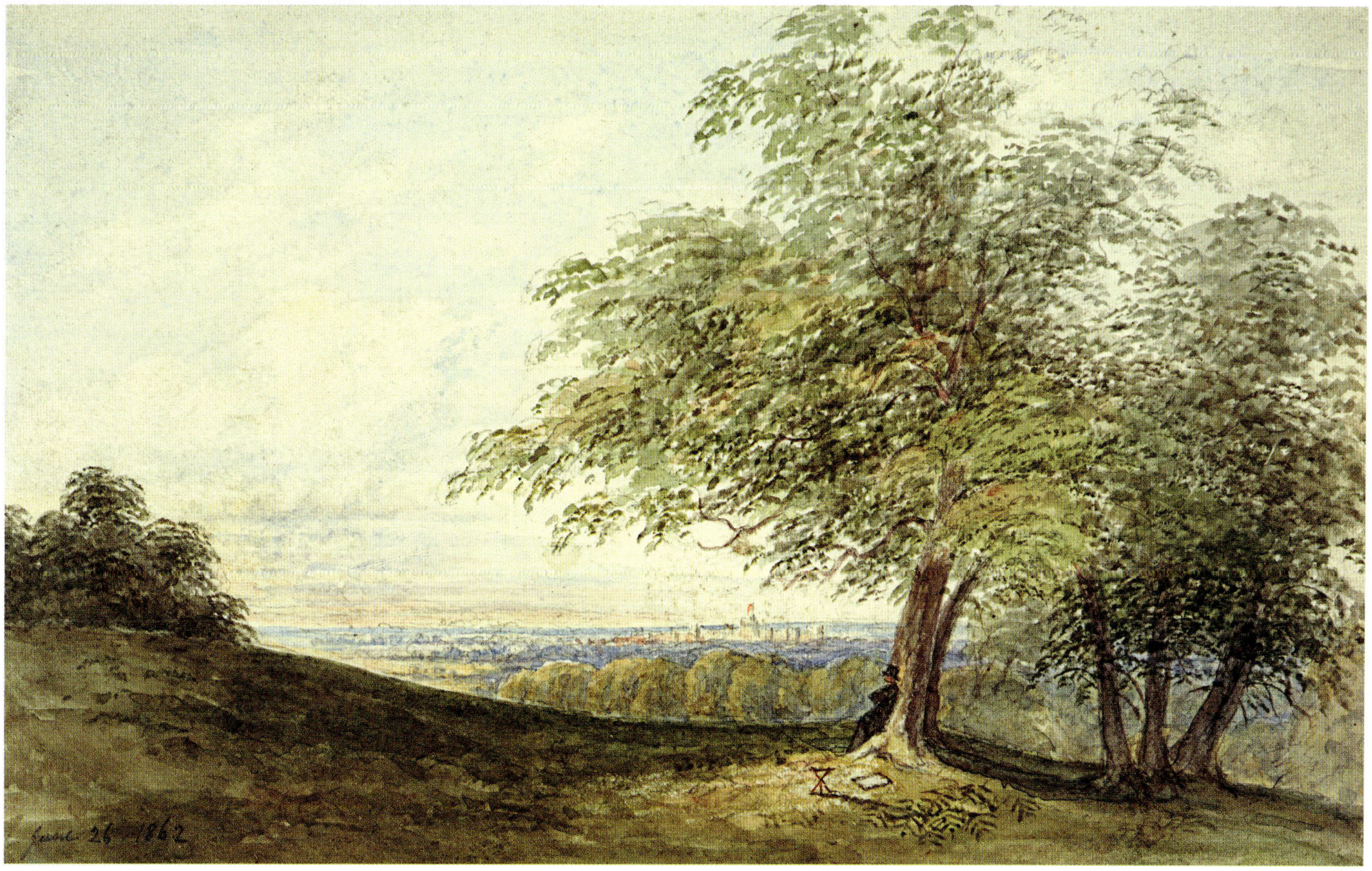
June 26 1862

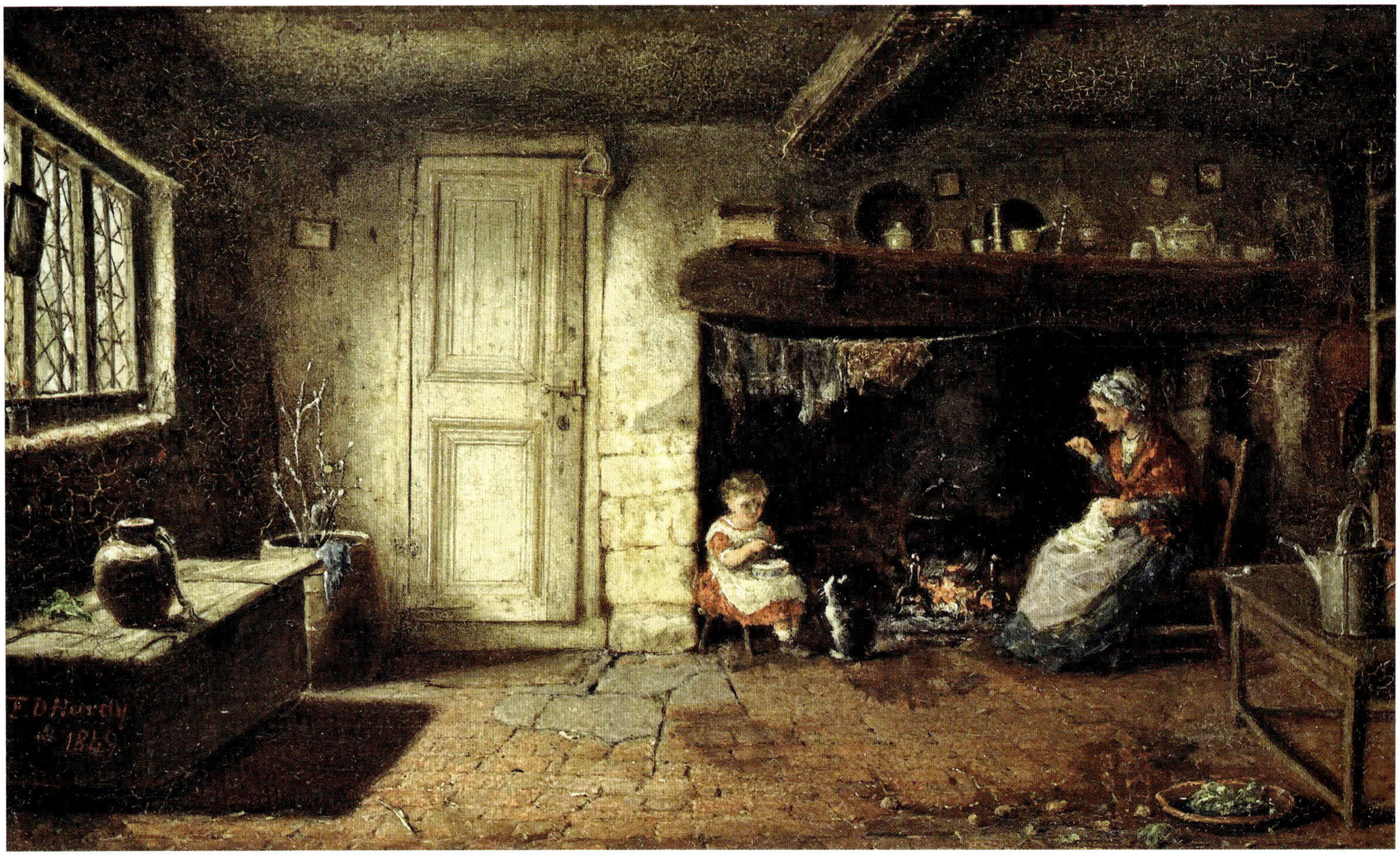

Plate 4: A Spoonful of Milk, 1849
Frederick Daniel Hardy. Oil on panel. 13.1 x 22.2cm. Private Collection

F.D. Hardy's working life may be divided into three parts. Firstly, in the 1850s, he began to produce carefully observed and detailed studies of cottage interiors. Initially, there were no people in the paintings, and then gradually he introduced one or two inhabitants. Secondly, in the 1860s, he achieved greater confidence in painting people, particularly children, which enabled him to produce pictures with a much higher content of narrative, activity and anecdote. Finally, from the 1870s towards the end of the century, most of his paintings depicted middle-class interiors. Many of these paintings are not as good as his paintings from the 1860s. His most interesting work in the 1870s comprised a few pictures that commented on social issues, particularly the hardships of domestic servants and seamstresses. In this chapter we will focus on the first period of his working life, when detailed domestic scenes dominated his output.

After taking up the study of art in 1849, Frederick travelled in the south of England to paint pictures of cottage interiors. His early paintings were studies of interiors with no figures at all, although perhaps there might be a cat by the fire.

The earliest attempt at painting by F.D. Hardy that is signed and dated appears to be an interior from 1849, *A Spoonful of Milk* (Plate 4). The figures were sketched in much later, in 1882, when his figure painting was rarely as good as it had been in the late 1850s and 1860s.[9]

A study made a year later, *Cottage Fireside* (1850) (Plate 5), shows that he had made progress in his ability to paint bricks, walls, floors and objects in an interior; the effect of light coming though the open door is entirely convincing. And he had already seen the potential of using a patch of red in his compositions; this was to be a hallmark of many of his later paintings. However, he did not feel confident enough to paint the features of a figure in the interior, apart from a well-drawn hand.

F.D. Hardy's early paintings are quiet, understated and unpretentious. In his cottage interiors, objects and people are equally carefully portrayed. Christopher Wood thought that F.D. Hardy was technically the best artist of the Cranbrook Colony.[10] The quality of Hardy's observation was apparent even in his earliest paintings; such as his picture of the cottage hearth, *Cottage Fireside* (1850):

> Some of his early works of this kind are beautifully observed, and quite unsentimental, omitting the usual children, pets and other familiar props of the cottage idyll painters. The old kitchen illustrated here, is delineated as dispassionately as a Dutch seventeenth century kitchen by Ostade or Brekelenkamp.[11]

In 1851 he had his first two pictures accepted for the Royal Academy exhibition, both entitled *Study from nature*. The corresponding address given with these Royal Academy submissions was his parents' house at 4 Gloucester Place, Windsor. In 1852 he had three pictures accepted (from the same address), *An Interior*, *Still Life* and *Afternoon*. These were similar titles to the first pictures accepted by the Royal Academy from his brother, George: *Study from nature* (1846), *An interior* (1847) and *Interior of a cottage* (1847).

One of F.D. Hardy's three exhibits at the Royal Academy exhibition of 1852 was a picture of a woman reading by a fire, *An Interior* (Plate 6). There were a few words about the painting in *The Art Journal*: "The humble home of an old woman, who sits reading by the fire. It is a small picture, worked up with much minute manipulation." [12]

Frederick Daniel married Rebecca Sophia Dorofield at Chorleywood, Herts, on 11 March 1852.[13] His paintings for the Royal Academy exhibition of 1852 were sent from an address at Snell's Wood in the Chilterns near Little Chalfont. This was three miles from where his wife's parents had their farm.

In the summer of 1853 F.D. Hardy moved to his house at 2 Waterloo Place in Cranbrook, Kent, a house that he kept all his life.[14] Waterloo Place is a terrace of six houses built early in the nineteenth century almost opposite to Cranbrook School (founded in 1518) that his sons attended. Presumably, F.D. Hardy was attracted to Cranbrook by the rural cottages that could be subjects for his painting. And there was the convenience of the recently opened railway line from London to Folkestone, with a station at Staplehurst, about five miles from Cranbrook. Photographs from F.D. Hardy's photograph album show the rural aspect of Cranbrook, including the extensive hop gardens, in the second half of the nineteenth century.[15]

Two small pictures from this period were bought by John Forster, close friend and biographer of Charles Dickens, and were bequeathed (along with his vast library) to the South Kensington Museum (now the Victoria and Albert Museum). The pictures are entitled *Cottage Interior* (1852)[16] and *Sunday Afternoon* (1852) (Plate 7). Both paintings are of cottage interiors near Snell's Wood in Buckinghamshire. *Cottage Interior* is presumably *An Interior* that was exhibited at the Royal Academy Exhibition in 1853, described by one reviewer as "Rather a blank interior, though in itself well painted. The only sign of life is a cat sitting by the fire."

At about the same time John Forster bought a small picture, *Cottage Interior,* by F.D. Hardy's cousin, David Hardy, which was also bequeathed to the South Kensington Museum.

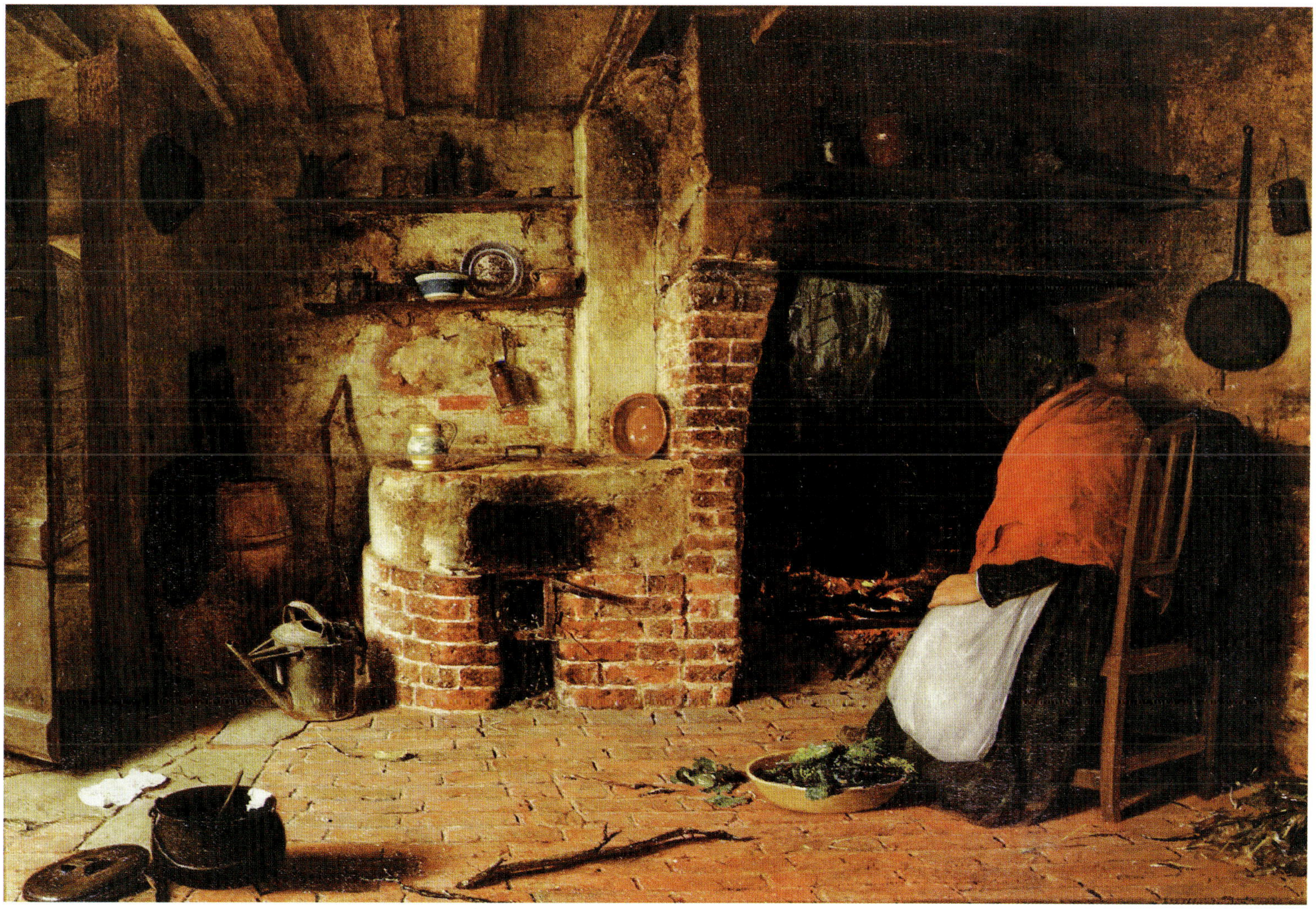

Plate 5: Cottage Fireside, 1850
Frederick Daniel Hardy. Oil on panel. 23.8 x 30.6cm. Private Collection

Several industrialists began collecting F.D. Hardy's paintings in the 1850s. A particularly important collector was Sidney Cartwright, a manufacturer of tin toys whose widow left his collection, which included several works by members of the Cranbrook Colony, to the Wolverhampton Art Gallery in 1887. Professor Samuel Cartwright FRS (unrelated to Sidney Cartwright) was an eminent London dental surgeon who commissioned several early works by F. D. Hardy, including three paintings (*Interior of a Kitchen, with Woman and Child*; *Interior, with Peasant and an Old Woman seated by the Fire*; and *Richard and Kate*) that were sold for 240 guineas at the Christie's sale of Cartwright paintings on 4 March 1865.[17]

F.D. Hardy's titles for his paintings were often puzzling. His first exhibit at the Royal Academy, in 1851, was a cottage interior entitled *Study from Nature*. *The Art Journal* commented: " ... a study from material with which nature never had anything to do – bricks and mortar, and hardware utensils".[18] However, the same publication did praise the "great cunning of execution" of the work. Perhaps in *Study from Nature* (also the title of George Hardy's first exhibit at the Royal Academy in 1846), Hardy was following Ruskin's recommendations about a careful, close study of any objects in "Nature", whether they are bricks or trees.

Similarly, his painting called *Still Life*, exhibited in 1852, was actually the study of a cottage interior. Despite the puzzling titles of his early paintings, they were being noticed by art critics for their fine execution:

> Among the pieces remarkable for minute accuracy of finish in the details, ... by Mr F.D. Hardy there is a small picture, of exquisite elaboration, called Still Life. It is a scullery, but a scullery of sculleries, with sink and dull glass window, kettle, bits of turnip-top on the sink and a bit of yellow soap upon the window. The scullery shelf furnished with its extraordinary lumber. The scullery hooks, supporting a rusty scale-beam, and other articles of furniture equally useful, and equally proper to that extraordinary apartment. A scullery is a great thing – a Poem, as the transcendentalists might say – to study; a great thing to paint; and Mr Hardy has proved great in painting it. By the same artist is another small interior called Afternoon, an old dame who has swept

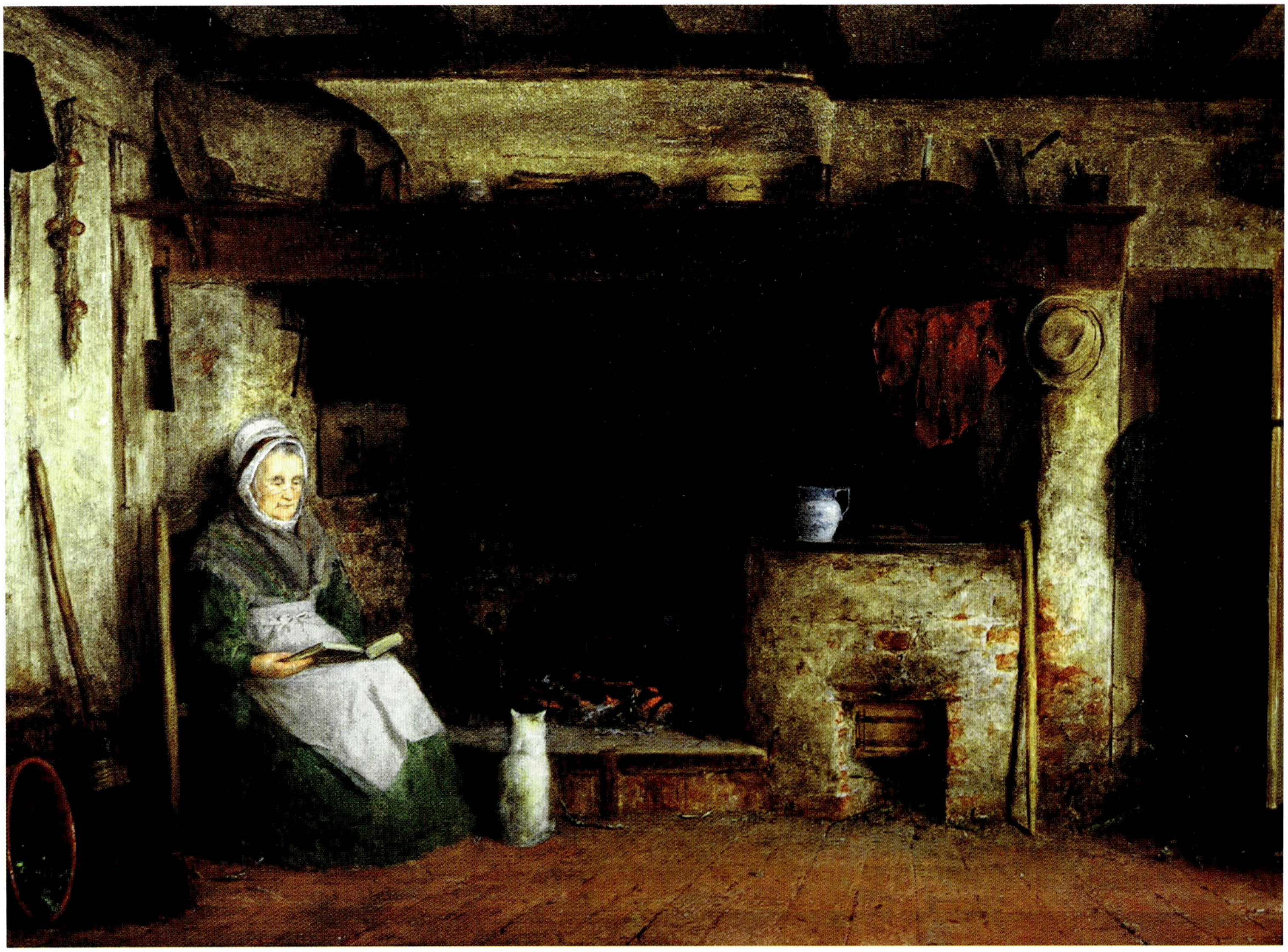

Plate 6: An Interior, 1852
Frederick Daniel Hardy. Oil on panel. 20.5 x 28cm. Private Collection

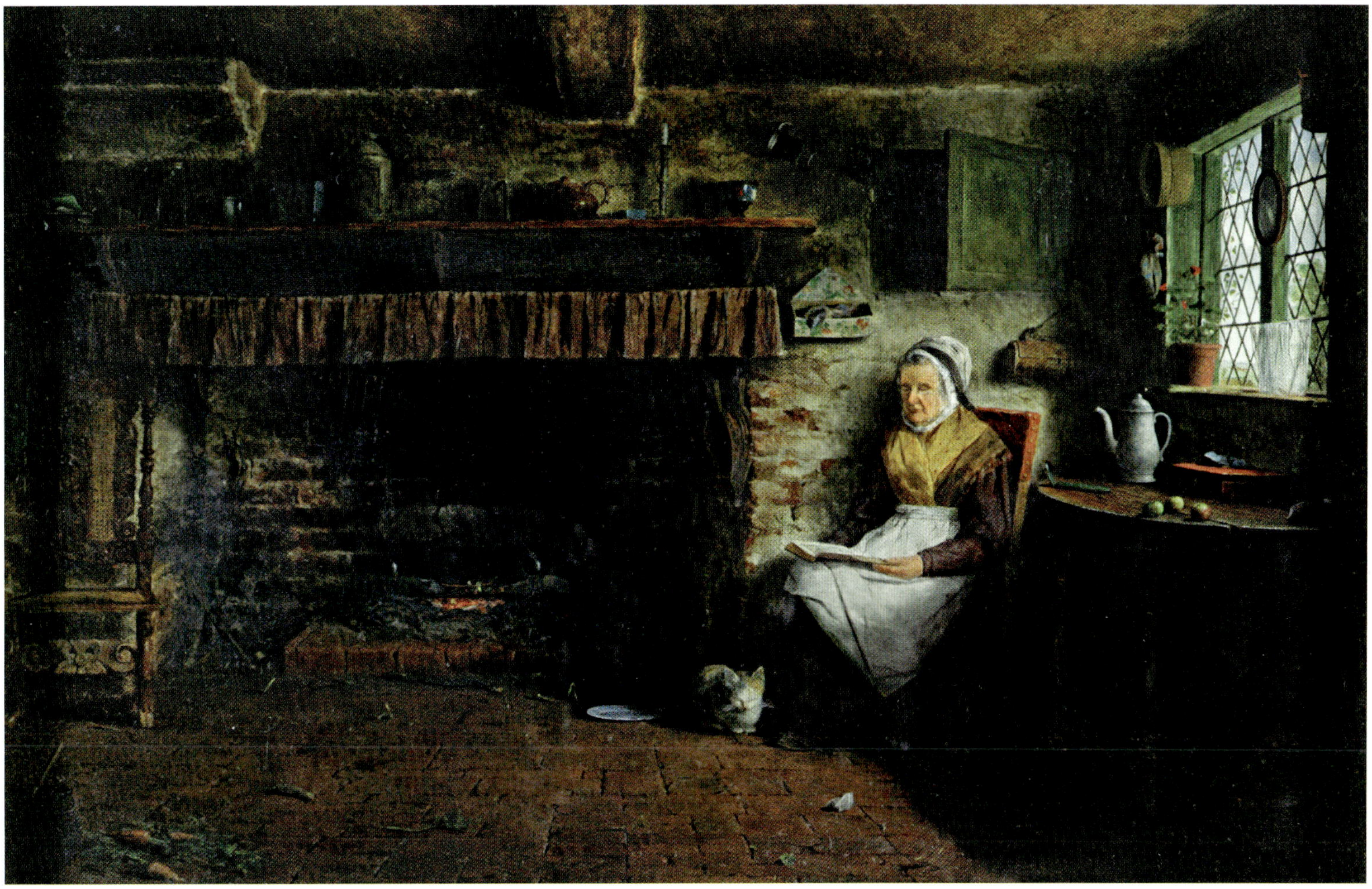

Plate 7: Sunday Afternoon,[19] 1852
Frederick Daniel Hardy. Oil on panel. 19 x 29.8cm. Victoria and Albert Museum
A photograph of a painting similar to *Sunday Afternoon* is in the photograph album of F.D. Hardy (Plate 8).

her cottage floor and sits tidily in the large chimney corner with her Bible, equally good in execution and in feeling: equally good in feeling, for we must maintain that a real scullery is a thing to be felt rather than talked about.[20]

F.D. Hardy called an exhibit at the 1853 Royal Academy exhibition *A Domestic Incident*, prompting *The Illustrated London News* reviewer to write: "This is a joke. We have here a very small interior, similar to many others we have already noticed; the only "incident" in which is an old woman, sitting asleep ... "[21]

The use of "incident" in the title might have been Hardy's sense of humour. But "incident" was probably used in the sense that he was painting an incident or "instance" in time in all its details, in the same way that the Pre-Raphaelites tried to capture a point in time. Holman Hunt in his painting *Fairlight Downs* captured the moment when a walking stick has been thrown and is seen hurtling through the air, to be retrieved by a dog.

When Hardy began making pictures of cottage interiors in the early 1850s, it was already a popular subject for painters. *The Art Journal* remarked: "These cottage firesides are coming in legion upon us. A cottage-interior mania seems to have set in, insomuch that there is no exhibition without them." [22]

Ten years later, paintings of cottage interiors remained popular even while comments were still being made about the

Plate 8: Photograph of a painting of a cottage interior, presumably painted by F.D. Hardy. From the photograph album of F.D. Hardy. Albumen siver print. 11.1 x 16.2cm. Private Collection

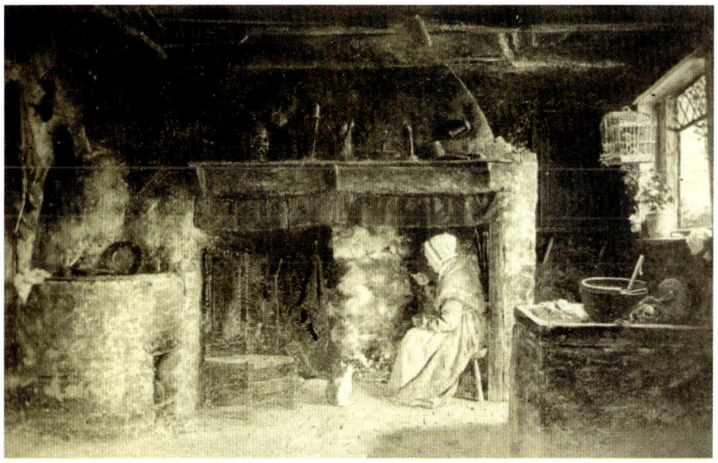

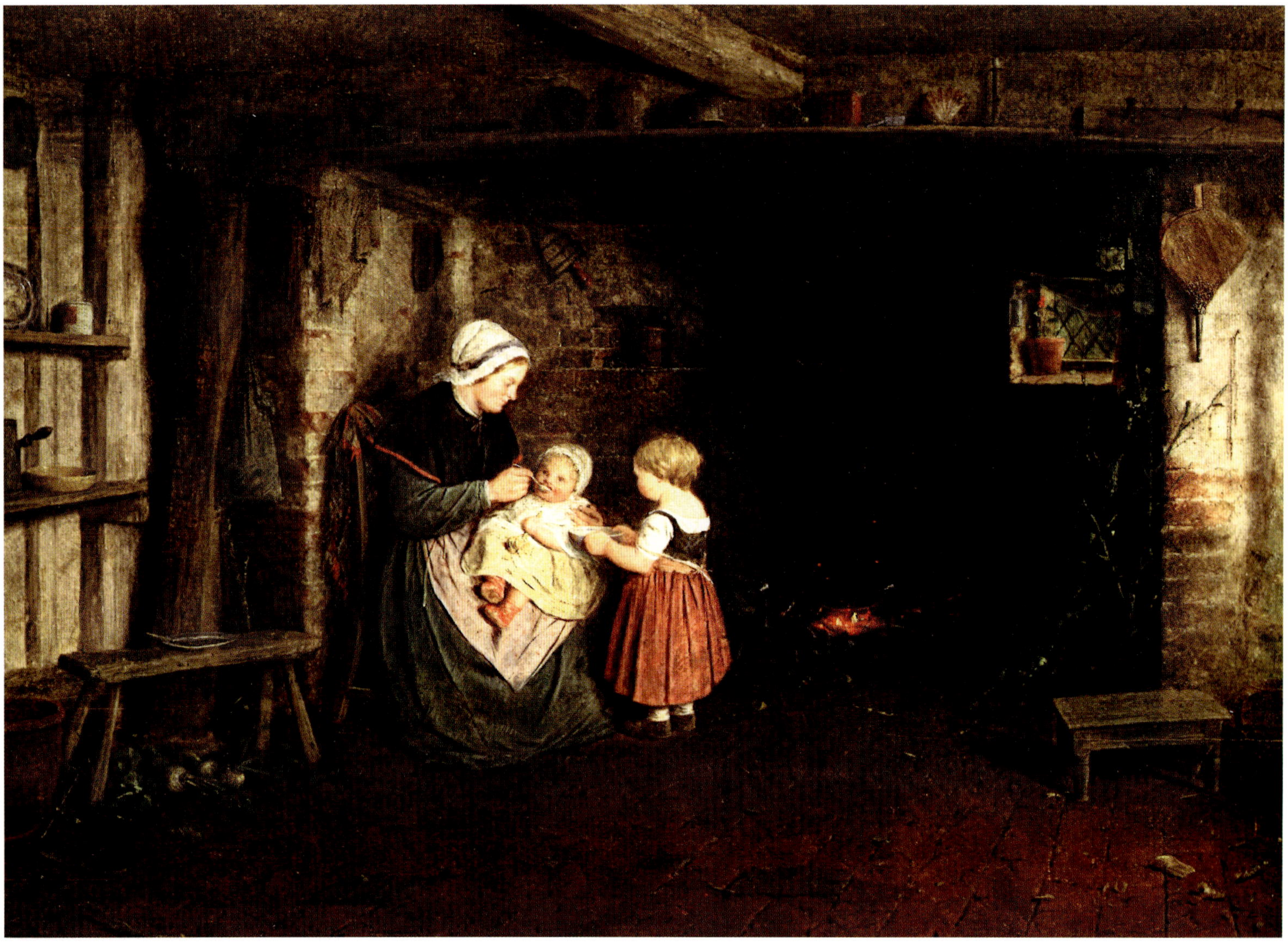

Plate 9: Expectation: Interior of Cottage with Mother and Children, 1854
Frederick Daniel Hardy. Oil on panel. 22.8 x 30.4cm. Royal Holloway, University of London

remarkable number of grandmothers sitting in inglenooks. Reviewing the International Exhibition in Paris of 1862, *The Art Journal* was full of praise for rustic genre painters: " ... that truly English school of home sympathies and rustic simplicity, to which the foreign galleries of the International Exhibition afford little or no parallel ... made sacred in the sphere of poetry by the writings of Crabbe and Wordsworth."[23]

From 1854 F.D. Hardy began to add more figures to his paintings and to begin to create narratives. His carefully observed interiors received increasingly favourable critical comment. His Royal Academy exhibit for 1854, *Expectation: Interior of Cottage with Mother and Children* (Plate 9) was a work of "unimpeachable exactitude" according to *The Art Journal:* "The walls and the brick floor have been most assiduously wrought into microscopic imitation of these surfaces ... The work is entitled to rank among the best of this class of subject."[24]

Always a stickler for detail, John Ruskin, who took a magnifying glass with him when he went to exhibitions, commented on Hardy's *Interior* exhibited at the Royal Academy in 1856:

> An exquisite little piece of interior painting; hurt only by some conventionality in finishing. For instance, how is it possible that, the sunbeams entering only by that one small window, the principal figures should be in full light, or the shadow fall at a steep angle from the knife-handle over the block in the left-hand corner? But, with his powers of execution, a little more faithfulness will make Mr. Hardy a perfect painter in this kind.[25]

F.D. Hardy seems to have followed the advice of Ruskin who believed that painters "should go to nature in all singleness of heart ... rejecting nothing, selecting nothing, and scorning nothing."[26] In the early 1850s F.D. Hardy probably completed many of his small pictures of interiors in the cottages themselves and did not make preparatory sketches to be worked up in the studio. This enabled him to give equal attention to each individual item and to paint them in great detail in line with the approach taken by Ruskin and the Pre-Raphaelites. Each item in the picture is in sharp focus.

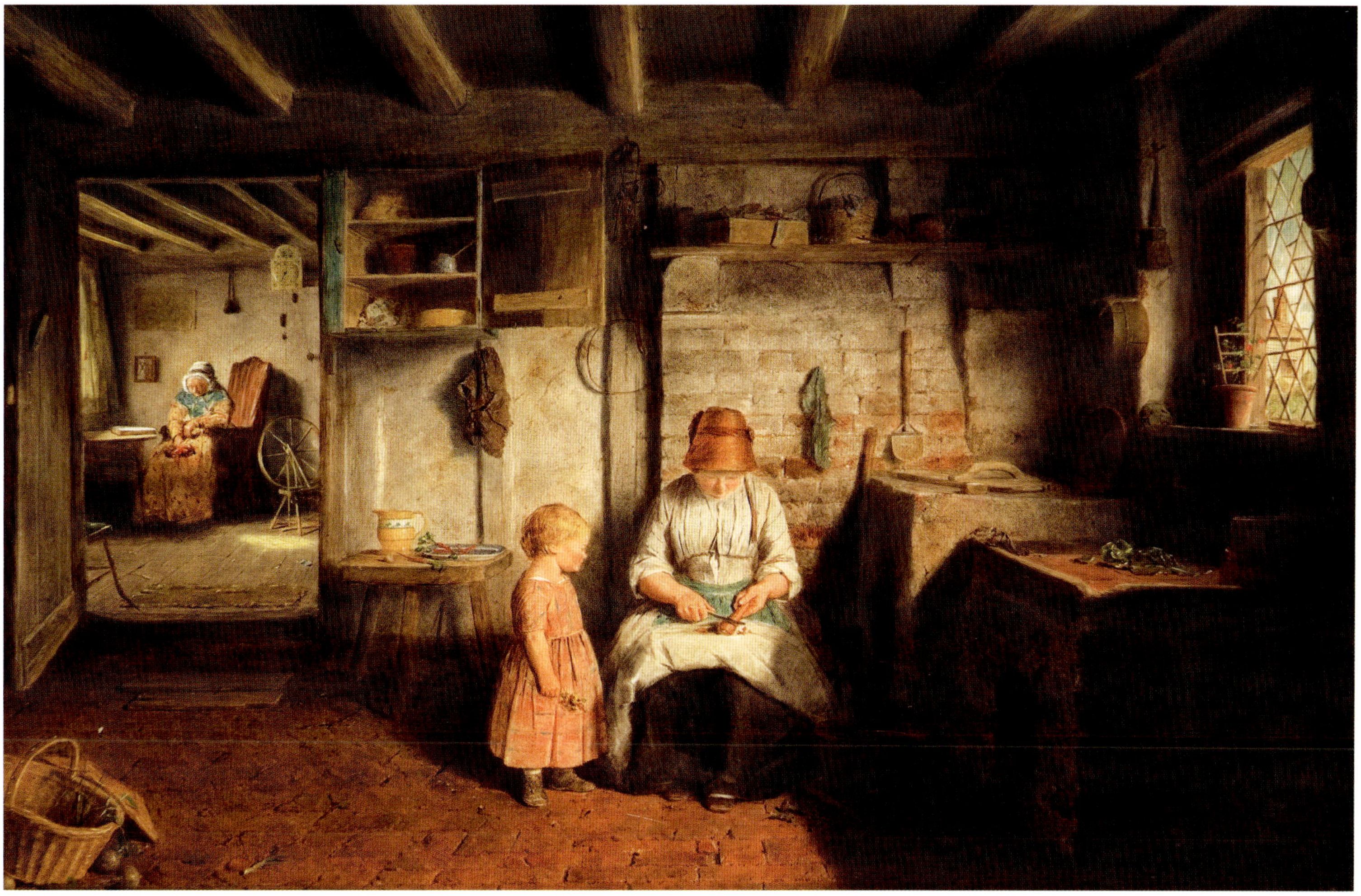

Plate 10: Preparing for Dinner, 1854
Frederick Daniel Hardy. Oil on panel. 22.5 x 33cm. © Wolverhampton Art Gallery

There are a few paintings by F.D. Hardy that are reminiscent of works by Nicolaes Maes and Johannes Vermeer, indicating that he was influenced by their paintings in The National Gallery in London. Dutch painting from the seventeenth century saw a considerable rise in popularity in England in the 1850s. However, the types of narrative that Hardy subsequently introduced into his Dutch-inspired cottage interiors were a particular feature of nineteenth-century genre painting. The colouring in paintings by F.D. Hardy and G.B. O'Neill (another member of the Cranbrook colony) resembles that of Dutch seventeenth-century genre paintings; there are muted colours often with an area of red as a central feature, as seen in many of F.D. Hardy's paintings and in G.B. O'Neill's *Market Day, the arrival of the Hippodrome* (1856).

Preparing for Dinner (Plate 10), which was called *Dinner Time* when exhibited at the British Institution in 1854, is particularly reminiscent of *A Woman Scraping Parsnips, with a Child Standing by Her* (Plate 11), painted by Nicolaes Maes in 1655. This was bequeathed to The National Gallery in 1838; The National Gallery had two of the best paintings made by Maes during the short period when he was a painter of genre pictures after leaving Rembrandt's studio.

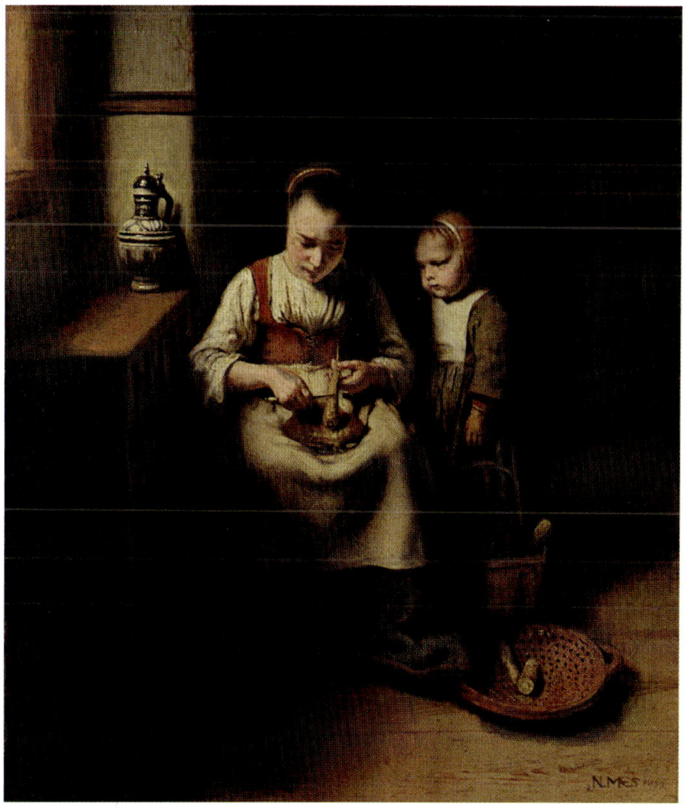

Plate 11: A Woman Scraping Parsnips, with a Child Standing by Her, 1655
Nicolaes Maes. Oil on panel. 35.6 x 29.8cm. The National Gallery, London

F.D. Hardy also uses the compositional technique favoured by Nicolaes Maes, Johannes Vermeer and Pieter de Hooch of an open door leading to another room beyond; this device was used to continue the narrative of the foreground scene into the background space. F.D. Hardy may have seen *The Idle Servant* (1655) by Nicolaes Maes, which has a view into a room beyond; it was bequeathed to The National Gallery in 1847.

From 1854 F.D. Hardy gradually began to introduce more figures into his paintings. His *Fireside Entertainment* (Plate 13) of 1854, featuring figures by the fire inside a large barn, resembles many of Adriaen van Ostade's paintings of vast interiors.

Around the year 1854, F.D. Hardy painted three pictures, *Old Soldier's Story* (1854), *Interior of a Sussex Farmhouse* (185?) (Plate 14) and *The Clergyman's Visit* (Plate 15), that all show the same interior with three figures. *Old Soldier's Story*, his 1854 Royal Academy exhibit, and *Interior of a Sussex Farmhouse* show an almost identical interior; there are only slight differences in the three figures near the fire.

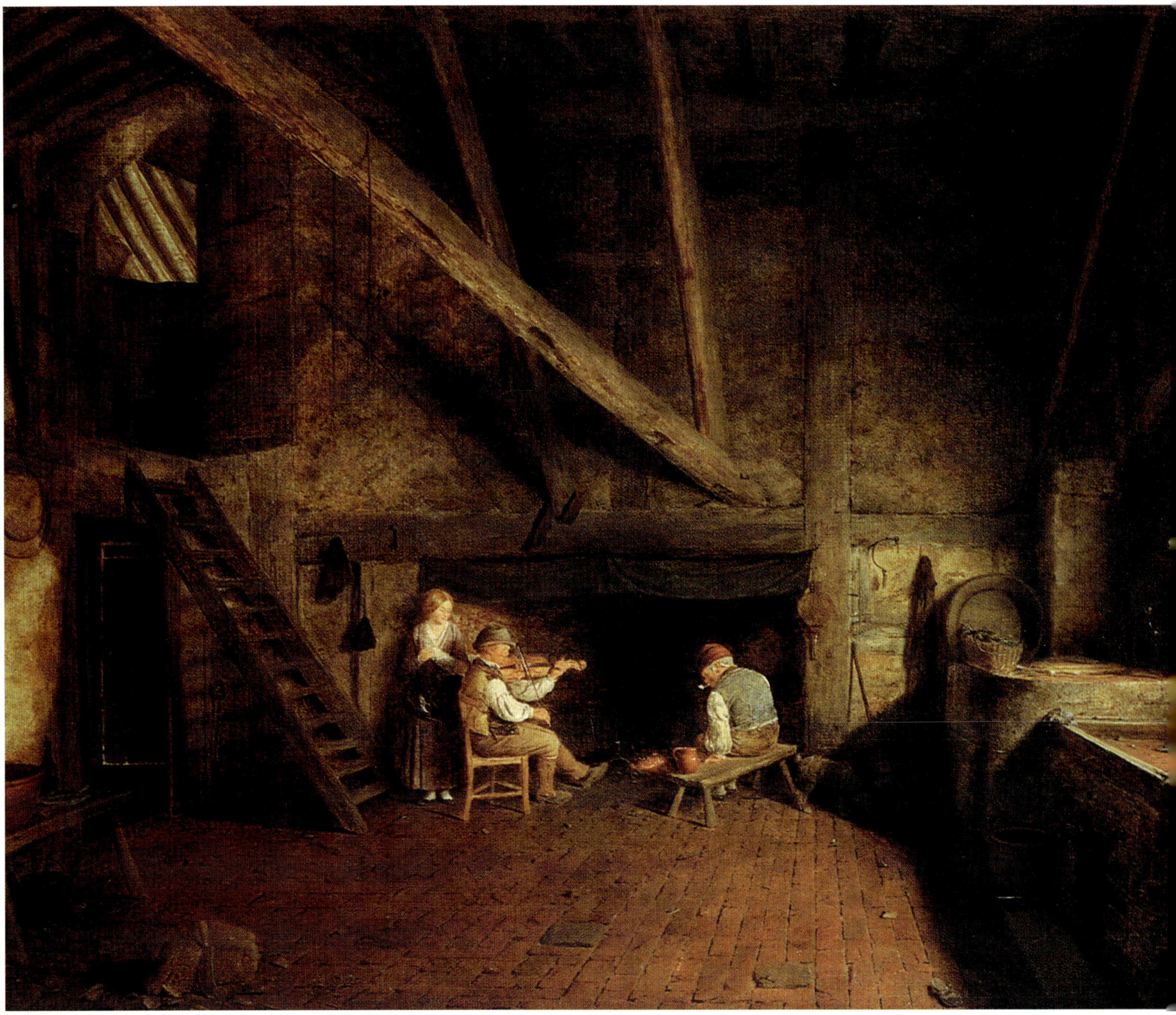

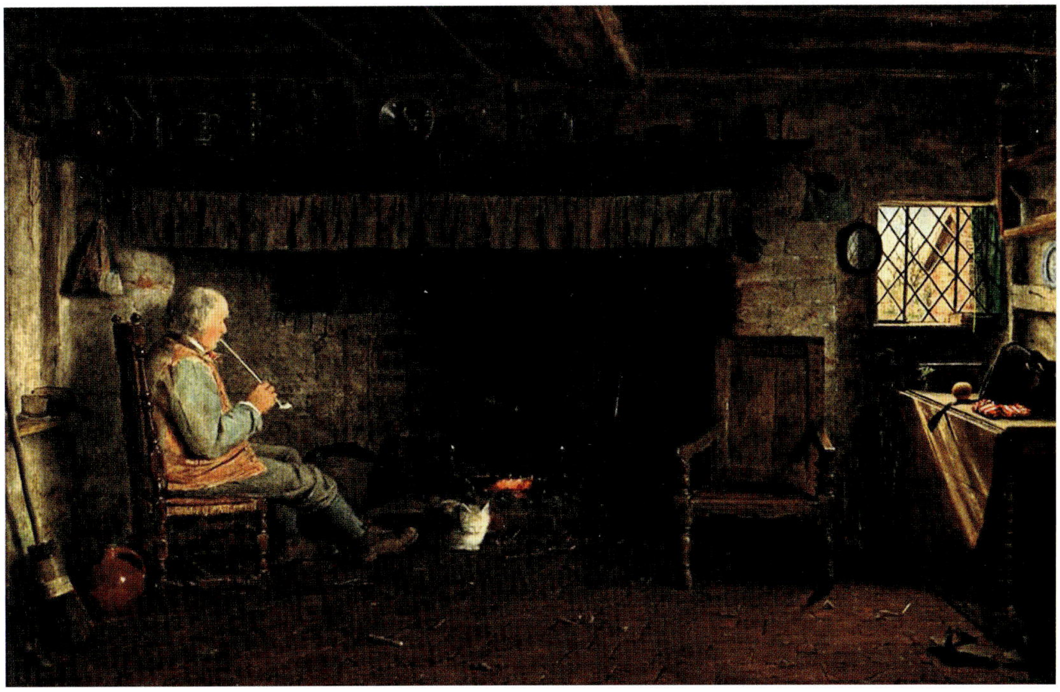

Plate 12: Quiet Evening by the Fire, 1853 [27]
Frederick Daniel Hardy. Oil on panel.
19.7 x 30.4cm. Private Collection

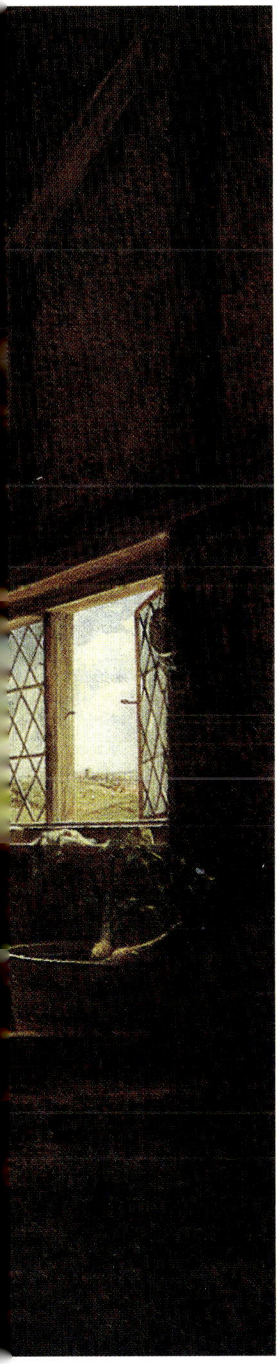

Plate 13 (left): Fireside Entertainment, 1854
Frederick Daniel Hardy. Oil on panel. 38 x 53cm. Private Collection

Plate 14 (below): Interior of a Sussex Farmhouse, 185?
Frederick Daniel Hardy. Oil on panel. 19.7 x 29.8cm. Leicester Arts and Museums Service

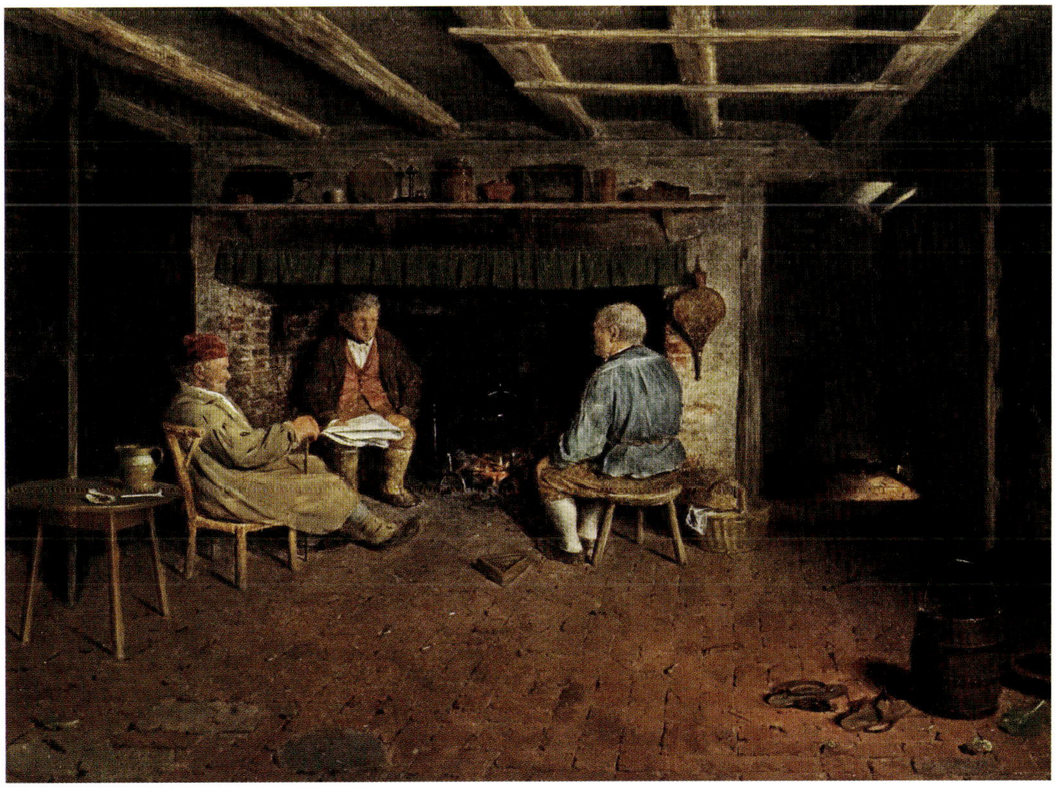

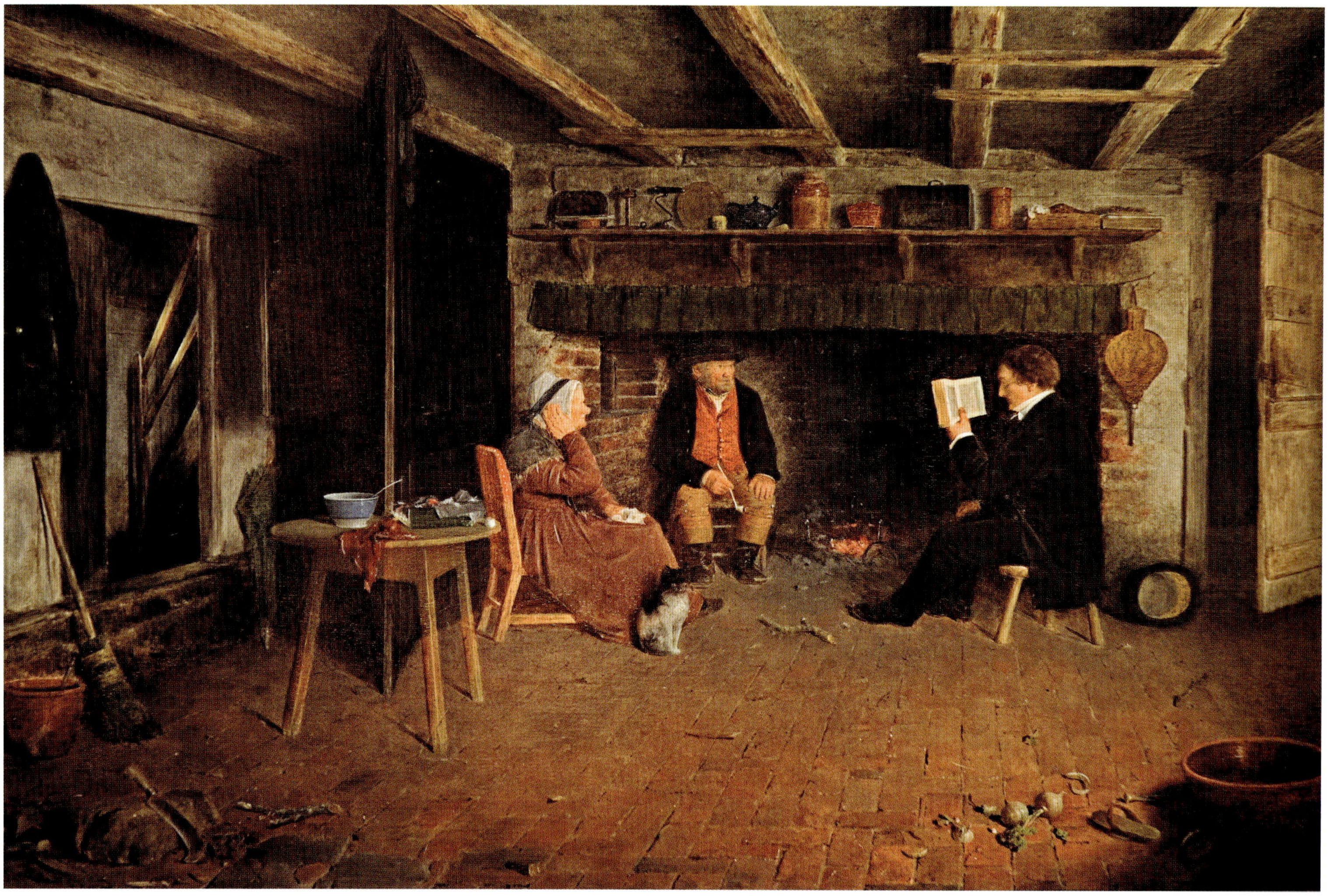

In his catalogue of the "The Cranbrook Colony" exhibition Andrew Greg compared the early work of F.D. Hardy with Thomas Webster's paintings:

> In a painting like *The Clergyman's Visit*, in which we have the first inkling of Hardy's venture from purely descriptive painting towards working in a more anecdotal framework, there are three people with scarcely a gesture between them, save the woman's hand raised to her ear. Yet we can realise for ourselves so much more of the atmosphere of the event than in a painting by Webster such as Sunday Evening in which emotional details are overemphasized. It is a little harder work looking at Hardy, but like most constructive work it is ultimately more satisfying. [28]

Plate 15 (above): The Clergyman's Visit
Frederick Daniel Hardy. Oil on panel. 22.5 x 33cm.

A photograph of a painting in F.D. Hardy's photograph album (Plate 16) has a similar grouping of three figures; the improved composition and the drawing of the figures suggests that this is a later work.

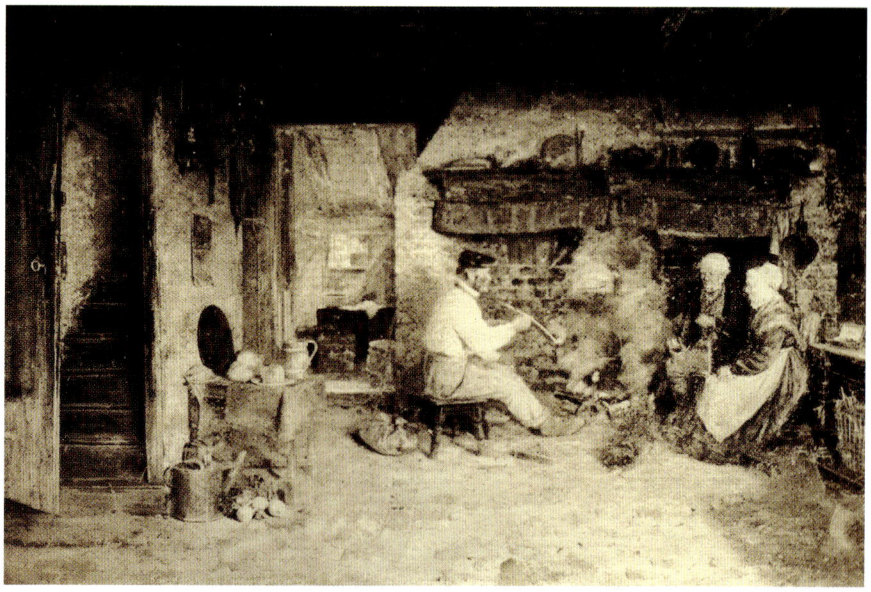

Plate 16 (right): Photograph of a painting, presumably painted by F.D. Hardy, in the photograph album of F.D. Hardy. Albumen silver print. 9.9 x 14.3cm.

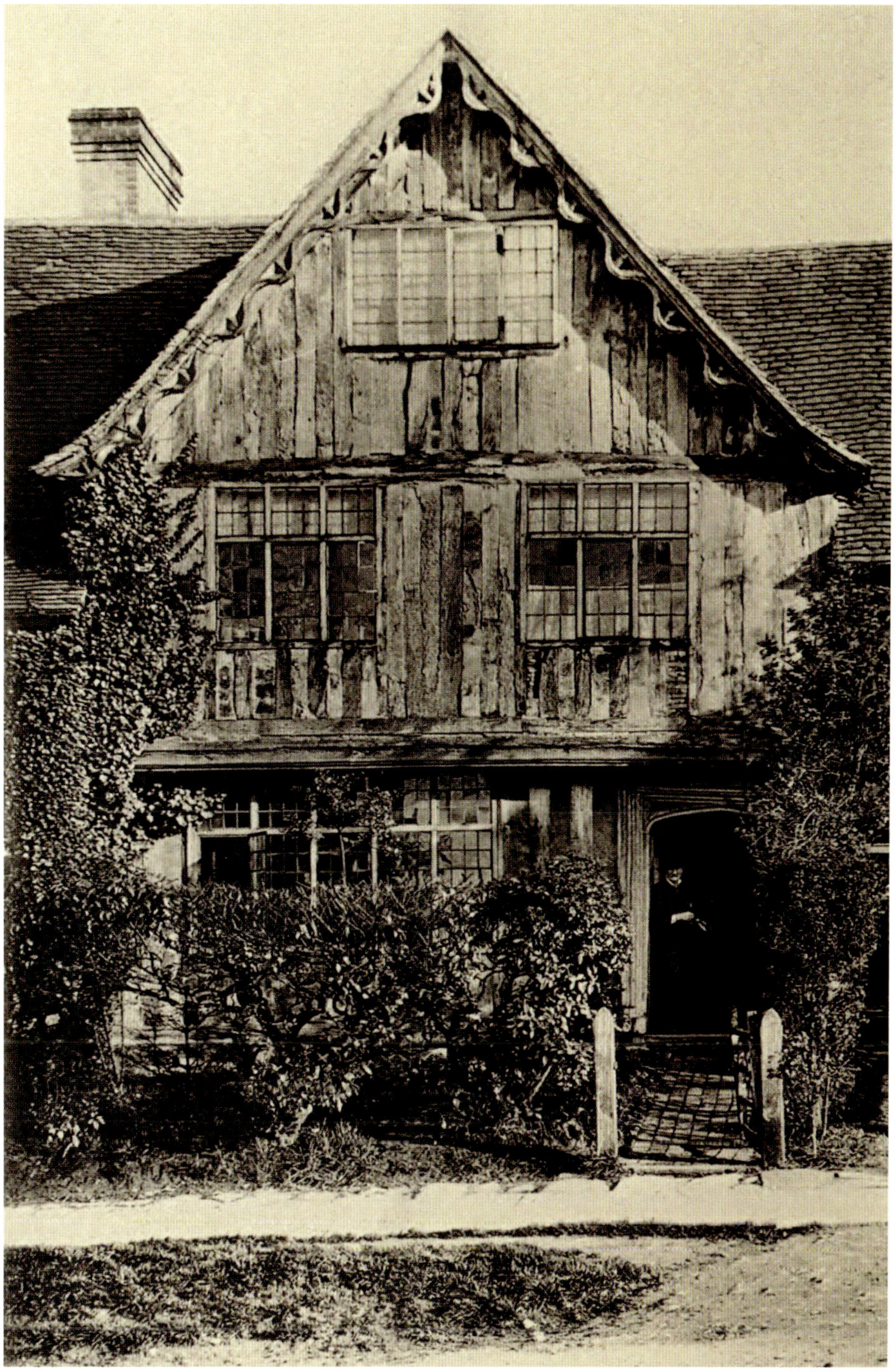

Plate 17: "Studio of Mr. F.D. Hardy, Cranbrook, Kent". Photograph by E. J. Holmes, Cranbrook. In *Old Cottages and Farm Houses in Kent and Sussex*, 1900, W. Galsworthy Davie & E. Guy Dawber, London: B.T. Batsford.

F. D. Hardy, holding his palette, is leaning against the sixteenth-century front door.

The Cranbrook Colony

As F.D. Hardy was the first of the "Cranbrook Colony" to live at Cranbrook, he could be considered the founder member, though Thomas Webster is often described as the group's mentor and its link with the genre tradition of David Wilkie. F.D. Hardy was living at Cranbrook for three or four years before other members of the Cranbrook Colony went to live there.

The Cranbrook Colony was a group of close friends and relatives.[29] Thomas Webster and John Callcott Horsley had been close friends for many years; they had been at the Royal Academy Schools together. Webster and Sir Augustus Wall Callcott RA (J.C. Horsley's great uncle) lived close to each other in the Mall, Kensington, for several years. George Bernard O'Neill had married Horsley's cousin, Emma Callcott. The artists George Henry Boughton and Augustus E. Mulready, friends of J.C. Horsley, were visitors to Cranbrook from London.

Thomas Webster and J.C. Horsley often visited F.D. Hardy at Cranbrook and by 1857 Webster was living there with his first wife, Betsy, who died at Cranbrook in 1859 (the following year Webster married Ellen Summerfield).

For his studio in Cranbrook, F.D. Hardy rented part of an old building in the high street, formerly the local cloth hall when the town was the centre of Kentish woollen cloth manufacture, in the sixteenth and seventeenth centuries. For their studios F. D. Hardy used the lower front room and Thomas Webster the upper front room[30] (Plate 17).

Horsley and his second wife, Rosamund, initially lived in lodgings at Cranbrook and then bought a house, "Willesley", in 1861, while keeping a house in London. Recalling his first visit to Cranbrook, Horsley wrote:

> "Where's Cranbrook?" I remember saying to old Tom Webster one day, when he told me he was going down into Kent to see the young artist F.D. Hardy who was painting the cottage interiors in the neighbourhood. This visit ended in Webster's taking rooms in a charming old farmhouse, which had been originally built and occupied by a prosperous Kentish cloth maker. Tempted by Webster's account of Cranbrook, we often went there and occupied lodgings, till the chance came of buying an old house standing about half a mile out of the town on a hill. [31]

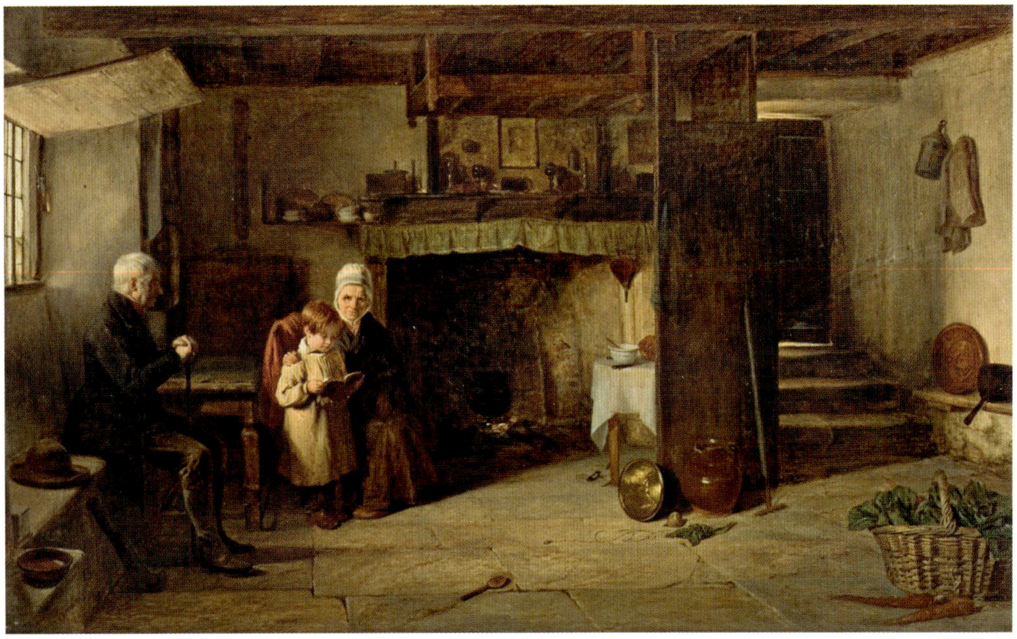

Plate 18 (left): The Lesson, 1831
Thomas Webster RA. Oil on canvas.
38.1 x 58.3cm. Victoria and Albert Museum

Plate 19 (below, left): Blossom Time, 1859
John Callcott Horsley. Oil on canvas.
90.2 x 69.2cm. Philadelphia Museum of Art

Plate 20 (below, right):
Showing a Preference, 1860
John Callcott Horsley. Oil on canvas.
68.6 x 53.3cm. Private Collection

F.D. Hardy's early paintings of interiors were influenced by Webster's early interiors such as *The Lesson* (1831) (Plate 18).

Most of J.C. Horsley's paintings were historical genre works set in the seventeenth century. But two of his finest works are *Blossom Time* (1859) (Plate 19) and *Showing a Preference* (1860) (Plate 20), which were painted a year or two after Horsley first visited Cranbrook. Victorian observers of *Showing a Preference* would no doubt have commented that the favoured companion walks on the right-hand side of the naval lieutenant next to a sunlit, ripe cornfield: the other girl, whose shawl is caught by brambles, is on the weed-covered, shady side of the path.

F.D. Hardy's *Writing a letter* (1856) (Plate 21) is reminiscent

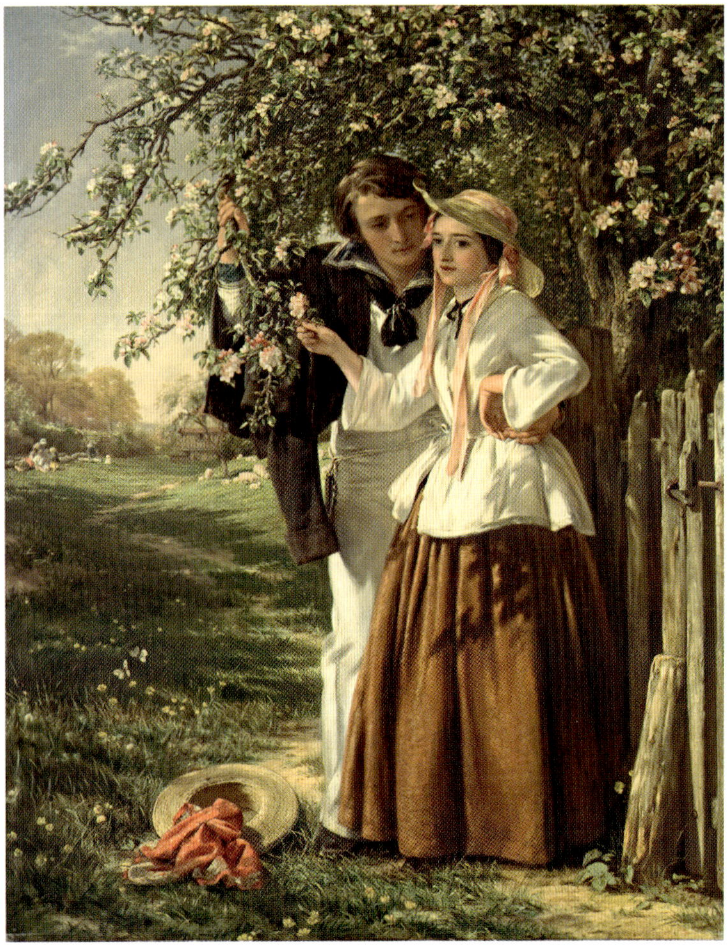

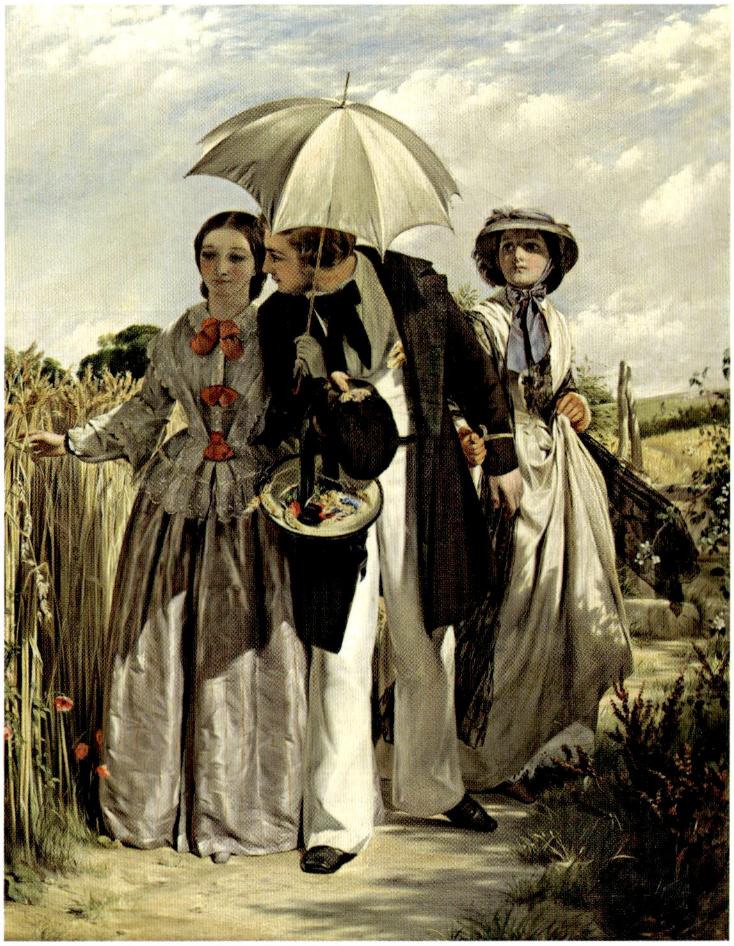

Plate 21 (right): Writing a letter, 1856
Frederick Daniel Hardy. Oil on panel. 22.9 x 17.8cm. Private Collection

Plate 22 (below): The Children's Party, 1871
George Bernard O'Neill. Oil on canvas. 77.5 x 114.3cm. Private Collection

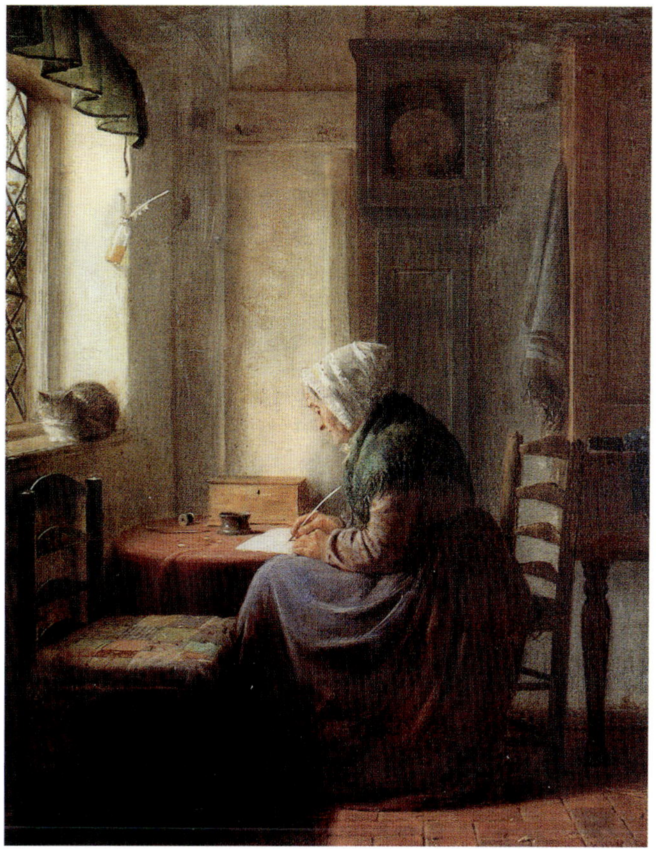

of Johannes Vermeer's pictures of people reading letters or writing near a window, but perhaps the influence is indirect, from J. C. Horsley who studied Vermeer's paintings closely.

In 1860 George Bernard O'Neill and his wife Emma rented a house in Cranbrook and kept it as a summer home and studio for many years. Many of O'Neill's paintings from the 1860s and 1870s used the house as a setting. Children of artists in the Cranbrook Colony appear in several paintings. G. B. O'Neill's *The Children's Party* (1871) (Plate 22) includes the artist's children in the foreground. And Andrew Greg noted that the bearded man in *The Children's Party* strongly resembles the man, believed to be George Hardy, in F.D. Hardy's *The Dismayed Artist* (Plate 46).[32] Perhaps G.B. O'Neill included a portrait of George Hardy holding his eldest daughter, Louisa, who would have been about two years old when the picture was painted.

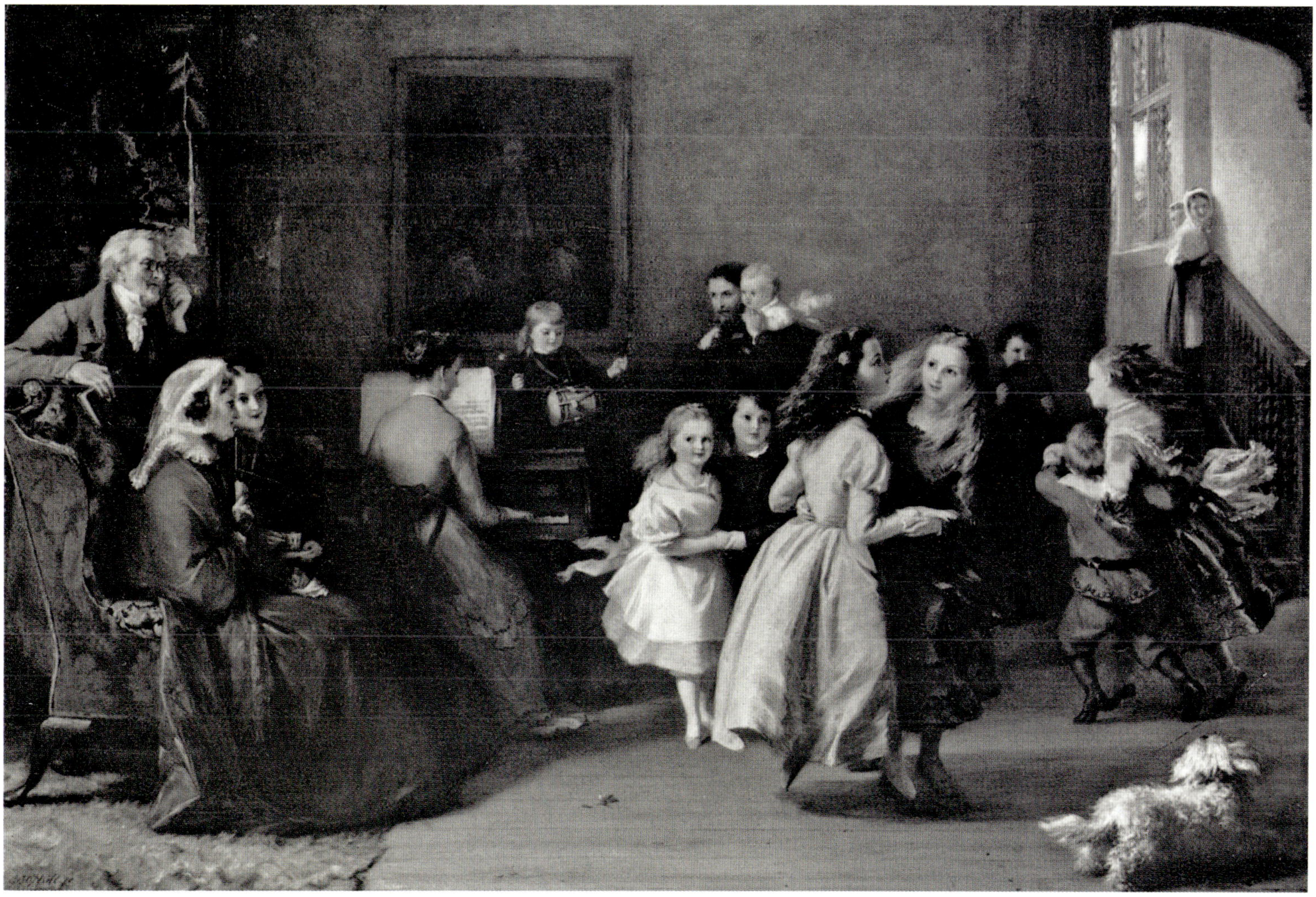

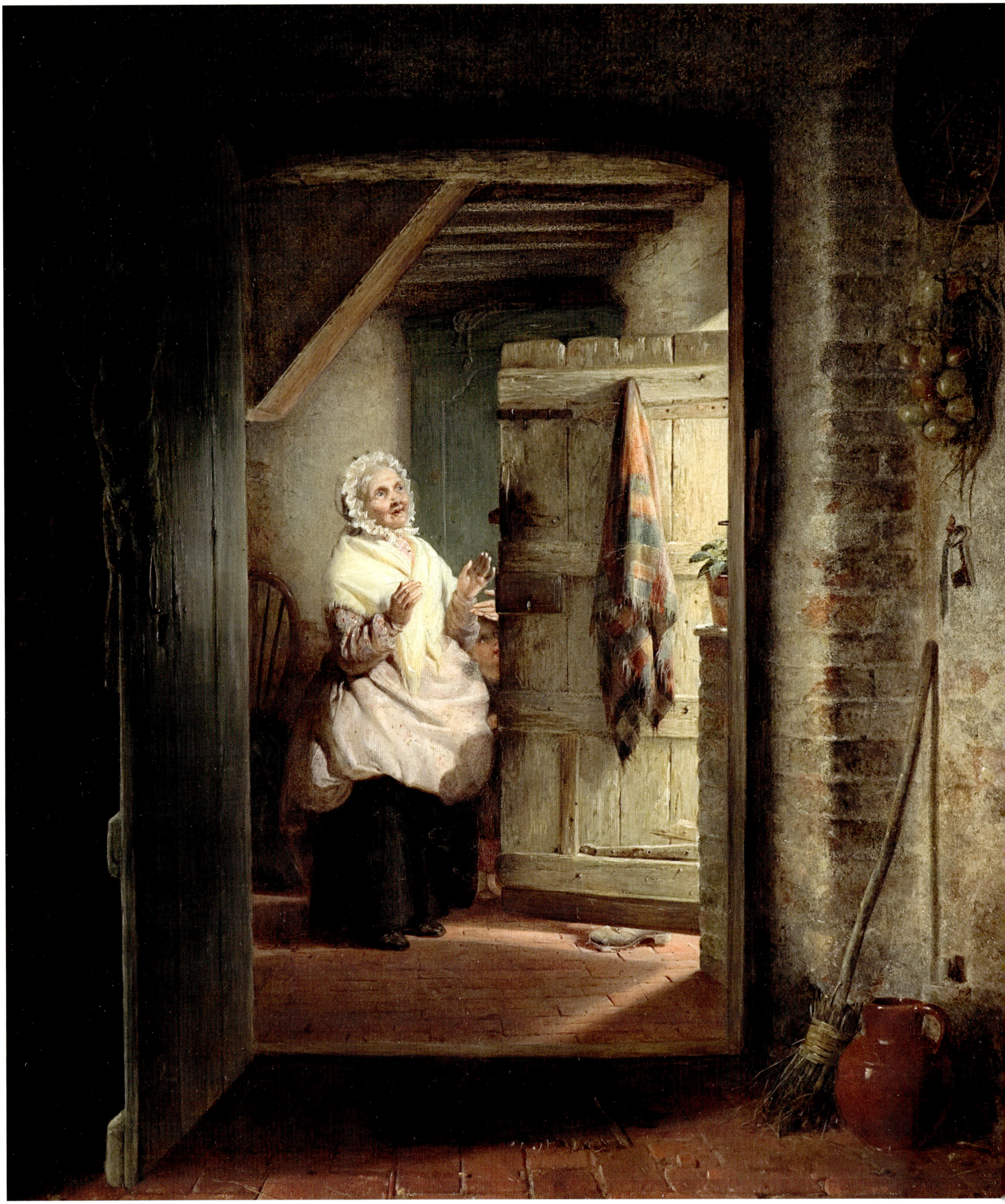

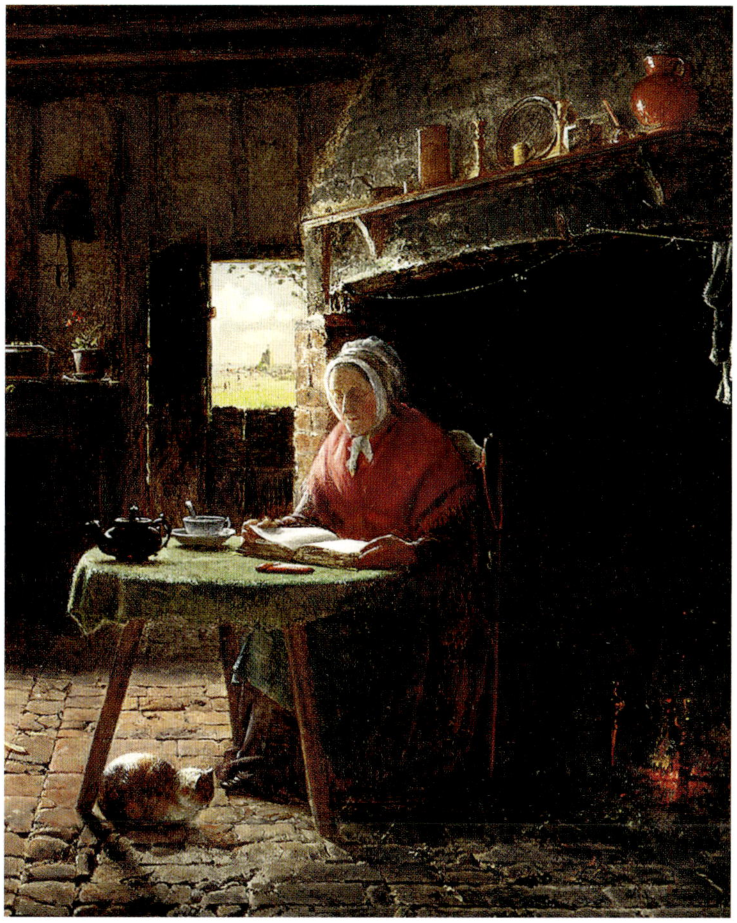

F.D. Hardy only gradually introduced narratives into his work as he became more confident in painting figures. Some of his early paintings had figures painted by G.B. O'Neill, for example *Returning Home,* inscribed "Interior by F.D. Hardy/ Figure by G.B. O'Neill/1856", and probably *The Surprise* (1856) (Plate 23)

At about the same time, F.D. Hardy collaborated with his brother George on a picture, *Reading by the Fire* (1857) (Plate 24), that appears to include a distant view of Cranbrook church.

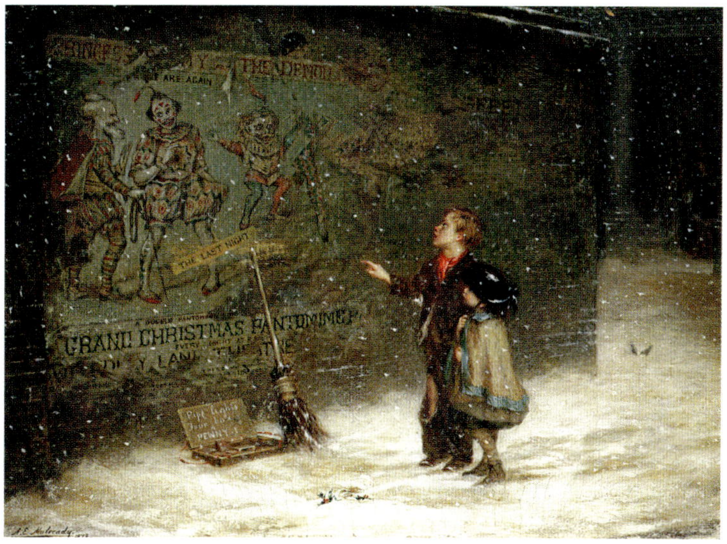

F.D. Hardy's photograph album has a print of a painting (Plate 25), made in the same year, depicting a woman preparing food (on a three-legged "cricket" table, well-suited to uneven cottage floors, that is in many of his paintings).

Members of the Cranbrook Colony shared an interest in music: Thomas Webster and F.D. Hardy had a musical education, as did J.C. Horsley who came from a renowned family of composers and musicians. Norman Houston O'Neill, youngest son of G.B. O'Neill, was a composer and conductor.

Augustus Mulready lived with the Horsleys at Cranbrook for a few years in the 1870s. His paintings were mainly pictures of the hard life and poverty of children in the streets of London. *Remembering Joys that have Passed Away* (1873) (Plate 26) shows a match girl and a London crossing sweeper, who swept paths clear of rubbish, horse droppings and snow for people walking on the pavements and crossing the roads.

By 1863, the group of artists at Cranbrook was well established and Horsley invited members of the Etching Club to join them for three days of walks around Cranbrook. In June 1863 Samuel Palmer replied to Horsley to say that unfortunately he would not

Plate 23 (opposite page): The Surprise, 1856
George Bernard O'Neill and Frederick Daniel Hardy.
Oil on Board. 35.2 x 29.8cm. © Wolverhampton Art Gallery

Plate 24 (above left): Reading by the Fire, 1857
Frederick Daniel Hardy and George Hardy. Oil on panel.
20.3 x 16.5cm. Signed and dated "FDH/&GH/1857" (upper right)

Plate 25 (right): Photograph of a painting by F.D. Hardy. Signed "FDH/1857" on the door. From the photograph album of F.D. Hardy. Albumen silver print. 4.7 x 7cm. Private Collection

Plate 26 (top right): Remembering Joys that have Passed Away, 1873 Augustus Edwin Mulready. Oil on canvas.
39 x 52cm. Guildhall Art Gallery

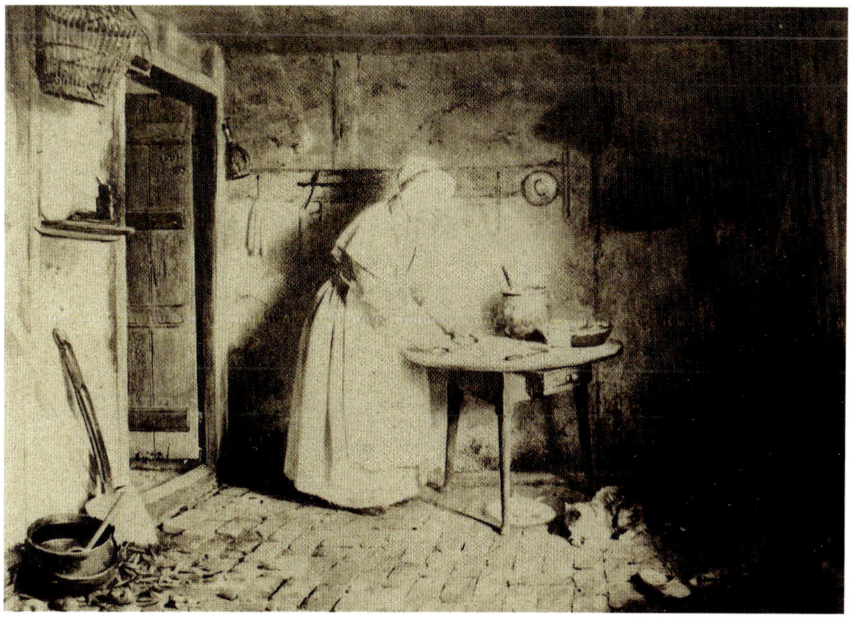

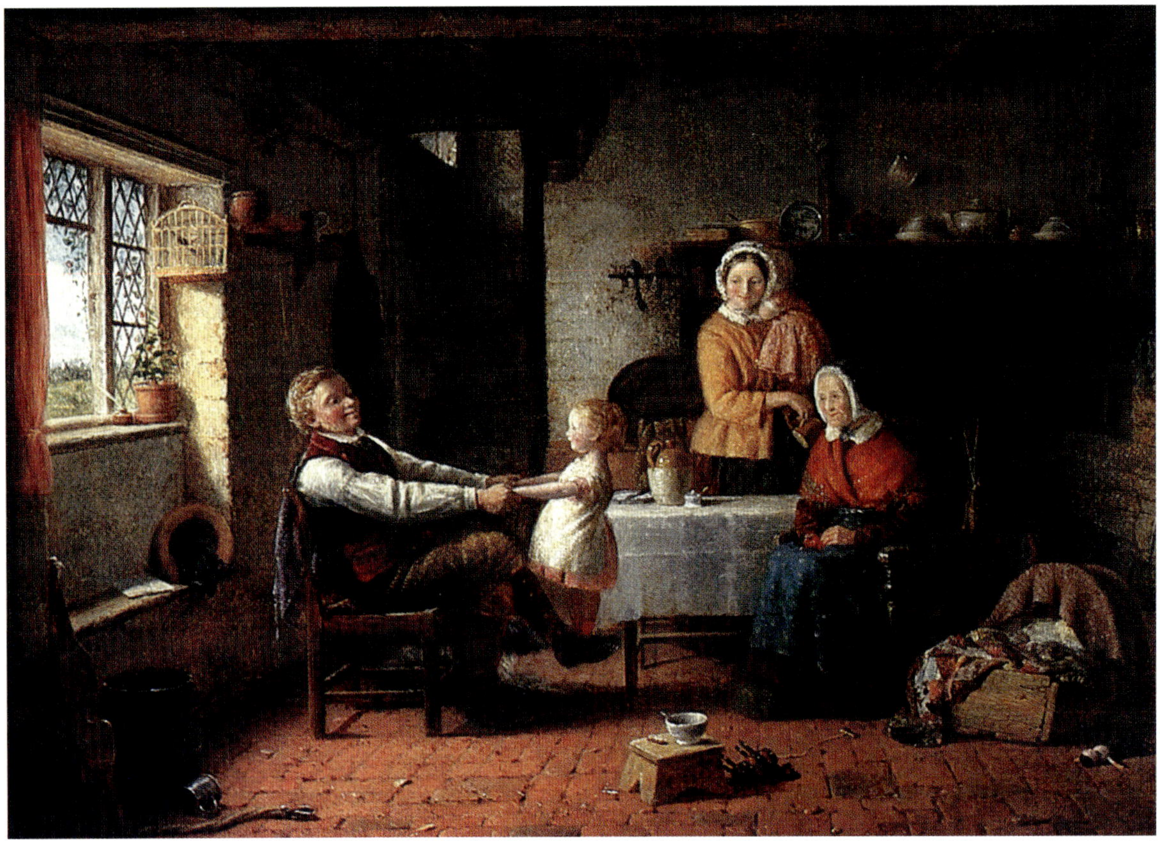

Plate 27 (opposite page):
A Kiss Goodnight, 1858
Frederick Daniel Hardy.
Oil on canvas. 40.6 x 30.5cm.
PRIVATE COLLECTION[33]

Plate 28 (left):
Happiness of Home, 1858
Frederick Daniel Hardy.
Oil on panel. 15.2 x 17.8cm.
PRIVATE COLLECTION

be able to visit the colony at Cranbrook because of his asthma: "I have read a good deal at one time or another about our colonies. You may suppose that I could not be indifferent to the institutions and productions of the colony at Cranbrook. It has been my frequent day-dream and I long to see it ... " In a postscript he added "Would that I also, albeit unworthy, were a settler at Cranbrook!" [34]

Other members of the Etching Club at this time, in addition to Horsley and O'Neill, included Holman Hunt and Millais. In fact, by 1863 Samuel Palmer preferred to stay at home and was always making excuses to avoid visits and meetings.

In the 1850s F.D. Hardy achieved a thorough understanding of the space and light in cottage interiors; this gave him a secure foundation for the pictures he painted in the 1860s in which the activities and the narratives of the cottage inhabitants are played out. Much of the appeal of F.D. Hardy's early paintings lies in their carefully balanced compositions, their treatment of light and shade and their subtle colour harmonies. *A Kiss Goodnight* (Plate 27) was painted 1858; the same setting of a child's bedroom was used many years later for several paintings including *A Bedtime Tale* (1871), *Ready for Bed* and *Sorrowful News* (1872). *Mother and Child*, a very similar picture to *A Kiss Goodnight*, was painted over thirty years later, in 1889.

The photograph album of F.D. Hardy contains photographs of several of his paintings; whether he made the photographs himself or had them made by a photographer is unknown. And we do not know whether F.D. Hardy made the photographs to keep a record of his pictures or if he used them in some way in his work. There are no photographs of cottage interiors in his album, apart from photographs of paintings that depict interiors. Several Victorian painters used photographs in their work, most famously William Powell Frith who commissioned a photographer to "photograph for him from the roof of a cab as many queer groups of figures as he could" for his picture *Derby Day*.[35]

Happiness of Home (1858) (Plate 28) is the only painting that the author has identified with a corresponding photograph in the album. It is a small painting measuring only 6 x 7 inches (15.2 x 17.8cm). The photograph does not match the painting exactly. Hardy sometimes painted small pictures and then modified the composition and colours slightly in a larger picture.

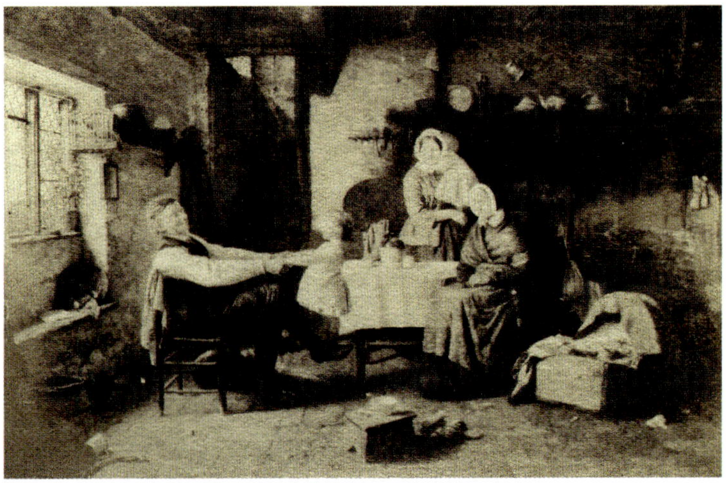

Plate 29: Photograph of a painting, similar to *Happiness of Home*, presumably by F.D. Hardy. From the photograph album of F.D. Hardy. Albumen silver print. 4.1 x 6cm. PRIVATE COLLECTION

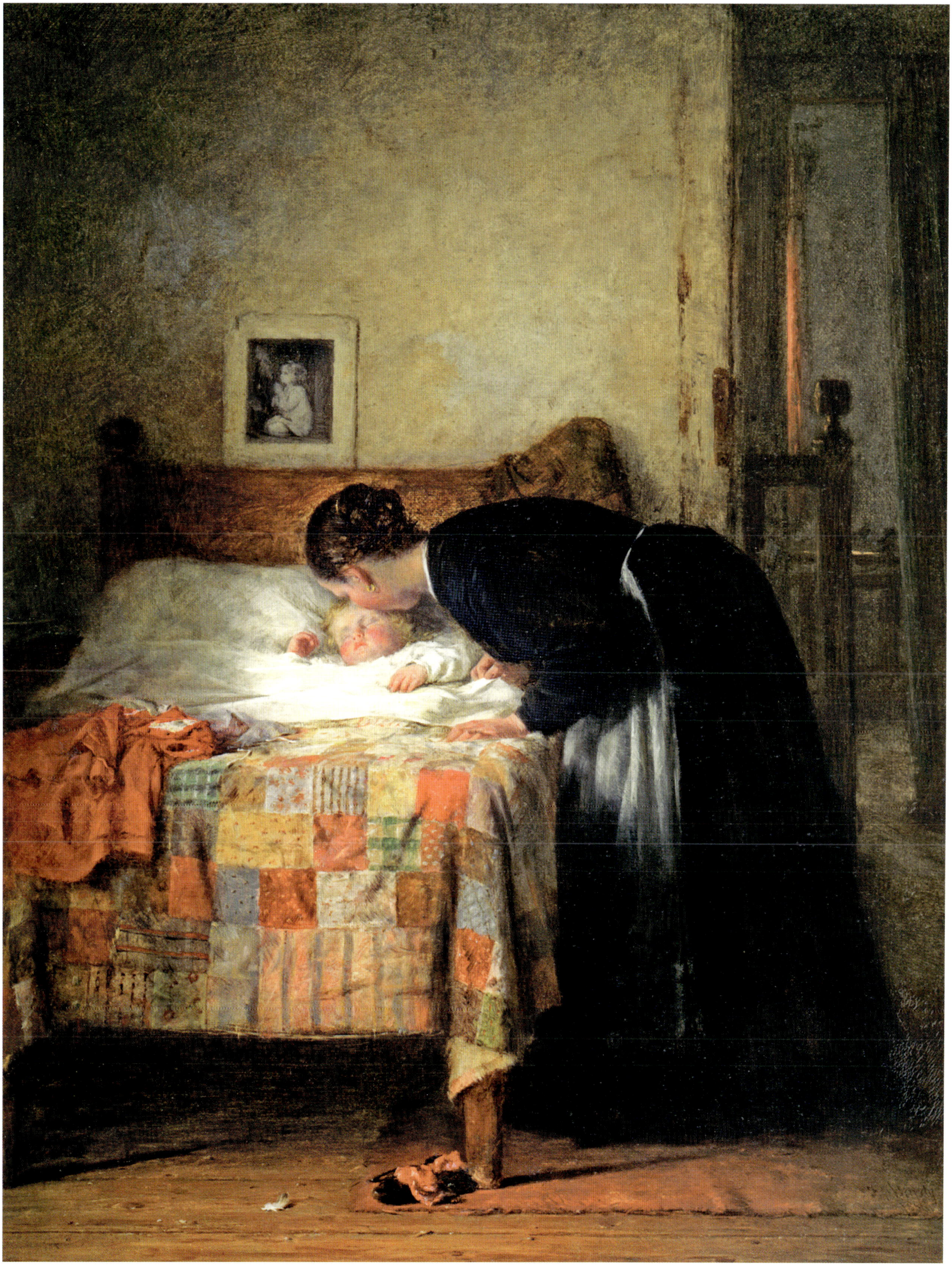

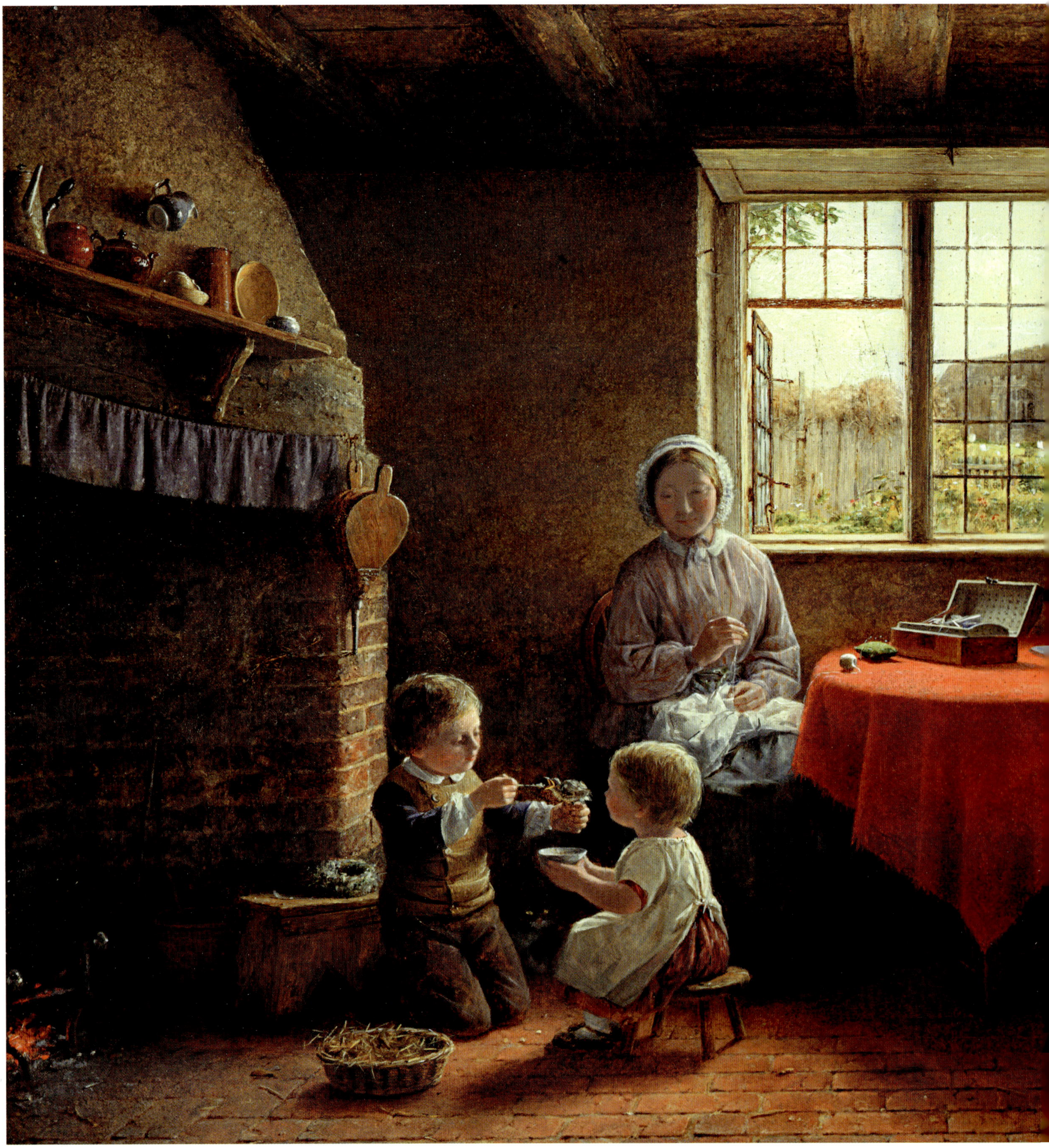

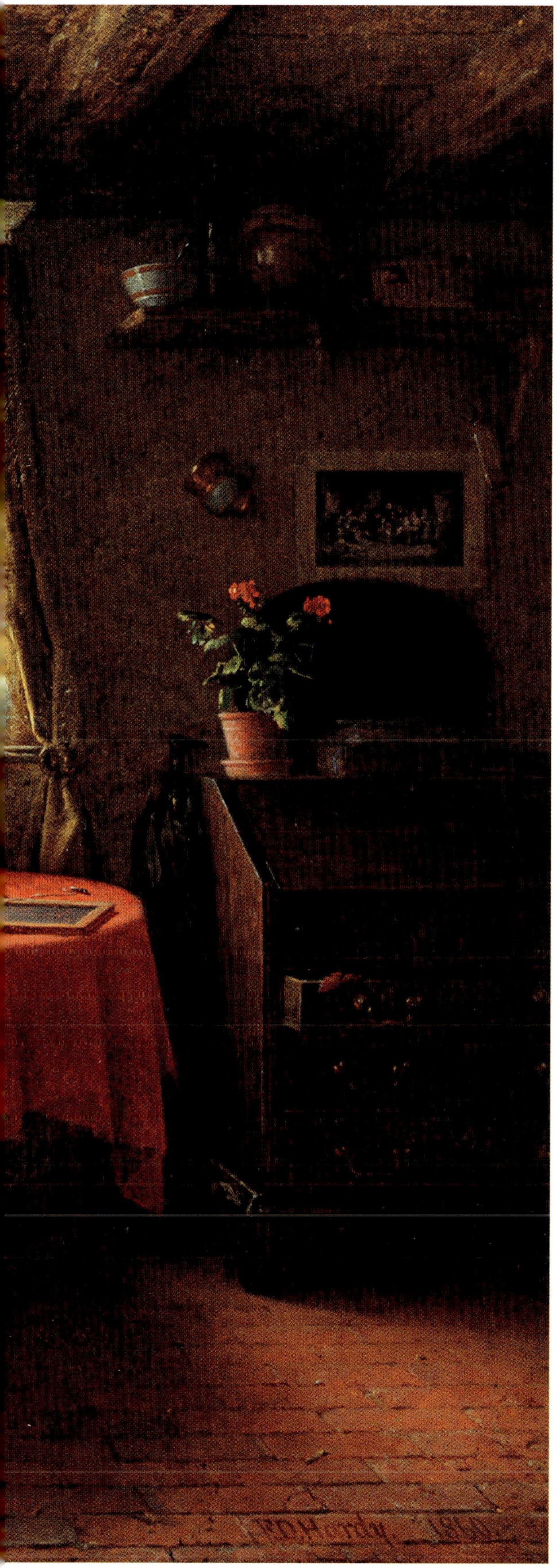

First Born (Plate 30) reportedly bears the date 1853, but the quality of the work on the figures suggests that it was painted in the late 1850s or early 1860s, when F.D. Hardy also painted pictures such as *The Happiness of Home* (1858) and *The Three Orphans* (1860).

The green-eyed cat is well positioned just behind two children feeding a nestling in *The Three Orphans* (1860) (Plate 31). The view through the window is of Cranbrook church as seen from a position close to the cottage that is now Cranbrook Museum. But the interior does not correspond to any of the existing cottages in the area.[37]

Plate 30 (below): First Born, 1853[36]
Frederick Daniel Hardy. Oil on panel. 23.7 x 30.5cm. Private Collection

Plate 31 (left): The Three Orphans, 1860
Frederick Daniel Hardy. Oil on wood panel. 26.7 x 35.6cm. Private Collection

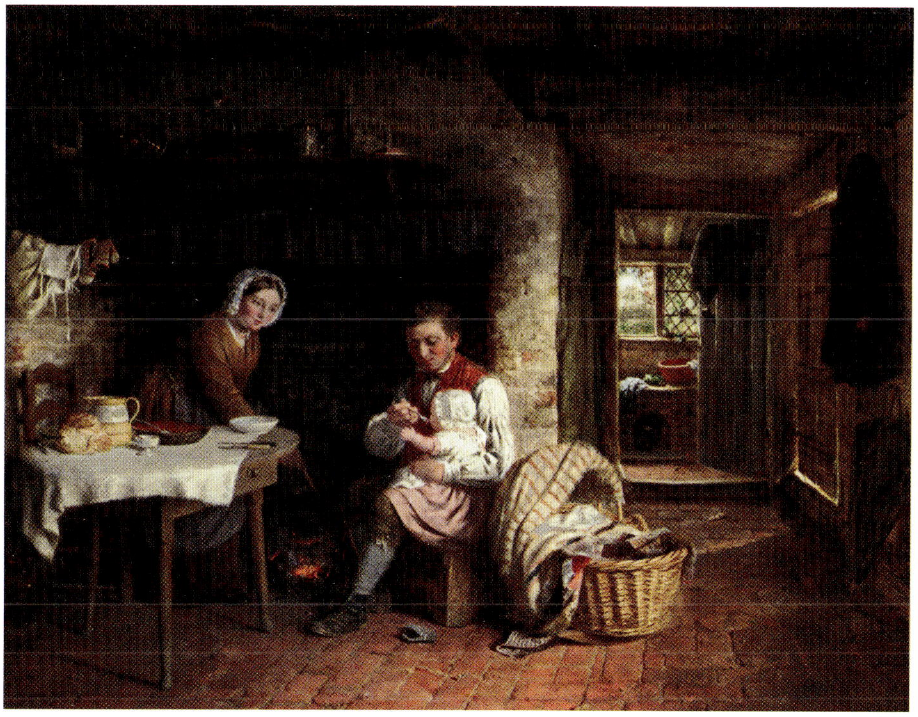

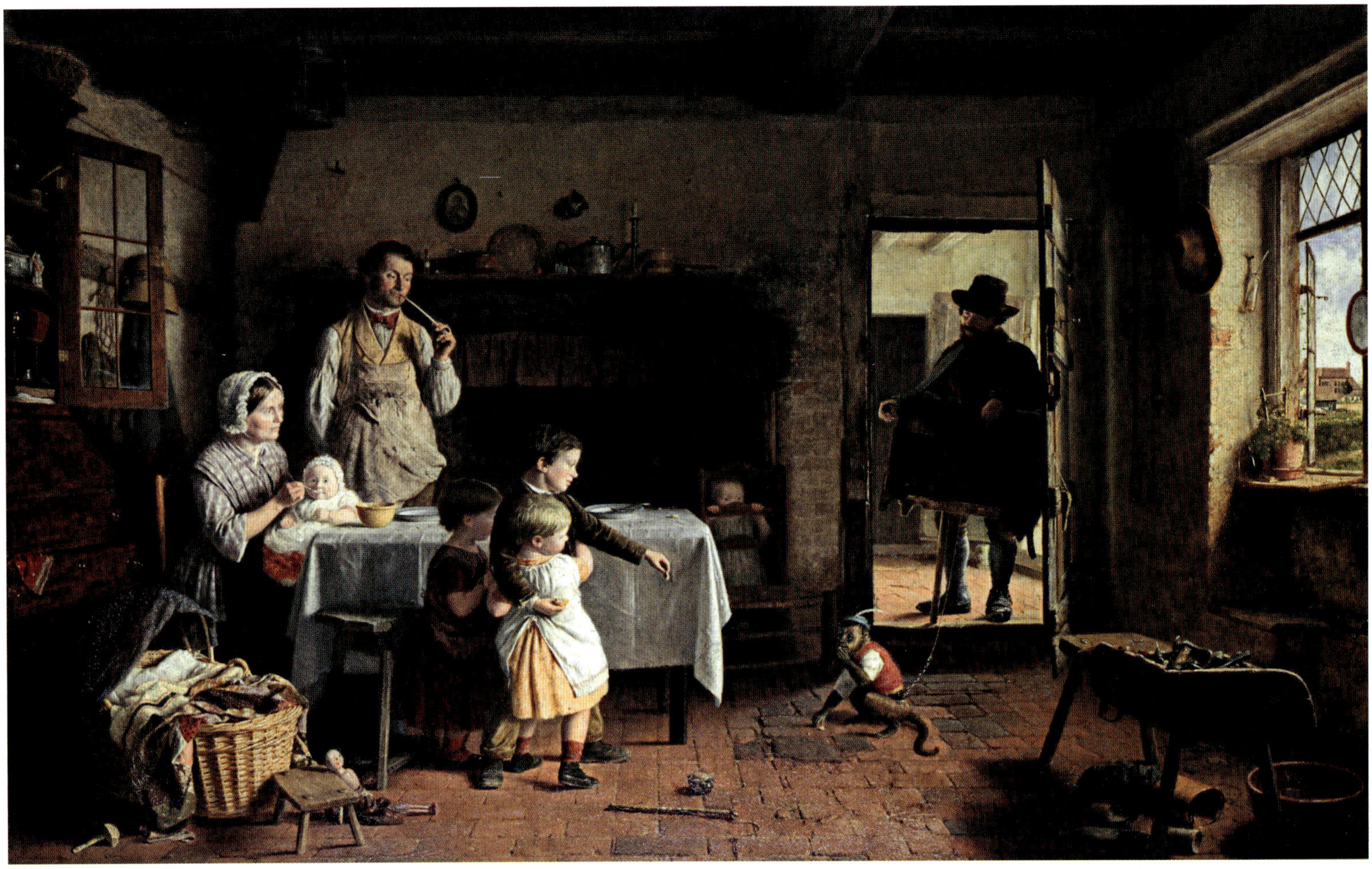

CHAPTER TWO

Frederick Daniel Hardy and George Hardy: after 1860

F.D. Hardy's Style Evolves

The Foreign Guest (1859) (Plate 32), a picture that includes an organ grinder and his monkey, marks a turning point in F.D. Hardy's artistic development; it appears to be the first composition in which he groups together a larger number of figures to produce a narrative.

It was one of three pictures he exhibited at the Royal Academy in 1859, as described by *The Art Journal*:

> The guest is the monkey of a peripatetic Italian musician and the scene of his entertainment is a cottage, the inhabitants of which – father, mother and children – welcome their visitor in the manner most acceptable to him, that is, by feeding him. It is equal to the author's best works.[38]

During the 1860s Hardy painted the pictures for which he is most well known, including *The Volunteers* (1860), *Early Sorrow* (1861), *The Sweep* (1862), *The Young Photographers* (1862), *The Doctor* (1863), *Try this Pair* (1864), *Baby's Birthday* (1865), *The Dismayed Artist* (1866) and *The Midnight Feast* (1866).

The Volunteers (Plate 33) shows children playing at soldiers and was exhibited at the Royal Academy in 1860, the year after the establishment of the Volunteer Corps, a home defence organisation made up of part-time volunteer soldiers. At first sight it is simply an amusing scene. But the serious expression and stiff pose of the Grenadier Guard in full-dress uniform, the woman whose back is turned, the long shadows of the children and the fallen skittles on the floor (the head of a broken skittle has rolled into the shadow of a table leg) reminded the Victorians of the reality of the soldier's life.

Although Thomas Webster was F.D. Hardy's mentor and teacher, Hardy became a significant influence on the work of Webster and helped him develop new themes in the latter part of his life, beginning in the early 1860s.[39] One of Webster's best paintings, *Roast Pig* (1862) (Plate 34), is significantly different to his previous work. It reflects the influence that F.D. Hardy's

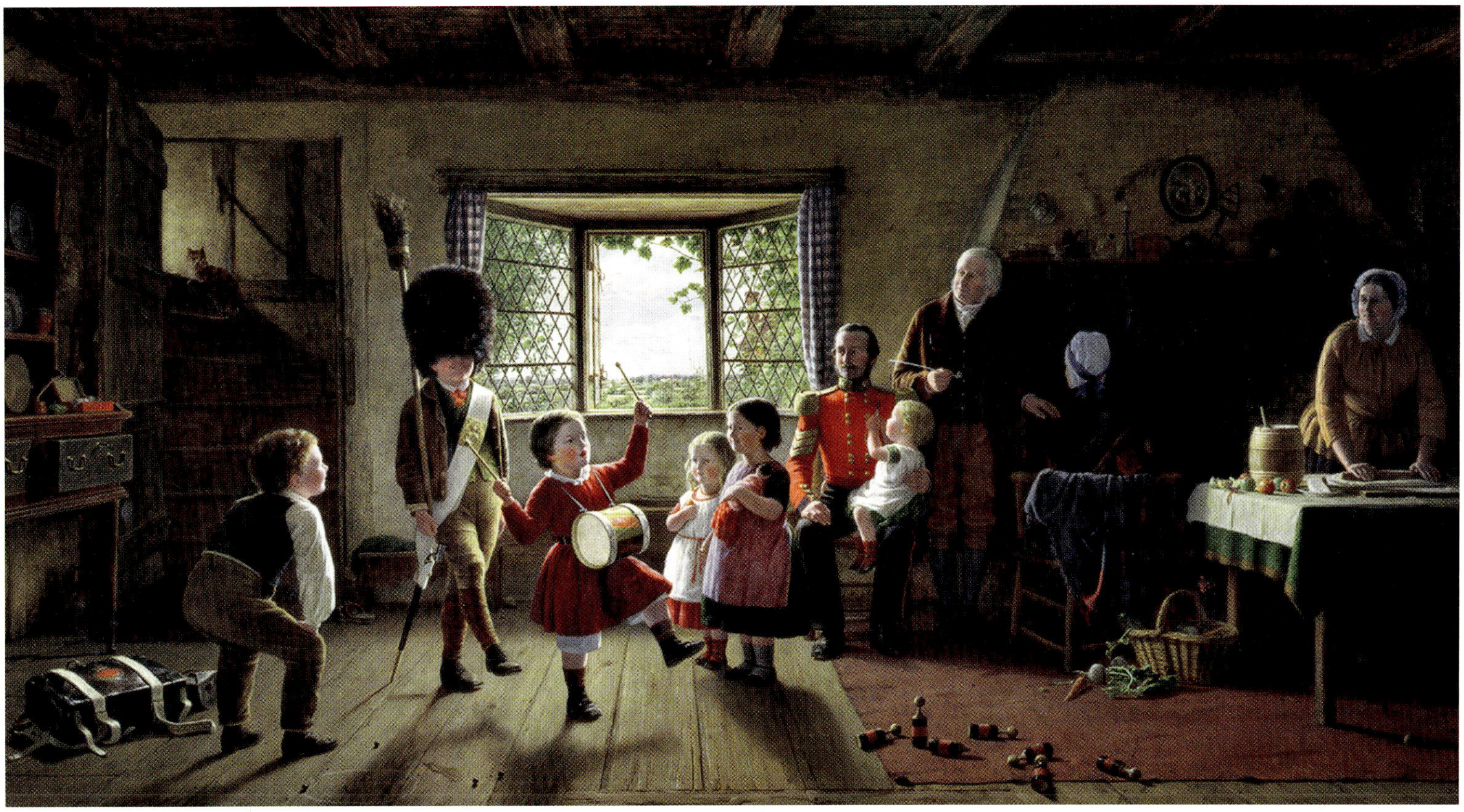

paintings, such as *The Volunteers,* had on Webster's work. Hardy was by this time painting more complex narratives than Webster and the figures were carefully arranged in a horizontal interior space with great attention to detail and lighting.

A reviewer's comment on *Early Sorrow* (Plate 35) probably indicates how many Victorians interpreted the picture's narrative:

... we must not pass without a word of recognition [for] Mr F.D. Hardy's cottage scene of *Early Sorrow*. The dead goldfinch taken from his empty cage, with the medicine cup and spoon still by its side, is drawn on a toy cart by the children in mock funeral procession; the eldest of the boys marching wand in hand at its head, and two little girls with

Plate 32 (opposite page): The Foreign Guest, 1859
Frederick Daniel Hardy.
Oil on panel. 35.4 x 51.3cm.
PRIVATE COLLECTION

Plate 33 (above): The Volunteers, 1860
Frederick Daniel Hardy.
Oil on panel. 63.5 x 113.5cm.
YORK MUSEUMS TRUST

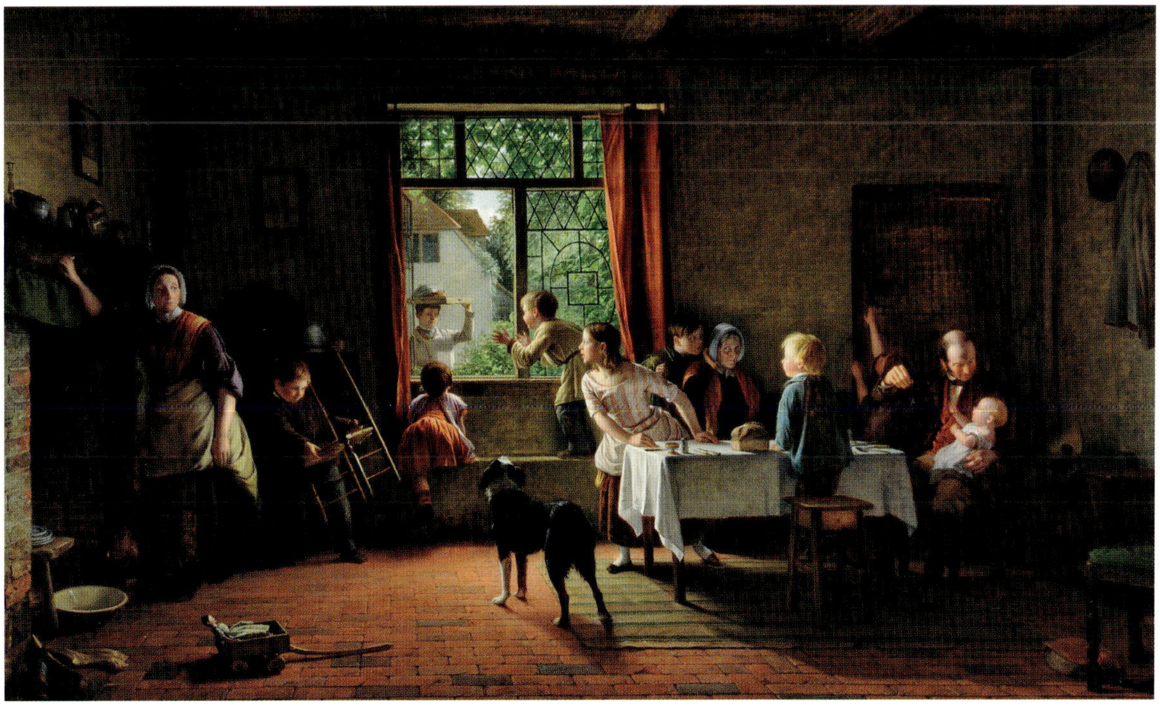

Plate 34: Roast Pig, 1862
Thomas Webster RA. Oil on canvas. 72.4 x 118.8cm.
MUSEUMS SHEFFIELD

their capes over their heads following as mourners. Another child is [a] grave-digger outside. Perhaps there should be (but perhaps there is, and we have overlooked it), in the father who pauses at his work, in the mother, or in some mute signs about the house, covert suggestion of a past reality, from which the children learnt the manner of their play. [40]

The Young Photographers (Plate 36) is one of Hardy's best pictures. By the early 1860s he was able to handle with greater confidence a more complex composition: the viewer's attention moves from the children playing in the foreground to their mother coping with her many tasks, then to their father who is outside the home talking to potential customers and finally to the photographic studio in the background. As always, attention to details such as the torn wallpaper gave clues for interpreting the narrative. Hardy and his wife both had a *carte de visite* made at about this time, by "Barns Bros., Ashford, Tenterden & Cranbrook". But the scene in *The Young Photographers* may be at Tunbridge Wells; the picture was bequeathed to Tunbridge Wells Museum by E.R. Ashton whose father, Alfred Ashton of Camden Park, Tunbridge Wells, acquired the painting in 1862.

F.D. Hardy seems to have been the only Victorian artist to paint a major picture about the work of photographers. From his photograph album, it appears that F.D. Hardy might have been an amateur photographer himself. Hardy painted his picture at a time when the relationship between art and photography was often discussed amongst artists and photographers such as Julia Margaret Cameron and Henry Peach Robinson. John Ruskin made large numbers of photographs, but declared that although photographs were popularly supposed to be "true" "...this truth of mere transcript has nothing to do with Art properly so called; and will never supersede it." In the 1850s Henry Peach Robinson produced pictorial narratives, in a style similar to paintings of domestic interiors, by combining several negatives. Prince Albert collected Robinson's photographs. Against the backdrop of debate about art and photography, Hardy produced a particularly imaginative composition and narrative. He selected the details with care and made particularly effective use of the internal space and the views outside the house. Hardy may have been especially interested in the relationship between photography and painting as his style was based very much on a detailed portrayal of interiors.

A typical contemporary comment on the narrative in *The Young Photographers* noted:

Among the Academy pictures let us add to our recognition of the excellence of Mr F.D. Hardy's *Sweep*, a word for his

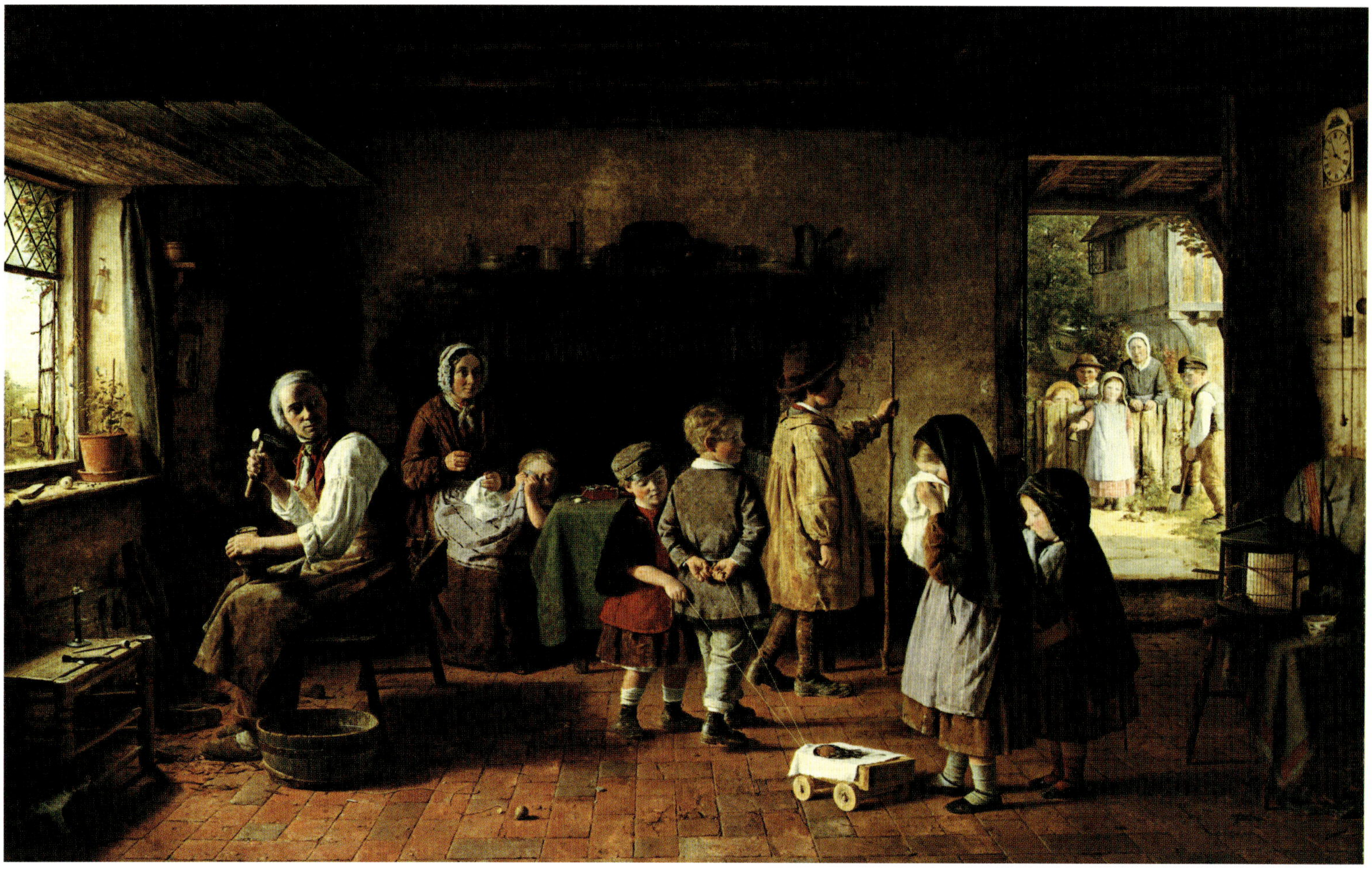

Plate 35: Early Sorrow, 1861
Frederick Daniel Hardy. Oil on canvas. 34.3 x 21.6cm. Private Collection

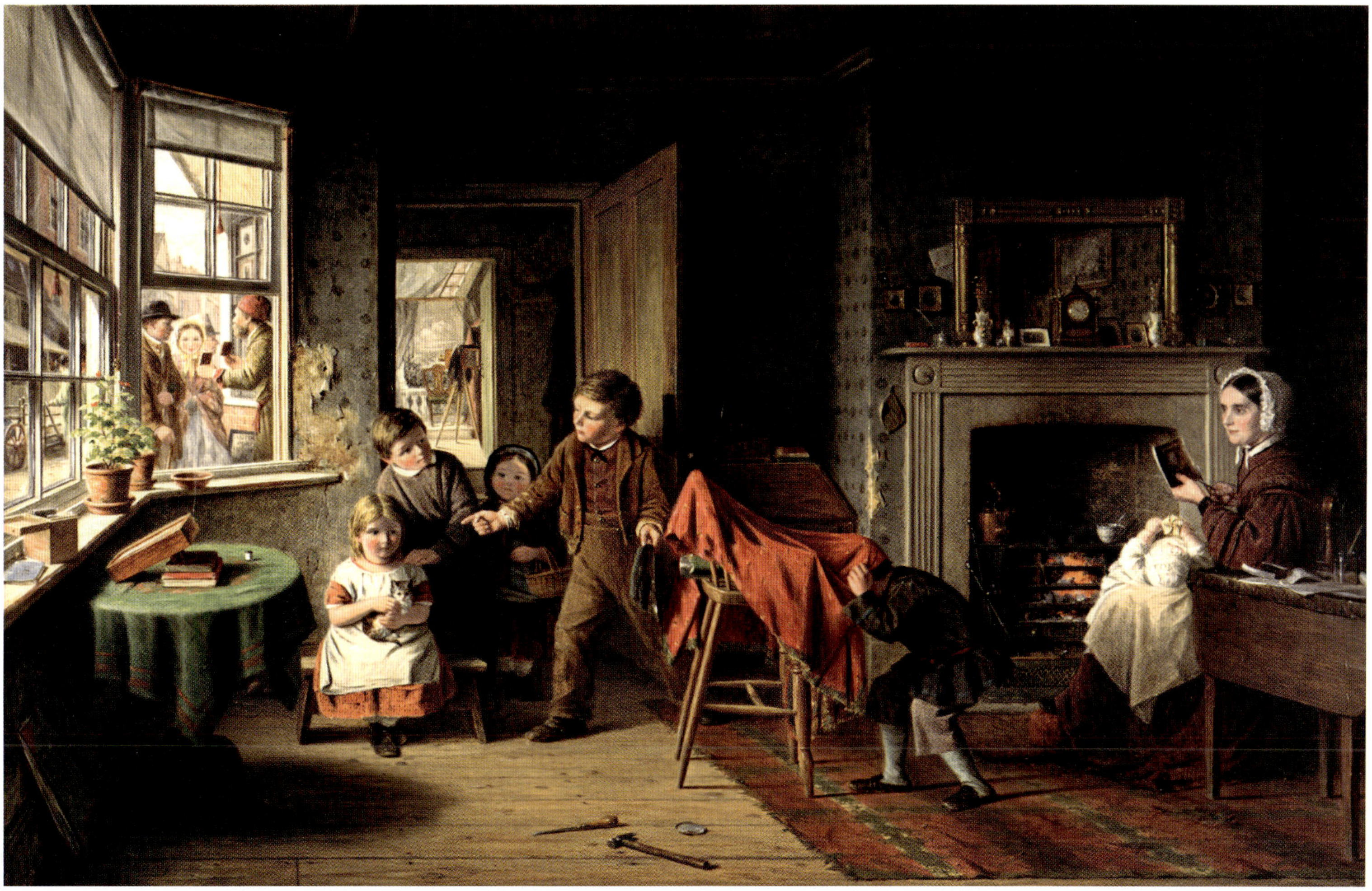

Plate 36: The Young Photographers, 1862
Frederick Daniel Hardy. Oil on canvas. 38.1 x 53.3cm. TUNBRIDGE WELLS MUSEUM AND ART GALLERY[41]

Young Photographers, which, though less good, pleasantly represents imitative sport in the children of a poor country photographer. The out-of-window suggestion of the noiseless summer street in a country town, with the photographer's man at the outer door, the father through a perspective of room visible in his den, the careful mother, near the light-hearted children, engaged in her household duty, are all pleasantly set forth, and the picture goes far to confirm the impression strongly made by his other work this year, that Mr Hardy is on the way up to high rank of his profession.[42]

Paintings such as *The Young Photographers* have retained their appeal; Christopher Wood wrote:

Playing at Doctors [The Doctor] and *The Young Photographers* are typical of Hardy's work – charming, humorous, rarely over-sentimental and beautifully observed. The details of his interiors are always scrupulously accurate too, a wonderful source of information about interior decoration. There is of course, a certain rosy unreality about all these pictures. The children are never noisy, cruel, or sick, like the peasants of Brouwer and Ostade; they never fight, or break things, as children always will. But they remain, as Baudelaire found them, "charming, intimate glimpses of home."[43]

And Lionel Lambourne thought *The Young Photographers* and *The Doctor* "so full of anecdote, are brilliantly successful in avoiding obvious humour because Hardy firmly and unpretentiously conveys a feeling of actuality, of surroundings which create the illusion of real space." [44]

The Sweep (Plate 37) was F.D. Hardy's most successful picture. It was exhibited at the Royal Academy in 1862. He painted at least ten versions in oils, three in pastels or coloured chalks and one in watercolour and body colour.[45] The version illustrated, dated 1866, is at the Wolverhampton Art Gallery, which has the finest collection of paintings by F.D. Hardy from the Cartwright bequest.

Hardy illustrates in *The Sweep* the striking contrasts in Victorian life – the spotless children in clean linen and the bare foot of the man who is no doubt covered in soot in the chimney. Though the chimney sweep is an adult, as can be seen from the size of his feet and his boots, some observers (including the art correspondents of *The Illustrated London News* and *The Morning Post*) assumed that the sweep was a child. The same mistake has been made in recent publications.[46] In fact, in 1862 thousands of children *were* still employed as chimney sweeps, despite this being

Plate 37: The Sweep, 1866
Frederick Daniel Hardy. Oil on canvas. 35.6 x 51.4cm.

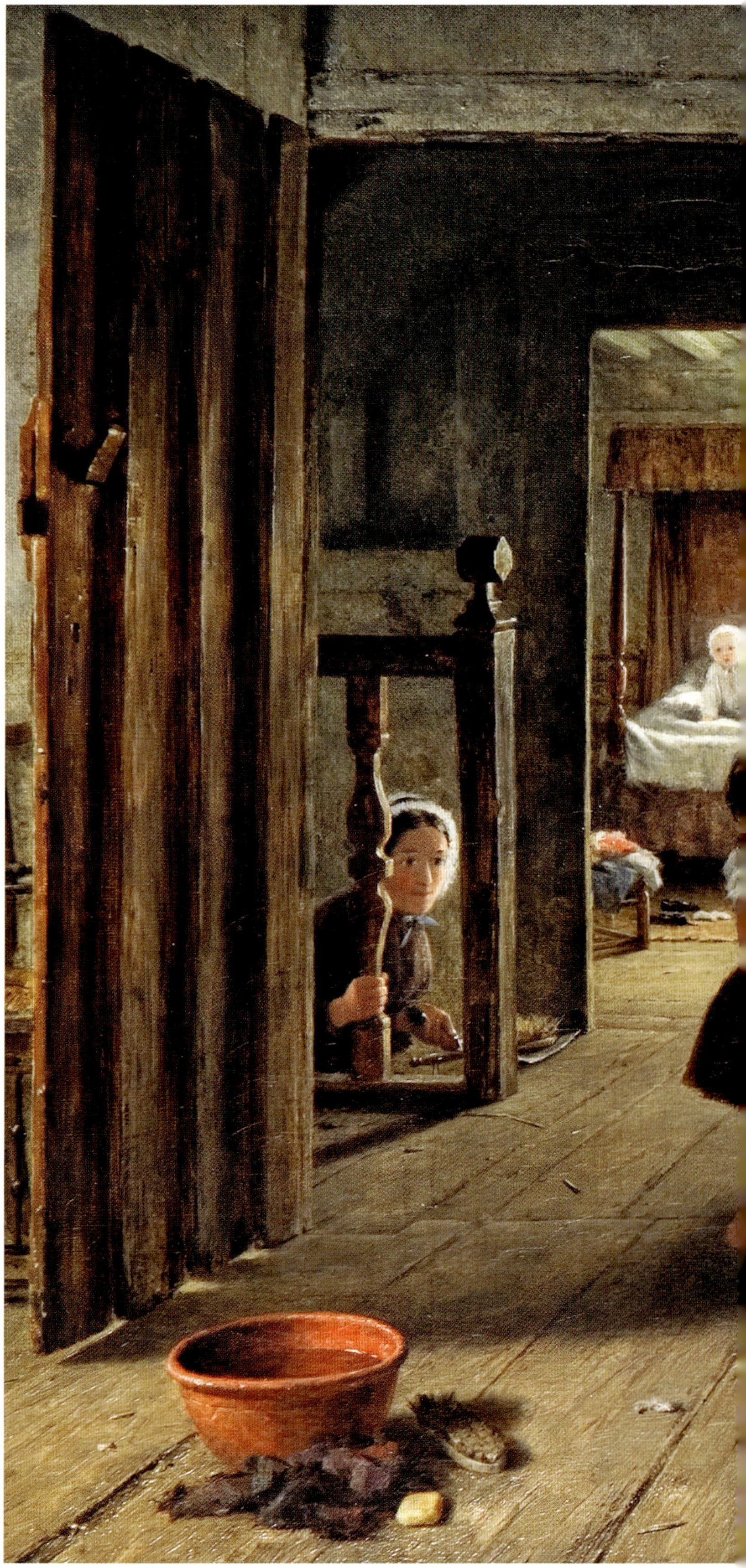

illegal under the 1840 Act. The numbers were only markedly reduced following the Act of 1864 that imposed heavy fines and imprisonment for non-compliance. The scene of the painting is in the building that is now the Cranbrook Museum, in the first floor room that is devoted to an exhibition about the Cranbrook Colony; the fireplace, door and banister are still as they were in Hardy's time. The Museum building also appears to be the setting for *The Mother* (1870) (Plate 49) and *A Crash*, a picture of children who have accidentally overturned a table, which was exhibited at the Royal Academy in 1860.

Contemporary comments on the painting reflect either the concerns or indifference of various reviewers to the conditions of sweeps and climbing boys. James Dafforne, an art critic for *The Art Journal* for more than 30 years, wrote in 1875 that the "subject may be classed among the humorous or the grave, as the spectator chooses". He continued:

> The picture had its origin in what the painter saw one morning in his own house: a man was preparing to sweep a chimney, and had, as usual, spread his cloth in front of the fireplace before commencing his operations, when two of the artist's young children, curious to see what was going on, stood in the room gazing with mingled wonder and fear at the sooty figure just disappearing behind the screen. Mr. Hardy chanced to get sight of the "situation" and subsequently transferred it to canvas: the amusing incident is most happily represented. At the sale of the late Mr. Eden's collection, a few months ago, "The Sweep" sold for 610 guineas, three times the sum the painter originally received for it.[47]

The Art Journal commented:

> *The Sweep* (108), F.D. Hardy, wherein we see, in the early morning, two children who have risen from their beds, and are surveying with awe and wonder the operations of the sweep, who is in the chimney just within the cloth that he has spread before the fireplace. A most natural incident, very happily told.[48]

And *The Illustrated London News* thought that F.D. Hardy,

> ... has made a great stride in his little picture "The Sweep". Two children, taking advantage of their mother's absence, get up and watch with timid awe ... A younger child is crawling out of a bed in a farther room, thus affording an opportunity of interior painting, which for brilliancy and perspective effect may compare with De Hooghe. "The Young Photographers" is also distinguished by many good qualities.[49]

In its review of the 1862 Royal Academy Exhibition *The Spectator's* art critic thought that the *The Sweep* "by Mr. F.D. Hardy, long known as a painter of delicately-finished interiors" was "one of the most charming, domestic pictures on the walls".[50]

The art correspondent of *The Morning Post* evidently thought

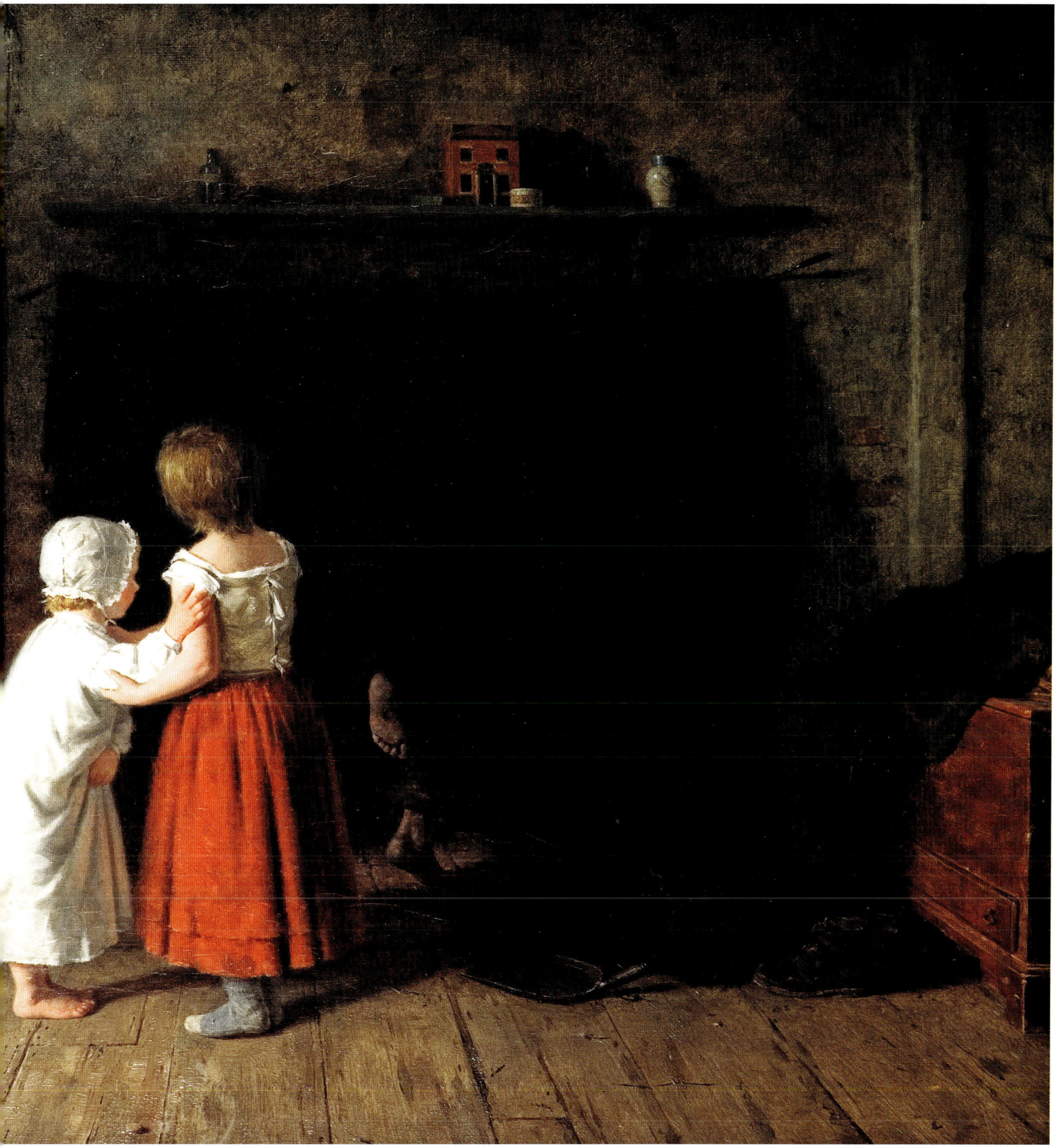

that the chimney sweep was a child. Although noting that a "climbing boy" was contrary to law, the correspondent called the scene a "simple homely incident". His only concern seemed to be the "discomfort [for the household] produced by a visit from a climbing boy". He wrote:

Amongst the most successful pictures in the Exhibition of the Royal Academy in 1862 was an attractive little work by Mr. F.D. Hardy, called "The Sweep." It represented the interior of a cottager's dwelling, with all the appearance of discomfort produced by a visit from a climbing boy, who is

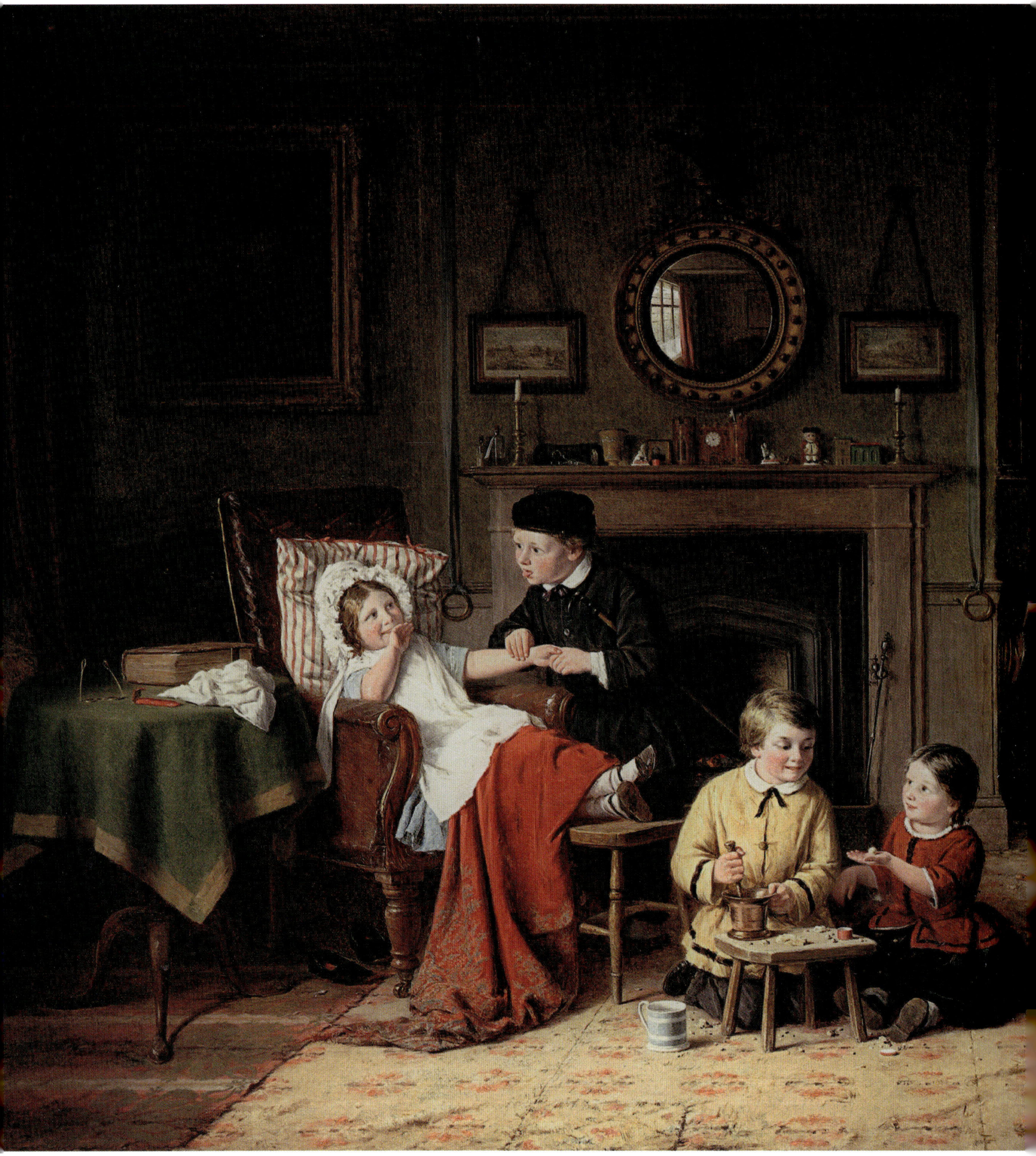

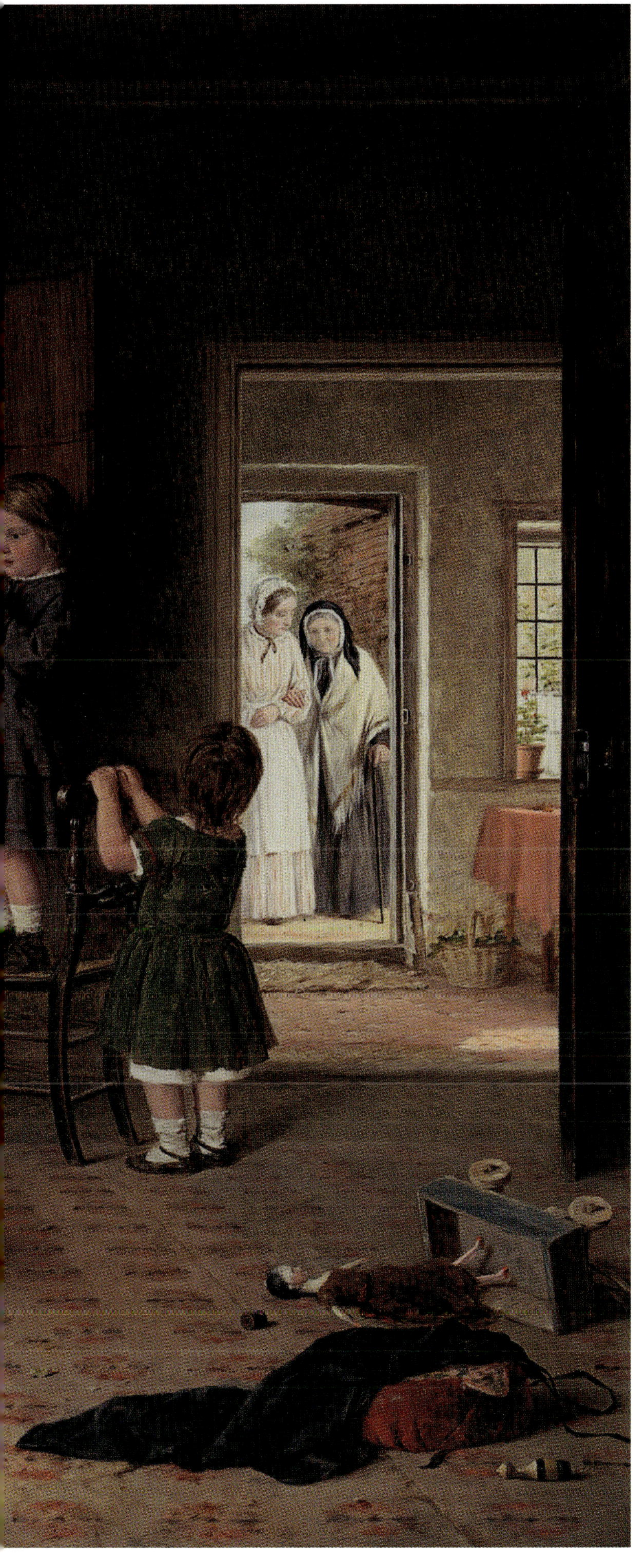

in the act of ascending the chimney (contrary to law even in those days), his begrimed feet and ankles just perceptible beneath the black cloth which has been hung in front of the fireplace to prevent the soot from doing any serious mischief. The children, sleeping in an adjoining apartment, have been aroused by the unusual noise and disturbance, and have hastened, half-clad, to bear witness to the movements of the little operator, their mother, who has risen with the lark — and the sweep — being visible on the stairs with her dust-pan, to be in readiness for subsequent purposes. There are three children prominently placed; and although the face of one of them is entirely concealed, and those of the other two are only partially exposed, the feeling of surprise and curiosity which they might be supposed to express, under the circumstances, is admirably conveyed, whilst a more juvenile urchin, who is not quite old enough to run about without assistance, is seen in the distance through a communicating door, endeavouring to crawl off the bed, to partake of the same happy privilege which the rest are enjoying.[51]

The Times art critic commented:

Small in dimensions, but very luminous and capital in character, Mr. Hardy's little picture, "The Sweep" (108), attracts and rewards an attention not deserved by many more ambitious canvasses. Two children, one of them an early truant from bed, watch with awe the mysterious disappearance of the sweep under the black sacking which hides the chimney-mouth. Through an open door is seen the nursery, with another little urchin, climbing out of bed, just in time to miss the sight. The childish sense of mystery is capitally expressed, and the picture is a natural and vigorous piece of simple interior painting, with a great deal of light and air in it.[52]

The Doctor (1863) (Plate 38) is another of F.D. Hardy's best paintings from the 1860s. Lionel Lambourne thought that,

The painting, so full of diverse anecdote, is brilliantly successful in avoiding obvious humour because Hardy firmly and unpretentiously conveys a feeling of actuality, of surroundings, which create the illusion of a specific sense of place. These qualities can also be seen in some of the artist's small still-life studies of virtually empty room interiors in the humble cottages around Cranbrook. They are intensely realized because he knew them so well.[53]

The Victorians' love of narrative in paintings is reflected in the newspapers of the time; a typical example is this commentary on *The Doctor* in a review of paintings at the Royal Academy exhibition of 1863:

Plate 38: The Doctor, 1863
Frederick Daniel Hardy. Oil on panel. 55.9 x 76.2cm. Private Collection

ROYAL ACADEMY. THIRD NOTICE. In his amusing picture, entitled "The Doctor", Mr. F.D. Hardy has treated a comic subject in a spirit of congenial drollery. A merry band of boys and girls, to whom life is a jest and the world simply a play-ground for children to disport in, have gained admission into their grandmother's bed-room during the temporary absence of the poor old lady, who has been ailing for sometime past, and is now taking a walk around the garden in company with her daughter.

The children, who have doubtless had many opportunities of witnessing the interviews between their venerable relative and her doctor, are now mimicking a scene of sickness with waggish humour. The eldest girl, who personates the grandmother, is decked out in a white-frilled night-cap and a red shawl, and, propped up with pillows, awaits in a huge arm-chair the visit of her medical attendant. This important personage is represented by the biggest boy in the party, who, swaggering pompously into the room with his father's walking-stick under his arm, feels the patient's pulse with a ridiculous affectation of learning and puts out his tongue to show his patient how she should perform the like ungraceful but indispensable feat.

This proceeding is too much for the gravity of the invalid, who throws herself back in her chair and bursts out laughing in the doctor's face, an irreverence which that learned pundit would resent with becoming indignation were it not that the spirit of fun is struggling hard within him, and he finds some difficulty in keeping his own countenance. About the room are grouped the other children, variously engaged in different departments of the healing art. A small boy and a still smaller girl are seated together on the floor, where they are busily employed in the innocent pharmacy of converting bread and butter into pills. They bray the bread and butter in a mortar, and produce pills about the size of thrushes' eggs. A third boy stands upon a chair near a cupboard and solemnly pours a dose of medicine out of a phial into a cup, while another child holds the chair steady and watches to give the alarm.

The opened door reveals a view of the garden, with the old lady placidly approaching. She leans upon her daughter's arm, and moves languidly along, little thinking, poor soul, how much her maladies have contributed to the enjoyment of her grandchildren. The scene is depicted with infinite humour and drollery, and all the details of the picture are painted with an accuracy that would do no discredit to the Dutch school. The threadbare carpet, the

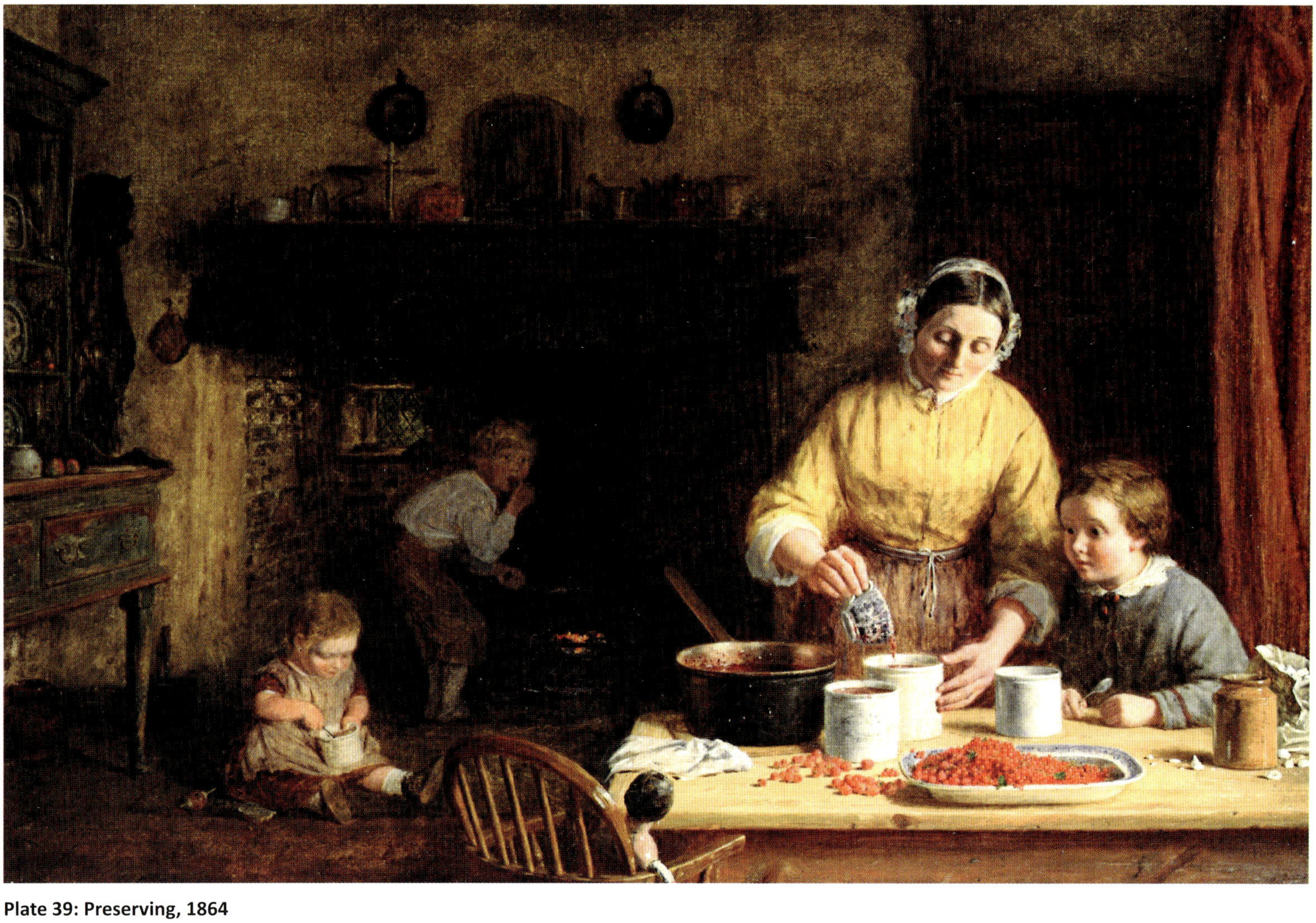

Plate 39: Preserving, 1864
Frederick Daniel Hardy. Oil on canvas. 47.5 x 66cm. Private Collection

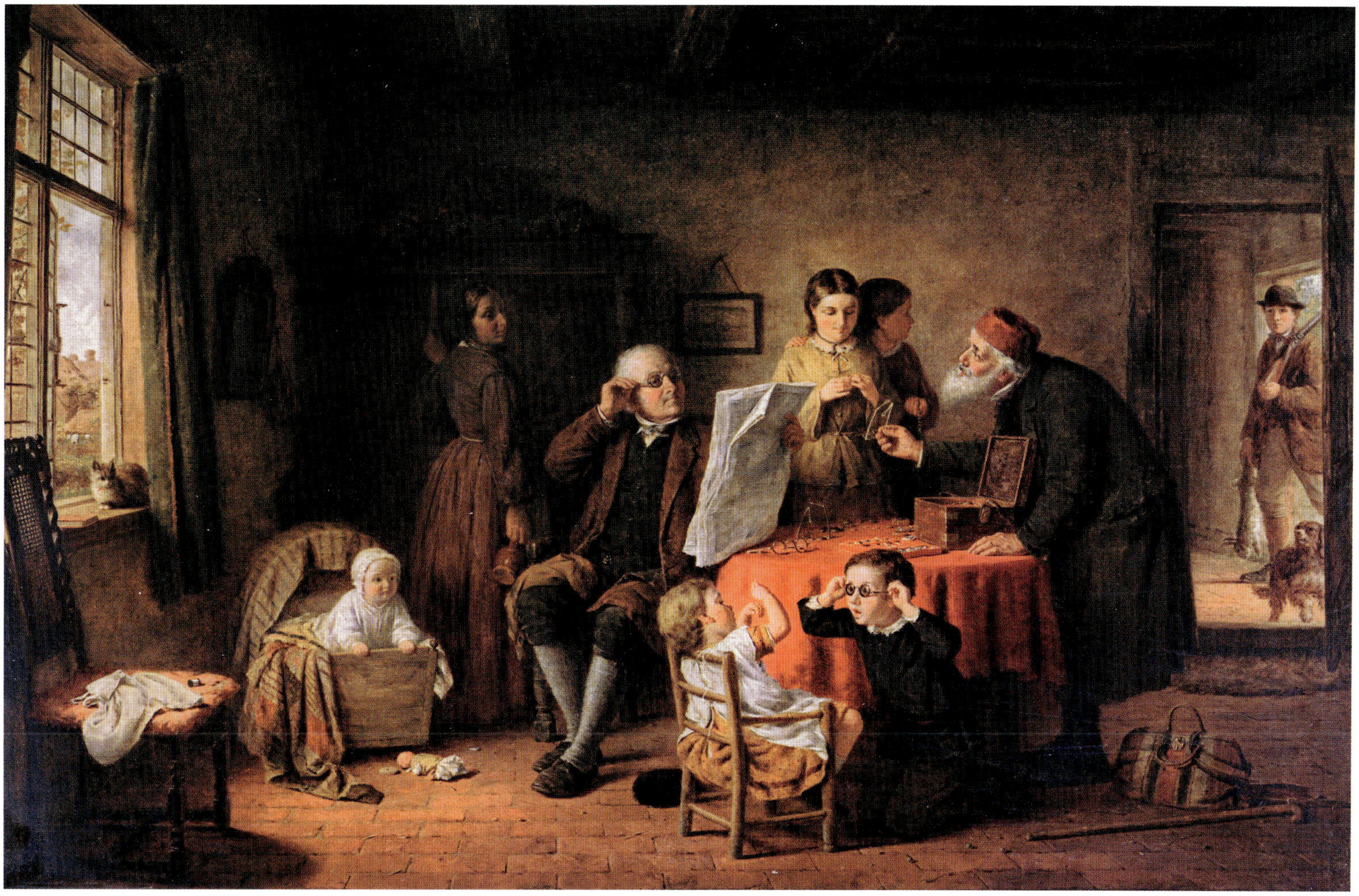

Plate 40: Try this Pair, 1864
Frederick Daniel Hardy. Oil on canvas. 27.9 x 40.6cm. GUILDHALL ART GALLERY. CITY OF LONDON CORPORATION[55]

various articles of furniture, the fragments of toys strewn about the floor, and the ornaments upon the mantelpiece, are all painted with absolute truthfulness of form and colour; and a convex glass over the fireplace has so illusive an appearance of transparency that it seems to reflect the interior of the apartment with the fidelity of a true mirror.[54]

The Art Journal was also impressed by *The Doctor*:

> But of all the pictures given up to Child's play, and they are legion, a little work called "The Doctor" by F.D. Hardy is certainly one of the best. A child shamming the invalid is bolstered up in a chair; another child invested with a cane and black cap, feeling the patient's pulse, acts as the doctor, while the two other little urchins, with pestle and mortar, are mixing and making the pills! The execution is sufficiently minute to give reality to the circumstantial narrative, without falling into excess of elaboration. The quiet humour and the quaint character which reign throughout so closely allied to Wilkie and Webster, and allied indeed to the wit and mirth which flow freely in our native literature ... [56]

In *Preserving* (1864) (Plate 39) the boy in the background is in charge of stirring the raspberry jam in a preserving pan and has apparently put his finger in the hot jam to try to taste it.

Several of Hardy's paintings of this period were relatively small pictures, such as *Try this Pair* (1864) (Plate 40). *The Leaky Roof* (Plate 41) was Hardy's Royal Academy exhibit for 1865. In the 1860s F.D. Hardy sometimes painted small versions of his Academy pictures before the final versions. An image of the smaller version of the painting is reproduced here (Plate 41); for the larger picture (Plate 42) Hardy decided to focus the composition more closely around the three figures.

The Leaky Roof was highly praised when it was exhibited at the Royal Academy and would prove to be one of F.D. Hardy's most successful paintings. It illustrates another side of life in a country cottage. Children were not always playing games or imitating their parents' activities, but often had to work hard to help their parents, in this case carrying as much water as they could. As in the case of *The Dismayed Artist* (see Plate 46), the family is portrayed as stoically dealing with the problem. There is no sentimentality, but there is a sympathetic portrayal of the characters. F.D. Hardy generates empathy and respect for the cottagers he portrayed. There is a touch of humour in the young boy carrying a large bowl up the stairs. The painting illustrates the more confident figure painting that Hardy had achieved by

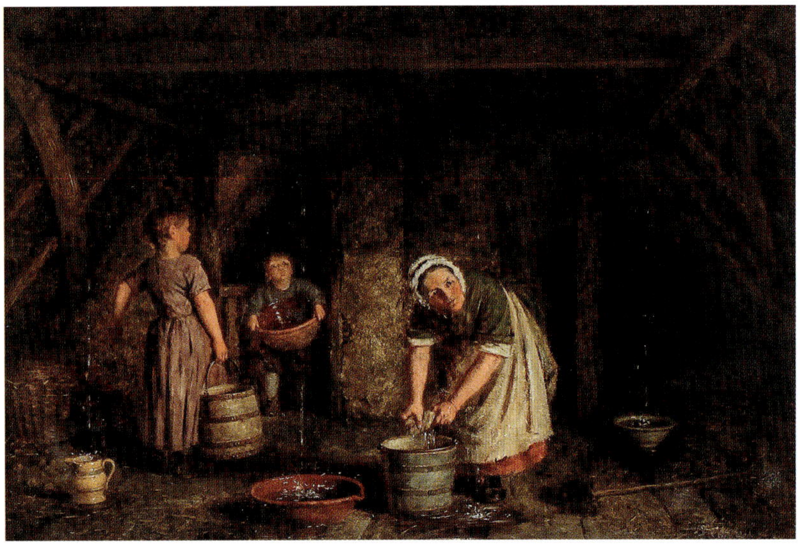

Plate 41: The Leaky Roof, 1865
Frederick Daniel Hardy. Oil on panel. 19 x 27cm. Author's Collection

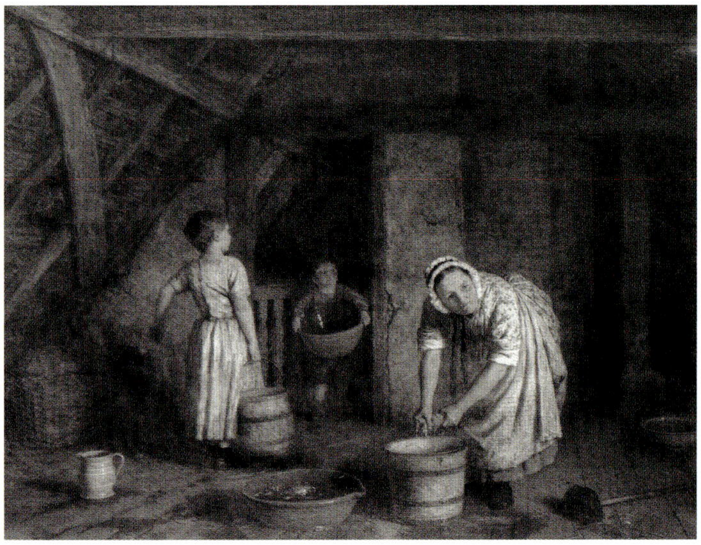

Plate 42: The Leaky Roof, 1865
Frederick Daniel Hardy. Oil on canvas. 66 x 84cm. Private Collection

the mid 1860s, as shown, for example, in the girl carrying a heavy pail, and the expression of the woman who is presumably looking out at the continuing rainfall.

The Spectator's review of the Royal Academy Exhibition included a favourable comment on *The Leaky Roof*:

Homely subjects are plentiful enough; as if our artists had taken to heart an old observation, that perpetual seeking after ideal forms and ideal beauty is in danger of producing disgust for common persons and things. The observation is probably a just one; but, allowing for difference of taste and talent in the artist, it must be concluded that it is no less difficult to treat homely subjects successfully than it is

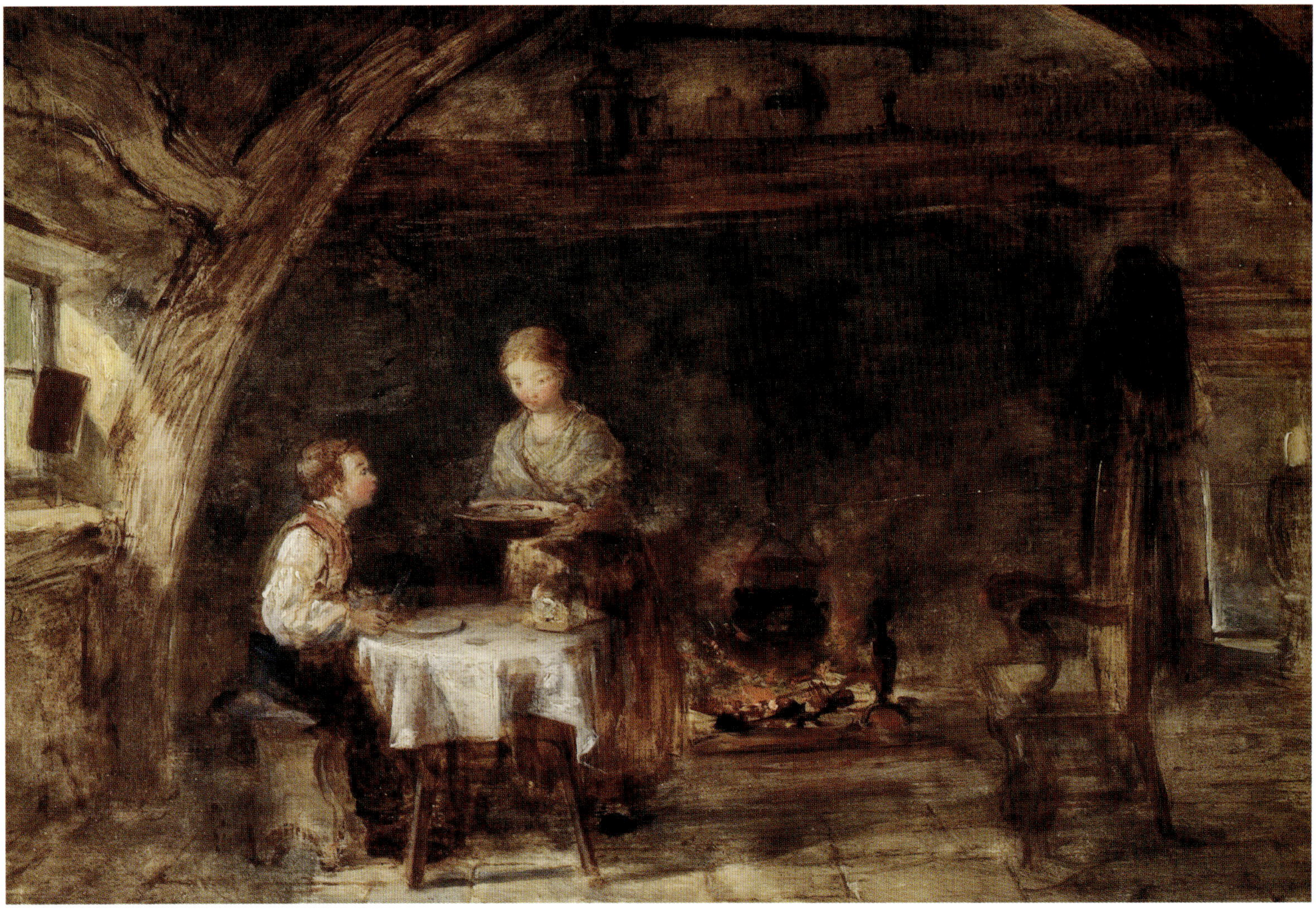

Plate 43: The Young Housekeeper
Frederick Daniel Hardy. Oil on panel. 22.5 x 33cm. © Wolverhampton Art Gallery

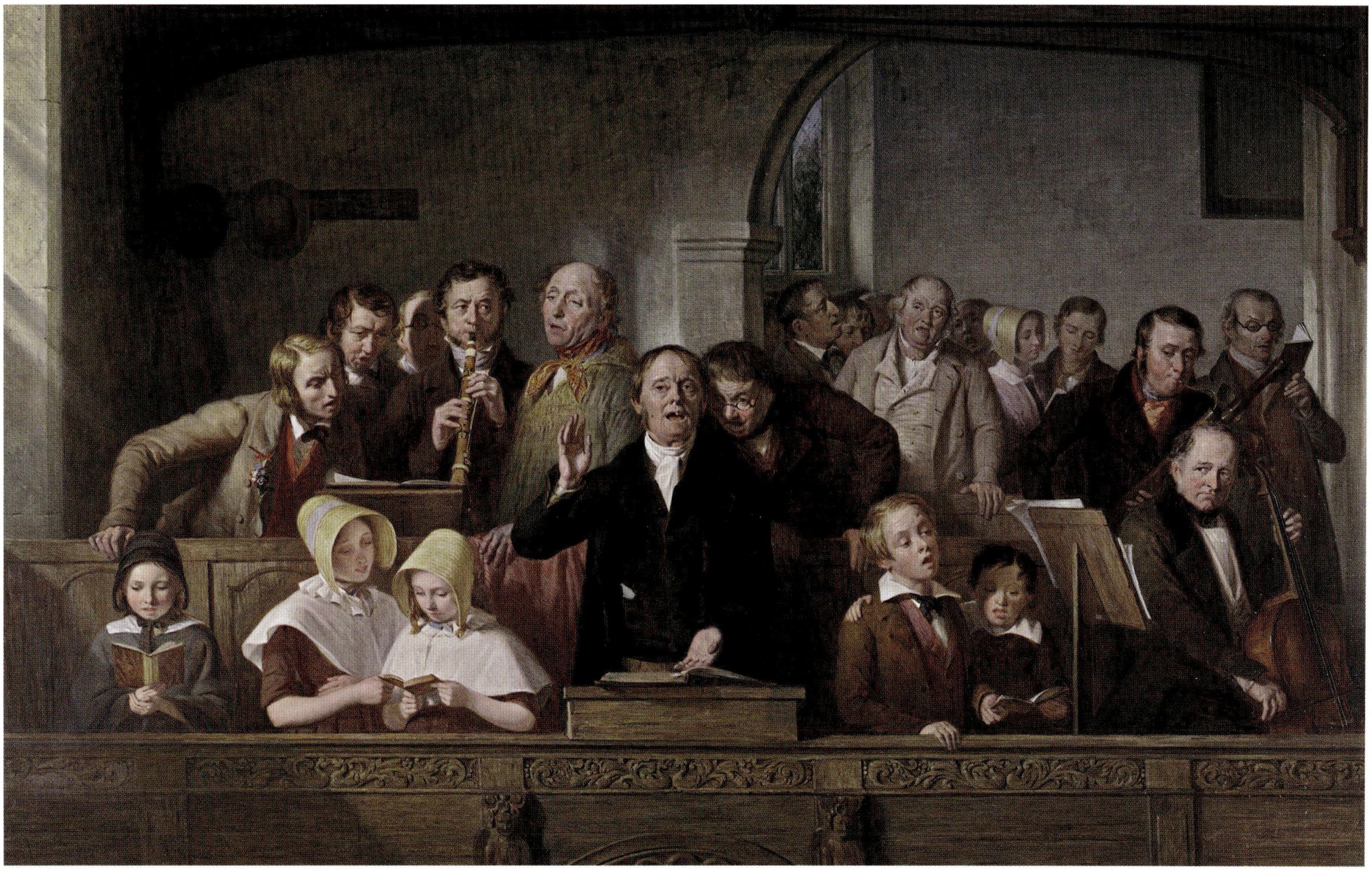

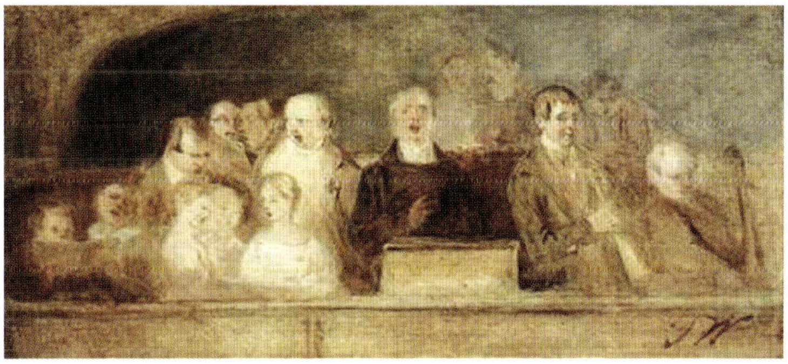

Plate 44 (above): The Village Choir, 1847
Thomas Webster RA. Oil on panel 60.4 x 91.5cm. Victoria and Albert Museum

Plate 45 (left): Study for "The Village Choir"
Thomas Webster RA. Oil on canvas. 22.9 x 46.4cm. Private Collection

to give outward shape to the creatures of imagination.

Among all the pictures taking every-day life for their subject that are annually exhibited, it is seldom that any one approaches the measure of success which Mr. F.D. Hardy has achieved in his "Leaky Roof" (265). It has more directness in the action, sobriety and simplicity in the treatment, and knowledge of the technical part of Art, than generally characterises English pictures of the same class. There is no attitudinizing, nor gaudiness of colour, none of that florid picturesqueness or "look-at-me if you please" immodesty which are the bane of half the works in the gallery, and which may be summed up in the one word vulgarity.[57]

The Art Journal thought the *The Leaky Roof* was "pre-eminent for knowledge, character and objective truth". [58] The first owner of the painting appears to have been Arthur C. Burnand of Hyde Park Gate, a wealthy insurance underwriter at Lloyds and friend of pianist and composer Clara Schumann; his extensive art collection was reviewed by The Art Journal in 1870:

"The Leaky Roof" is the title of F.D. Hardy's best picture. It is comparatively large for him; that is, much larger than the small interiors whereby he is best known. It represents a house-wife and her little maid endeavouring vainly to mop up an inundation which has burst in upon them through the thatch of their cottage.[59]

A preliminary sketch, *The Young Housekeeper* (Plate 43), suggests that Hardy's technique was similar to that of Thomas Webster, who also sketched out his compositions in brown tints. An example is Webster's oil sketch for one of his most famous paintings, *The Village Choir* (Plate 44). The Victoria and Albert Museum has a number of similar small sketches made by Webster.

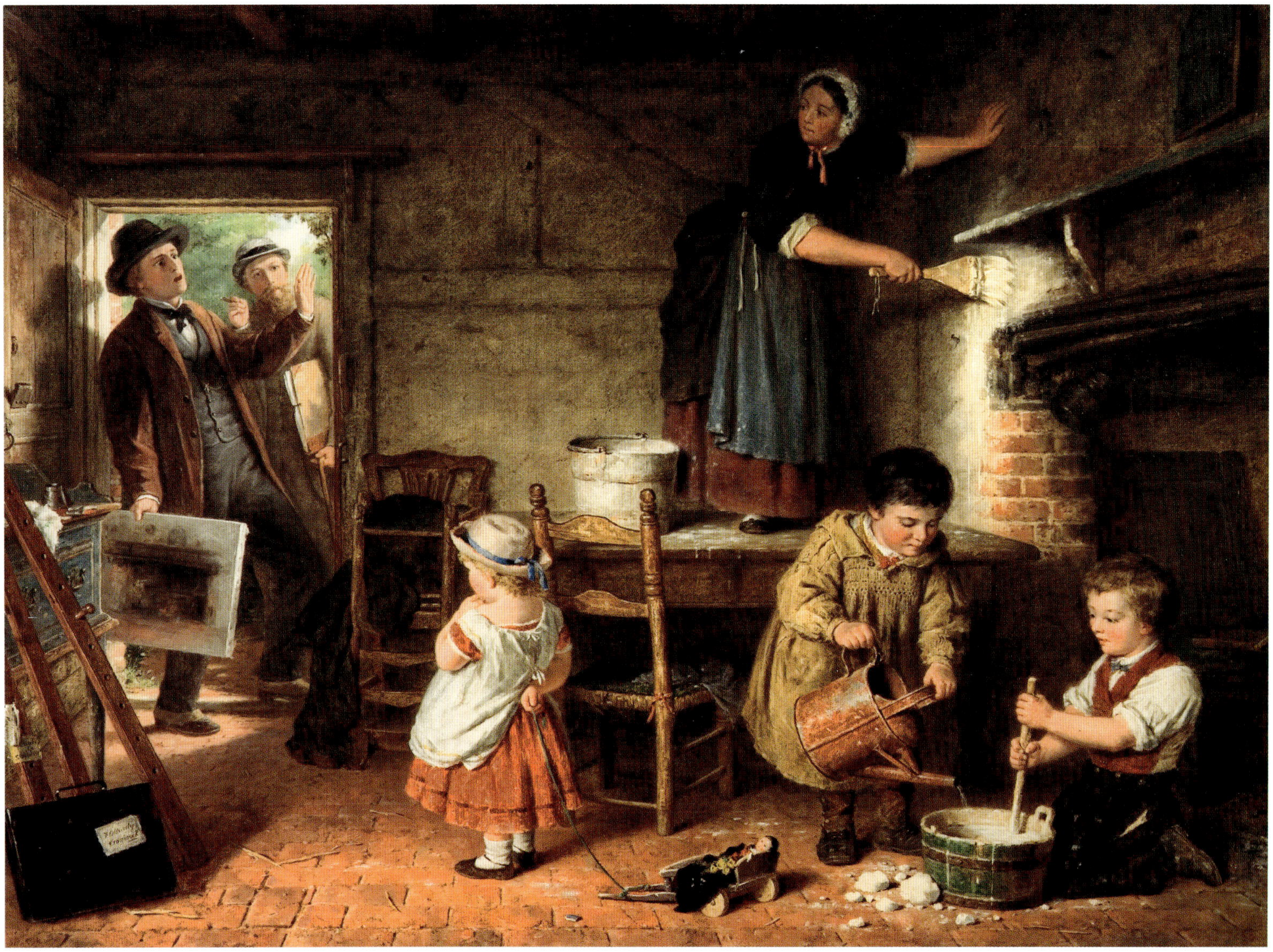

Plate 46: The Dismayed Artist, 1866
Frederick Daniel Hardy. Oil on canvas. 45.7 x 61.3cm. © Wolverhampton Art Gallery

The Dismayed Artist (1866) (Plate 46) was exhibited at the Royal Academy in the year after Hardy had exhibited *The Leaky Roof*. It is a picture of F.D. Hardy, who is thought to be accompanied by his brother George; there are similarities to photographs of both artists. They have just arrived to continue their painting, only to find that the family is intent on freshening up the walls around the inglenook, covering the picturesque, dirty surface with fresh whitewash.

George Hardy might have had a particular dislike for white-washed walls around fireplaces after *The Art Journal* had criticised one of one of his earliest pictures, *Interior of an English Cottage* (1849): "Every brick in the floor is marked; it is a successful story in all but the white round the fire-place." [60]

Baby's Birthday (1867) (Plate 47), in which the portraits of the participants are particularly well painted, is set in a tailor's cottage. The first birthday of the youngest daughter is being celebrated. Cranbrook's St Dunstan's Church is visible through the doorway.

During the 1860s, F.D. Hardy's most productive decade, his paintings received much praise and by the end of the decade he was recognised as the pre-eminent artist in painting narratives such as *Baby's Birthday*. According to the art critic of *The Times*:

> F.D. Hardy works up the cottage interiors in which his simple little dramas pass with a perfection never surpassed in our school, and his figures are always nicely introduced, and painted with good taste and a sense both of beauty and effect which are rare among English painters of this kind of subject.[61]

The same commentator was critical of Joseph Clark's paintings of interiors:

> It is a pity Mr. J. Clarke [*sic*] cannot acquire something like Mr. Hardy's nice touch and clever execution to bear out his unaffected sentiment and honest intention; but we cannot report progress in the technique of this most disappointing of young painters. ... woolly, heavy in the shadows, and unlovely in all points of execution. Mr. Clarke's choice of

models, like his execution, seems to indicate a deficient sense of what is picturesque and pleasing.

In fact, Joseph Clark continued to paint interiors for many years and was sufficiently successful to maintain a house in London and in the country.

Reading a Will (Plate 48), painted in 1869 and exhibited at the Royal Academy in the following year, marked a change in subject matter towards interiors of middle-class households, but only a few such pictures were as successful as his earlier interiors. *The Art Journal* commented:[62]

On the same wall, is "Reading a Will" (913), a first-rate specimen of the Anglo-Dutch school by F.D. Hardy. Wilkie threw into the same subject action and incident, Hardy has struck out a line on his own, and within the limits of his Art is little short of perfect.

Perhaps the culmination of critical comment on F.D. Hardy's work from 1860 to 1870 was the following assessment by Tom Taylor, art critic of *The Times,* who commented on Hardy's *The Mother* (Plate 49) and *Reading a Will*. During the 1860s Taylor, a controversial critic, had been particularly uncomplimentary about "domestic" art. Indeed, he remained highly critical of other painters of domestic scenes, such as Erskine Nicol, George Smith and Joseph Clark. But Tom Taylor thought that Hardy's *Reading a Will* was "the most complete work the artist has yet produced":

... we have no right to limit our definition or conception of art by the kind of work we may happen to like. The duty of catholic criticism is to appreciate all genuine expressions of the human imagination through the medium of form and colour. The only thing we have a right to exclude from toleration is falsehood and insincerity ...

Those who find their ideal of art in such work as Mr. A. Moore's will be apt to deny the right to the name of art to such homely painting of life as F.D. Hardy's. But it is not the less true that no pictures give more pure and innocent gratification to the crowd of visitors to the exhibition than this artist's pictures, so conscientiously and completely wrought out, and so straightforward in their appeal.

And there is genuine imagination, if of the novel-writer's order rather than the poet's, in this capital picture

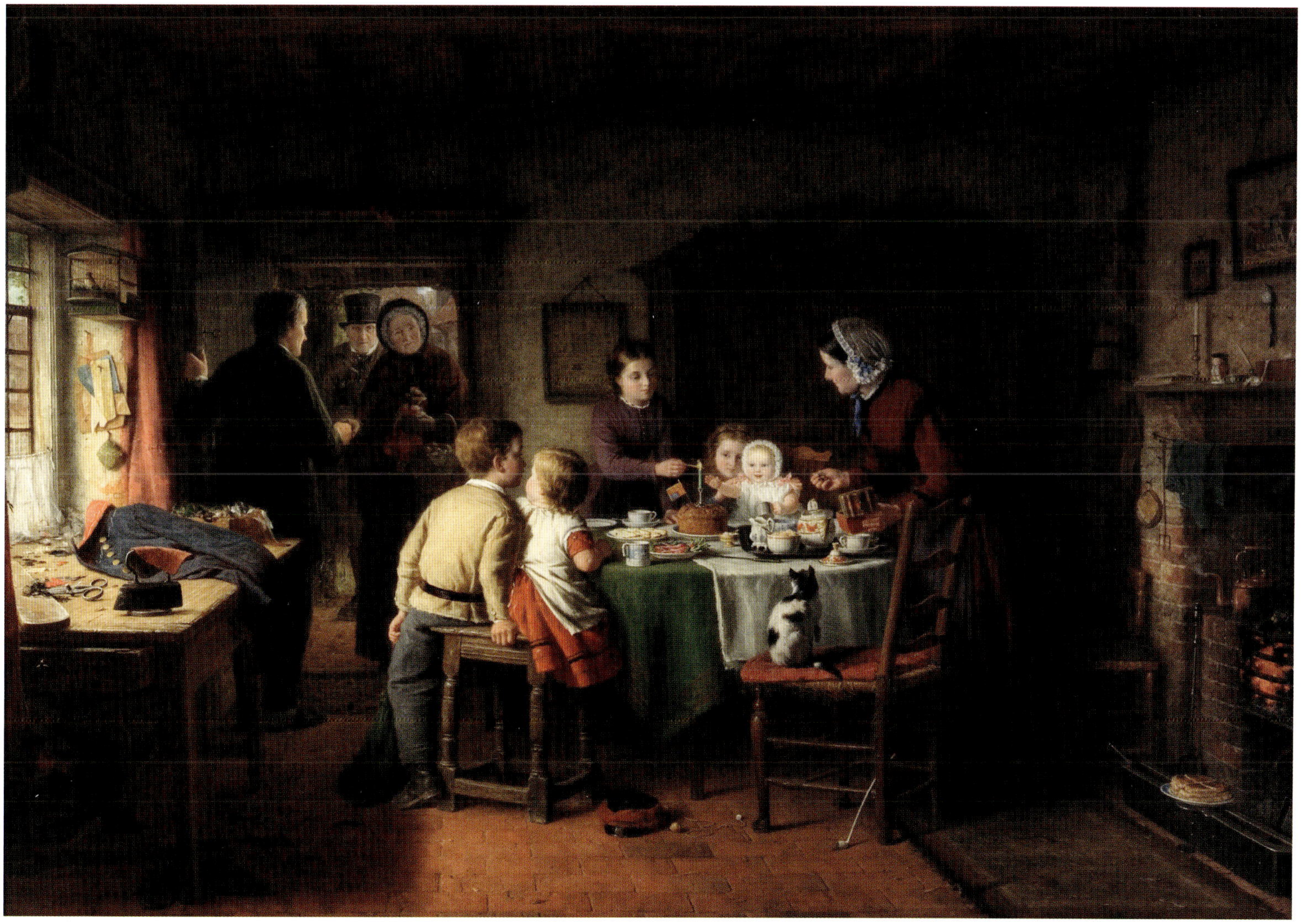

Plate 47: Baby's Birthday, 1867
Frederick Daniel Hardy. Oil on canvas. 66 x 91.5cm. © Wolverhampton Art Gallery

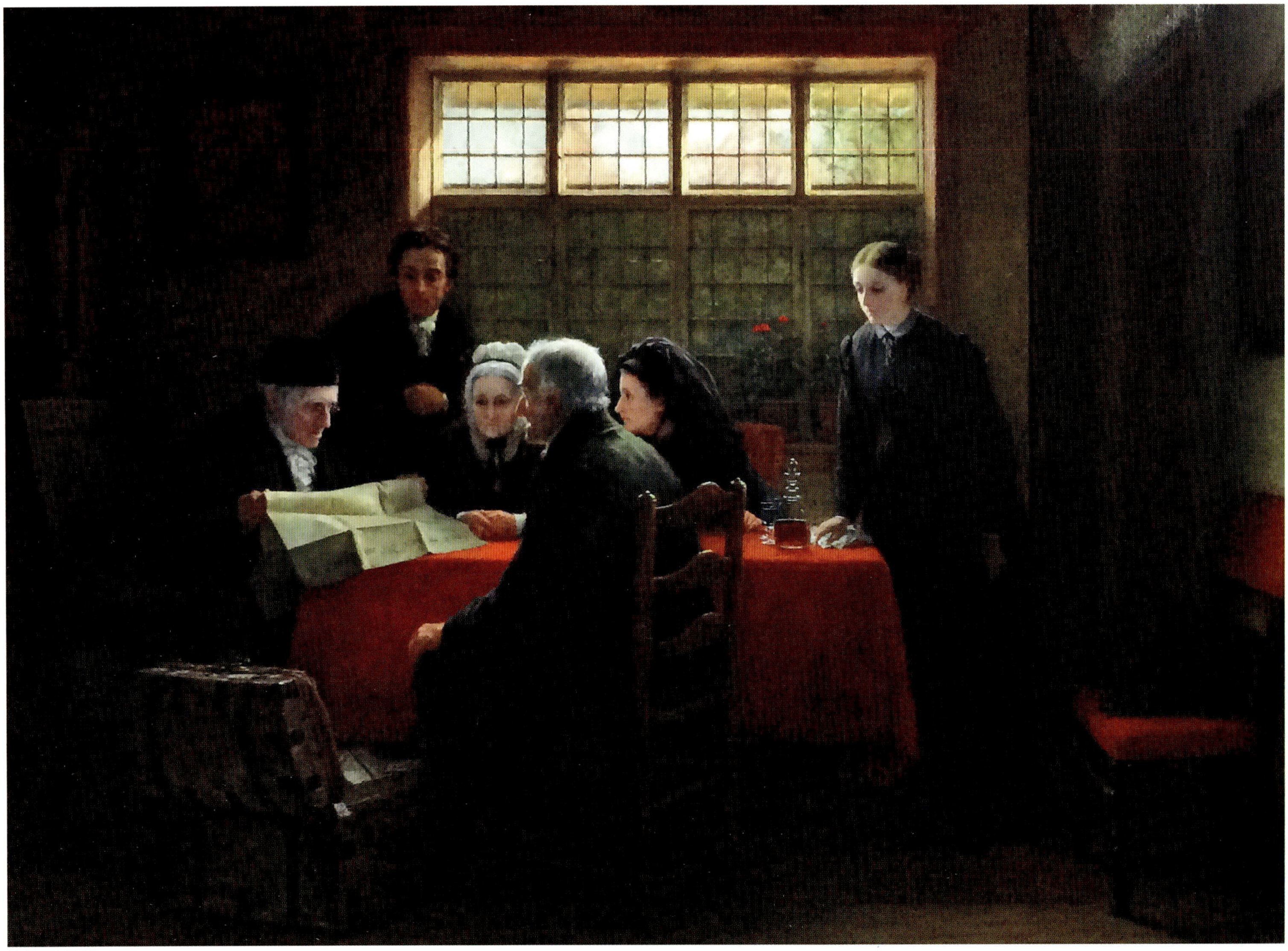

Plate 48: Reading a Will, 1869
Frederick Daniel Hardy. Oil on canvas. 66 x 86.4cm. Alexander A Bove Jr. Collection

of "The Reading of the Will" (915), in which, by judicious concentration of interest, and distribution of natural character within natural limits, and without the least suggestion of the stage, or that kind of caricature which offends us in the clever work of E. Nicol, not to speak of pictures like G. Smith's, the painter has given a new interest, both pictorial and incidental, to about the most hackneyed of all conceivable subjects. Taking it altogether, we should say this is the most complete work the painter has yet produced. Nothing can be better than the light – the way in which it is made to lead the eye to the right points without any forcing or falsification – and the quiet truth of expression in faces and attitudes, from that of the old man and woman, who are deeply interested, but without any objectionable motive for their attention, the hungry look of the woman in the black bonnet, so evidently a greedy expectant for more than she has a right to hope for, and the gentle girl who has risen in unselfish surprise at the mention of her name for bequest or legacy ...

Mr. Hardy has the rare merit, among English painters of this kind of subject, of being able to make a picture, as distinct from the ability to paint the separate objects before him. He has the cultivated instinct of art.[63]

Hardy's picture *The Mother* (Plate 49) was also a successful exhibit at the Royal Academy in 1870; *The Times* commented:

> ... surely there is ... domestic poetry, at least, in the intense happiness of the pretty young mother (260), who is kissing her baby as she carries it to its bed after its undressing, with the help of the happy little handmaiden who trots at her side.

Another reviewer echoed these remarks:

> One of the sweetest little pictures in this room, or, indeed, in the whole exhibition, is "The Mother," by Mr. F.D. Hardy (260). Surely the true maternal kiss, with its homely joy and deep love, was never illustrated with more true sentiment, nor with less of mere sentimentalism.[64]

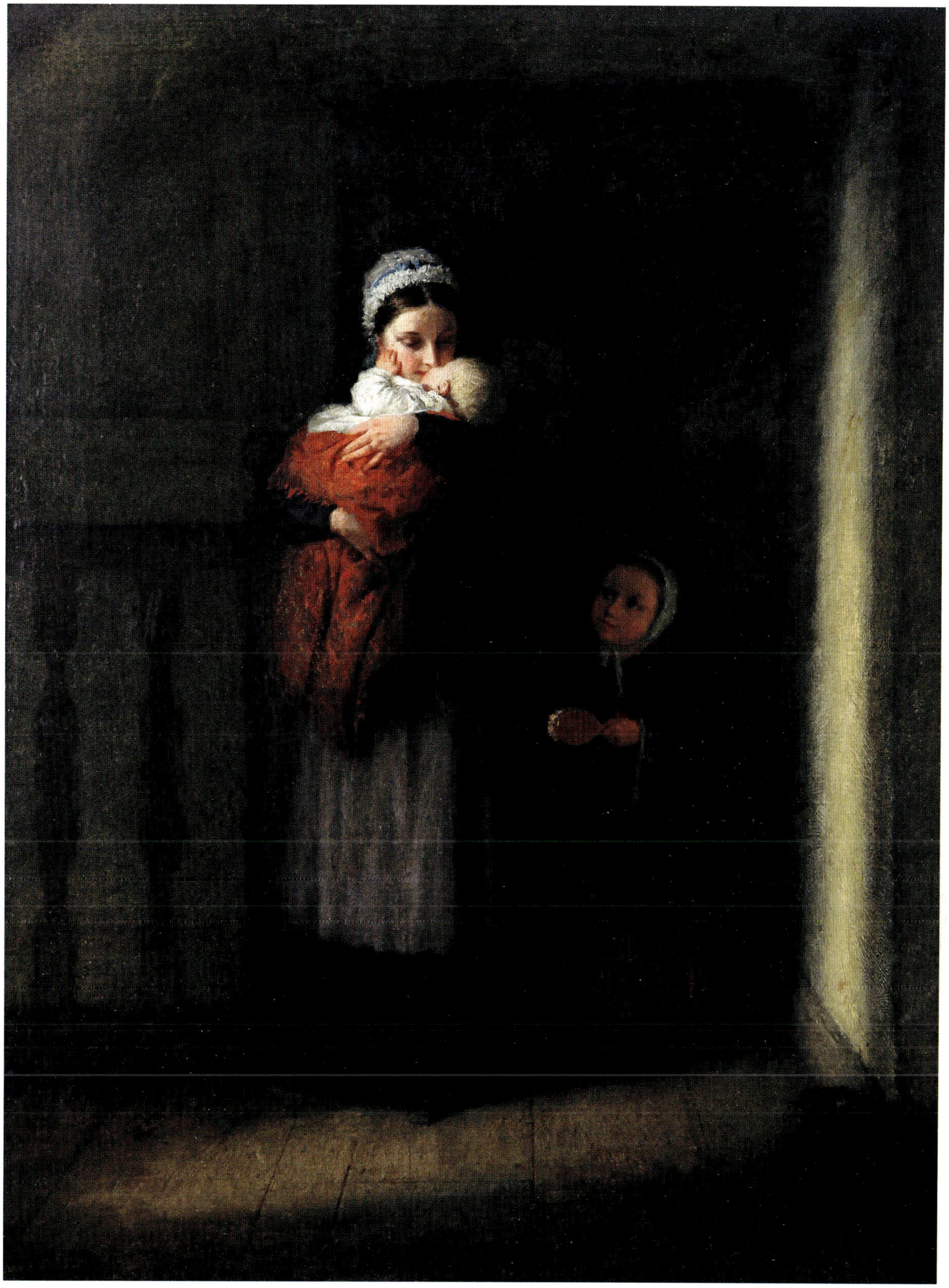

Plate 49: The Mother, 1870
Frederick Daniel Hardy.
Oil on canvas. 57.5 x 42cm.
Private Collection

The scene for *The Mother* appears to be at the top of the stairs in the building that is now the Cranbrook Museum; *The Sweep* includes a similar view.

The Art Journal commented on the other two pictures that Hardy exhibited at the 1870 Royal Academy, *Mrs Herne and her grand-niece, Miss Fanny Homan* and *Christmas visitors*: "two small pictures by F.D. Hardy are, as usual, among the best examples of the Anglicised Dutch school to be found in the Academy." [65]

In the early 1870s, pictures such as *The Wedding Breakfast* (Plate 50) were still being highly praised by many commentators. For Hardy it must have been an important achievement to be able to paint such a picture. But it is ironic that just when he reached this level of accomplishment, the culmination of 20 years of work, there were an increasing number of critical comments about this type of painting. By 1870 some critics had seen quite enough blushing brides, shy young husbands, bluff old fathers making speeches and servants making merry in the background – no matter how well they were painted.

The Graphic was one such voice:

> Illustrators of cottage life and nursery situations still abound. It may be assumed, therefore, that a continuous demand regulates the plentiful supply of pictorial renderings of the "goody" and the "namby pamby" class, with which our exhibitions annually teem. With many of these works artistic painstaking has done much to countervail the vapidity of their subjects. It is impossible to withhold admiration from the skill in expression, the sense of beauty, the refined colour and the careful finish displayed in the "Wedding Breakfast" of Mr. F.D. Hardy, and "The Children's Party" of Mr. G. B. O'Neill [Plate 22]. Yet there is something depressing in these elaborate portrayals of smug benevolence and exuberant amiability. One suspects geniality so unmeasured, and simplicity so pronounced. The figures here limned are, perhaps, "too bright and good for human nature's daily food." And they are gifted with a sort of consciousness of their own excellence, which is somewhat afflicting to spectators. In this respect, foreign artists have an advantage over natives in dealing with themes of this character. [66]

The popularity of F.D. Hardy's paintings is reflected in the prices paid at auction; the sale prices reached a peak in the 1870s and then declined. The prices paid at auction for *The Wedding Breakfast* declined from a peak of £798 in 1877 to £535 10s. (1882), £293 10s. (1884) and to £115 10s. (1909). *A Quartette Party* (1872) was sold at Christie's in 1873 for £850, apparently the highest price paid for a picture by F.D. Hardy in the nineteenth century.

In the 1870s Hardy decided to paint several pictures that made a direct social comment. In marked contrast to *The Wedding Breakfast*, some of F.D Hardy's most interesting paintings from that decade highlighted social issues of the day. The 1870s was the decade when social realism was most popular, or at least acceptable; the paintings of Frank Holl, for example, received a good deal of

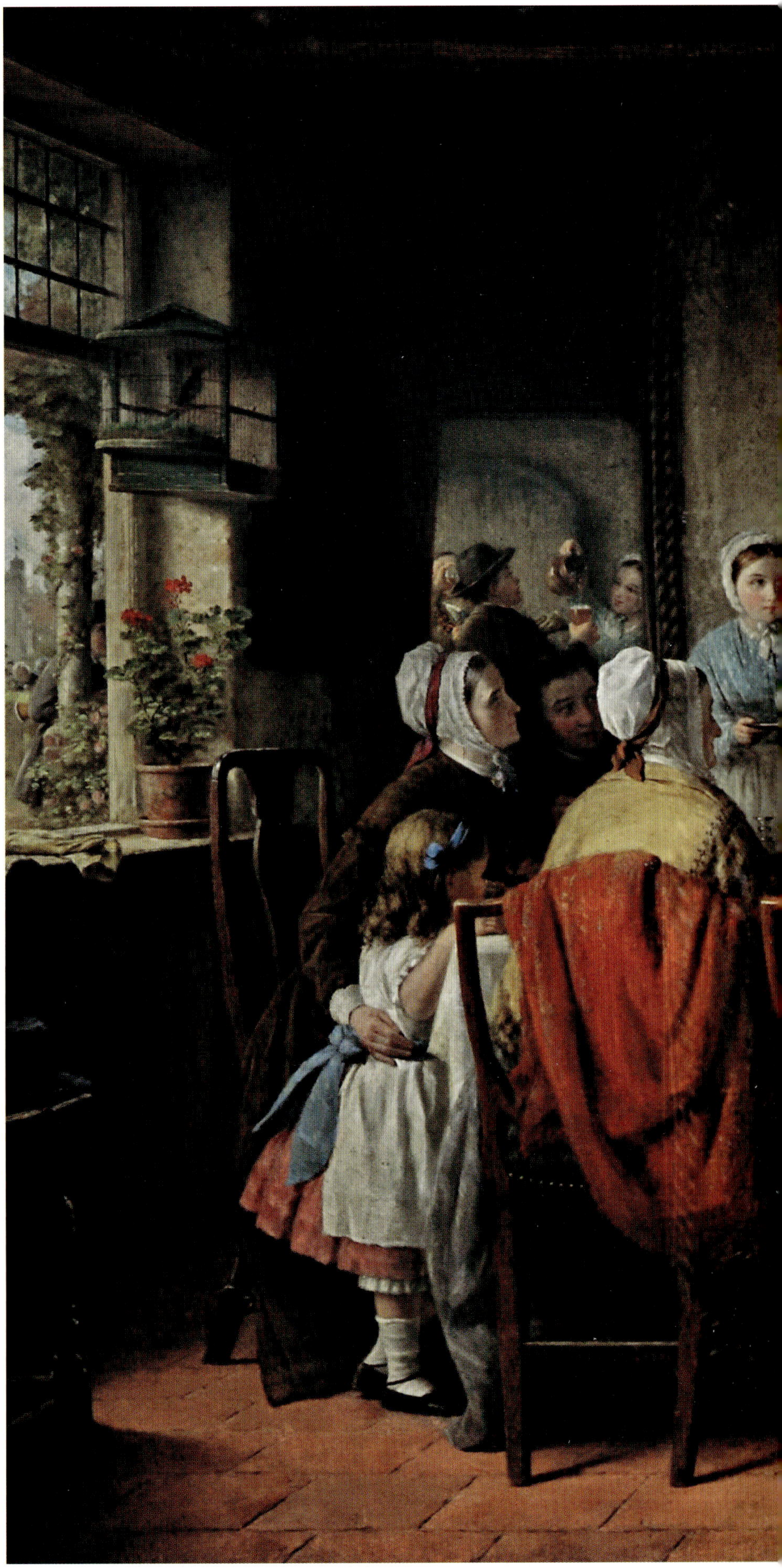

Plate 50: The Wedding Breakfast, 1871
Frederick Daniel Hardy. Oil on canvas. 88.9 x 124.5cm.
Atkinson Art Gallery Collection

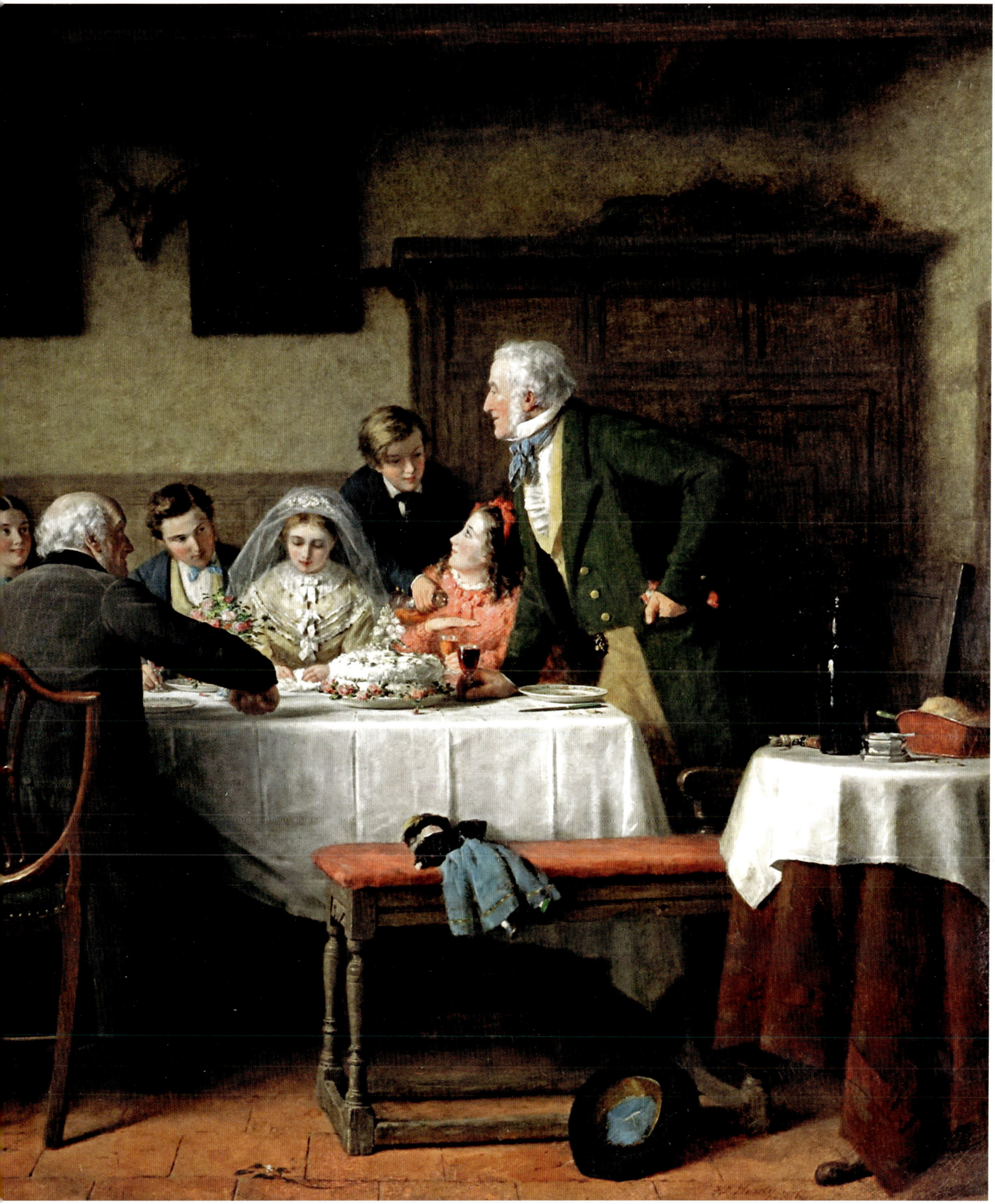

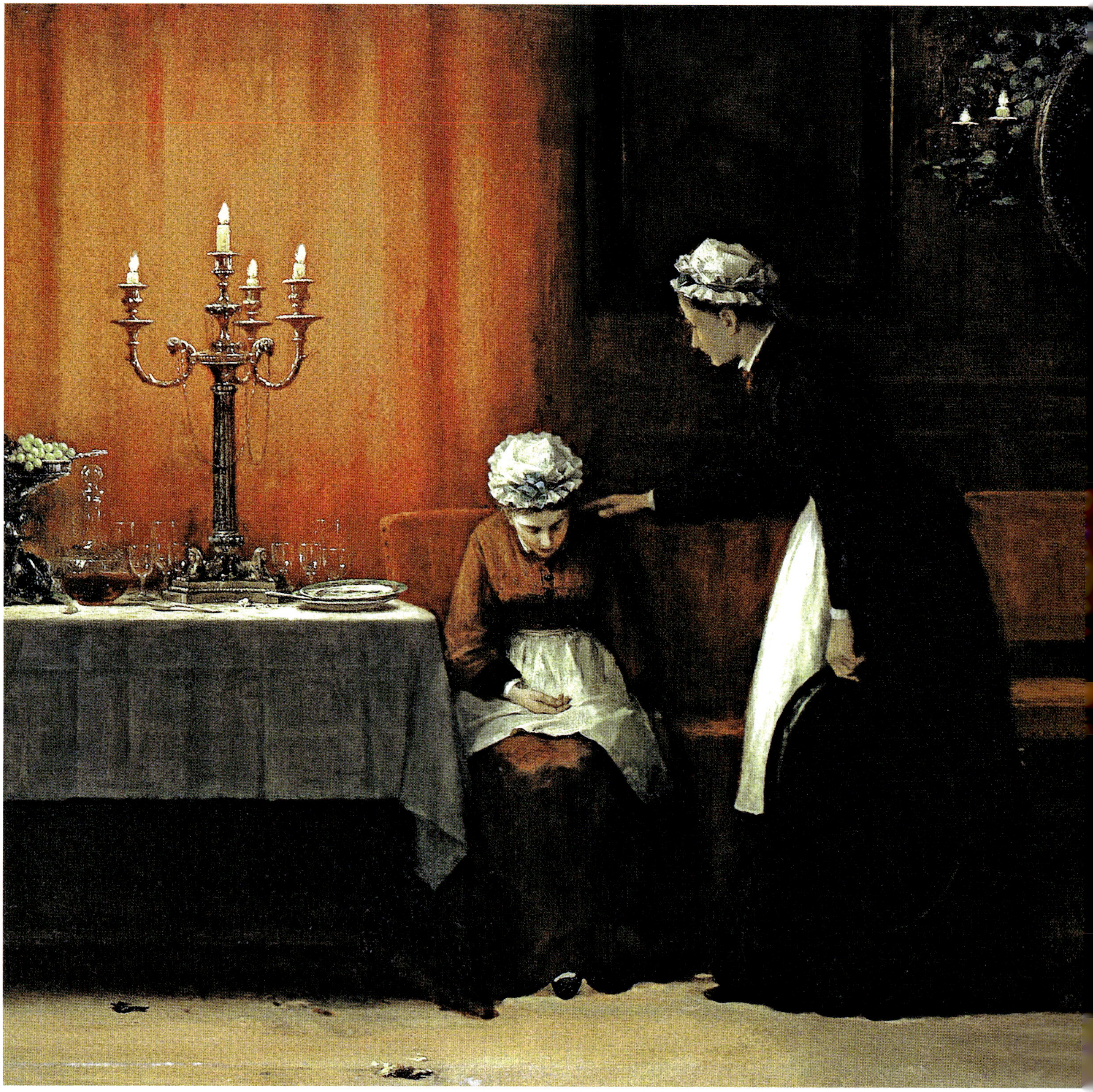

attention at Royal Academy exhibitions. F.D. Hardy made his contribution, highlighting social issues when the public were most receptive. The whereabouts of several Royal Academy exhibits that presumably addressed social questions – *Rent* (1874), *Hunger* (1874) and *Fatherless* (1876) – are unknown. But we know that *Looking for Father* (1873) (Plate 51), one of his Royal Academy exhibits for 1873, shows a young girl, standing in the snow, looking into an alehouse. *The Times* commented:

> In this room hang two of F.D. Hardy's scenes of humble life (164), one painful, of a poor little neglected drunkard's child, looking fearfully for her father through the panels of a public house door, through which the red light of the gas gleams till they glow like the red eye of the drunkard whom the poor little waif is in quest of ... [67]

The Athenaeum thought the narrative in *Looking for Father* was "... capitally told, simple as it is, there is nothing left to tell which the visitor cannot supply ... It certainly produces the effect desired without trial or pretence." [68]

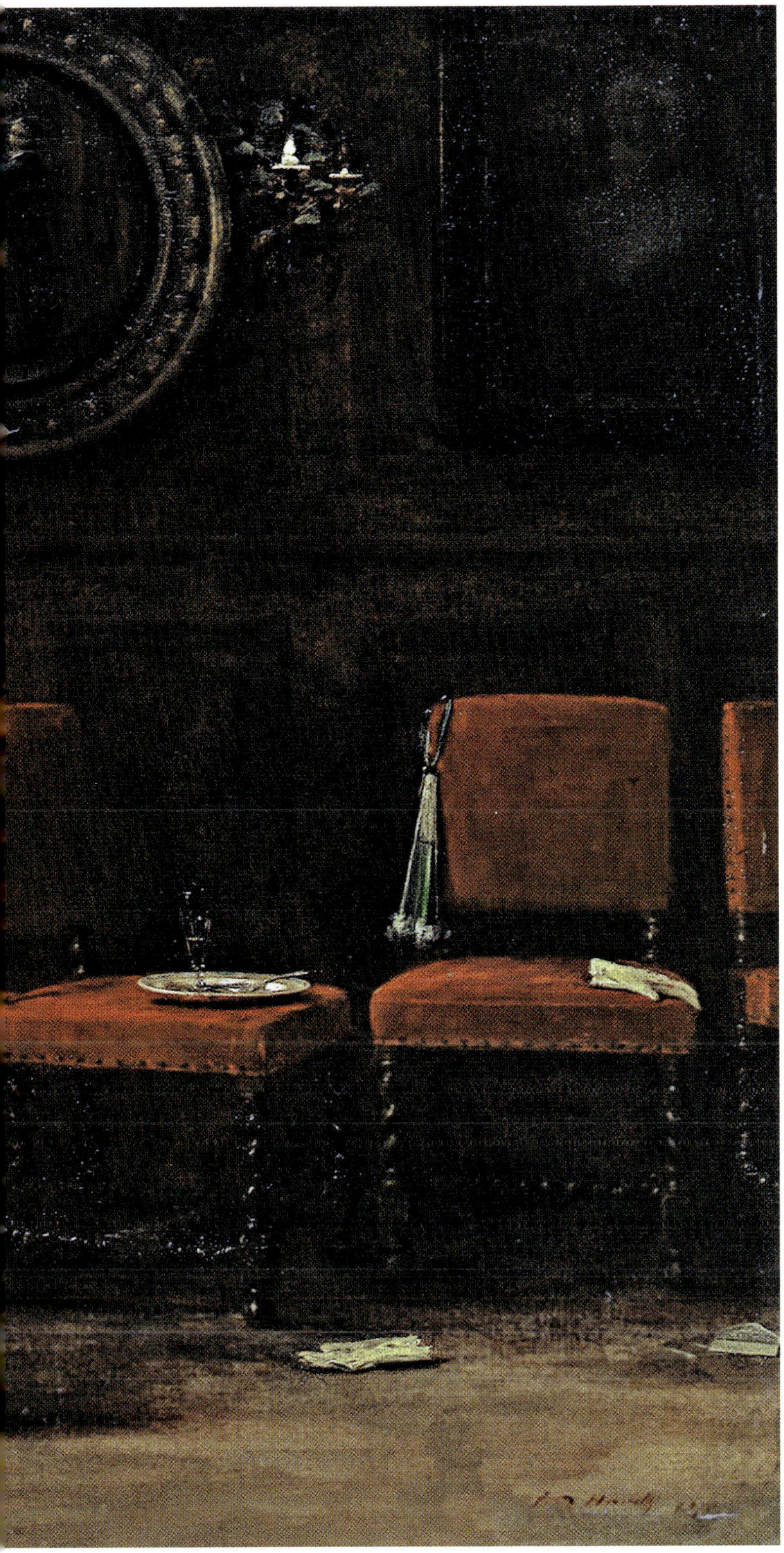

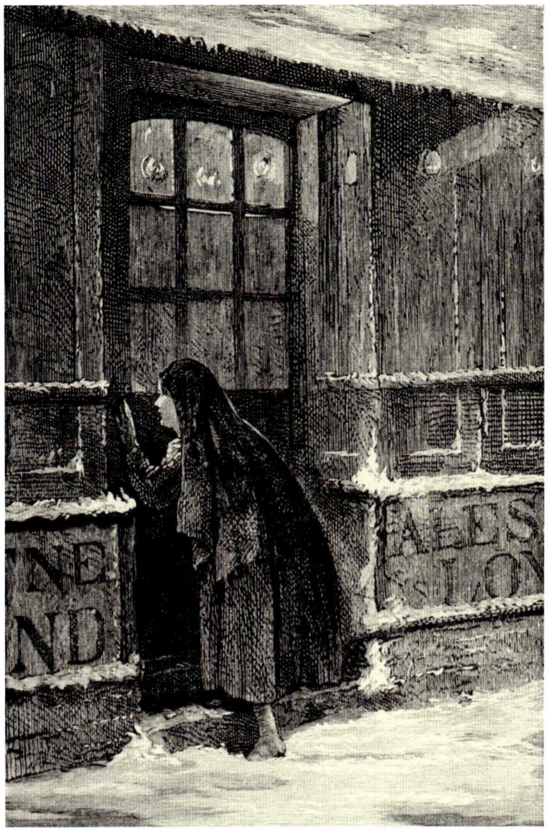

Plate 51 (above): Looking for Father, 1873
After Frederick Daniel Hardy. From *The Trial of Sir Jasper: A Temperance Tale in Verse.*

Plate 52 (left): After the Party, 1875
Frederick Daniel Hardy. Oil on canvas. 69.2 x 108.9cm. PRIVATE COLLECTION

An engraving of the picture appeared in a book *The Trial of Sir Jasper: A Temperance Tale in Verse* (1873) published by Samuel Carter Hall [69], with an accompanying verse:

> "Looking for father", *that* the artist saw;
> And *that* some guiding spirit bade him draw.

Samuel Hall was a barrister and editor of *The Art Journal*. A teetotaller, he commissioned wood engravings of works from many of the leading artists of the day. *The Spectator* enthused:

> Mr. S. C. Hall has been most ably seconded. The little shilling book, a marvel of cheapness, is profusely illustrated by drawings by our best artists – there is hardly a name of distinction missing from the list – engraved by the leading engravers.[70]

After the Party (1875) (Plate 52), which was exhibited at the Royal Academy in 1876, is a sympathetic portrayal of an exhausted servant. Reflected in the mirror is a boy putting glasses on a tray in the morning light near a window. The servant girl who had fallen asleep after the party is being gently woken up.

Servants worked long hours in the 1870s; in a letter to her grandmother, a fourteen-year-old housemaid called Harriet described how tired she felt:

> I have been so driven at work since the fires begun I have ardly [*sic*] any time for anything for myself. I am up at half past five and six every morning and do not go to bed until nearly twelve at night and I feel so tired sometimes. I am obliged to have a good cry ... [71]

Three contemporary responses to *The Wedding Dress* (1875) (Plate 53) indicate how "painful" the Victorians found such paintings:

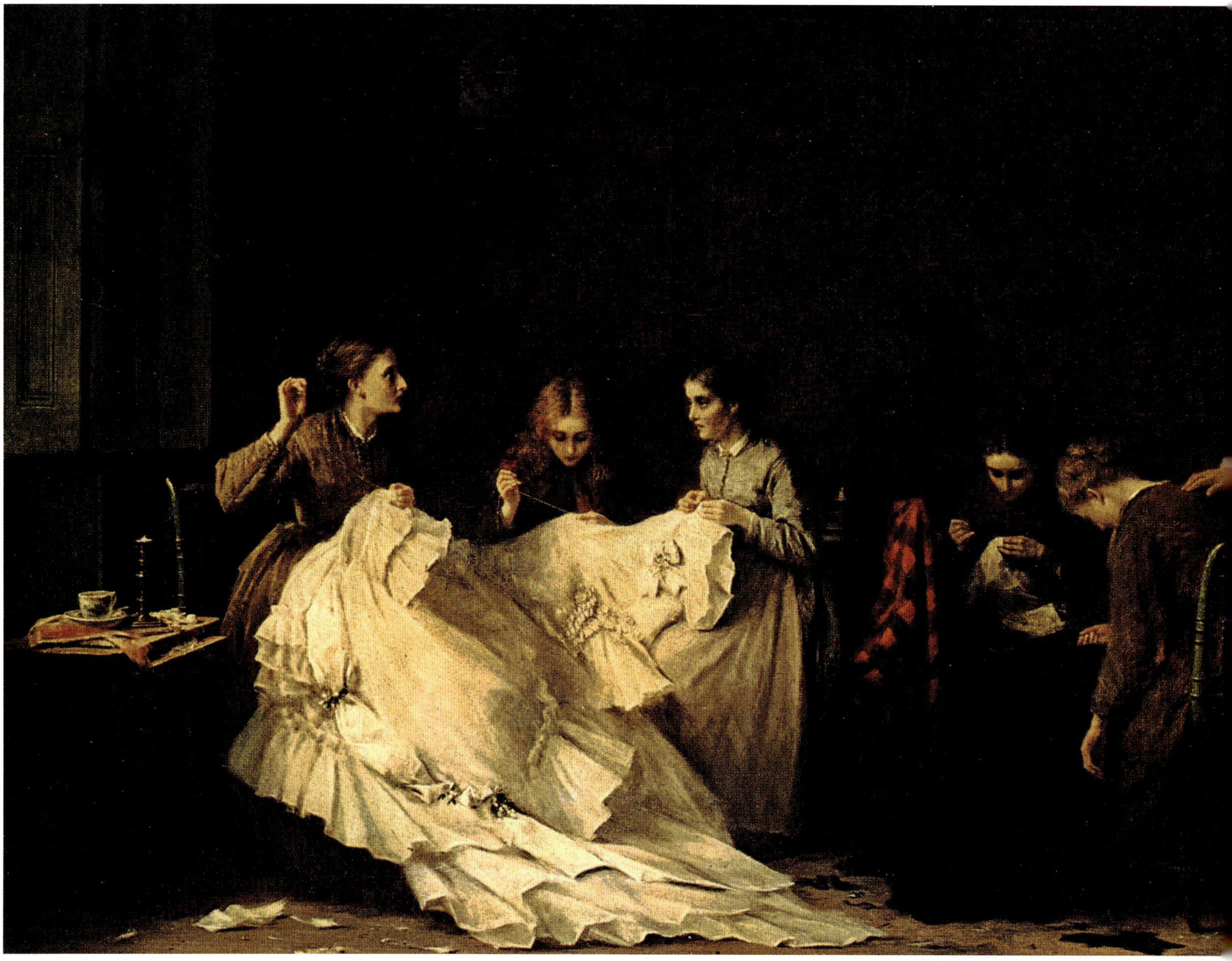

Another painful subject is treated with a terrible realism in Mr. F.D. Hardy's "Wedding Dress", also from the Academy. The idea is taken from Hood's poem, "The Lady's Dream."

> And, O! those maidens young,
> Who wrought in that dreary room,
> With figures drooping and spectres thin,
> And cheeks without a bloom; —
> And the voice that cried, 'For the pomp of pride,
> We haste to an early tomb!'

A group of weary pinched and pale-faced seamstresses are seated round a white muslin dress, upon which they are bestowing the finishing touches. The hands of the clock, the extinguished and nearly burnt out candles, and the faint light of the breaking dawn are all indications that the weary eyes and aching fingers have been strained to their fullest extension though the livelong night. We turn with relief from this painful, though thoroughly artistic work to … [72]

An American commentator made similar remarks, quoting from the same poem by Thomas Hood:

> … would that we could treat "The Wedding Dress" (F.D. Hardy) with all the cheerful respect it deserves. But orange-blossom and satin are not always typical of unalloyed happiness and pleasure, as we may learn from the following lines of Hood …
>
> We heartily commend this picture to the notice of some Society for relieving Distressed Needlewomen, not with a view to mitigating the distress brought about by want of work, but the ill health, suffering, and ultimate want constantly being provoked by too much of it. And, as there are quite as many ladies interested in such subjects on the American as on the English side of the Atlantic, we take leave to print the number of the picture in the catalogue, which is number 1177 [73].

A comment on *The Wedding Dress* from Tom Taylor of *The*

Times, previously highly complimentary about F.D. Hardy's work, is a good example of the response of many Victorians to paintings that made critical social comments. Taylor thought the theme was as painful as ever, but that it was also an unsuitable subject for a painting as there was an Act of Parliament regulating hours of work:[74]

> [There are] subjects of common life which carry their mood and moral implicitly, like Mr. Robertson's "Winter," and those which thrust it in your face like, say, Mr. Hardy's "Wedding Dress" ... a party of haggard, hollow-eyed milliner's girls, after a long night's toil, still working on the bright bridal robe introduced to point the contrast between the lots of workers and that of wearer. The subject was a very good one for Hood when he wrote his "Lady's Dream", but we have an Act of Parliament now regulating such workwomen's hours of labour, and while the painfulness of the subject as a theme for painting is as great as ever, its point as a rebuke and a reminder no longer exists.

Undaunted by comments in *The Times*, Hardy reworked the theme in *The Seamstresses* (1875) (Plate 54), in which two figures in *The Wedding Dress* are shown near a window in the early morning light. The exploited seamstress was the subject of paintings by several Victorian artists who were inspired by *The Sempstress* painted by Richard Redgrave in 1844; Anna Elizabeth Blunden painted *The Song of the Shirt* (1854) and Frank Holl painted *Seamstresses* (ca. 1875).

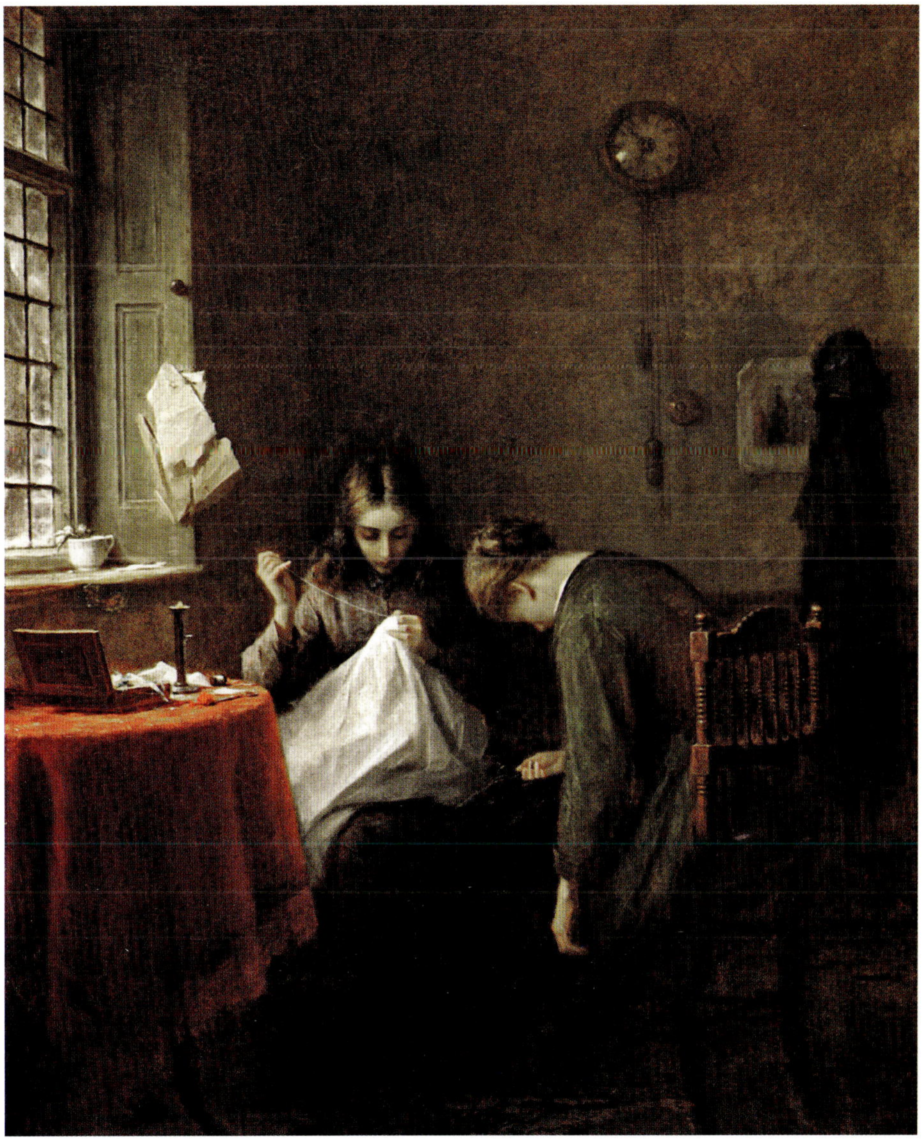

Plate 53 (above): The Wedding Dress, 1875
Frederick Daniel Hardy. Oil on panel. 25.5 x 38cm. Private Collection

Plate 54 (right): The Seamstresses, 1875
Frederick Daniel Hardy. Oil on canvas. 61.9 x 46.7cm. Private Collection

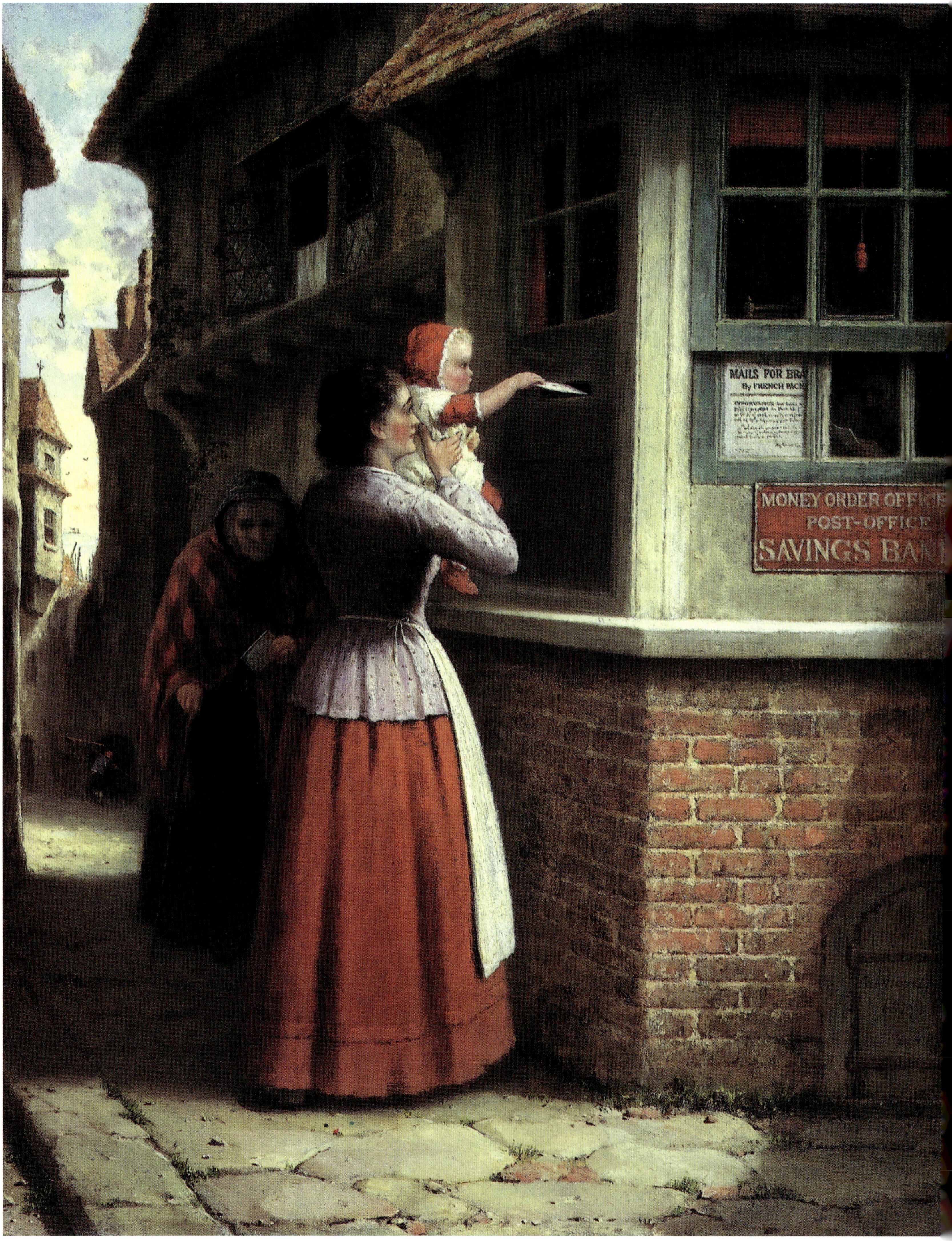
MONEY ORDER
POST-OFFICE
SAVINGS

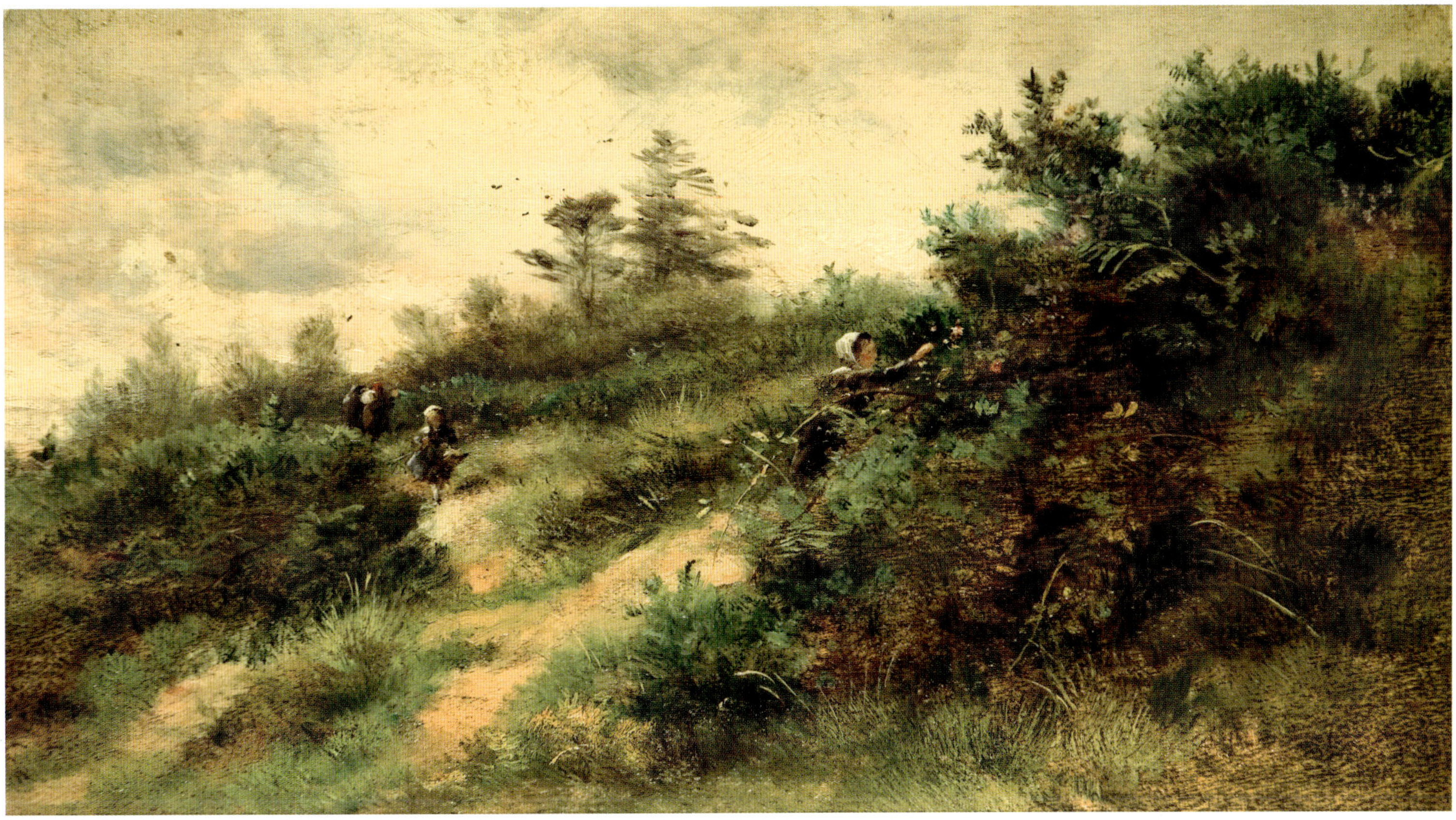

By 1876 F.D. Hardy was able afford a house in London at 17, Brunswick Gardens, Kensington, which he kept until at least 1881. He also had a studio in London at 13a Pembridge Place, a narrow three-storied house in Bayswater that had three studios for artists.

His later works included the carefully painted *Posting a Letter* (1879) (Plate 55)[75] and *Near Windermere Lake* (1887) (Plate 56), his only known landscape, in which the free brushwork is reminiscent of the work of his cousin Heywood Hardy. Surprisingly few pictures from members of the Cranbrook Colony make reference to the agricultural life of the area around Cranbrook. Thomas Webster painted a picture of hop-pickers, *The Hop Garden* (1858). And there seems to be only one such picture by F.D. Hardy, *Fresh from the Orchard* (1883).

Plate 55 (opposite page): Posting a Letter, 1879
Frederick Daniel Hardy. Oil on canvas.
86.5 x 66cm. Private Collection

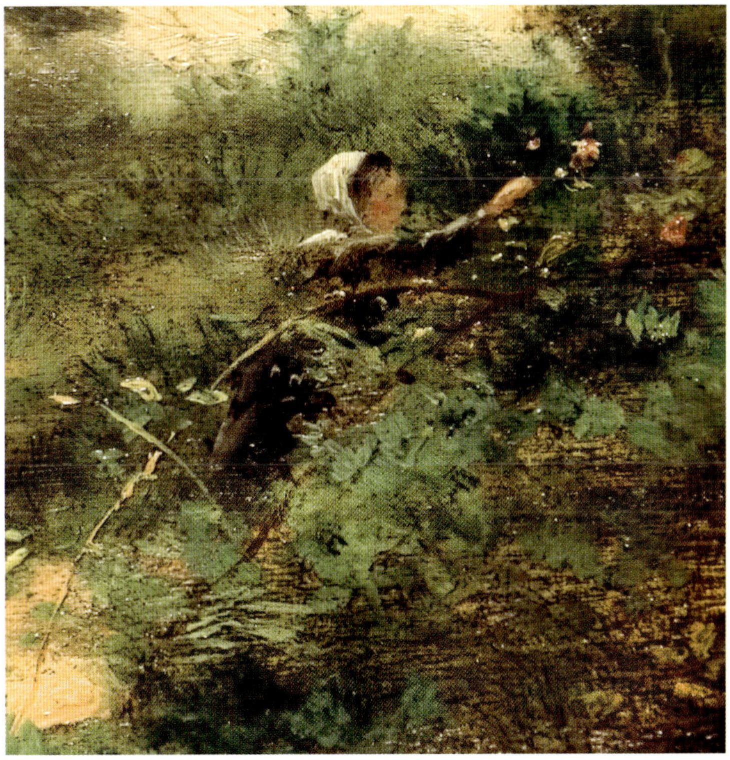

Plate 56 (above, and detail right): Near Windermere Lake, 1887
Frederick Daniel Hardy. Oil on canvas.
12.7 x 21.6cm. © Wolverhampton Art Gallery

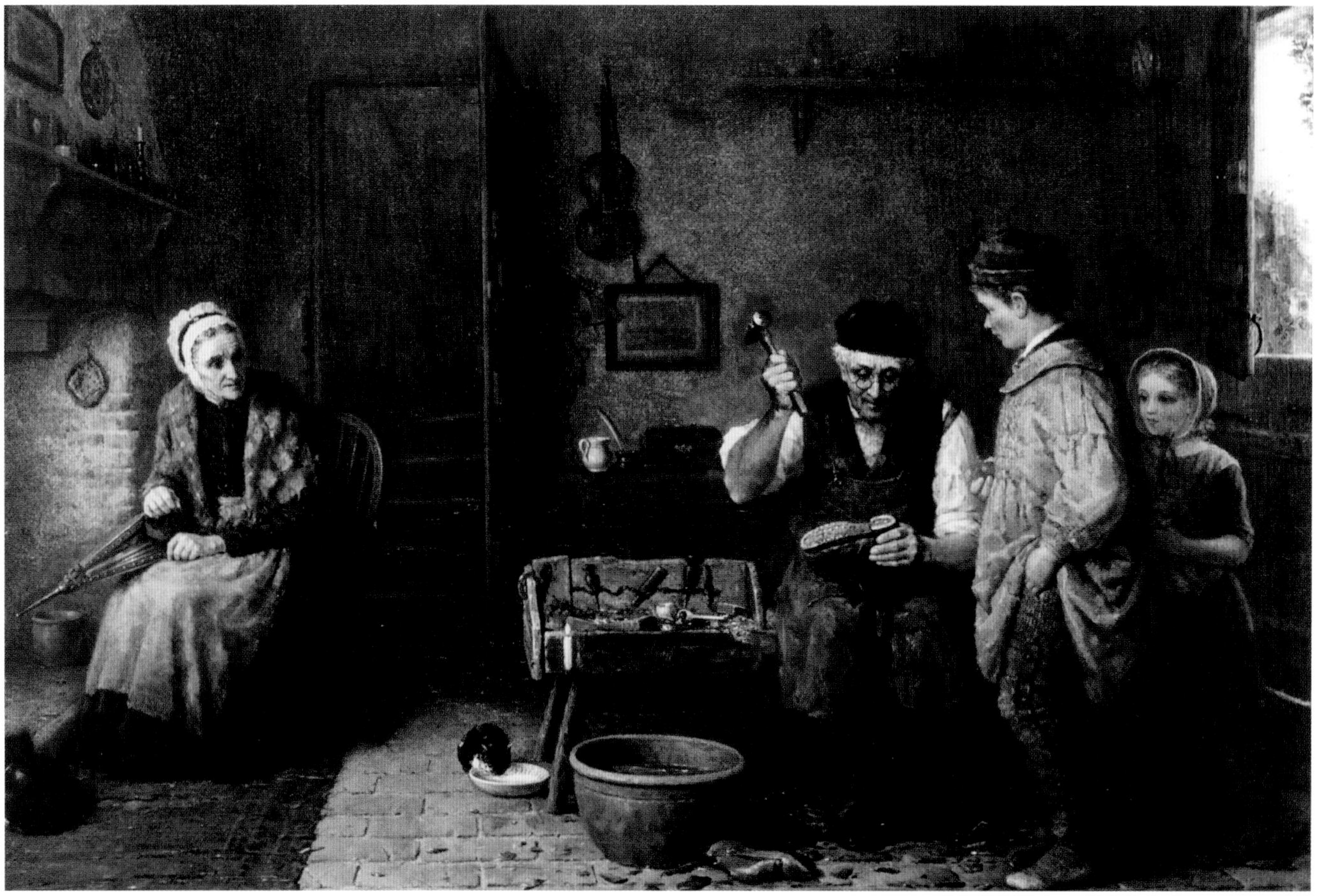

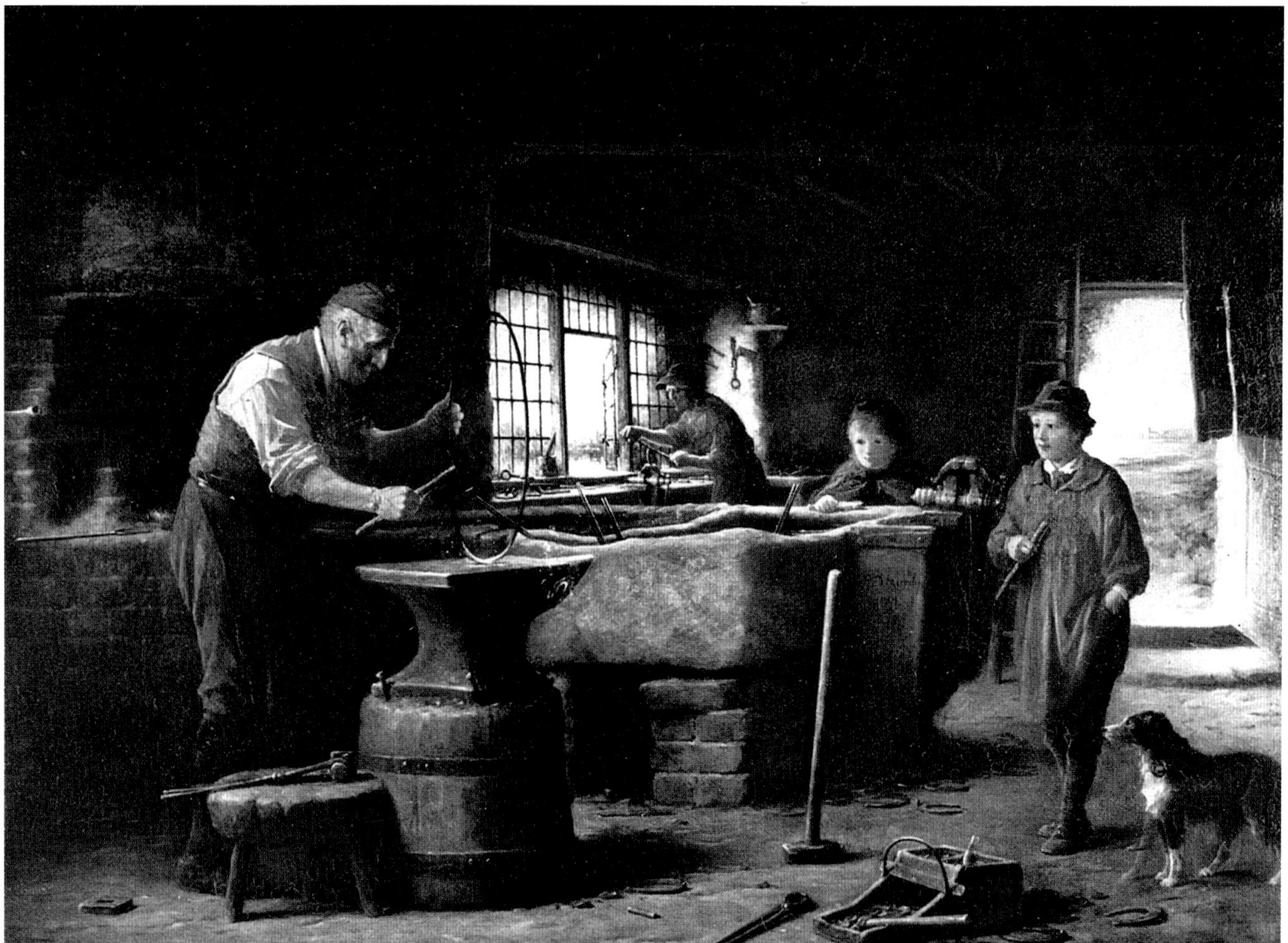

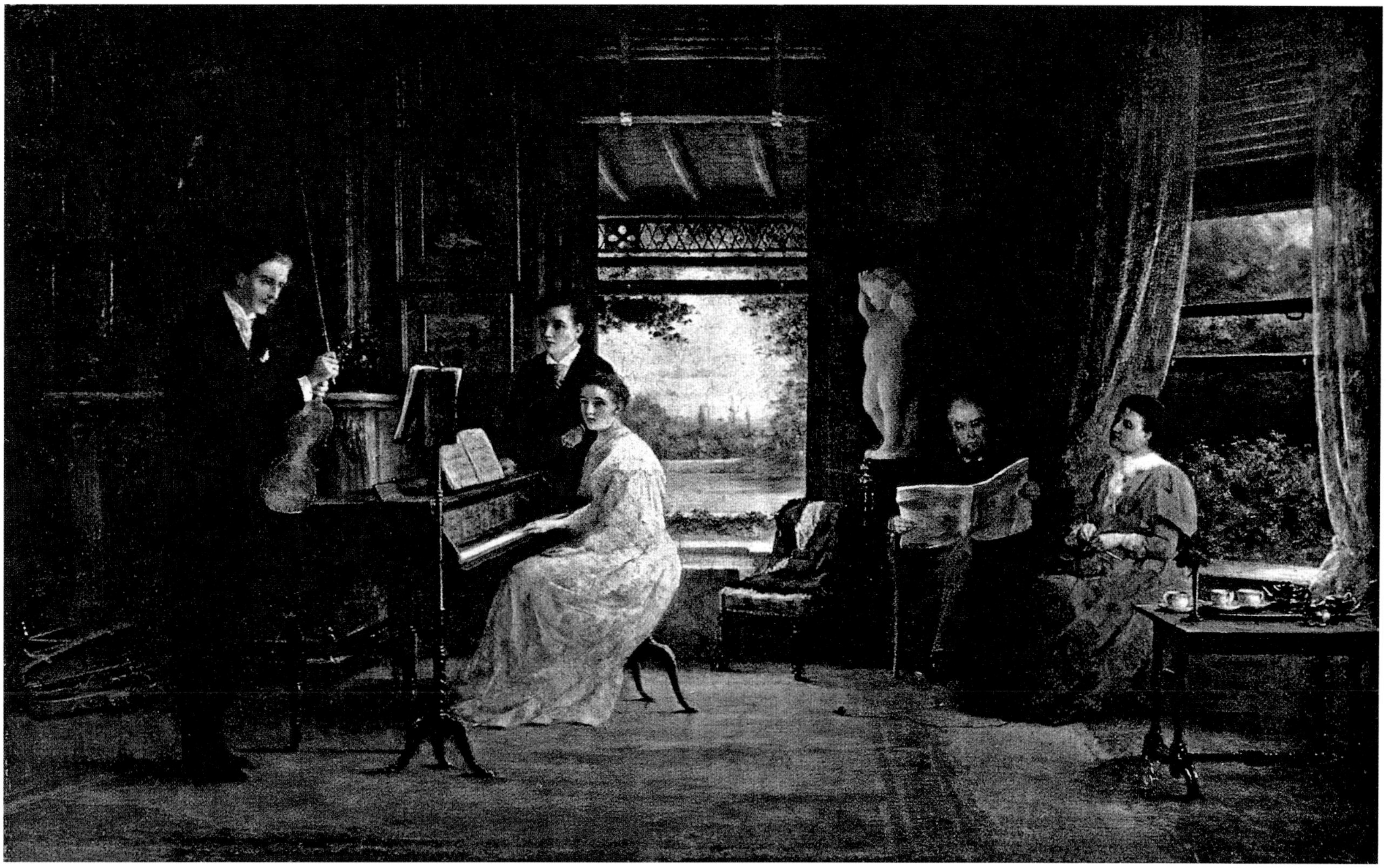

Plate 59: A Family Group, 1890
Frederick Daniel Hardy. Oil on panel. 36.5 x 56cm. Private Collection

Some of Frederick Daniel's most successful paintings of the 1880s and 1890s were those in which he returned to his more traditional themes of village life and the work of village craftsmen, such as *The Old Shoemender* (1882) (Plate 57) and *The Broken Hoop* (1891) (Plate 58).

Of his later works, one of the best is *A Family Group* (1890) (Plate 59). Graham Reynolds, art historian, one time Keeper of the Department of Paintings at the Victoria and Albert Museum and author of *Painters of the Victorian Scene* (1953), thought that this picture:

> ... shows that unpretentious informality was second nature to him. It is hardly possible to believe that such a picture could have been painted so late in the nineteenth century. It has the charm of a slice of life arrested for all time, and we feel convinced when we see it that many late Victorian drawing-rooms looked just like this. [76]

F.D. Hardy's title for the last painting he exhibited at the Royal Academy, in 1898, is as enigmatic as several of the paintings he submitted almost 50 years earlier. *My Studio* (1898) (Plate 60)

Plate 57 (opposite page, top): The Old Shoemender, 1882
Frederick Daniel Hardy. Oil on canvas. 45.7 x 60.9cm.

Plate 58 (opposite page, bottom): The Broken Hoop, 1891
Frederick Daniel Hardy. Oil on canvas. 49.5 x 67.3cm.

depicts three convex mirrors and a sword. He frequently included convex mirrors in his paintings; the first example appears to be in *The Doctor* (1863). In *My Studio*, the left-hand mirror shows a table being laid. In the central mirror a man, seemingly F.D. Hardy, looks up from his writing towards the window. In the mirror on the right there are wisps of smoke from a candle that has just been extinguished. Beneath the mirror on the right is a flame. Perhaps the sword dates from F.D. Hardy's days as an officer in the Volunteer Corps. In all, he exhibited 93 paintings at the Royal Academy between 1851 and 1898.

Hardy painted another picture of his studio, in 1896, showing him painting on the ground floor of the old cloth hall in Cranbrook that he used as a studio. He frequently painted figures at the open window (on the left looking at the house from the road) and would sit at his easel behind the right-hand window, from which he hung a cloth to prevent too much light shining on his painting.

There are at least ten paintings by F.D. Hardy dated in the twentieth century; the last painting appears to be *Exchanging News*, painted in 1905.

F.D. Hardy's father, George Hardy senior, the musician and amateur artist, came to live with Frederick Daniel and his family at Cranbrook in 1873 and died there on 6 October 1877. F.D. Hardy's sister, Emily (Plate 63), was a frequent visitor to Cranbrook and was often photographed with Hardy's wife, Rebecca.

F.D. Hardy died at Cranbrook on 1 April 1911. He is buried at St Dunstan's Church, Cranbrook. His wife, Rebecca, had died on 25 December 1906.

F.D. Hardy's place in the tradition of genre painting

Frederick Daniel Hardy represented the last generation of British artists who specialised in domestic interiors, in a line that went back to William Hogarth and to the seventeenth-century Dutch masters. "Domestic painting" arguably reached its peak of popularity in the 1860s at a time when F.D. Hardy himself was at his best.

The domestic painters were followers of David Wilkie, the founder of the Victorian domestic style in the early years of the century. And Wilkie himself was seen as the successor to the eighteenth-century painter Hogarth. As *The Illustrated London News* put it, it was Hogarth who "gave the domestic character to British art".[77]

Wilkie and his successors were seen as producing original "English" art (even though Wilkie was of course a Scot) that reflected the national character. Their domestic paintings were in contrast to the "high art" and history painting in the grand manner that had been promoted by Sir Joshua Reynolds, and which was more influenced by continental art.

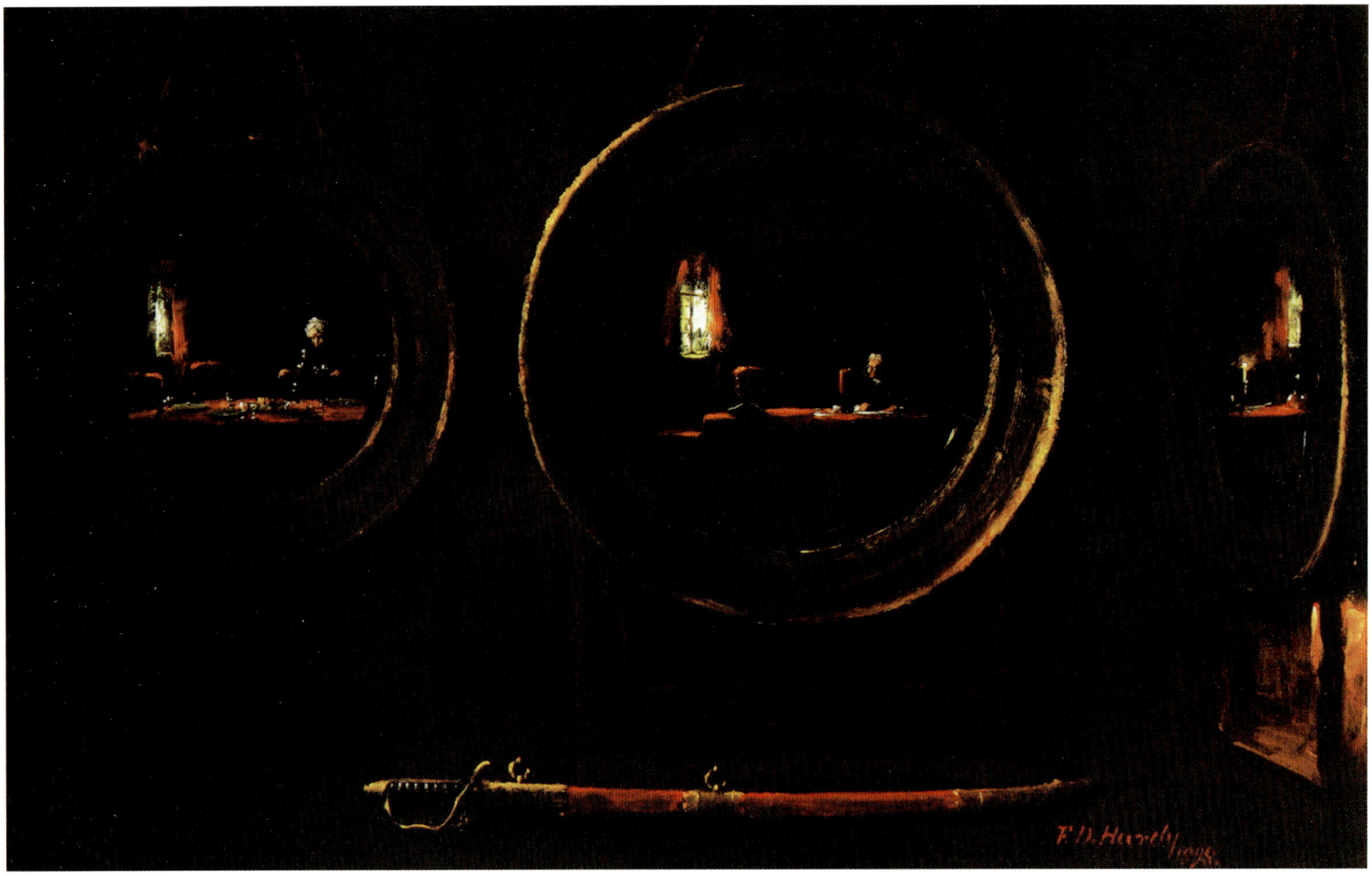

Plate 60: My Studio, 1898
Frederick Daniel Hardy. Oil on board, laid down on panel. 25.4 x 39.1cm. Private Collection

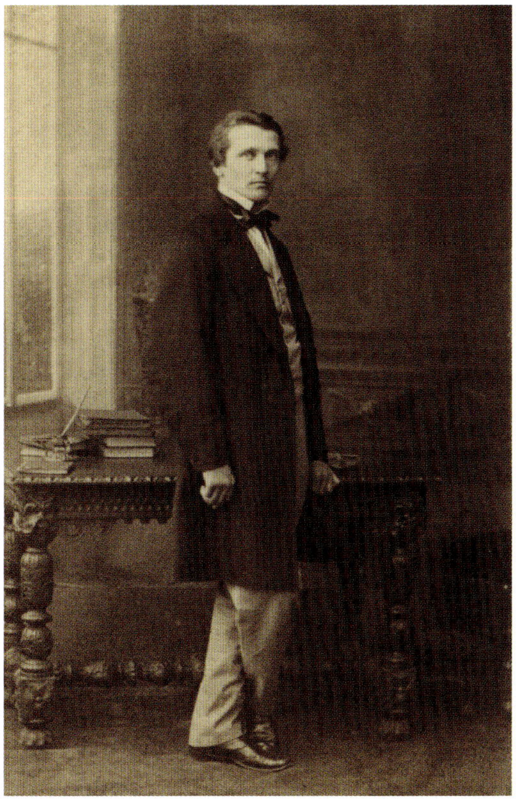 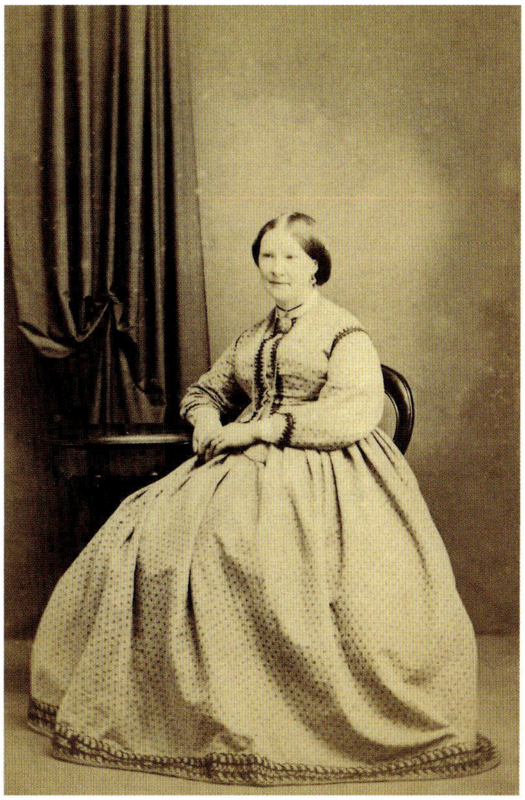 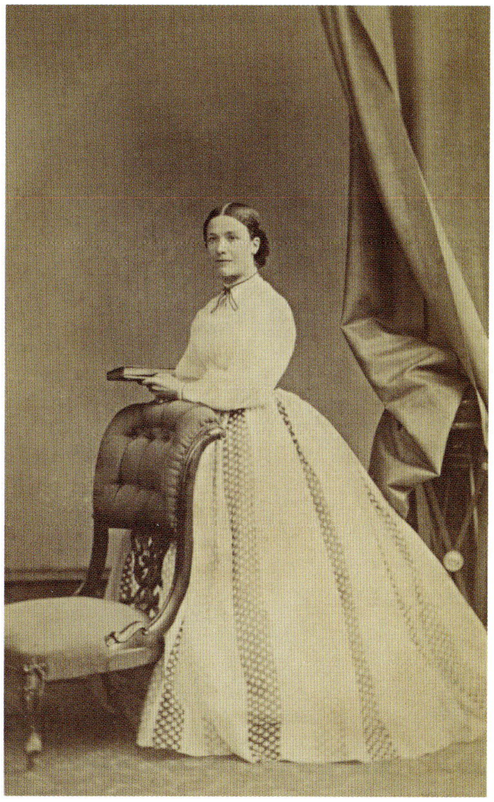

Above, left to right:
Plate 61: Frederick Daniel Hardy
Photograph by Caldesi & Co., London. NATIONAL PORTRAIT GALLERY

Plate 62: Rebecca Hardy, wife of F.D. Hardy
Photograph by Barns Bros. of Ashford, Tenterden & Cranbrook.
FROM THE PHOTOGRAPH ALBUM OF GEORGE AND SARAH HARDY

Plate 63: Emily Hardy
Sister of Frederick Daniel Hardy and frequent visitor to the Hardy family at Cranbrook. PHOTOGRAPH BY HILLS AND SAUNDERS

J.C. Horsley, a member of the Cranbrook Colony, wrote that the English Domestic School comprised painters who "derived from Hogarth the prince of story-tellers on canvas, followed by David Wilkie, William Mulready, C.R. Leslie, and others."[78] And John Ruskin, the foremost art critic of the day, believed that, "whatever is to be truly great and affecting must have on it the strong stamp of the native land".[79] By 1855 Thomas Webster's domestic paintings were regarded as examples of a "class of Art" that had no "counterpart in any nation of Europe", that were "indigenous to the English soil".[80]

In their search for more realistic themes, and in contrast to the grand manner and romanticism of the preceding decades, Wilkie and his immediate successors looked towards the great tradition of genre painting in the Low Countries. The Dutch genre painters of the seventeenth century provided the model for the British Victorian genre painters, particularly those like F.D. Hardy who painted domestic scenes of village life.[81] J.C. Horsley wrote how he had studied the works of Peter de Hooghe and Gerard Terborch. And there are paintings by F.D. Hardy that resemble works by Maes, van Ostade and Vermeer (see pages 19, 20, 24 and 25).

However, the earthiness and scenes of raucous drunkenness that were a prominent feature of Dutch genre paintings and to some extent of Hogarth's work had no part in paintings of the English Dutch School in the nineteenth century. In its place there were well-observed, often subtle, contemporary narratives, as in the work of F.D. Hardy for example. And there was humour, and a more sympathetic approach to the people who lived in country cottages.

In 1860 the art critic of *Blackwood's Magazine* wrote:

> Our English and Scotch art in this department has certainly always been more refined than its kindred Dutch. Instead of placing our characters in a dirty back kitchen wallowing in mire, with pigs as playmates, we have an eye for comfort and cleanliness, sweep the floor, put the furniture in order … Provis and Curnock and Hardy, with others, still paint a simple subject with unpretending truth.[82]

This "domestic" style of painting was strongly supported by the new patrons of art in the nineteenth century. The domestic genre paintings of F.D. Hardy and his friends of the Cranbrook Colony were usually bought by self-made Victorians. Wary of imitating aristocratic tastes for Old Masters (and their imitators and fakes), they wanted pictures whose subjects, narratives and humour they understood and that were painted with an objectivity and professionalism that they could appreciate. Typical of the new type of collector was Sidney Cartwright who acquired the largest collection of pictures painted by members of the Cranbrook colony (see page 16).

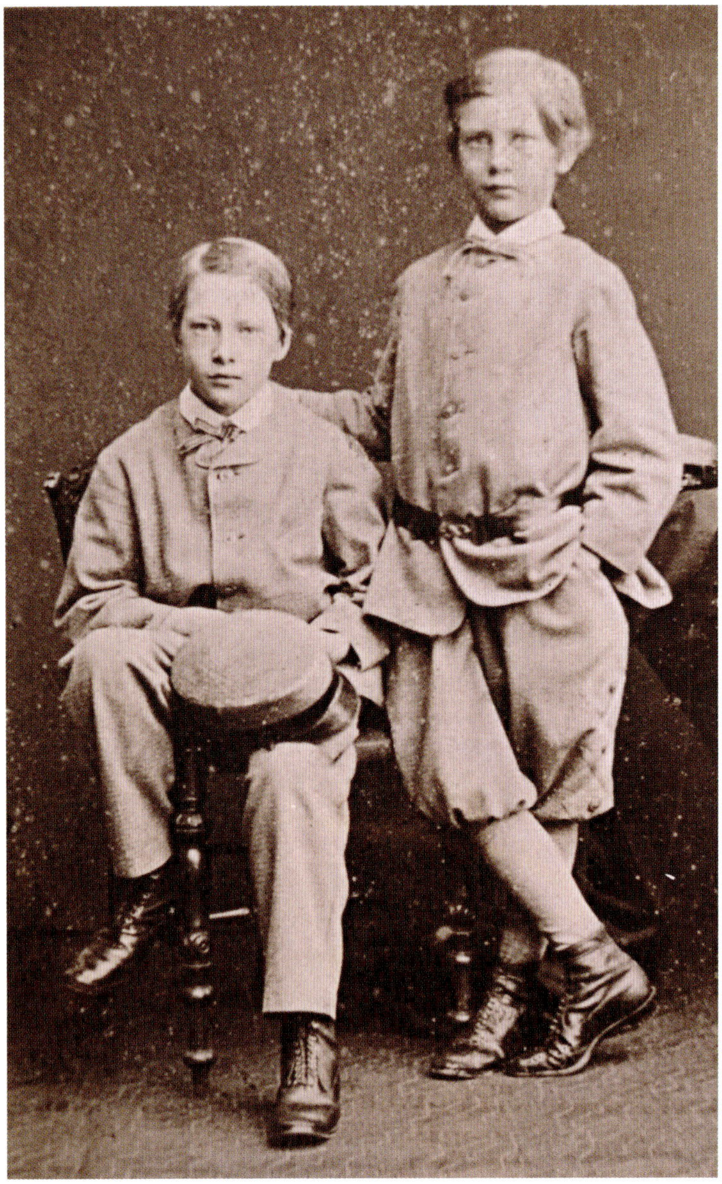

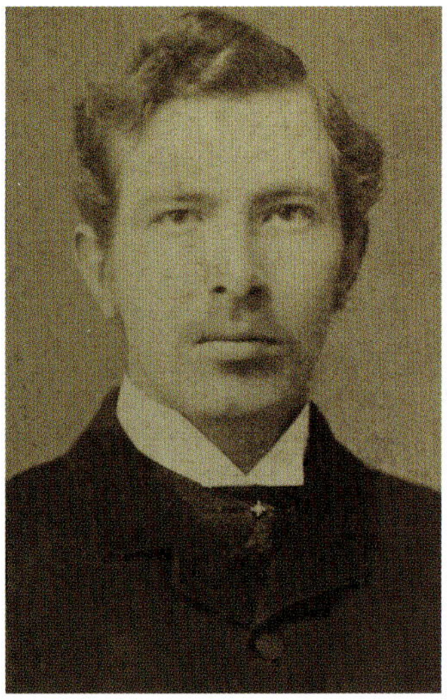

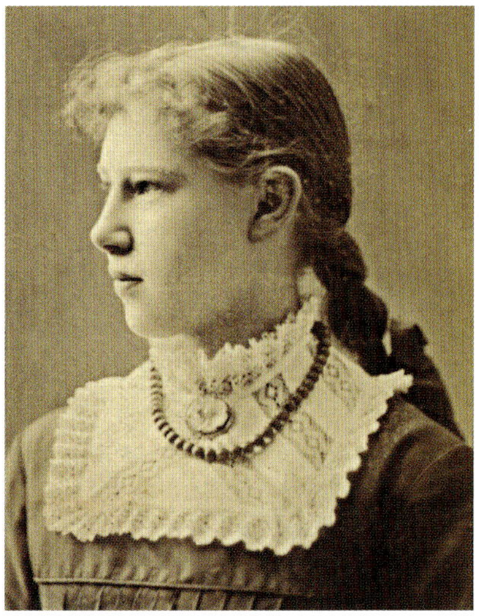

Left to right:
Plate 64: Lewis and Frederick, Edwin and Amelia Gertrude Hardy, sons and daughter of Frederick Daniel and Rebecca Hardy.
FROM THE PHOTOGRAPH ALBUM OF GEORGE AND SARAH HARDY

Events abroad during the 1850s – the Crimean War, the Indian Mutiny and the potential threats from France that led to the formation of Volunteer Corps – contrasted with a more peaceful Britain as reflected in its domestic pictures and may have reinforced the popularity of such pictures that depicted homes in a tranquil England.

Commenting in 1859 on the Paris "Exposition Universelle" of 1855, Richard Redgrave, artist and Special Commissioner for Fine Arts at the Exhibition observed:

> To pass from the grand salons appropriated in the Palais des Beaux Arts to French and Continental works, into the long gallery of British pictures, was to pass at once from the midst of warfare and its incidents, from passion, strife and bloodshed, from martyrdoms and suffering, to the peaceful scenes of home; – it was said of our pictures that they reflected the life of a people who had long been permitted to dwell safely.

Redgrave argued that art in England,

> ... has flourished from the demands of those who love it as a home delight, therefore our pictures are small, and suited to our private residences, while the subjects are such as we can live by and love; and hence, they have been largely illustrative of the feelings and affections of our kind.

Whereas in France,

> Church and State are the great patrons of art, and pictures are largely commissioned for town halls, palaces, and churches. These are constantly of large dimensions, and calculated by their mere size to make an impression on those who do not reflect that all the highest qualities of art may be contained in pictures of moderate size.[83]

In 1863 *The Art Journal* commented on the popularity of domestic art:

> ... pictures technically known as genre, or, as they are commonly termed, domestic subjects, seem to promise well for the future ... [the pictures] are unquestionably most popular with the public. The reason they are so is obvious enough. We are emphatically a domestic people; other nations may equal us in their love of country, but they have not the same regard for their homes. An Englishman ... feels pride in his home and household, whether he be wealthy or in humble circumstances; his sympathies are in unison with everything which speaks of home-affections, home-influences, home-pursuits. England, happy in her homes, and joyous in her hearty cheer, and peaceful in her snug firesides, is equally fortunate in a school of Art sacred to the hallowed relations of domestic life.[84]

Commenting on the work of Wilkie, Webster and Hardy, *The*

Art Journal noted that "painting follows in the wake of a nation's literature", in this instance the works of Wordsworth and Crabbe. The *Journal* even argued that the British liking for domestic paintings might be due to the weather; the colder weather in the north of Europe made the British more appreciative of comfortable homes. The following comment from the same publication in 1866 summarised what the Victorians wanted to see in domestic art and why they appreciated F.D. Hardy's work:

> ... domestic scenes have in the "great-coat" weather of England found special favour. Such homeish themes are in every way suited to the adorning of our houses. They are as cheerful as the domestic hearth and varied as life itself. In fact, no apology can be called for in extenuation of the known predilection of our people for small cabinet pictures of this humble and essentially materialistic class. Truth, simplicity, tenderness, humour, fun, sparkling satire, these are the qualities and harmless sensations which fittingly find a place.
>
> To speak more generally, such subjects are either serious or comic. This last element, however, is found more sparingly, and when present, it serves for the most part as minor by-play, as a pinch of salt or of pepper to give flavour and pungency ... Character and detail are also essential to this school. The faces should be individual, they should each tell a story, contain lines of history, and marks of joys and sorrow. The details too – the furniture, for example, in a room – must have a meaning and even point a moral. Hogarth's "Rakes Progress" was written upon walls and floors, every object had its tongue and spoke of folly. As for the execution, the more real the better; detail gives verisimilitude to the narrative, and local truth enables the mind to realise the situation. The handling, indeed, as in the glib telling of an anecdote, is in itself a prime element in success. Cleverness, dexterity, neatness, sparkle, and a keen edge, should mark every touch. An English Academy is never wanting in numerous examples of such felicitous work. [85]

This idyllic view of life in the country, as seen in many paintings by Hardy, was hardly a realistic or comprehensive representation of the lives of many people who lived in English villages; many villagers lived in poverty. Commenting in 1868 on David Hardy's cottage interior *News from Afar* (1857) (see endnote 307), *The Illustrated London News* wrote:

> We should not conclude without confessing that there is a sad reverse to this picture of cottage comfort and content. Large numbers of our rural population are steeped in ignorance; their lives are a dreary scene of misery and depravity; the "homes" in which dwell large families are fit only for brutes; the cottagers are virtually serfs to their landlords. Look to it, ye Reformers – Conservative, Liberal, Radical, whatever ye style yourselves – for ye are alike responsible for this stain on our beloved country. [86]

The more carefree aspects of country life certainly predominate in Hardy's paintings of village life. George Eliot wrote in 1856 that:

> The notion that peasants are joyous, ... that cottage matrons are usually buxom, and village children necessarily rosy and merry, are prejudices difficult to dislodge from the artistic mind, which looks for its subjects into literature instead of life. The painter is still under the influence of idyllic literature, which has always expressed the imagination of the cultivated and town-bred, rather than the truth of rustic life. [87]

Indeed, this may well have been true for many painters, and perhaps it is equally true for their patrons. Many of them were industrialists who wished to see representations of the more pleasant aspects of village life, as they imagined or remembered from an earlier, less industrial age. Hardy had to sell his paintings in a market that had well-defined limits about what was acceptable.

Though his pictures were not representative of the lives of many villagers, Hardy was not moralising and most of his paintings did not make a direct appeal to sentimental feelings. His characters are depicted as capable and self-reliant. And there is no hint of caricature. His close involvement over many years with the lives of people in his community led to a directness of observation and sympathy of approach in his paintings, with a good deal of empathy and a lack of pretension.

By the end of the 1860s, although domestic art was still popular with the public and many reviewers, there were more critical voices. Hardy's *The Wedding Breakfast* and George Bernard O'Neill's *Children's Party* were criticised as "pictorial renderings of the 'namby pamby' class".[88]

When Social Realism, to use Graham Reynold's description, became more acceptable and marketable for a few years in the 1870s, F.D. Hardy painted several pictures illustrating the working conditions of women servants and workers.

F.D. Hardy and the Cranbrook Community

The families of the Cranbrook artists were close friends; they often dined and had tea together, were members of the Cranbrook Croquet Club,[89] and attended local dances and concerts together.[90] They attended the Volunteer Balls at the Town Hall [91] and the Fancy Dress Balls at Angley Park, Cranbrook, which once included Mrs F.D. Hardy as "Lady Blushrose", Miss Gertrude Hardy as "Chloe", Mrs George Hardy as "lady of the 18th century" and Miss M. Hardy (George Hardy's daughter, Madeleine) as "Titania". [92] The local newspapers recorded that the Christmas Ball of the "nobility and gentry of the weald of Kent and Sussex" at Cranbrook Town Hall was attended by Mr and Mrs F.D. Hardy.[93]

F.D. Hardy's sons were particularly good friends with J.C. Horsley's boys, who were about the same age; F.D. Hardy's son Lewis would go on long treks with his friend Victor Horsley (later Sir Victor), including a 40-mile walk when they were about 14 years old.[94] Graham Reynolds commented that the Cranbrook Colony "had so homogeneous an attitude towards the

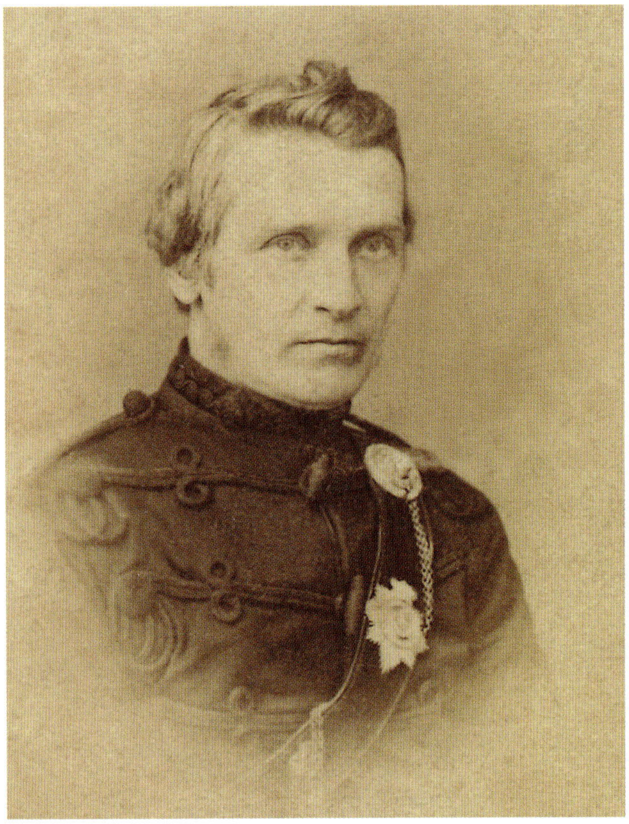

Plate 65: Frederick Daniel Hardy as an Officer in the 37th Kent Rifle Volunteer Corps.
From the photograph album of George and Sarah Hardy

interpretation of village drama that it seems an oversight that they did not choose a village called Cranford as their home".[95] Indeed, Cranbrook is portrayed as an idealised, quiet, country community. However, as in Elizabeth Gaskell's novel, the narratives often include clues to real concerns, which were not lost on their Victorian audience. Poor housing, disease and old age were underlying issues that were evident even in pleasant paintings such as F.D. Hardy's *The Doctor*, *Early Sorrow, The Leaky Roof* and *The Volunteers*.

Hardy also attended the Annual Dinners of the Cricket Club, which were held at the Bull Inn.[96] A report of the Cranbrook Cricket Club Concert gives a glimpse of F.D. Hardy's social life in the village, playing a duet on a "wretchedly tuned piano" at the club concert:

> In spite of adverse weather quite a fashionable audience assembled at the Vestry Hall, on Thursday, to do honour to local cricket, prominent in the goodly gathering being a strong muster of the fair sex, who had braved the pitiless rain to give support to the good old English game. For the occasion, the decoration of the hall was at once pretty, tasteful, and effective, not the least attractive portion being a characteristic trophy of the implements of the game neatly arranged above the stage within a circle of coloured lights, and having in the centre the monogram of the Cranbrook Cricket Club. The adornment of the stage and hall, together with all the arrangements of the concert, reflected great credit on the joint labours of Messrs. Manwaring, Burnham, Dr Harris, Delves, and the indefatigable secretary of the club, Mr. F. Winch.
>
> The programme, which was an excellent one, was opened by Messrs. Hardy and Joyce, who, in spite of a wretchedly tuned piano, gave a skillful rendering of Boggetti's pianoforte duet, entitled "Bewitching Gavotte," and the same wretched instrument marred the fine efforts of M. Sidney Leppard ... [97]

F.D. Hardy was an officer in the 37th Kent Rifle Volunteers (Plate 65) from when the Corps was formed in 1860 until he resigned his commission in 1873. The volunteer movement began in 1859 when there was a remote possibility of invasion by France. In 1859, war had started between France and the Austrian Empire and there were concerns that Britain might become involved in a European conflict. The "home guard" volunteers were part-time soldiers; F.D. Hardy would have had to buy his own uniform, gun and equipment. It was a popular movement; many enjoyed the comradeship, exercises and patriotic parades of the Volunteer Corps.

Hardy was appointed an ensign in 1860[98] and was a lieutenant from 1867.[99] There were occasional "sham fights by moonlight" between the Tenterden and Cranbrook rifle corps (it was decided beforehand who would win "after some harmless shooting").[100] Ensign F.D. Hardy provided a prize of 10s. 6d. for the rifle contest of the volunteer rifle corps[101] and led visits to the Hawkhurst Company for joint drills.[102] In the evenings, following drill inspections, there were dinners and songs in the Bull Inn with music played by the Band of the Corps.[103]

F.D. Hardy was more closely linked to the community in Cranbrook than other artists in the colony. He was a church-warden, a member of the cricket club, a member of the Kent Archaeological Society and was on the Committee of the Literary Association of Cranbrook. Along with Webster, Horsley and O'Neill, F.D. Hardy was a subscriber to the Cranbrook Soup Society, which, as the name suggests, established a soup kitchen in the town. Together with his sons, he performed at musical concerts that the Literary Association occasionally organised, usually playing the piano.

F.D. Hardy's Family

Frederick Daniel and Rebecca Hardy had five sons, Frederick ("Dorofield"), Lewis, Arthur, Edwin and Herbert [104], and a daughter, Amelia Gertrude. All their sons attended Cranbrook School.

Their eldest son, Frederick Rembrandt Hardy (1853-1937), studied at the Royal Academy School and became an artist using the pseudonym "Dorofield Hardy". He exhibited seven pictures at the Royal Academy, including portraits of J. C. Horsley and Mrs Horsley, and at several galleries in London. He lived in Kensington[105] and most of his commissions were for carefully made copies of paintings, usually portraits.

Edwin George Hardy (1859-1896), F.D. Hardy's fourth son, became an architect after studying at the Royal Academy School. As a student in 1883 he won a Royal Academy gold medal for design in architecture and a travelling scholarship (for £200), which he used to make drawings of buildings in Florence and elsewhere in Italy. These were shown at the Royal Academy Exhibitions and were published in various journals.[106] He exhibited 14 works at the Royal Academy between 1881 and 1887. Edwin's prize work in architecture, a design for a museum, was published in *The Illustrated London News*.[107]

Edwin worked initially in the office of the architect Richard Norman Shaw. Shaw became a friend of the Cranbrook Colony; he worked on Horsley's house in 1864 and, in addition to Edwin Hardy, employed a son of J.C. Horsley and a son of G.B. O'Neill in his office.

Edwin was a founder member of the St George's Art Society, one of the groups that contributed to the emergence of the Arts and Crafts Movement. The society, formed in 1883 to discuss art and architecture, was established by a group of young architects who had worked in Shaw's offices: Edwin Hardy, Gerald Horsley, Ernest Newton, Mervyn Macartney, Reginald Barratt, William Lethaby and E.S. Prior.

After working in Shaw's office, Edwin Hardy worked in the office of (Sir) Mervyn Macartney. Macartney, another pupil of Shaw's, was also responsible for some restoration work on Old Wilsley, the house in Cranbrook rented by George Bernard O'Neill. Ernest Newton wrote about Edwin Hardy:

> I was in partnership with Mervyn Macartney for some years. He was surveyor to St. Pauls at the time. The Clerk of Works told me he never went near his office in the Cathedral, quite unlike his predecessor, Somers Clarke. He was also surveyor to Durham Cathedral, but only looked in there on his way to salmon fishing in Scotland. He never took things seriously. His great mainstay had been another Norman Shaw pupil or assistant, one Hardy, who was undoubtedly a genius. But he was always going on the razzle-dazzle, returning shame-faced to take up his designing again.[108]

In his biography of Richard Norman Shaw [109], Andrew Saint quotes Shaw's son, Robert, saying about Edwin George Hardy: "He seemed very capable at first, but got into some financial trouble, and I believe committed suicide early in the nineties." Edwin Hardy took his own life in 1896 at the age of 37.[110]

After F.D. Hardy's death, his daughter, Amelia Gertrude, an amateur artist, sold much of his antique furniture at an auction at Waterloo Place on 3 October 1911 and lived until 1952 in her father's former studio in Cranbrook High Street. She died on 11 March 1952 and was buried at St Dunstan's Church in Cranbrook.

George Hardy

George Hardy, eldest brother of F.D. Hardy, was born on 21 November 1822 and baptised at St Nicholas Church less than a month later. On the recommendation of family friend Thomas Webster RA, George entered the Royal Academy Schools in 1841. His lived at Windsor until 1848, but for Royal Academy exhibit for 1849 he gave his address as 7 Marylebone Street in London. By 1861 George Hardy was living at White Barn in Brenchley, Kent, and then after his marriage he resided firstly at Rose Cottage, Waterloo Road, Cranbrook, close to where his brother F.D. Hardy lived, and then at Fernside Villa, also in Cranbrook.

Few pictures by George Hardy exist, compared to the hundreds by his brother Frederick Daniel and cousin Heywood; only some 50 pictures by George Hardy are owned by galleries or have been sold in the past 20 years.

George Hardy exhibited 41 paintings at the Royal Academy between 1846 and 1892. The first was *Study from Nature* (1846). Several paintings of interiors were exhibited between 1847 and 1849. As mentioned previously, there was a comment about *Interior of an English Cottage* (1849) in *The Art Journal*: "Every brick in the floor is marked; it is a successful story in all but the white round the fire-place."[111] Another early painting, *The Leisure Hour* (1855) (Plate 67), reflects the influence of seventeenth-century Dutch interiors and his mentor, Thomas Webster.

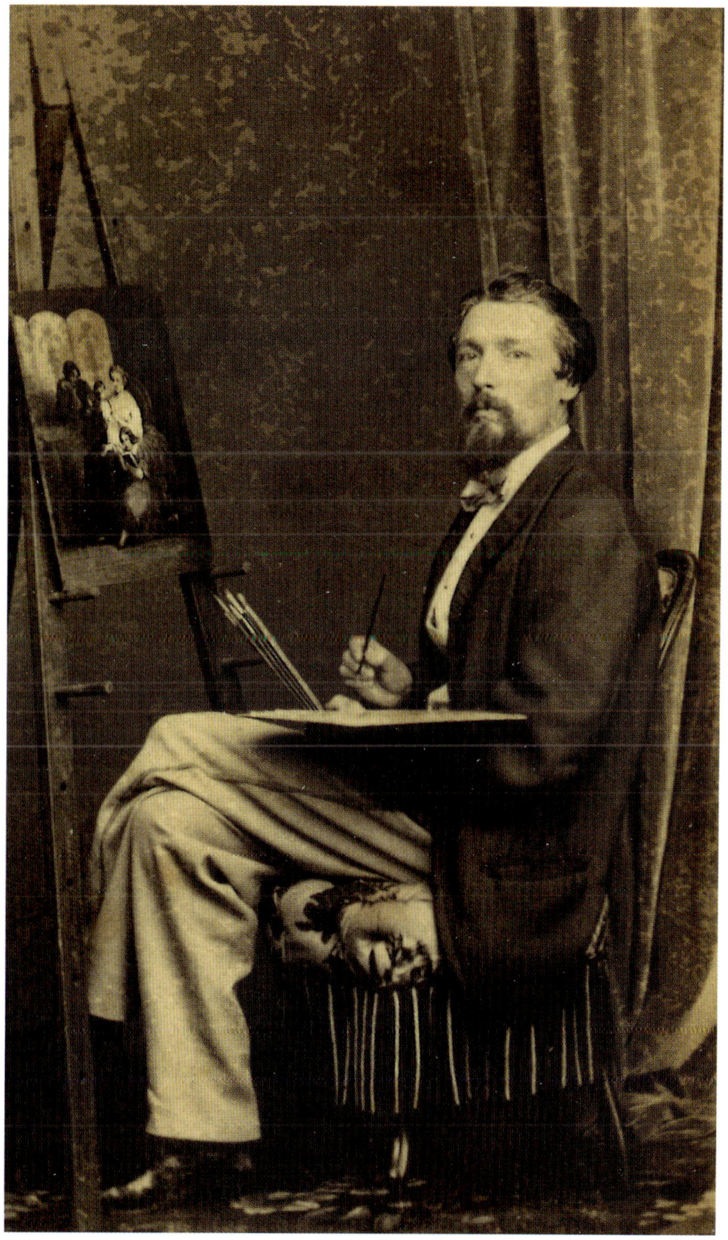

Plate 66: George Hardy, elder brother of F.D. Hardy. Original image taken by Verneuil Photography.
FROM THE PHOTOGRAPH ALBUM OF GEORGE AND SARAH HARDY

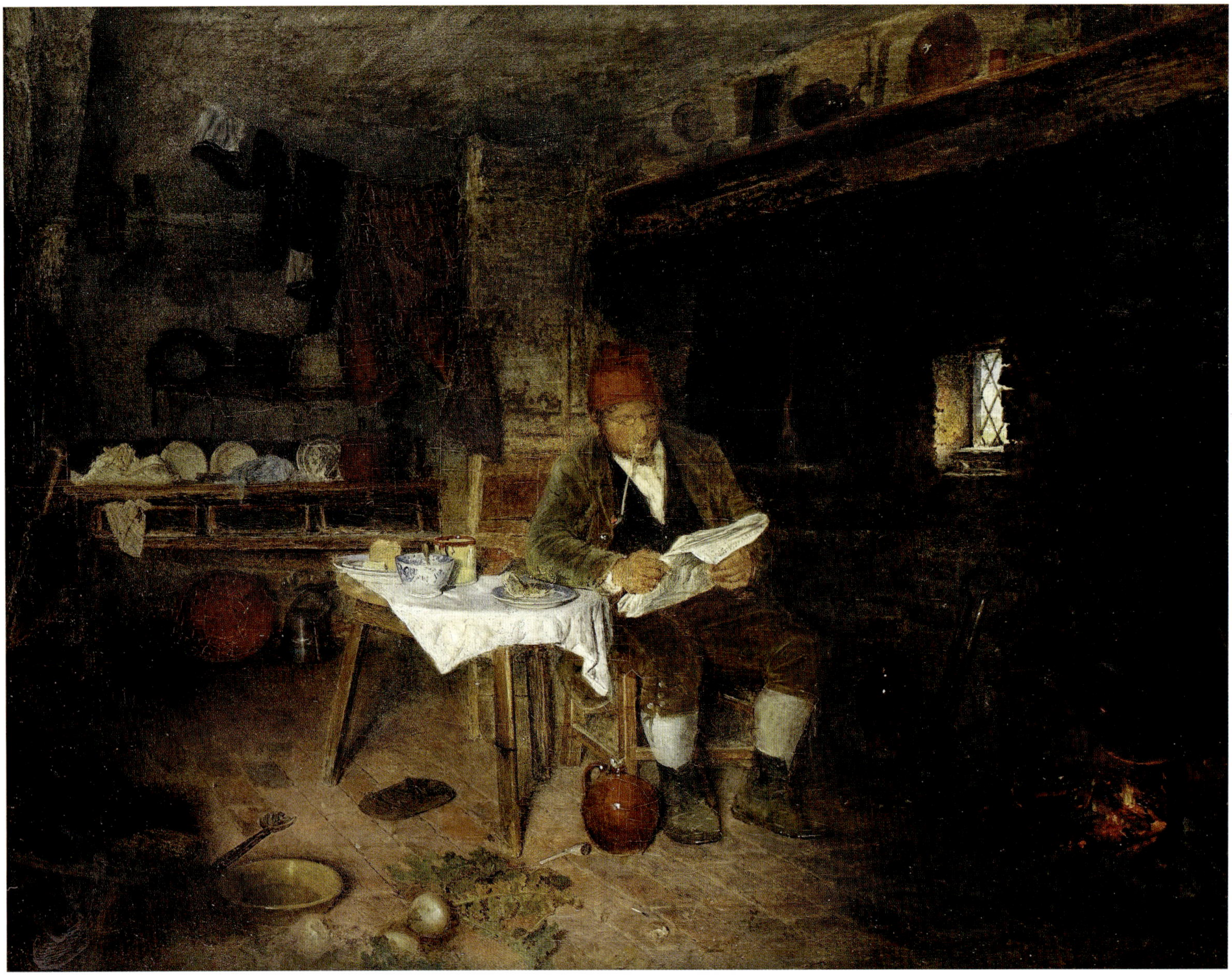

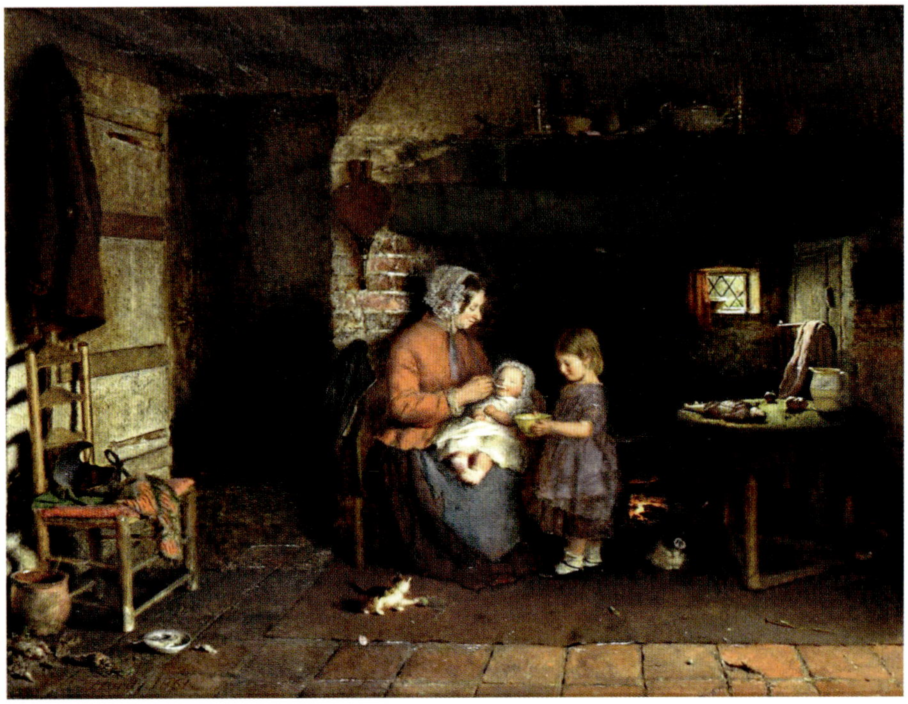

Plate 67 (above): The Leisure Hour, 1855
George Hardy. Oil on panel. 17.5 x 21.5cm.
Private Collection

Plate 68 (left): Pap, 1861
George Hardy. Oil on panel. 20.5 x 25.5cm.
Private Collection

George Hardy helped to teach his younger brother Frederick, but their paintings indicate that by the mid-1850s Frederick could paint as well as George. In 1861 George painted *Pap* (Plate 68), which is similar to Frederick's *Expectation: Interior of Cottage with Mother and Children*, painted in 1854 (Plate 9).

George travelled to France during the 1850s; he exhibited several interiors of French cottages at the Royal Society of British Artists exhibitions, including *Cottage Interior – Dieppe* (1852) and *A Peasant's Cottage – Normandy* (1852). Perhaps the four paintings with French titles that he exhibited at the Royal Academy after he was married in 1862 were based on these earlier studies. *La Soeur de Charité* (Plate 69), a Royal Academy exhibit of 1866, is an interior of a fisherman's cottage. George subsequently painted the right-hand side of the painting again as *Early Teaching* (Plate 70), possibly as a commission from Sidney Cartwright who owned the picture.

The Art Journal commented on *La Soeur de Charité*:

The Dutch School of Teniers and Ostade and the cognate Scotch school of Wilkie, have many adherents and successful imitators. Hardy, Clark, Hunt, Lucas, Provis and Smith, are names which have been, for some years past, identified with small cottage interiors peopled by peasants, pots, pails and pans. There are two artists rejoicing in the name of Hardy: the one, F.D. HARDY, remembered as the painter of "The Sweep" and "The Leaky Roof" in former exhibitions. ... G. HARDY, the second artist of the name, is represented by one

Plate 69: La Soeur de Charité, 1866
George Hardy. Oil on canvas. 44 x 69cm. Private Collection

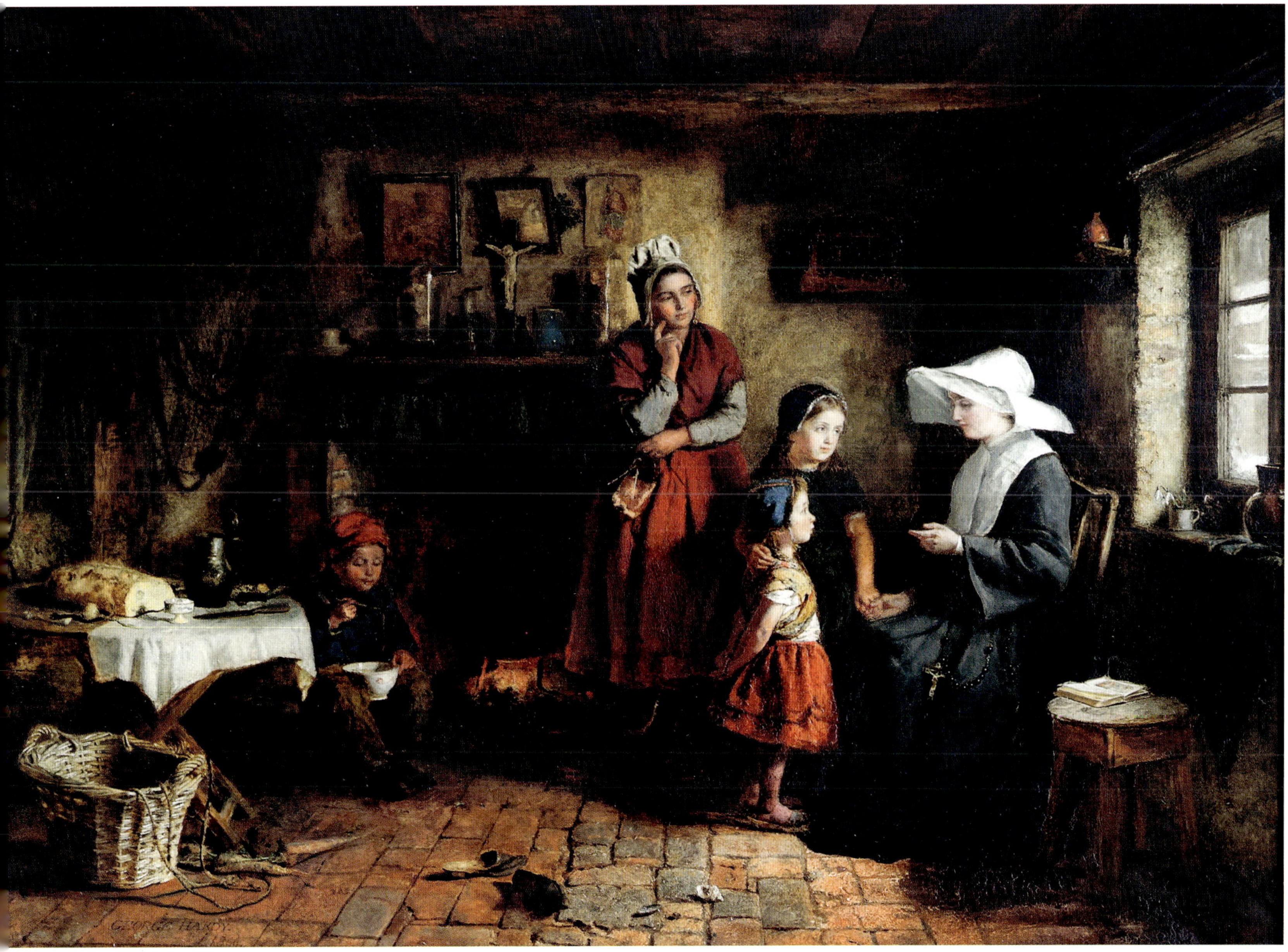

Plate 70 (opposite page): **Early Teaching**
George Hardy. Oil on panel. 45.4 x 37.5cm.
© Wolverhampton Art Gallery

of the best examples of our English revival of the small Dutch school. The composition has the skillful distribution of Ostade, the details are circumstantial, the execution is certain and minute, and the colour has a rich harmony. Those are just the qualities we look for in such small interiors, where manner has to make amends for lack of weighty argument.[112]

Following the death of his wife, Ellen, George Hardy lived with his daughter Louise and her husband, Rev. Charles Pratt, firstly at Eastbourne and then at The Rectory, Warbleton, Sussex, where he died on 20 November 1909, aged 86.

George Hardy's second daughter, Marguerite Ellen, was an artist. She made paintings of the Kent countryside and exhibited "Studio of Thomas Webster, R.A." at the Society of British Artists (Suffolk Street Gallery) in 1893. Following her marriage to Mr Llewelyn Tipping M.A., the first principal (and one of the founders) of Islamia College, Peshawar, she painted watercolours of mountain scenes in the Khyber Pass.

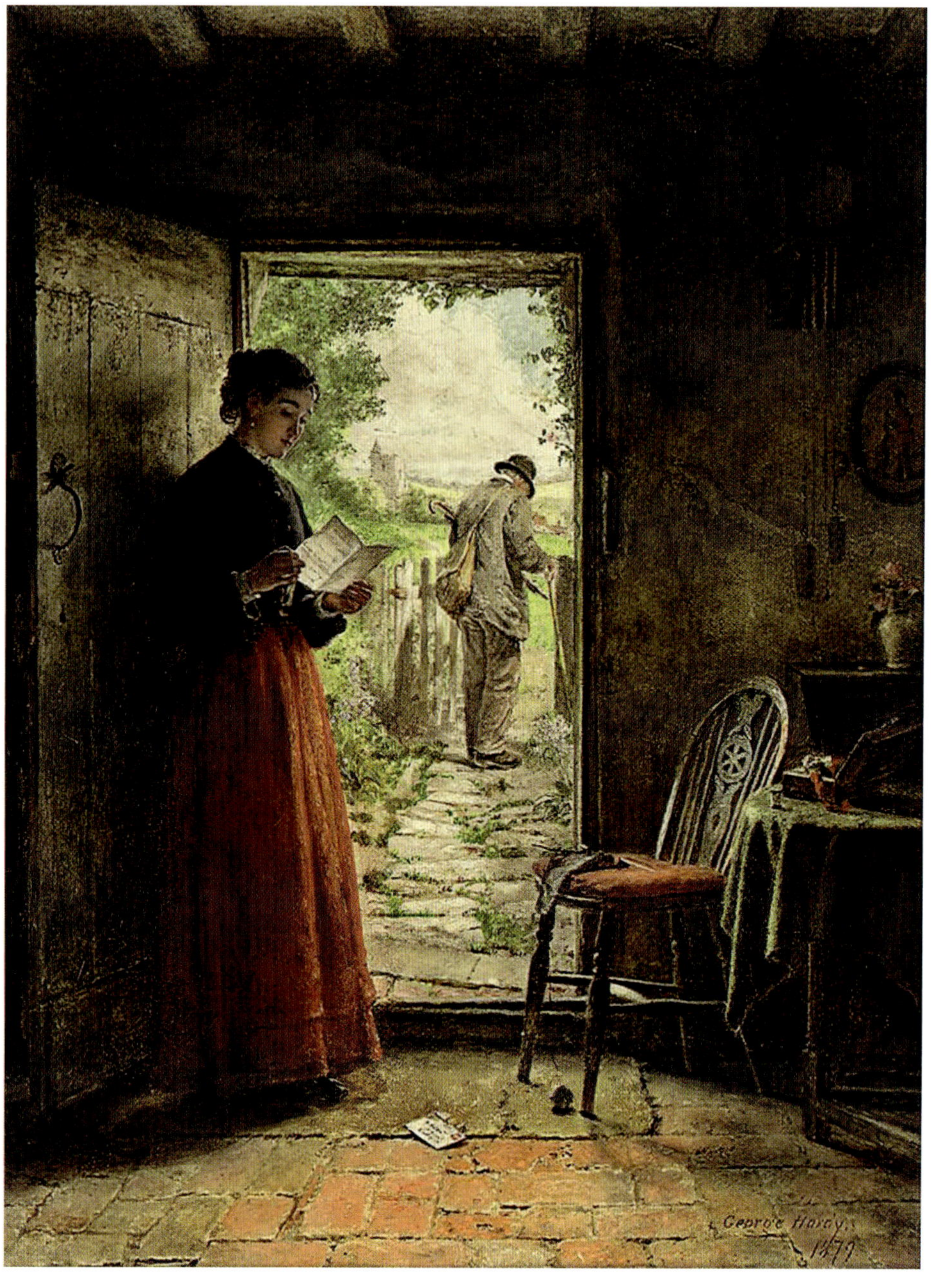

Plate 71: The Welcome Letter, 1879
George Hardy. Oil on board. 46 x 34.9cm. George Hardy painted several pictures of this view of the open door and garden path. Private Collection

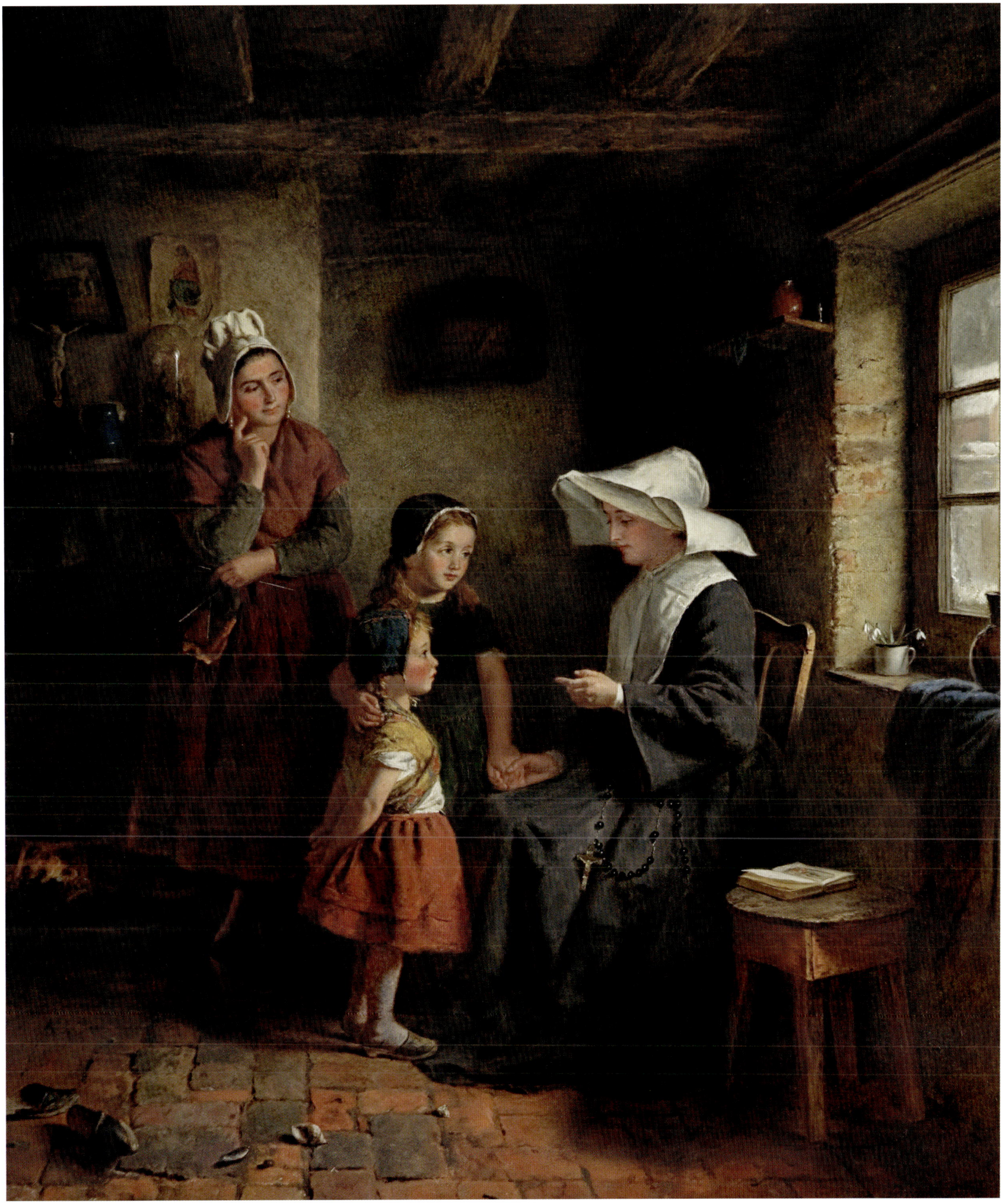

CHAPTER THREE

Heywood Hardy, Early Years: Keynsham and Paris

Heywood Hardy, cousin to Frederick Daniel and George, was born in Chichester, Sussex, on 25 November 1842, the youngest of ten children of the artist James Hardy senior and his wife, Elizabeth (née Vinson). In 1846 the family moved from their home at 55 Westgate, Chichester, to Bath; all their belongings were loaded onto a farm cart and they spent four days on the road, camping at night. In Bath they lived firstly at 8 Lower East Hayes, a three-storey terraced house on the London Road. And from 1851 they lived at 30 Henrietta Street, a Georgian crescent close to the centre of Bath.

In 1927 Heywood Hardy wrote that he often looked back to his boyhood when he began painting at their house in Henrietta Street.[113] There were studios from basement to garret. Young Heywood's studio was on the ground floor, where he would bring in dogs, donkeys and goats as models for his paintings. On the first floor his brother James had his studio. His father, James Hardy senior, occupied the drawing room for painting portraits and miniatures. Above that was his brother David's studio, and in the attic his sister Ada had her studio for painting portraits and miniatures in watercolour. By the time Heywood was ten years old his elder brother James was already receiving praise for the paintings he exhibited in Bristol and Bath.[114]

A few of Heywood Hardy's earliest paintings survive, dating from 1858 and 1859.[115] Painted when he was 15 or 16 years old, they are oil paintings of animals, such as *Waiting for Master* (1859) (Plate 72). Although they reflect some influence of his elder brother James, who was a specialist in still-life studies of game birds in the 1850s, it seems that Heywood quickly established his own interests. He spent much less time than James painting in watercolours; his primary interest was animal painting in oils followed a few years later by landscapes.

Heywood had fond memories of his family home when his brothers and sisters were there, but by 1860 all except his brother Thomas had left home; Thomas remained as assistant to his father while Ada, Georgiana, David and James Hardy junior had all become artists or art teachers.

Heywood left home when he was 17 years old. He was unable to live with his quick-tempered father; after a furious argument Heywood left for Keynsham, five miles from Bristol, where his sister Ada lived. Many years after his father had died, Heywood Hardy painted a portrait of him (Plate 79), which may be compared with his father's self-portrait (Plate 200) on p.156.

After he left his home in Bath, Heywood lived most of the time at Keynsham (in a house on the Bath Road), but in 1861 he stayed for a time with his brother James Hardy junior and his wife who were living with her parents in Tewkesbury, Gloucestershire. At Keynsham he tried to earn a living as an animal and landscape artist. Typical of his early works are pictures of shepherds, for

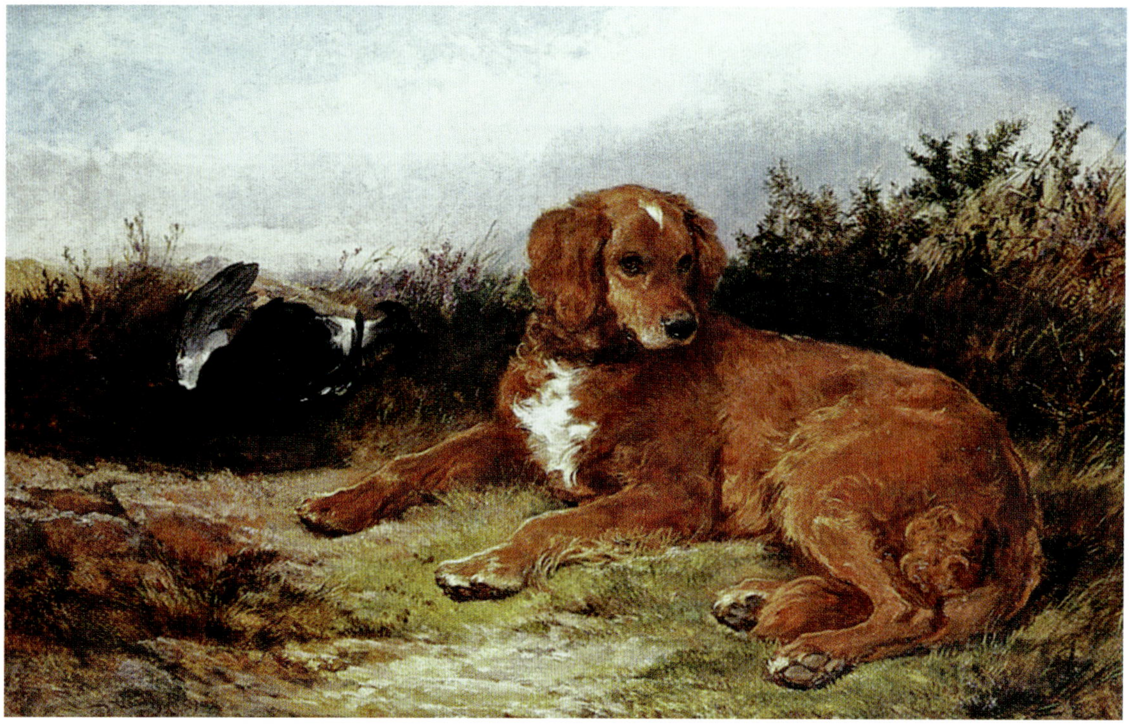

Plate 72: Waiting for Master, 1859
Heywood Hardy. Oil on canvas. 47 x 71.1cm. Private Collection

Plate 73 (opposite page): Fetch Them In, 1860
Heywood Hardy. Oil on canvas. 36.8 x 31.5cm.[116] Private Collection

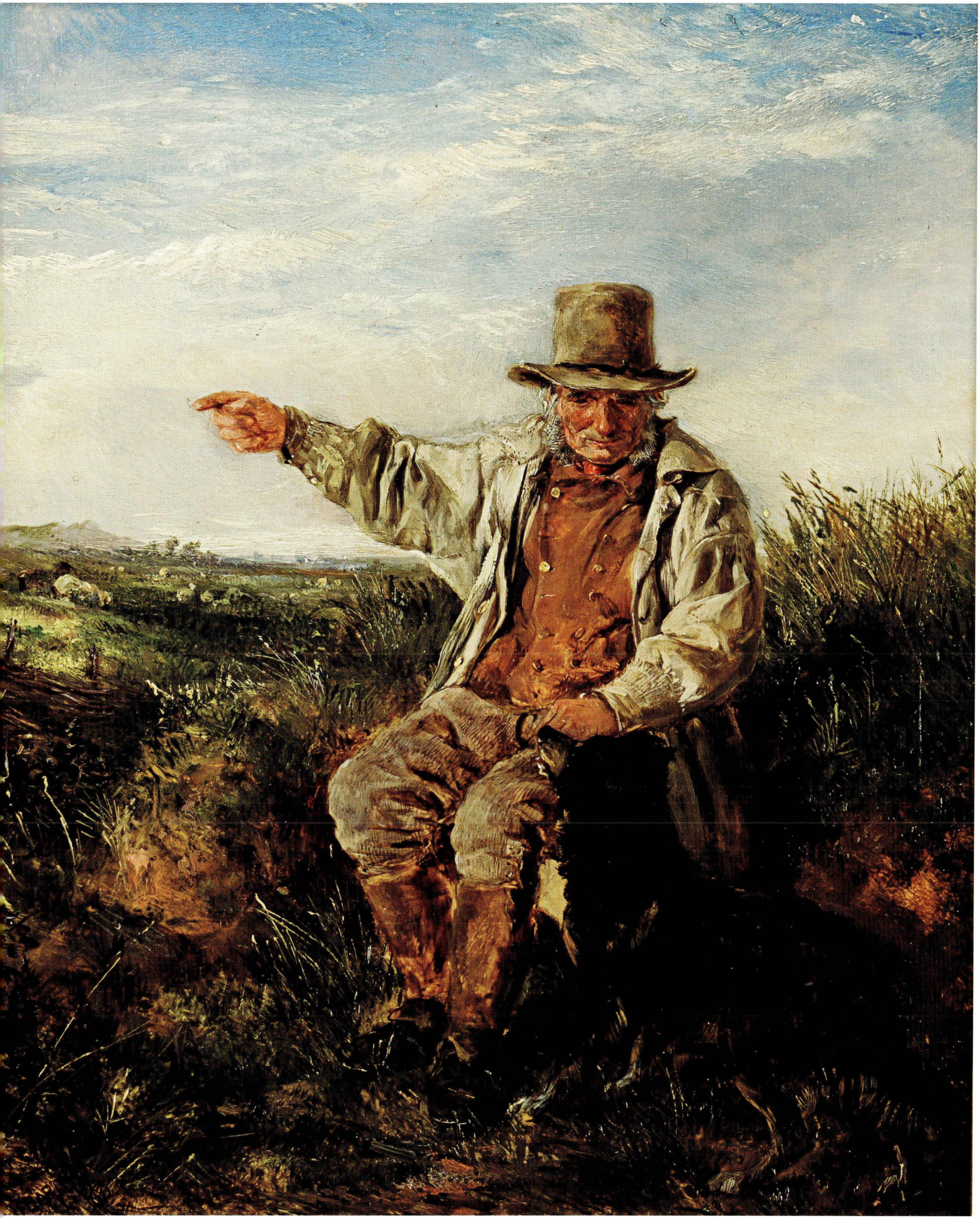

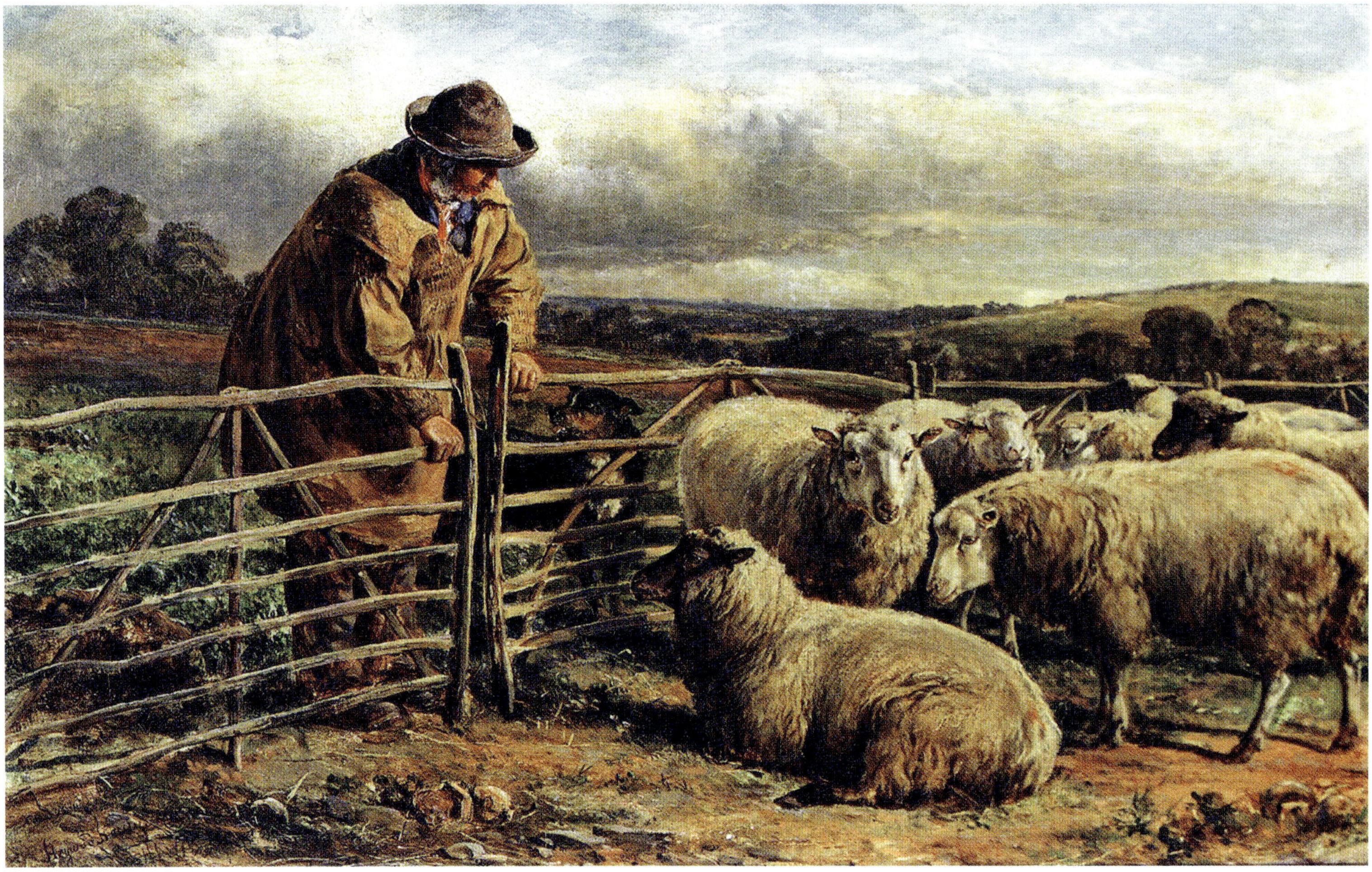

Plate 74: At the End of the Day, 1863
Heywood Hardy**.** Oil on canvas. 40.7 x 63.2cm. Private Collection

example *Fetch Them In* (1860) (Plate 73) and *At the End of the Day* (1863) (Plate 74), and paintings of dogs such as *A Jack Russell Terrier Rabbiting* (1865) (Plate 75).

One of his earliest landscapes is *At Keynsham, Gloucestershire* (1866) (Plate 76); the Church of St John the Baptist is in the distance.

Heywood Hardy found it very difficult to earn a living as a painter in the West Country. Some years later, when he was living in London as a successful artist, he "dreamt one night that he was back in Bristol and woke up in a frightful tremor of alarm as he had never experienced before, the prospect being so distinctly unpleasing".[117]

Despite the difficulties of his early career, he persevered and began exhibiting at the Royal Academy when he was 21 years old; two landscapes were accepted in 1864, one of which was painted near Cork when he visited Ireland.[118] However, neither painting raised comment in reviews of the exhibition.

Heywood became a close friend of William Henry Hopkins (1825-1892), who lived near Keynsham and specialised in pictures of horses and the surrounding countryside. In 1863 Heywood collaborated with Hopkins on a commission from Queen Victoria to paint pictures of two of the late Prince Albert's favourite horses. Another friend at this time was local landscape artist John Syer (1815-1885); they collaborated to paint *Summer Landscape with Drover and Cattle* (1864).

Heywood and William Henry Hopkins were both members of the 7th Somersetshire Rifle Volunteer Corps that had been formed in Keynsham in February 1860. In February 1864 Heywood Hardy was appointed an officer of the Corps, holding the same rank as his cousin, F.D. (see page 62). He replaced Hopkins who was promoted from ensign to lieutenant and who shortly thereafter became Captain of the Corps.[119] A photograph of Heywood Hardy in 1864 shows him in his ensign's uniform (Plate 78). Hardy was an officer for only a few months; he resigned later in 1864 just before he left for Paris.[120]

In 1864 Heywood Hardy borrowed money from his brother James and went to Paris to study at the École des Beaux-Arts. It is unlikely that his brother was able to lend him much; in March 1859 James had appeared at the Bath County Court as an insolvent debtor with debts of about £240 and assets of £50 available for the creditors.[121] The debt was a considerable sum; for example, his father, James Hardy senior, paid an annual rent of £32 for their house at 30 Henrietta Street in Bath.[122]

Heywood was ambitious and may have decided to study in Paris as he recognised his limited prospects as a landscape and sporting artist in the West Country. Also, the debts accumulated by his elder brother might have prompted Heywood to pursue a different path. And no doubt the idea of enjoying two or three years in Paris played its part in his decision; Heywood was very sociable and enjoyed music, the arts and travel.

Some of the leading artists of the day, including John Everett Millais, one of the founders of the Pre-Raphaelite Brotherhood, were against the idea of British painters learning their trade abroad, but in the 1860s an increasing number of artists went to Paris. The 1863 reforms to the curriculum at the École des Beaux-Arts meant that instruction in painting as well as drawing was included for the first time, adding to the school's attraction for young artists. And there were an increasing number of private schools and studios run by French artists who catered for foreign painters. British artists often preferred the free and spontaneous approach to painting that was taught in some of the private schools.

Heywood Hardy's studies were supervised by Isidore Pils (1813-1875), who had been appointed Professor of Painting at the École des Beaux-Arts in January 1864. Pils had specialised in religious scenes earlier in his career, but in the 1850s, with the start of the Crimean war, he received commissions from the French government to paint military pictures.[123]

From records in the archives of the École, it appears that Heywood was not registered as a full-time student nor as a graduate of the school. But some professors allowed artists to attend their courses as part-time students. Heywood apparently spent much of his time copying in the Louvre; his inscription as a "copyiste" is in the Louvre archives. Many students copied paintings in the Louvre in the 1860s; often it was part of their training and for some an important source of income.

The bohemian Heywood Hardy had little money in Paris and usually ate in Pierre-Louis Duval's popular "Bouillons"; these restaurants had just opened in the 1860s, serving cheap soup and bread. He occasionally "dabbled in the occult" with the help of a visiting medium and two friends who shared his apartment and studio.

After studying under Pils at the École, Heywood continued his studies in the studio of Henri Coroënne (1822-1909) at 112 rue du Faubourg-Poissonnière in Paris. He became friends with

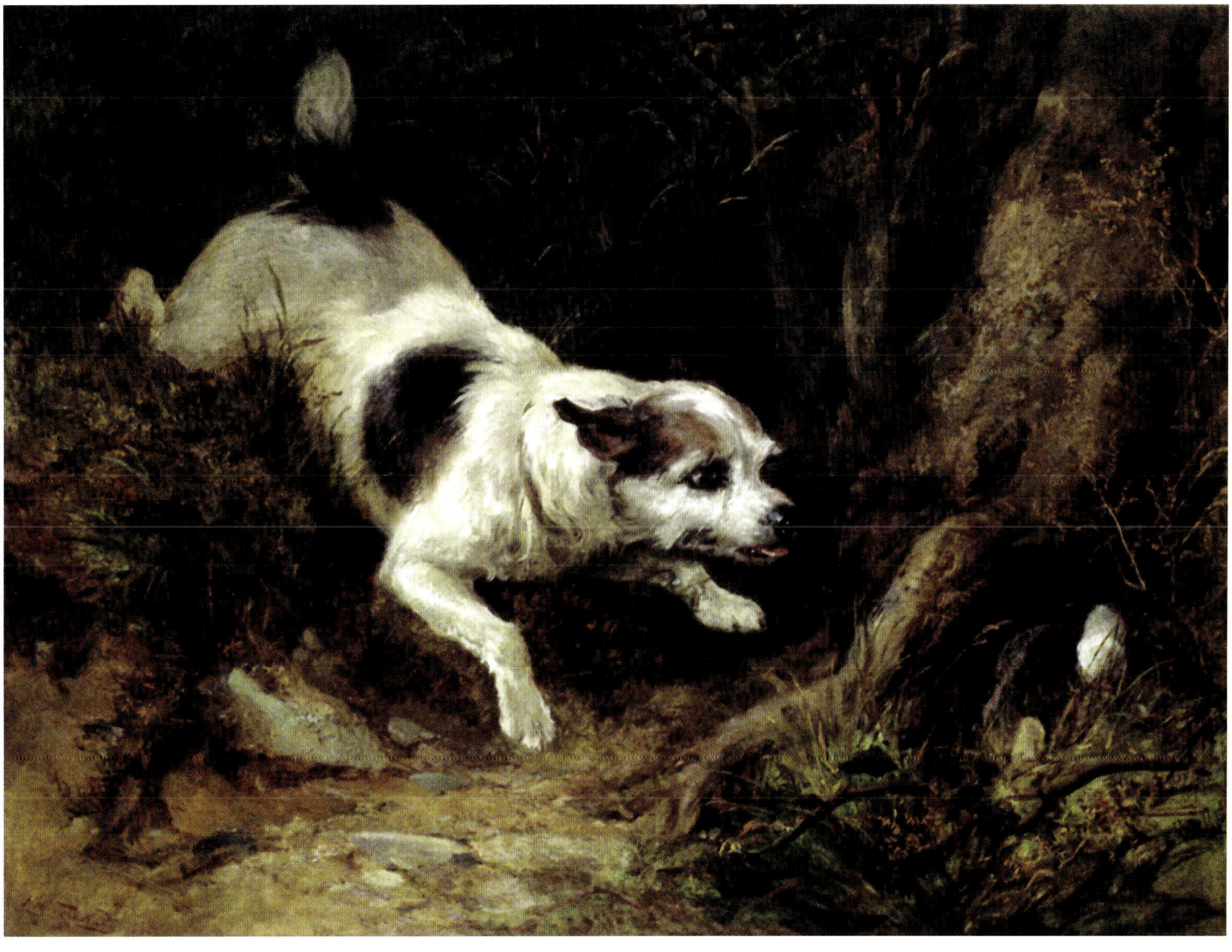

Plate 75: A Jack Russell Terrier Rabbiting, 1865
Heywood Hardy. Oil on canvas. 70.5 x 90.8cm. Private Collection

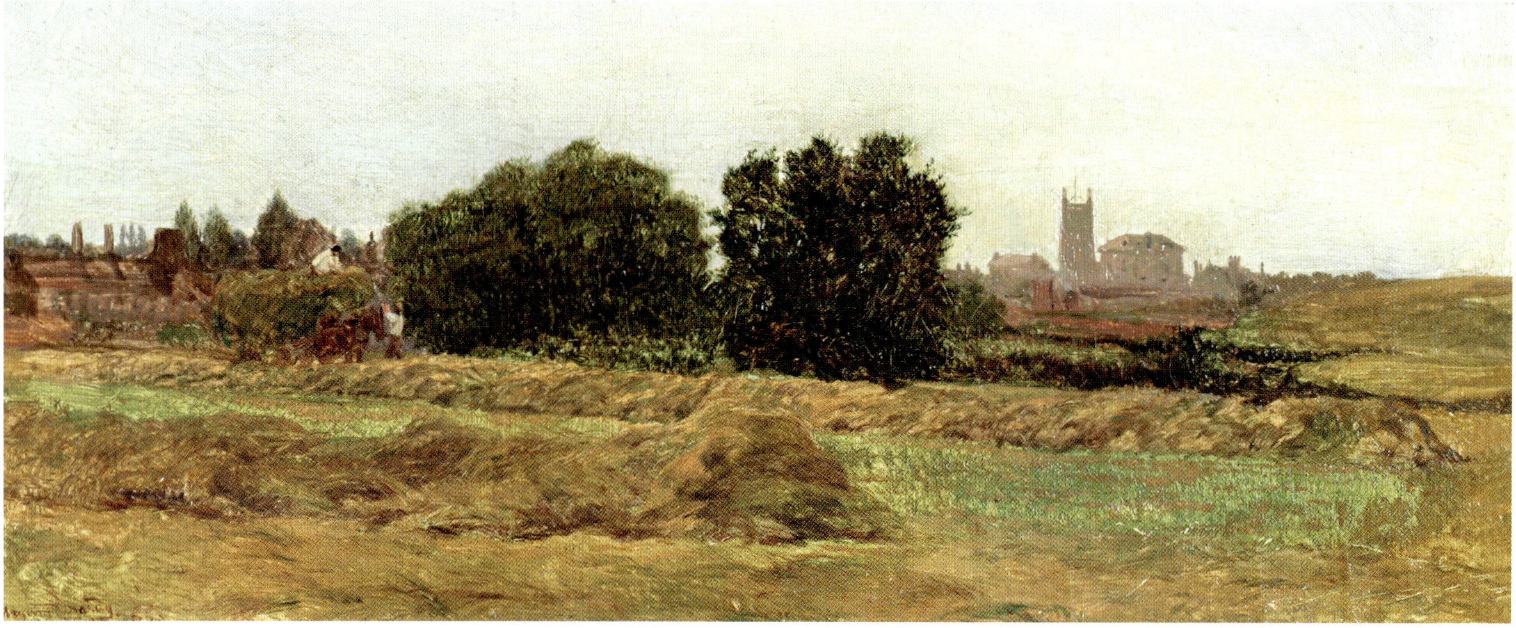

Plate 76: At Keynsham, Gloucestershire, 1866
Heywood Hardy. Oil on canvas, 16 x 37cm. Private Collection

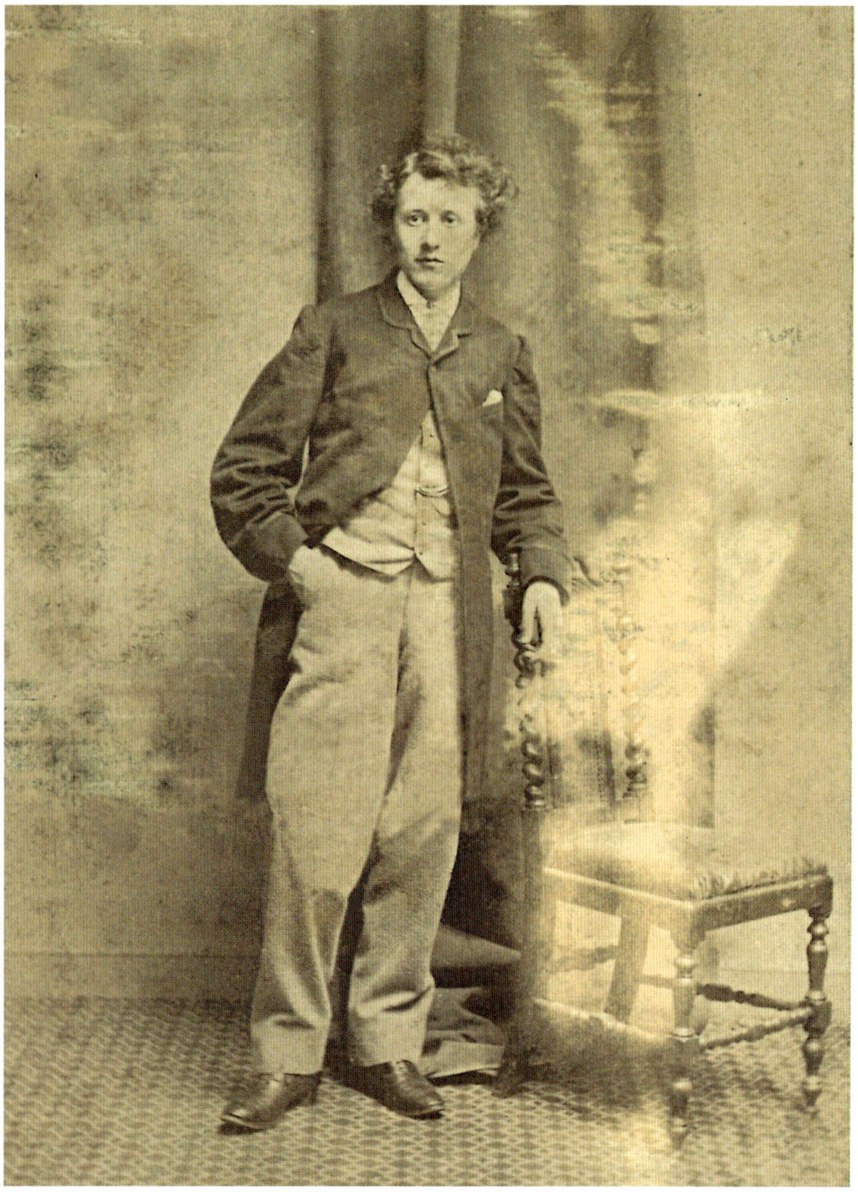

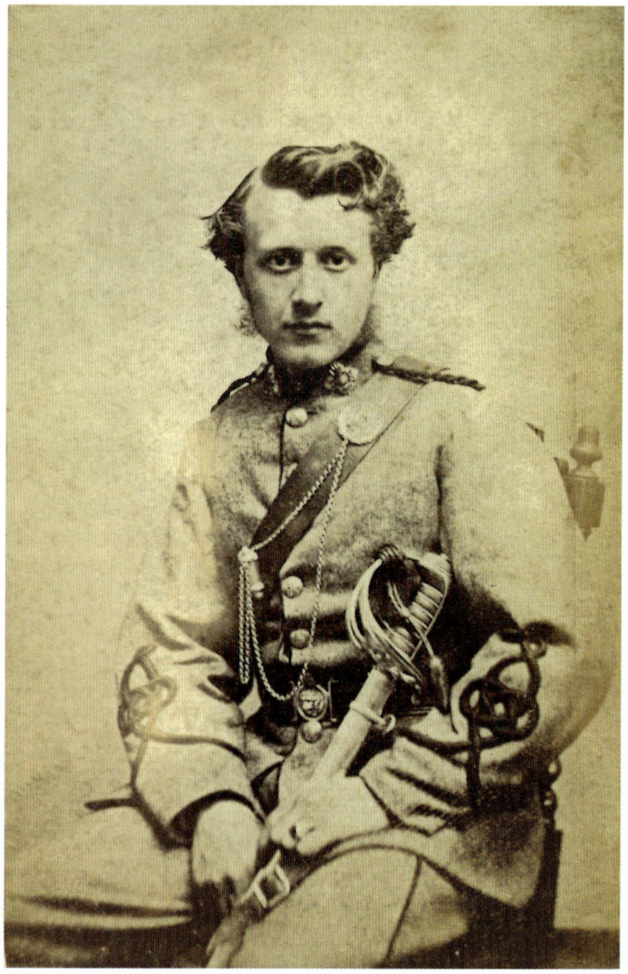

Plate 77 (left): Heywood Hardy in 1863.
From the photograph album of George and Sarah Hardy

Plate 78 (above): Heywood Hardy in 1864, as an ensign in the 7th Somersetshire Rifle Volunteer Corps.
From the photograph album of George and Sarah Hardy

two artists who were too old to join the École des Beaux-Arts and all three worked in Coroënne's studio. Henri Coroënne was mainly a portrait painter; he had studied under François-Édouard Picot and had made many copies of paintings of Rembrandt and Rubens. After two years in Paris, Heywood returned to England via Antwerp where he presumably studied the works of Rubens and other Flemish painters.

While he was in Paris and Antwerp, Heywood Hardy continued to send pictures to the Royal Academy. *Windsor Park* was accepted for the Royal Academy exhibition in 1865 and *Au Soir* in 1866. There were no comments about either painting in reviews of the exhibition.

Heywood and his brother James Hardy junior contributed numerous paintings to the exhibitions of the Society of British Artists; in 1865 Heywood contributed *Views of Wales* (Langland Bay and Swansea Bay), and in 1866 *Cornfield near Tintagel* and three other paintings (giving his address as c/o Mr W.H. Hopkins, Willsbridge, Bristol).

Heywood Hardy continued to send pictures to exhibitions in the West Country; in the 1867 exhibition of the Bath and West of England Society his father and the three brothers, James, David and Heywood exhibited 40 pictures in all. A year later he exhibited *The First Crop – Scene at Keynsham* and *The Reaper* with the same society.

Eventually, in 1867, a landscape by Heywood received some recognition from an art correspondent. *The Art Journal's* review of the exhibition at the British Institution noted: "We have been exceedingly pleased with a thoroughly truthful study, 'The Mowers', by Heywood Hardy. If the artist goes on in this way, he will do well."[124]

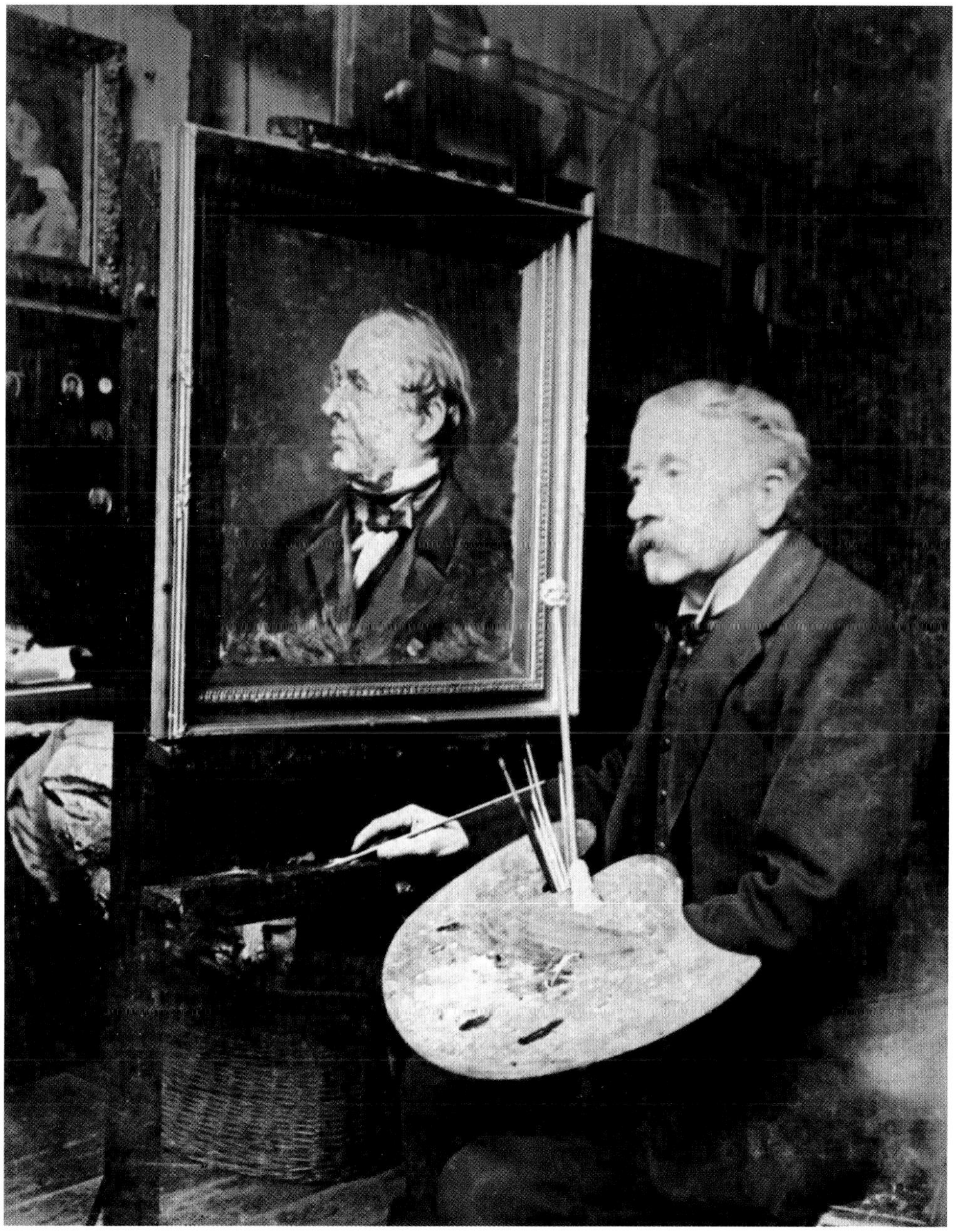

Plate 79: Heywood Hardy and a portrait of his father, James Hardy Senior. Ca. 1910.
Photograph courtesy of David Hardy Ivens

CHAPTER FOUR

Heywood Hardy, London: New Directions

By 1868 Heywood Hardy had returned to England from Paris and Antwerp. He found lodgings at Goring in Oxfordshire, near the bridge over the Thames, which was ideal for his purpose; he was still primarily interested in animal and landscape painting at this time. He rented rooms in a building that is now part of the Miller of Mansfield inn. And he also rented a nearby orchard, with a barn that he converted into a studio.

He kept his links with the Bristol artist John Syer; both Heywood and his brother James contributed to the picture of Betws-y-Coed painted by Syer in 1868 that was later given as a wedding present by the City of Bristol to the Duke and Duchess of York (later King George V and Queen Mary) in 1893.

However, Heywood's circle of artist friends had by then expanded beyond his West Country connections and included several painters he had met in Paris. Visitors to his house shortly after his return to England included Frederick (Fred) Walker, who returned to London on 11 June from a visit to the Continent. Fred and his mother spent about a month with Heywood Hardy in the summer of 1868 before Walker continued on his journey to Somerset.[125] At Goring, Walker started painting a garden scene, *Lilies*, and he worked on his sketch for a large oil painting, *The Old Gate* (now in the Tate Gallery), his highly acclaimed exhibit at the Royal Academy exhibition of 1969.

At this time Heywood Hardy began his association with the art dealer William Agnew, a close friend of Fred Walker's. This was an important step in his career; Agnew commissioned several paintings and had numerous engravings made.

Having settled in Goring, Heywood Hardy married Mary Beechey on 30 June 1868. The first of their four daughters, Nina,

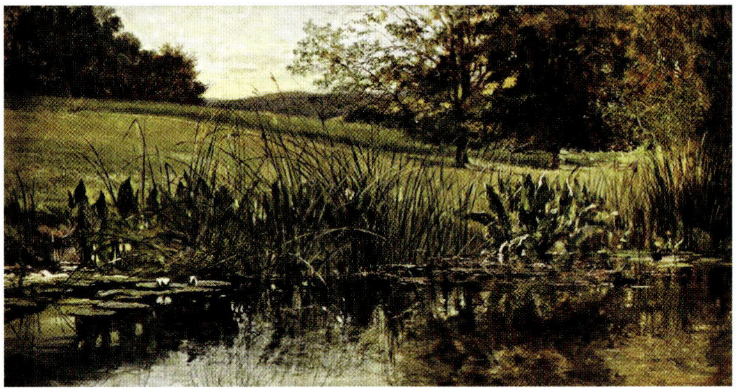

was born the following year. Mary's family included several professional and amateur artists. Mary was the youngest daughter of Rear Admiral Frederick William Beechey, a Fellow of the Royal Society and President of the Royal Geographical Society. He was also an accomplished amateur artist who had illustrated several accounts of his voyages. Mary's grandparents were the portrait painter Sir William Beechey (portrait painter to Queen Charlotte) and Lady Beechey (née Miss Anne Phyllis Jessop), an accomplished painter of miniatures. Two of Mary's uncles were artists, George Duncan Beechey and Richard Brydges Beechey. Her sister, Frances Anne Hopkins, was an artist who travelled extensively in Canada; several paintings made on her travels in canoes to fur-trading outposts with her husband are in Canadian museums.

Hardy painted several scenes around Goring, such as *By the Riverbank* (Plate 80) ("No 1 Backwater, Goring/August 1869/H. Hardy" is written on the back of the painting) and *Barge on the upper Thames* (Plate 81). And in 1872 he painted *Corn Stooks by*

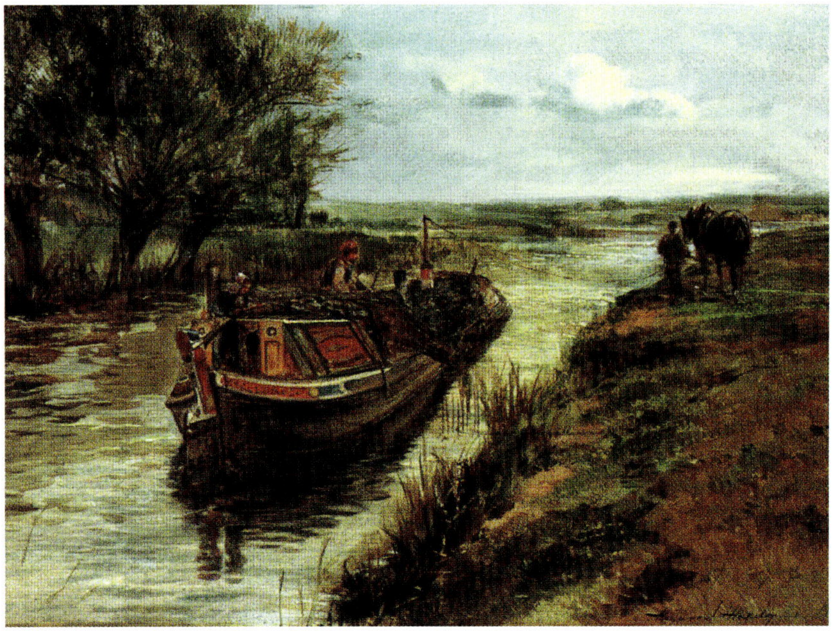

Plate 80 (above): By the Riverbank, 1869
Heywood Hardy. Oil on canvas. 21.6 x 39.4cm. PRIVATE COLLECTION[126]

Plate 81 (left): Barge on the Upper Thames
Heywood Hardy. Oil on canvas. 23 x 30.5cm. PRIVATE COLLECTION

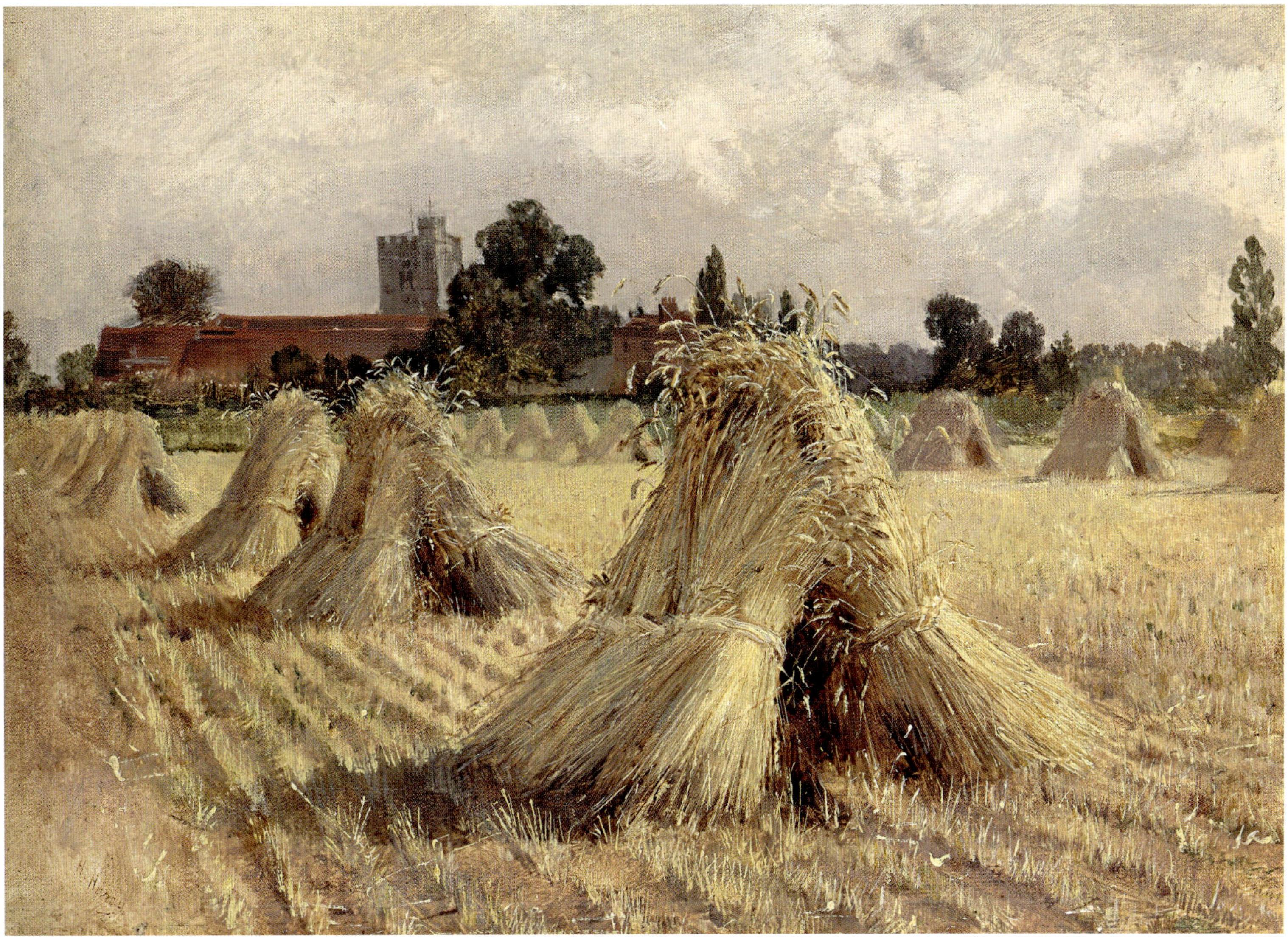

Plate 82: Corn Stooks by Bray Church, 1872
Heywood Hardy. Oil on paper laid on board. 20.3 x 27.9cm. Yale Center for British Art, Paul Mellon Collection, USA

Bray Church (Plate 82); Bray is close to the Thames near Maidenhead.

By 1870 Heywood Hardy had moved to St John's Wood in London, firstly to 42 Grove End Road and later, from 1872, to 19 St John's Wood Road. He shared a studio for a short while with the animal painter Briton Rivière. St John's Wood was a popular address for artists; perhaps the most famous resident of Grove End Road was James Tissot, who lived in grand style at number 17 after he moved to England following the collapse of the Paris Commune that he supported.

To support his family and home in St John's Wood (by 1871 Heywood and Mary Hardy had two daughters and three servants) Hardy had to produce pictures that would sell at higher prices than his landscapes and animal paintings. When he moved to London he immediately began to paint new subjects. He greatly expanded the range of themes and tried many new ideas in the 1870s, though animal painting always formed an important element of his work.

Heywood used his skills in drawing and painting animals as a basis for pictures that would appeal to the Victorian public and art collectors. Heywood Hardy and Briton Riviére, the other prominent animal painter in the 1870s, both experimented with classical and mythological scenes (Rivière's paintings of classical subjects were more successful than Hardy's), and with sentimental pictures of children and dogs. As artists who followed the highly successful animal painter Sir Edwin Landseer, who died in 1873, Rivière and Hardy took different paths: Rivière was Landseer's direct successor and became a master of the archetypal Victorian sentimental picture. He was also Landseer's successor in his technical mastery of animal painting. Heywood painted a few sentimental pictures, but he avoided painting pictures of children and animals that were designed to generate strong feelings of pity and he did not succumb to Landseer's tendency to imbue his animals with human feelings and emotions.

Heywood and Rivière were often mentioned together, and compared, as the two young, promising animal painters of the day:

> Landseer's mantle as an animal painter was believed to have fallen on Mr. Briton Rivière: but within the last few

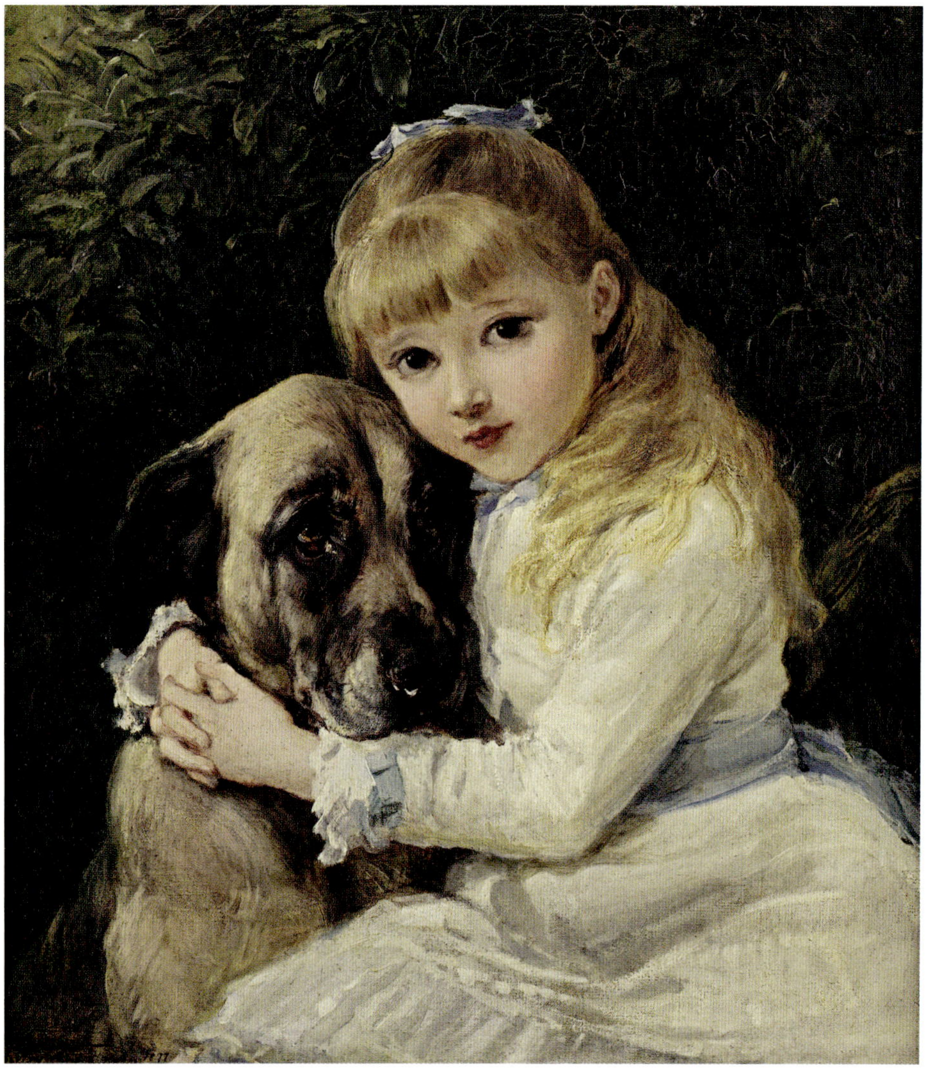

Plate 83 (left): Best Friends, 1877
Heywood Hardy. Oil on canvas. 56 x 78cm.
Private Collection

Plate 84 (below): He Won't Hurt You, 1875
After Heywood Hardy. Engraving.
From The Illustrated London News. [127]

Plate 85 (opposite page): Her Only Playmates, 1870
Heywood Hardy. Oil on canvas. 37.5 x 32.4cm.
Private Collection

> years it has been made evident that if it has not, like St. Anthony's, been divided, Mr. Heywood Hardy has at least a good a right to wear it as the first named artist. M. Briton Rivière and Mr. Heywood Hardy have both fortunately some important works here, and an examination of these may assist the public to form an opinion as to which is most natural in his treatment of animals subjects. [128]

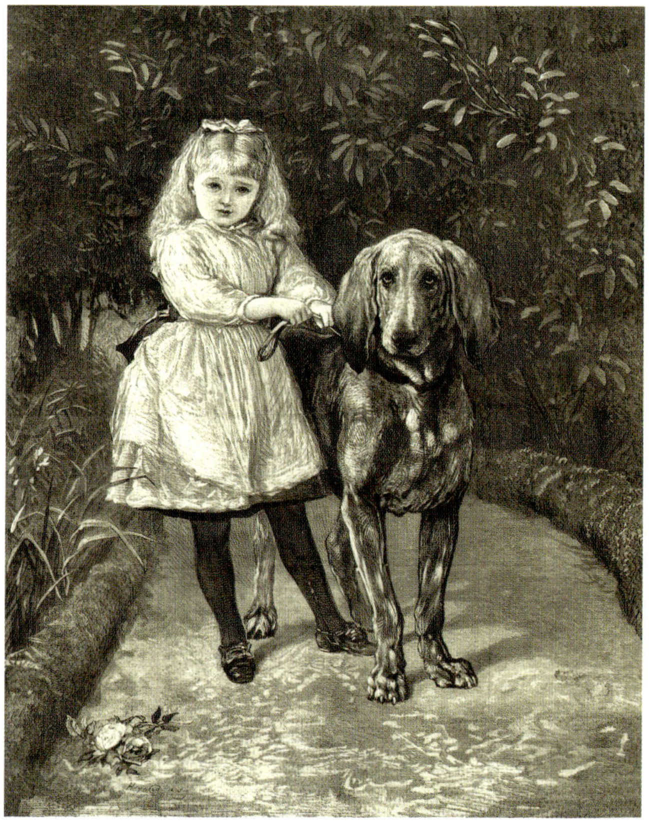

And a reviewer of the Winter Exhibition at the Dudley Gallery noted:

> "The Stricken Lioness", by Heywood Hardy, has much of the vigour of the famous fighting lions of the Academy. In "A Prince of Orange", by Briton Rivière, the puppy might be stamped "Landseer".[129]

In the 1870s Hardy's pictures of girls with large dogs were an immediate success, particularly *Her Only Playmates* (1870) (Plate 85), *He Won't Hurt You* (1874) (Plate 84), *Best Friends* (1877) (Plate 83) and *In the Lap of Luxury* (1880). *Her Only Playmates*, a picture of girl with a pug and a St Bernard, was exhibited at the Royal Academy in 1870. It was the first of many of his paintings to be reproduced as popular mezzotint engravings, by George H. Every in England and by William Wellstood in America.

A typical contemporary comment on *He Won't Hurt You* was: "a clever study of a child with a bloodhound – something of a sober version of one of John Leech's most admired contributions to Punch".[130] And another reviewer thought it "A nineteenth century edition of Una and the Lion is

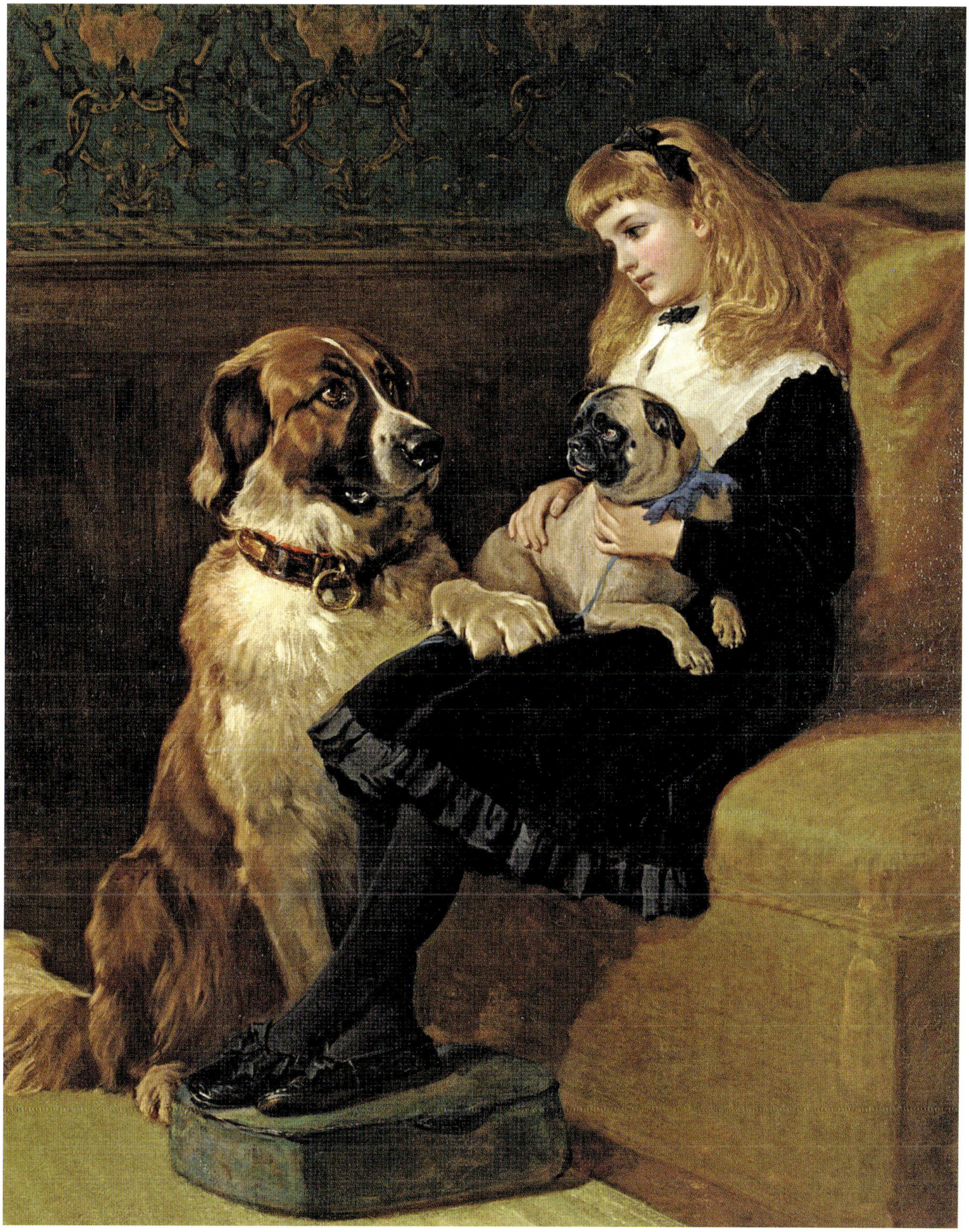

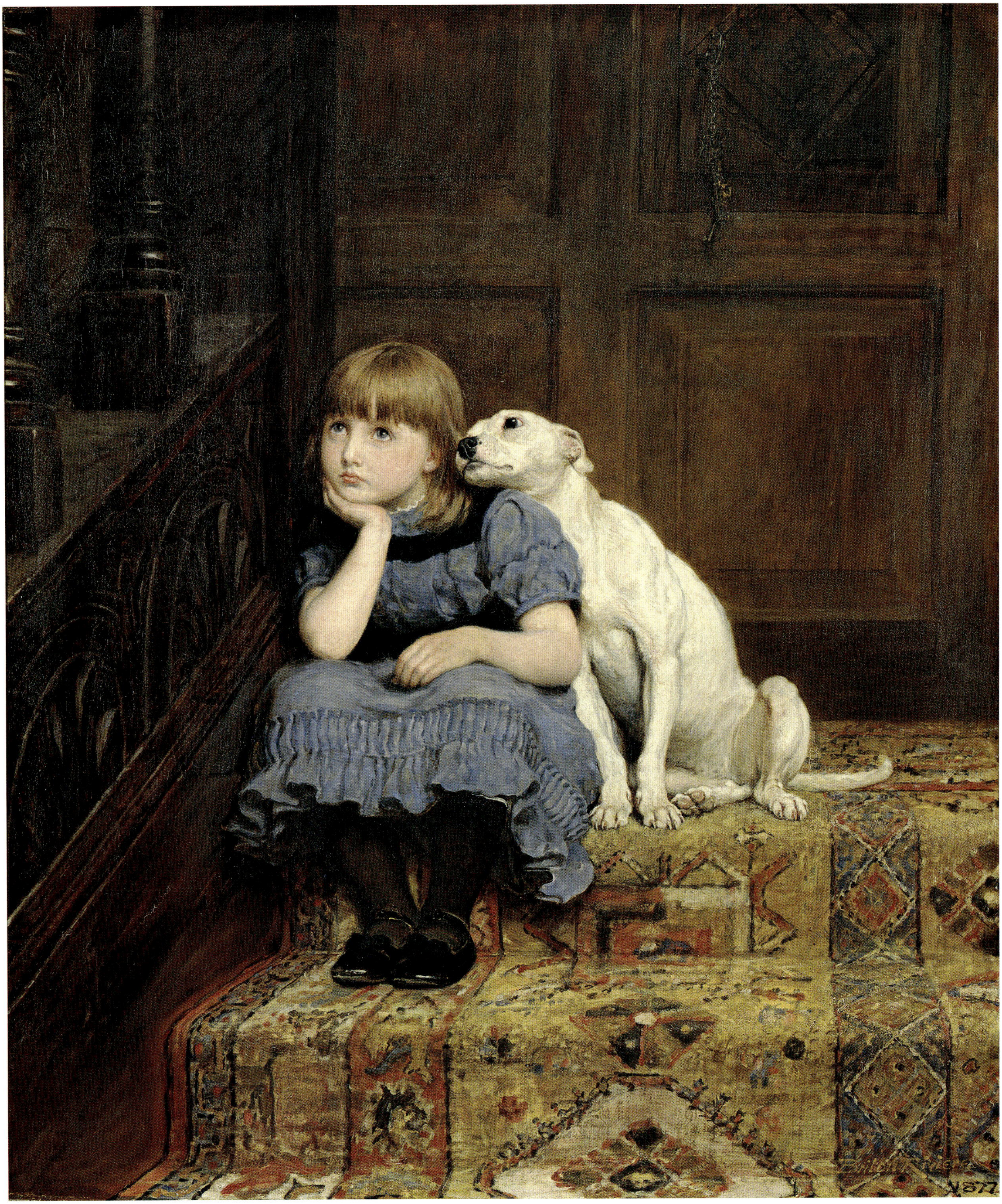

Plate 86 (opposite page): Sympathy, 1877
Briton Rivière. Oil on canvas 76.2 x 63.5cm.[131]
ROYAL HOLLOWAY COLLEGE, UNIVERSITY OF LONDON

Mr. Heywood Hardy's "He won't hurt you," a superb mastiff held in check by a pretty little damsel, both damsel and dog being evidently portraits, and charming portraits as well."[132] *The Spectator's* reviewer judged *He Won't Hurt You* one of the best paintings in the Dudley Gallery exhibition of 1874 and marked Heywood Hardy as a rising young artist.[133]

The paintings were very popular in Britain, America and Australia, judging from the number of engravings and mezzotints published in *The Graphic* and other magazines; new engravings of *He Won't Hurt You* were still being made in the 1890s.

Briton Rivière also achieved a notable success at the 1870 Royal Academy exhibition. His painting was *Charity*, a starving girl sharing her last crusts of bread with her two dogs. This was also Rivière's first painting to be engraved and is characteristic of his animal paintings that focus on the pitiful to generate a response. Rivière began exhibiting at the Royal Academy before Heywood Hardy, from 1858, but recognition of their work came at about the same time. Rivière's 1869 Royal Academy exhibit was *The Long Sleep*, portraying an old man dead in a chair, looked over by his two dogs.

In comparison to Heywood's *Her Only Playmates* (1870), Rivière's *His only friend* (1871) is much more directly aimed at achieving an emotional response, depicting a poor, prostrate boy next to his dog with its pink tongue hanging out:

> One of the popular pictures of the gallery is Mr. Heywood Hardy's "Road to Gretna Green" ... Still more popular, we suppose, will be Mr. Briton Riviere's "His only Friend" (62). Mr Riviere does these subjects of pauper and animal pathos with undeniable talent, and sometimes with touching felicity; but he must be careful of their becoming hackneyed under his hand.[134]

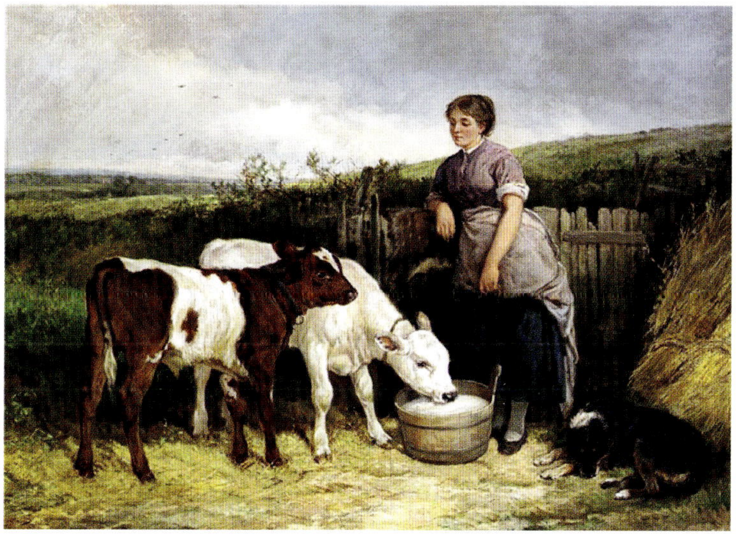

Plate 87: Feeding the Calves, 1871
Heywood Hardy. Oil on canvas. 56 x 78cm. PRIVATE COLLECTION

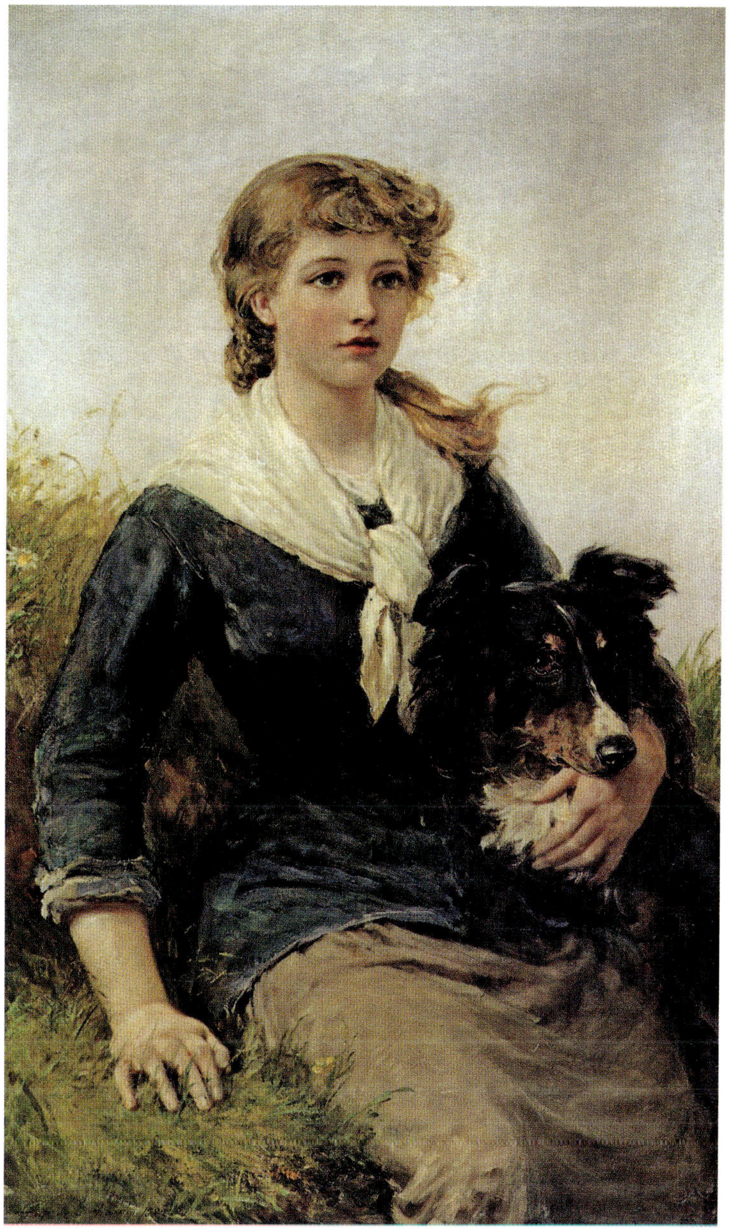

Plate 88: The Good Companion, 1882
Heywood Hardy. Oil on canvas. 101.6 x 62.2cm. PRIVATE COLLECTION

Rivière followed Hardy's lead in painting children with their canine companions and produced the very popular sentimental picture *Sympathy* (1877) (Plate 86), a painting of his daughter Millicent and a bull terrier. It was described as the "picture of the year for sentiment" by *The Graphic*.[135] He painted several versions of *Sympathy* and continued to paint similar pictures for many years.

Not all Heywood's paintings of animals in the early 1870s were sentimental. *Feeding the Calves* (1871) (Plate 87), exhibited at the Royal Academy, is a highly finished pastoral scene. And in his pictures of children with animals painted after 1880, for example *The Good Companion* (1882) (Plate 88), Hardy's approach appealed less to sentiment.

Heywood Hardy's other painting at the Royal Academy in 1871, *A Scene from Barnaby Rudge*, was also recognised in reviews:

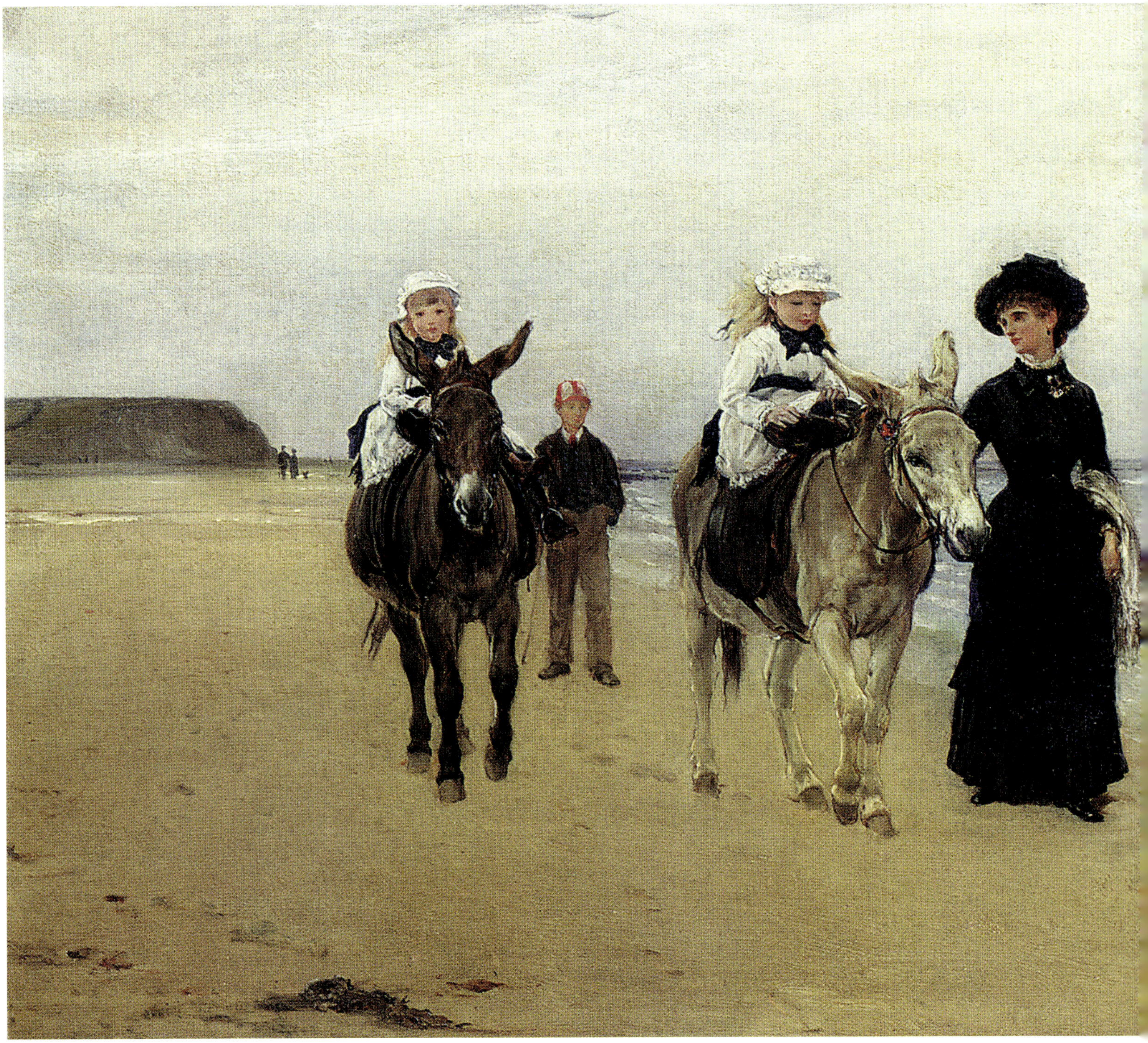

H. Hardy also surpasses his previous efforts in an effective scene taken from "Barnaby Rudge" (62). The famous raven is alighting on Barnaby's hand, around are a score of vagabond dogs belonging to the neighbours.[136]

No. 62, A Scene from "Barnaby Rudge," by H. Hardy, is a picture of uncommon merit, which, considering the number of the author's admirers, ought not to remain long unsold. ... We fancy this picture has not as yet attracted the notice it deserves, but we feel sure if any of our readers will examine it carefully, and take notice of the remarkable power the artist has displayed in the wild, crazy look he has given to Barnaby's eyes, they will leave it with the impression that it is the work of no ordinary man. The dogs are also skilfully painted, and the raven "Grip" upon Barnaby's arm is very lifelike.[137]

There was a reaction against "sugary" English painting in the 1870s, the decade when social realism was more popular; English pictures were sometimes contrasted with the Realism of French painters such as Léon Lhermitte. A critic writing in 1875, however, thought that even such a picture as Hardy's *Gaining Health* (1875) (Plate 89), a painting of two young girls riding sidesaddle on donkeys, was full of Victorian "manly honesty and healthiness" compared to the sugariness of much English painting:

At all events, one feels the grimness and gravity of M. L'Hermitte's picture, refreshing among so much English softness and sugariness and over-obvious aim at tickling the presumed taste of the market. Not that these faults are by any means universal. It is always pleasant to come upon Heywood Hardy's work for its freshness, frankness, and manly honesty and healthiness.

Here are three examples of it. A Norfolk gamekeeper and his little girl [*A Norfolk Gamekeeper*] on his feeding-round of the hutches where the pheasants are being reared under their foster-mother fowls; "Gaining Health", two sweet little girls taking their seaside constitutionals on donkey-back along the sands of Littlehampton or Bognor, one of the prettiest motives imaginable for a group of children's portraits; and "Not to be Caught with Chaff"[Plate 90], a girl trying to attract a pony in the field to the halter. Trivial as the subjects may seem, they are sufficient for a painter with such a true feeling as Heywood Hardy's at once for landscape, humanity, and animals other than human. We note with pleasure several examples here, besides those of the higher interest with which subjects of animal life are being again invested, since the loss of Landseer, by a new generation of animal painters, among whom Heywood Hardy and Briton Riviere are among the most prominent.[138]

There was a similar comment in *The Illustrated London News*: [139]

Among "outsiders," Mr. Heywood Hardy has greatly modified his style in the direction of minute finish, and now reminds one, by his dainty execution and colour, of some of the French genre-painters. See "A Norfolk Gamekeeper", a charming group of children on donkeys on the sea-beach, called "Gaining Health", and "Not to be Caught by Chaff", a girl trying to capture a loose pony.

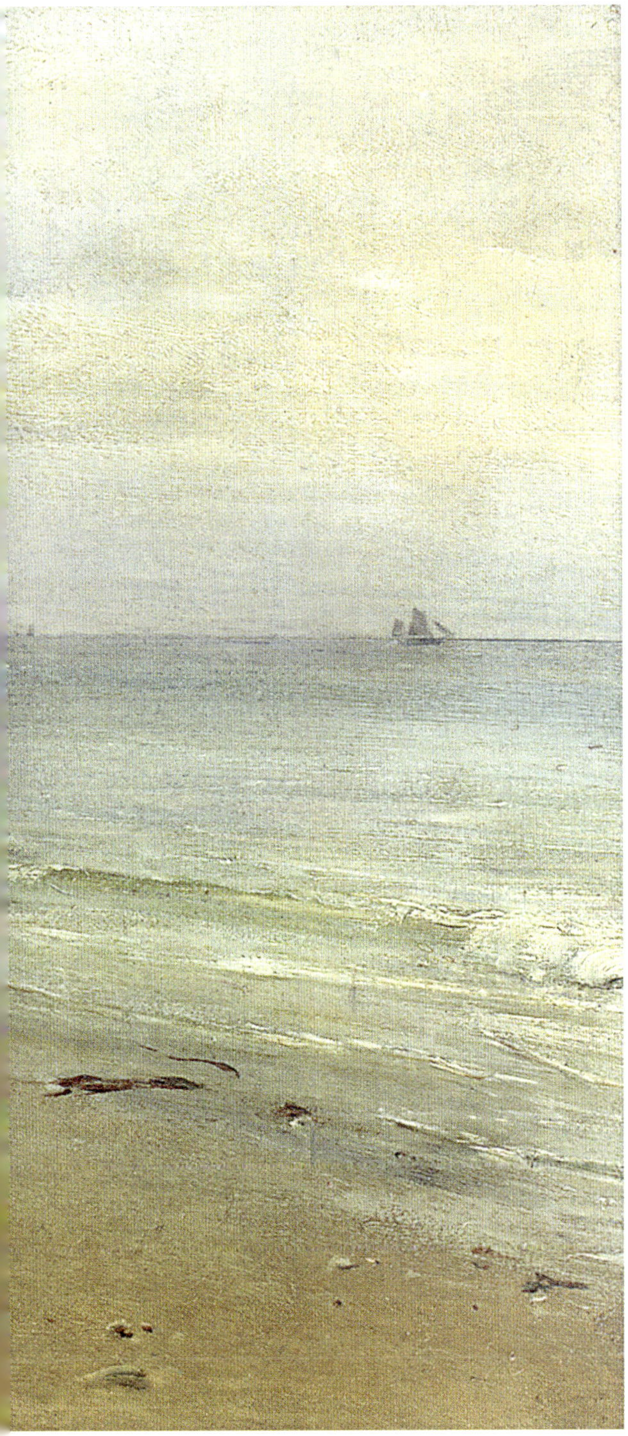

Plate 89: Gaining Health, 1875
Heywood Hardy. Oil on panel. 29.5 x 45.5cm.
Private Collection

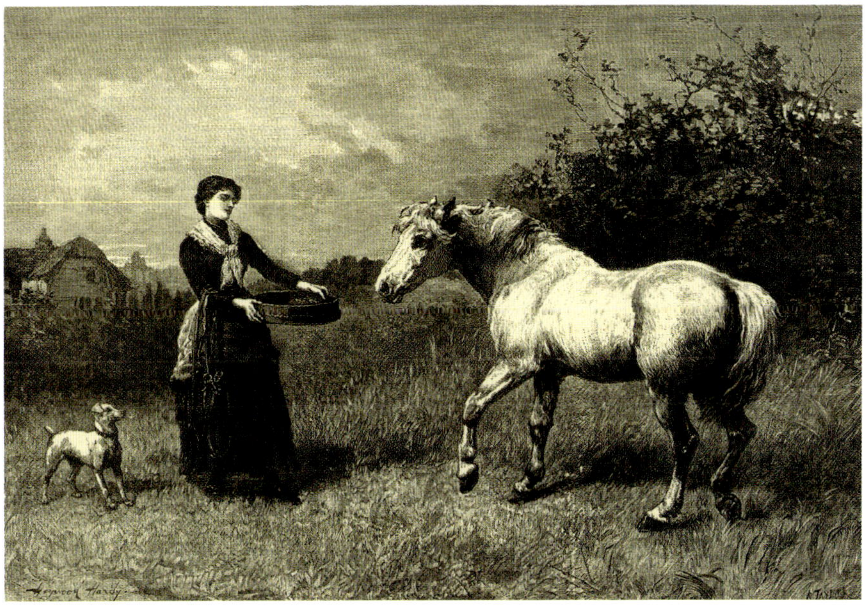

Plate 90: Not to be Caught by Chaff, 1884
After Heywood Hardy. From *The Illustrated London News*. Engraving by Richard Taylor from the painting of the same name painted by Heywood Hardy in 1875.[140]

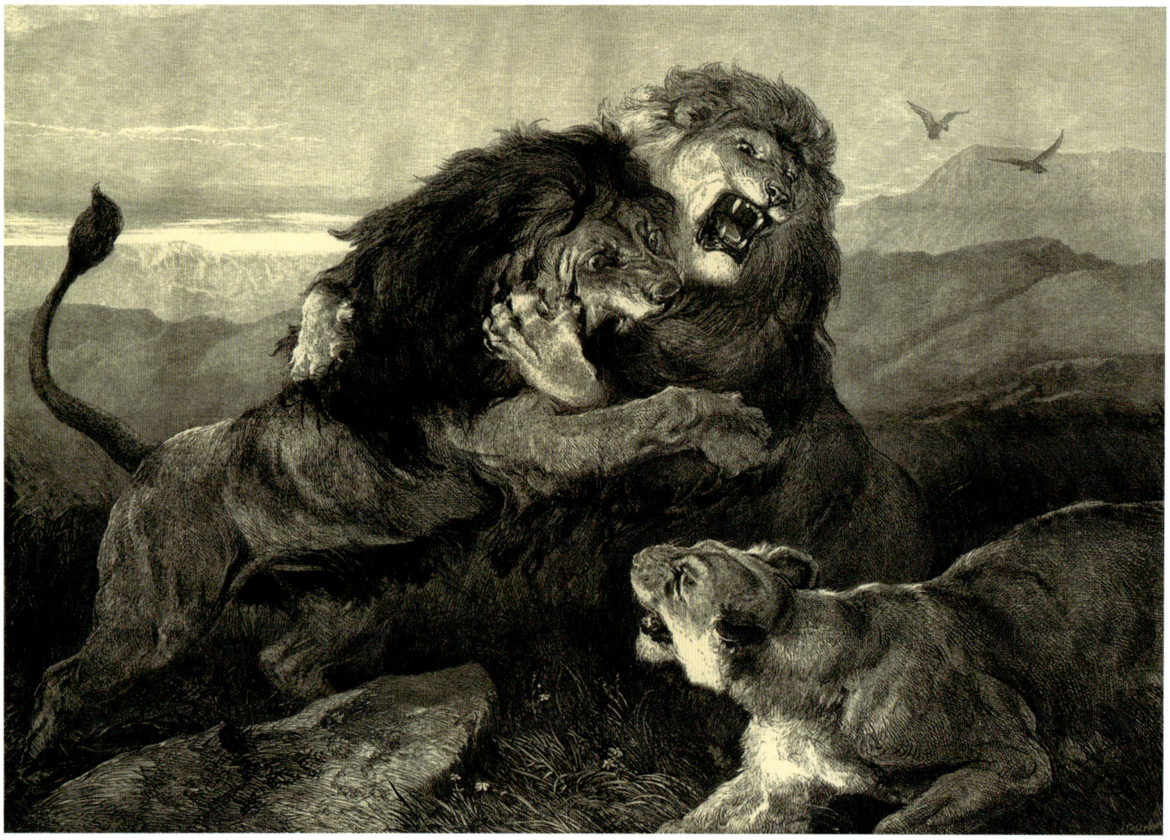

Plate 91 (left): "Fierce as conflicting fires the combat burns ... "
After Heywood Hardy. Wood engraving by John Greenaway after the painting by Heywood Hardy.
FROM THE ILLUSTRATED LONDON NEWS[141]

Plate 92 (below): Lion and Lioness Hunting, 1902
Heywood Hardy. Oil on canvas. 43 x 65cm. PRIVATE COLLECTION

Plate 93 (opposite page): Lion and Lioness, 1877
Heywood Hardy. Oil on canvas. 44 x 65cm. PRIVATE COLLECTION

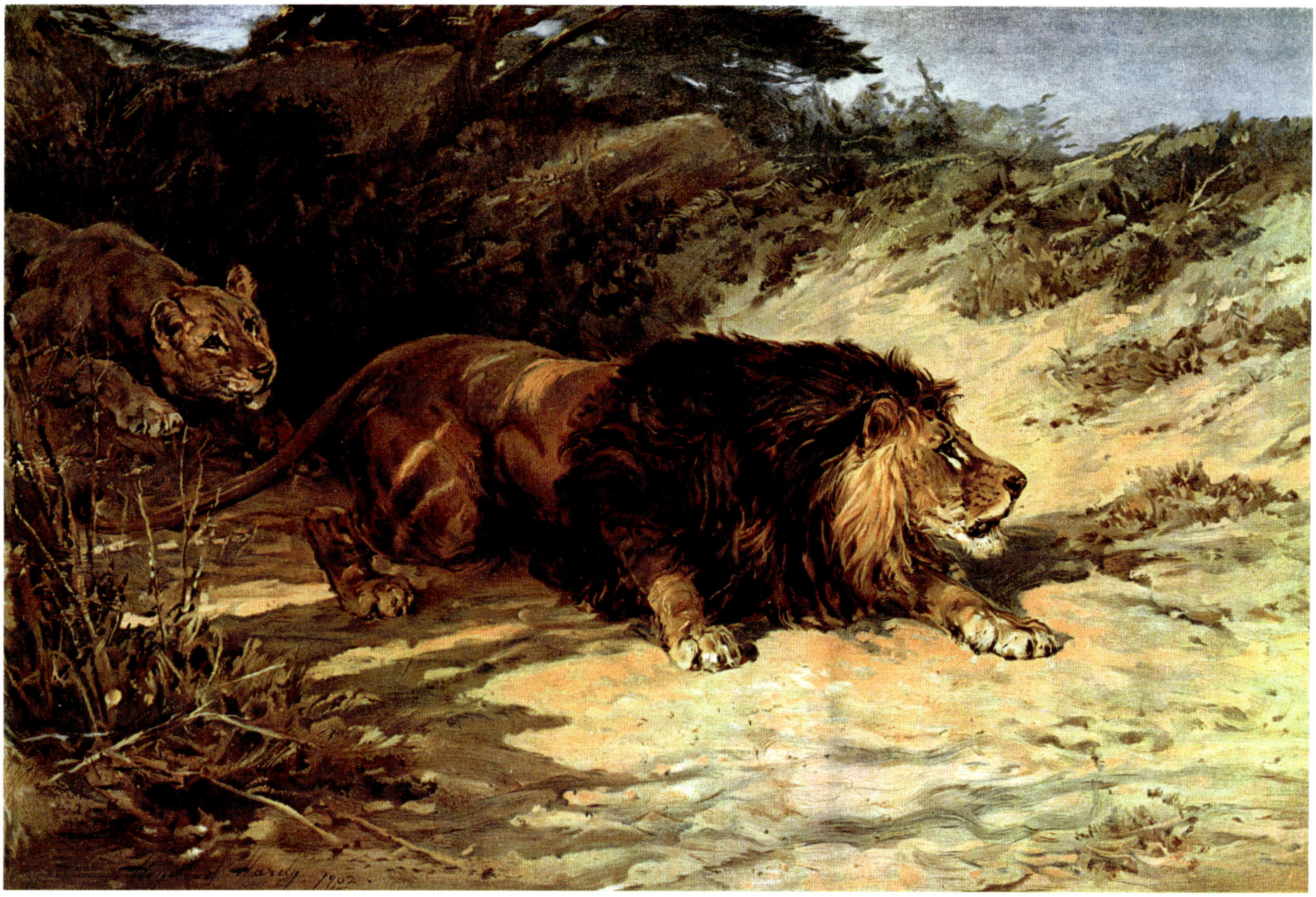

Lions

Soon after moving to London, Heywood Hardy exhibited his first pictures of lions. They were an immediate success and he returned to the subject occasionally over the next 30 years. His first exhibits were a picture of fighting lions exhibited at the Royal Academy in 1873, *Fierce as conflicting fires the combat burns ...* [142] (Plate 91), and *Stricken Lioness* (1873), which was shown at the Dudley Gallery. Subsequent pictures of lions included *Camp Followers* (1875*), Lion's Head* (1875), *Study of Lion's Head* (his Royal Academy exhibit of 1880) and *A Lion and Lioness Hunting* (1902) (Plate 92). *Lion and Lioness* (1877) (Plate 93) was based on a drawing and engraving made by John Frederick Lewis in 1825.[143]

Reviewers of the 1873 Royal Academy exhibition were full of praise for Hardy's life-size picture of fighting lions. *The Times* commented: " ... we do not remember such a daring and determined piece of savage animal life from an English hand – few from any hand since Rubens. The picture at once gives a great rise in artistic rank to the artist."[144]

Indeed, when he was in Antwerp, presumably Hardy had seen the pictures of lions and fighting wild animals painted by Peter Paul Rubens, Frans Snyders and Paul de Vos. Other reviewers commented in dramatic prose to match the picture's theme:

Taking for his text this couplet from the "Iliad"— "Fierce as conflicting fires the combat burns, And now it rises, now it sinks by turns"— Mr. Heywood Hardy applies it to a fight between two lions, whose frantic rage and desperate encounter he depicts with something of Homeric spirit. Locked in deadly conflict, their eyes flashing fire, their cavernous mouths wide open, and the claws of one embedded in the other's bleeding jaws, the rampant brutes carry on their combat with terrific frenzy. The scene of their conflict is a rugged mountain landscape with scenery as savage as themselves; but the adversaries are not without witnesses of their strife. A lioness looks on with fierce sympathy, and overhead hovers the vulture — ill-omened bird attracted by the scent of carnage, and little recking upon which combatant he shall sate his appetite. It is for lawyers to point the moral. Mr. Hardy, heretofore known only for his water-colour drawings of small size, though of no inconsiderable merit, displays in this colossal work a breadth and boldness of handling, a brilliancy of colour, and a dramatic vigour of expression for which his most ardent admirers could hardly have given him credit. The picture, No. 129 in the catalogue, occupies the position in the second gallery assigned last season to Mr. Davis's fine cattle-piece, "The Panic," to which it is no unworthy successor.[145]

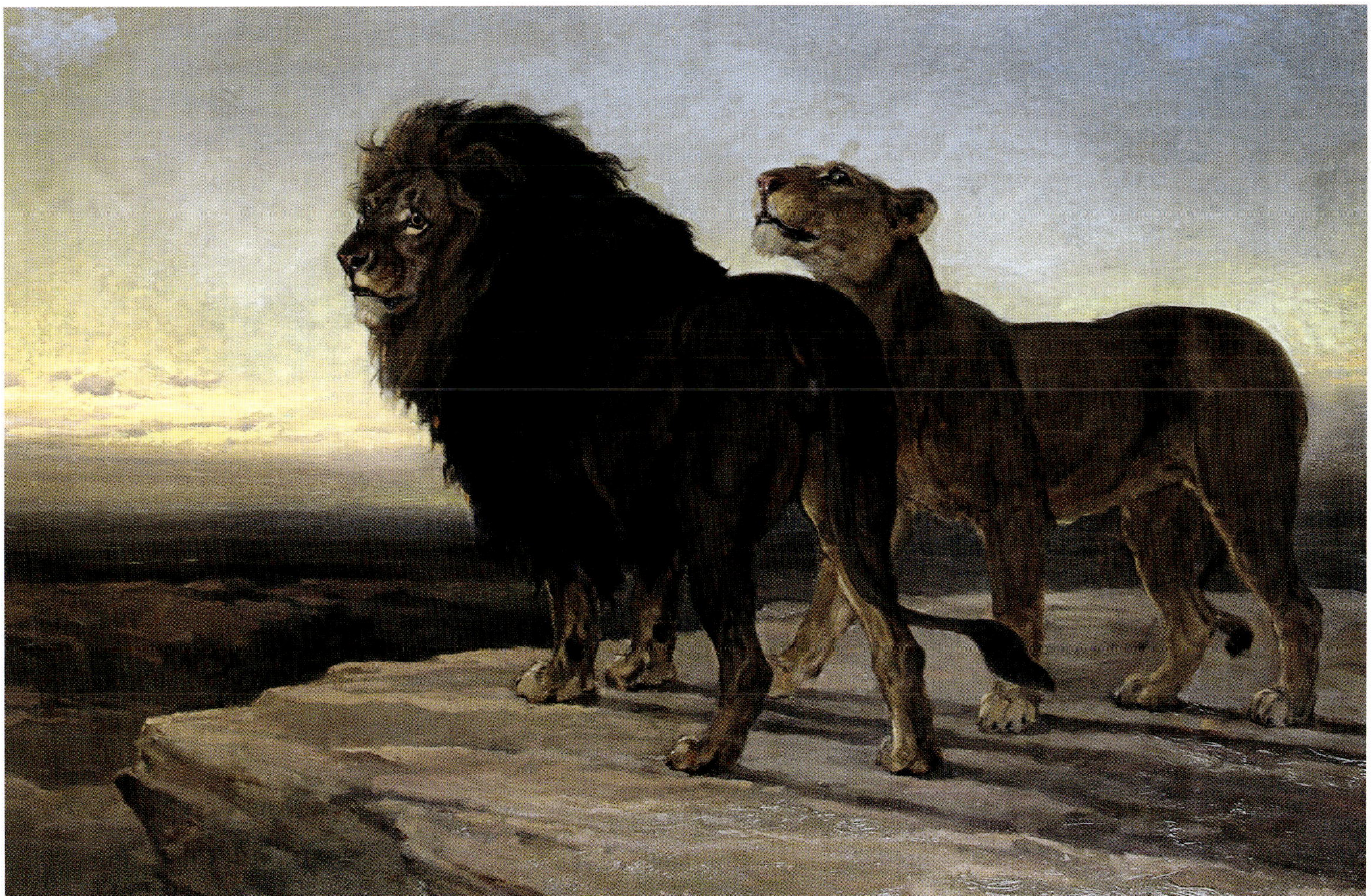

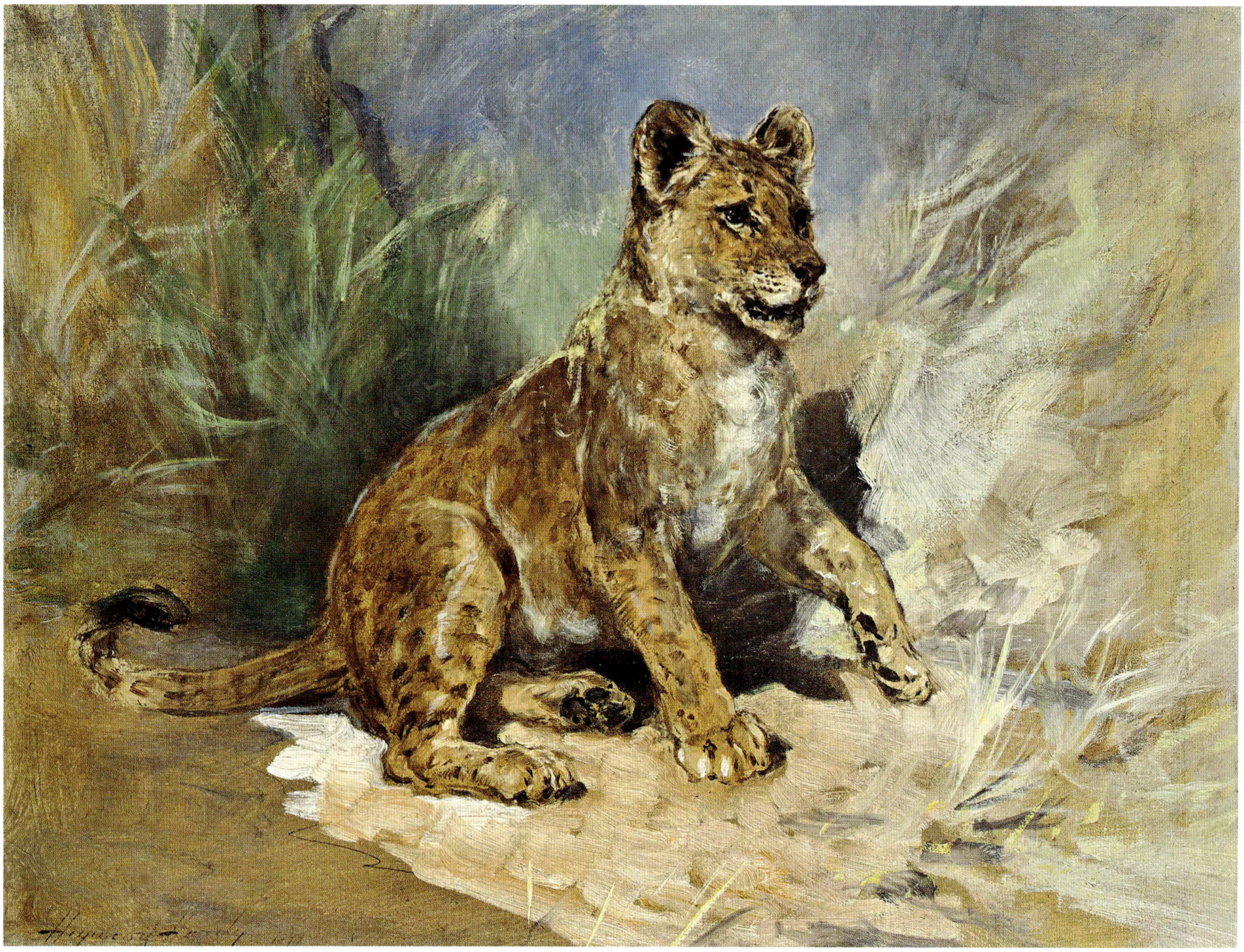

Plate 94: A Lion Cub, 1877
Heywood Hardy. Oil on Canvas. 36.8 x 47cm. Private Collection

The Illustrated London News commented on the engraving, included in their *Extra Supplement*:

> A word of warm praise is due, in conclusion, to the painter for the knowledge of animal character, the vigour and mastery of execution displayed in this picture, and that on a scale seldom attempted by contemporary artists. It is unquestionably one of the most admirable works by a young painter exhibited in recent years, and holds its own even besides our recollection of similar subjects by Rubens, Snyders, and other great animal painters.[146]

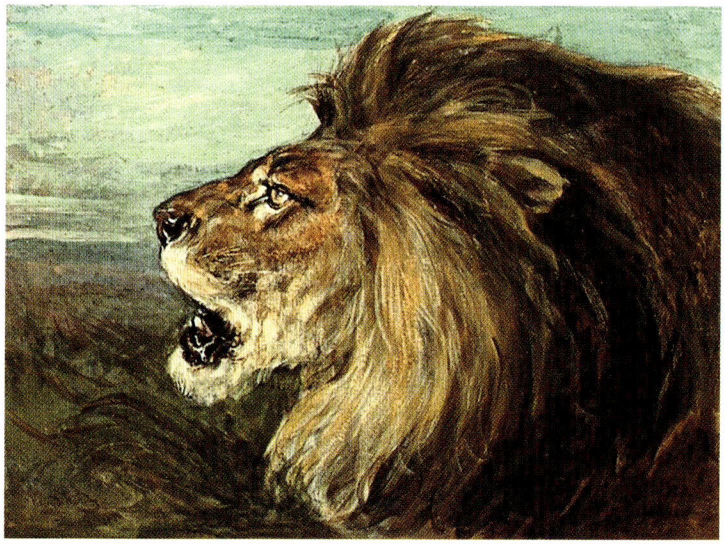

Plate 95: Head of a Lion
Heywood Hardy. Watercolour and body colour. 32 x 42.5cm.
Private Collection

Heywood frequently sketched lions at the London Zoological Gardens which were not far from St John's Wood. He studied comparative anatomy there, under Professor Garrod, Head of the Scientific Department. The Superintendant of the Zoo, Abraham Dee Bartlett (a zoologist often consulted by Charles Darwin), was a friend of Heywood's and allowed him access when the Zoo was closed to the public. Another model for his

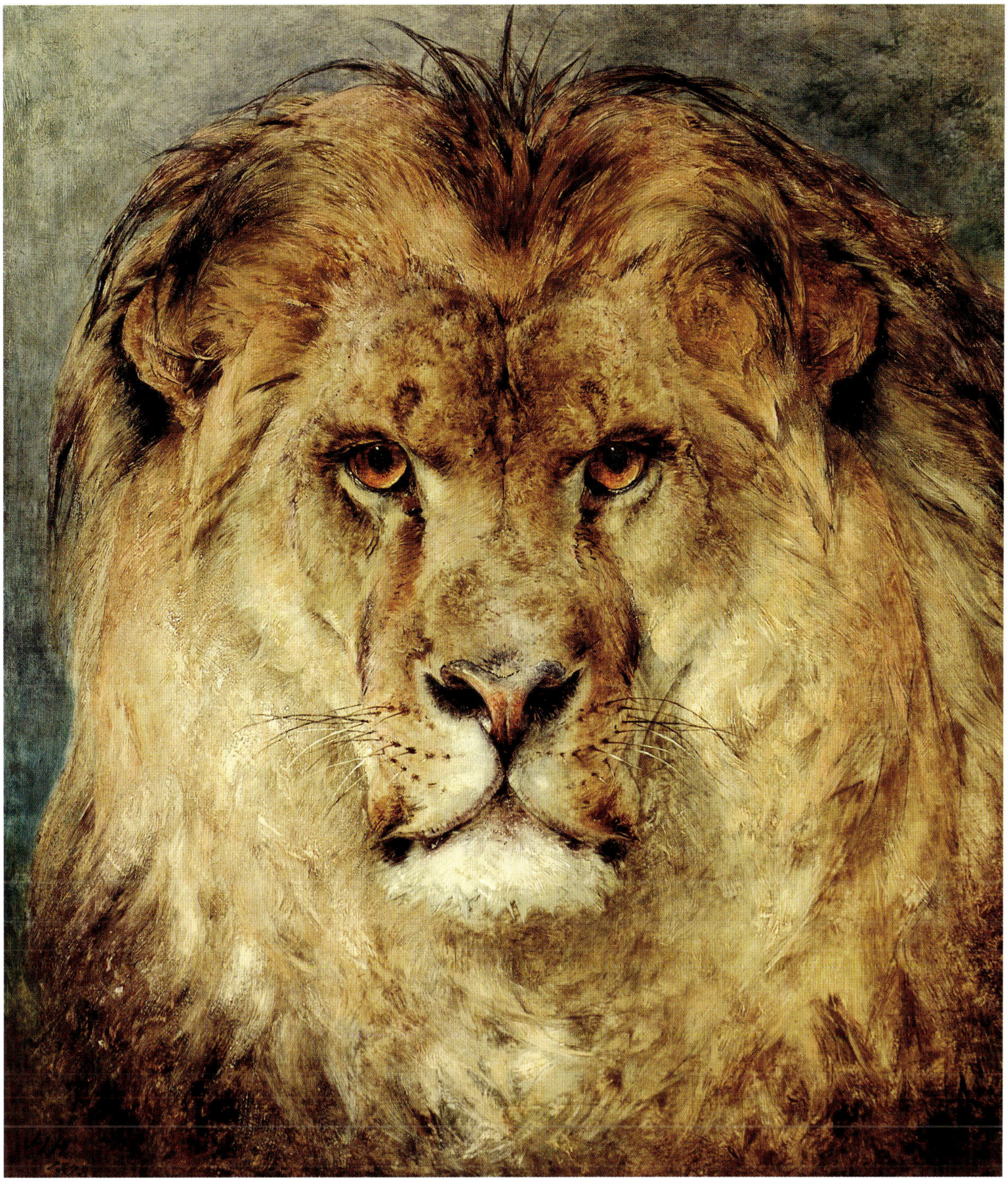

Plate 96: A Lion's Head, 1878
Heywood Hardy. Oil on canvas. 76.5 x 63.5cm. Russell-Cotes Art Gallery and Museum, Bournemouth

lion studies was Hannibal I, bred by the Clifton Zoological Society at Bristol.[147]

Heywood Hardy's successful paintings of lions were no doubt helped by his acquisition of a lioness that had died at the London Zoological Gardens in January 1873. He had it mounted by Rowland Ward, who had worked as a taxidermist with his father for many years and had just started his own business.[148] Heywood and Ward became close friends and Ward collected several paintings by Hardy. Ward was probably the foremost taxidermist of his time and a pioneer in the study of modelling and making casts of the structure of the muscles rather than just stuffing animal skins. Ward was also a good animal artist. The lioness was on view for a while at Ward's premises at 158 Piccadilly before being installed in Heywood's studio in St John's Wood. Hardy painted several studies of lions' heads. One was described as "thoroughly leonine in form...and alarmingly life-like in expression. It is grandly modelled, and altogether would do no dishonour to Madlle. Rosa Bonheur,[149]" a description that could also apply to *Head of a Lion* (1878) (Plate 96). Based on sketches made at the Zoological Gardens, this was a gift to Rowland Ward.

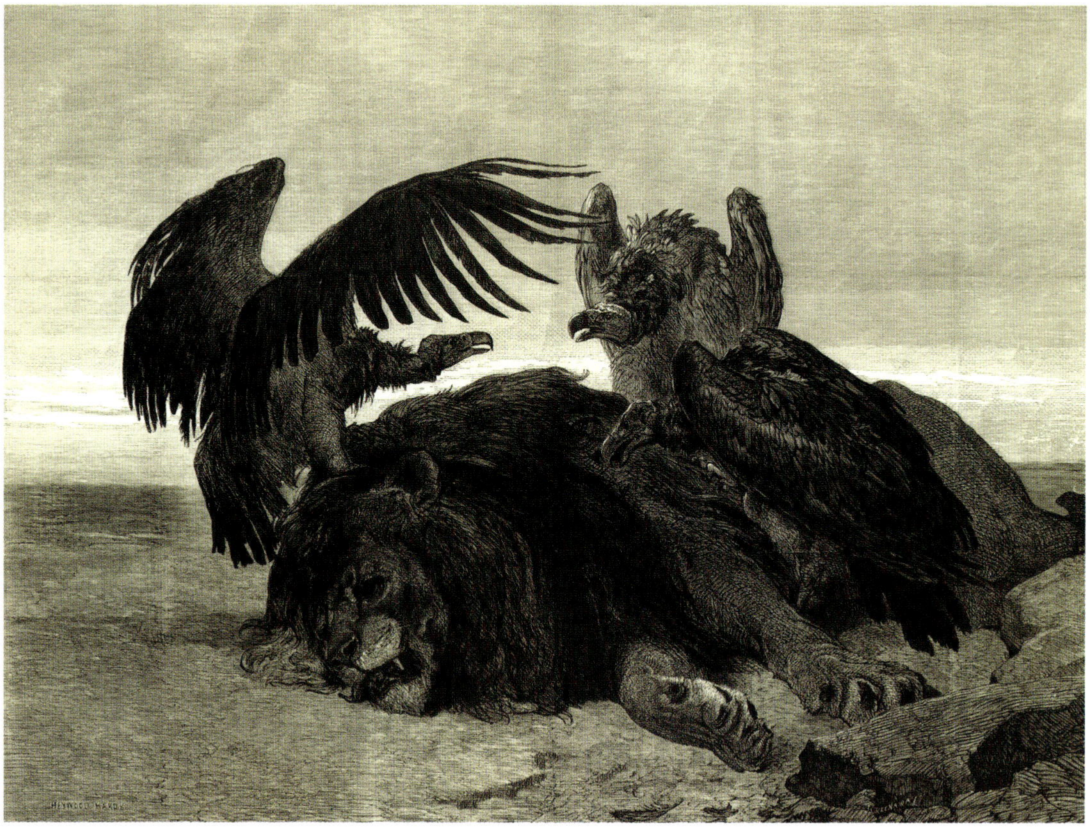

Plate 97 (right): How are the Mighty Fallen
After Heywood Hardy. Wood Engraving by J. Greenaway.
FROM THE ILLUSTRATED LONDON NEWS.[150]

Plate 98 (below): Vulture on a Rock
Heywood Hardy. Watercolour, pen and ink on paper. 31 x 22.2cm.
PRIVATE COLLECTION

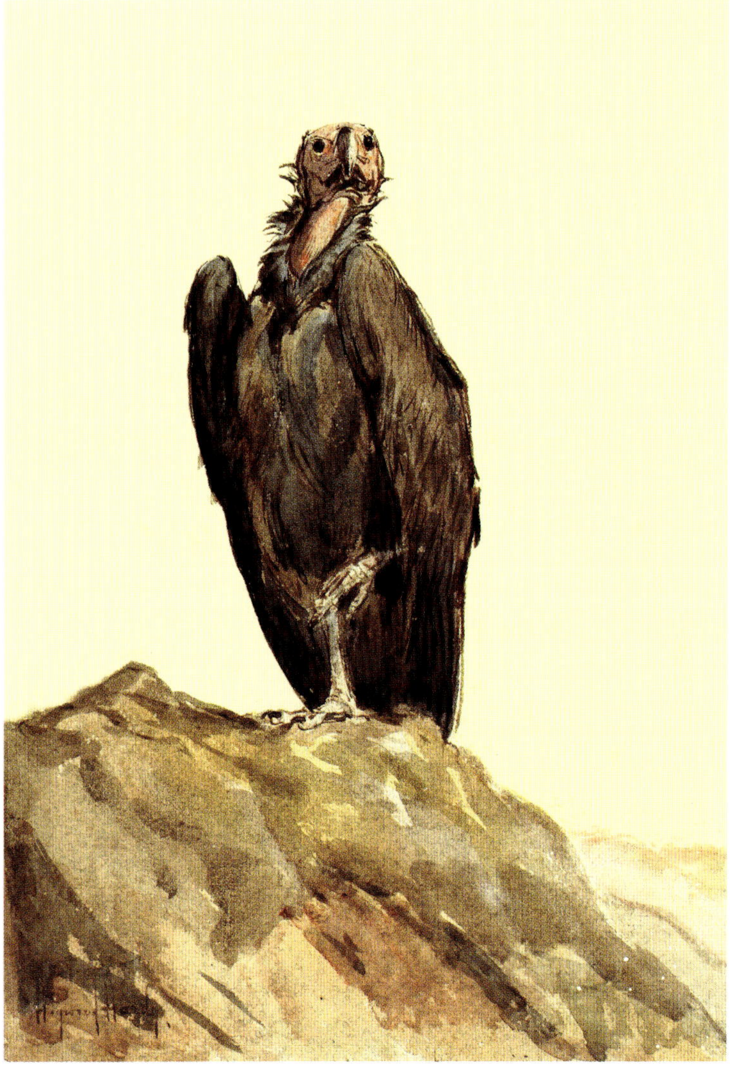

How are the Mighty Fallen (1875) (Plate 97) was described by *The Art Journal* as "a spirited representation of foul, hungry, and quarrelling vultures tearing at a dead lion in the desert."[151] Similarly, William M. Rossetti praised Heywood's study of a lion and vultures shown at the Dudley Gallery: "a grand piece of work, full of observation, strength and firm design, entitling the artist to rank among the foremost animal painters of our time."[152] Hardy's exhibits at the first annual exhibition of The Society of Painter Etchers was described by *The Portfolio* as "a capital study of vultures – obscene *Camp Followers* – in ghastly row on a branch awaiting their prey."[153]

Egypt

Following the success of the "fighting lions" at the Royal Academy in 1873, Heywood Hardy visited Egypt later that year.[154] His well-travelled friend John Varley junior built his own boat at Gravesend and sailed to Egypt in the same year ("where he remained some two years painting, at times living in rock-hewn tombs, and so acquiring his exceptional knowledge of Arabic"[155]). But we do not know whether Heywood and Varley sailed together. The pair later shared a studio at 10 Abbey Road, St John's Wood, and collaborated on several paintings of Egyptian scenes, including *Falconers* (1887) (Plate 99) and *A Courtyard of*

Plate 99 (opposite page): Falconers, 1887
Heywood Hardy and John Varley junior. Oil on panel. 63.5 x 48.3cm. PRIVATE COLLECTION
The dog in the centre appears to be based on Hardy's watercolour *Two Lurchers* (Plate 163, page 136).

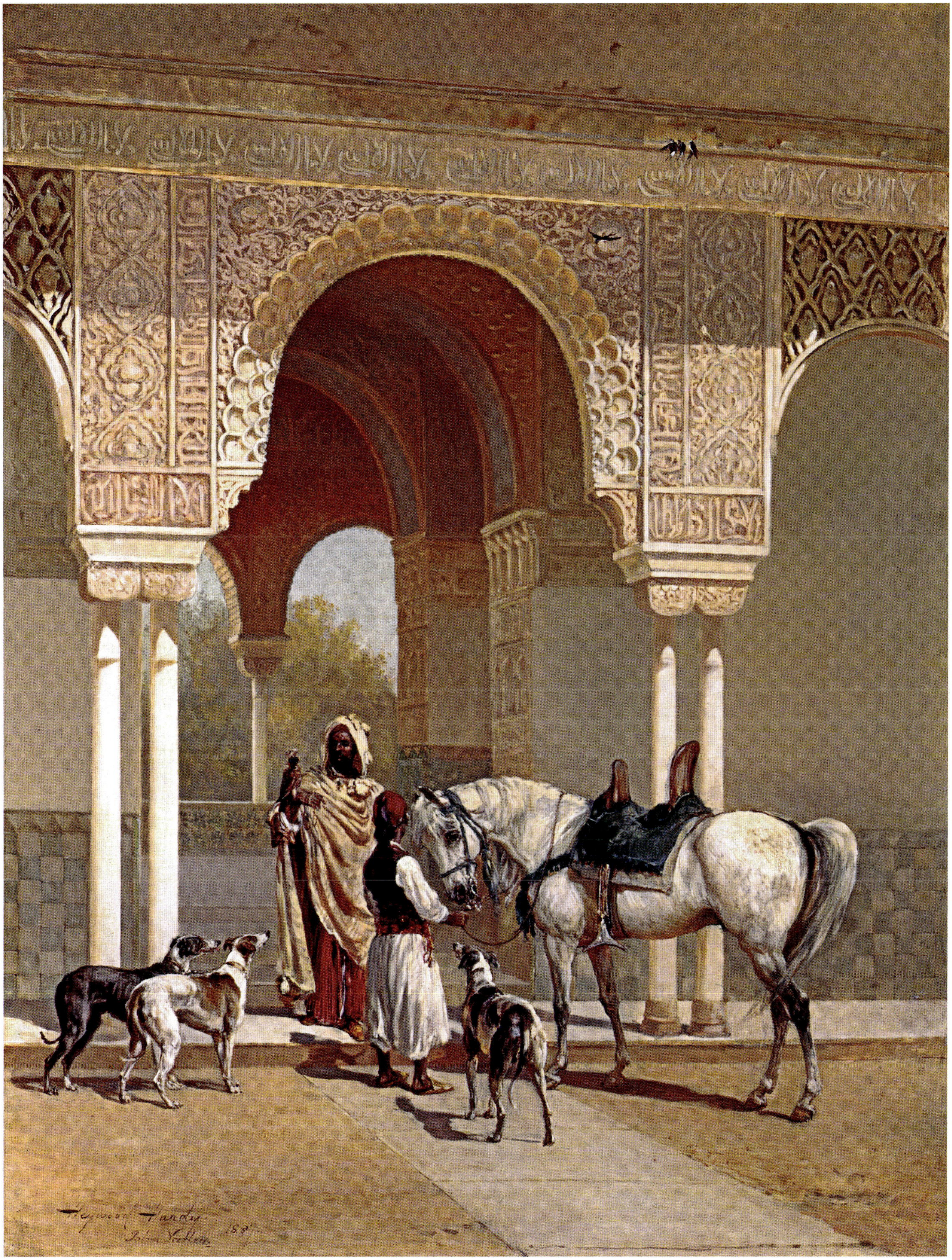
Heywood Hardy
John Varley

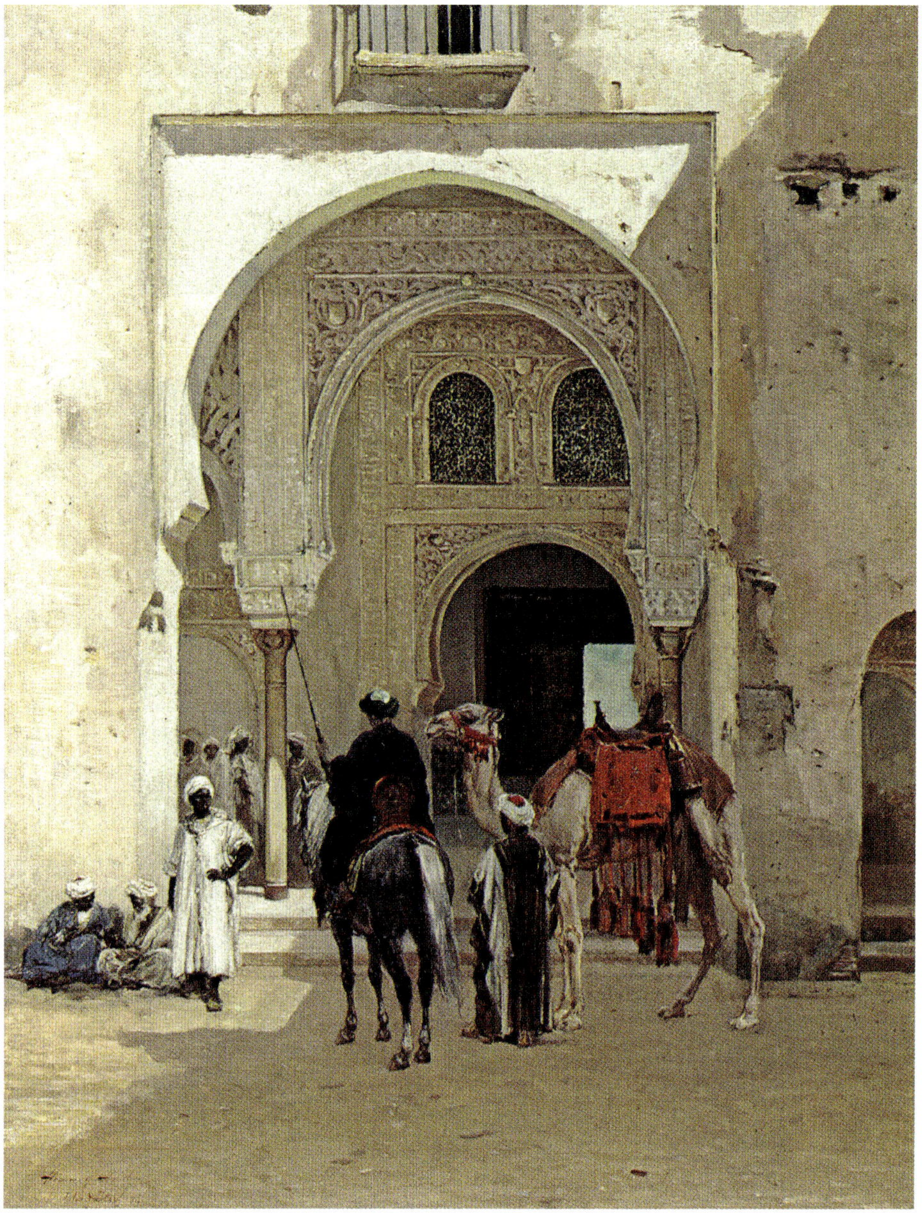

Plate 100: A Courtyard of a Mosque, Cairo, 1889
Heywood Hardy and John Varley junior. Oil on canvas. 68.5 x 52cm.
PRIVATE COLLECTION

a Mosque, Cairo (1889) (Plate 100). Hardy visited Naples, Rome and Florence on the return voyage from Egypt. He later travelled in Germany, Spain, Portugal and Holland, but there are no records of pictures painted there.

Heywood Hardy was by now well established as an animal painter and many reviews drew attention to the studies he produced in Egypt or that were based on sketches he made there, such as *The Travellers* (Plate 101), *Cairo Donkey Boy*, *Fishers of the Nile* and *Field Labour in Upper Egypt*.

The Times reviewer of the Dudley Gallery exhibition commented:

> ... we must select certain drawings as in their way scarcely to be surpassed. These are Mr. Heywood Hardy's "Fishers of the Nile" – a group of pelicans on a sand bank, with one of the mountain escarpments that hem in the "father of rivers" in the distance. Mr. Hardy has caught the very essence of the oddity, the gravity, cumbrousness in repose and scrutinizing self-importance which make pelicans among the grotesquest and most human of birds.[156]

However, on Heywood's return from Egypt, in 1874, his Royal Academy exhibit for that year did not quite repeat the success of the "Fighting Lions" from the previous year. Indeed, the few pictures that Hardy painted that had classical or mythological themes were never particularly successful. *Ulysses Ploughing the Seashore* (1874) (Plate 102) was begun before he went to Egypt and was completed after he returned, just in time for the Royal Academy exhibition.

The Art Journal was impressed by the work:

> It is quite a relief to the general monotony of subject-matter... when one meets with a canvas that shows the painter has moved out of the beaten track; has set his mind, as well as his hands, to work, and gives to the world some thing that is not only novel in subject, but of manifest pictorial interest: such was the impression Mr. Hardy's 'Ulysses Ploughing the Seashore' made on us when it hung in the Academy in 1874. The story related of him is that very soon after his marriage with Penelope he was summoned

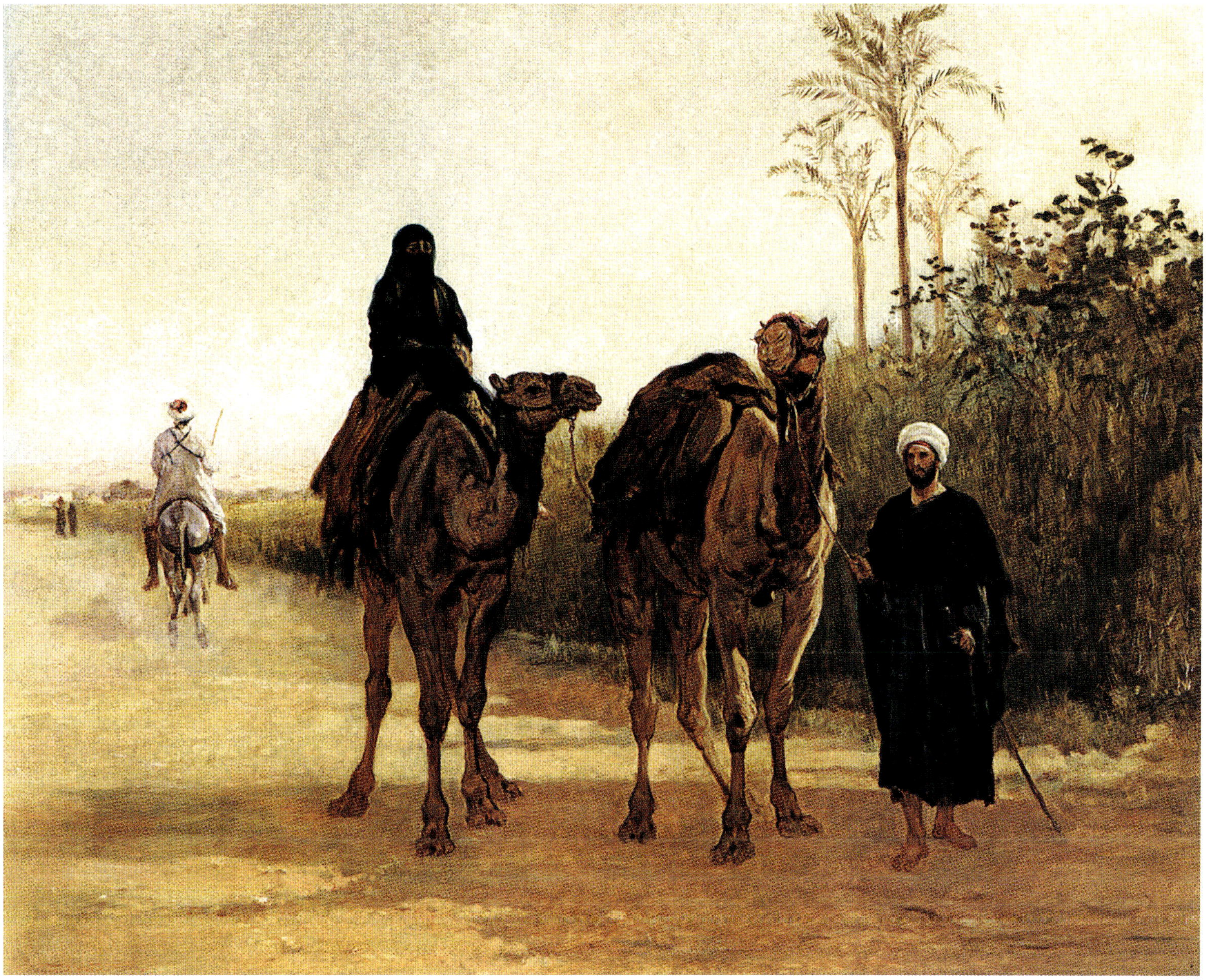

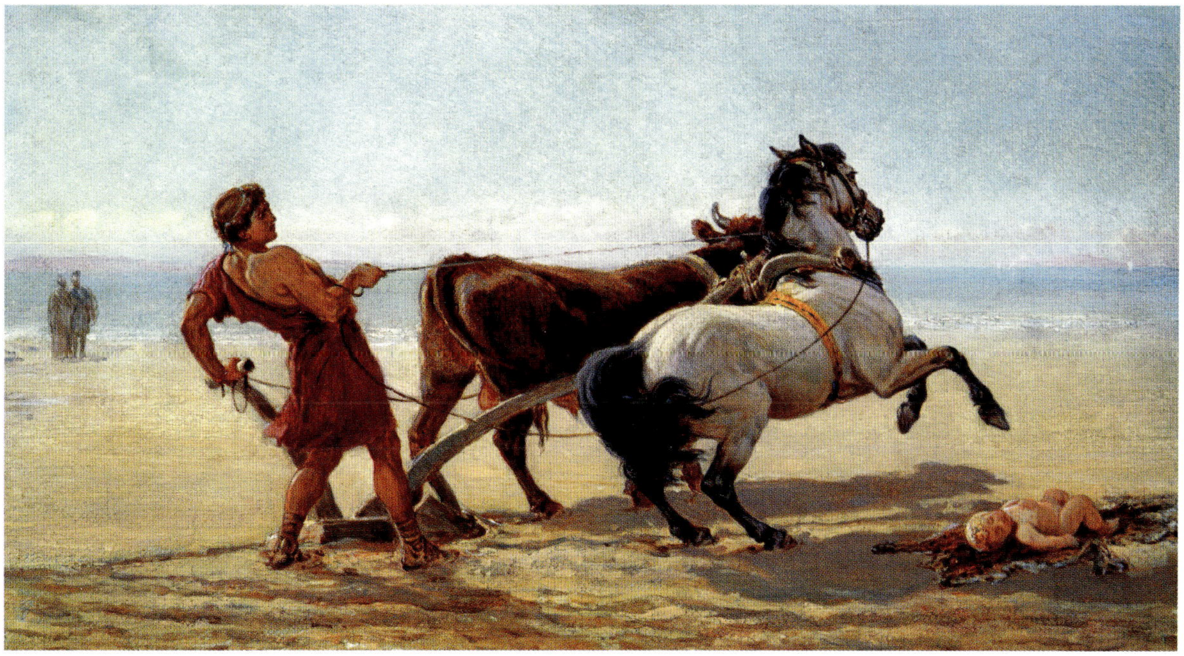

Plate 101 (above): The Travellers, 1874
Heywood Hardy.
Oil on canvas. 48.3 x 58.4cm.
PRIVATE COLLECTION

Plate 102 (right): Ulysses Ploughing the Seashore, 1874
Heywood Hardy. Oil on canvas.
49.1 x 95.5cm. PRIVATE COLLECTION

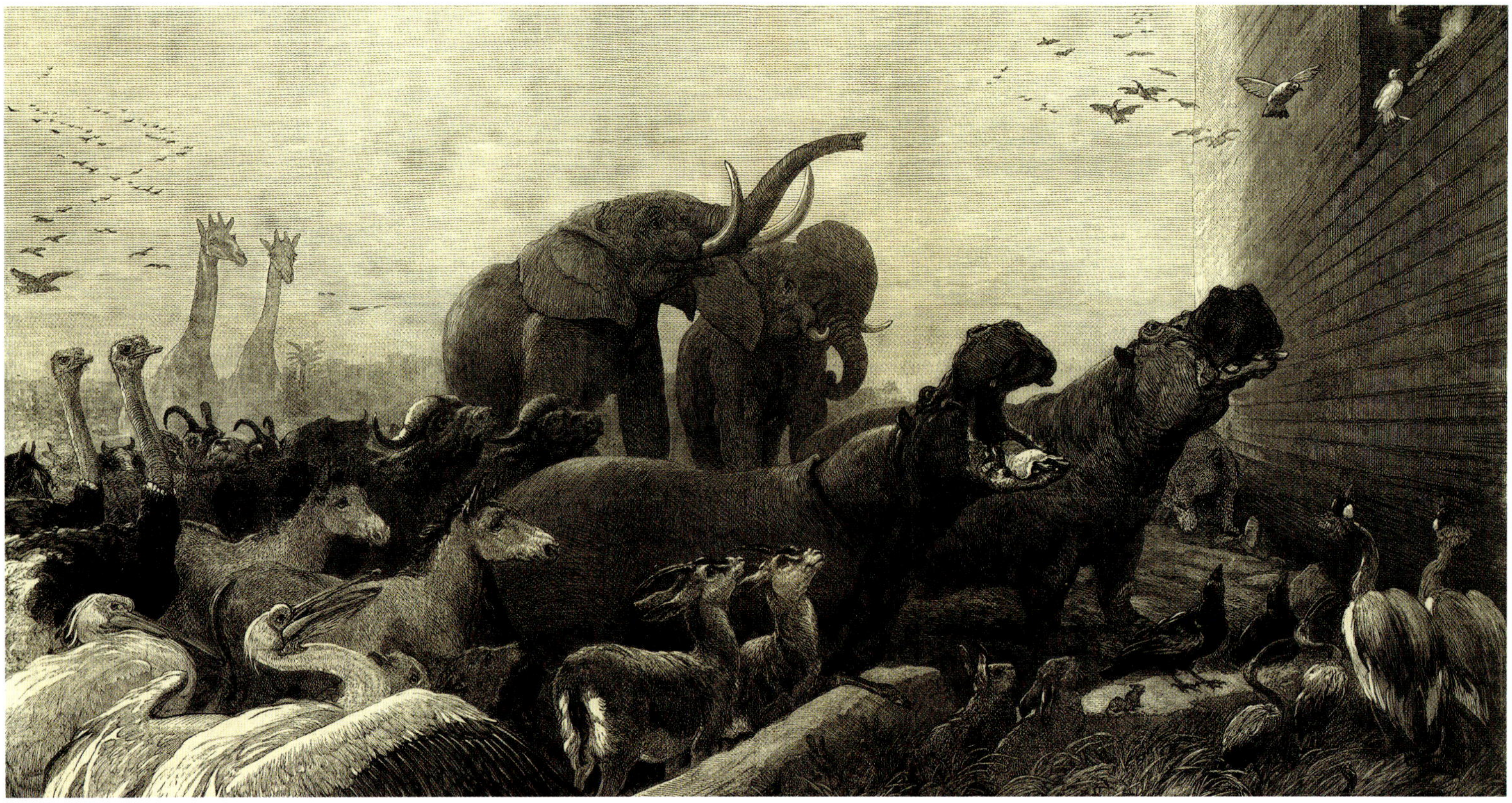

Plate 103: God's Covenant with Noah, 1876
After Heywood Hardy. Wood engraving by J. Greenaway. *Illustrated London News*. 28 October 1876

> with the rest of the Grecian princes to take part in the Trojan war: unwilling to leave his young wife, he pretended to be insane, and yoking a bull and a horse together he ploughed the seashore, sowing therein salt instead of corn. The dissimulation, however, was soon detected by Palamedes, a Greek chieftain sent to bring Ulysses to the camp, who contrived to get possession of Telemachus, the infant son of the latter, and placed him in the track of the ploughshare. The sanity of the father was proved to the satisfaction of the Greek leaders by his turning the plough aside to avoid injuring the child. This is the point of Mr. Hardy's capital picture: by the exercise of considerable strength, apparently, he has managed to turn the animals from the course they were taking, as evidenced by the ridges of turned-up sand, on the edge of which the boy lies asleep on a leopard's skin. Near the waterside stands Palamedes with a companion watching the effect of their stratagem. The composition is very spirited, and the drawing both of the figures — Ulysses and his child — and the animals is excellent. The picture, when exhibited, received, as it deserved, marked attention as well from the critics as from the public, and this was due no less to the novelty of the subject than to the truly artistic manner in which it is carried out.[157]

The Illustrated London News was more critical:

> Mr. Heywood Hardy's picture representing Ulysses in feigned madness ploughing the seashore with a horse and bull yoked together, is a little opaque and dry technically. Here again the painting of the dun-coloured horse – studied apparently, and very properly, from the Elgin frieze – is more admirable than that of the human figure, the sudden and violent effort of Ulysses to avoid trampling on his infant son being somewhat ungainly.[158]

God's Covenant with Noah: a Critical Response

Heywood Hardy's studies of animals were generally successful. A notable exception, however, was *God's Covenant with Noah* (Plate 103), his exhibit at the 1876 Royal Academy exhibition. The picture had been commissioned by William Agnew from a sketch Hardy had shown him. Presumably they thought it would be a subject well-suited to Hardy's abilities as an animal painter. Many animals and birds that he had studied in Egypt or at the Zoological Gardens were included. But artists had to be careful in their treatment of biblical subjects in Victorian England. It was difficult to be sufficiently reverential for Victorian taste while depicting a scene like Noah's Ark, which was a sensitive topic in the 1870s. In December 1872 George Smith of the British Museum announced at a meeting of the Society of Biblical Archaeology that he had found the story of the Flood and the Ark on a cuneiform tablet from Nineveh that was much older than the account of the Ark in the Book of Genesis. Smith's discovery, which questioned the truth of biblical history, was so important that the Archbishop of Canterbury and Prime Minister W.E. Gladstone attended the meeting.

The Graphic questioned Hardy's taste:

> A mistake, we cannot but think. This gathering of hippo-

potami with gaping jaws, elephants, giraffes, buffaloes, gazelles, wild asses, hares, ostriches, pelicans, ibises, ravens and demoiselle cranes, under the bellying quarter of the Ark, is of questionable taste as regards subject, while neither in colour nor relative proportion do the creatures seem right. Heywood Hardy, like Briton Rivière, this year, seems a clever painter gone rather astray.[159]

Journals and newspapers competed to criticise the painting. *The Spectator* concluded that:

> This is certainly a very extraordinary picture, but that an artist so clever as Mr. Hardy should waste his time upon such an incongruous composition is still more wonderful. On the extreme right of the picture is a portion of the Ark, and two large feet, apparently intended for those of the Patriarch. The two enormous hippopotami who are standing with their mouths wide open are evidently disquieted as to their means of transit, and indeed the manner in which they are to be hoisted into the exceedingly small window where Noah (or rather his feet) is standing does not seem very evident. Very evidently there was in this case but one step from the sublime to the ridiculous, and the artist has taken it.[160]

The Times added its contribution to the general criticism and suggested that the picture could have been entitled "Hailing the Gangway":

> Another eminent animal-painter, Heywood Hardy, strikes us as, like Briton Rivière, below his best this year in "God's Covenant with Noah", but which might more fittingly have been called "Hailing the Gangway," for that is what is suggested by the open mouths of the hippopotami, the principal figures in the group of animals gathered below the entrance port of the Ark, on which we see the feet of Noah or one of his family … At the same time it is a very original conception for a zoological picture, but rather comic than scriptural in its suggestions, and calling up associations, unavoidable, perhaps, rather with the Zoological gardens than Genesis.[161]

The Illustrated Sporting and Dramatic News lampooned *God's Covenant with Noah* in a cartoon entitled *Royal Academy 1877 – Pictures Prophesied* (Plate 104), suggesting that his next submission to the Academy might be entitled "A visit to Jamrach's". Charles Jamrach was the owner of Jamrach's Animal Emporium and Menagerie in London. (A Bengal tiger once escaped from his Emporium and carried off eight-year-old Jaffy Brown in its mouth; Jamrach ran after it and with his bare hands forced the tiger to release him.)

Hardy might, perhaps, have taken some comfort from *The Sporting and Dramatic's* similar treatment of works by the renowned artists Lawrence Alma-Tadema and Sir Luke Fildes. An *Audience at Agrippa's* (1876), one of Alma-Tadema's paintings of ancient Rome, suggested to *The Sporting and Dramatic* that his next exhibit would be "Playing with Marbles".

The Sporting and Dramatic was also unimpressed by the "tender pathos and sentiment"[171] in Sir Luke Fildes' picture of *The Widower*; it suggested that his next picture might be "The Bachelor".

A letter[162] from Heywood Hardy to William Agnew describes the origins of the controversial *God's Covenant with Noah* commissioned by Agnew. It seems that both Hardy and Agnew misjudged how critics would respond to the painting.

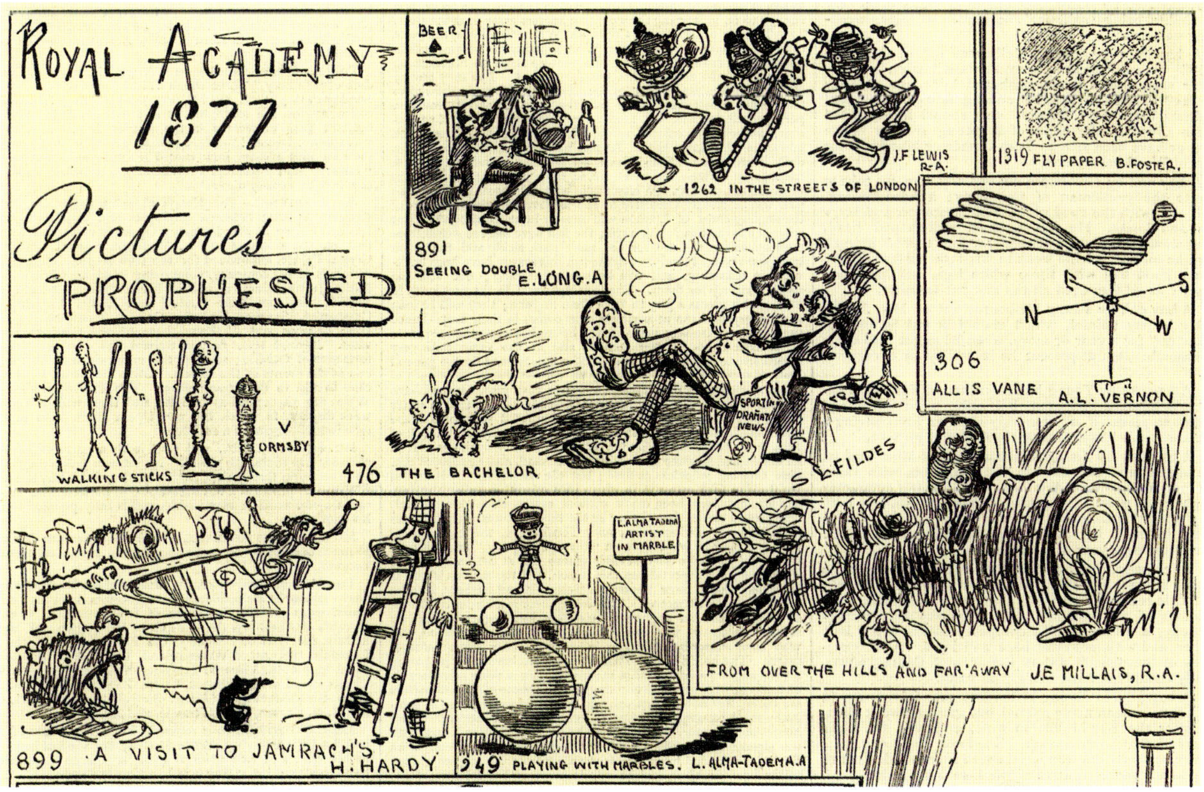

Plate 104: Royal Academy 1877 – Pictures Prophesied. *The Illustrated Sporting and Dramatic News.* 10 June 1876 p.268

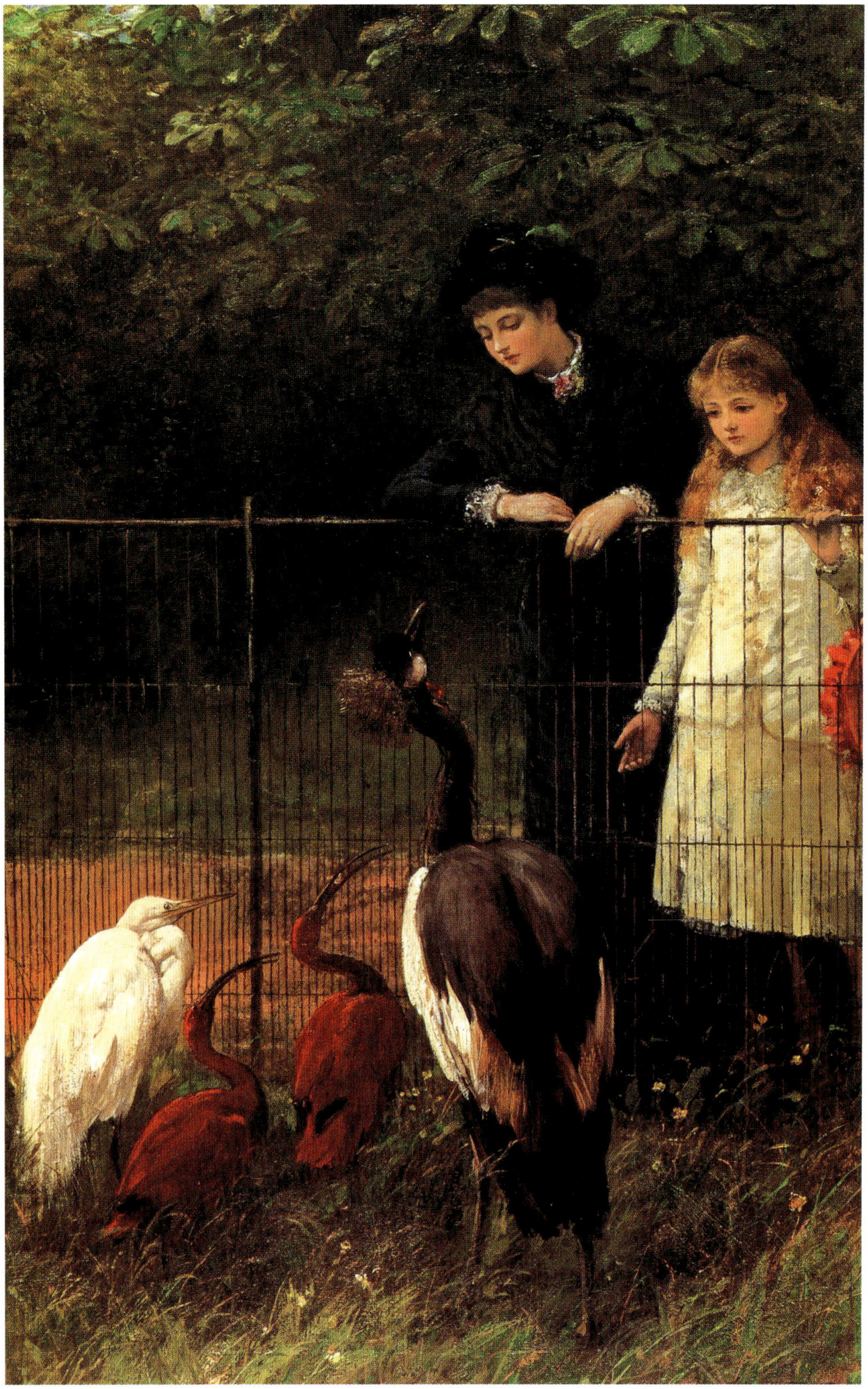

Plate 105: At the Bird Cage, 1890
Heywood Hardy. Oil on canvas.
102.9 x 63.5cm. Private Collection

Many years later Hardy used the studies of birds he had made for *God's Covenant with Noah* for another picture, *At the Bird Cage* (1890) (Plate 105). In this study of birds at the zoo, the two ibis and the crane are almost identical to birds on the far right of *God's Covenant with Noah*. *The Graphic* noted that Hardy had no doubt spent many hours sketching pelicans and other birds at the zoo as well as in Egypt:

> … there is no drawing we remember so distinctly and pleasurably as Heywood Hardy's admirable "Fishers of the Nile," a cluster of solemn, sententious-looking pelicans on a sandbank among reeds. Thanks to the Zoological Gardens, the artists of this generation have opportunities of studying nature denied to their predecessors. Mr. Hardy is one of those who has turned such opportunities to the best account. He has studied the habits of the pelican at home on the Nile, and has, no doubt, worked up the details of his pouched and piscatory sitters at the Zoo. He has got at the heart of their mystery, and has painted his pelicans as if he loved them.[163]

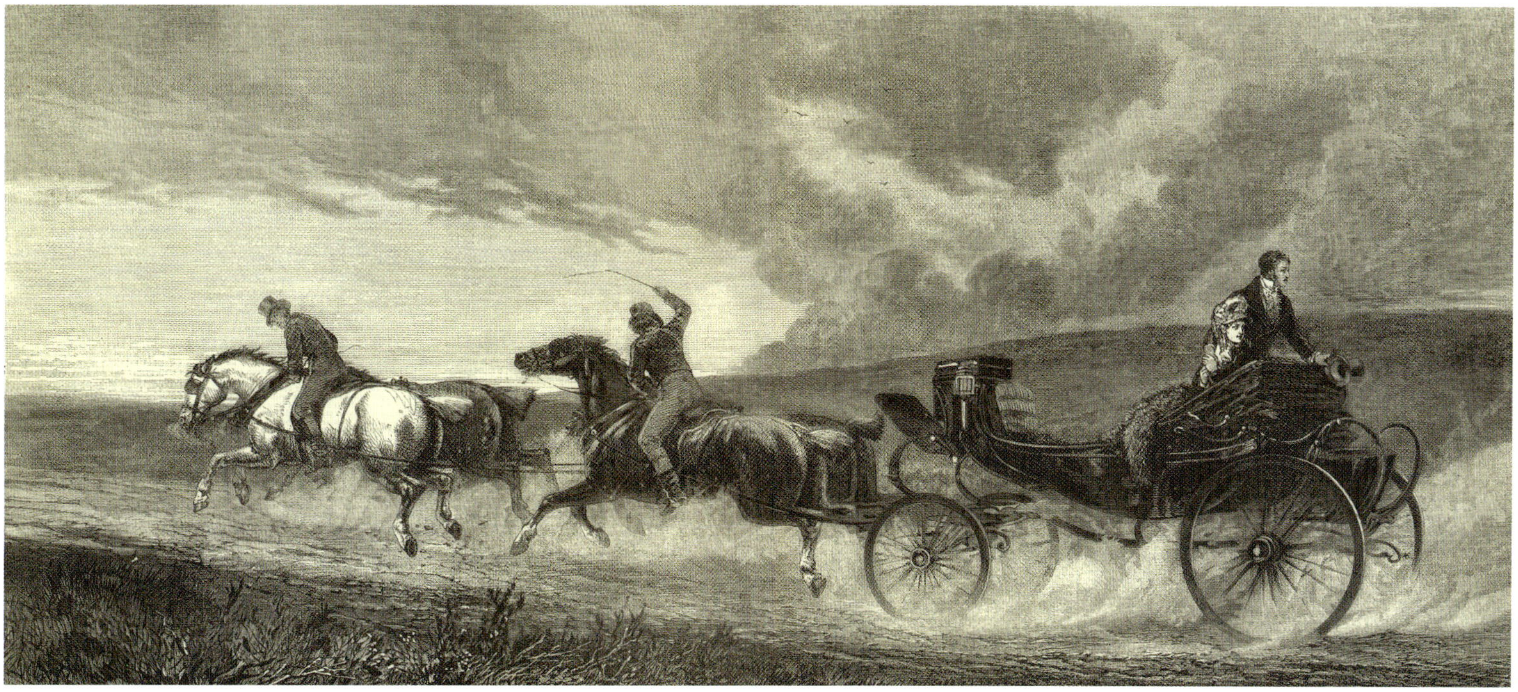

Plate 106: The Road to Gretna Green
After Heywood Hardy. Wood engraving from *The Illustrated London News*.[164]

Horses

Heywood Hardy eventually became one of the best equestrian artists of the latter half of the nineteenth century, in the period after J.F. Herring senior and before Sir Alfred Munnings, both renowned in the genre.

Heywood's studies of horses, begun early in the 1870s, were to provide the basis for many paintings in his long career. His early pictures included *The Belated Traveller* (1871) (Plate 107), *The Road to Gretna Green* (1871) (Plate 106), *The Lost Track* (1873) and *A Match* (1873) (Plate 132), which was the first of many paintings of horse-riding on beaches.

Engravings of all four paintings were published in *The Illustrated London News* and evidently appealed to Victorian taste:

> One of the popular pictures of the gallery is Mr. Heywood Hardy's "Road to Gretna Green"; ... the incident is kept in its place, and the point of the work lies in the clever action of the galloping, nearly spent horses, and the very pleasant rendering of landscape and atmosphere, with an open moorland road curving away into the distance. The qualities of Mr. Hardy's smaller second picture are almost identical with these.[165]

Similarly, whilst *The Times* art critic (presumably Tom Taylor) was unimpressed by two of Briton Rivière's exhibits in 1871 ("M. Rivière has fallen into a rank yellow, which pervades his backgrounds."), he was fulsome in his praise for *The Road to Gretna Green*:

> Another rising young animal painter, who first won his spurs at the Dudley [Gallery], Heywood Hardy, has two pictures here ... the other, more important, of a calèche and four at full gallop to Gretna, with the Lothario looking back for pursuers, the lady nervously clasping his hand, and the boys getting as much out of their team as stout thonging and Ripon steel can do. If there is dark cloud and danger of pursuit behind, there is a bright horizon before the runaways. How far off seems the subject now, and yet some of our fathers carried off our mothers so. Mr. Hardy has told the story with great spirit and capital choice of incidents and accompaniments.[166]

In commentating on *The Road to Gretna Green, The Illustrated London News* called Hardy "a young artist of marked promise"[167] and included the following note:

> A few rising oil painters present stronger claims; and prominent among them is Mr. Heywood Hardy, with "The Road to Gretna Green", a posting-carriage tearing along a country road, as the friendly shades of evening are coming on, with an anxious pair in the costume of the Regency inside; the man looking over the back of the carriage to see if they are pursued, the woman clinging to his hand. The lovers are desperately in earnest, but there is no false sentimentality. The fast, whirling haste of postilions and horses is capitally expressed, and the whole suggests a story of romantic love and elopement, as well as – nay, that would be a poor compliment, far better than – many a three-volume novel.[168]

The Belated Traveller (Plate 107), shown at the Dudley Gallery, also attracted the attention of art critics. *The Illustrated London News* gave a characteristictly enthusiastic narrative on its supplementary engraving:

> This vigorous drawing by Mr. Heywood Hardy, which we have engraved from the exhibition at the Dudley gallery, has a capitally managed effect of evening, with man and horse, trees and hedgerow, relieved against a still, luminous sky. Nor is the draughtsmanship in the action of the figures a whit less admirable. The powerful horse dashes along at a pace which, for his bulk, is tremendous; doubtless he has his own private reasons for putting on the steam; and the man is made to sit him perfectly – a thing more easy to do in nature than in a picture. The night promises to be bitterly cold, for it is winter; the trees are leafless; the sky is clear. And to find oneself straying from the road; perhaps stumbling about over a moor on a frosty night, with only starlight to direct, would be awkward as well as romantic. But supposing there is no danger of losing the way, one might guess at various other reasons why the traveller should quicken his pace, without supposing him liable to a recontre with Dick Turpin, or to be pursued by the imaginary terrors of Tam o'Shanter. The jolly farmer may have a very important engagement to keep; or, more serious still, he may be expecting a cold reception from a scolding wife. All our surmises are, however, overthrown by the lines from "Macbeth" inscribed on the frame of the picture:-
>
> The west yet glimmers with some streaks of day.
> Now spurs the belated traveller apace,
> To gain the *timely inn*.
>
> The italics, if you please, being ours, not Shakespeare's.[169]

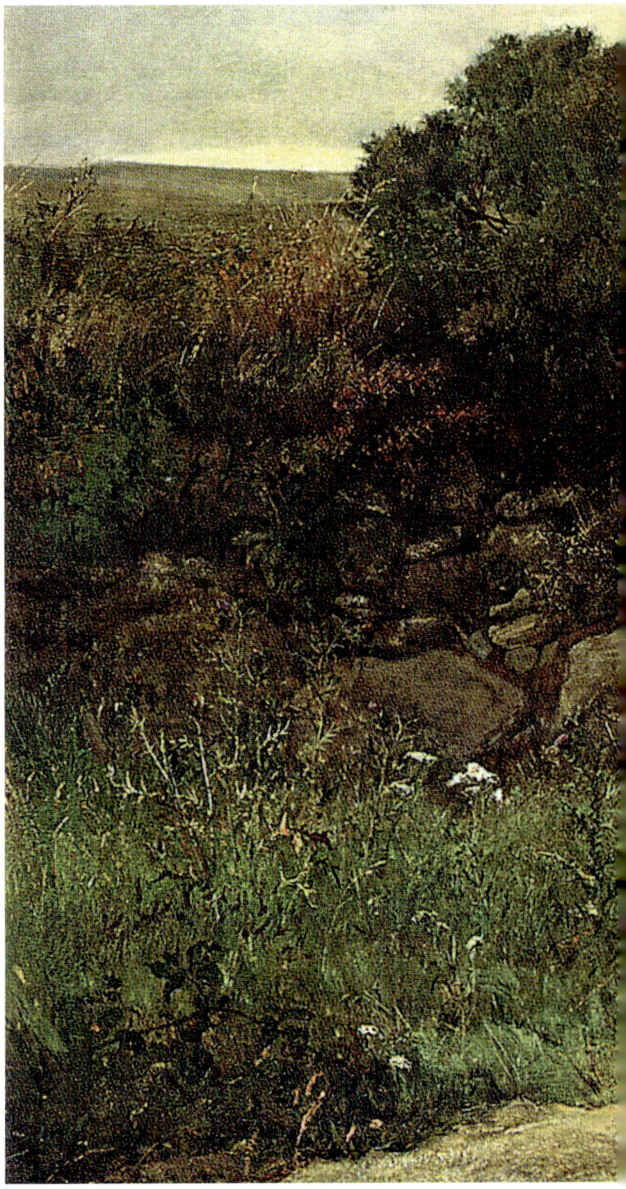

Heywood Hardy was one of the first artists to highlight the plight of cab horses. *The Last Days of the Old Hack,* shown at the Dudley Gallery in 1872, alongside *The Dilemma* (Plate 107), stimulated a response from *The Times* reviewer that could have been written by Anna Sewell (*Black Beauty* was published a few years later in 1877):

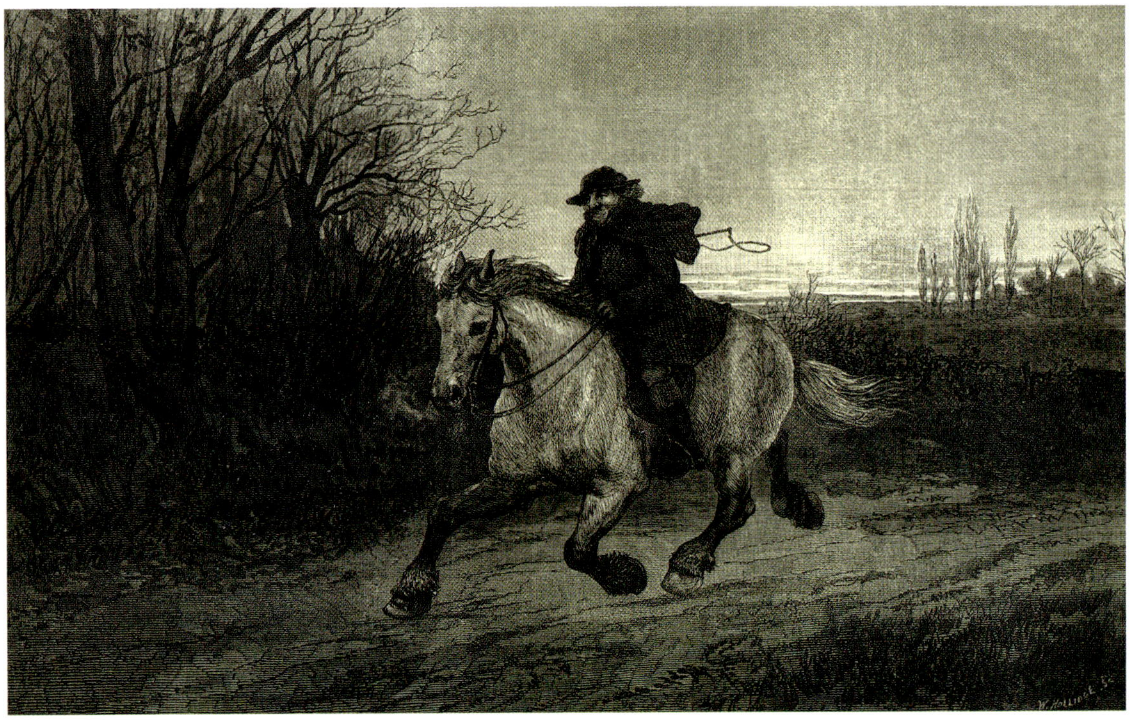

Plate 107: The Belated Traveller
After Heywood Hardy. Wood engraving from The Illustrated London News.

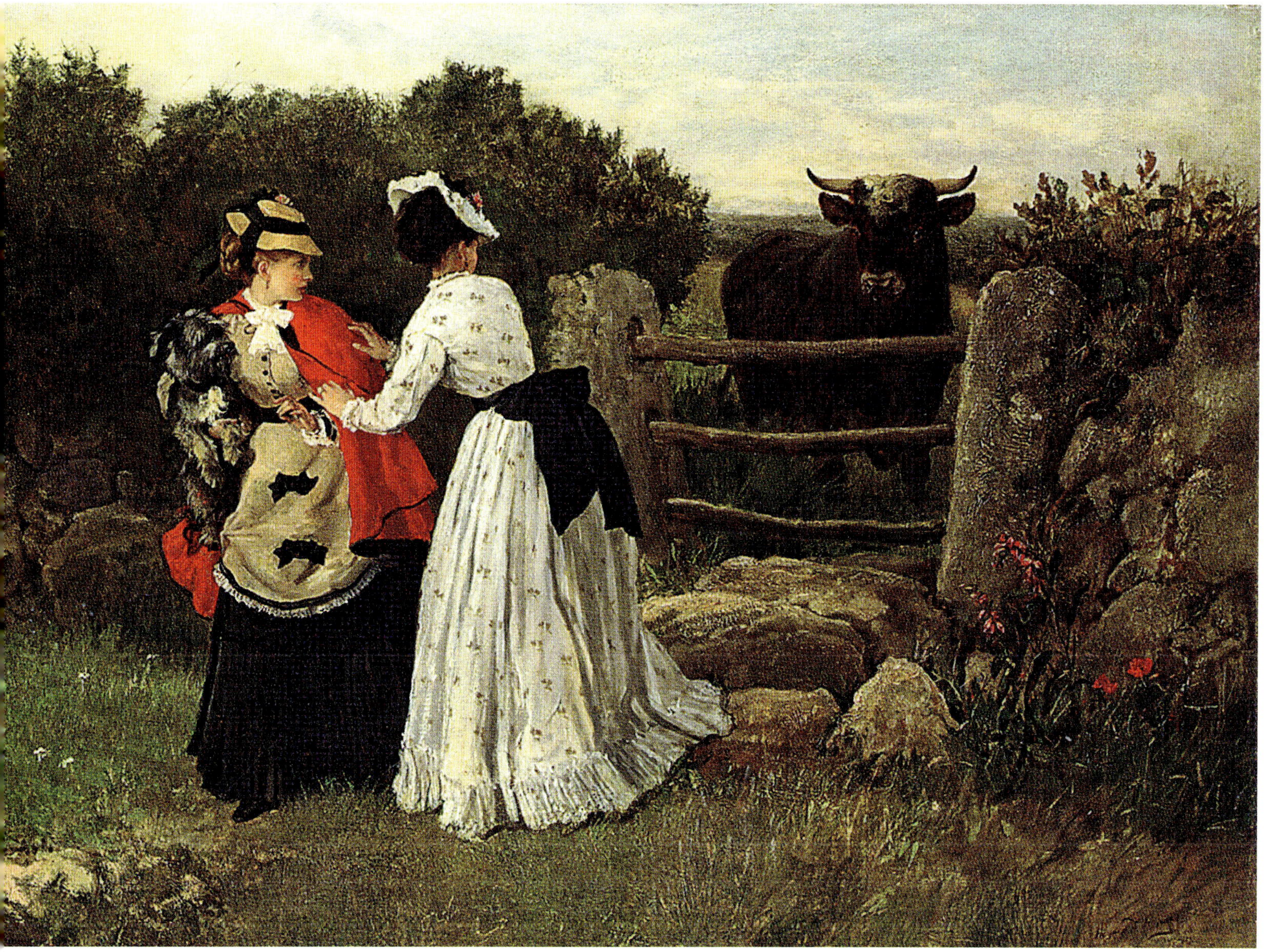

Plate 108: The Dilemma, 1872
Heywood Hardy. Oil on canvas. 54 x 106.4cm. Private Collection

> ... in this capital sketch of Heywood Hardy's (71) "The Last Days of the Old Hack" – come down from the glories of the ring, the course, and the stud-stable, to the cab-shafts, and left on a wet day, after a long drive in the mud to shiver through a long waiting outside a suburban villa entrance. This little picture, if slight, is full of feeling and meaning, and infinitely more precious than the same painter's larger but less interesting "Dilemma" (101), two girls interrupted in their walk by a young bull on the other side of a stile.[170]

Heywood Hardy's picture of cab horses was painted several years before John Dollman's celebrated picture of 1888, "Les Misérables (A London Cab Stand)". Another commentator noted that:

> Though Mr. Heywood Hardy's pictures, dealing as they do with familiar topics, may not perhaps belong to the sublime region of what is termed "high art" — a phrase almost as ambiguous as the "legitimate drama" — they display singular delicacy of execution, and are to be commended for their interesting fidelity of representation in all that relates, not alone to form and colour, but also to character and expression ... "*Manum de tabula*," a precept which has come down to us from the old masters, is duly appreciated by Mr. Hardy, who, having carried "finish" to the highest point desirable, knows when to take his hand off his picture and never sacrifices general effect to excessive elaboration of details.
>
> Mr. Hardy exhibits another picture, entitled "The Dilemma" [Plate 108] whimsically descriptive of the dismay of two girls who are crossing a field, and who, on arriving at a stile, find themselves confronted by a bull on the other side, who, resenting as a personal indignity the red cloak of one of the ladies, glares at the offender with a rage thoroughly

oxine. The terror of the girls and the majestic indignation of the brute, whose honour they have wounded on so sore a point, are capitally depicted, as also is the fussy alarm of a terrier whom his mistress has snatched up to keep him out of the way of harm.[171]

Heywood Hardy's paintings of *The Village Doctor* (1872) (Plate 109) and *Duty* (1880) (Plate 110) are rare portrayals of Victorian general practioners. *The Village Doctor* was exhibited at Agnew's Gallery in Pall Mall in 1872, described thus: "We see the gaunt, dark, bent form of 'The Village Doctor' (by Heywood Hardy). He is on his way through the snow, summoned by night to attend at an old mansion, walled in like a fortress, suggestive of romance and human grief." [172]

Heywood reworked the theme for *Duty*, shown in 1880 at the Royal Academy. An engraving of the painting was produced, bearing the title *The Village Doctor* (though it was not the same as *The Village Doctor* painted in 1872), and appeared in *The Graphic* and in *L'Univers Illustré* in 1881.

Vincent Van Gogh collected illustrations from *The Graphic* and similar publications; in 1882 he wrote to his friend Anthon van Rappard to ask if he could send him a copy of an engraving of Heywood Hardy's *The Village Doctor*, as published in *L'Univers Illustré* of 10 December 1881. [173]

The figure of the young shepherd in *Duty* resembles the shepherds in Hardy's pictures from 1862, in which the sheepdogs are instructed to fetch the sheep. In *Duty* the sheepdog is perhaps unsure whether it should follow the directions the boy is giving to the doctor.

Duty was a successful exhibit at the Royal Academy in 1880. Several reviewers praised the work. A reviewer who mistook the doctor for a clergeyman wrote:

> As an animal painter, Mr. Heywood Hardy has not often risen to Mr. Riviere's popularity, but then he has kept in his pictures the human element distinct from the animal ... Now the comedy in Mr. Hardy's pictures is in the human character alone, and in human adventure. This year the work is called "Duty." A faithful horse, contented in his daily task, and just as innocent as is his rider of thoughts of "promotion," carries the old clergyman — it is in bygone days — over the breast of the moor ... the discreet figure, closely wrapped, as the beast stumbles on over wild country and in sight of threatening storm. There is genuine truth to character — truth to a vivid effect of English landscape such as Mr. Hardy, we think, has nowhere before depicted, and animal drawing to boot, of the quality we are accustomed to look for.[174]

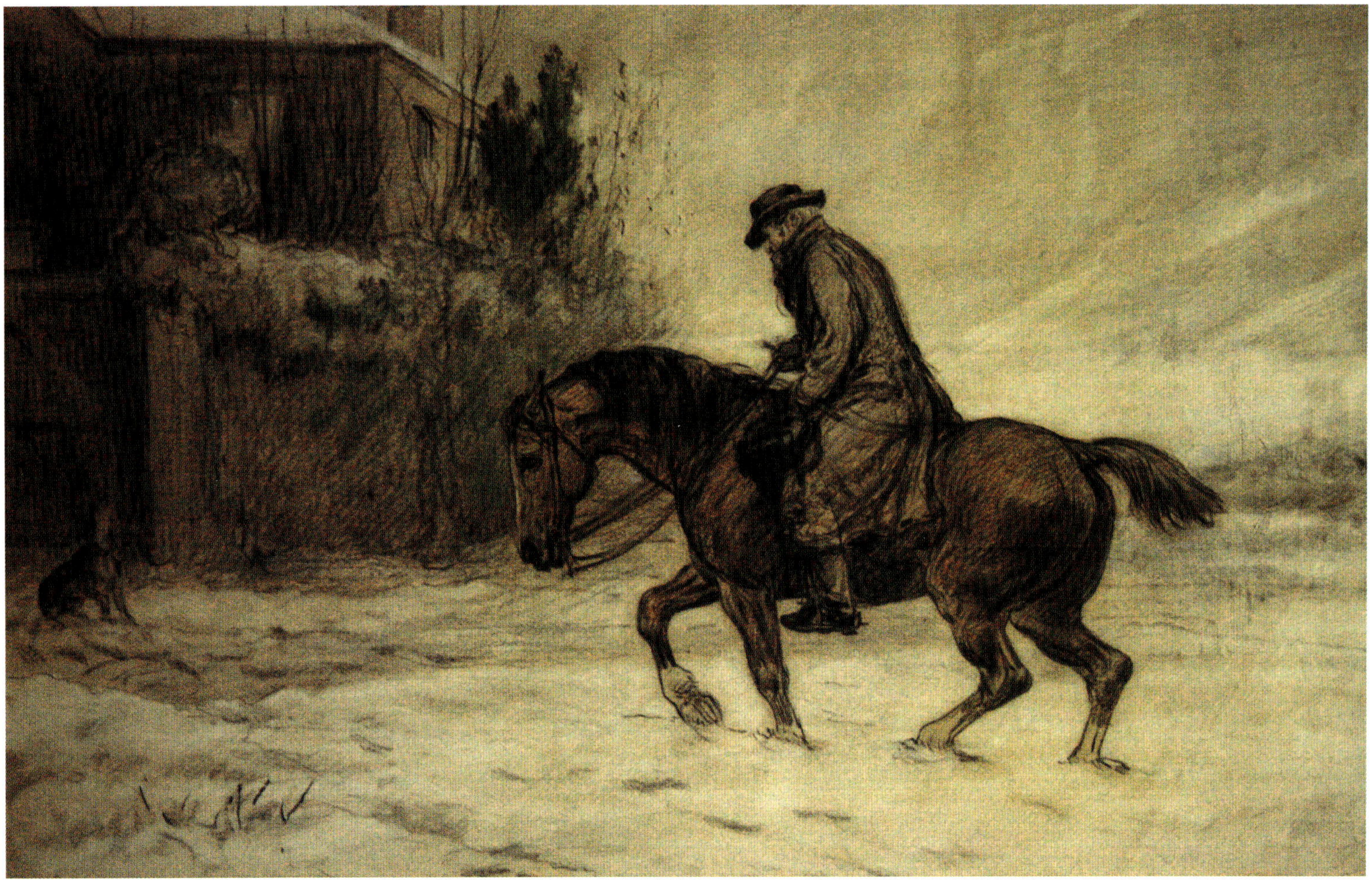

Plate 109: The Village Doctor, 1872
Heywood Hardy. Pencil and watercolour. 23.6 x 36.7cm. Private Collection

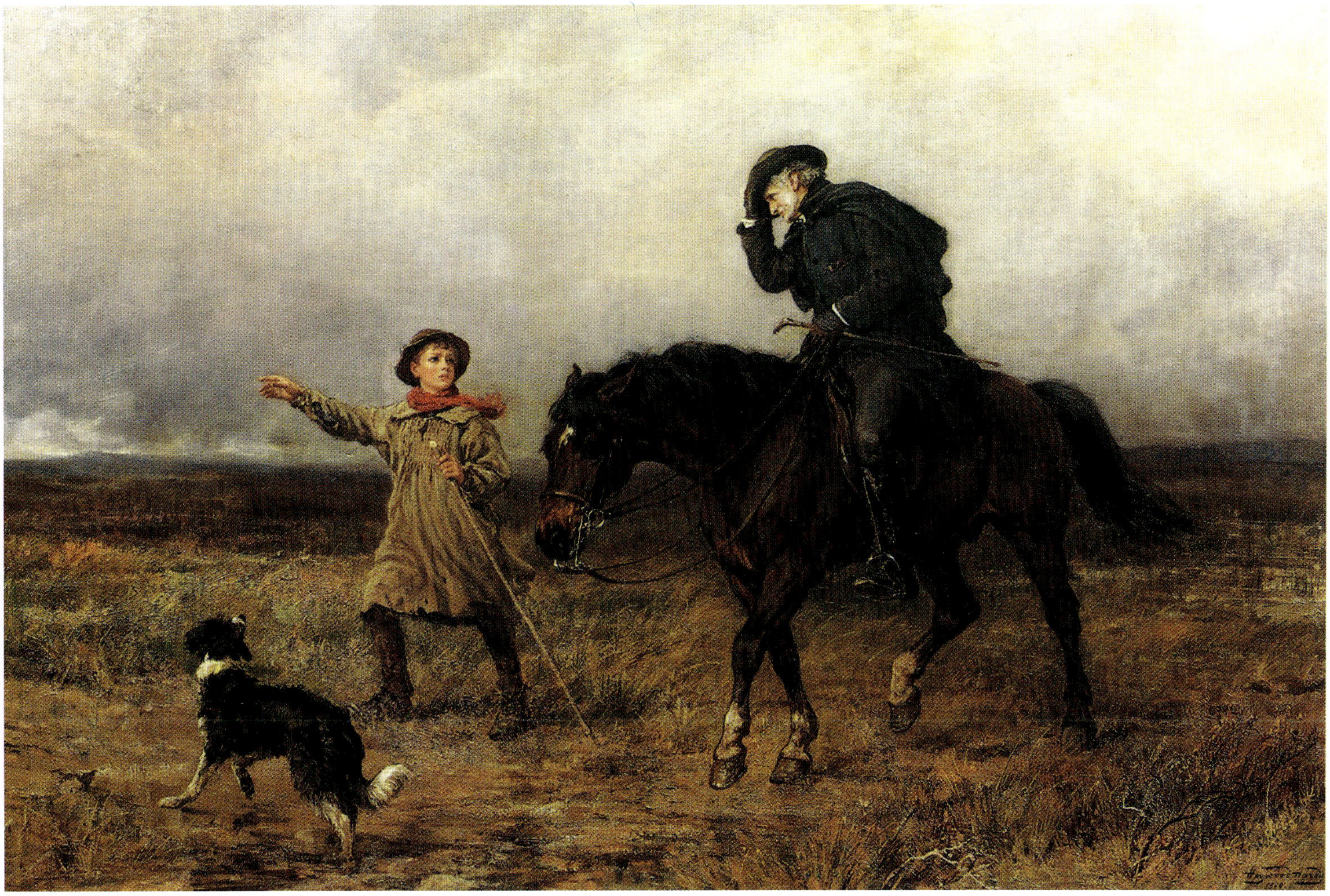

Plate 110: Duty, 1880
Heywood Hardy. Oil on canvas. 83 x 118cm. Guildhall Art Gallery, City of London Corporation

Dr David Huskie was a typical village doctor at about the time Hardy painted *Duty*. From his home in Moffat, Scotland, the area of his practice extended over 20 miles in all directions. Having begun his practice in 1891, he reflected at the end of his working life:

> It has been a hard and strenuous life, and for years I seldom got to my bed on the same day that I left it; and frequently two or three nights in the week I never got to my bed at all – arriving home only in time to have a bath and breakfast and start my rounds again ... [175]

Hardy's Royal Academy exhibit for 1877, *Christmas Eve: He comes, the herald of a noisy world etc.* (Plate 111)[176], had a similar theme. *The Times* wrote:

> Heywood Hardy's "Christmas Eve" is another suggestive, though less pathetically and dramatically suggestive, subject. We have the cross-country postman in his mail-gig, caked with snow, his horse scarcely able to make his way over the thickly-covered, bleak moorland. Woe to the man if the wind rises and he is overtaken by the night. There is pathos in the suggestion of his cold labour, while those he works for sit by the fire; and a suggested contrast of the pace he is able to travel and the eagerness with which the contents of his mail cart may be awaited.[177]

The Spectator's art correspondent – presumably Harry Quilter who wrote for *The Spectator* from 1876 – was similarly impressed:

> "Christmas Eve," by Heywood Hardy, No. 464, is one the most complete and spirited of this artist's works. It represents a postman in his mail-cart making his way across a desolate high-road, in the teeth of snow and wind. The drawing of the horse is particularly good, and the whole picture tells its story thoroughly well.[178]

Heywood Hardy's exhibit at the 1878 Royal Academy exhibition, *Tipping* (Plate 114), is a unique representation that shows how horses were used to pull wagons of ballast in enormous quantities to make Victorian railways. The picture was commissioned by Sir John Aird, a collector of modern British art.[179] He was chairman of John Aird & Co. one of the most important

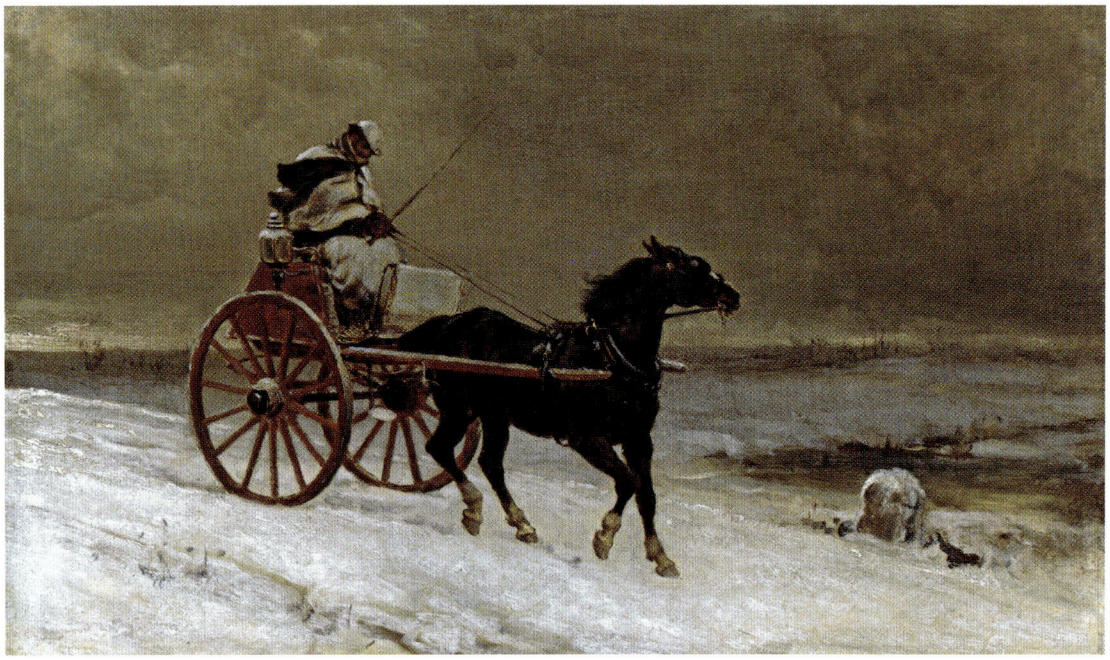

Plate 111: Christmas Eve, 1877
Heywood Hardy. Oil on panel. 27.4 x 45.8cm. Private Collection

companies engaged in railway construction and civil engineering work in the late nineteenth and early twentieth centuries.

Henry Blackburn, author of *Academy Notes*, commented on the "skilful rendering of an every-day event not often seen on canvas".[180] *The Art Journal* "would have the visitor note ... the clever way in which H. Hardy has made pictorial use of the common operation of 'Tipping' as pursued by navvies in the making of a railway[181] ... the picture shows contractors' trucks at work, laying ballast, with the horse, at the critical moment, stepping out from between the metals, a familiar illustration of animal docility and intelligence ... "[182].

Heywood Hardy's studies of horses always received favourable comment, though in the 1870s his drawing of human figures was sometimes seen as less assured. His acknowledged skill in painting horses provided a cornerstone for a variety of different subjects – pictures of racehorses, equestrian portraits, hunting scenes and horses at work.

Heywood's realistic and lively portrayal of horses in motion may have benefited from the drawings he made during the 1870s to illustrate the lectures of Professor Alfred Garrod FRS "On the Locomotion of the Horse". Hardy was a friend of Professor Garrod from the time when Hardy began sketching at the Zoological Gardens in London. Garrod was prosector to the Zoological Society and Hardy studied the comparative anatomy of birds and animals with him.

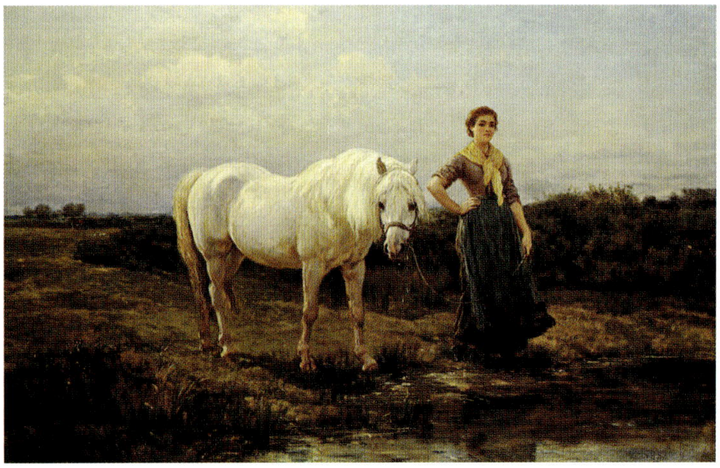

Plate 112: Noonday. Taking a Horse to Water, 1877
Heywood Hardy. Oil on canvas. 66 x 99.1cm. Private Collection

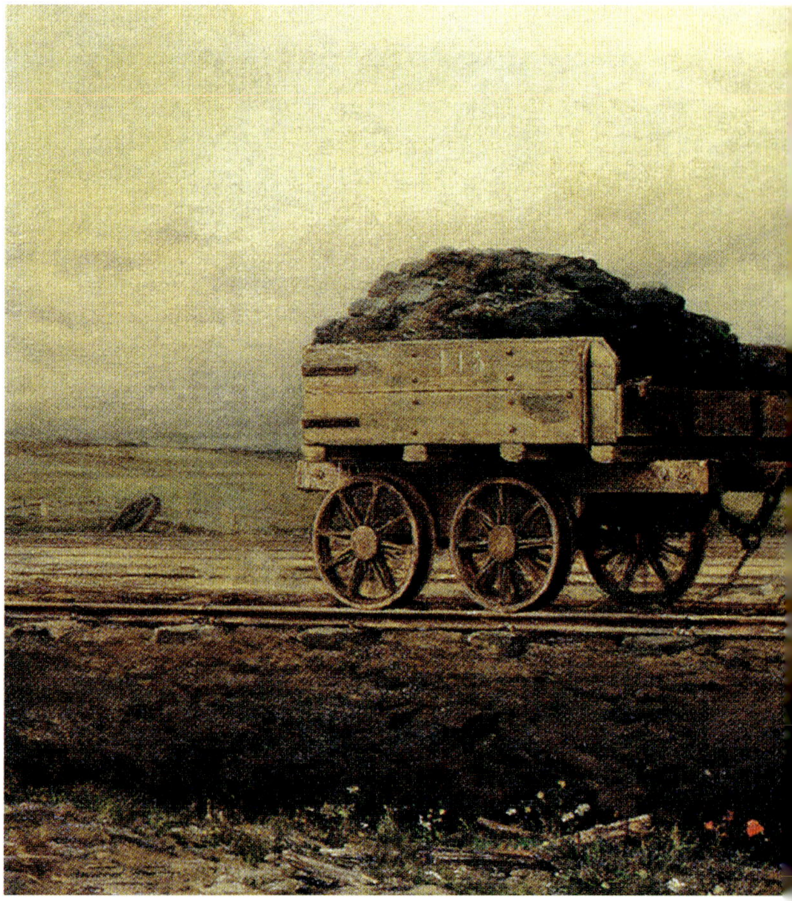

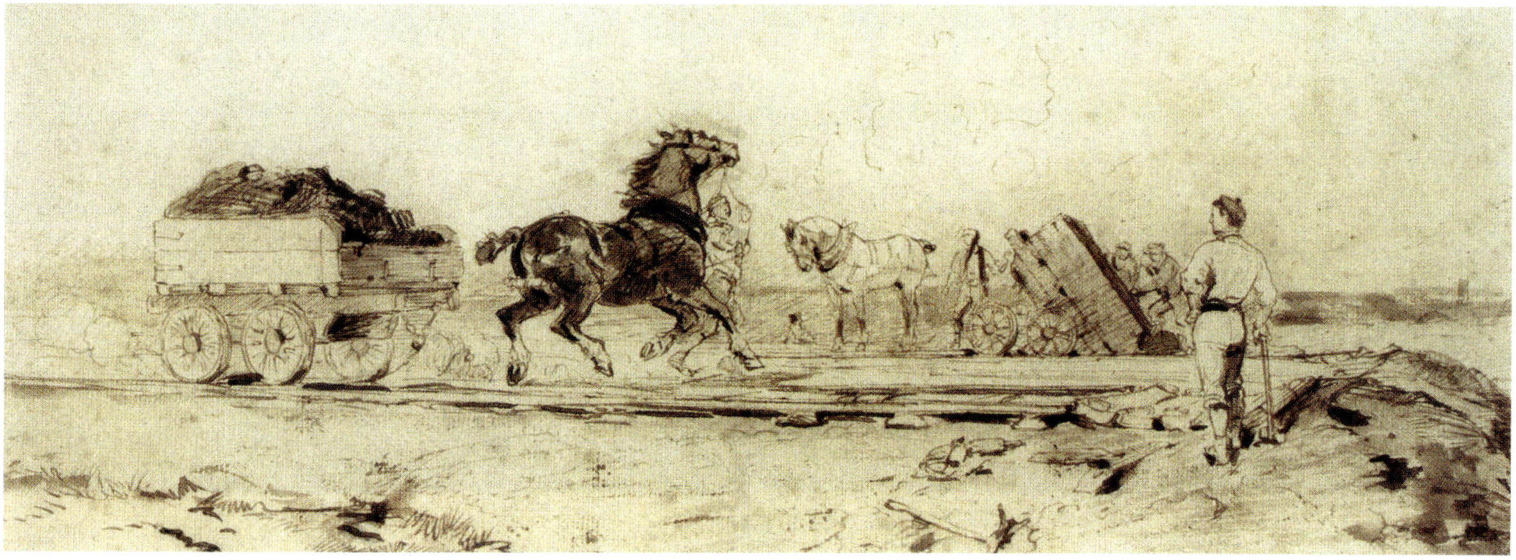

Plate 113 (above): Sketch for Tipping, ca.1878
Heywood Hardy. Pen and brown ink on paper. 14 x 36.2cm. Private Collection

Plate 114 (below): Tipping, 1878
Heywood Hardy. Oil on canvas 79.4 x 205.7cm. Private Collection

Professor Garrod published a paper in the scientific journal *Nature* on studies of the horse's gait, the sequence and pattern of foot-falls during walking, trotting etc., in part based on the recent work of the French physiologist Professor Étienne-Jules Marey. Marey's apparatus consisted of a rubber ball attached to a horse's hoof; the ball was compressed when the hoof touched the ground and the event was registered by means of the compressed air entering a tube that was attached to a recording device.

Garrod gave several lectures at the Royal Institution and Philosophical Societies.[183] Although Garrod and his assistant

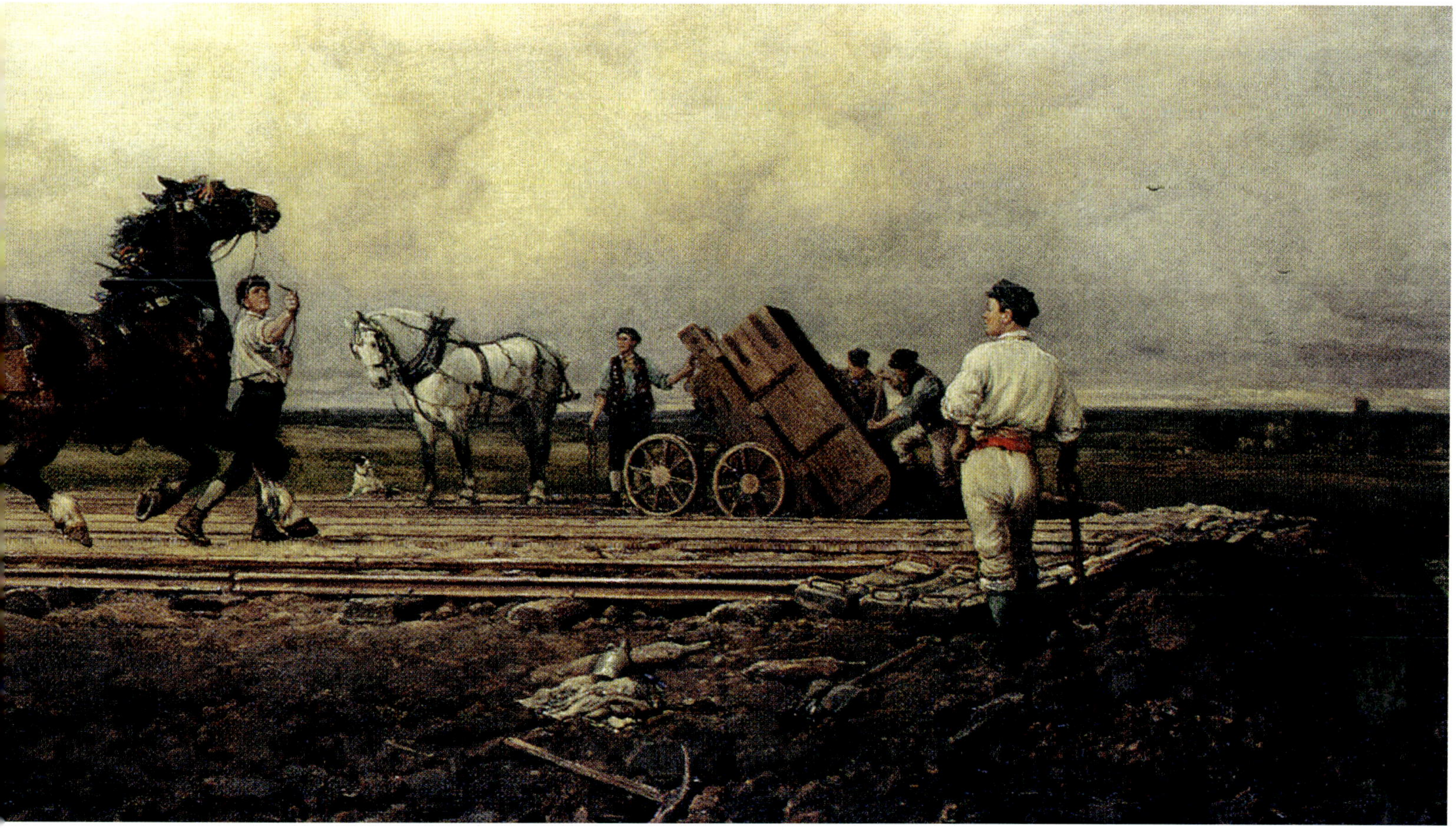

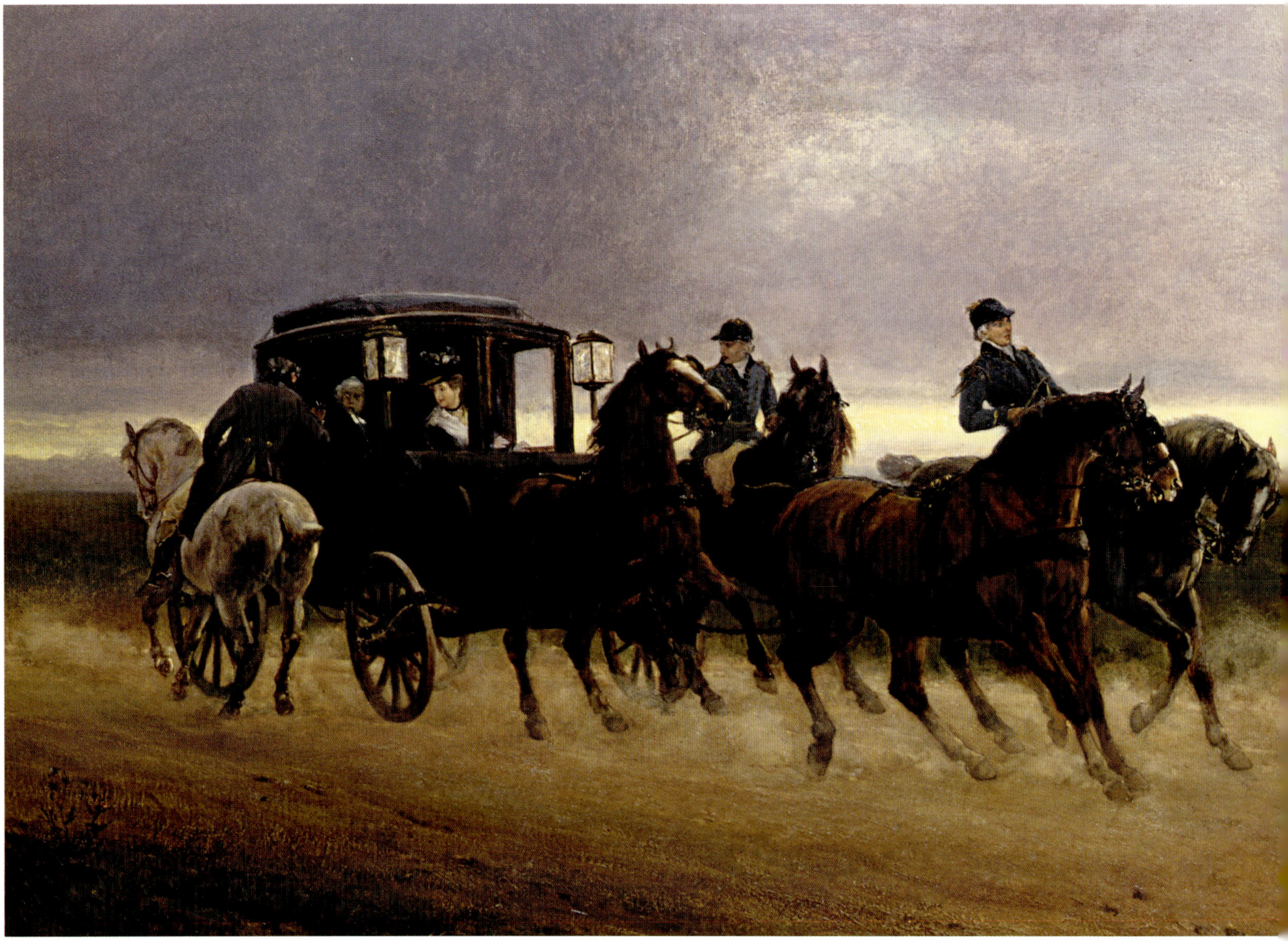

Plate 115: A Hold-up on Hounslow Heath, 1875
Heywood Hardy. Oil on canvas. 57 x 122cm. Private Collection

illustrated the lectures by walking behind each other, looking like a pantomime horse, it seems that it was impossible to understand without the help of Heywood's drawings:

> Nothing was apparently more puzzling than to understand the coordination of the steps of the horse ... The method invented by Professor Marey was next described at great length. Without the aid of the diagrams used by the lecturer any attempt to reproduce this portion of the lecture would be practically unintelligible. The illustrations and diagrams were numerous, and drawn by Mr Heywood Hardy. Incidentally, adverting to the discussions which took place some time ago respecting one of the horses in Miss Thompson's famous picture ("The Roll Call"), the lecturer observed that the question whether she was right or wrong was definitely settled by appeal to Professor Marey's method, which proved that Miss Thompson was slightly wrong, but the error was very slight indeed.[184]

Once images of horses in motion, taken by pioneering photographer Eadweard Muybridge, were published in 1878, it became clear that Lady Butler (Elizabeth Thompson) was correct.[185] In *An Autobiography* (1922) Lady Butler wrote that she "had told many people to go down on all fours themselves and walk, noting the sequence with their own hands and knees, which was sure to be correct instinctively". Publication of Muybridge's photographs did not completely solve the problem of how best to represent a galloping horse in a painting. A drawing based on the photographs does not usually give an impression of the horse's action; selecting the right vewpoint and particular stage of the horse's gait was crucial to representing the animal's movement.

Heywood Hardy's grandson, Alastair Hardy Ivens, recalled how Heywood loved to go to the cinema to watch cowboy films, to study the movements of horses:

> You might think it would have been rather dull for a small boy like myself to spend summer holidays in an old

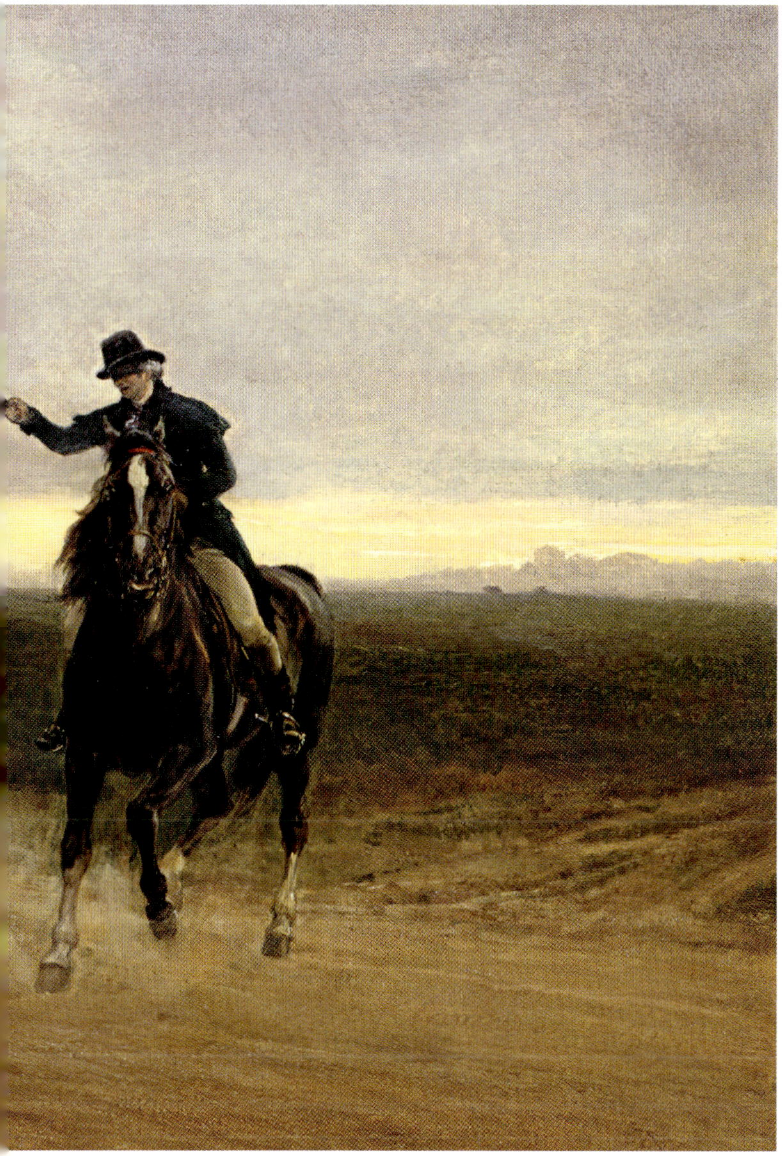

gentleman's house, but in fact he was great fun and always ready for a walk or an adventure. He loved cowboy films. He used to say to me, "If we set off early we shall just have time to have a cup of tea and see another film before the bus returns home". He used to tell us that he visited the cinema to study the movements of the horses, but we all knew he loved the shooting in cowboy films as much as we did.[186]

No doubt Hardy enjoyed cowboy films as much as his grandson – according to Alastair he kept a pile of cowboy magazines on a small table beside his fireside chair.[187] The first moving pictures must have been fascinating for someone who had spent so much of his life studying horses and knew all about the controversy in the 1870s about the horse's gait.

Horses and Riders – Eighteenth-Century Style

Shortly after he settled in London, Heywood Hardy started to paint country scenes populated by horses and riders in eighteenth-century or Regency costume. The pictures remained so popular with Victorian and Edwardian collectors, and with the wider public through the sale of prints, that he continued to paint them for almost the next 40 years. For the Victorians, his paintings and prints helped to establish the romantic view of the eighteenth-century countryside, populated with squires and hunt followers on horseback drinking outside country inns.

When Hardy returned to London from the Continent in the late 1860s there was already a revival of interest in eighteenth-century painting by artists such as Millais who, in turn, had been especially interested in the portraiture and painting styles of Joshua Reynolds and Thomas Gainsborough. Millais' painting of *Vanessa* in 1868 marks the date when he began his portraits depicting eighteenth-century costume employing more dramatic and visible brushwork.

Other artists who painted eighteenth-century costume pictures included James Tissot, who became established in London in the early 1870s. And Hardy might also have been familiar with pictures of figures in period costumes by Henri Coroënne, in whose studio he studied in Paris (see page 73). In the 1850s John Frederick Herring senior, one of the best horse painters of the previous generation, painted several costume pictures of cavaliers and horses, such as as *The Rose, The Baron's Charger, Soldiers Resting, Cavalier Taking Refreshment* and *A Letter of Intent*. The popularity of the eighteenth century in the latter half of the nineteenth century was also reflected in literature, fashion and china.

One of Hardy's first pictures with figures in eighteenth-century costume was *Hold-up on Hounslow Heath* (1875) (Plate 115); eighteenth century travellers who crossed the Heath on the road from London to Windsor and Bath were frequently subject to highway robbery.

I'm Going a-Milking, Sir, She Said (Plate 116), was shown at the Dudley Gallery in 1877. *The Morning Post's* note on the picture is typical of contemporary comment:

> "I'm going a-milking, sir, She said", is the title given by Mr. Heywood Hardy to a brilliant little picture (285) charmingly illustrative of the old ballad.
>
> *Where are you going, my pretty maid?*
> *I'm going a milking, sir, she said.*
> *May I go with you, my pretty maid?*
> *You're kindly welcome, sir, she said.*
> *What is your father, my pretty maid?*
> *My father's a farmer, sir, she said.*
> *What is your fortune, my pretty maid?*
> *My face is my fortune, sir, she said.*
> *Then I won't marry you, my pretty maid.*
> *Nobody asked you, sir, she said.*
>
> Mounted upon a grey hunter, and sprucely dressed in a blue coat, three-cornered laced hat, and shining jack-boots, the young squire is carrying on his supercilious flirtation with the milkmaid, the prettiest and most espiègle of little country wenches, who views him with an air of the sauciest

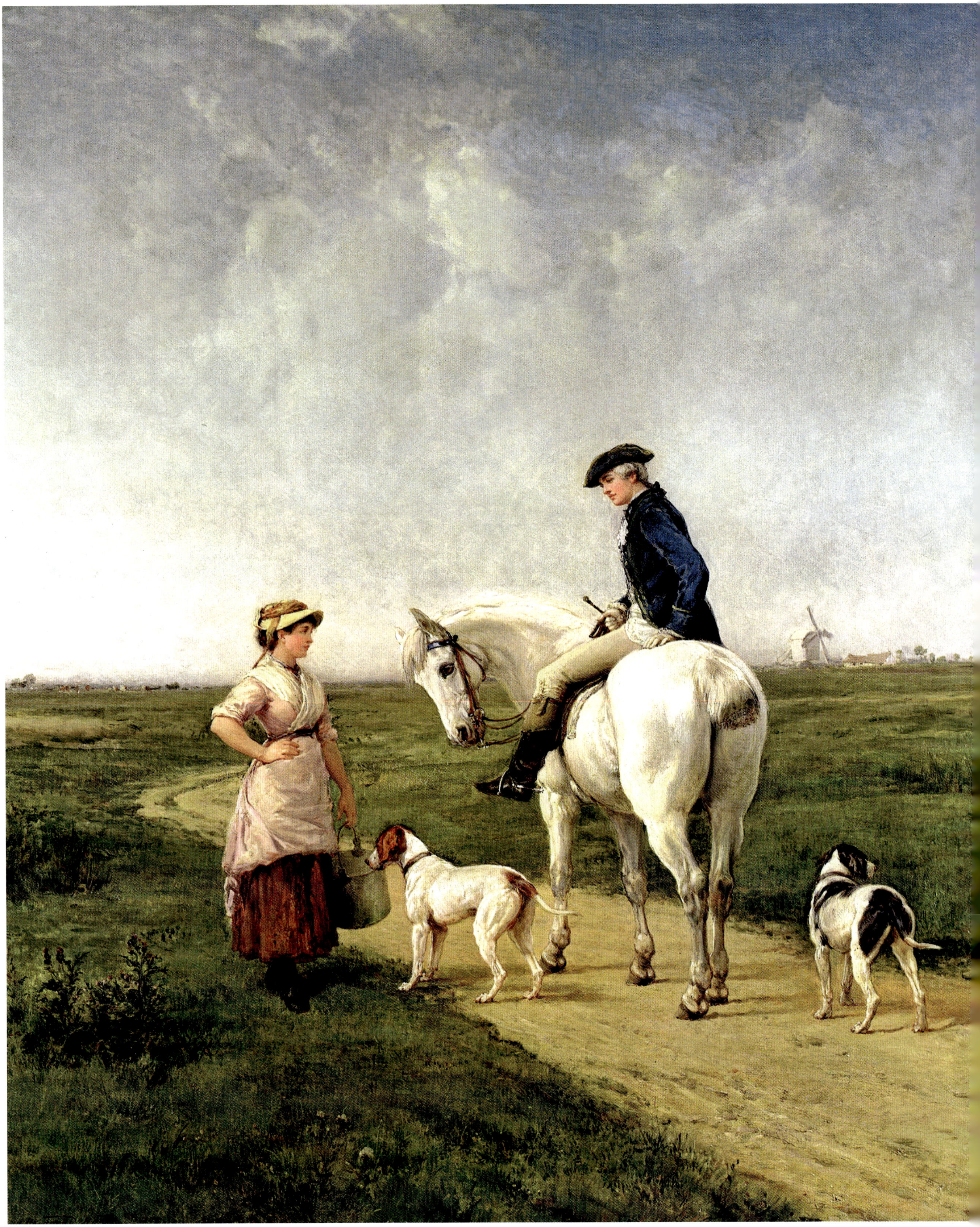

Plate 116 (opposite page): I'm Going a-Milking, Sir, She Said, 1877
Heywood Hardy. Oil on canvas. 57.6 x 38cm. Private Collection

disdain. Meanwhile one of the squire's dogs is peering with a droll expression of canine curiosity into one of her milk pails. The place is a stretch of pasture, intersected by a road leading to a mill; and the cows are grazing in the distance. The figures are admirably drawn and full of character, and the story is told with dainty humour.[188]

A similar picture to *I'm Going a-Milking*, *Forced Company,* was exhibited at the Dudley Gallery in 1878. *The Graphic* describes "a dashing young squire, on his gallant grey, ranging up alongside a broad-backed farm horse, which carries a pretty girl on a pillion behind her rustic swain".[189] The *Pall Mall Gazette* appreciated the "unforced humour" of *Forced Company*:

Mr. Heywood Hardy's "Forced Company" (284) is a good specimen of quiet, unforced humour, not too frequently found in modern English art. A country lover and his lass are riding homeward on a stout cob, when they are joined by the gallant squire, who evidently is struck with the charms of the buxom damsel. Whether she in return appreciates his compliments is left somewhat uncertain; but there is, on the other hand, no mistake about the feelings of the young rustic who persistently turns his back on the intruder.[190]

Heywood's exhibit at the 1879 Royal Academy exhibition was *Meg Merrilies and the Laird of Ellangowan* (Plate 117). The scene is from Sir Walter Scott's novel *Guy Mannering*, in which Meg Merrilies suddenly appears to curse the Earl of Ellangowan and his servant, Guy Mannering, after her gypsies were evicted from the Earl's land. *The Art Journal* was impressed by the painting, but thought the figure of Meg Merrilies could have been more dramatically portrayed: "The honours of the Lecture Room are given to ... Meg Merrilies and the Laird of Ellangowan."[191]

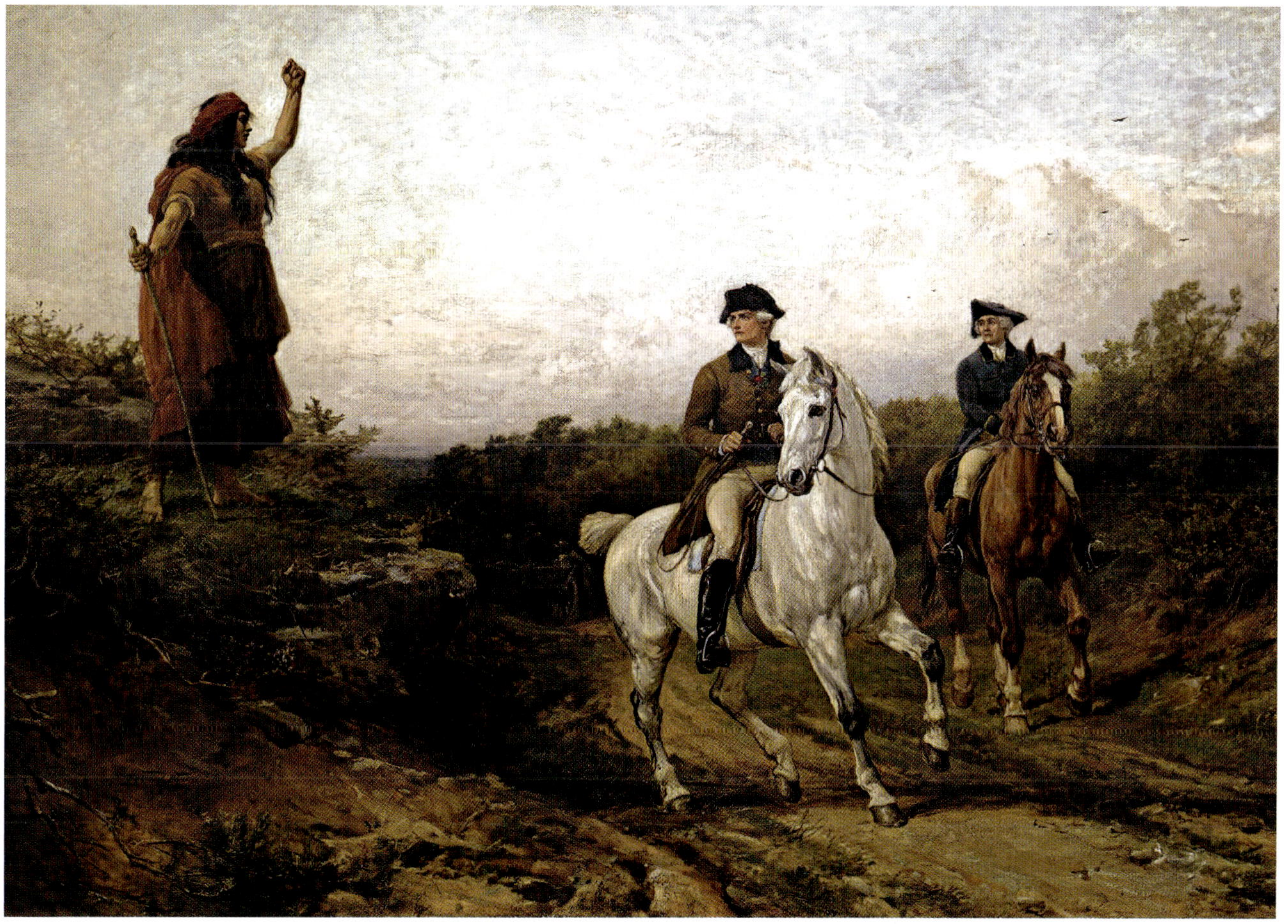

Plate 117: Meg Merrilies and the Laird of Ellangowan, 1879
"As he was about to turn his horse's head to pursue his journey Meg Merrilies unexpectedly presented herself."
Heywood Hardy. Oil on canvas. 122 x 167cm. Private Collection

Painting in France

The Sale of Cavalry Horses (1884) (Plate 118) is a good example of Hardy's ability to portray a galloping horse. He spent several months living in France in 1883 and 1884, part of the time at Dinan in Brittany. Annual fairs for selling horses were held at Carhaix and Pont Aven. These were favourite places for artists from Paris to spend the summer months. Two of the equestrian studies Heywood made in Brittany were exhibited at the Royal Academy in 1884: *The Rear Guard*, showing dragoons gently riding along a country road in Brittany, and *The Sale of Cavalry Horses*.

Heywood's paintings were well-drawn, animated scenes:

> A very interesting animal as well as genre painter should be mentioned here ... Mr. Heywood Hardy. His studies of animals, lately published as etchings, heads of lions, horses, etc., are popular in the print-shops, and every year his pictures are on the Academy walls. For the last year he has been living in France, and has sent home some admirable studies of French horse-soldiers.
>
> The "rear-guard" of dragoons riding up a quiet road in Brittany, in rather free-and-easy fashion; the last man, saluting a peasant-girl leading a cow by a string, has an air of *vraisemblance* seldom achieved. Mr. Hardy gives exact portraits of the style and accoutrements of the men; they "sit on their horses" unmistakably, the road is a French road, and there are ease of manner and an open-air effect which are so often missed in similar subjects. All this we may see in the foregoing sketch, which Mr. Hardy has made for us; also in the spirited drawing of the central figure in his second picture, "The Sale of Cavalry-Horses" a dragoon, in undress, riding through the fair. The large annual sales of horses in the interior of Brittany are great opportunities for artists.[192]

The Times' reviewer of the Royal Academy exhibition of 1884 made similar comments:

> In Room VII, besides the pictures of which we have already spoken, there are several excellent works of Messrs. Heywood Hardy... Mr. Hardy is well known as a painter chiefly of animals, and his "Sale of Cavalry Horses" (793) is a very animated and well-drawn scene of French military life.[193]

Hardy's picture depicts a scene much as described a few years later by his friend, the artist Randolph Caldecott, when he was at Carhaix:

> The horse fair was held in a large square or *place*. Under the trees was a crowd of men and women in the dust and heat; horses, cattle, pigs and dogs, in confused movement; with much drinking and shouting at the booths which lined one side of the enclosure.[194]

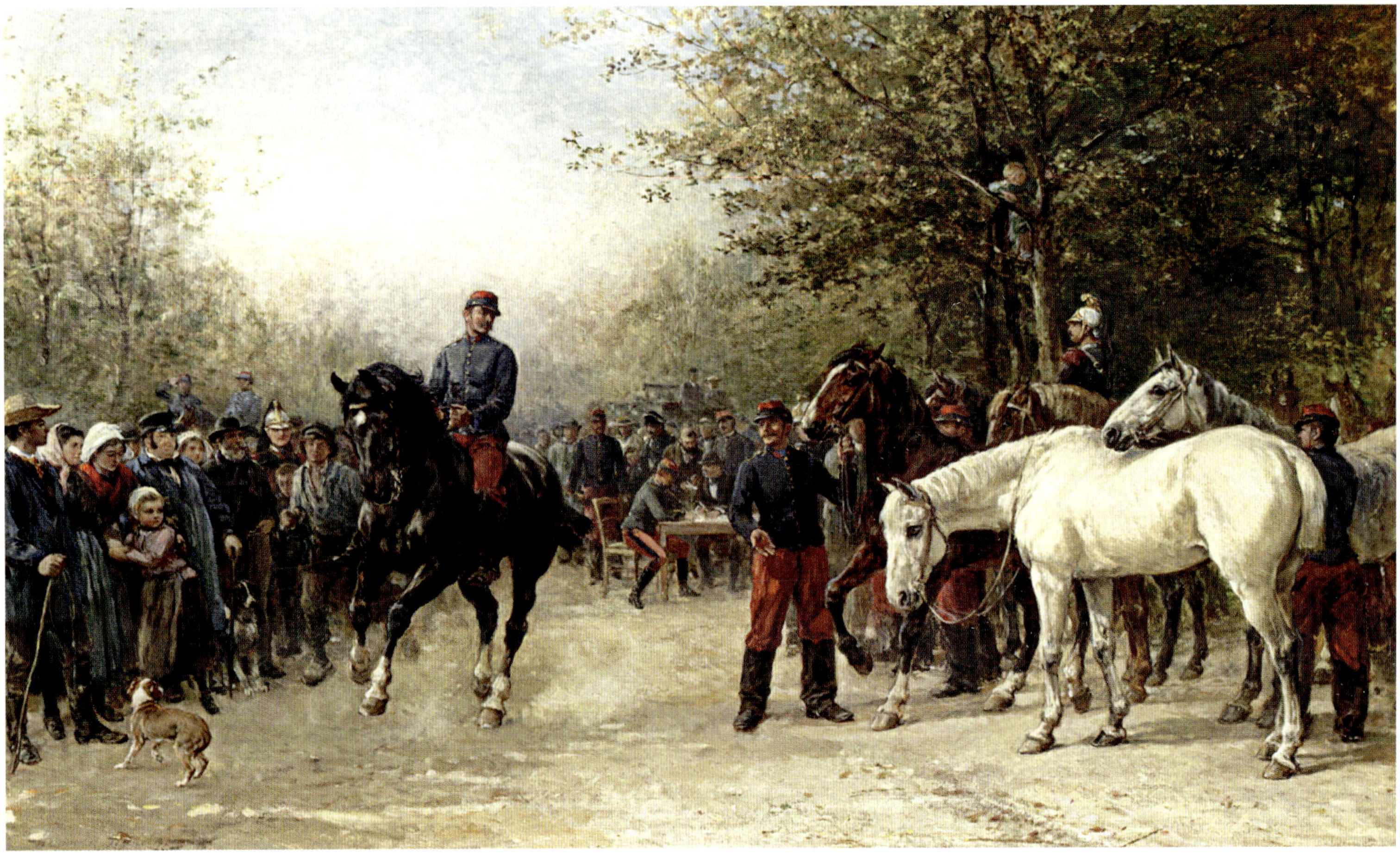

Plate 118: The Sale of Cavalry Horses, 1884
Heywood Hardy. Oil on canvas. 45.4 x 73cm. Private Collection

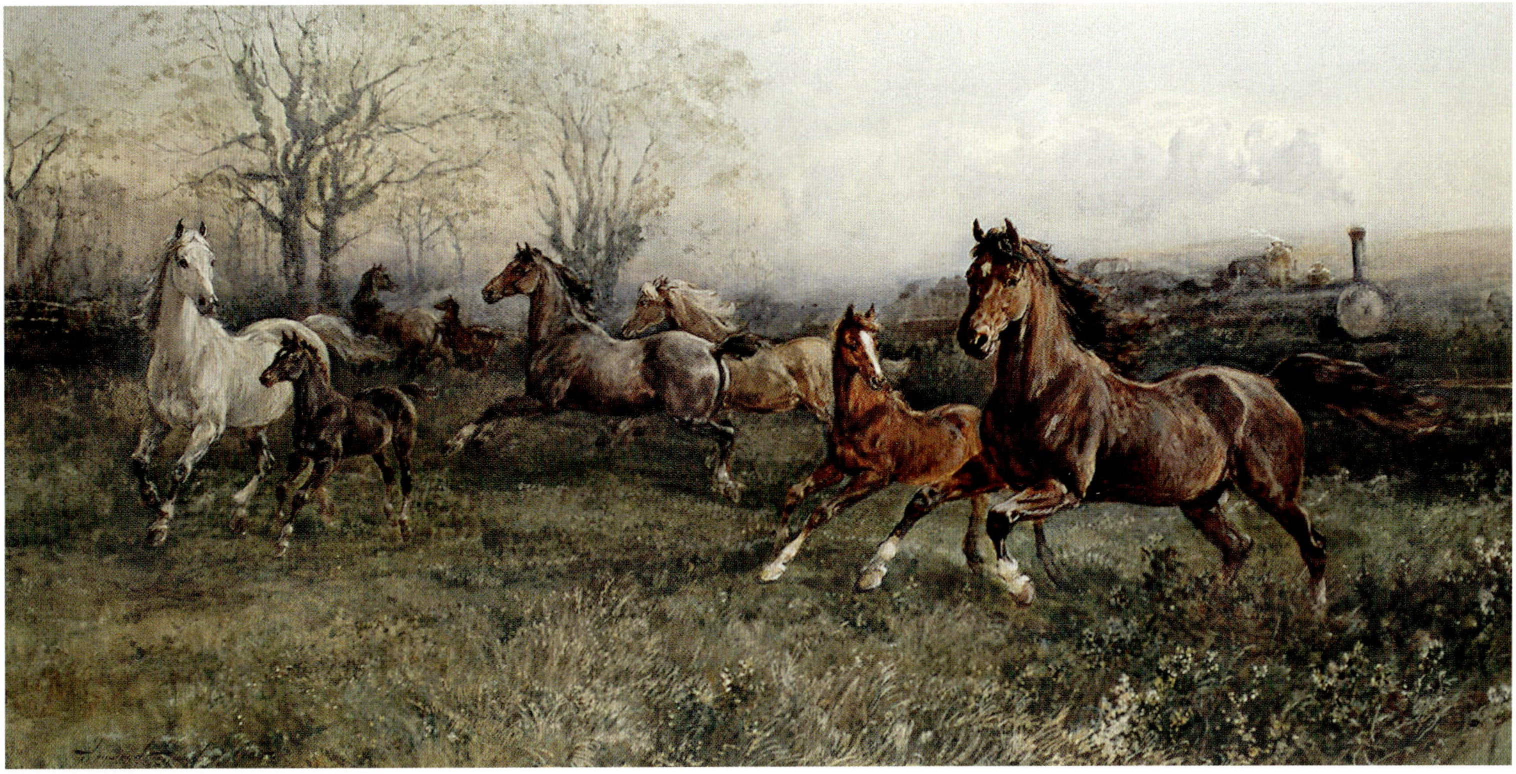

Startled (1885) (Plate 119), a study of horses painted at about the same time, in watercolour and gouache, also illustrates his ability to paint animated pictures of horses.

By the time Hardy had returned from France in the mid-1880s, his methods of painting were characterised by their free and spontaneous brushwork, which had much in common with French naturalist painters of the period. To English critics this was sometimes seen as a fault, though Heywood Hardy would no doubt have seen it as a compliment.

A critic in 1885 commented on one of his beach scenes:

> Mr Heywood Hardy has become, *pro tem.* at least, a disciple of the school of Bastien Lepage and Leon Lhermitte.[195] The result is scarcely satisfactory, Mr Hardy's "Over the Sands" and "Wonders of the Deep" having simply a "washed-out" appearance compared with previous efforts, though they possess, of course, all the conspicuous merits of Mr Hardy's accomplished style.[196]

After Heywood returned from France in 1885 it appears that he and his wife, Mary, increasingly led separate lives. Their grandchildren understood that Mary "was considered a very strong-minded person". Following an application for a legal separation in 1891, Mary had custody of their youngest daughter, Sylvia May Hardy, then aged seven.[197]

Plate 119 (above): Startled, 1885
Heywood Hardy. Watercolour and gouache. 45.5 x 87.5cm. PRIVATE COLLECTION

Plate 120 (right): Love's Barrier, 1891
After Heywood Hardy. Mezzotint by Thomas Appleton, published by I. Mendoza.

Romance and Horseflesh

Heywood Hardy's pictures of horse riders in eighteenth-century costume – "Romance and Horseflesh" pictures as George Bernard Shaw called them[198] – were popular as paintings and prints for several decades.

During the 1880s and 1890s pictures by Heywood were often shown at Isaac Mendoza's St James's Gallery. Mendoza commissioned several paintings from Heywood Hardy for the purposes of making prints, for example *Love's Barrier* (Plate 120), *Forgiven* (Plate 122) and *Too Late* (1885).[199] Mendoza also bought the copyright to *Not to be Caught by Chaff* (1875) (Plate 90) and *The Toast* (1886). Some of Hardy's pictures of figures in eighteenth-century or Regency costume that were painted for Isaac Mendoza, for example *Too Late*, resemble the paintings of Marcus Stone RA, which became popular from the mid-1870s onwards.[200]

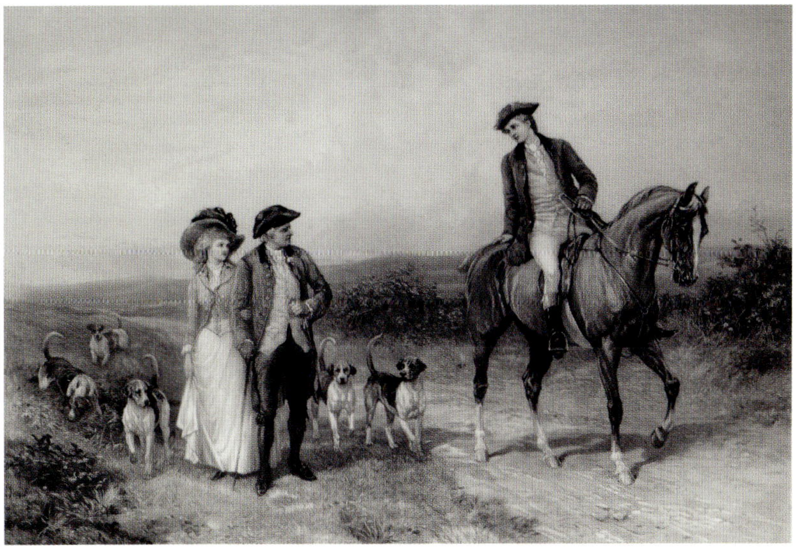

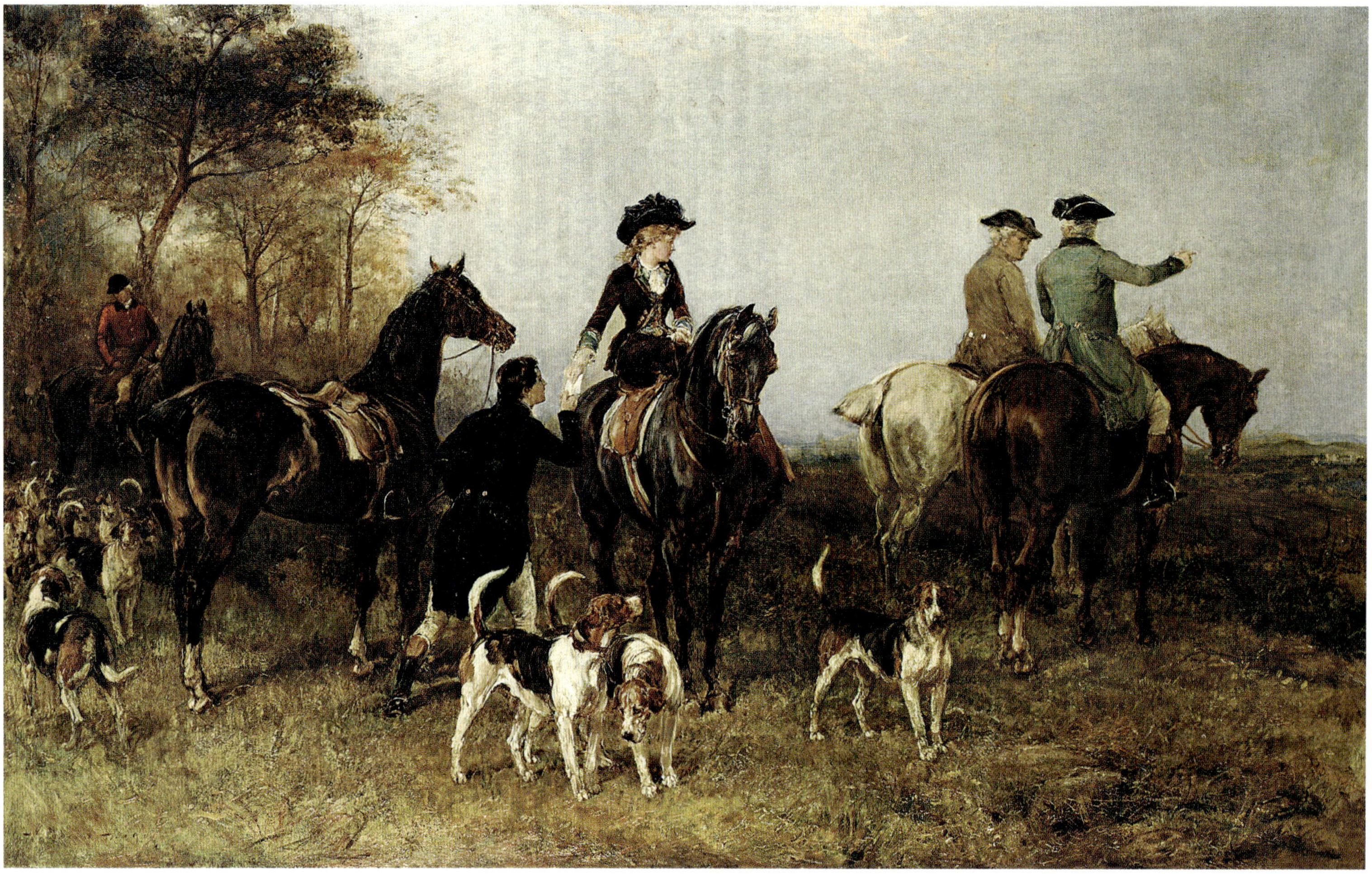

Plate 121: Love's Stratagem
Heywood Hardy. Oil on canvas. 86.6 x 133.4cm. Private Collection

Mezzotint engravings of Hardy's paintings were made by Thomas Appleton and William Simmons, and his pictures were reproduced as photogravures by major printmakers including Goupil & Co., and Boussod Valadon & Co. in Paris and The Berlin Photographic Company, which produced numerous photogravures from the early 1880s. The prints were published by leading British-based art publishers Arthur Lucas, B. Brooks, the aforementioned I.P. Mendoza, Tooth & Sons, Léon Henri Lefèvre and Thomas Agnew and Sons, as well as publishers in the United States, Germany and France.

Hardy took a keen interest in the making of prints from his paintings, an important source of income. He was one of five painters on the Fine Arts Committee of the London Chamber of Commerce, which was organised in 1890. Other painters on the committee were George Boughton ARA, Luke Fildes RA, Briton Rivière RA, and Marcus Stone RA.[201] The chairman was William Agnew and all the leading art dealers and publishers of the day were members of the Committee. It was established mainly to deal with the widespread piracy of valuable engravings. Pirated copies of Hardy's *Too Late* were on sale in London[202]. The Victorian artists' reference book on copyright law, *The Law of Artistic Copyright*, written by John Routh in 1881,[203] was dedicated to Heywood Hardy "at whose suggestion a practical explanation of the working of the Copyright Statutes, in relation to works of art was attempted, the book is affectionately inscribed by the author."

George Bernard Shaw commented on an exhibition at the Grosvenor Gallery in 1889:

> Mr Lefèvre's neighbour, Mr. Mendoza, has also snatched a pair of pictures by Mr. Heywood Hardy from the Grosvenor Gallery. The usual bit of romance and bit of horseflesh, which make Mr. Heywood Hardy the Whyte-Melville[204] of the studio, are in both works.[205]

Victorian newspapers, in this instance *The Morning Post*, delighted in spelling out the narrative in such pictures:

> Love's Barrier [Plate 120], by Mr. Heywood Hardy, is one of those pictures of sweet-hearting, which may be relied on to retain their popularity at least as long as the sentimental themes they illustrate. What may happen in the event of the unification of the sexes – an object apparently dear to some ladies – is, of course, another matter; but while the human race continues to be divided between men and women, love-making and pictures descriptive of it will certainly enjoy much public favour. In the present case, a

handsome young horseman who, to judge from the style of his costume, must have flourished, and that luxuriantly, about the middle of last century, is on his way home along a country road, after exercising his trencher-fed pack – for those were the days before regular kennels – when he meets not only his lady-love, but a less welcome personage – her father, as well, who evidently regards the suitor with keen antipathy. Not so the comely lady, who bestows upon him a sweet, though rather timid, smile. Mr. T. G. Appleton's fine mezzotint after this attractive picture leaves nothing to be desired. It is brilliantly lighted, and represents with the fidelity of the original, the wild mountain landscape, the human figures, the horses and dogs, and all the incidents and accessories of the romantic scene. Both painting and engraving are in continuation of the series including "Twixt Love and Duty," "Too Late," "The Runaway Match," and "Forgiven."[206]

Love's Stratagem (Plate 121) (which was entitled *The Secret Letter* when the picture was last sold at auction) was Hardy's exhibit at the 1890 Royal Academy exhibition. *The Graphic* noted:

"Love's Stratagem," by Heywood Hardy, introduces us to a pretty landscape, horses, dogs, and brightly-clad figures, the interest, moreover, being heightened by the introduction of a dramatic little incident, the clandestine delivery of a *billet doux* by the lover to his sweetheart, the vigilance of the elders being temporarily turned in another direction.[207]

Forgiven (Plate 122) was a popular painting and print. *The Morning Post's* correspondent gave his views on the reasons for the work's popularity with Victorians:

With sentimental people, a class destined to survive as long as the human race, it is a matter of inevitable though unavailing regret that improvement in the practical and realistic often involves decay of the picturesque and romantic. Steamships are not half so beautiful as sailing vessels; a railway is not so pretty a spectacle as a well horsed mail coach; elopements to Gretna Green, with all their concomitant circumstances of races between the post-chaises of the runaways and those of the angry fathers in hot pursuit of the fugitives, are ... so much more ... exciting

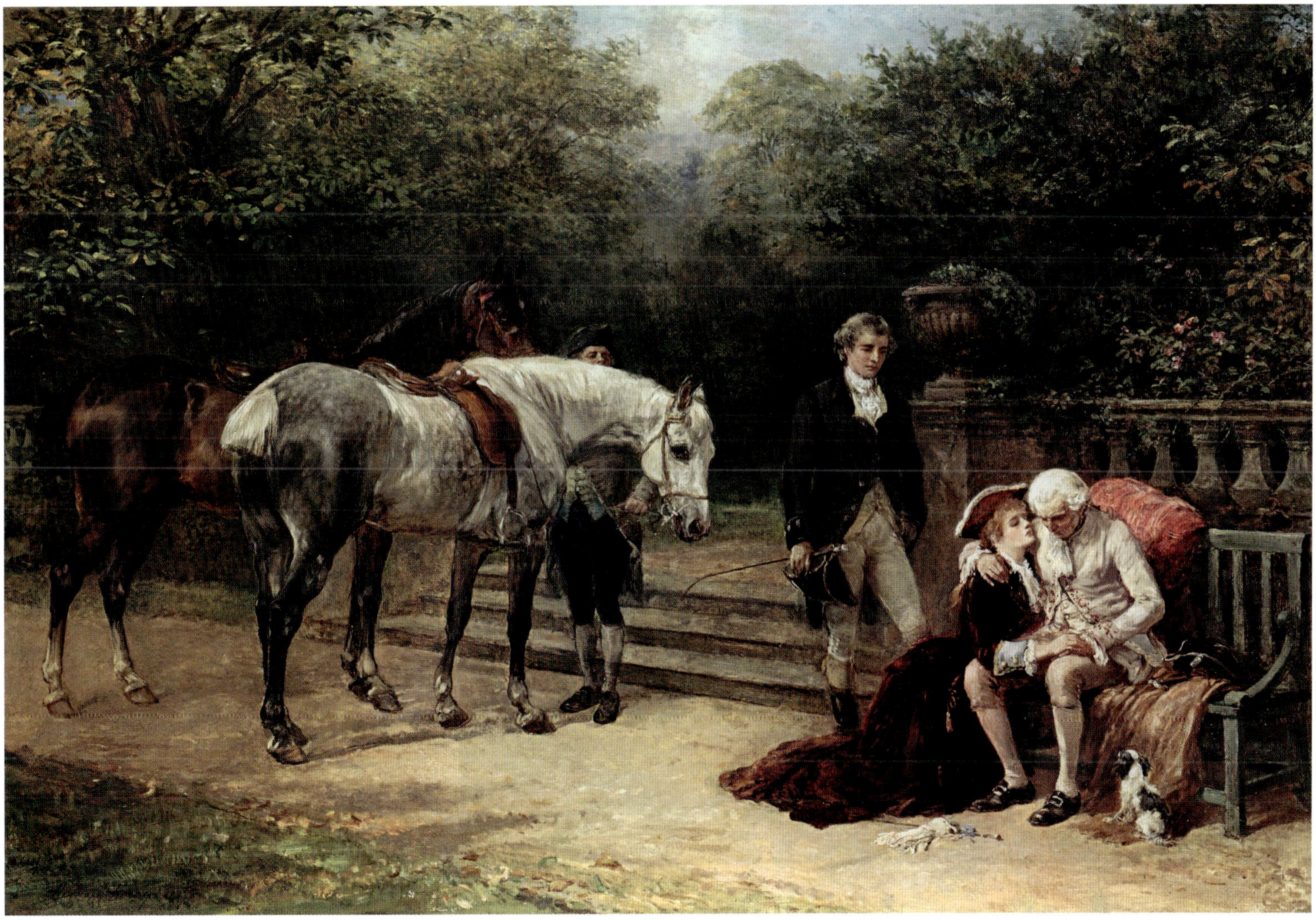

Plate 122: Forgiven, 1887
Heywood Hardy. Oil on canvas. 75 x 106.5cm. Private Collection

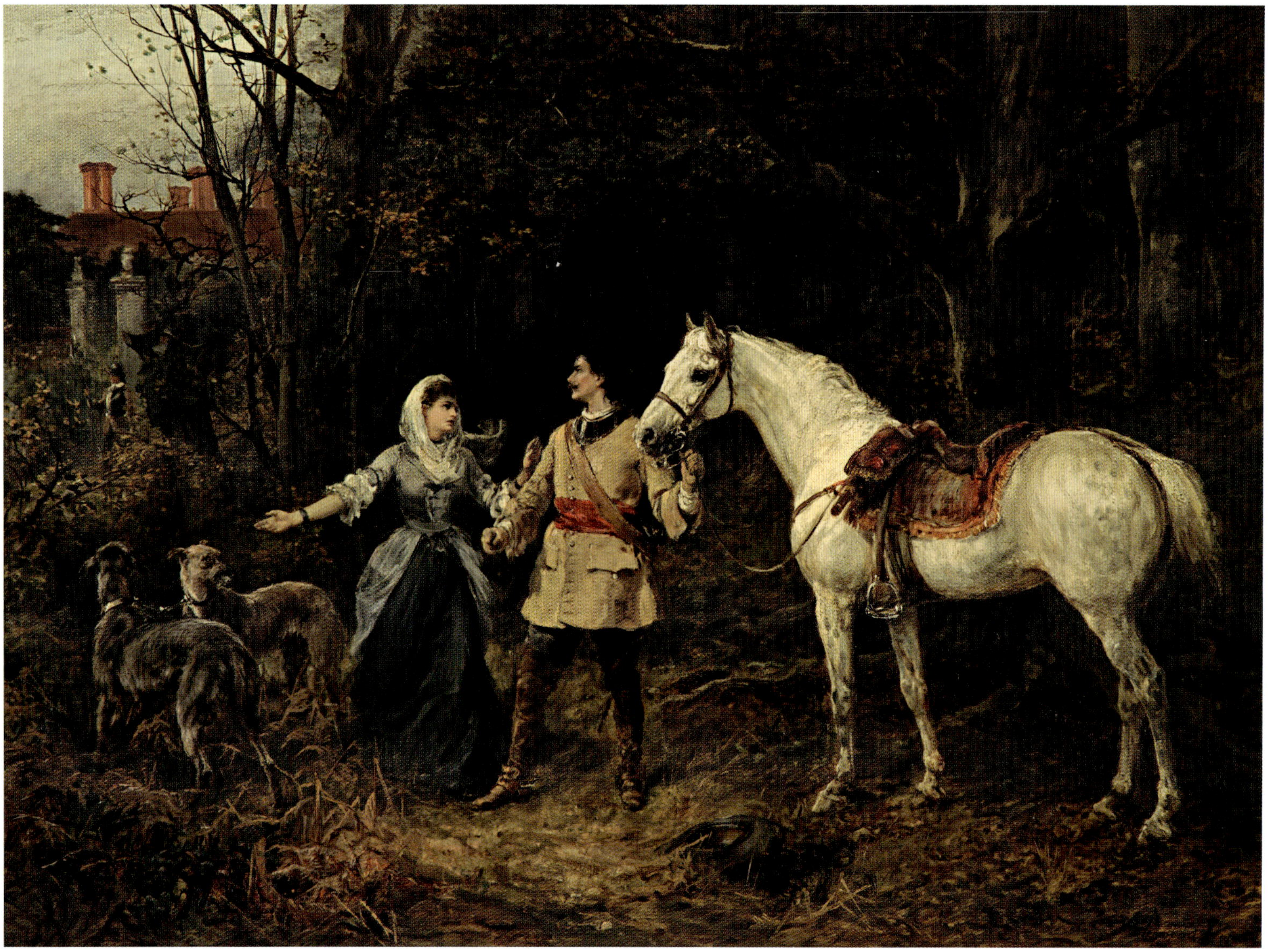

Plate 123: The Warning, 1887
Heywood Hardy. Oil on canvas. 77 x 104cm. © Bury Art Museum, Greater Manchester, UK

to the imagination ... than the sight of Edwin and Angelina quietly mingling with the crowd of commonplace voyagers on board the Calais packet. Even highway robbery, as practised of old by the Knights of the Road, was not without its picturesque uses.

Happily it is the province of Art, unmindful of the "worser part," to preserve and perpetuate in pictorial representation whatsoever of brilliant, elegant, and impressive may have vanished from the realms of Fashion. Elopements in particular, and all their dramatic sequels, are still favourite topics with painters. Of this fact the popular painting, "'Twixt Love and Duty", (painted by S.E. Waller) is a notable example. Another and a still more remarkable instance is Mr. Heywood Hardy's attractive picture bearing the terse title "Forgiven."

Here the lovers who, as may be inferred from their costume, flourished, and that luxuriantly, in the eighteenth century, have become man and wife. In that (occasionally) indissoluble character they have ridden on horseback to the country seat of the bride's father. Swiftly dismounting the young and beautiful lady throws herself at the feet of the poor old gentleman, who, seated on the terrace before his ancient mansion, receives her with open arms, and, melted to tears, of course bestows both his pardon and his blessing. Meanwhile, the bridegroom looks on with silent but delighted attention, wisely leaving to his better-half the duty of pleading their joint cause. Both are "Forgiven," and so the name of the painting is clearly justified. The only other spectators of the scene are the horses and their attendant groom. The pleasure grounds are in front; the park furnishes a sylvan perspective very pleasant to the eye. A mezzotint plate after this interesting picture, executed with all his wonted skill and taste by Mr. Appleton, has been just published by Mr. I. P. Mendoza, of the St. James's Gallery, and will prove an appropriate companion for "'Twixt Love and Duty."[208]

The Warning (Plate 123) was another popular painting and print:

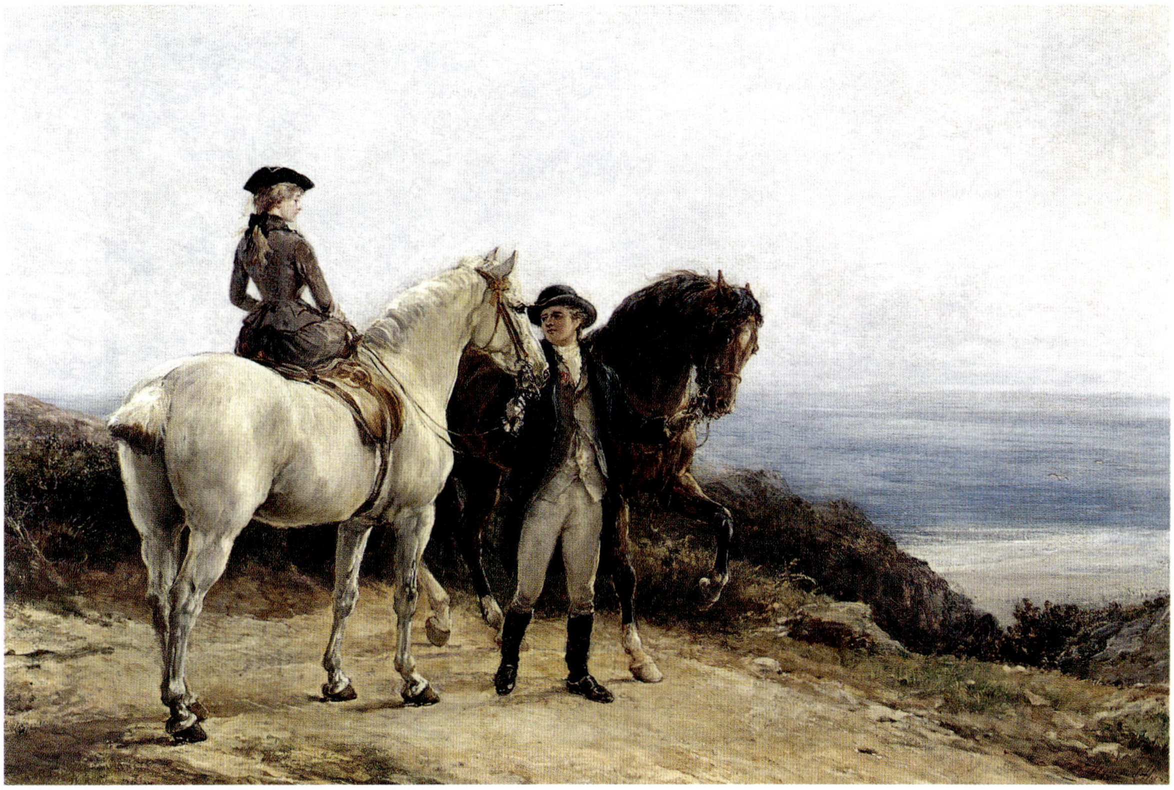

Plate 124: The Morning Ride, 1886
Heywood Hardy. Oil on canvas. 62.2 x 90.2cm. Private Collection

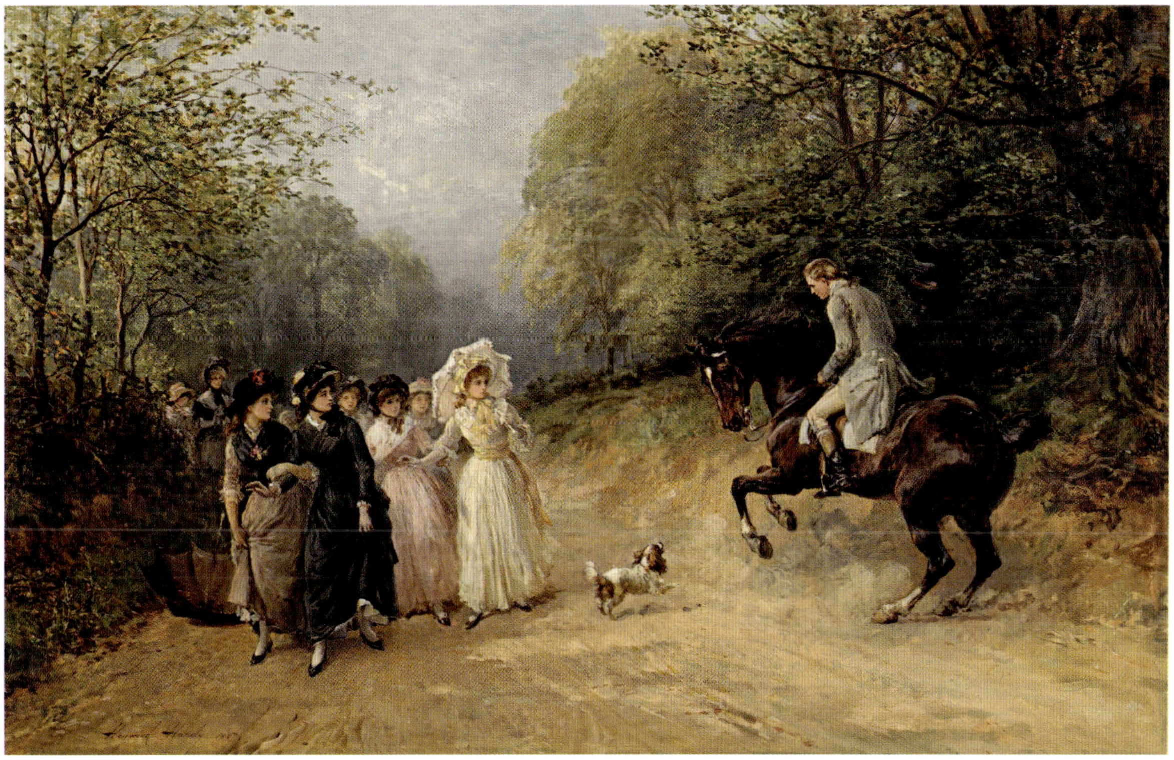

Plate 125: The Unwanted Chaperone, 1887
Heywood Hardy. Oil on canvas. 19.7 x 29.9cm. Private Collection

At the St. James's Gallery in King-street Mr Mendoza has on view some three score oil paintings by British and foreign artists. Mr Heywood Hardy sends a dramatic little subject, skilfully handled, in "The Warning." A cavalier is riding at the close of day up to his park gates, when his lady emerges from the bracken, and lays her hand on his bridle. He must not return to the house; already a sentinel is at the gate. The story may be amplified *à discrétion*.[209]

Other examples of pictures in this style are *The Woodland Meeting* (1882), *The Morning Ride* (1886) (Plate 124), *The Unwanted Chaperone* (1887) (Plate 125), *The Squire's Daughter*, *Welcome Home* and *The Meeting in the Forest* (1903) (Plate 126). Heywood Hardy's models for these paintings included Cora Potter, the celebrated American actress who appeared in several stage productions in England, and was the model for "an attractive young ward" in *Welcome Home.*[210]

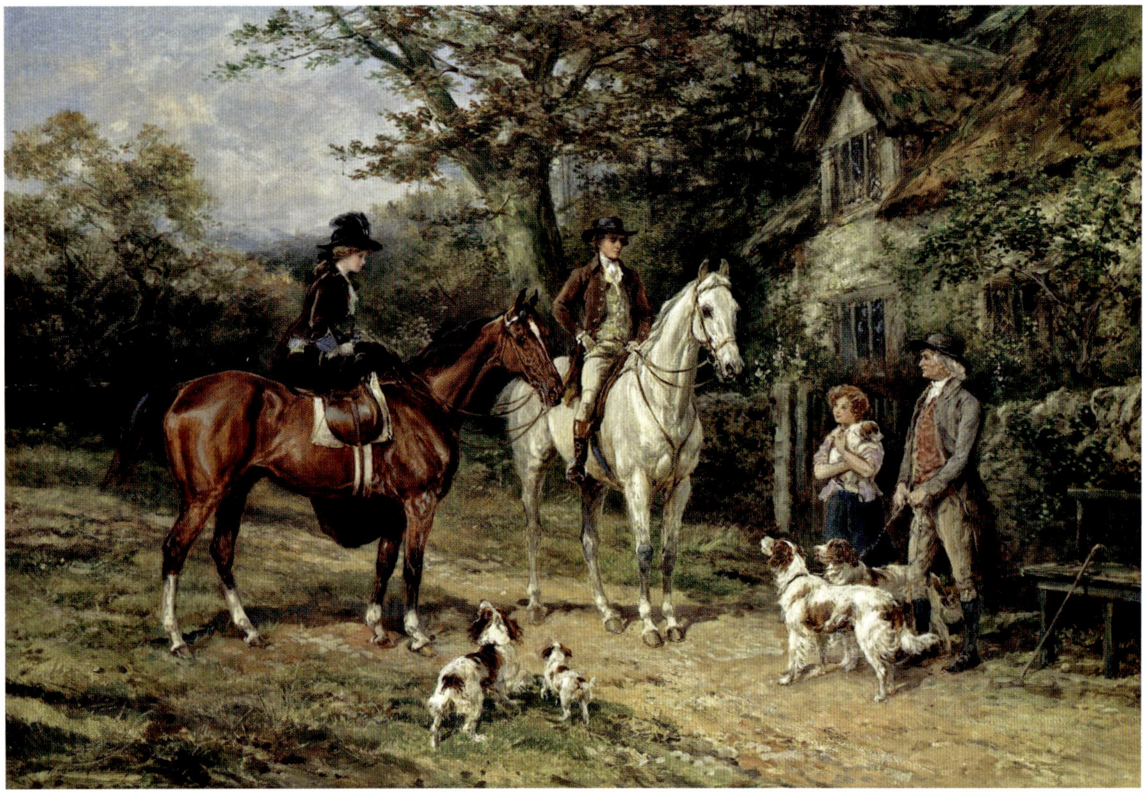

Plate 126 (opposite page): The Meeting in the Forest, 1903
Heywood Hardy. Oil on canvas. 104 x 84cm. PRIVATE COLLECTION

Plate 127 (left): A Convivial Greeting, 1906
Heywood Hardy. Oil on canvas. 61 x 84cm. PRIVATE COLLECTION

Also popular, judging from the numerous engravings made from them, were scenes of village life such as *Country Scene* (1905) and *A Convivial Greeting* (1906) (Plate 127).[211]

Most pictures by Heywood Hardy represent an idyllic view of the country in the nineteenth and eighteenth centuries. But a few highlight the differences between rich and poor. Hardy's depiction of gypsies in *Far from the Madding Crowd* (Plate 128) recalls *The Vagrants*, a study of a gypsy family painted by his friend Fred Walker. The supercilious rider receives an unfriendly response from the gypsy girl standing by the fire.

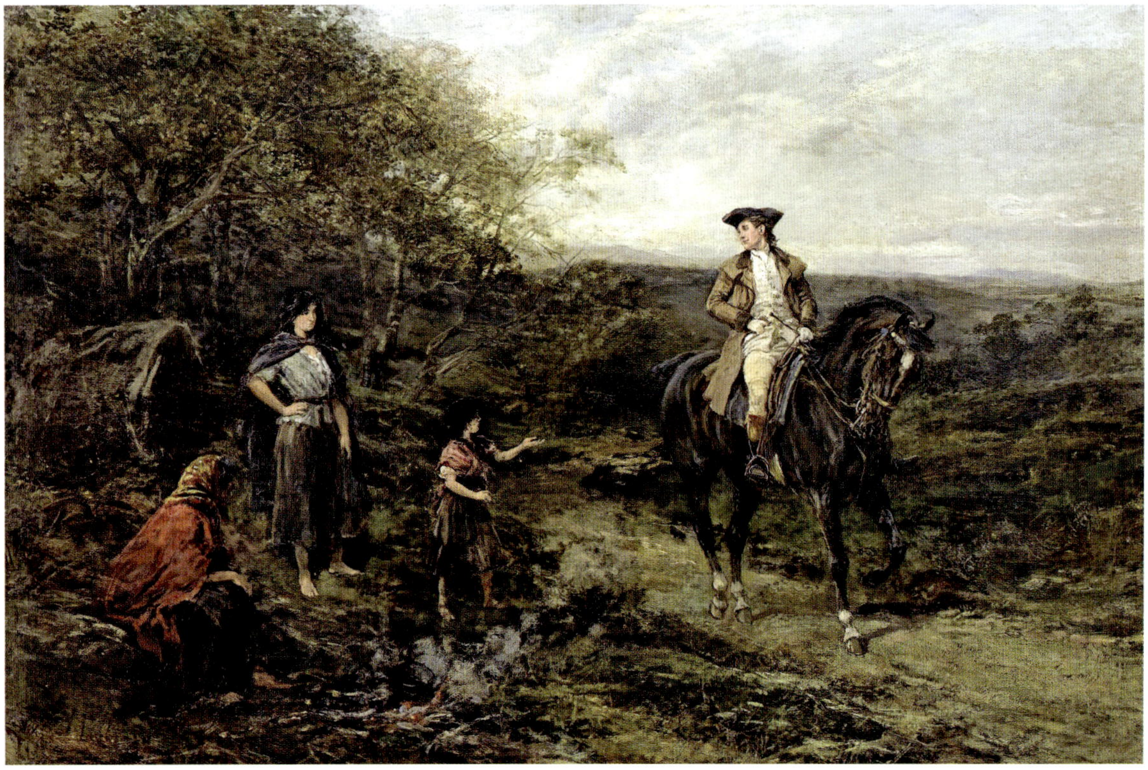

Plate 128 (left): Far From the Madding Crowd
Heywood Hardy. Oil on canvas. 53 x 73cm. PRIVATE COLLECTION

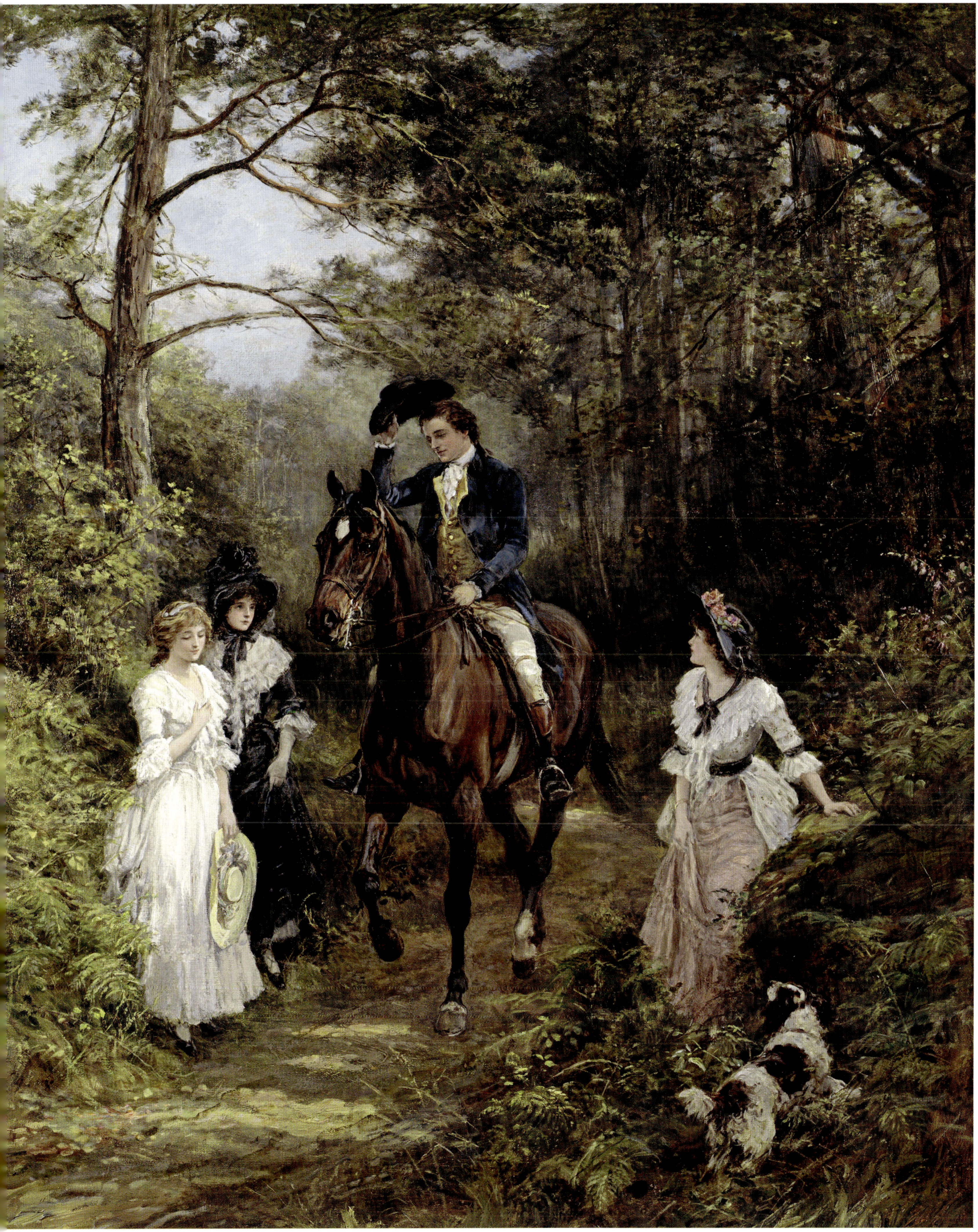

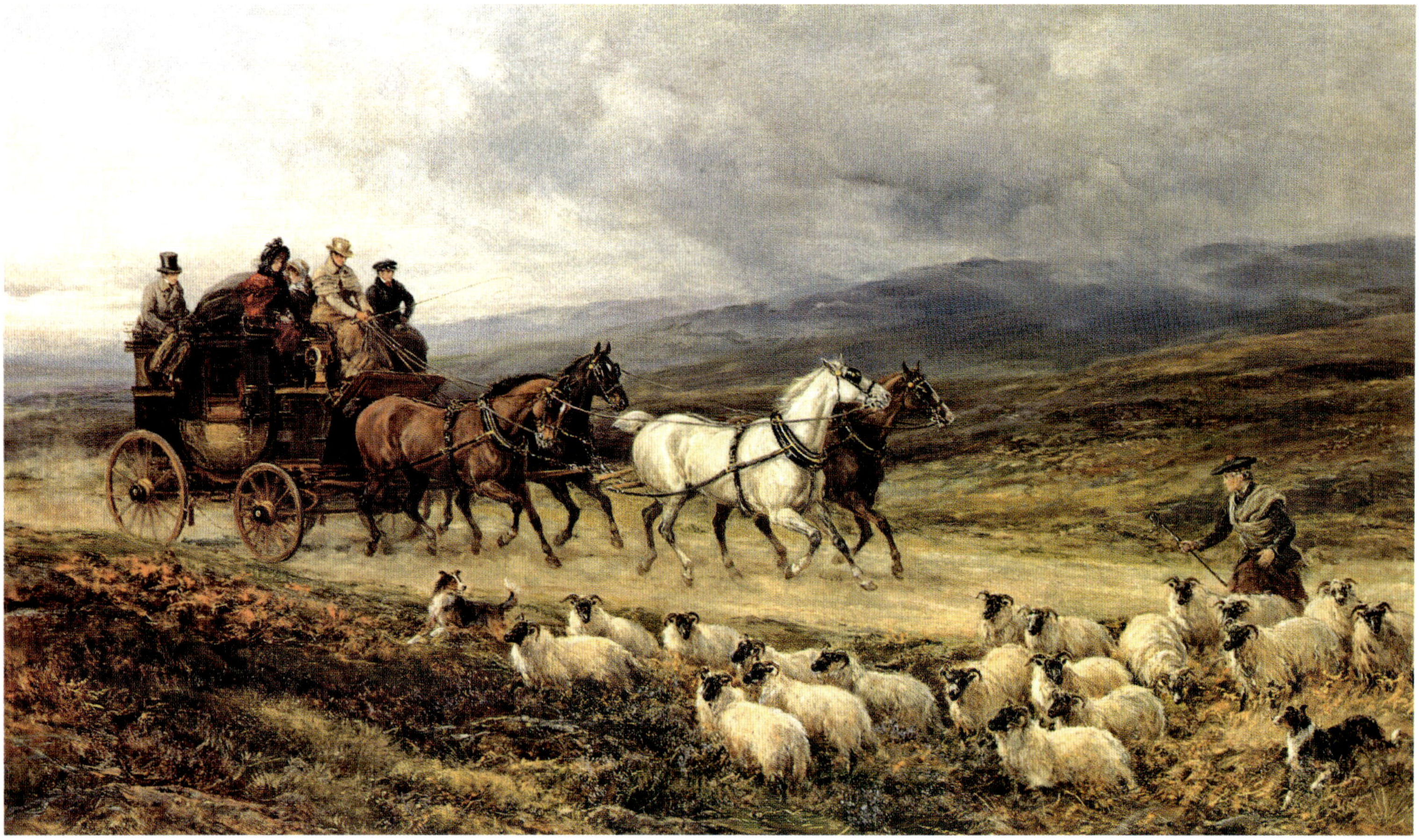

Plate 129: Highland Coaching, 1904
Heywood Hardy. Oil on canvas. 87 x 142.9cm. Private Collection

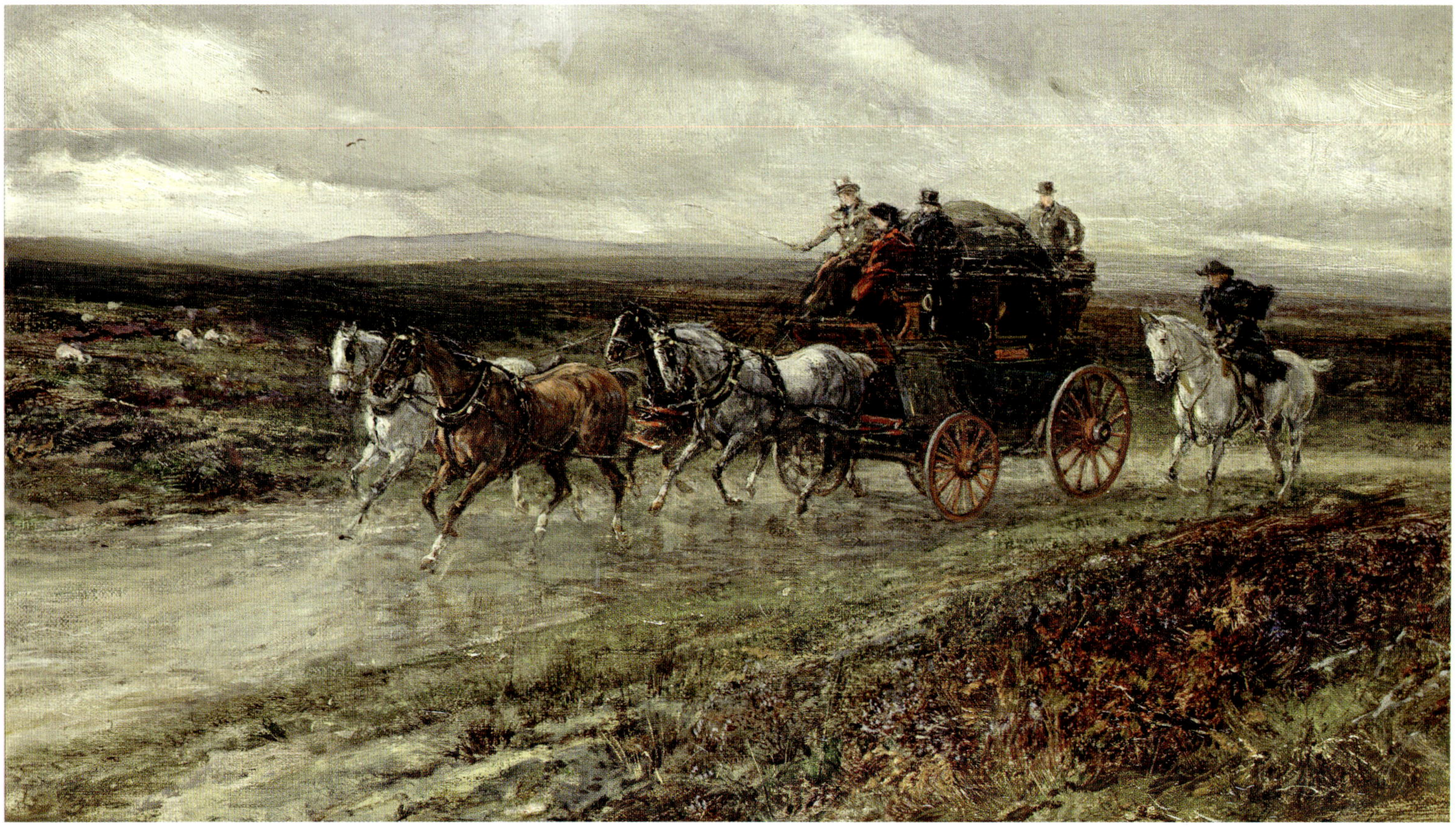

Plate 130: Welcome Company
Heywood Hardy. Oil on canvas. 27.5 x 47.5cm. Private Collection

Plate 131 (right): A Timely Arrival, 1891
Heywood Hardy. Oil on canvas. 76 x 66cm.
PRIVATE COLLECTION

Plate 132 (below): A Match, 1873
After Heywood Hardy. Wood engraving in *The Illustrated London News*.[212]

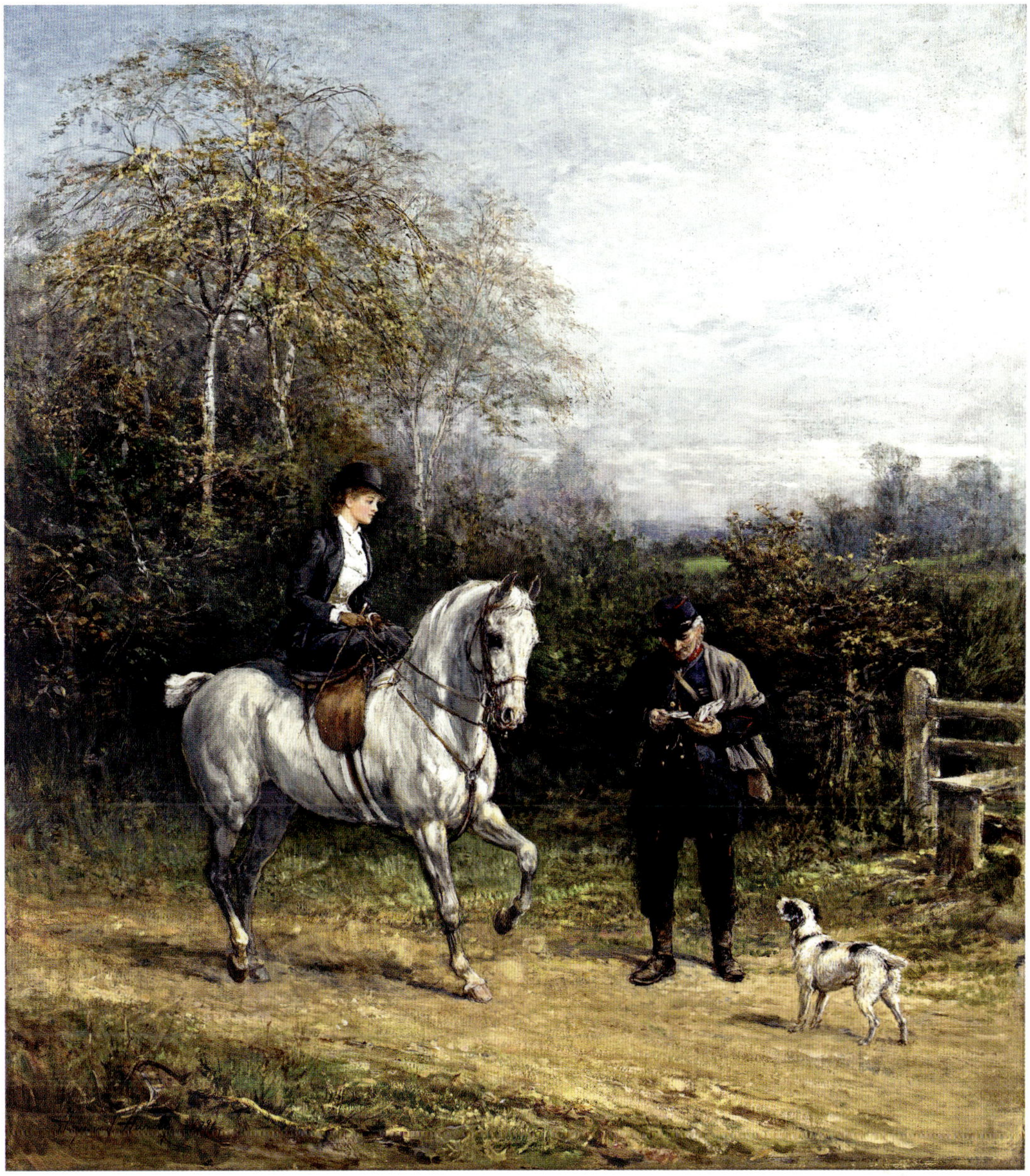

Hardy also painted numerous coaching scenes, such as *Highland Coaching* (1904) (Plate 129) and *Welcome Company* (Plate 130), a small, freely painted sketch.

Less commonly he painted scenes of contemporary country life, aside from sporting pictures, as in *A Timely Arrival* (1891) (Plate 131), which includes a carefully painted postman, complete with three "good conduct" stripes on his coat.

By the Sea

Heywood Hardy painted many pictures of horse-riding on beaches. In the first of these, *A Match* (1873),[213] the horses were depicted in a "rocking horse gallop" at full stretch with all four hooves off the ground. This was the conventional way of drawing galloping horses, as seen in pictures by John F. Herring and other nineteenth-century sporting artists. By the late 1870s, however, Hardy had a much better understanding of how a horse galloped; he studied the problem carefully with his friend Professor Garrod, and by the end of the decade, Muybridge's photographs of galloping horses had been published.

The Illustrated London News noted: "Mr. Heywood Hardy has a spirited drawing, under the double entendre of the title "A Match" (310), representing a young couple galloping along seaside sands."[214]

However, judging from the engraving (Plate 132) that was published in *The Illustrated London News*, the criticism in *The Times* of this early sketch seems appropriate:

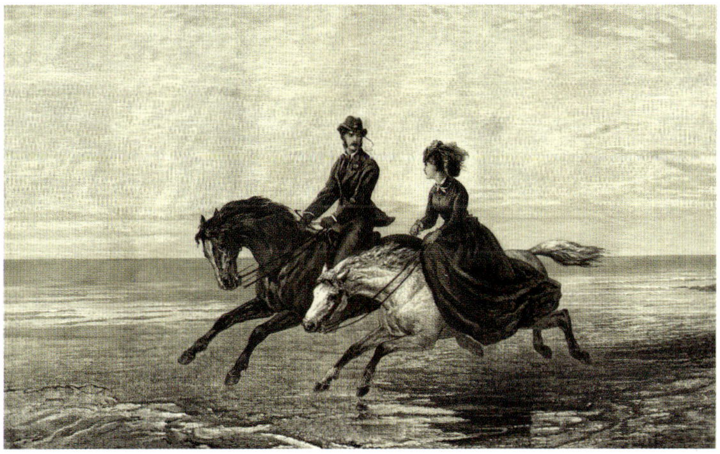

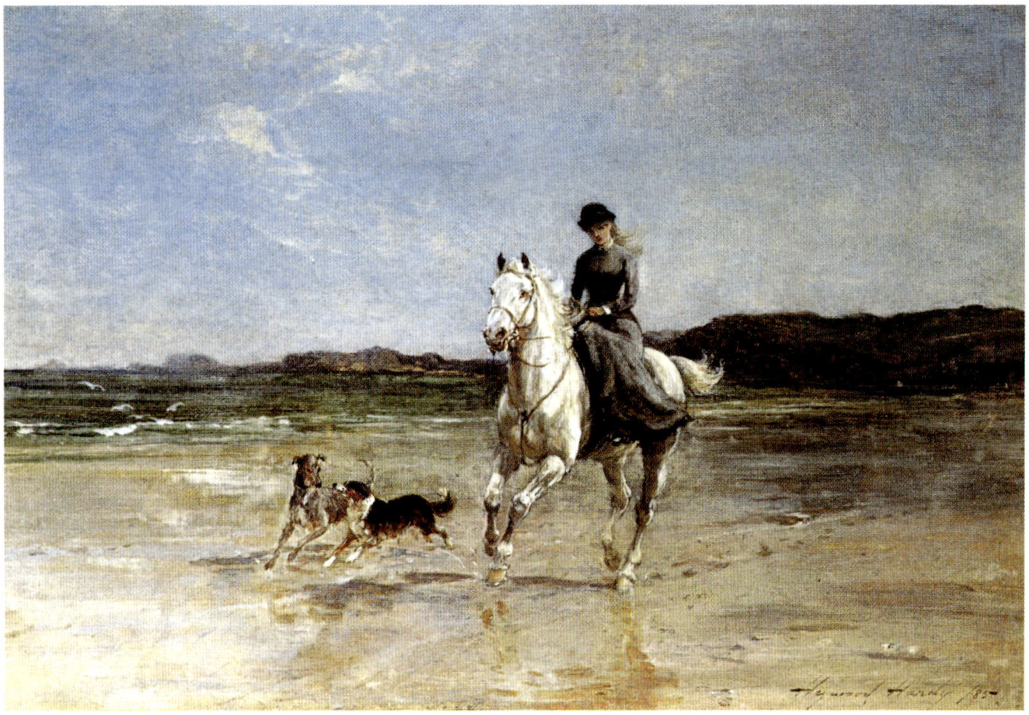

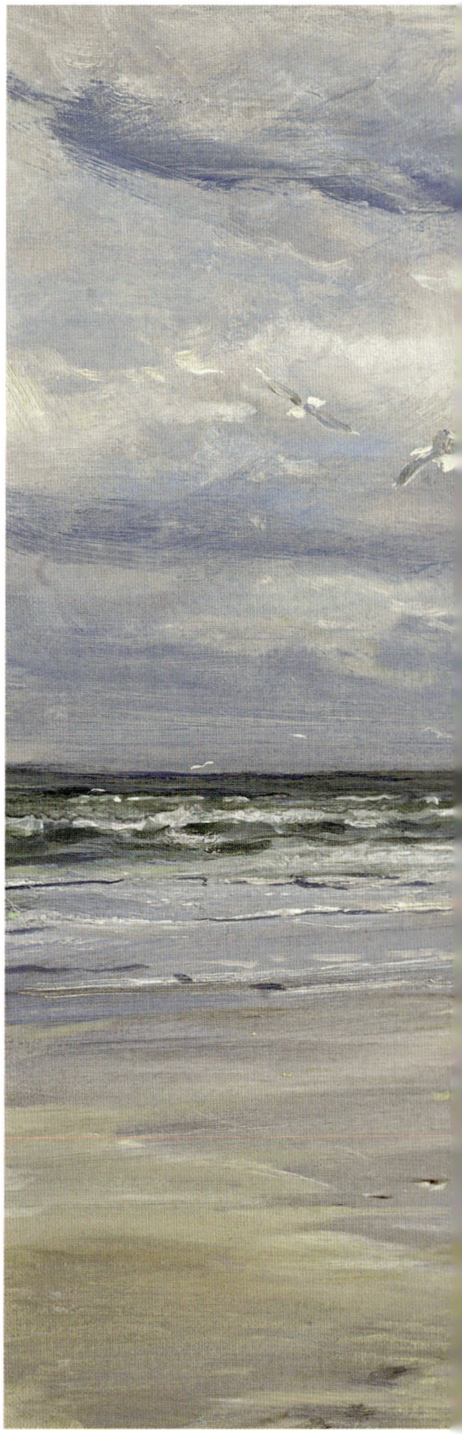

Plate 133: Horse and Rider on a Windswept Beach, 1885
Heywood Hardy. Oil on canvas. 25.4 x 35.6cm. Private Collection

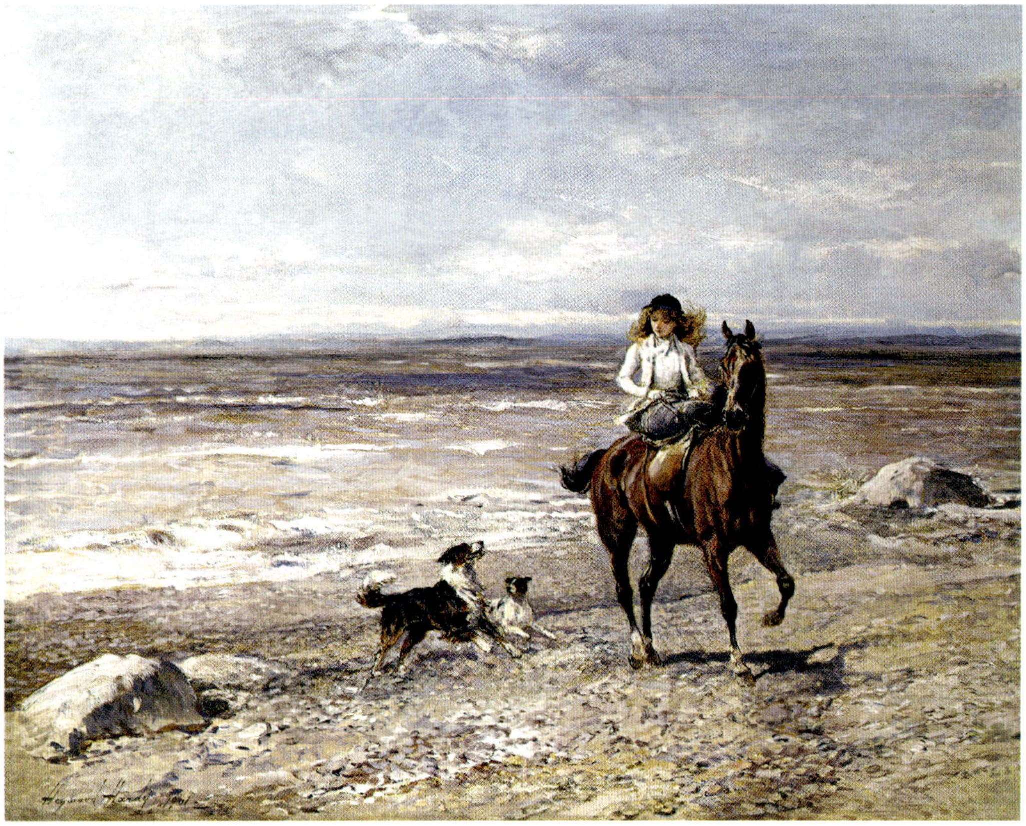

Plate 134: Pony Ride on the Beach, 1901
Heywood Hardy. Oil on canvas. 43 x 56cm. Private Collection

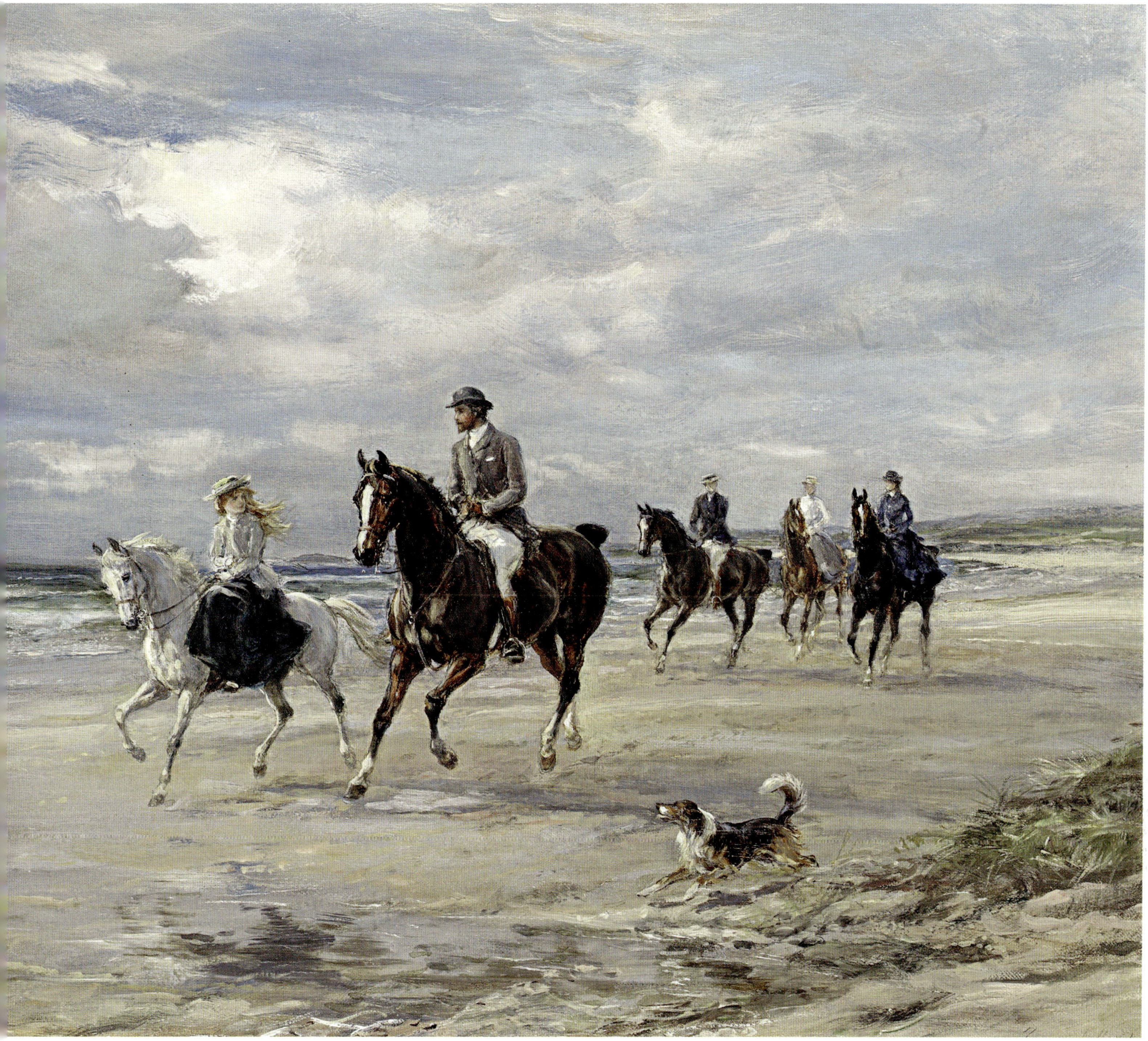

Plate 135: A Morning Ride
Heywood Hardy. Oil on canvas. 45 x 66cm. Private Collection

Mr Heywood Hardy's sketch of a happy young couple enjoying a gallop on the beach, with the appropriate title, "A Match," is better in intention than execution. So competent a painter has no right to exhibit work so slight and incorrect. Want of finish is quite allowable in, and in no way detracts from the merit of, a sketch or study; but here there is palpable bad drawing, both in man and horses.[215]

Hardy returned to the theme of horse-riding on beaches in the 1880s and continued painting such pictures into the Edwardian era. After his visit to France in 1885, by which time he was much better at rendering galloping horses, he painted *Horse and Rider on a Windswept Beach* (1885) (Plate 133).

Later pictures with the same theme included *Pony Ride on the Beach* (1901), *Pleasant Company* (1906), *A Morning Ride*

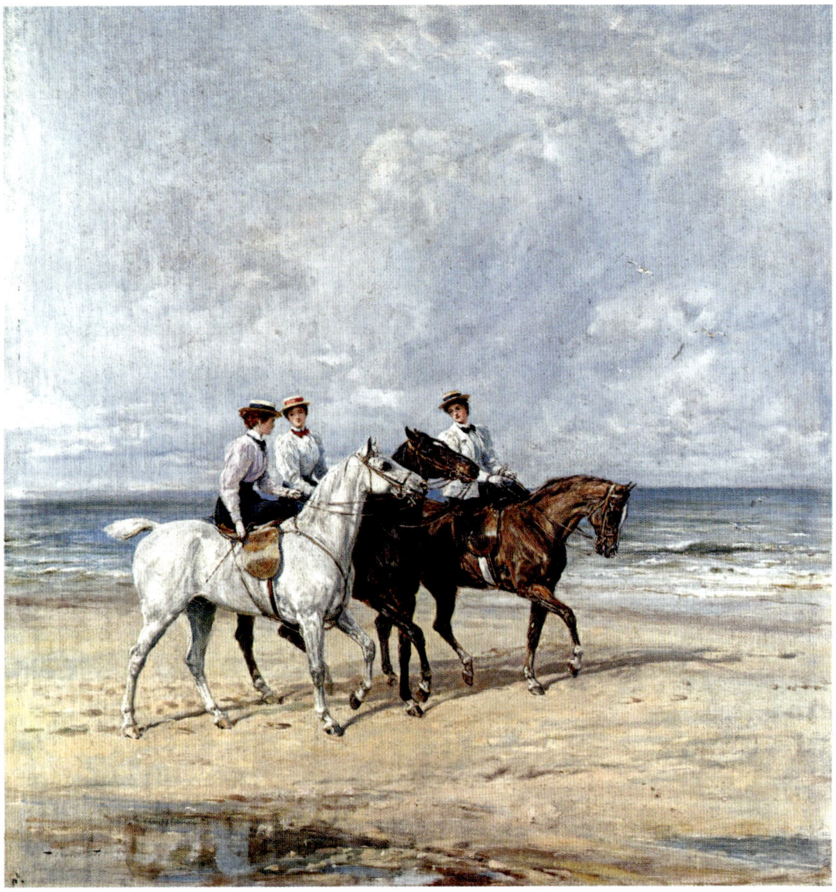

Plate 136 (left): Riding on the Dunes
Heywood Hardy. Oil on canvas. 84 x 75cm. Private Collection

Plate 137 (below): Holiday Time, 1908
Heywood Hardy. Oil on canvas 45.5 x 61cm. Private Collection

Plate 138 (opposite page, top): Morecambe Sands
Heywood Hardy. Oil on canvas. 45.7 x 83.8cm. Private Collection

Plate 139 (opposite page, bottom): The Plough Team
Heywood Hardy. Oil on canvas. 50.8 x 86.4cm. Private Collection

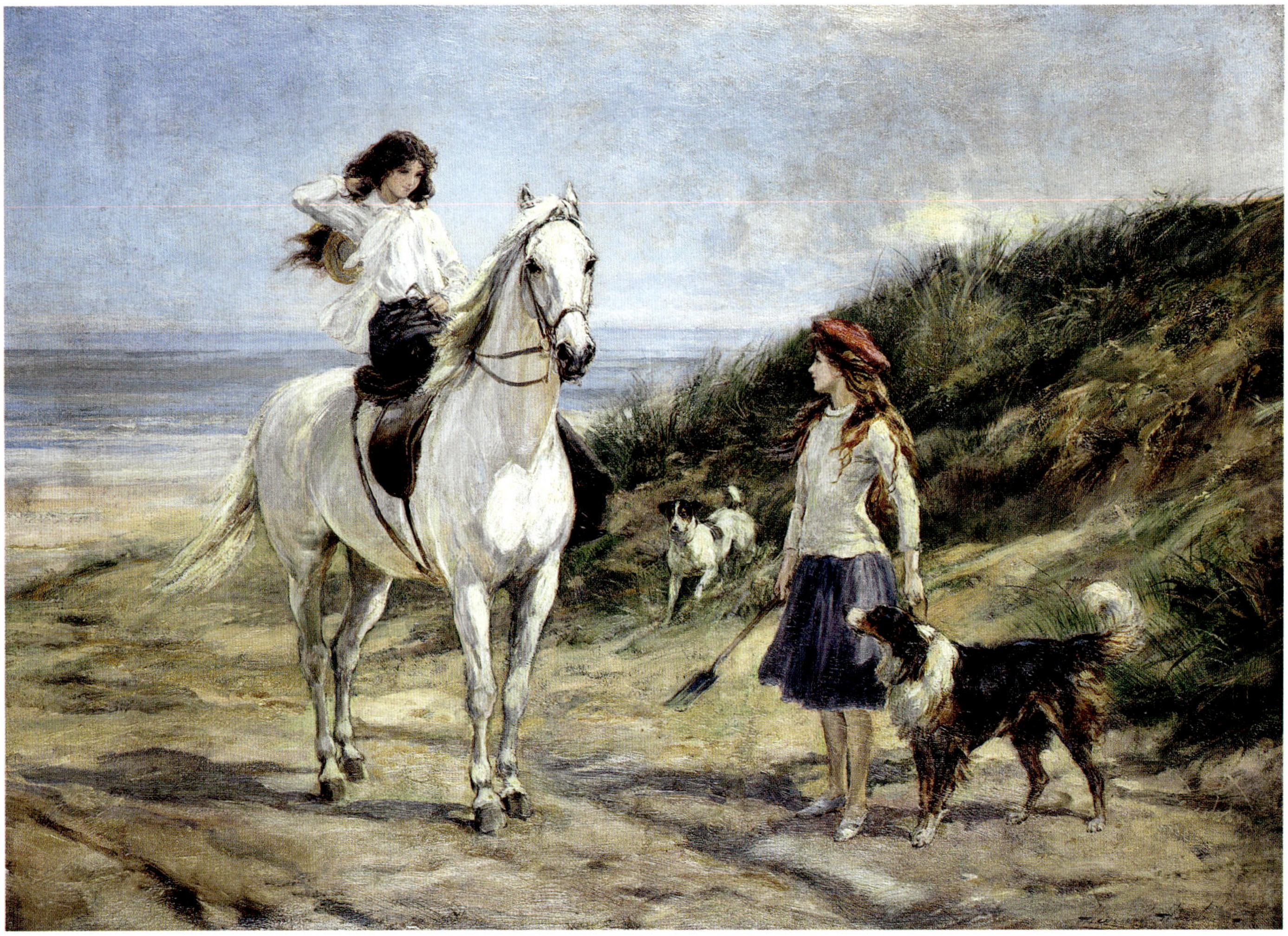

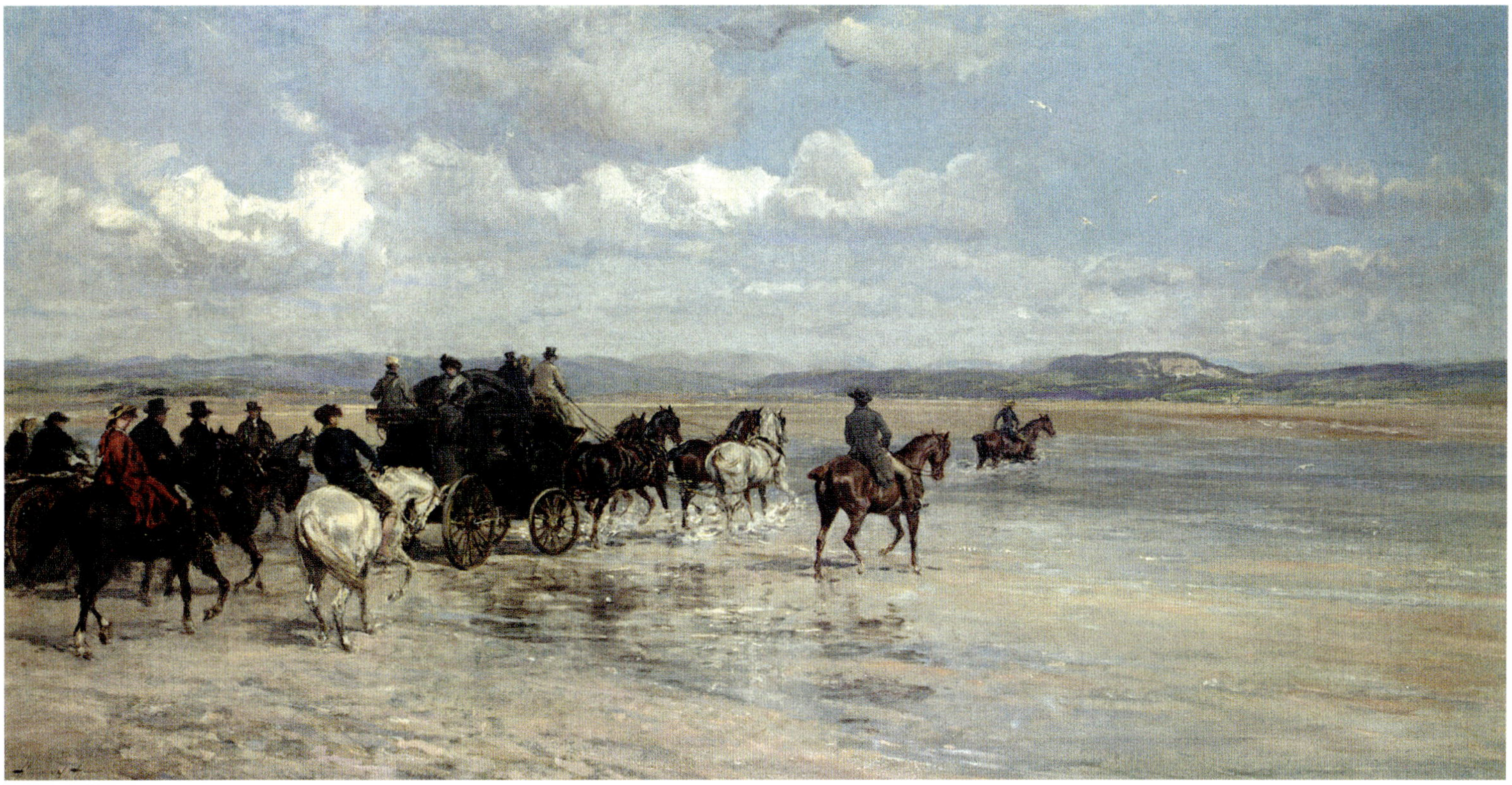

(Plate 135), *Riding on the Dunes* (Plate 136) and *Holiday Time* (1908) (Plate 137).

An effective treatment of sea and sky also features in *Morecambe Sands* (Plate 138) and *The Plough Team* (Plate 139). The scene at Morecambe Sands was made famous by paintings made earlier in the nineteenth century by J.M.W. Turner and David Cox. Travellers crossed the treacherous sands with a guide at low tide to shorten the route between Lancashire and the Lake District.

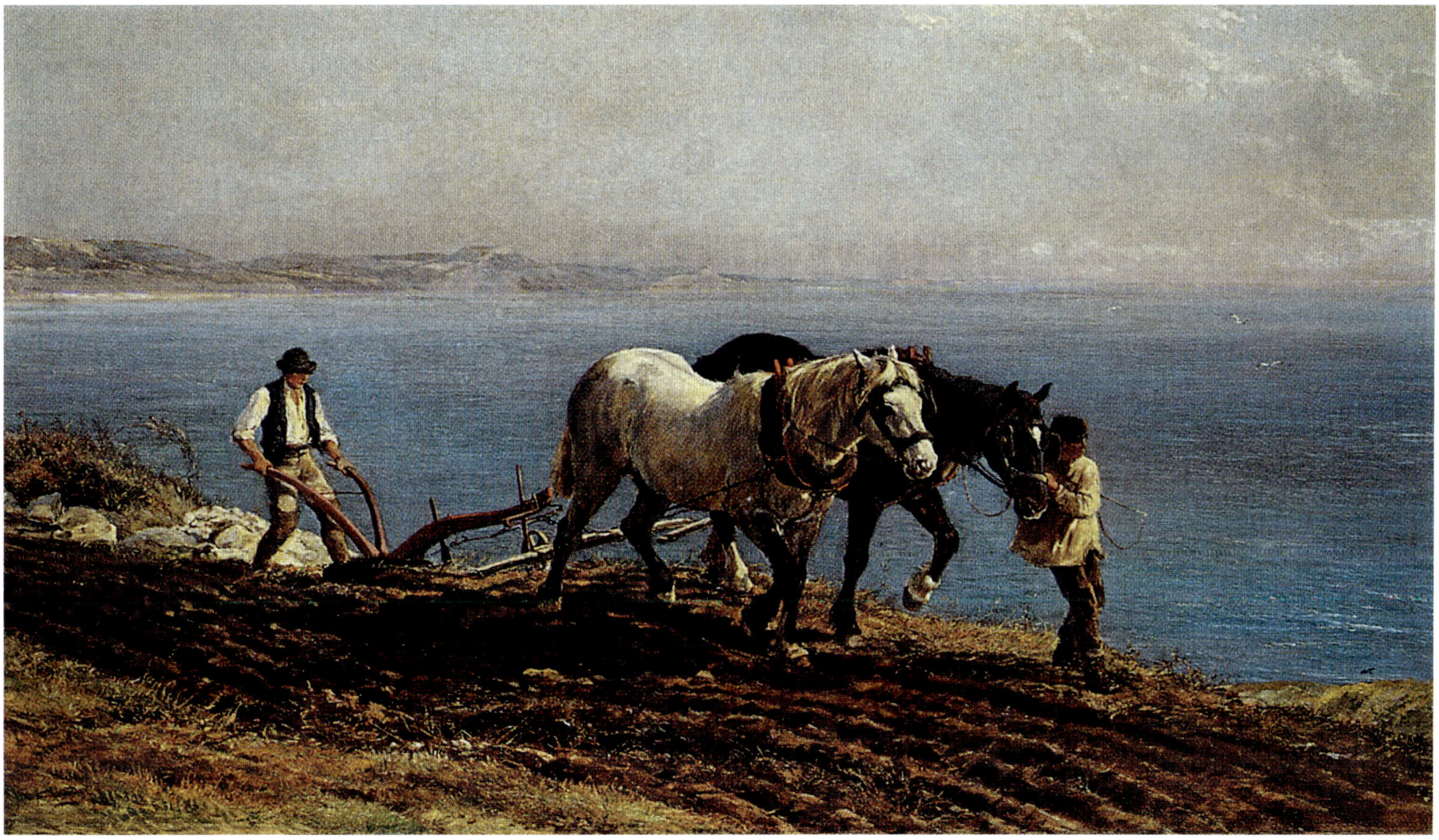

CHAPTER FIVE

Heywood Hardy, The Later Years: Field Sports and Portraits

In the 1880s Heywood Hardy began painting equestrian portraits, particularly of hunt followers in the north of England. These commissions became an increasingly important part of his later work as he formed friendships with country families; in addition to equestrian portraits he painted pictures of hounds, dogs of all kinds, horses and hunting. He became one of the foremost equestrian and sporting artists of his day.

His first commission for a group of equestrian portraits was from members of the Zetland Hunt (Plate 140). The commission was to present the Earl (later Marquis) of Zetland with a large oil painting (measuring 4 x 10 feet) showing the Earl's family and several followers of the Hunt "as a recognition of the excellent sport he has afforded them while he has been master". The Prince and Princess of Wales paid a visit to Aske Hall at the end of January 1889 and members of the Hunt proposed to ask the Prince of Wales to present the painting to the Earl of Zetland "if the picture is finished in time."[216]

In fact, it was more than a year before the picture was completed and presented. Heywood began painting the picture in March 1888; portraits of the Earl of Zetland and Lady Hilda Dundas were made first. Then later, in March 1888, he stayed for two weeks in Richmond, Yorkshire, to take the likenesses of several people closely connected with the Hunt, before travelling to Darlington for two weeks to paint individual portraits for the work. By March 1888 over 1,300 guineas had been raised by members of the Hunt towards the cost of the picture.

The local newspaper described Hardy making a sketch for the painting:

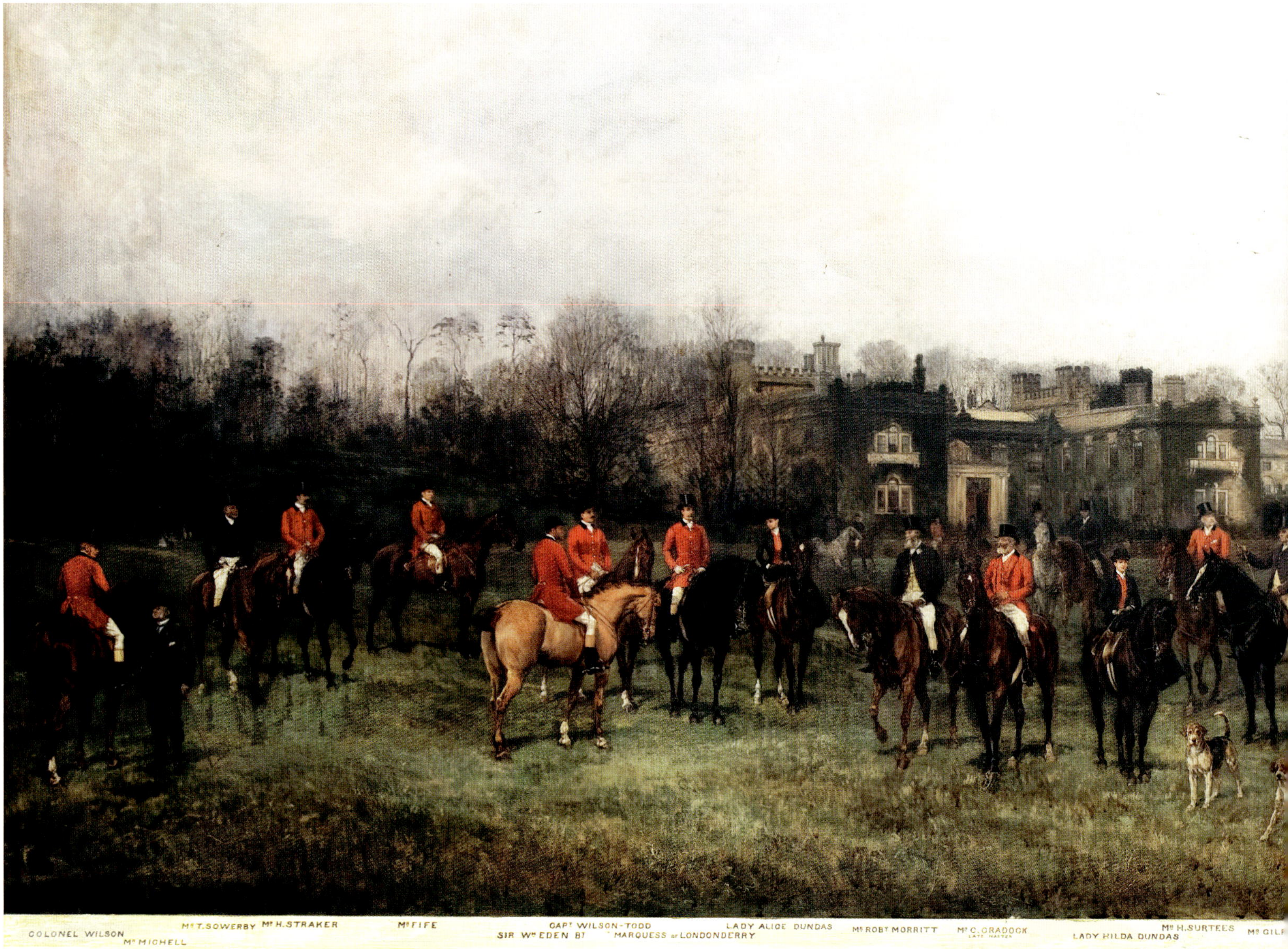

> Weather of the most delightful kind was associated with the Aske Park meet of the Earl of Zetland's famous pack yesterday. Many old hunting men turned up at the rendezvous ... in the picteuresque park midway between the ivy-mantled hall and the swan pond. Such was the scene which met the gaze of Mr Heywood Hardy, the celebrated painter, who has come to Richmond for the express purpose of painting a picture of the hunt. As soon as the painter had taken in a general view of the group and its surroundings the signal was given, and shortly before mid-day the party cantered over to Sedbury Park.[217]

The picture was eventually presented on 5 November 1889, in the grounds of Aske Hall:

> Not only, however, were the regular followers of the hunt present, but by the kindness of the Earl of Zetland there was a large gathering of farmers and others, who were entertained to breakfast in a tent specially erected near the hall. Altogether about a thousand persons sat down to breakfast.
>
> It was a breakfast of the old-fashioned order, substantial and vinous, The tables were laden with toothsome viands, and the bottle of sparkling champagne stood cheek by jowl with the tankard of foaming ale. At one end of the marquee the picture was hung, somewhat dangerously subjected to atmospheric influences. The Earl of Zetland said: "Looking at this picture, I may say, in the presence of the artist who painted it, that it is a beautiful picture, and I may go so far as to say I believe it to be unrivalled as a work of art. (Cheers.) As such it will be very highly appreciated by myself and by my family, and it will be, I am sure, appreciated and looked at with interest by my successors."[218]

Plate 140: The Zetland Hunt at Aske Hall, 1890
Heywood Hardy. Oil on canvas. 182.9 x 304.8cm. PRIVATE COLLECTION
First Whipper-in Tom Harrison is in the foreground with the hounds. Huntsman Thomas Bridger Champion is just behind the hounds to the right of Tom Harrison. Bridger Champion was described as a "brilliant man after a fox, a fine horseman, with a good voice, and keen to show a gallop at any hour of the morning or evening; according to my view he was an ideal Huntsman". [219]

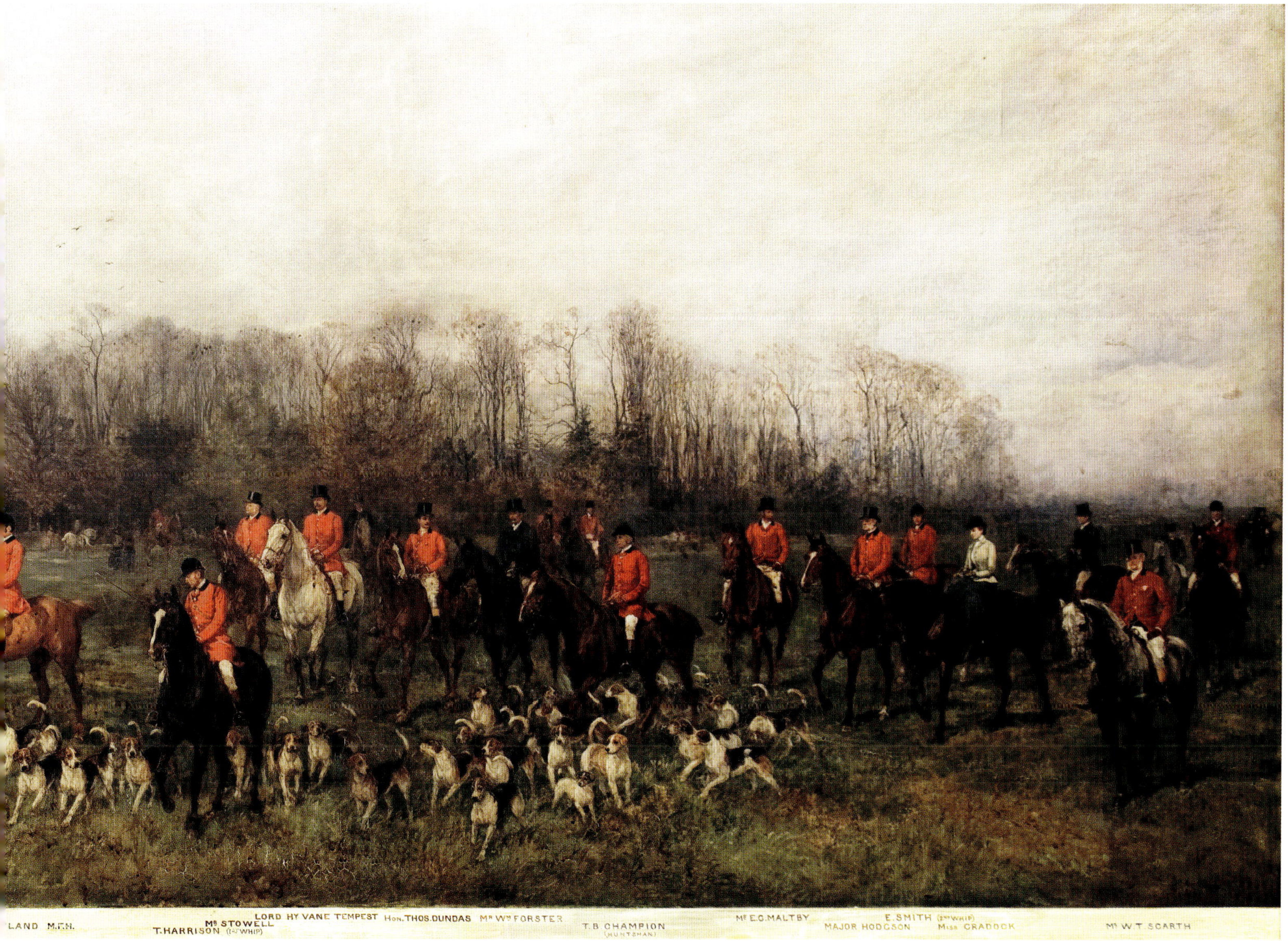

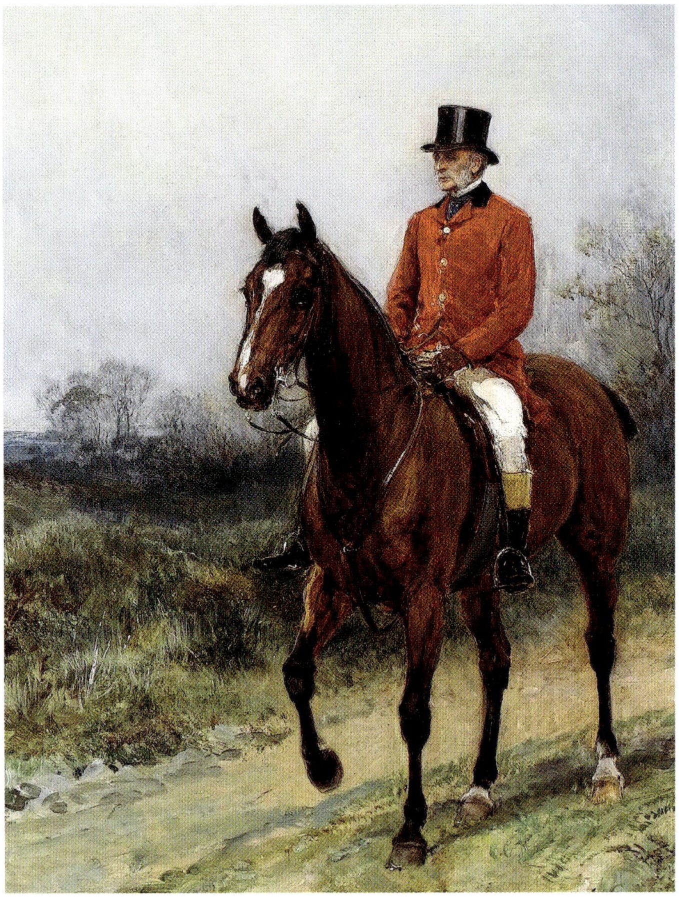

Plate 141 (above): Major George Hodgson's Morning Ride, 1888
Heywood Hardy. Oil on canvas. 47 x 36.5cm. Detail

Plate 142 (below): Miss Lavender Pease on "Zaccheus", 1898
After Heywood Hardy. From: Sir Alfred E. Pease. "Hunting reminiscences". London: W. Thacker

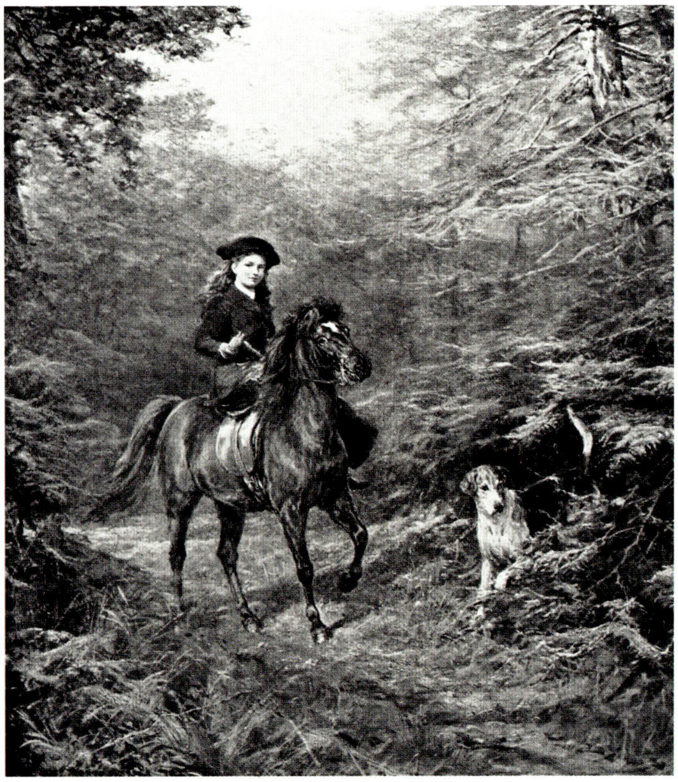

After the picture was engraved in 1890, it was sent to Dublin and hung in the Viceregal Lodge during Lord Zetland's period of office as Lord Lieutenant of Ireland.[220] The painting is now at the top of the main staircase in the recently renovated Aske Hall.

When the Hunt painting was exhibited in London, George Bernard Shaw, in his role as art critic for *The World* periodical, commented: "58 Pall Mall is now called the "Land and Water" Gallery. The chief thing to see there is Mr. Heywood Hardy's picture of Lord Zetland's pack. The horses are capital and the bit of landscape and sky not bad."[221]

Heywood Hardy took the opportunity to paint several individual equestrian portraits of members of the Zetland Hunt; a portrait of Mr William Scarth of Staindrop was Hardy's 1889 Royal Academy exhibit (Mr Scarth is on the grey on the extreme right of the Zetland Hunt picture): "Mr. Heywood Hardy's portrait of Mr. Scarth gives a good idea of the hearty old hunting-man, a survival of the age John Leech so aptly illustrated, and who looks as if he meant to have many a good day yet".[222]

Other individual portraits painted in 1888, which were then used for the large picture of Zetland Hunt, were portraits of Major George Hodgson (1888) (Plate 141), Charles Stewart Vane-Tempest-Stewart, 6th Marquess of Londonderry, and Mr Stowell (1888).[223] Mr C. Cradock of Hartforth Hall had a portrait painted by Heywood Hardy of the celebrated huntsman Thomas Bridger Champion.[224]

Like the great equestrian artist of the previous generation, John Ferneley, Hardy was invited to many country houses to paint pictures of hunts, hounds and equestrian portraits. Among the many equestrian portraits he painted were those of *Miss Lavender Pease on "Zaccheus"* (1897) (Plate 142), daughter of Alfred E. Pease; *Alfred Pease* (Member of Parliament for Whitby (1880-1885) and for Darlington (1895-1898); *E.C. Baron Lethbridge and Harriers* (Mr Baron Lethbridge had a pack of harriers at his residence in Tregeare, in Cornwall); *The Lethbridge Family* (1891); *The Leney Family out Riding on the Kentish Coast* (1898); a portrait of *W.E. Rigden Esq.* (one of two Royal Academy exhibits for 1896; W.E. Rigden was Master of the Tickham Hounds); *Lady Ferguson of Kilkerra, Ayrshire, on Horseback* and *Gerald Holbech Hardy, Master of the Meynell Hunt with Three of the Hounds of the Meynell Hunt,* which was painted jointly with John Collier in 1913; and *The Meynell Hunt, with Charles West on Comet and George on Red Prince* (1915). He painted a large equestrian portrait, measuring four by six feet, of Mr George Brendon, Master of Fox Hounds at Bude in Cornwall (Plate 143), which was presented to Mr Brendon by members of the Hunt in June 1904. He painted *Rev. Edgar A. Milne, Master of the Cattistock Foxhounds, Drawn Blank – Lord and Lady Daresbury with the Cheshire Hounds* (1899), *Colonel and Mrs William Wharton at Skelton Castle* (1889) and *Mr Watson Master of the Darlington Beagle Hunt*. Hunt followers paid for several of the portraits, including Mr Watson's; Hardy often arranged for engravings of the paintings (in the case of Watson's portrait, produced by Gimpel of Paris) to be made available to subscribers.[225]

Hardy painted several studies of horses and hounds exercising at the water's edge, beginning with *The Morning Bath* (1872), described by *The Illustrated London News* as: "horses being ridden by grooms into the sea margin – a work distinguished by great spirit and truth in the action of the animals and excellent draughtmanship." A similar study painted for Colonel Wharton of Skelton Castle, *A Summer's Day in Cleveland* (Plate 142), was Hardy's Royal Academy exhibit for 1889. The picture shows Colonel William Wharton in the foreground, his

Plate 143 (right): Mr George Brendon (MFH) and Family with his Pack of Hounds, Bude, Cornwall, 1904
Heywood Hardy. Oil on canvas. 134.6 x 188cm.
MR RUPERT BRENDON, BUDE, CORNWALL[226]

Plate 144 (below): A Summer's Day in Cleveland, 1889
Heywood Hardy. Oil on canvas. 54.5 x 104.6cm. PRIVATE COLLECTION

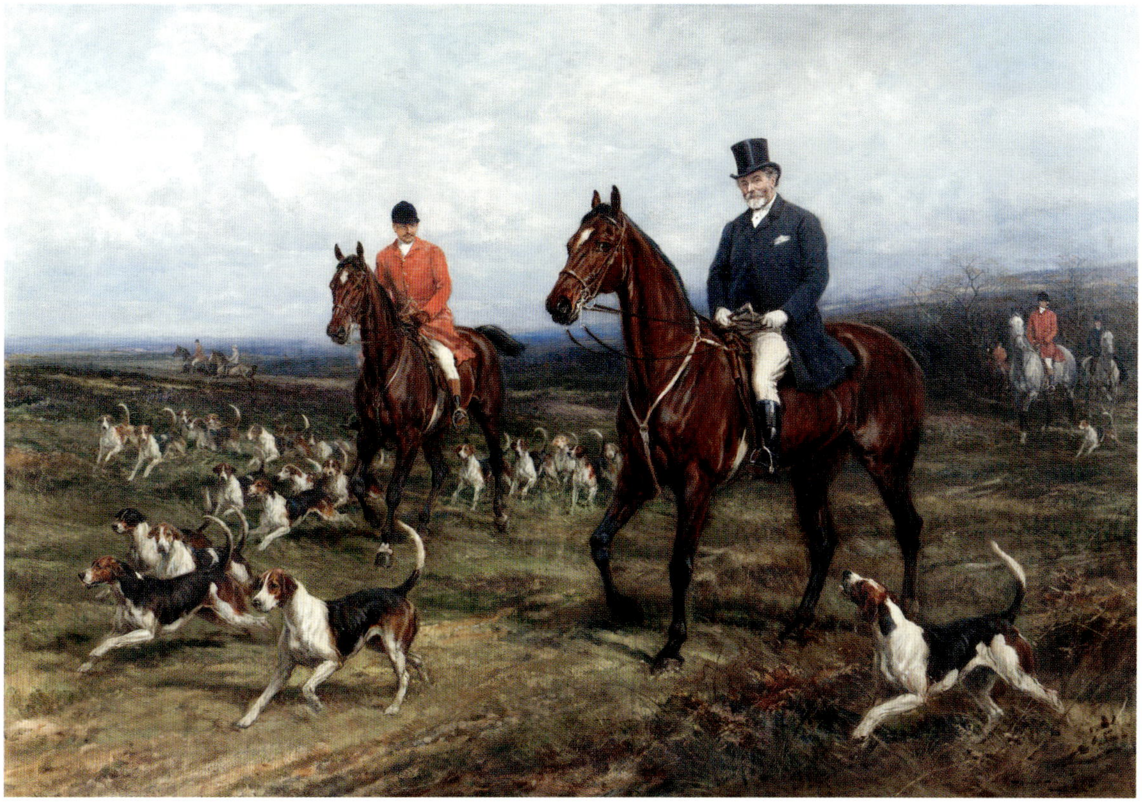

father John Wharton (the previous Master) to the right, Harry Pacey (Huntsman) behind and Dick Gibson (Whipper-in) on the left. Colonel Wharton was Master of the Cleveland Hunt from 1886 to 1919 and owned the Cleveland pack for 52 years.

From the mid 1880s to almost the end of his life, hunting scenes and equestrian portraits formed an important part of Heywood's work. Captain Forester was probably his most significant patron. Heywood Hardy became close friends with Forester and with the Milbank family from about 1889. Hardy was frequently a guest of Captain Forester; he joined his shooting parties and was an enthusiatic participant at musical entertainments. Forester inherited estates and a large fortune from the Duke of Cleveland. In 1905 he became Master of the Quorn Hunt.

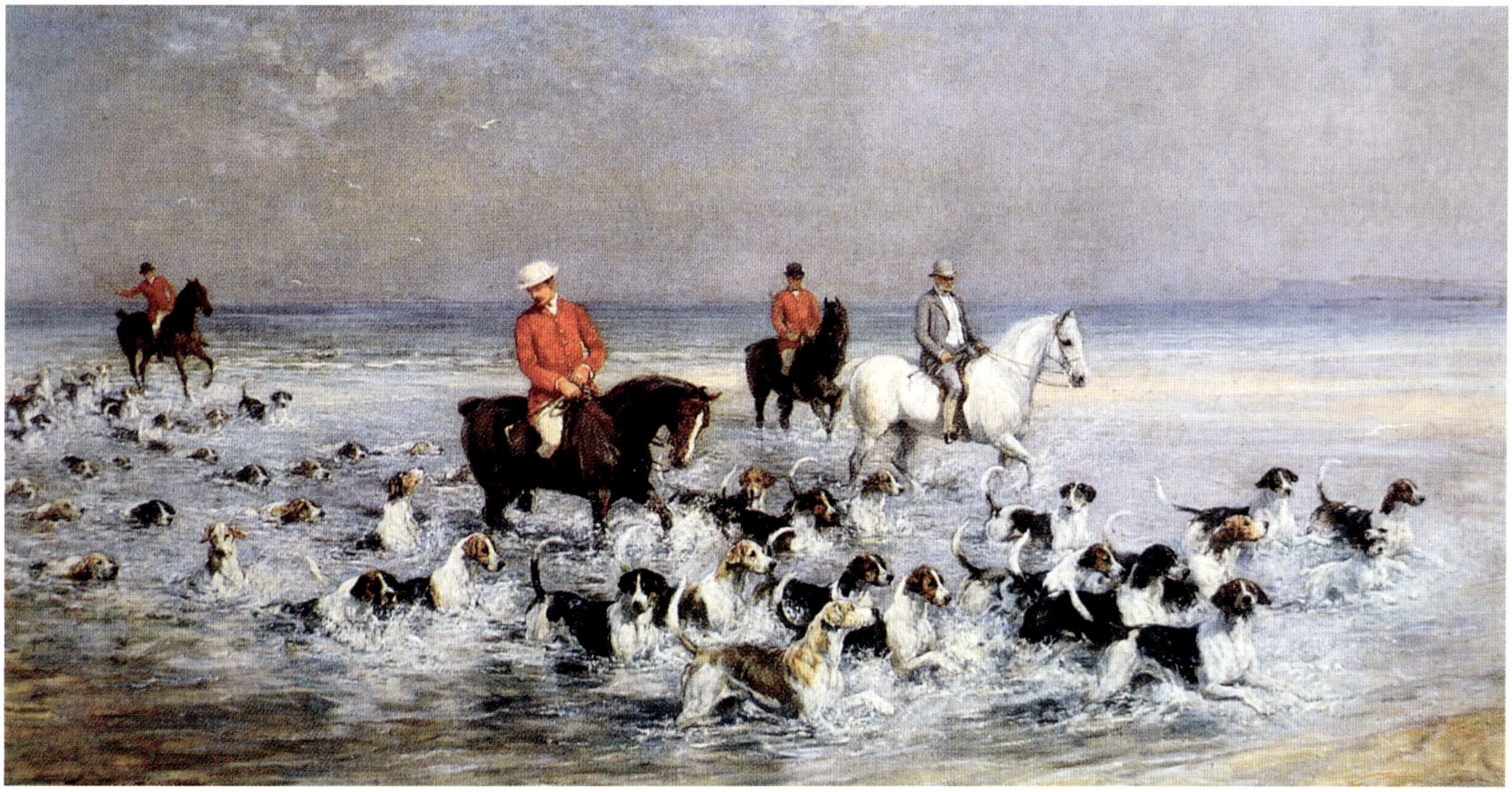

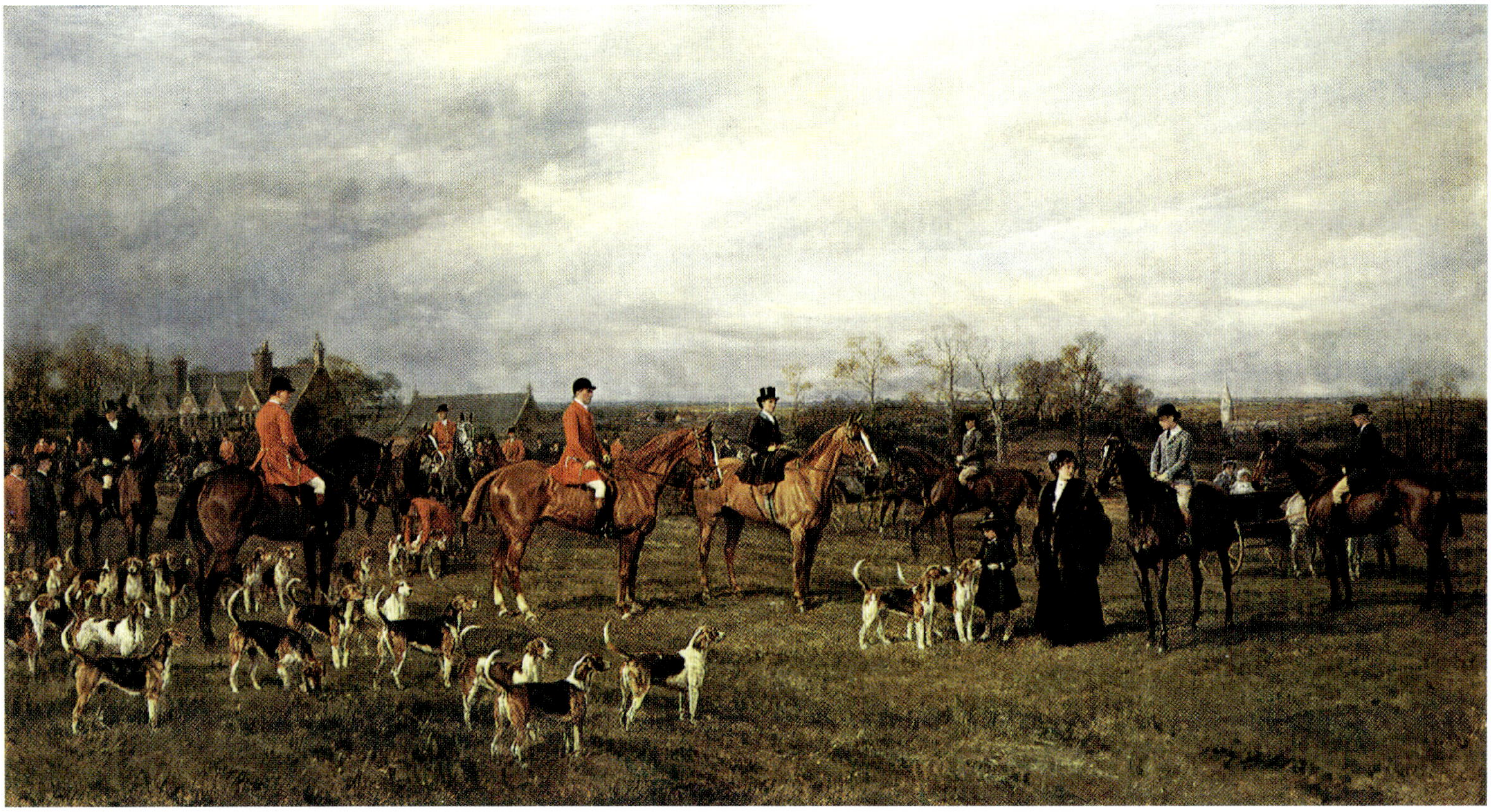

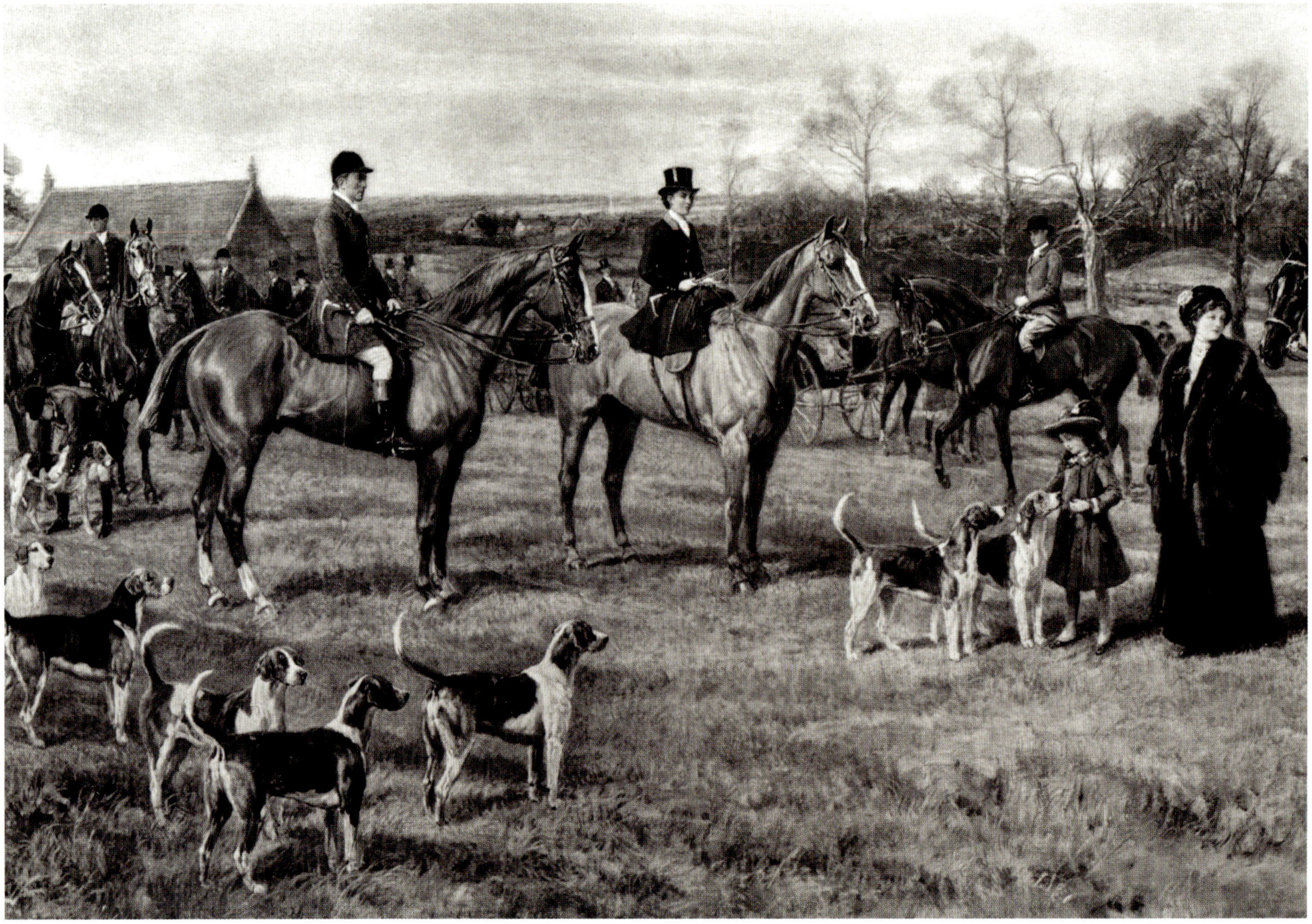

Plate 145 (opposite page, top): The Meet of the Quorn Hunt at Kirby Gate, November 7, 1910, with Asfordly Church in the Distance.
Heywood Hardy. Oil on canvas. 96.5 x 170.2cm. Private Collection

Plate 146 (opposite page, bottom): After Heywood Hardy. The Meet of the Quorn Hunt at Kirby Gate, November 7, 1910. Detail.
Berlin Photographic Company, Germany

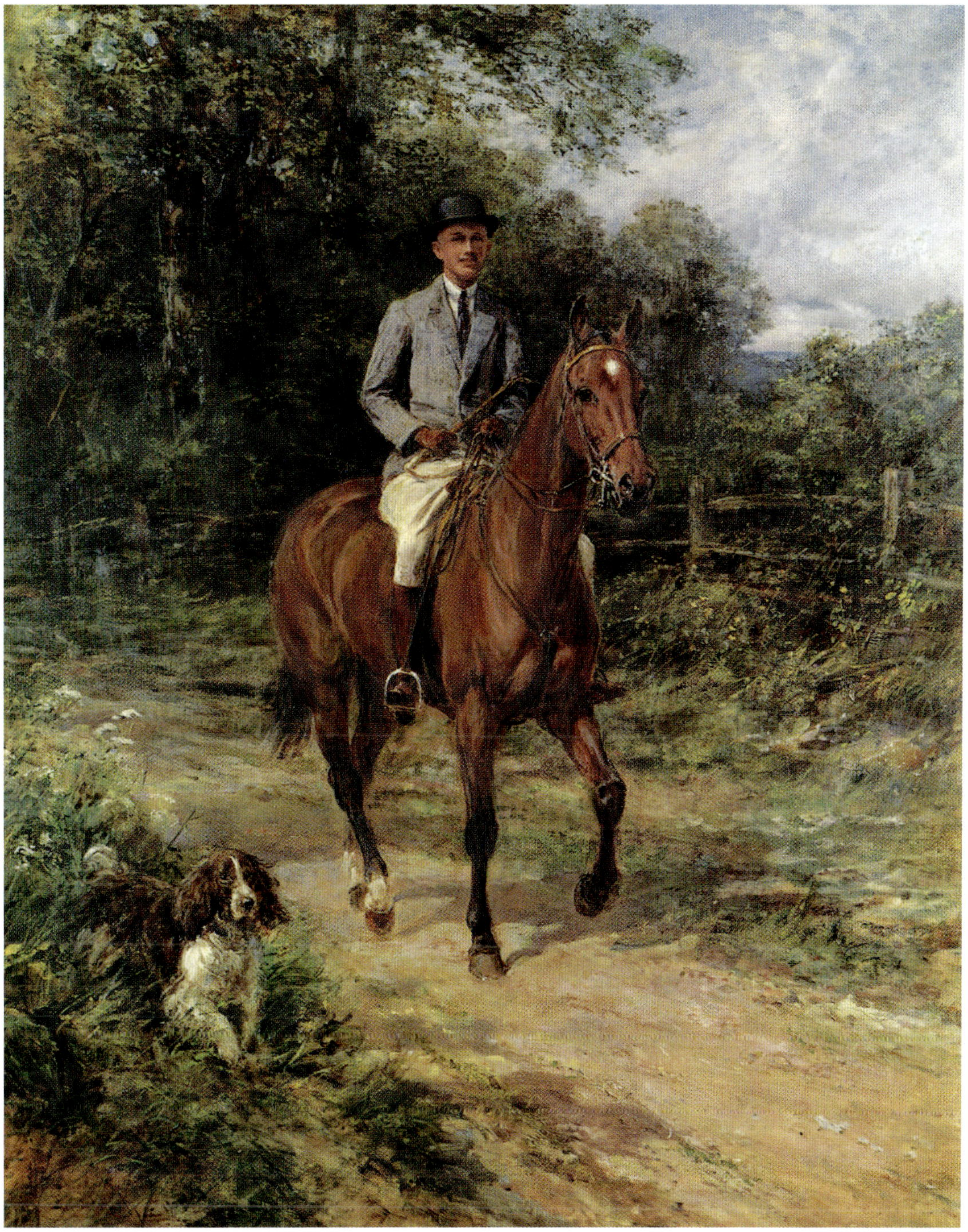

Plate 147 (right): The Morning Ride, 1925
Heywood Hardy. Oil on canvas. 139 x 107cm. Private Collection

Probably Hardy's best painting of a hunting meet is *The Meet of the Quorn Hunt at Kirby Gate, November 7, 1910, with Asfordly Church in the Distance* (Plate 145). The scene is Kirby Gate, near Melton Mowbray, where the Quorn has held its opening Meet for over 200 years. On horseback in the centre are Captain F.W. Forester and Miss Mary Forester. On foot are Miss Aline Forester with two favourite hounds and Mrs Forester who is next to Henry Forester on horseback. To the left of Captain Forester is Nimrod Capel, 1st whip, removing a thorn from a hound's foot; Capel later became a renowned huntsman with the South Staffordshire Hunt. According to Major Henry Forester, all those portrayed sat individually for Hardy; the picture took some two years to complete and all except one of the horses were thoroughbred racehorses. A detail of the photogravure of this painting made by the Berlin Photographic Company (Plate 146), printed in Berlin just before the First World War, shows how Heywood Hardy's portrayal of horses and his portraiture had developed since his first picture of a Hunt, the Zetland, painted 20 years earlier.

In 1913 Hardy painted *Portrait of Capt. F.W. Forester on Denis Aubern 6 years, Winner of the Hunters Sweepstakes at Croxton Park, April 10, 1913*. Forester won many steeplechases and was regarded as one of the best horsemen of his day. Hardy's 1918 Royal Academy exhibit was *An Incident with the Quorn Hounds*, "a scene that occurred at the Asser Drybrook Reservoir with the Quorn Hounds on March 29th 1910. The fox having been killed in the middle of the Reservoir, one of the foot people swam out and dived to bring him up." Hardy's last equestrian portrait seems to have been *The Morning Ride* (Plate 147), which he painted in 1925 at the age of 83.

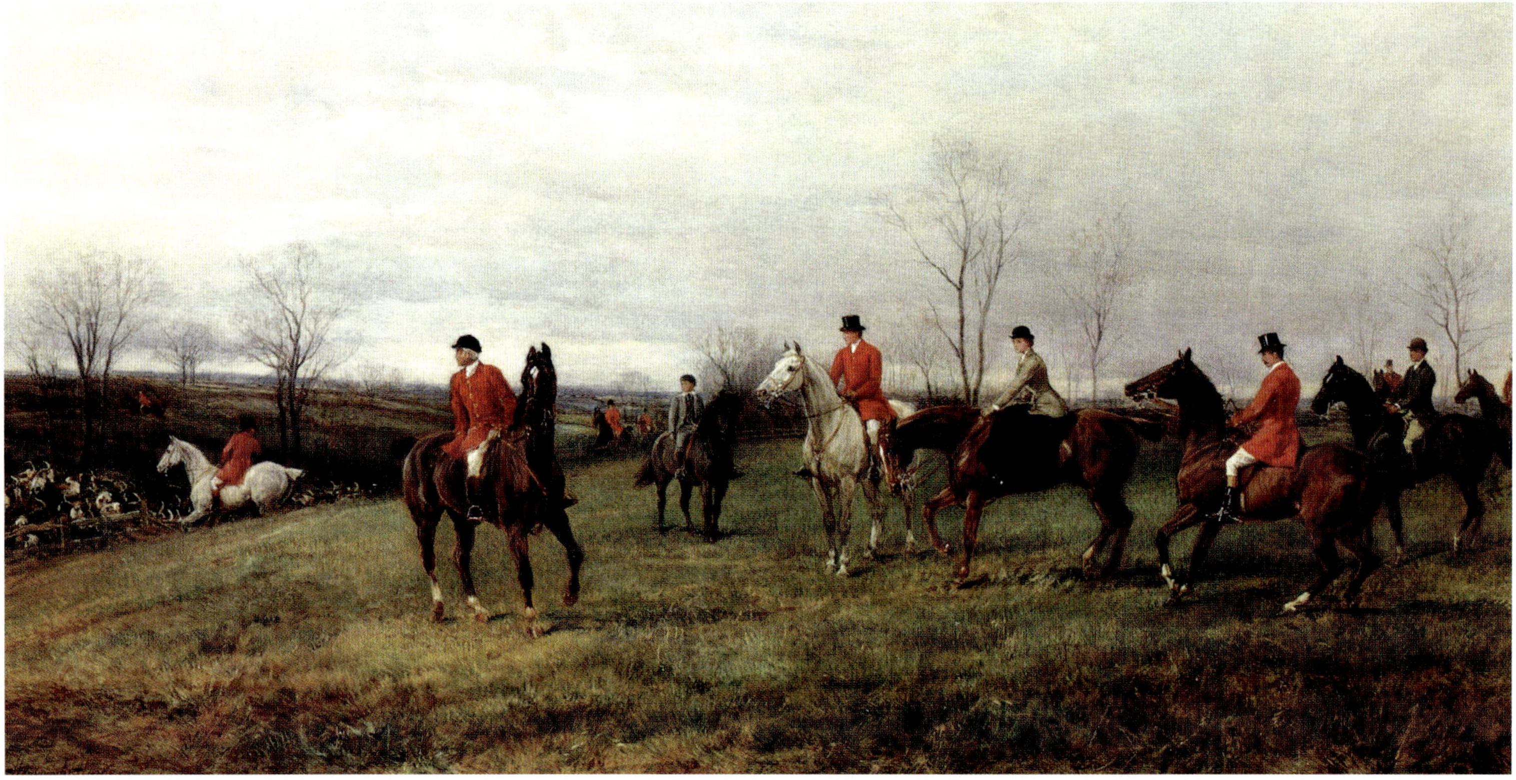

Hunting Scenes

Heywood Hardy's picture of the Zetland Hunt (Plate 140), painted from 1888 to 1890, was the starting point for many pictures of hunts and hunting. It immediately established him as a skilful painter of equestrian portraits and hunting scenes. He had by this time mastered the elements needed for a good picture of horses and hounds; his accurate drawing and confident brushwork expertly captured the movements of both. And he already had extensive experience of landscape painting.

Hardy made full use of the expertise he gained in painting horses and riders for *The Zetland Hunt*; in the same year (1890) he painted the first of many pictures of hunting scenes. Indeed, he used his sketches of the Zetland Hunt as a basis for the pictures, and his skill in painting hunting scenes was quickly recognised. For example, *The Illustrated News* commented:

> There are few artists who can paint horses and their riders with so much truth and taste as Mr. Heywood Hardy. As a rule he does not venture upon a very large canvas, but the three pictures now on view at the St. James's Gallery (King street, St. James's) prove that he need have no misgivings as to his powers ... It is obvious at first sight that this present series of hunting episodes has grown out of Mr.

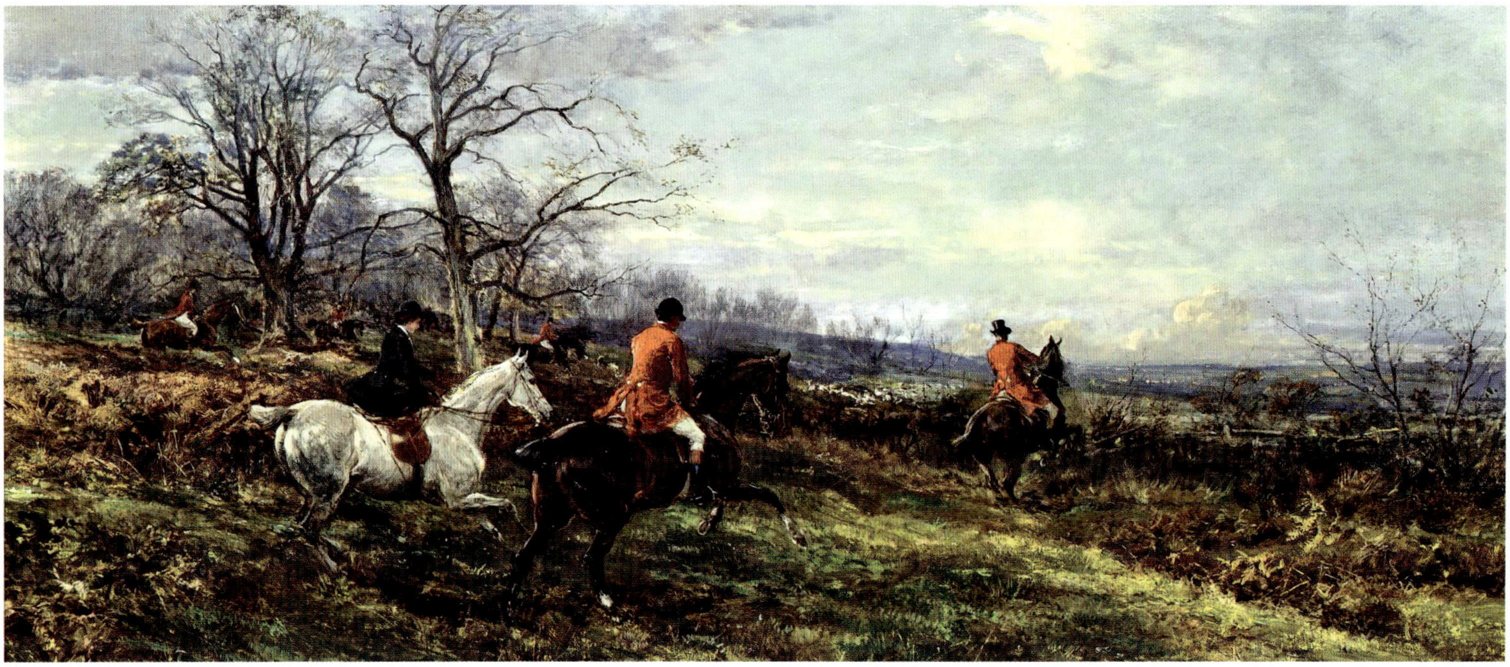

Plate 148 (opposite page, top): Picking up the Scent, 1894
Heywood Hardy. Oil on canvas. 50.2 x 91.4cm. Private Collection

Plate 149 (opposite page, bottom): On the Scent , 1902
Heywood Hardy. Oil on canvas. 45 x 92cm. Private Collection

Plate 150 (right): Picking up the Scent, 1903
Heywood Hardy. Oil on canvas 91.5 x 70.5cm. Private Collection

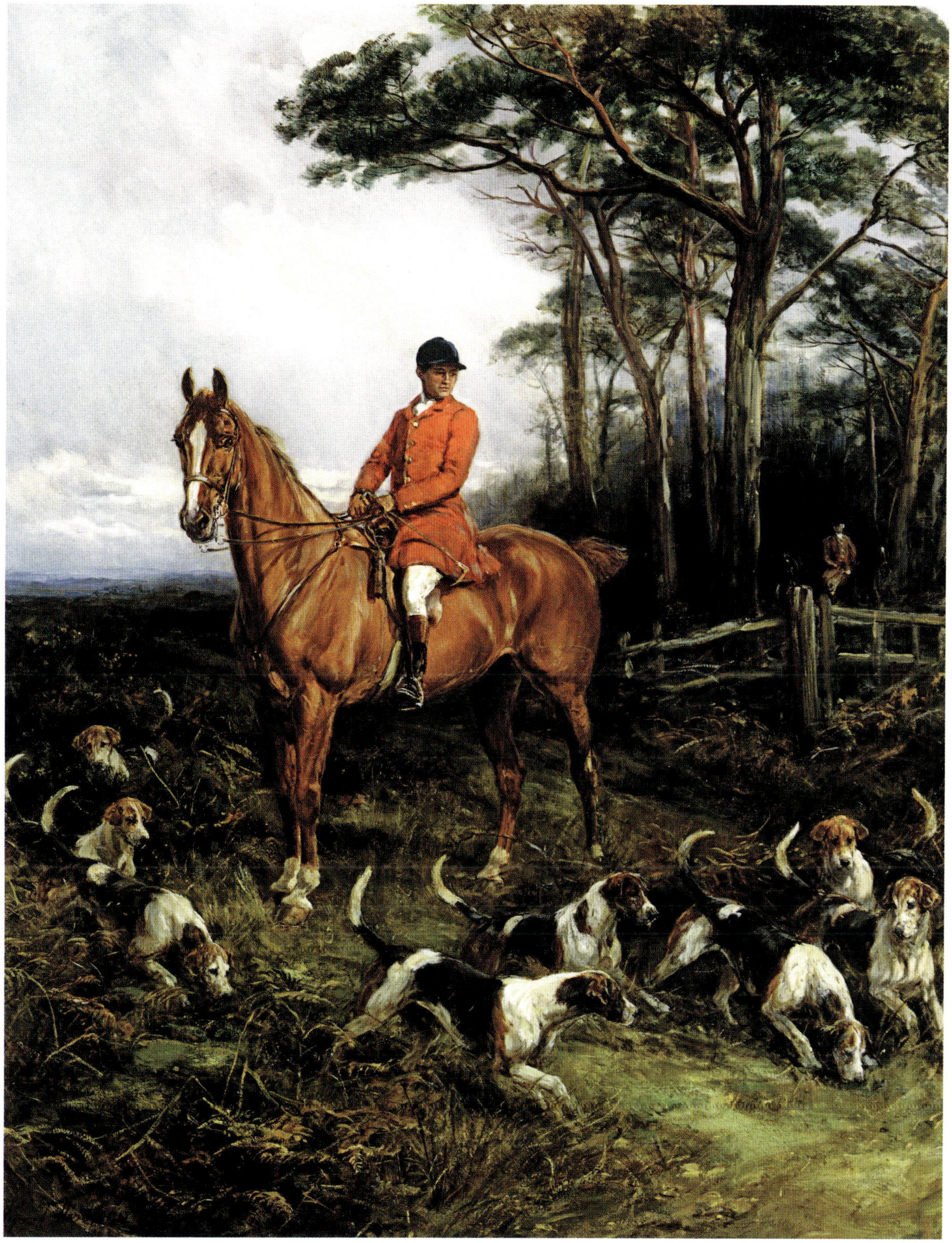

Heywood Hardy's successful picture of the Zetland Hunt. We can recognise a corner of Aske Hall in the first scene, a stretch of the North Riding moor in the second, and the faces of more than one of the actors in the last scene. The pictures give an admirable as well as a truthful idea of English hunting in a thoroughly typical English county, and the artist has done ample justice to horses, dogs, riders, and scenery. Not by any means the least satisfactory part of the work is the rendering of the dull November day at different hours of the run, and others besides hunting men or hunting ladies will realise the charm which the sport offers to all lovers of the country when to the rest of the world Nature seems so cold and lifeless.[227]

Examples of his later hunting pictures include *Picking up the Scent* (1894) (Plate 148), *On the Scent* (1902) (Plate 149), *Picking up the Scent* (1903) (Plate 150), *Drawing Cover* (1903) (Plate 151), *Drawn Blank* (1906) (Plate 152), *Hounds on the Scent Leaving a Covert* (1907), *Drawing the Covert* (Plates 153 and 154) *and The Presentation.*[228] After he painted *Picking up the Scent* in 1894, his pictures became more animated and the hounds featured more prominently.

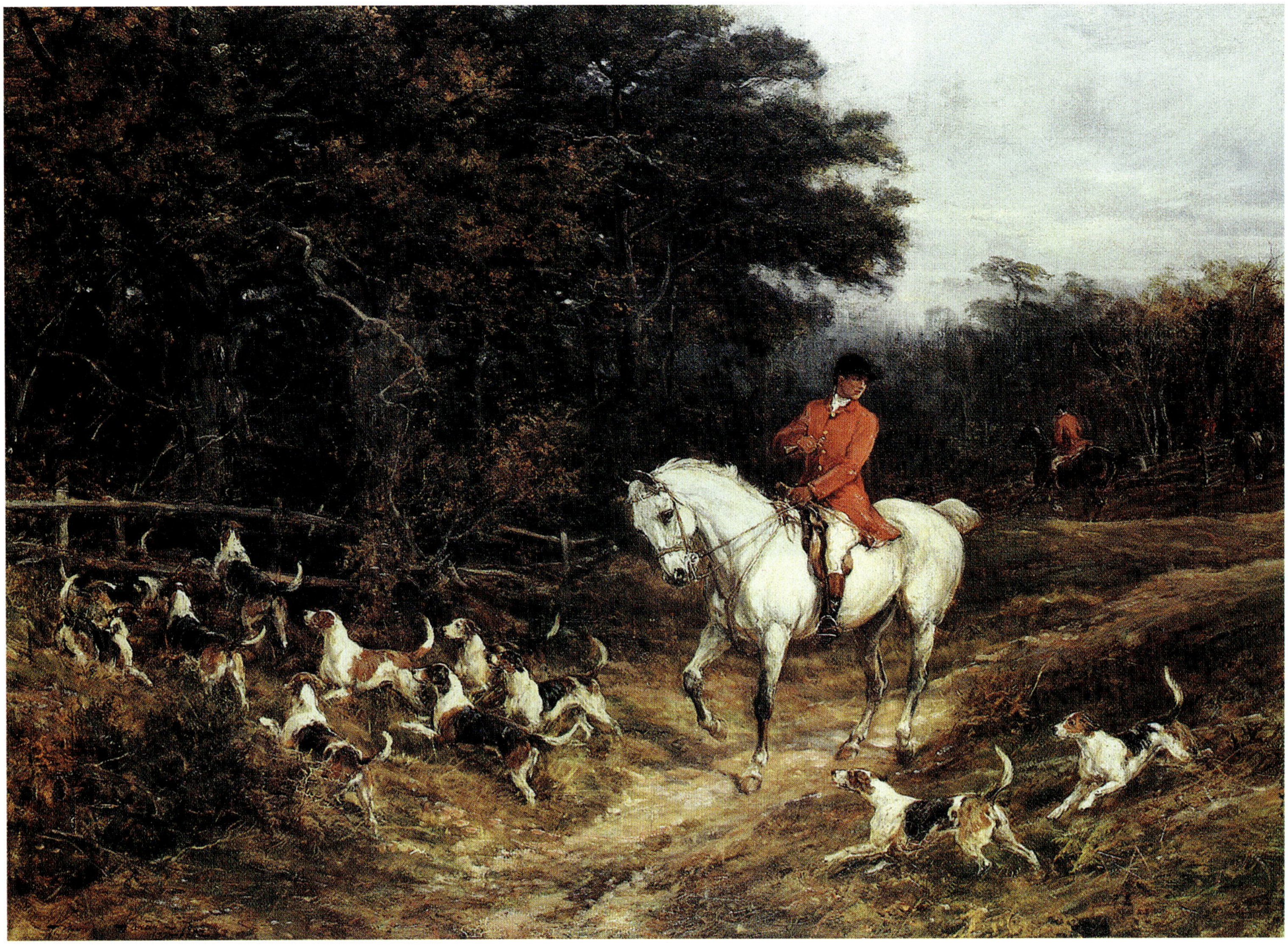

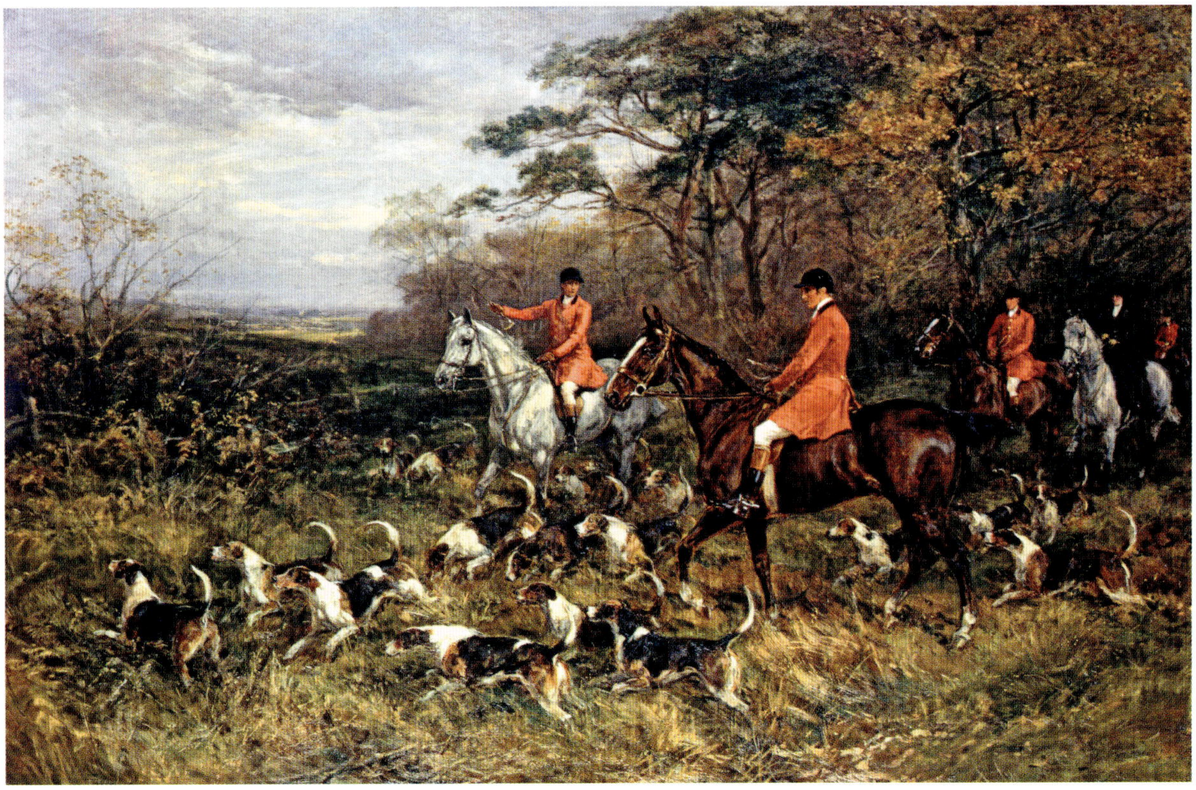

Plate 151 (above): Drawing Cover, 1903
Heywood Hardy. Oil on canvas. 66 x 85cm.
Private Collection

Plate 152 (opposite page): Drawn Blank, 1906
Heywood Hardy. Oil on canvas. 61 x 51cm.
Private Collection

Plate 153 (left): Drawing the Covert
Heywood Hardy. Oil on canvas. 61 x 91.4cm.
Private Collection

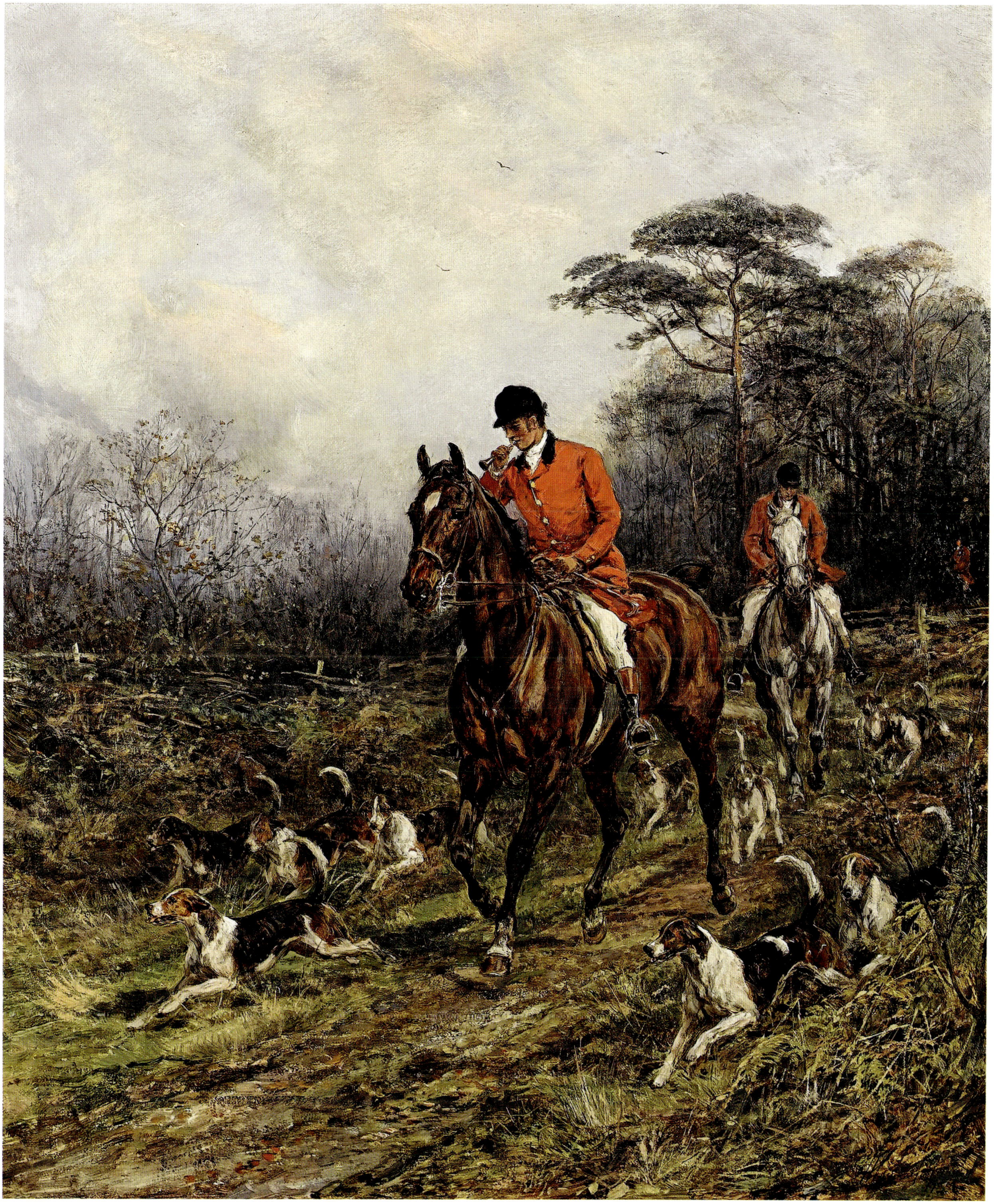

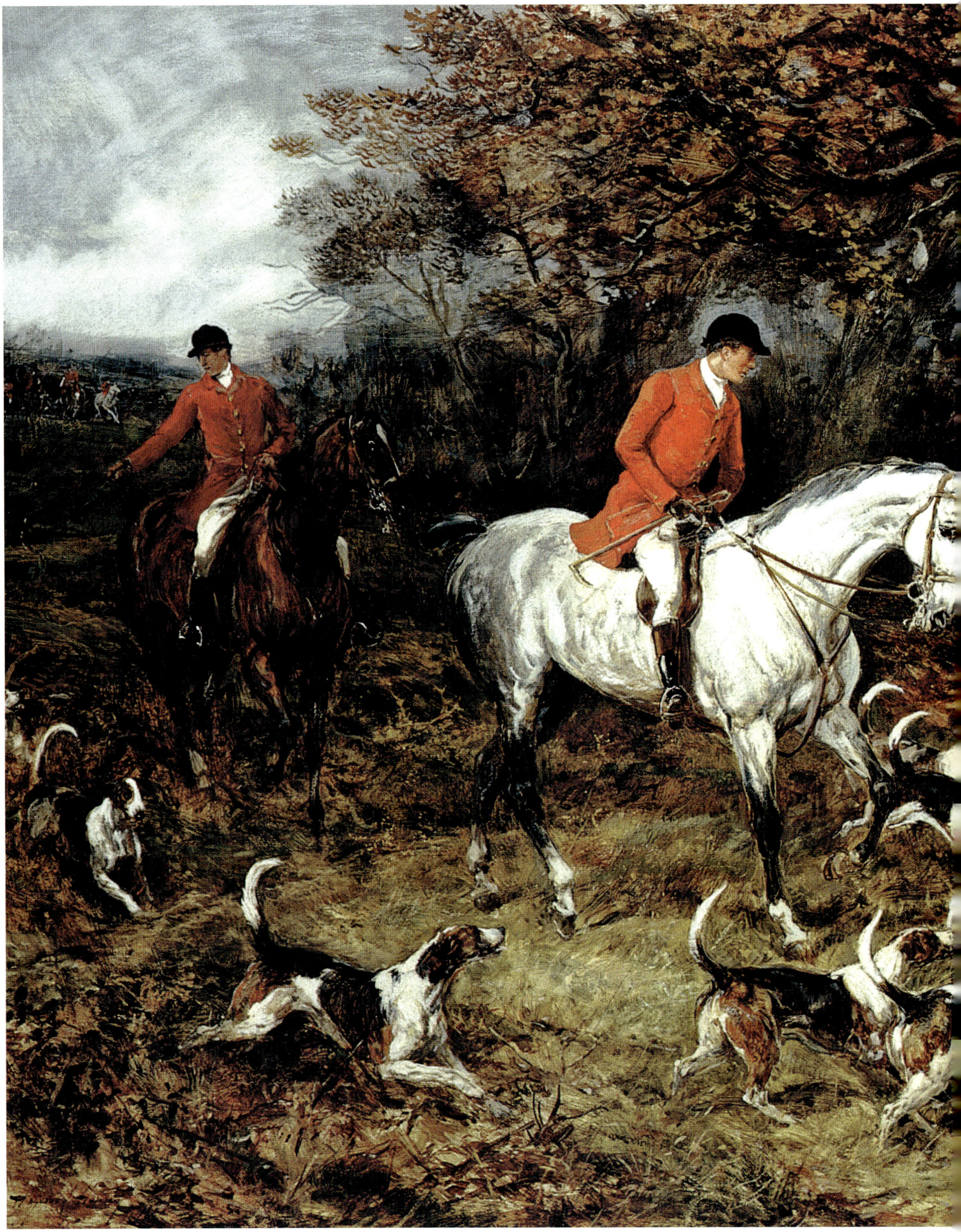

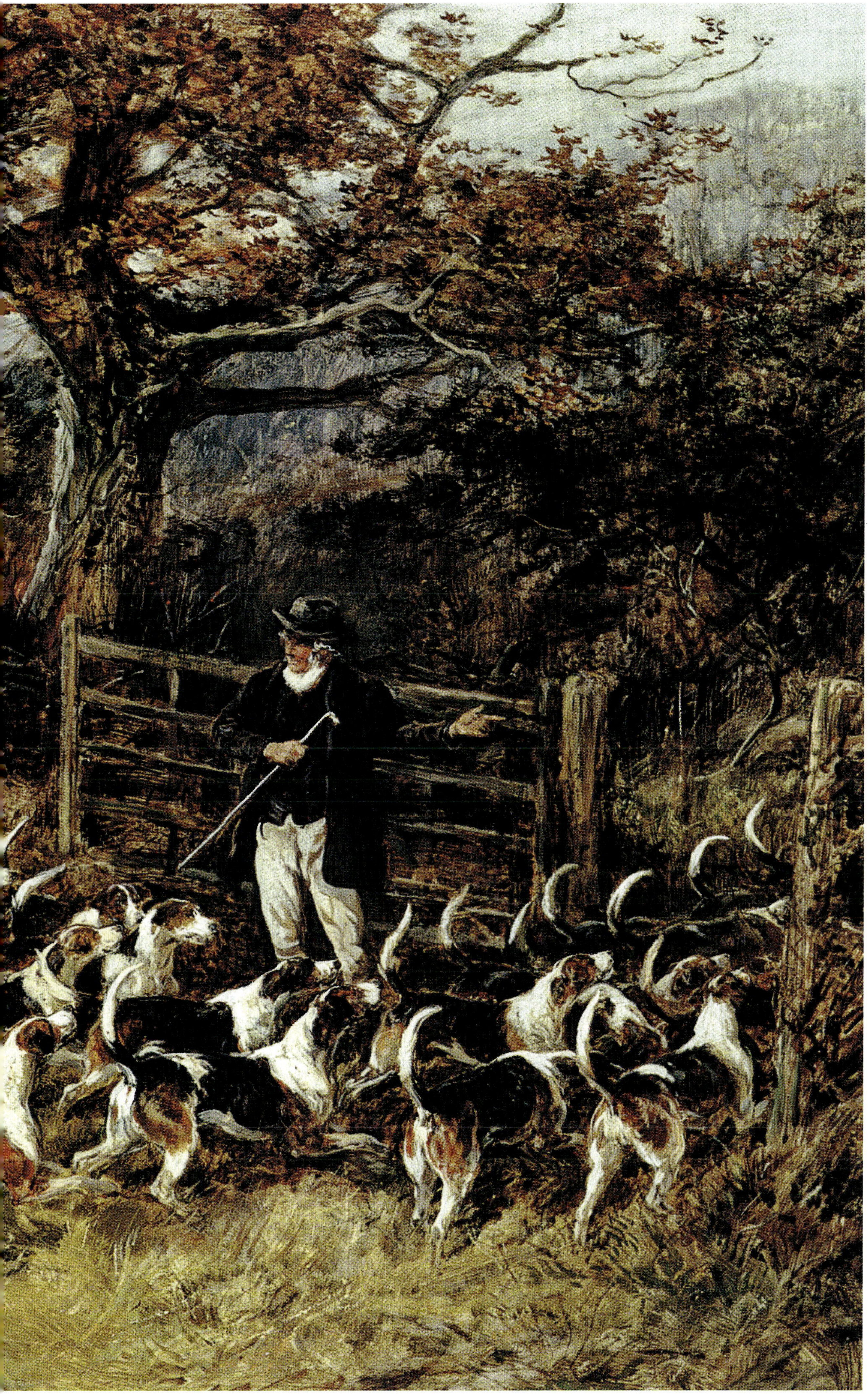

Plate 154:
Drawing the Covert
Heywood Hardy.
Oil on canvas.
81 x 117cm.
PRIVATE COLLECTION

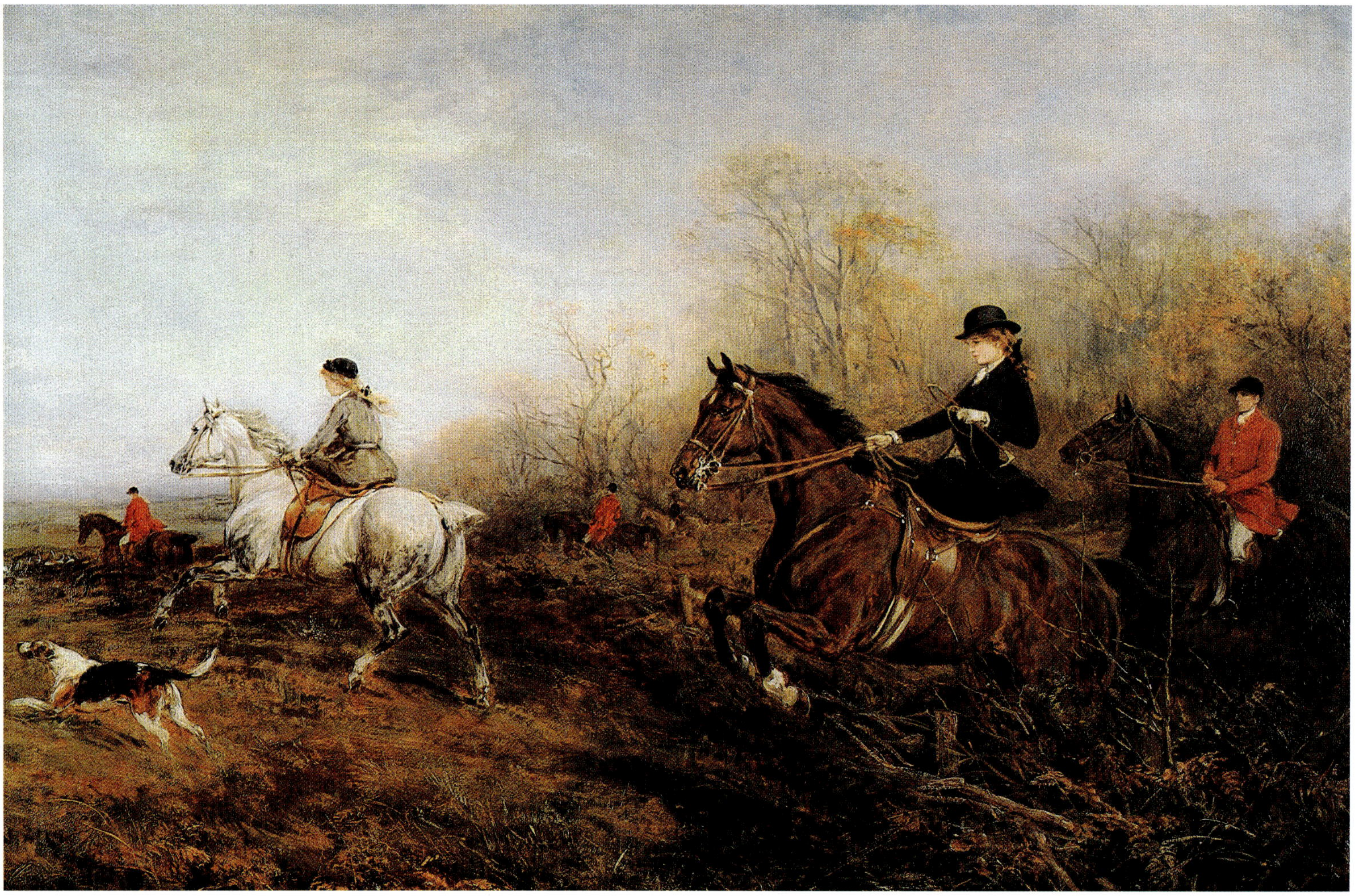

Plate 155 (above, and detail below): Out for a Scamper
Heywood Hardy. Oil on canvas. 60.5 x 91cm. Private Collection

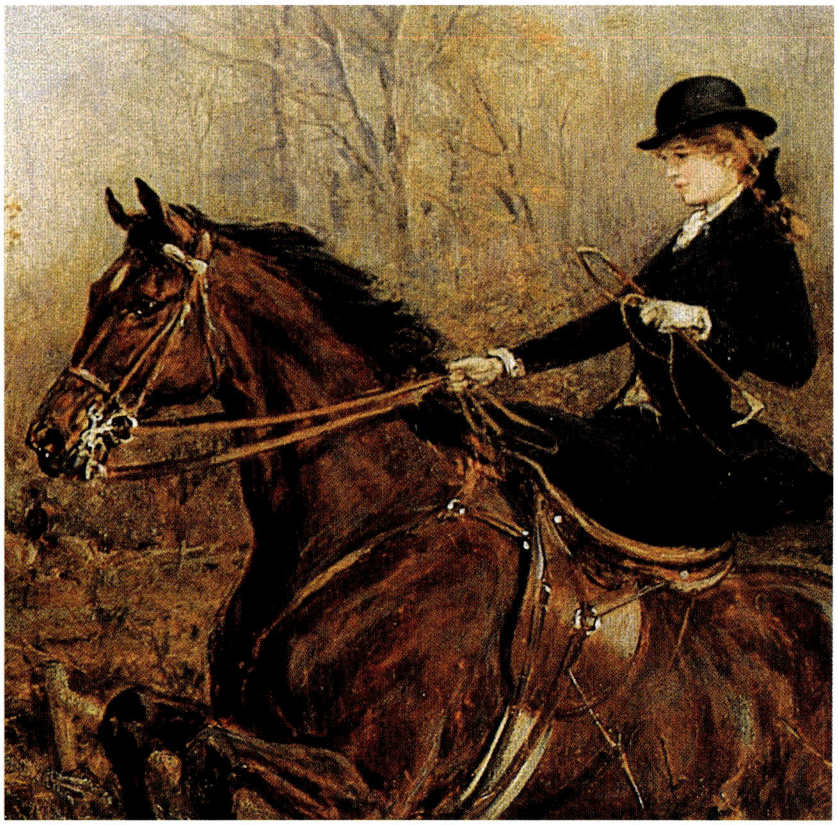

Ladies confidently riding side-saddle was a favourite subject of Hardy's, as in *Out for a Scamper* (Plate 155). *Hunters and Hounds* (Plate 156) is an unusual, perhaps unique, picture for the times; a girl who is upset at the killing of a fox is the centre of attention. The model for the girl may have been his daughter, Sylvia, who had red hair. Hardy sometimes had one of his daughters sit for pictures on a model horse in his studio.

Hardy produced many paintings of hunt followers outside inns and country houses, such as *The Stirrup Cup* (Plate 157) (probably his only painting that also includes a motor car); they are some of the artist's most popular paintings.[229]

Plate 156 (opposite page, top): Hunters and Hounds
Heywood Hardy. Oil on canvas. 91.4 x 121.9cm. Private Collection

Plate 157 (opposite page, bottom): The Stirrup Cup
Heywood Hardy. Oil on canvas. 50.8 x 76.2cm. Private Collection

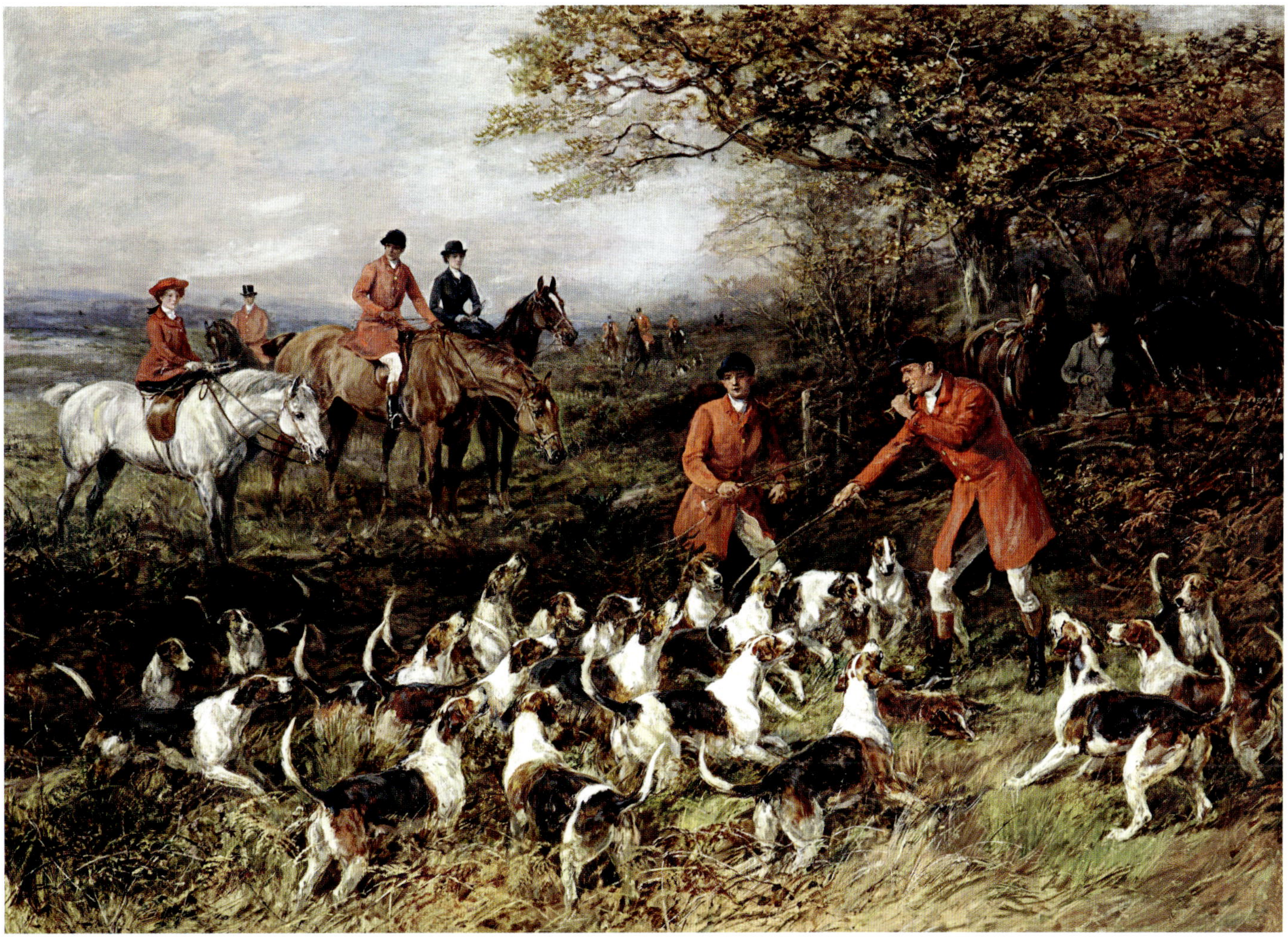

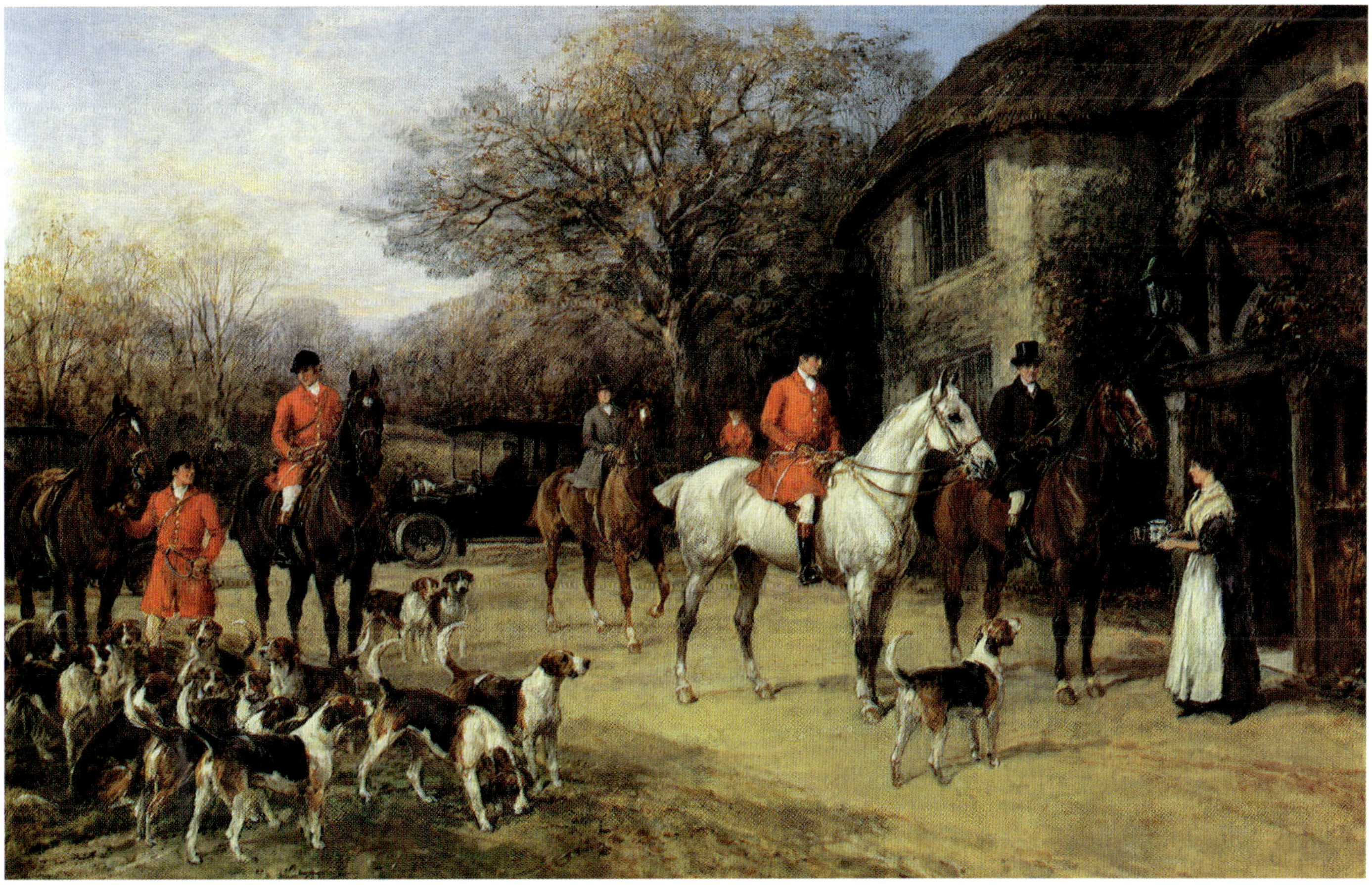

Hounds and Sporting Dogs

Heywood Hardy always enjoyed painting dogs – from his first attempts when he lived with his parents at Bath to the foxhounds and regimental mascots that he painted after the First World War. Heywood's association with numerous foxhunts led to several commissions for pictures of hounds and sporting dogs. He began by painting Mr S. Lang's prize-winning Gordon Setters; a woodcut of the painting was reproduced in *The Field,* which remarked that Mr Lang "spared neither money nor trouble to get together the finest kennel of this magnificient breed in existence".[230] This was followed by such pictures as the curiously named *Couple of Australian Kangaroo Hounds, Bull Terrier, and Pug Dog, the Property of E. Homan, Esq.*, exhibited at the Dudley Gallery in 1870.

The dogs for some pictures apparently came from a dog dealer in Seven Dials (near Covent Garden); Hardy wrote that "...he always "knew of" the very dog I wanted. Where he got them I do not know, but he always brought the dogs at the time appointed, and had a wonderful way of managing them too."

Head of a Foxhound (Plate 158) and *Dandy, Sapphire and Nigel: North Shropshire Foxhounds* (Plate 159) are good examples of the later, free style of brushwork that enabled him to paint such animated scenes of horses and hounds. One of his last pictures of a foxhound was *Sunshine, a Foxhound of the Quorn,* painted in 1917.

He also painted several pictures of packs of foxhounds, including *The Hounds of the Tickham Hunt* (Plate 160), *The*

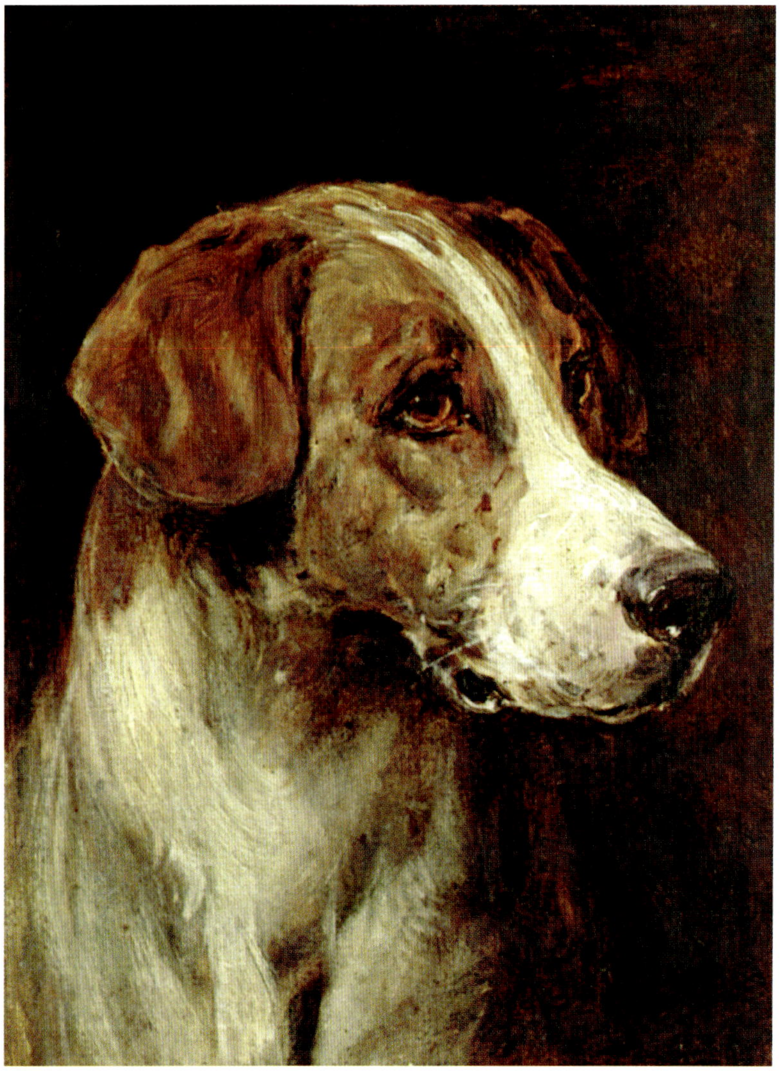

Plate 158: Head of a Foxhound
Heywood Hardy. Oil on canvas. 45 x 32.5cm. Private Collection

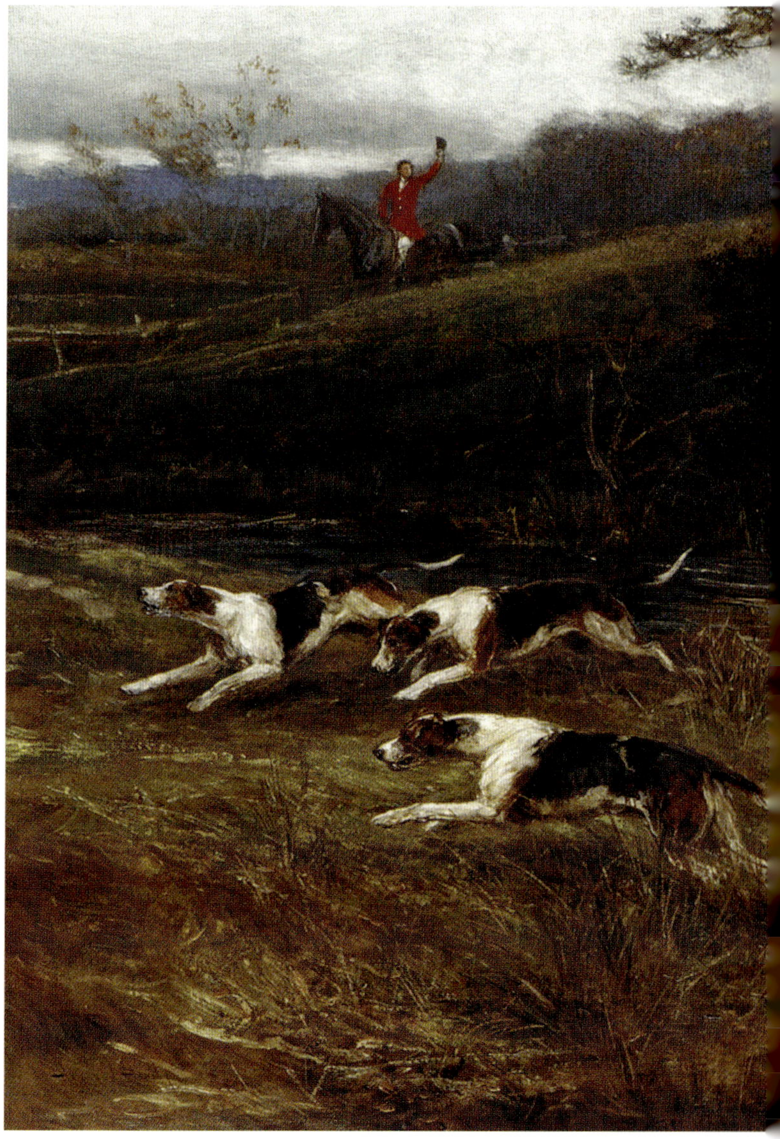

Plate 159 (right): Dandy, Sapphire and Nigel: North Shropshire Foxhounds, 1906[231]
Heywood Hardy. Oil on board. 34.3 x 43.8cm.
Private Collection

Plate 160 (below): The Hounds of the Tickham Hunt, Kent, Crossing a Brook
Heywood Hardy. Oil on canvas. 76.5 x 165.2cm.
Private Collection

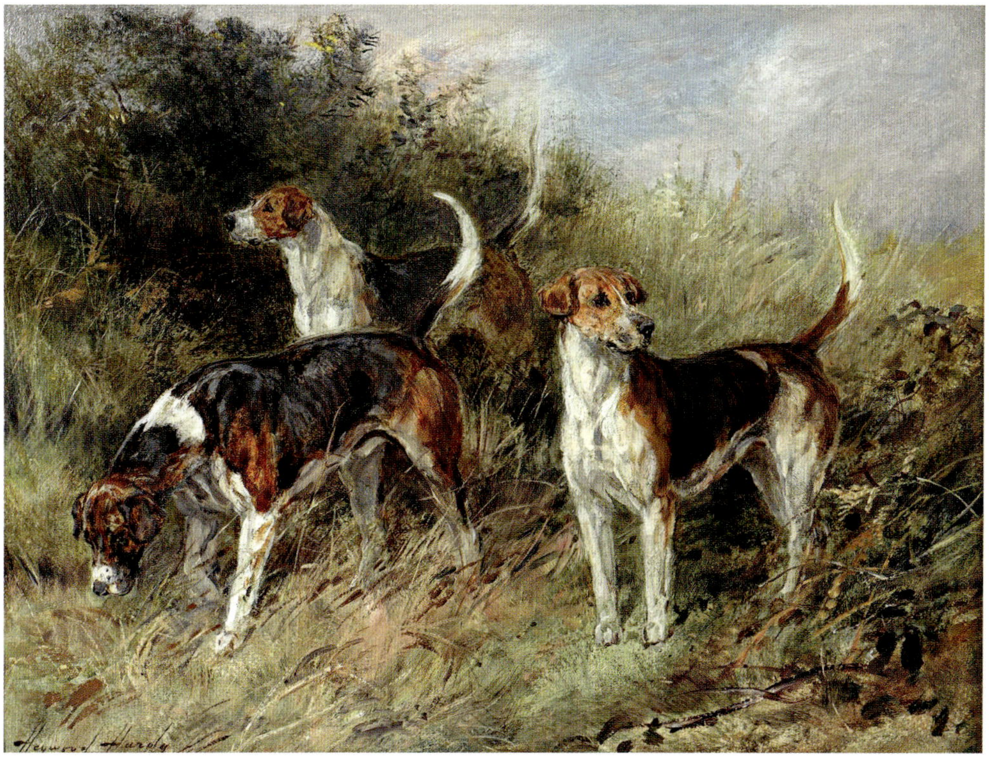

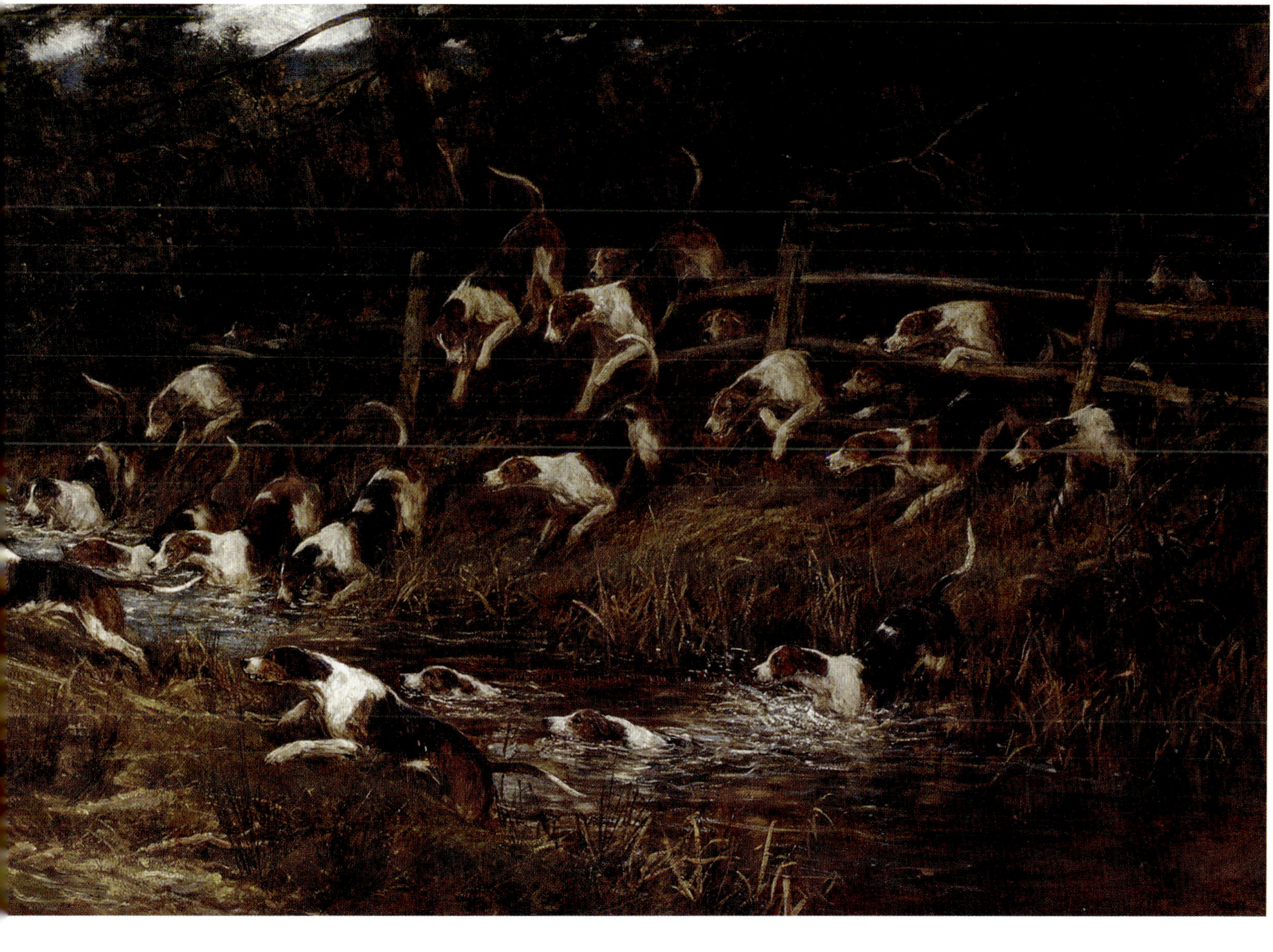

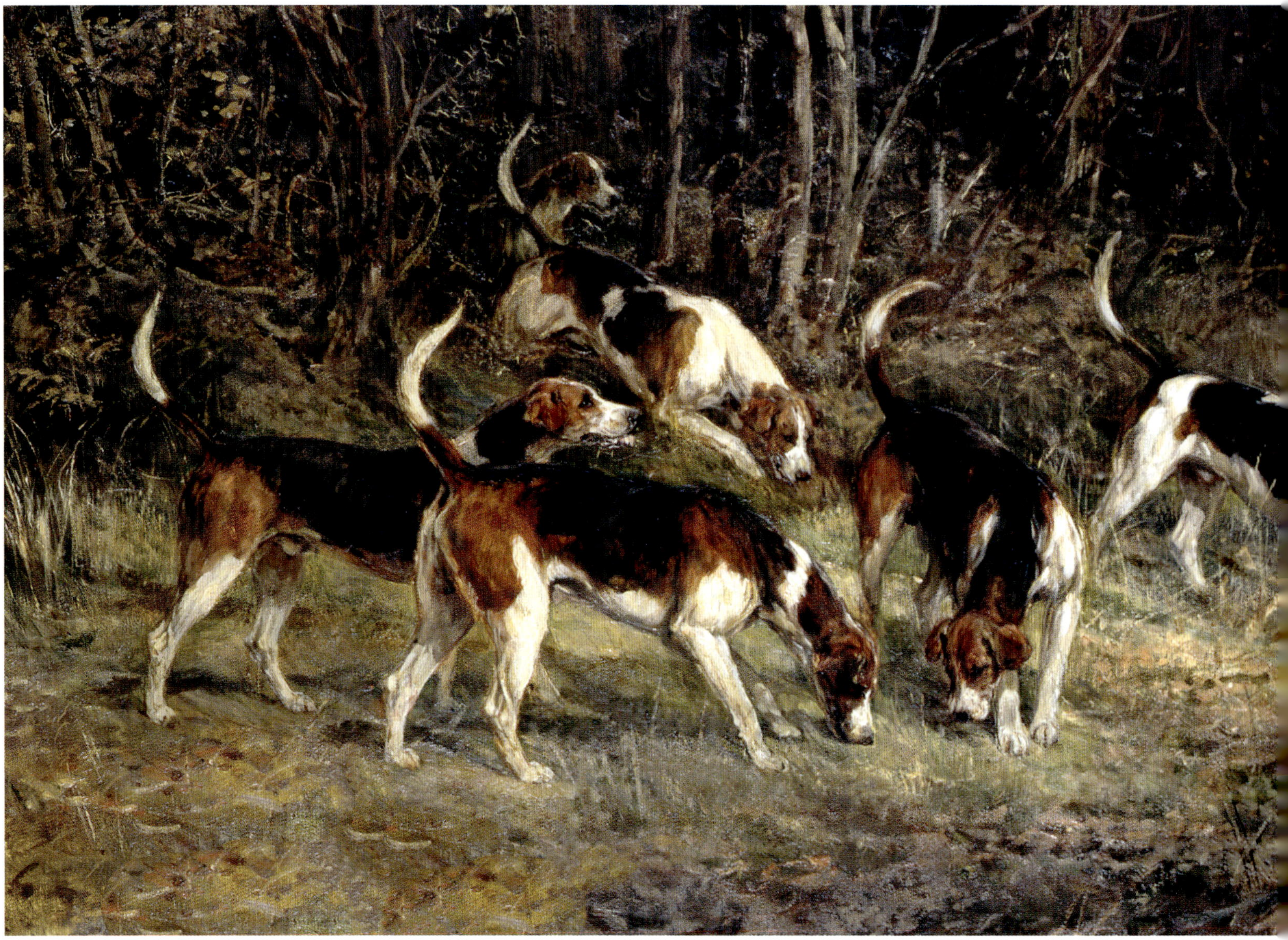

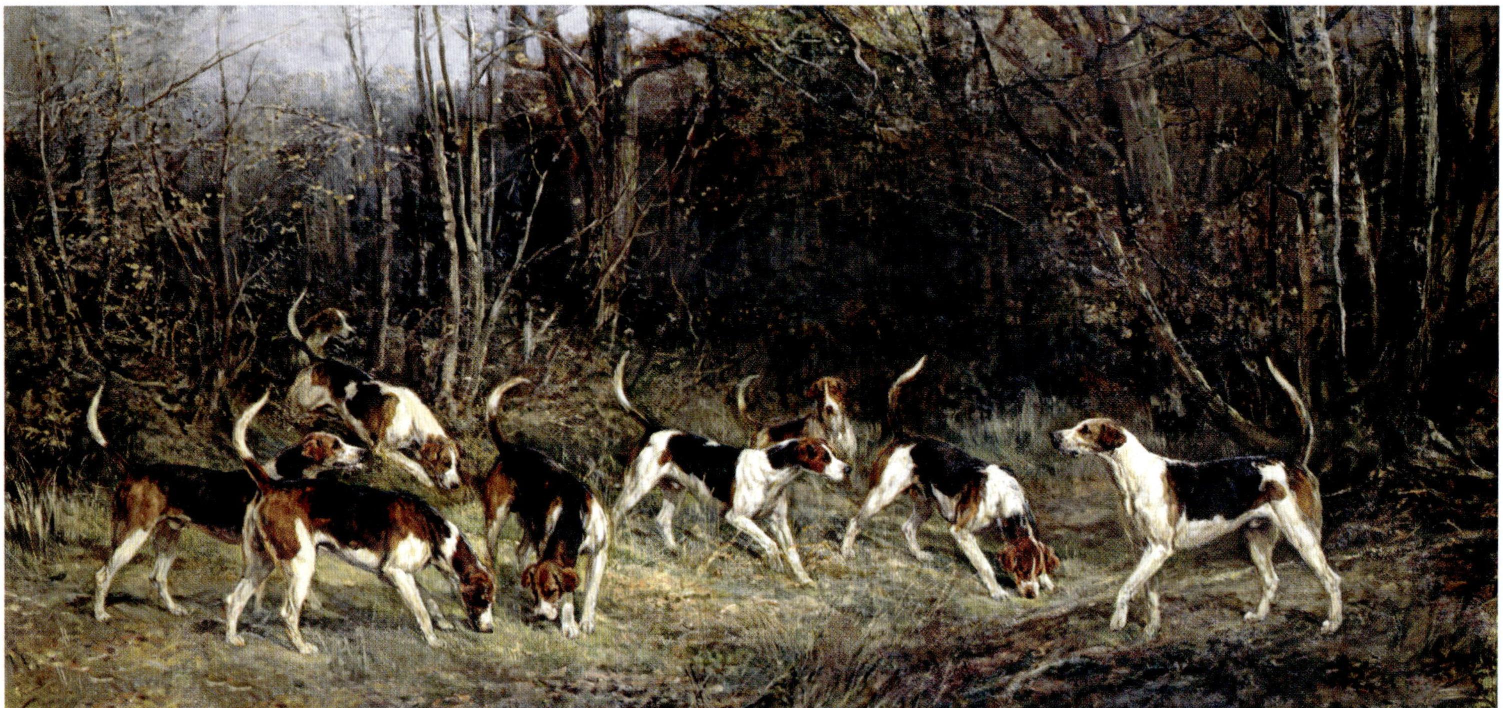

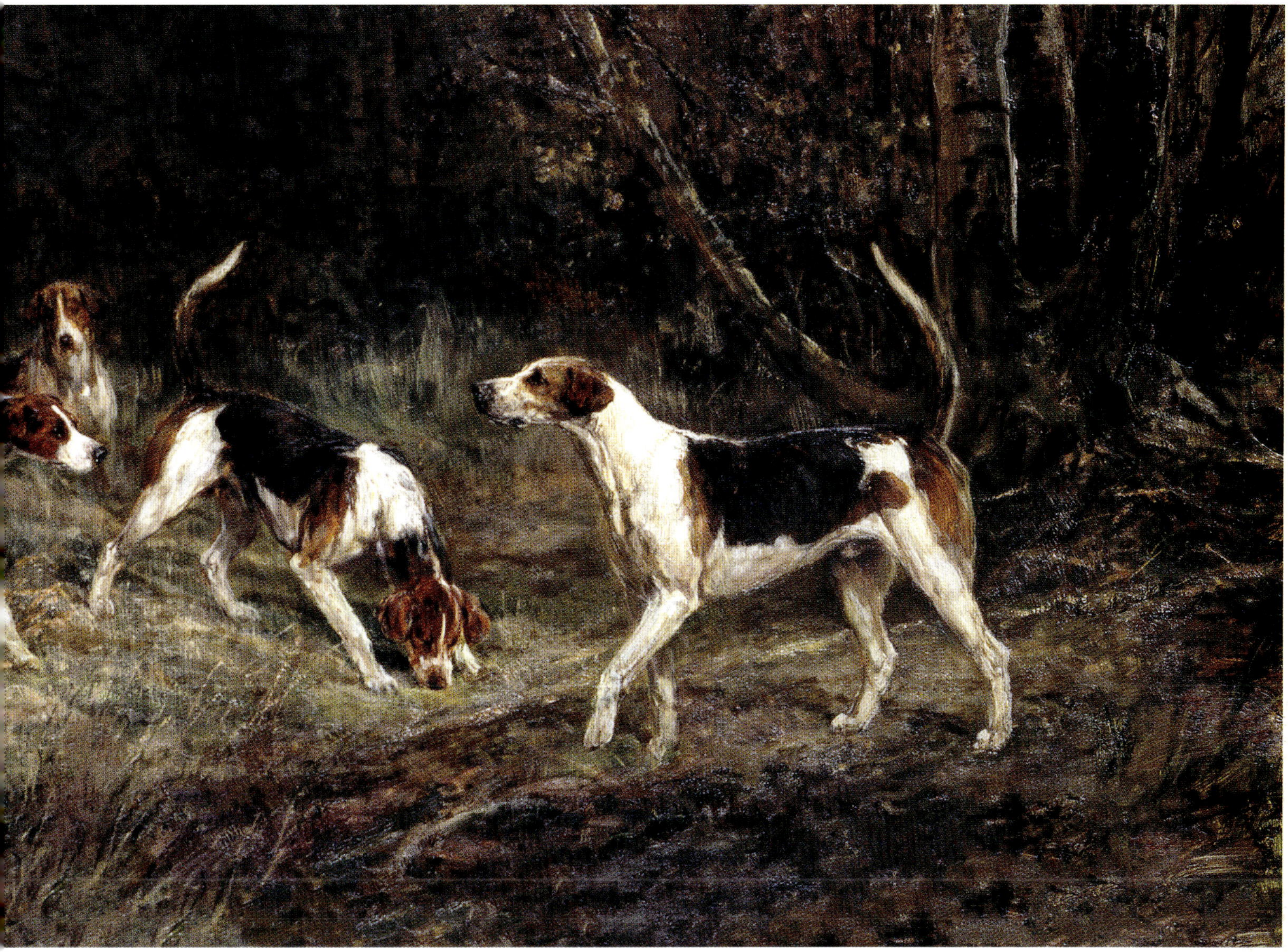

Plate 161 (left, and detail above): The Blankney Hounds, 1895
Heywood Hardy. 61.0 x 121.9cm. Private Collection

Plate 162 (right): Waiting for the Master
Heywood Hardy. Oil on canvas 55.8 x 45.7cm. Private Collection

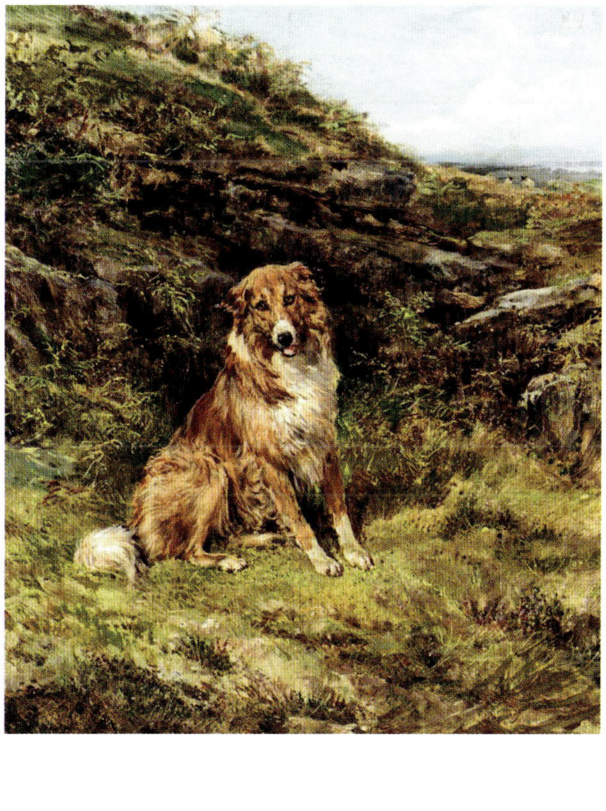

Blankney Hounds (1895) (Plate 161), *The Belvoir Hounds* (1894) and *The Meynell Hounds* (1916).

Heywood Hardy was also in demand to paint portraits of highly prized greyhounds, including *Sweet Sauce and Roulette VII* and *Fellow from Wales and Silvery Sand, Greyhounds*, and portraits such as *Pointers Alden Fluke and Bride II of Pilerog*. He painted several pictures of collies, with or without their owners; for example *Waiting for the Master* (Plate 162).

Heywood Hardy painted portraits of the first three Irish Wolfhound

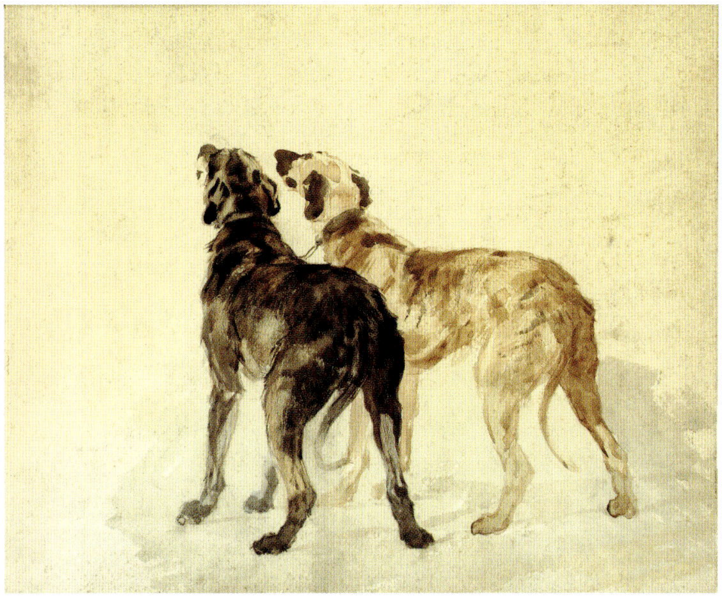

Plate 163 (left): Two Lurchers
Heywood Hardy. Pencil and watercolour on paper. 30 x 35cm. Private Collection
This study appears to have been the basis for the central dog in *Falconers* (Plate 99)

Plate 164 (below left): Brian Boru. 1st Mascot of the Irish Guards 1902-1910
Heywood Hardy. Oil on canvas. 58.2 x 47cm.
Officers' Mess of the Irish Guards

Plate 165 (below right, top): The Pick of the Pack, Stormer and Grasper
After Heywood Hardy. Mixed method engraving by Joseph B. Pratt, published 1901 by Thomas Agnew & Sons. 55 x 67.5cm.

Plate 166 (below right, bottom): A Pair of English Setters at Work
After Heywood Hardy. Mixed method engraving by Joseph B. Pratt, published 1904 by Thomas Agnew & Sons. 55 x 66cm.

mascots of the Irish Guards. The first mascot, *Brian Boru* (Plate 164), named after the Irish King, was presented to the regiment just after it was formed in 1902. Brian Boru was succeeded by Leitrim Boy in 1910 and Doran in 1917. All three portraits hang in the "Dog Room" at the Officers' Mess of the Irish Guards (Mons Barracks, Aldershot).

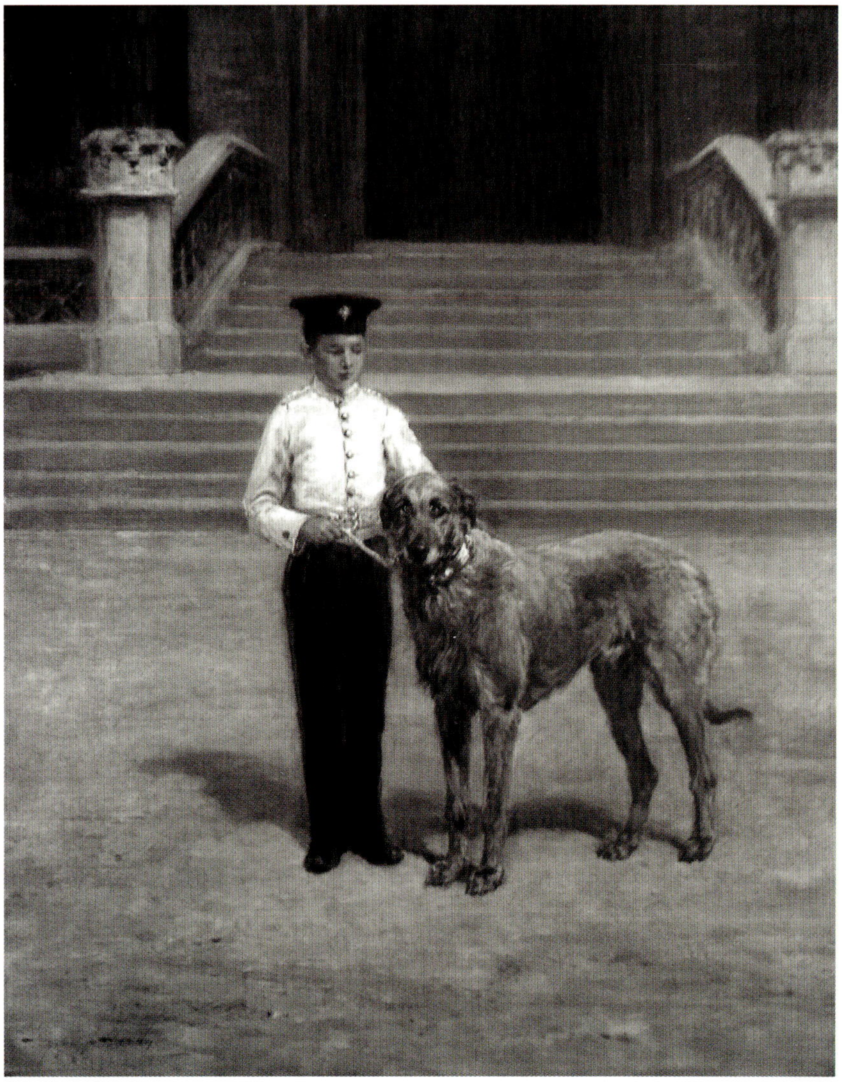

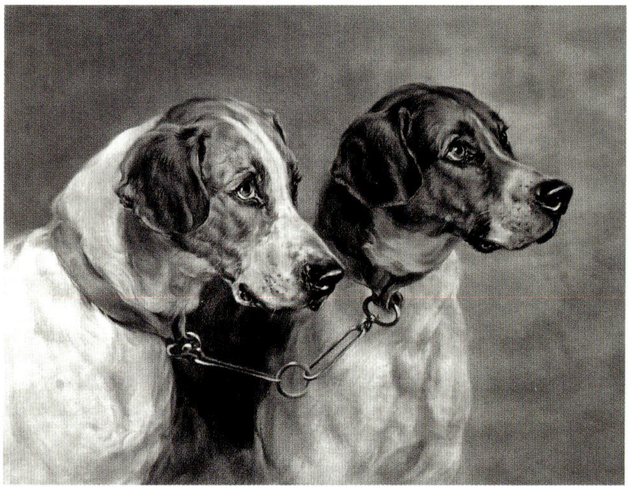

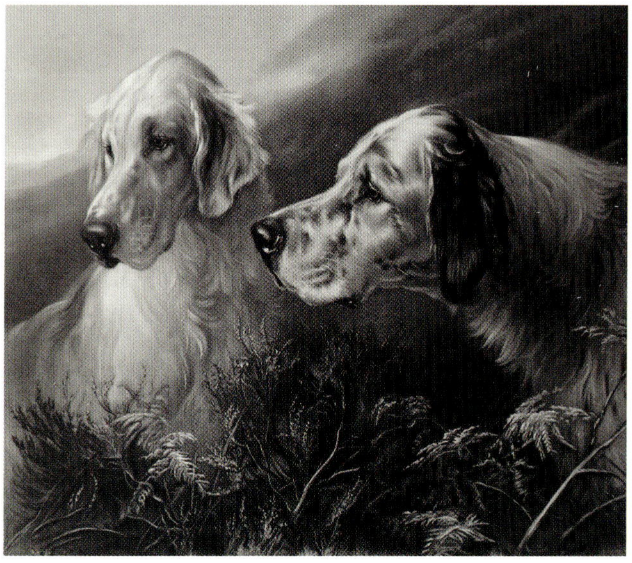

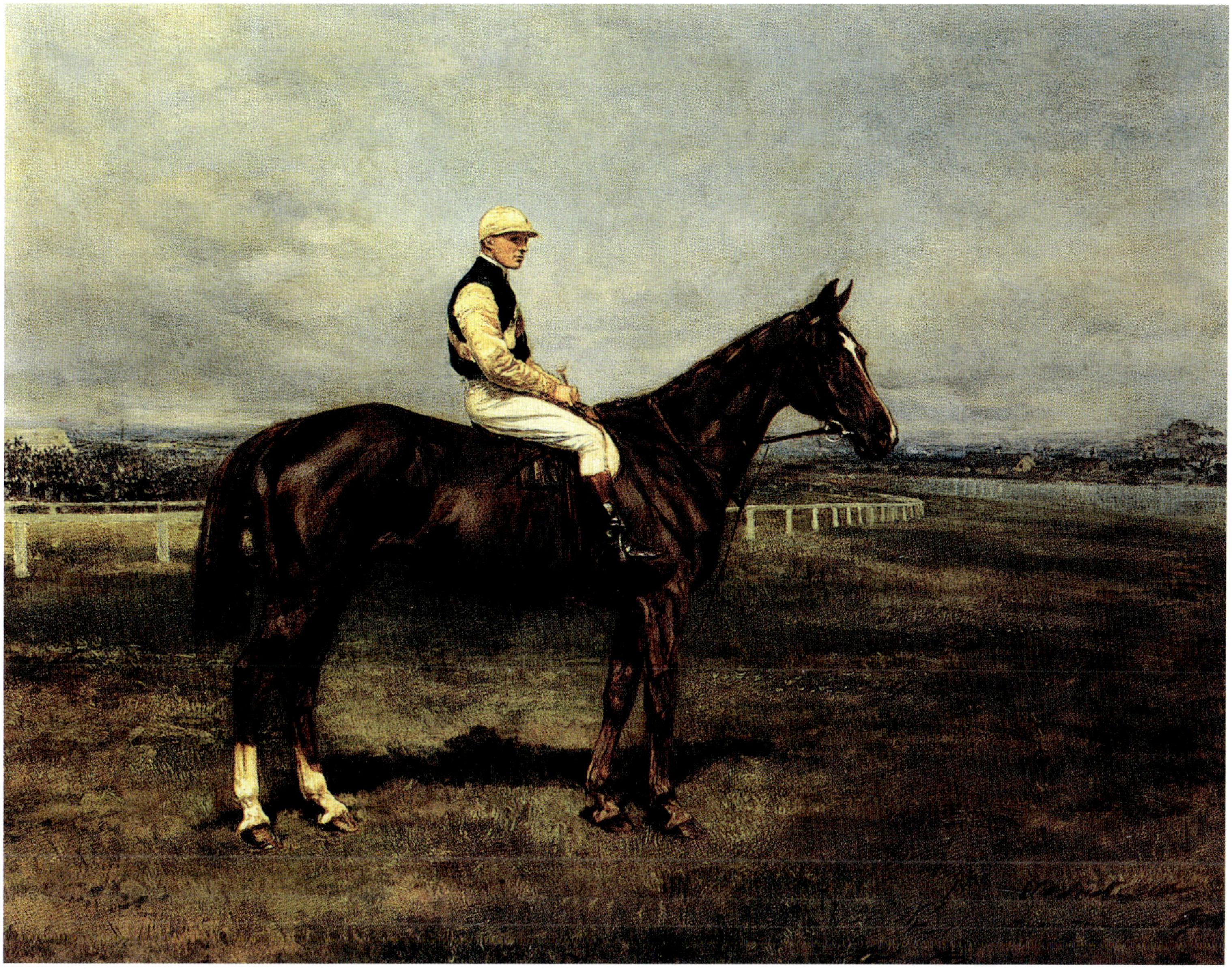

Plate 167: Portrait of "Tich" Mason on "Kirkland", 1905
Heywood Hardy. Oil on canvas. 69 x 86cm. Private Collection

Racehorses

Hardy painted three winners of the Grand National: "Kirkland" (Plate 167), winner in 1905 with Frank "Tich" Mason; Glenside (Plate 168), winner in 1911 with Jack Anthony; and "Why Not?", winner of the race in 1894.

Owner Frank Bibby and jockey Frank "Tich" Mason came close to winning the Grand National several times; Kirkland was fourth in 1903 and second in 1904. They finally won the race in 1905; Frank Bibby was so eager to take all possible precautions that he paid Mason £300 not to ride for a fortnight before the race at Aintree, in case he might fall and injure himself.

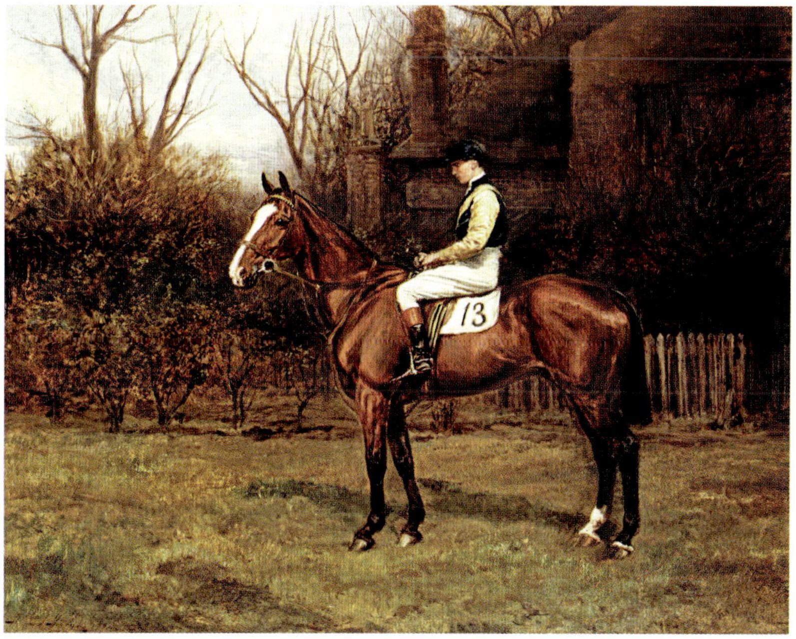

Plate 168: Glenside, Winner of the 1911 Grand National, 1911
Heywood Hardy. Oil on canvas. 45.7 x 55.9cm. Private Collection

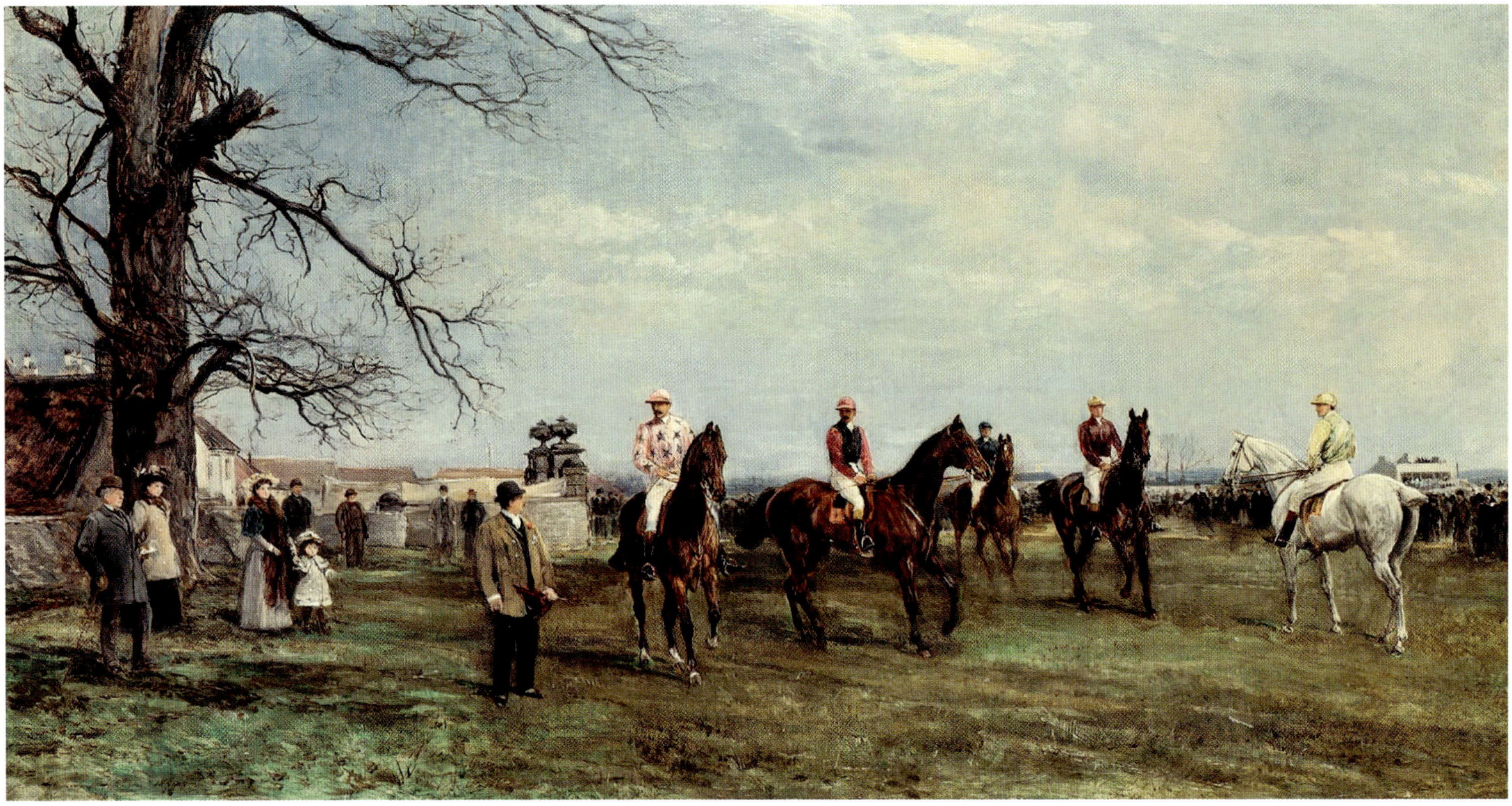

Plate 169: The Start of Catterick Steeplechase, 1894
Heywood Hardy. Oil on canvas. 49.5 x 91.5cm. Private Collection

Jack Anthony was fortunate to win on Frank Bibby's "Glenside" in the 1911 Grand National; Anthony got the ride because Mason broke his leg shortly before the race. Glenside won by 20 lengths.

Hardy may have won the Grand National commissions through his hunting connections. Captain C.H. Fenwick, owner of "Why Not?", at 13 one of the oldest winners of the Grand National, hunted with the Cottesmore. And Frank Bibby, owner of the Bibby shipping line of Liverpool, was Master of the Shropshire Hunt 1898-1900.

Hardy's painting of the *Start of Catterick Steeplechase* (Plate 169) in 1894 shows the five runners in the "Catterick Steeplechase Plate of 30 sovereigns", a race of two and a half miles. From left to right the horses are: "Highway", a bay gelding ridden by his owner, Mr J.B. Dale; "Forlorn Hope" (probably), a brown gelding ridden by his owner, Mr W. L. Christie; "Firefly", a chestnut gelding ridden by his owner, Mr R. Johnson; "Cast off" (probably), a brown gelding owned by Mr W. Hardcastle and ridden by Mr Menzies; and "Bridesmaid", a grey mare ridden by her owner Mr Illingworth.

As the race was for amateur riders, the jockey's colours were not recorded so there is uncertainty about which of the two brown geldings in the picture is "Forlorn Hope" and which is "Cast off".

The race was for horses " ... which have been fairly hunted during the current season with the Marquis of Zetland's, the Bedale, the Hurworth, South Durham or Cleveland Foxhounds". Although there were only five runners it seems to have been an eventful race. The strong favourite, "Highway", led all the way and won the race by a length. "Firefly" finished second but was disqualified for following the wrong course, so "Bridesmaid" was awarded second place. "Forlorn Hope" fell and "Cast off" refused. The painting was probably commissioned by the winner of the race, Mr James Dale of Carlbury Hall, Piercebridge; Mr and Mrs Dale sometimes followed the Marquis of Zetland's hounds.

The painting shows the horses coming towards the starter, who holds a red flag, before they turn for the start and race towards the spectators and the white flag man who is in the distance, to the left of the grey mare "Bridesmaid".

Hardy's last exhibit at the Royal Academy was *In Training* (1919), a string of racehorses at exercise.

Shooting Parties

Heywood Hardy painted several shooting parties, particularly those associated with Sir Frederick Milbank. Hardy participated in grouse shoots at Barningham Park and Thorp Perrow in the 1890s. He was in distinguished company:

> During the past fortnight Sir Frederick and Lady Milbank have been entertaining at Barningham Park for the grouse shooting. Prince and Princess Ferdinand Radziwill and Princess Margaret Radziwill, General Herbert and Mrs Herbert, Mr Milbank, M.P., Mr Fred. Milbank, Capt. and Mrs Forester, Mr and Mrs Dale, Mr Rouse, Colonel Worsley, Mr Copley, Mr Alfred Pease, M.P., Mr Heywood Hardy, &c. The sport has been good, though the high winds interfered with it.[232]

Plate 172 (opposite page, bottom): Grouse Shooting: After the Drive, 1901
Heywood Hardy. Oil on canvas. 83.8 x 106.7cm. Private Collection

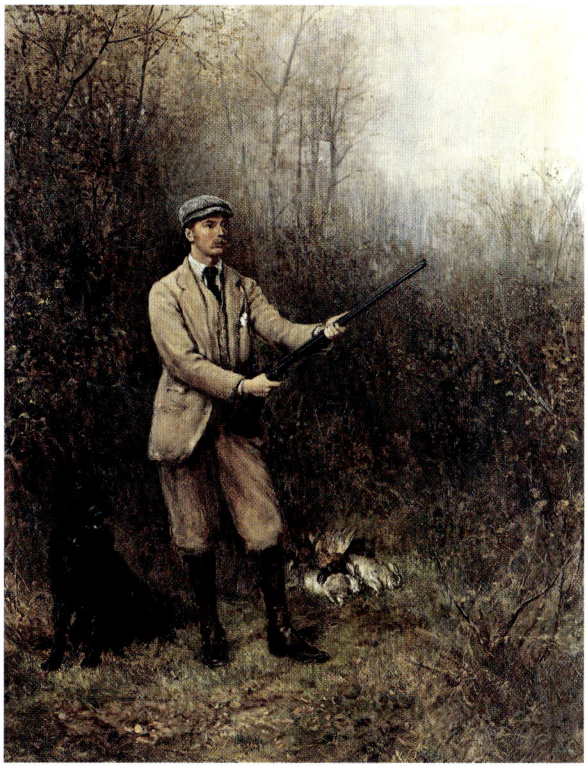

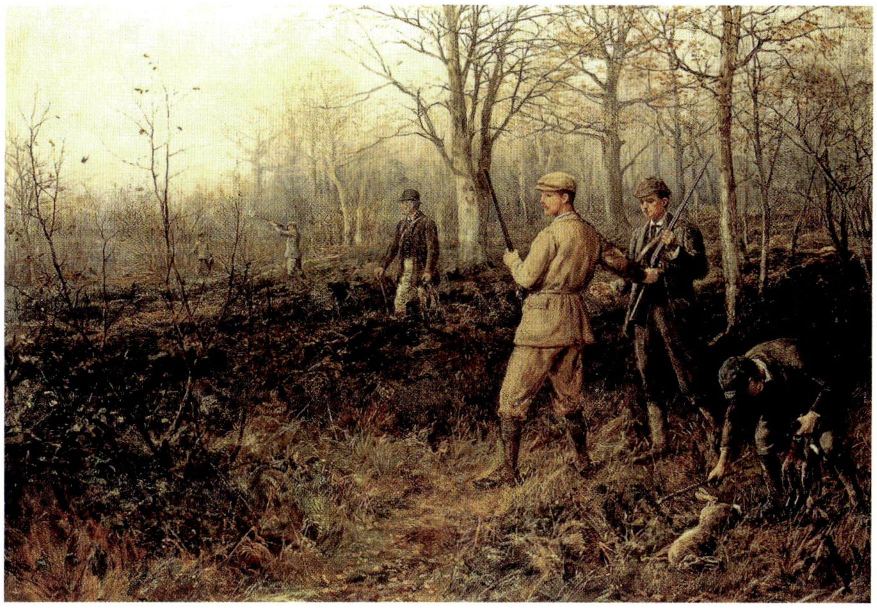

Plate 170 (left): A Waiting Gun, 1890
Heywood Hardy. Oil on canvas. 101.6 x 76.2cm. Private Collection

Plate 171 (above): The Shooting Party, 1892
Heywood Hardy. Oil on canvas. 76 x 108.5cm. Private Collection[233]

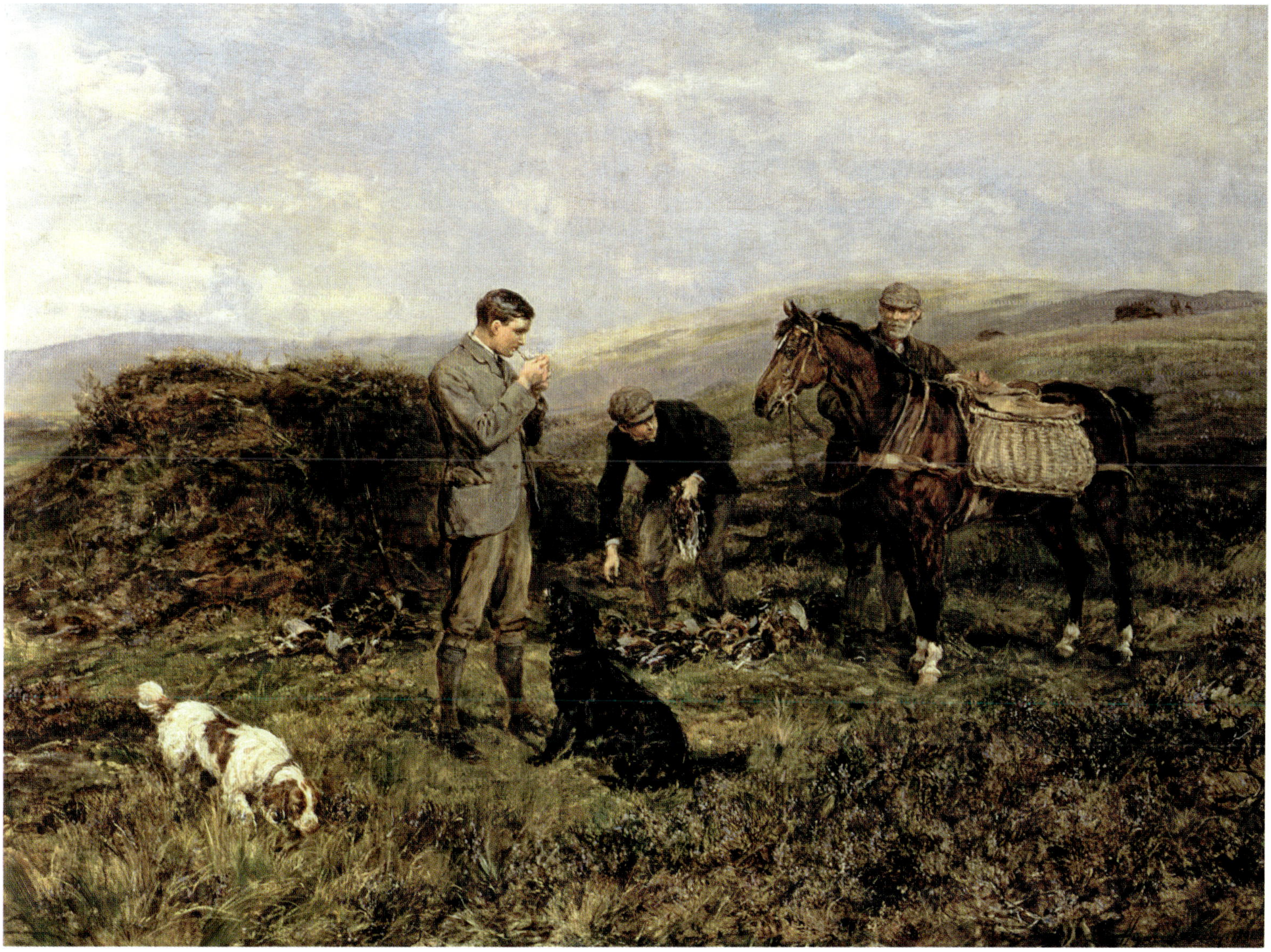

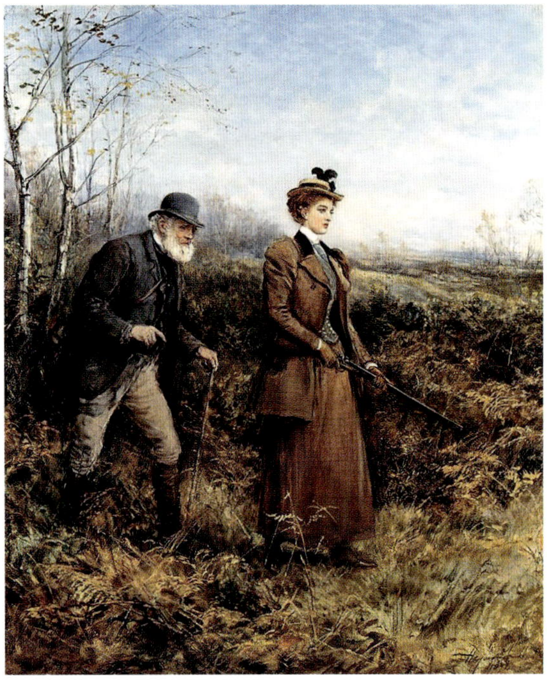

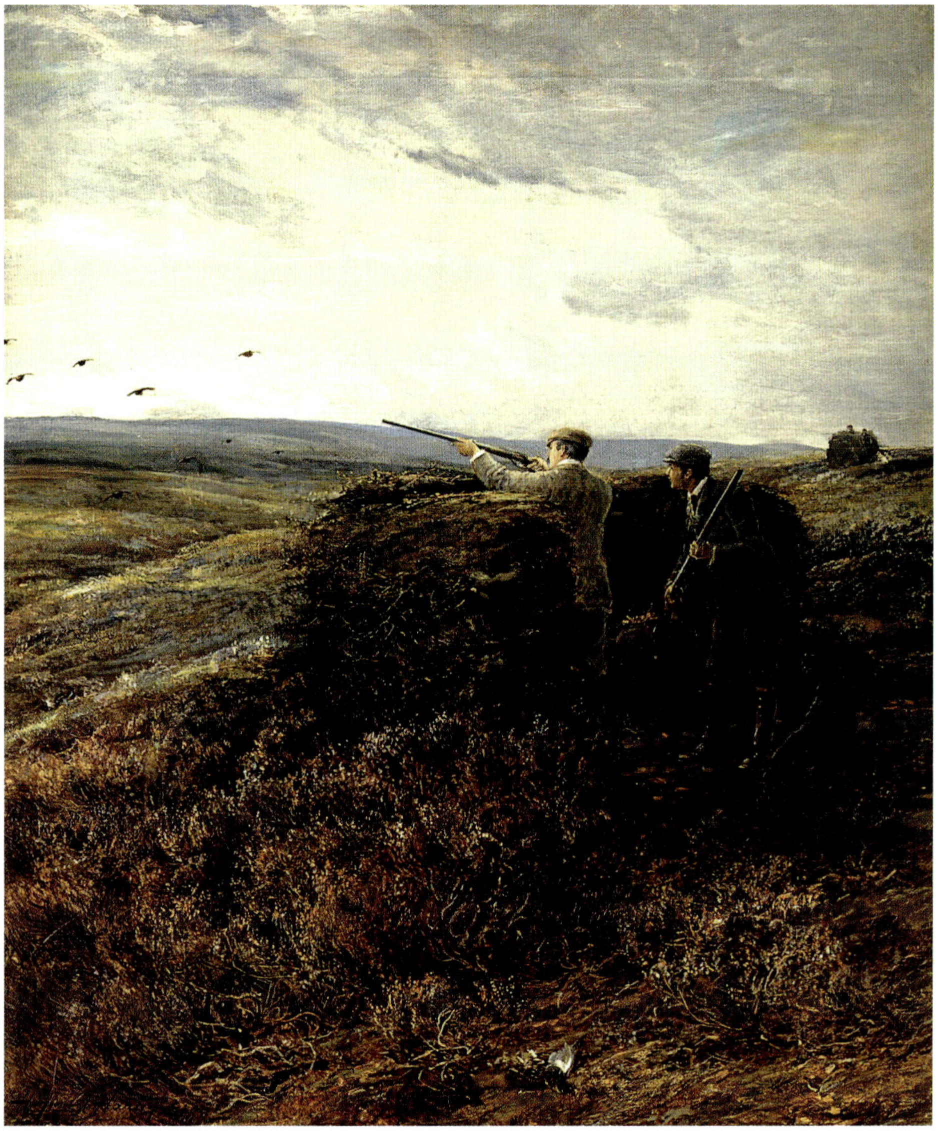

Plate 173 (above): The Gun Shot, 1894
Heywood Hardy. Oil on canvas. 77.5 x 64.1cm.
Private Collection

Plate 174 (right: The Grouse Shoot, 1898 [234]
Heywood Hardy. Oil on canvas. 77.5 x 64.5cm.
Private Collection

Plate 175 (below): A Figure Out Shooting with his Dog
Heywood Hardy. Oil on canvas. 48.3 x 91.5cm.
Private Collection

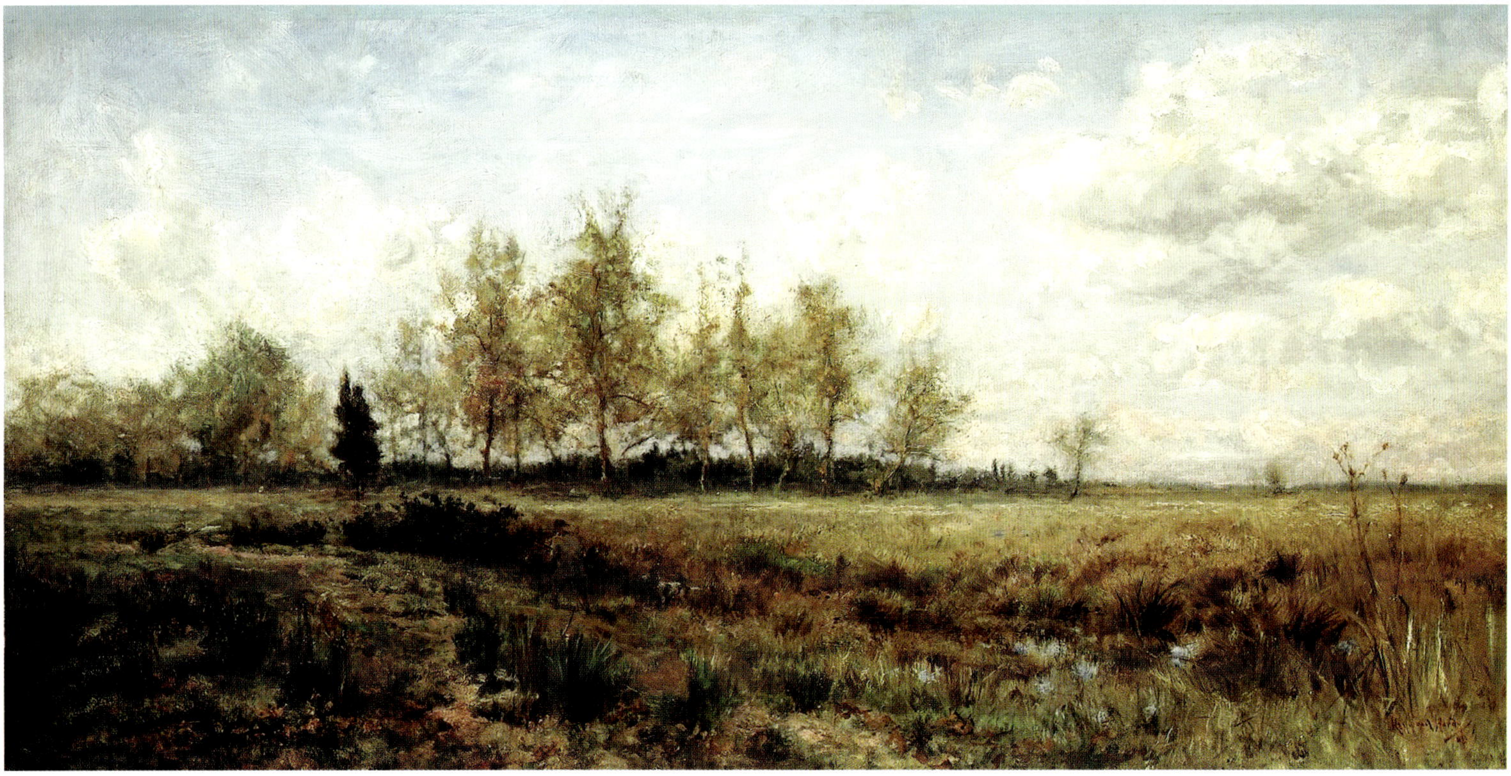

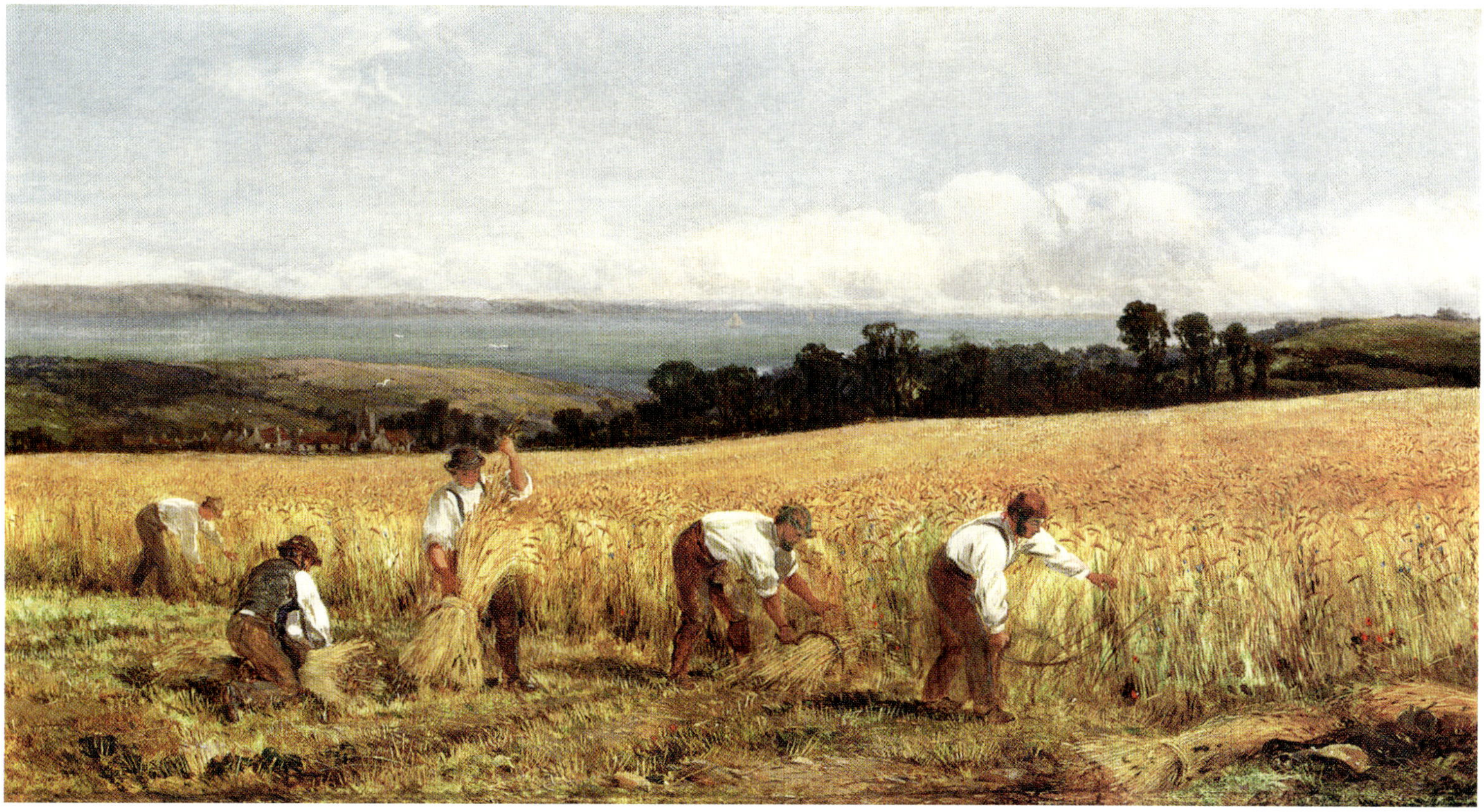

Grouse shooting. Reports from the moors. Barningham Moors. On Tuesday Sir Frederick Milbank's party shot over Barningham Moors. The party included General the Hon. Herbert, Mr G.H.V Milbank, Capt. Forrester [*sic*], Mr J.B. Dale, Mr Heywood Hardy, and the Rev. J.P. Hales. The party enjoyed good sport, and bagged 160 brace of grouse. On Thursday, with his unfailing generosity, Sir Frederick sent out to each of his tenants three brace of grouse. To all his upper servants he gave three brace of grouse, to all servants staying in the house three brace, and to all other servants at Barningham Park two brace each. This has been the annual custom of Sir Frederick ever since he came into possession of Barningham Moor.[235]

Shortly after this shoot, Heywood Hardy wounded a hare while shooting in Ireland on the Earl of Zetland's estate. When he went to pick it up he had the impression that it "looked at him with imploring eyes, tears trickling down its face". He was so much moved that he never shot again; he sold his gun and bought a pair of binoculars.[236]

There is an impressionistic treatment of the landscape in *A Figure Out Shooting with his Dog* (Plate 175). *An Extensive Landscape with a View Towards Mountains* (Plate 177) was painted with broad, free brushstrokes near the Earl of Zetland's estate in Connemara. Hardy painted many harvesting scenes; *A Golden Harvest* (Plate 176) dates from 1884.

Plate 176 (above): A Golden Harvest, 1884
Heywood Hardy. Oil on canvas. 42.2 x 79.3cm. Private Collection

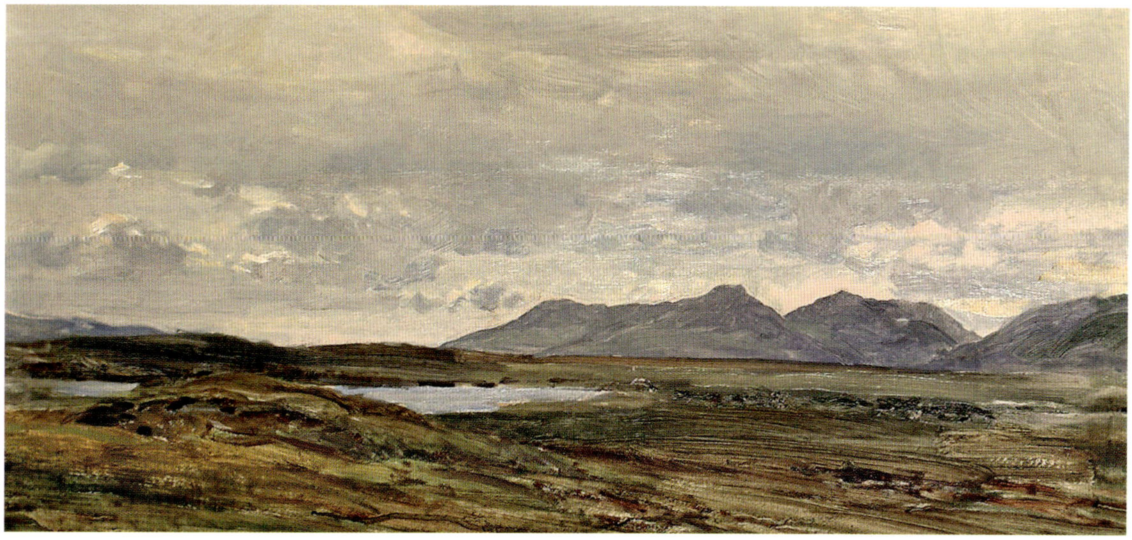

Plate 177 (right): An Extensive Landscape with a View Towards Mountains
Heywood Hardy. Oil on panel.[237] 39.7 x 54.7cm. Private Collection

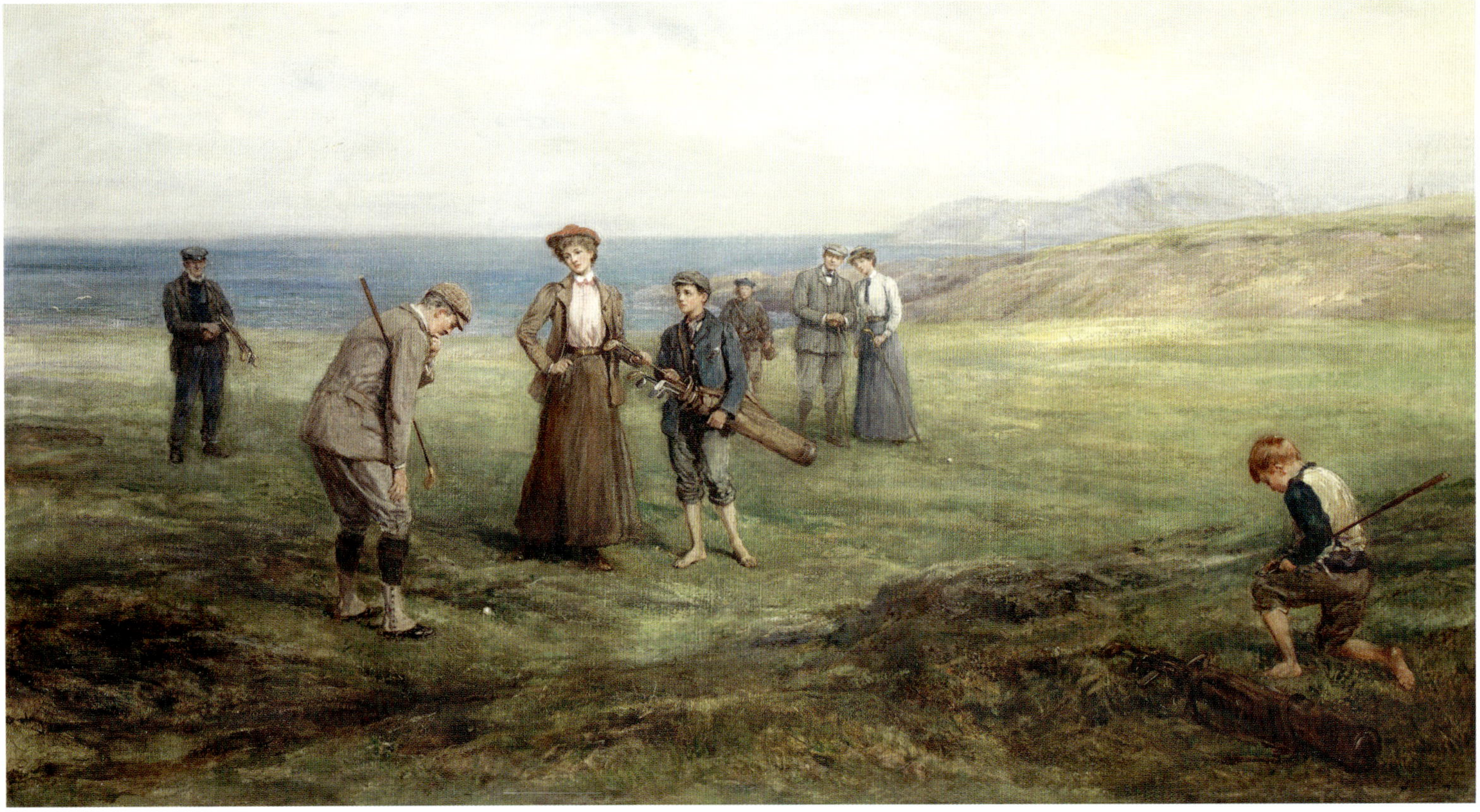

Plate 178: A Doubtful Lie, 1900
Heywood Hardy. Oil on canvas. 101.6 x 179.1cm. Private Collection
The scene is at North Berwick Golf Course in Scotland; the island of Craigleith in the Firth of Forth is in the distance.

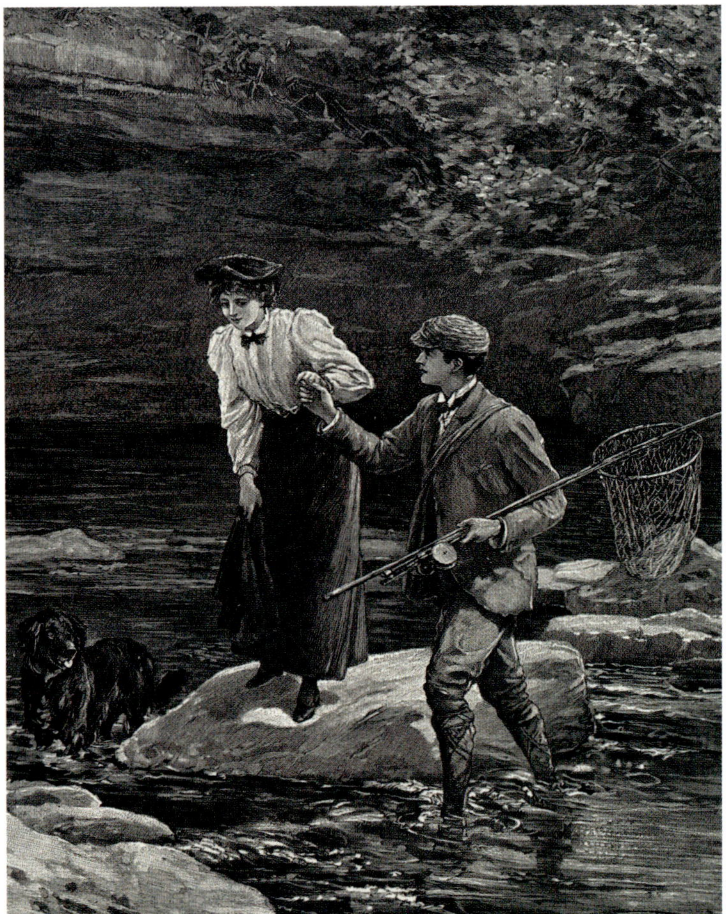

Other Sports

Heywood Hardy painted a few pictures of golfers and anglers. George Glennie was probably the most successful golfer of the Royal Blackheath Club, the oldest golf club in England, formed in 1608. Heywood Hardy's painting, *George Glennie Putting at Blackheath with a Putting Cleek* (1881) (Plate 180) shows Glennie on the first green in a foursome with his caddie, Dick Steer. A red coat was obligatory when playing on the Heath. The picture was presented to Blackheath Golf Club by Sir John Aird in honour of George Glennie at a dinner on 27 October 1884, at the Ship Hotel in Greenwich. Glennie was a civil engineer, born in Glasgow. Aird was a civil engineering contractor who commissioned Heywood Hardy's *Tipping* (Plate 114), his exhibit at the Royal Academy in 1878, which showed how horses were used in railway construction.

Hardy's *A Doubtful Lie* (Plate 178), showing golfers with their caddies, was exhibited at the Royal Academy in 1900. (The corresponding photogravure was entitled *A Difficult Lie.*) Hardy's composition, which has a caddie kneeling in the foreground, emphasises that some caddies were barefoot in 1900.

Hardy's pictures of fishing included *The Gentle Art* (1896),[238] *Salmon Fishing* (1895) and *A Friend in Need* (1899) (Plate 179).

Plate 179: A Friend in Need (detail)
After Heywood Hardy. From Die Gartenlaube. 1899. p.712.

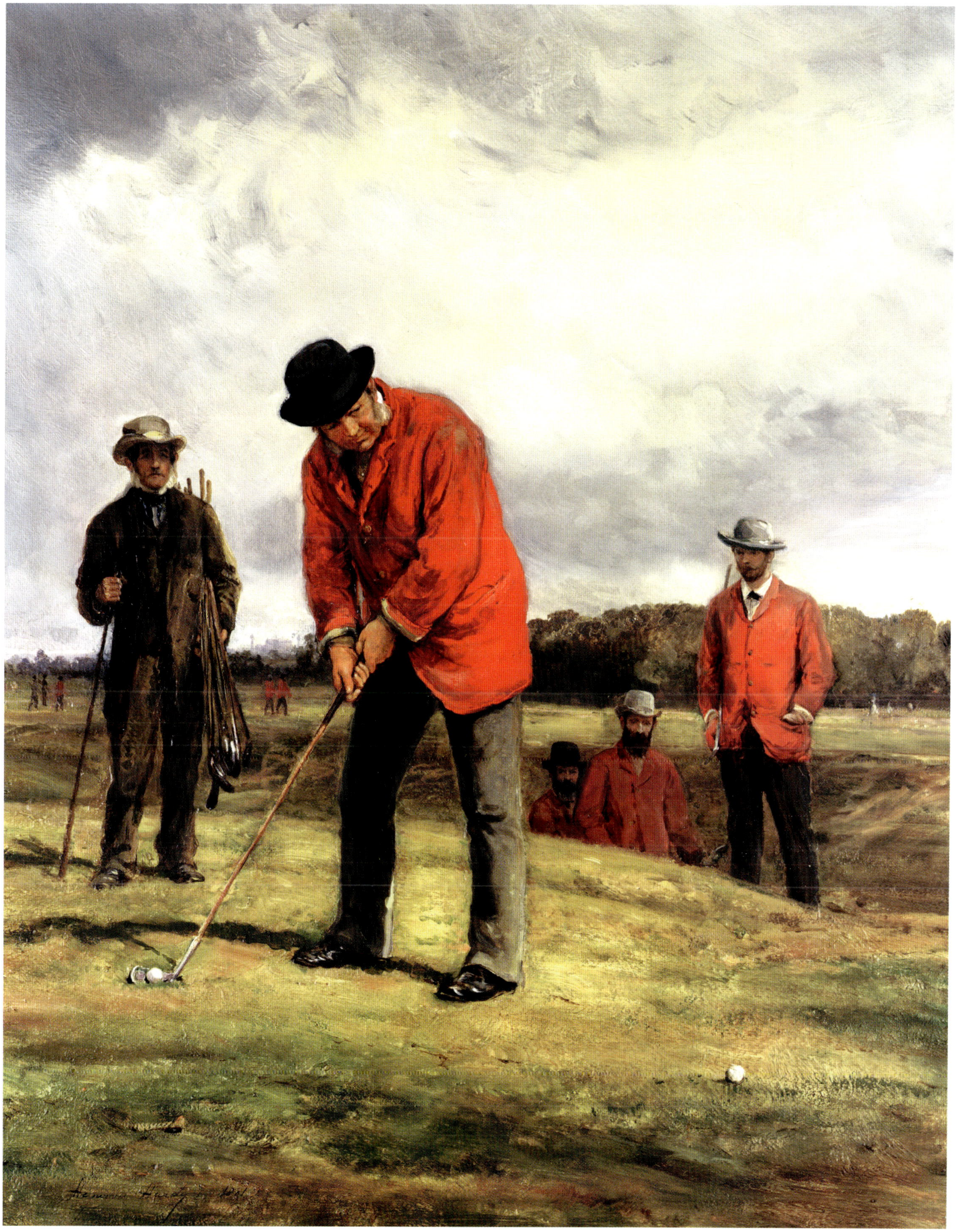

Plate 180: George Glennie Putting at Blackheath with a Putting Cleek, 1881
Heywood Hardy**.** Oil on canvas. 92 x 71.6cm. Private Collection

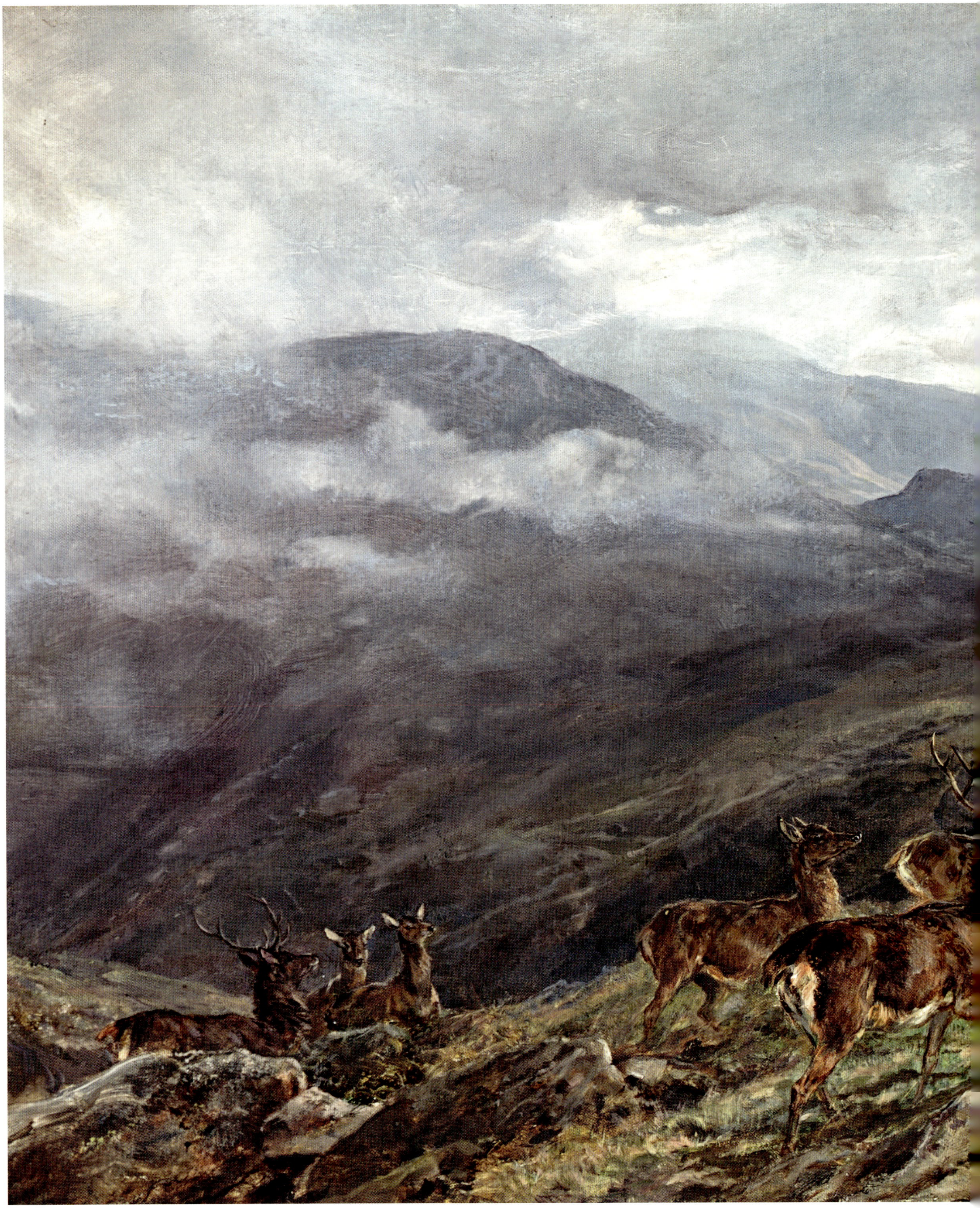

Plate 181: Deer in Mountains
Heywood Hardy. Oil on canvas. 63 x 101.5cm. Russell-Cotes Art Gallery & Museum

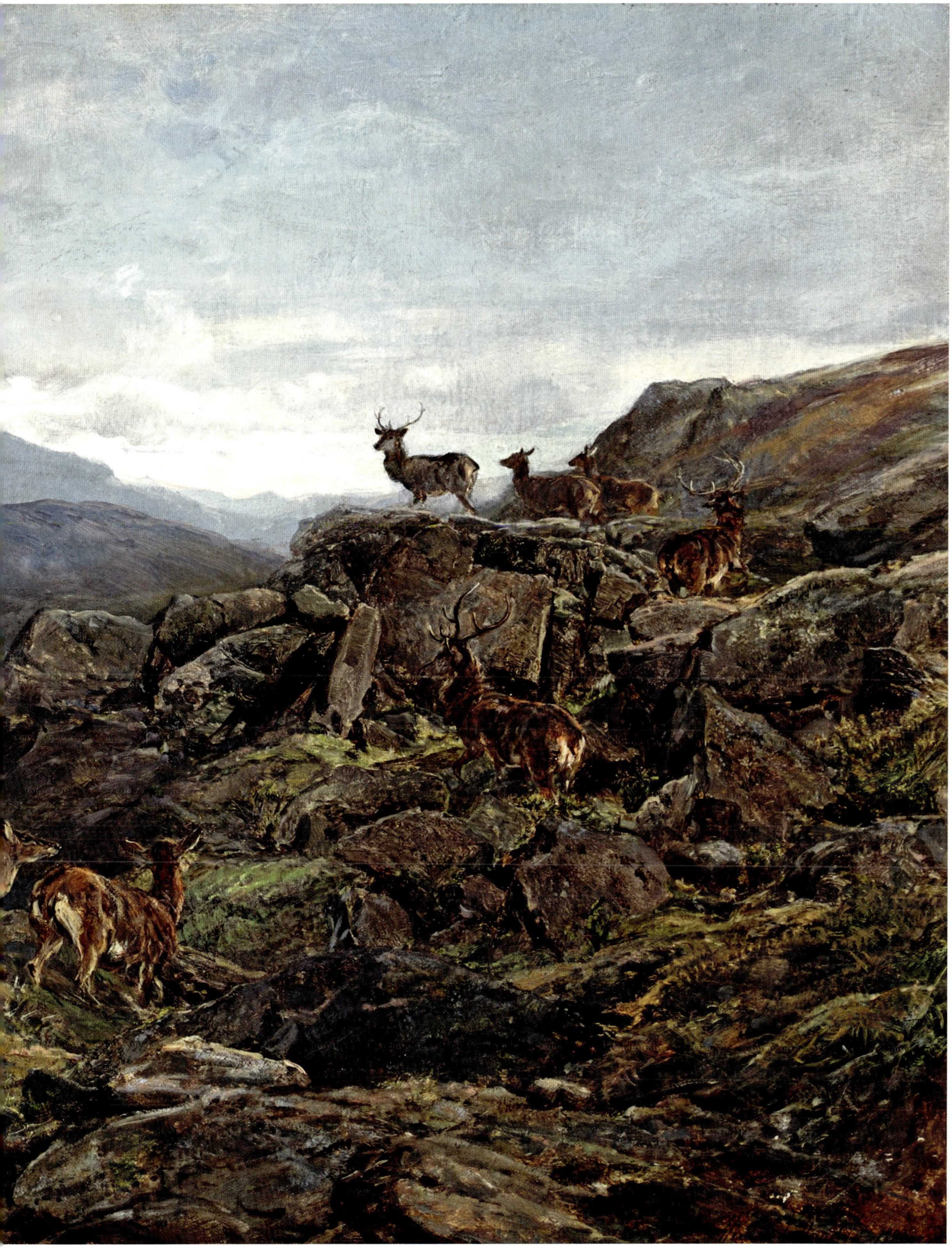

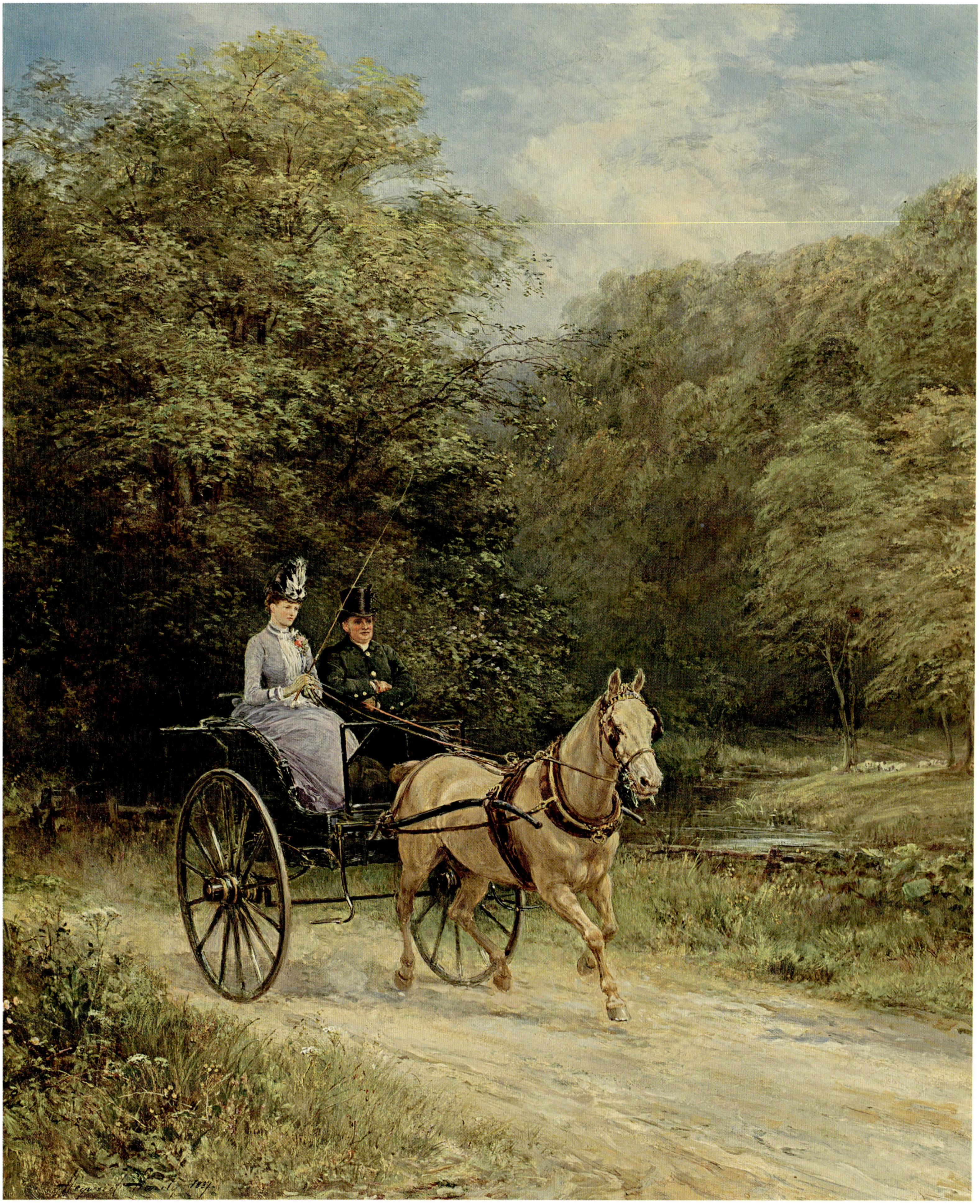

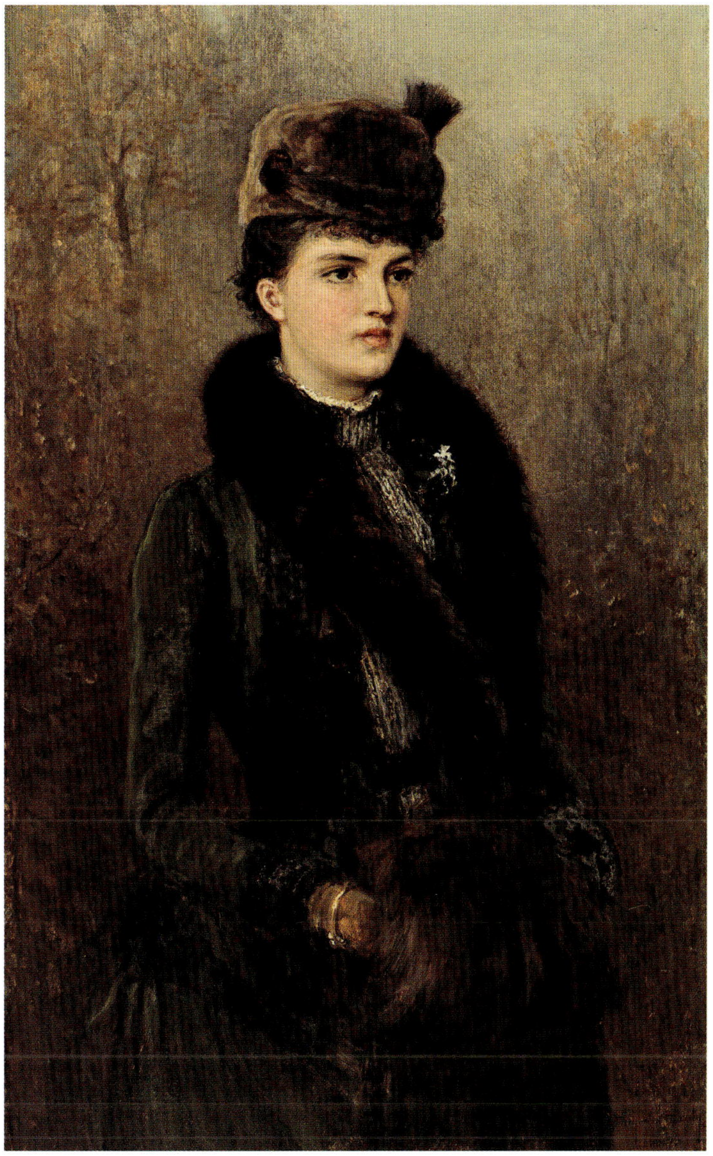

Plate 182 (opposite page): Lady Ida Sitwell in a Pony and Trap, 1887
Heywood Hardy. Oil on board.
56 x 46cm.

Plate 183 (right): Portrait of Lady Ida Sitwell in a Fur Cap, 1888
Heywood Hardy. Oil on board.
40.5 x 24.5cm.

Portraits

Most of the portraits Heywood Hardy painted during the 1880s were equestrian portraits of families associated with fox hunting, often in the north of England, but there were a few exceptions. He painted two portraits of Lady Ida Sitwell (née Denison) following her marriage at the age of 17 to Sir George Sitwell in 1886. Lady Ida was a daughter of the 1st Earl of Londesborough and a granddaughter of Henry Somerset, 7th Duke of Beaufort, who was descended from the Plantagenets. As a wedding present, Sir George commissioned a portrait of *Lady Ida Sitwell in a Pony and Trap* (Plate 182). Hardy also painted a small portrait, *Lady Ida Sitwell in a Fur Cap* (Plate 183), which is in the Red Dining Room at Renishaw Hall. From correspondence between Hardy and Sir George Sitwell, it seems that the painting of the pony and trap was completed in the summer of 1887 (Hardy was paid in July). Hardy wrote that he would visit Renishaw again in the Autumn of 1887, possibly to paint the portrait of *Lady Ida Sitwell in a Fur Cap* (Hardy was paid for the portrait in March 1888).[239]

According to Lady Ida's son, Sir Sacheverell Sitwell, his mother "had only met his father twice at luncheon before their marriage; within a few days of the wedding she ran home to her parents, but was firmly sent back to her husband".[240] However, contrary to some accounts, it seems that they were happy in the first years of the marriage.

Heywood Hardy's 1887 portrait was the first of several of Lady Ida Sitwell commissioned by Sir George. William Blake Richmond painted a fine portrait of Lady Ida with a zither on her lap, an instrument that Osbert Sitwell said she had never seen before.[241] But perhaps Heywood Hardy had taken his zither to Renishaw when he painted Lady Ida's portraits and she had taken a liking to the instrument. Osbert Sitwell thought the painting by Richmond was "hideous" and said his father, Sir George, considered cutting out the head to place in a small oval frame and burning the rest.[242]

Correspondence between Sir George and Hardy in August 1887 indicates that they had discussed the possibility that Hardy's friend, Hubert von Herkomer, might be commissioned to paint portraits of the Sitwells. Hardy wrote about making arrangements for Sir George to visit Herkomer and sent directions about travelling to Bushey where Herkomer lived. Hardy and von Herkomer were founder members of the Royal Society of Painter-Etchers and the Royal Society of Portrait Painters. They also shared an interest in playing the zither; Herkomer painted a picture entitled *A Zither-Evening with my Students in my Studio* (1901).

CHAPTER SIX

Heywood Hardy: Societies, Music and Artistic Children

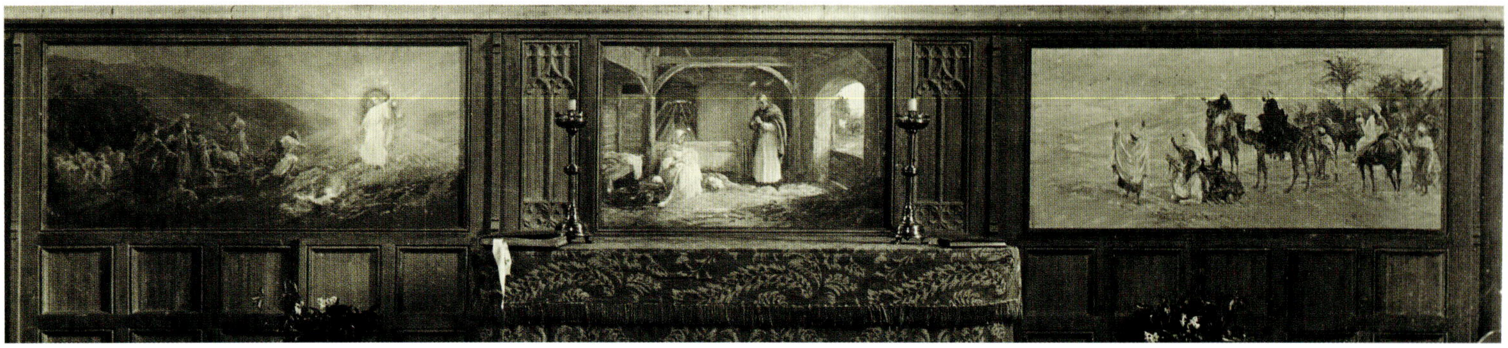

Returning to Sussex: Altar Pieces at Clymping and Haslar

In 1909 Heywood Hardy returned to live in Sussex, not far from Chichester where he was born; he moved to "The Rosery" in East Preston. Next to his house there was a thatched flintstone barn that he used as a studio.[243] His house was a few minutes walk from a sand and shingle beach, which is still used for horse riding at low tide; even today the scene evokes Hardy's paintings.

He kept a studio at 10 Abbey Road until at least 1921, but this might have been primarily for his daughter, Nina, or his granddaughter, Daphne Maugham, who completed her studies at the Slade School of Art in 1922.

From 1925 to 1928 (by which time he was 86 years old) Heywood produced a series of eight paintings encased by oak panels for the Church of St Mary at Clymping (Plates 184 and 185), which is about five miles from where he lived at East Preston. The paintings were dedicated in commemoration of the seventh centenary of the church by the Archdeacon of Chichester on 3 February, 1925.

The paintings are still in the church, most of them in the north transept. Originally, three of the panels were in the beautiful thirteenth-century, Early English chancel, beneath the lancet windows (see Plate 184). The setting for the Nativity seems to be a Sussex barn or cowshed with tie beams, struts and queen post; outside there are grazing cattle – perhaps Sussex reds. The last painting in the series, an allegory on "I am with you all the days until the end of the world", depicts several local people: war wounded, scouts, a farmer with his dog, and his friend Rev. E.F. Leech, the rector of Clymping, were all portrayed in contemporary dress in the Sussex countryside beside the river Arun, with Arundel Castle in the background. The girl who is shown receiving Christ's blessing was a member of the church congregation until the 1980s.

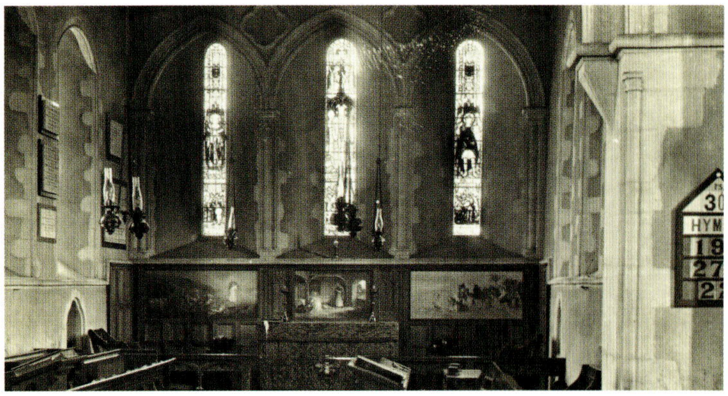

Heywood's last major commission was an altarpiece, *The Healing of Blind Bartimaeus,* painted in 1928 for St Luke's Church at the Royal Naval Hospital Haslar at Gosport. The painting is now in the baptistery of the church.[244] Hardy charged a nominal sum of £50 for the work, most of which was raised through an appeal in the *Royal Naval Medical Journal* in 1928 and from residents of Haslar.

Heywood Hardy remained at the The Rosery in East Preston until 1930, when he moved to live with his daughter, Mrs Curtis, at Epsom. He died there at the age of 90 on 20 January 1933. His ashes were buried at Clymping Church.

Family, Friends and Societies

Heywood Hardy was a member of several societies, but was not elected a member of the Royal Academy. His thoughts about the Royal Academy were published in the *Pall Mall Gazette* in 1886. At the time, the *Gazette* was agitating for reform of the Academy. Several artists had questioned the privilege of Royal Academicians to have up to eight of their pictures shown at the annual exhibition, even though not all availed themselves of the privilege. Critics of the Royal Academy argued that much of the best space "on the line" (a dado rail, positioned about eight feet from the ground, on which the paintings were most easily viewed by the jostling crowds) was occupied by large pictures painted by Academicians that were of little interest to the public. There was a suggestion that the number of such pictures exhibited in the best places should be limited in some way or that there should be a national exhibition that was more representative of British art.

Plate 184 (left): St Mary's Church, Clymping. Ca. 1930. Photograph by John White & Son, Littlehampton.

Plate 185 (above): Paintings by Heywood Hardy in St Mary's Church, Clymping. Ca. 1930. Photograph by John White & Son, Littlehampton.

Plate 186 (right): A Private View at the Royal Academy, 1881, 1883
William Powell Frith. Oil on canvas.
60 x 114cm. Private Collection

Plate 187 (below left): Study of a Lion
Heywood Hardy. Pencil on paper.
23.5 x 22cm. Private Collection

Plate 188 (below right): Sidi Ahmed ben Avuda and the Holy Lion, 1881
Heywood Hardy. Oil on canvas,
221 x 153.4cm. Private Collection

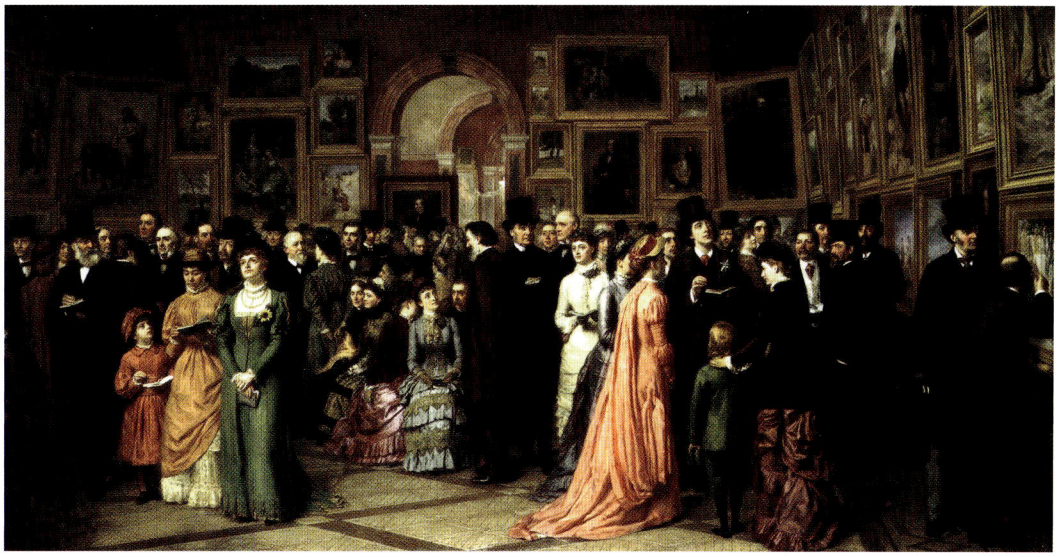

In response to a request from the *Gazette*, Heywood Hardy gave a frank reply, encouraging young painters:

> *In answer to your communication I can only echo Mr. Walter Crane's letter of the 20th inst. I have no hope of any real reform in the Academy. Nearly all its members have in their turn protested against its management, before they were elected – after which all action has ceased. I have no personal feeling. I am only answering your question as to my views frankly. I heartily support Messrs. Holman Hunt, George Clausen, and Walter Crane, in their proposed national exhibition. I do not grudge the Royal Academicians their good fortune, but I feel certain that if the strong young painters of England want to assert themselves they must not wait for the reform of the Royal Academy; they must make a way for themselves. They have the press and a great part of the picture-loving public on their side, and if they are true to themselves they have nothing to fear. They only want the courage to wait and combine and they must win.*[245]

Throughout his career Hardy seemed to have little trouble in getting his pictures accepted for the annual Royal Academy exhibitions or to have his pictures exhibited in good positions. For example, *Grouse shooting*, his 1893 exhibit, was shown "on the line", one of only two painters of sporting art who had that privilege.[246] His exhibit in 1881, *Sidi Ahmed ben Avuda and the Holy Lion* (Plate 188), though not exhibited "on the line", was hung in the largest and grandest gallery of Burlington House, Gallery III. It is the largest picture on the left in *A Private View at the Royal Academy, 1881* (1883) (Plate 186), painted by William Powell Frith. Plate 187 shows a preparatory drawing for "The Holy Lion".

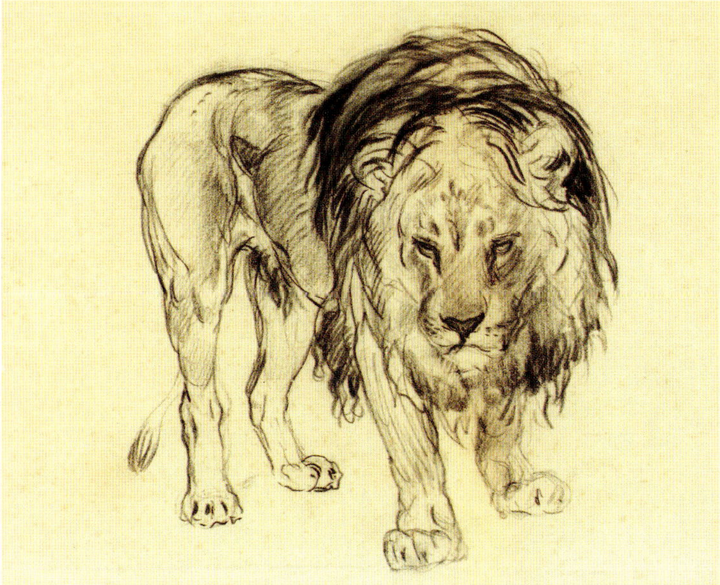

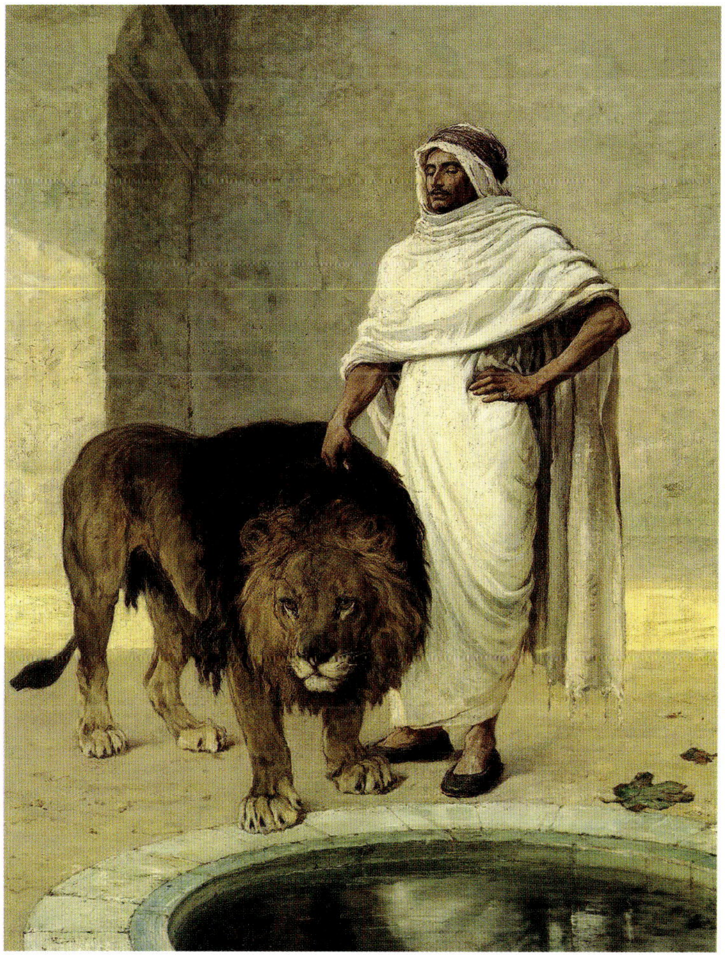

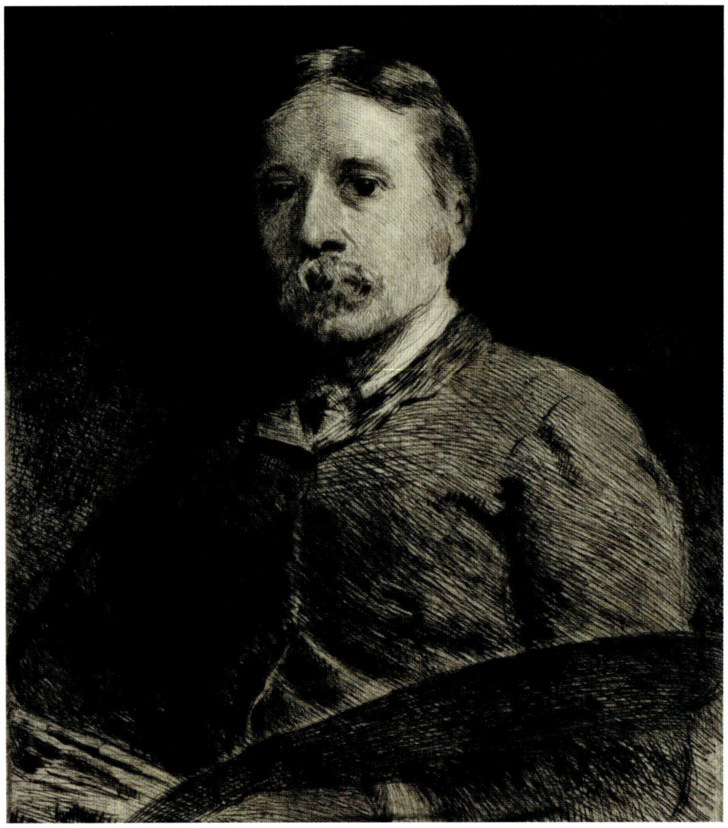

Plate 189: Portrait of Heywood Hardy, 1884
Frank Holl. Dry point. Ashmolean Museum, Oxford

William Agnew, the art dealer who helped Heywood Hardy's early career, also features in Frith's painting; he is the bare-headed gentleman with white whiskers just to the right of the Archbishop of York who is in the centre, wearing a top hat. Oscar Wilde is on the right, holding a catalogue and looking up at a picture.[247]

Though not elected to the Royal Academy, Hardy was rumoured to be among the proposed candidates. In 1881 an apparently well-informed source mentioned Hardy as well as Frank Dicksee, Henry Moore, John Brett, James Archer and C.E. Johnson as favourites for two vacancies at the Academy.[248] In fact, Frank Dicksee and H. Thorneycroft were elected Associates of the Academy on 20 January, and John Brett was elected eight days later.

Another commentator was surprised that Hardy had not been elected:

> The election of Messrs. F. Dicksee and H. Thorneycroft to the position of Associate is not by any means calculated to excite one's ire. As for Mr. Frank Dicksee, he eminently deserved the honour: indeed, he may be said to have won his Associateship when he painted "Harmony." Mr. Thorneycroft, who, like Mr. Dicksee, is young, probably owes his elevation somewhat to honourable family considerations. ... Who is to be next? The list of outsiders might be stronger, but surely Mr. Brett's turn has arrived! Is he for ever to be kept out because he happens to be eccentric in his views of landscape-painting? And Heywood Hardy? How much longer is he to wait? As for Colin Hunter, and Seymour Lucas, and William Hughes—greatest of fruit-painters—their turn must come sooner or later. Meanwhile let us congratulate the Royal Academy on their recent elections.[249]

Heywood Hardy became a member of the Royal Institute of Oil Painters in 1883. In the 1890s Hardy collaborated on several sporting paintings with Frank Walton, who became President of the Royal Institute of Oil Painters in 1898.

Hardy was one of the 24 founder members of the Royal Society of Portrait Painters, established in 1891. The founding members felt that the selection process excluded their work from Royal Academy exhibitions. And he was elected an Associate of the Royal Society of Painters in Water Colours on 16 March 1885.

Francis Haden, James Tissot, Alphonse Legros, Robert Macbeth, Hubert von Herkomer and Heywood Hardy founded the Royal Society of Painter-Etchers in 1880. The society quickly established itself in London and secured royal endorsement (Queen Victoria and Prince Albert both made etchings).

Hardy was commissioned to make etchings of some of his own oil paintings for *The Portfolio* in 1881 and 1885. His etchings were also exhibited at the Dudley Gallery. In 1880 a reviewer noted:

> Mr. Heywood Hardy's etchings "Village Doctor" (288), "Head of a Buffalo" (297) and "Idols of the Home" (620); also the dry-points "Head of a Horse" (36), and "Lion's Head" (52), display marvellous knowledge and most accomplished manipulation. "Old Battersea Bridge" (3I4) is a superb etching, exhibiting the artist's [Whistler's] best qualities, by Mr. Whistler.[250]

Most of Heywood Hardy's etchings were studies of animals – horses and elephants or the deer in Windsor Park. *The Times* commented on his etching at the Royal Academy exhibition: "A head of a lion in dry-point, by Heywood Hardy, has attracted special notice by its finish and force, remarkable in the work of one to whom an etching-needle is a comparatively a new tool". [251]

Frank Holl was elected a member of the Society of Painter-Etchers in 1882; apparently he exhibited only one etching, a portrait of Heywood Hardy (Plate 189).

Hardy was also a member of the Arts Club, which was originally at Hanover Square (next door to the Royal Academy of Music), from 1873 to 1901. He joined in the same year as his cousin, Frederick Daniel Hardy, who was a member until 1888. Heywood's brother, James Hardy, was a member from 1884 to 1888. Heywood was a member of the Hogarth Club (his friend Whistler was also a member).

Heywood Hardy had a wide circle of artist friends, many of whom were members of the Arts Club, including James McNeill Whistler, John Everett Millais, Fred Walker, John Singer Sargent, Frank Holl and Lawrence Alma-Tadema. Hardy was often called "HH" by family and friends. James McNeill Whistler was a

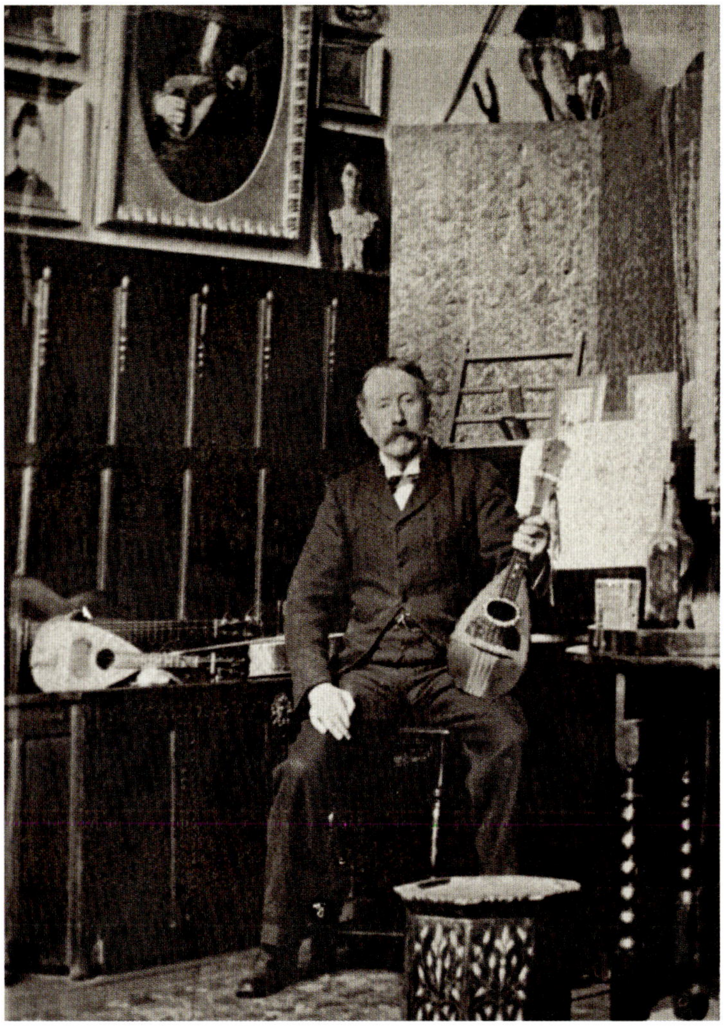

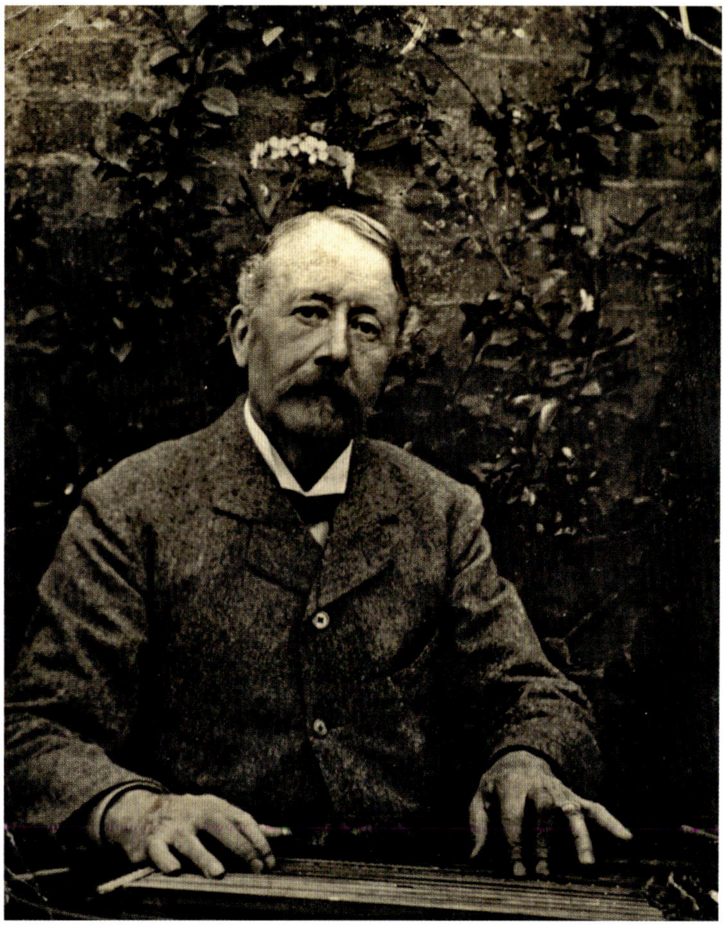

Plates 190 and 191: Heywood Hardy playing the zither (above) and (left) in his studio, with his musical instruments.
PHOTOGRAPHS COURTESY OF DAVID HARDY IVENS

frequent visitor to Heywood Hardy's home in St John's Wood. Hardy's daughter, Mabel ("Beldy"), remembered that when she was eight years old Whistler looked at her drawings and watercolours, giving her some encouraging words: "We shall certainly hear of her one day."

Heywood Hardy took the artistic education of his daughters seriously and gave them marks for their work in drawing and painting. His daughter "Beldy" could remember that when she was a young girl he once asked her to copy a drawing of a sow with her litter of piglets and that she burst into tears when he pointed out that she had forgotten to draw one of the piglets.

Heywood's granddaughter, Mrs Clarisse Farrell, remembered him with great affection. She visited his studio in St John's Wood and played with his other grandchildren in the garden:

> He was such a lovely person and used to keep us all amused by drawing pictures of animals and dragons. He had a good sense of humour, was kind, intelligent, thoughtful and understanding. He was always good with children, was very fond of animals, and enjoyed reading, writing and music. Indeed he was a wonderful man and charming in every way – we all adored him. My mother and her sisters were devoted to him.[252]

Heywood Hardy, the Musician

Heywood was well known amongst his fellow artists for his musical skills (Plates 190 and 191). The artist Charles S. Keene,[253] one of Heywood's musical friends, was a founder member of the Arts Club and the subject of many anecdotes about the institution and its members. In 1878 Keene, one of the principal illustrators for *Punch*, wrote to his close collaborator, Joseph Crawhall:

> *I was at Heywood Hardy's, the animal painter, last Sunday night. He's very clever musically too – plays the penny whistle, the zither (have you heard this instrument? – charming, but difficult). I'm trying to resist the desire to have one – foresee I shall cave in; and he plays the old English guitar exquisitely – the same instrument that the Newcastle dealer had and sent me a sketch. I have a very pretty one in the original case, A.D. 176-, which Hardy is stringing for me.*[254]

Hardy's grandson Alastair Hardy Ivens, whose portrait was painted by Heywood Hardy's daughter, Nina (see Plate 195), remembered him as a good musician who "encouraged us with his enthusiasm to take up the guitar and the mandolin; evenings

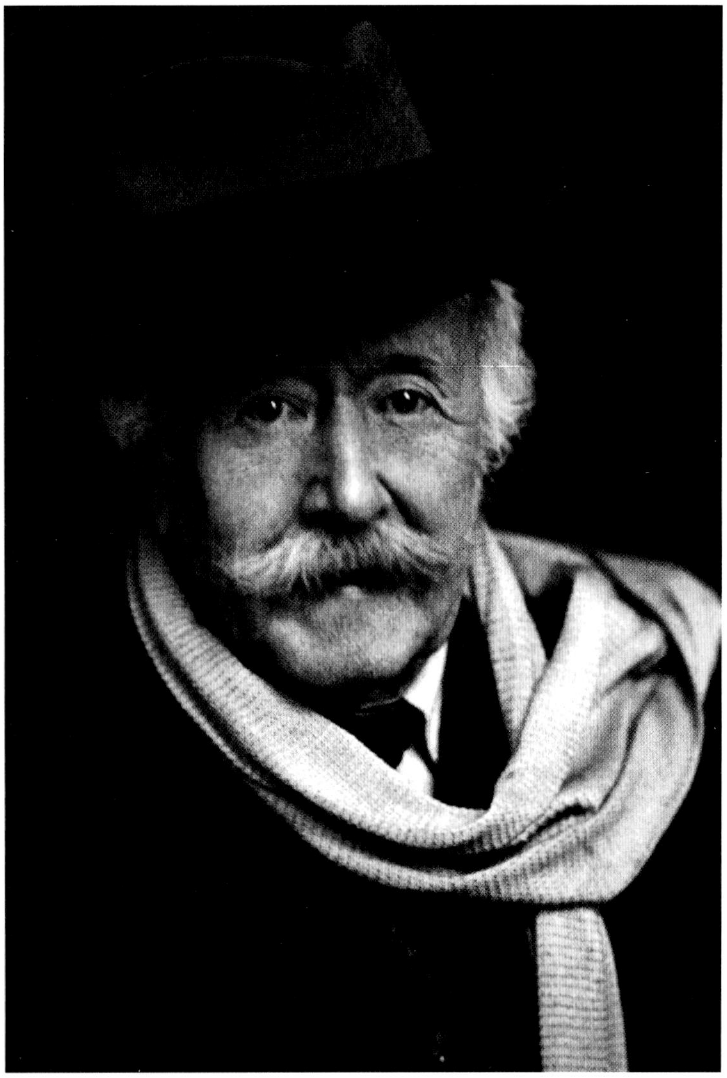

Plate 192: Heywood Hardy. Ca. 1920. Photograph by John White & Sons, Littlehampton. Photograph courtesy of David Hardy Ivens

at his house often rang with the sound of the family orchestra playing old music hall songs and popular French tunes".

Hardy's musical talents were much appreciated by his patrons and friends in the country families of northern England. He took part in musical entertainments that the Milbank family enjoyed in Yorkshire, such as the:

> Concert in the Reading Room at Snape, in aid of the funds of the Institute, by Lady Milbank. There was a capital attendance, and those who took part in a first class programme were:— Vocalists, Miss Cookson, Mr. Dundas, Mr. Wilson, and Mr. Heywood Hardy; and instrumentalists, Lady Milbank, Miss Milbank, the Misses Pease, and Mr. Hardy.[255]

And again:

> At Christmas 1897 Captain and Mrs Forester gave a concert at Cresswell Hall, inviting over 200 parishioners. Among those present were Captain Forester, Mrs. Forester, Mrs. De Capell Brooke, the Misses de Capell Brooke, Mr. Spofforth, Mr. Heywood Hardy, ... The Ashington Orchestral Band opended the concert with "Life on the Ocean Wave". Miss de Capeli Brooke charmingly sang the "Skye Boat Song" and the "Bunch of Cowslips", while Mr. Heywood Hardy greatly amused the audience with his humorous "West Country Love Song", and the song of "The Plough Boy."[256]

An account of late-Victorian entertainment in the village hall at Snape in 1897 noted Heywood Hardy's contribution; he played the zither, mandolin and English guitar. And his humorous songs were much appreciated:

> Mr Heywood Hardy, who is a great favourite at Snape, followed with "Betsy Varing," whose whimsical cry, "Drat them rheumatics, What's caught in damp attics," raised the risible faculties of the audience to the highest pitch, and fairly brought down the house. There was a loud demand for an encore.
>
> A humorous recitation in the Yorkshire dialect having been given by Mr Wilson, Mr Hardy played two soft and pleasing airs on the zither; after which the Hon. John Dundas sang "True unto Death," and, being encored followed with the pretty song "Turnham Toll" ...
>
> A guitar solo, by Mr Hardy, in imitation of the Portuguese mandolin players, was followed by "Close to the Threshold," from Miss Cookson, with a violin and pianoforte accompaniment. Mr Hardy then sang "The Suffolk Ploughman," a comic song, which being loudly encored, he responded with a pleasing negro melody, which brought the concert to a close. The room was crowded and the proceedings throughout were of the heartiest character. The sum of seven guineas was realised."[257]

Nina and Mabel "Beldy" Hardy, and Daphne Maugham Casorati

Two of Heywood Hardy's four daughters became artists, Nina and Mabel (or "Beldy" as she was always known) (Plates 193 and 194).

Nina Charlotte Elizabeth Hardy (1869-1949) was born at Goring and was taught drawing and painting by her father. Nina continued to paint after her marriage, but always signed her paintings "Nina Hardy" and usually gave her father's studio addresses at 10 Abbey Road or 6 Finchley Place, although she lived in Windsor.[258] Her first exhibit at the Royal Academy was in the year of her marriage, 1891. She showed a total of 15 paintings at the Royal Academy between 1891 and 1919, mostly portraits of women and children. She continued to paint and exhibit until she was over 60 years old.

Nina painted in oils, watercolours (including miniatures) and also in pastels; and exhibited at The Pastel Society, Royal Institute Galleries, Piccadilly, until the 1930s. She also exhibited 22 pictures at the New Gallery and several works at the Royal Institute of Oil Painters, the Royal Society of Portrait Painters, the Royal Society of Artists, the Walker Art Gallery (Liverpool) and the Grosvenor Gallery.

Mabel Frances Hardy ("Beldy"), Mrs Charles Maugham, (1874–1971), was a talented musician like her father and studied at the Paris Conservatoire. She won first prize for the harp at the age of seventeen, and the report of a recital in Paris in 1891 noted that

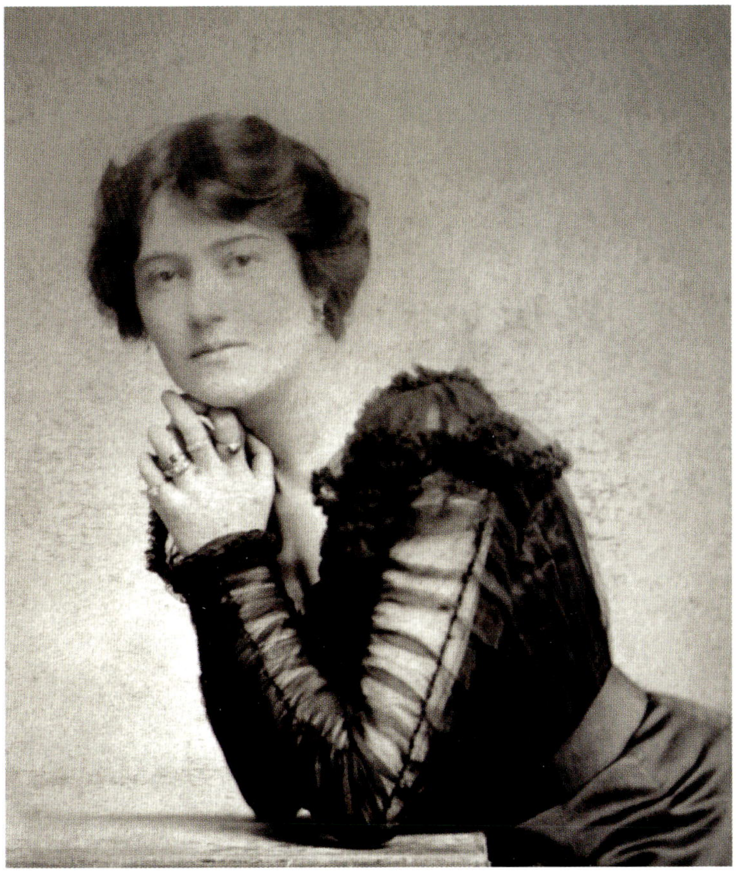

Plate 193: "Beldy" as a young woman.
PHOTOGRAPH COURTESY OF DAVID HARDY IVENS

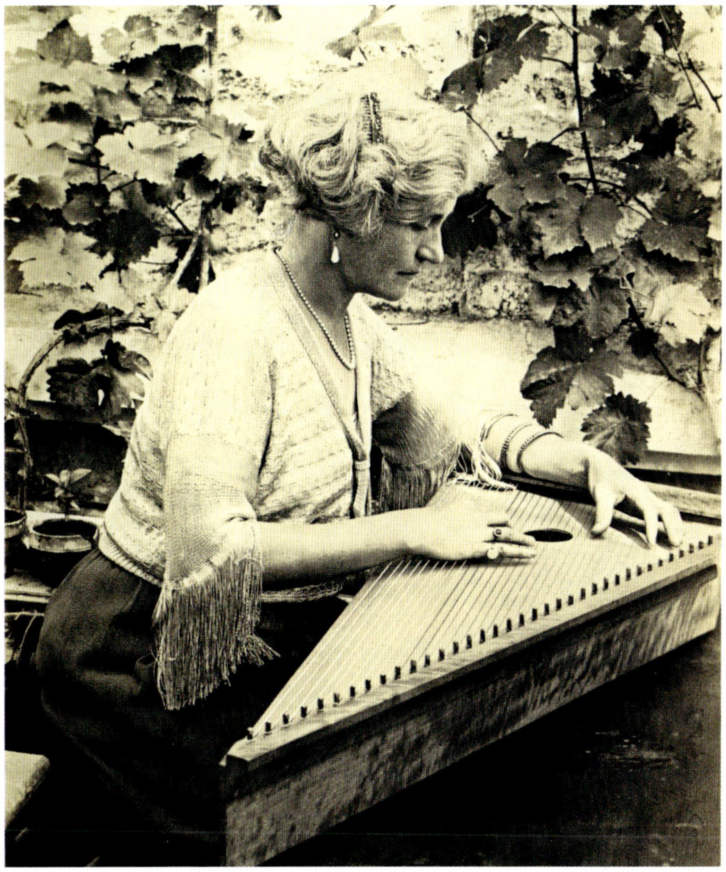

Plate 194: "Beldy" playing the kantele.
PHOTOGRAPH COURTESY OF DAVID HARDY IVENS

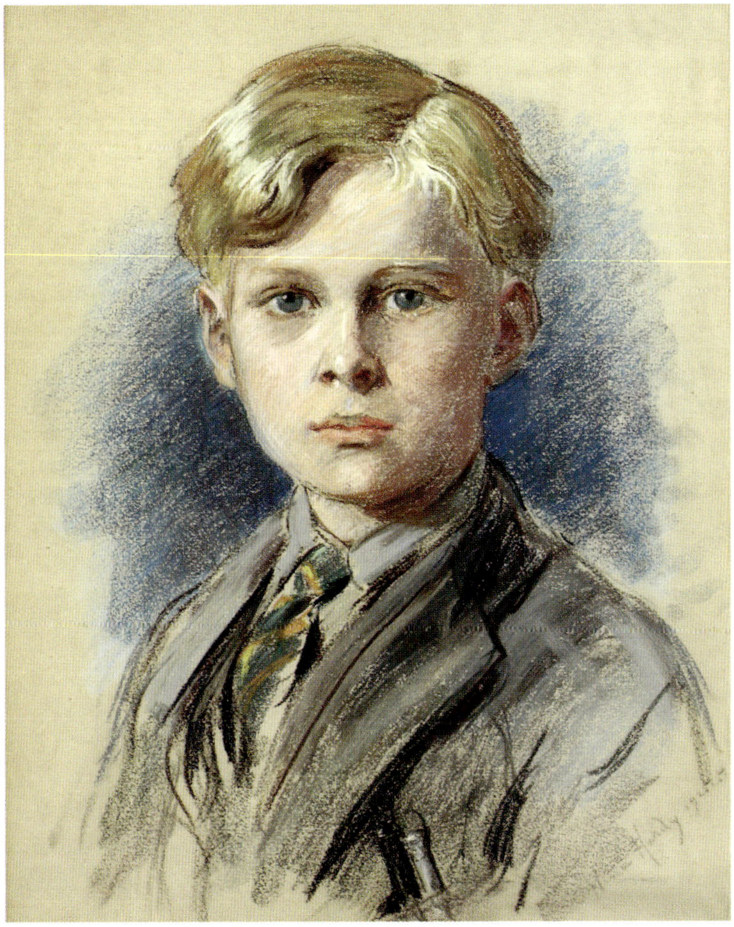

"Mlle Mabel Hardy a remarquablement exécuté plusieurs morceaux de harpe." [259] She played a variety of instruments including the zither and guitar (both favourites of her father), the kantele (a Finnish zither) (Plate 194), harp and piano. From her student days in Paris she was always known as "Beldy", a blend of Ma**bel** and Har**dy**.

While Beldy was studying at the Conservatoire, during which time she was described as "vivacious and fun",[260] she met Charles Maugham, a partner in his family's law firm in Paris and brother of author Somerset Maugham. In June 1894, when she was 19, she married Charles at St Stephen's Church in Bayswater, the church where her parents had been married in 1868. They returned to Paris after the wedding. Later, when she lived near Versailles, she became a close friend of Sir Gerald Kelly's wife and introduced Gerald Kelly to Somerset Maugham; Kelly played an important role in building Somerset Maugham's collection of eighteenth-century theatrical paintings.

When Heywood Hardy had just completed his final paintings for the churches at Clymping and Haslar in 1928, Beldy and his

Plate 195: Portrait of Alastair Hardy Ivens (grandson of Heywood Hardy)
Nina Hardy. Indistinctly dated 192?. Pastel on paper. 43.5 x 33cm.
PRIVATE COLLECTION

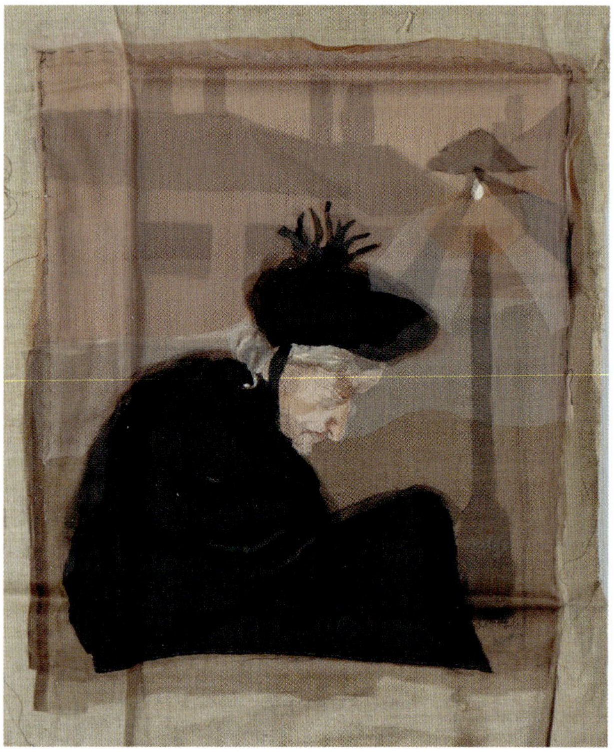

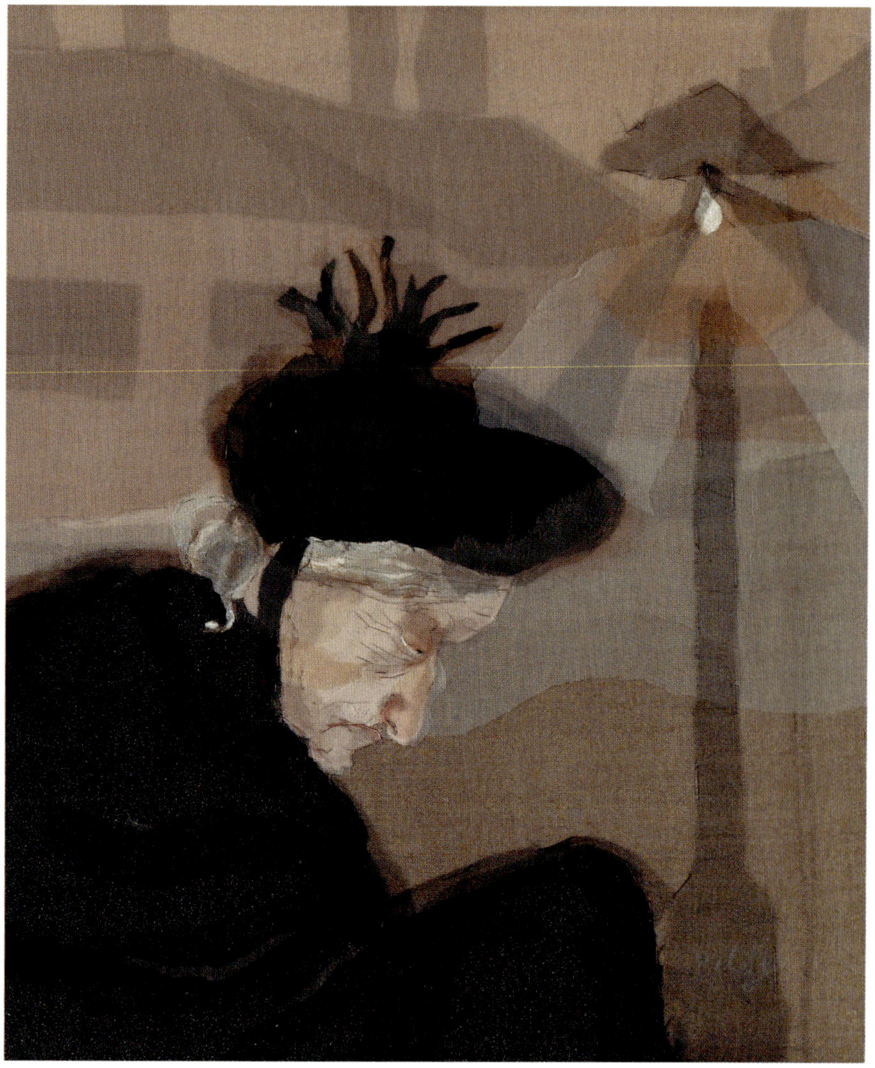

Plate 196: La Vieille, 1936
Mabel Maugham ("Beldy"). Silk crepeline sewn on linen. 37.8 x 30.8cm. The unframed picture above illustrates the technique she used. LE CENTRE POMPIDOU, PARIS.

Plate 197 (below): Felice Casorati and Daphne Maugham Casorati, ca. 1950. ARCHIVIO CASORATI. TURIN

granddaughter, Daphne Maugham (see below), were just having their first paintings exhibited. Beldy developed the art of "fabric painting"; pieces of fabric were laid on canvas as if put on by a brush (Plate 196). The artist Felice Casorati first saw the potential of Beldy's designs and suggested they should be exhibited. Her work was shown first at the Salon des Arts Décoratifs in Paris in 1929. Beldy subsequently had numerous exhibitions of her work, in Europe and the USA. She had nine exhibitions in London (including six at the Leicester galleries). Her last exhibition was

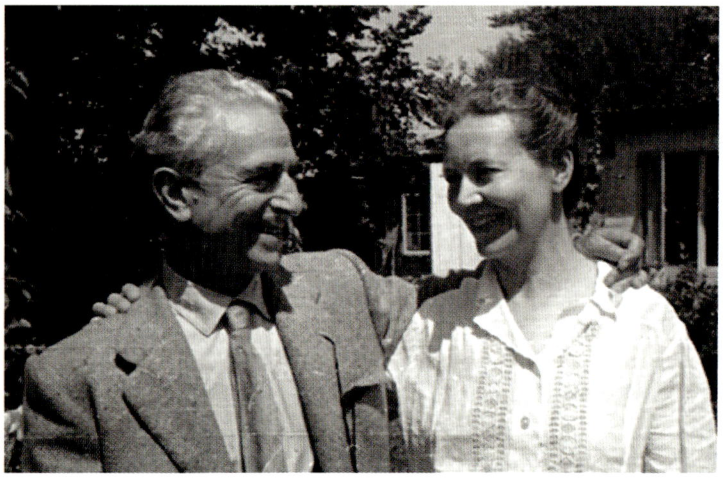

held at the Grosvenor Gallery in 1966 when she was 92 years old. A visitor to her exhibition at the Leicester Galleries in 1936 commented:

> ... she has developed the art of using a blending materials of all kinds, thinking of them as media for a picture, and "painting" with them without any idea of needle work, as if they were indeed oil, water-colour or gouache ... The delicacy of execution of these pictures made of scraps of silk and chiffon adjusted to the background, sometimes with a single stitch, created so remarkable an illusion, that at ten paces the spectator is often unaware that the picture is not painted in an ordinary medium.[261]

Beldy's daughters, Daphne and Clarisse, were also artists. Daphne Maugham (1897-1982), who was also a talented pianist, began her training at the Académie Ranson, Paris, in 1914, when she was seventeen. She studied under Maurice Denis and Paul Sérusier, an associate of Paul Gauguin and a founder of Les Nabis, a group of post-Impressionists inspired by Paul Gauguin's use of colour and pattern. From 1916 she studied in the Paris studio of the Polish painter, Mela Muter, and from 1918 to 1921 attended the Académie Notre Dame des Champs, where her teacher was the cubist painter and sculptor André Lhote. Finally,

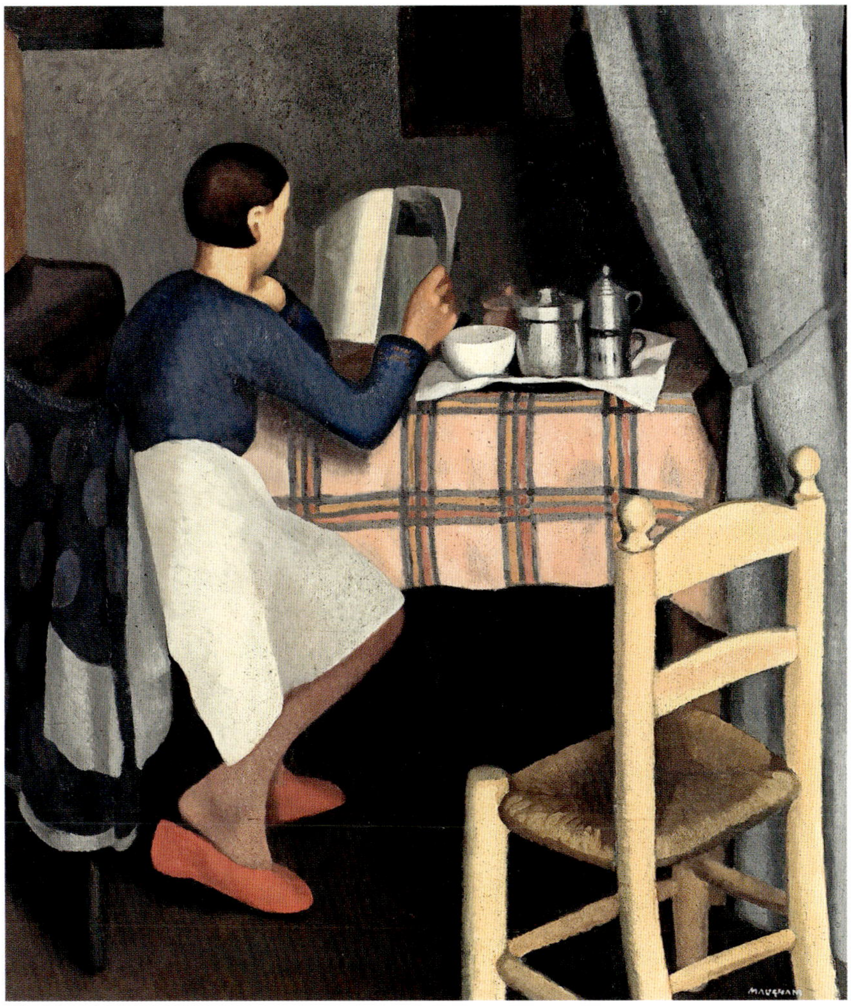

Plate 198 (left): La Colazione, 1929
Daphne Maugham Casorati. Oil on canvas. 120 x 100cm.
PRIVATE COLLECTION

Plate 199 (below): In Giardino, 1935
Daphne Maugham Casorati. Oil on canvas. 91.4 x 62.2cm.
MUSEO DEL NOVECENTO, FLORENCE

she studied at the Slade School of Fine Art until 1922. In 1921 her first painting was accepted at the Salon d'Automne in Paris.

Daphne went to live in Turin in 1925, where her sister, Cynthia, was a dancer with the Sacharoff Company and whose portrait had been painted by Felice Casorati, who was already a prominent artist in Italy. Daphne became a pupil of Felice (Plate 197) and they married in 1931. Though perhaps somewhat overshadowed by the work of her more famous husband, there were numerous exhibitions of Daphne Casorati's work, at the Venice Biennale, at the Rome Quadriennale, in Florence, Turin, London and the USA. Daphne also featured in several paintings by Felice.

Their son, the artist Francesco Casorati, described how his mother worked: " ... she held several brushes in her hand and sometimes even in her mouth. She had a controlled frenetic approach to painting in which overlapping colours brought unity across the canvas." The compositions reflected the teaching of Felice. But the subjects were often enlarged, seeming to expand beyond the confines of the canvas, as in *La Colazione* (1929) (Plate 198) and *In Giardino* (1935) (Plate 199), which shows the one-year-old Francesco in their garden at Pavarolo in the Piedmont. Francesco Casorati (1934–2013) lived and worked as an artist in Turin all his life. He represented the fifth generation of artists descended from James Hardy senior. Among the numerous presentations of his work was a joint exhibition with the work of his late mother in Turin in 2011.

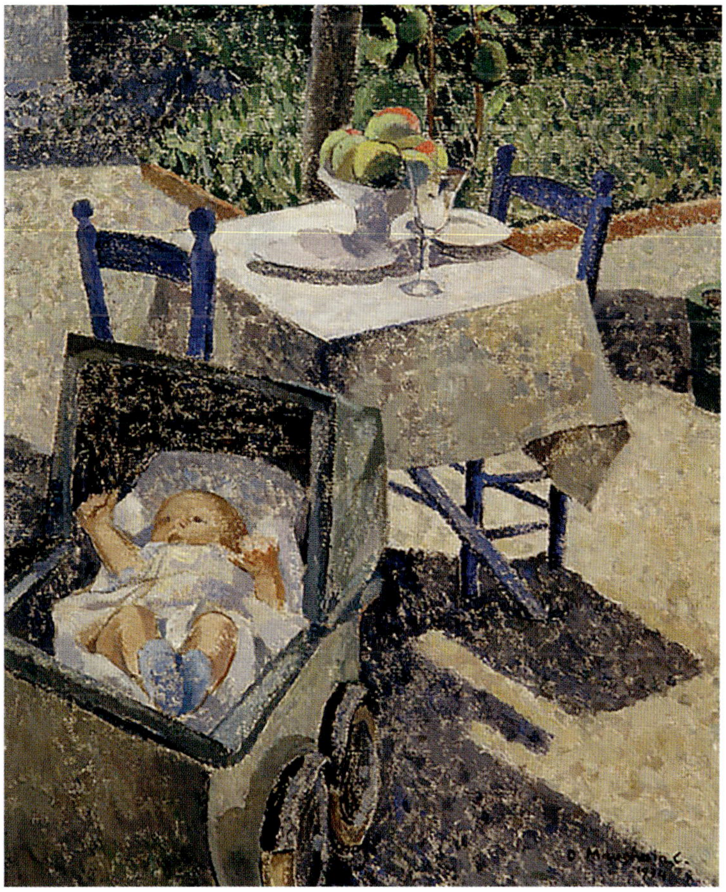

CHAPTER SEVEN

James Hardy Senior and James Hardy Junior

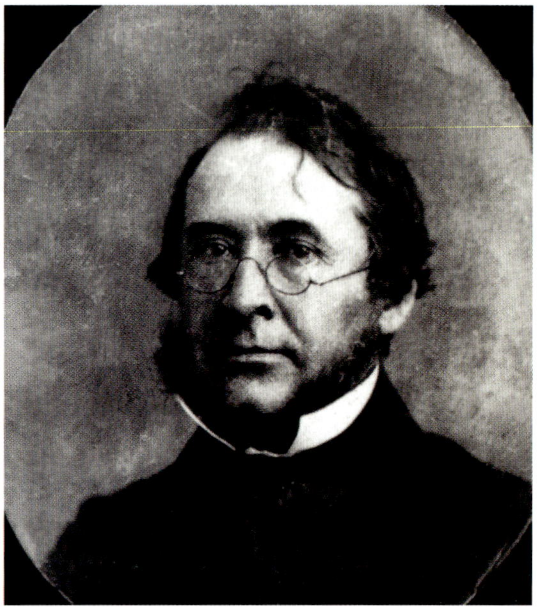

James Hardy Senior (1801-1879)

James Hardy senior (Plate 200) was born on 23 August 1801 at Hounslow, Middlesex, in the Cavalry Barracks where his father, William, was stationed with the 10th Hussars. He was the sixth of nine children of William and Jane Hardy. James originally trained as a musician; with his three elder brothers he joined the boys' band associated with the 10th Hussars and like them he was subsequently appointed a member of the Prince Regent's Private Band of Music. The Prince Regent was Colonel of the 10th Hussars, "The Prince's Dolls".

In his early twenties James Hardy senior was principal trumpet in the Royal Private Band of Music. James's position in the Band ended abruptly. Gertrude Madeline Hardy, his granddaughter, wrote: "Originally his taste was music and he became 'chief' trumpeter to George IV. Failing to obtain his way in some little adventure of his profession, one day in a fit of temper, of which he had an abundance, he threw his trumpet to the ground, stamped on it, and made a vow to earn his living by portrait painting." [262]

By 1824 James Hardy is listed in *Baxter's Stranger in Brighton Guide* as a "Profilist" at Grenville Place in Brighton. He married Elizabeth Vinson (Plate 201) the following year, on 31 August 1825 at St Nicholas Church, Brighton. *The Watering Places of Great Britain and Fashionable Directory,* 1831 lists James Hardy senior as an "Artist & Drawing Master" of 143, North Street, in Brighton. In 1832 he was still in Brighton, listed as a "Portrait & Miniature artist" at 163 Royal Colonnade, North Street, in *Pigot's Directory of Sussex* (1832-1834). Three of James and Elizabeth's ten children were born in Brighton: Henry Hine Hardy (in 1831), James Hardy junior (1832) and Georgiana Hardy (1834).

James Hardy senior apparently accumulated significant debts in Brighton; in 1833 he was imprisoned briefly in Horsham Gaol as an insolvent debtor:

> WHEREAS the Assignee of the estate and effects of James Hardy, formerly of Windsor, in the County of Berks, Musician, then of Windsor aforesaid, and of the Colonnade and Down-Cottage, Brighton, in the County of Sussex, Musician and Artist, then of Clarence-Place and the Colonnade aforesaid, and late of No. 8, Devonshire-Place, all in Brighton, in the County of Sussex, Artist, an Insolvent Debtor, lately a Prisoner in the Gaol of Horsham, in the County of Sussex, has caused an account of the said estate and effects, duly sworn to, to be filed in the Court for Relief of Insolvent Debtors; the Creditors of the said Insolvent are

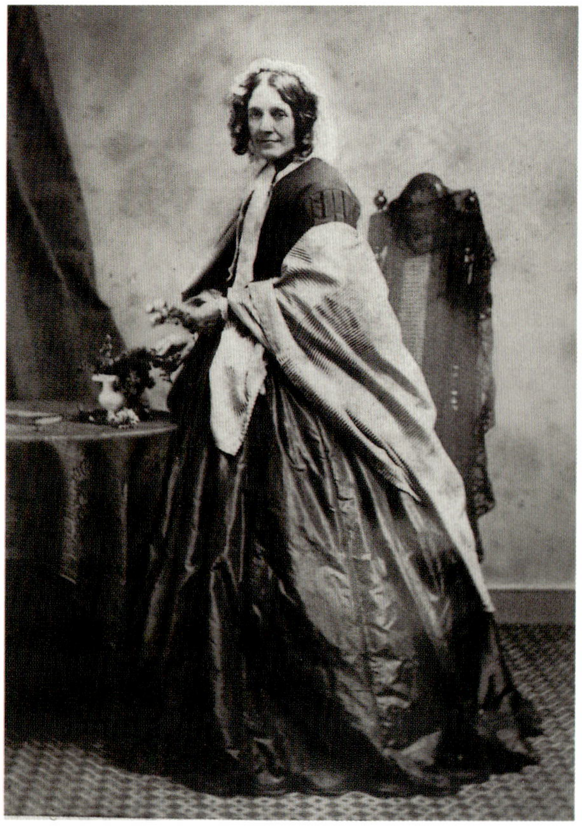

Plate 200 (above): Self portrait, ca. 1850
James Hardy senior. Private Collection

Plate 201 (right): Elizabeth Hardy, wife of James Hardy senior
Photograph by H.E.Hobson.[263] From the photograph album of George and Sarah Hardy

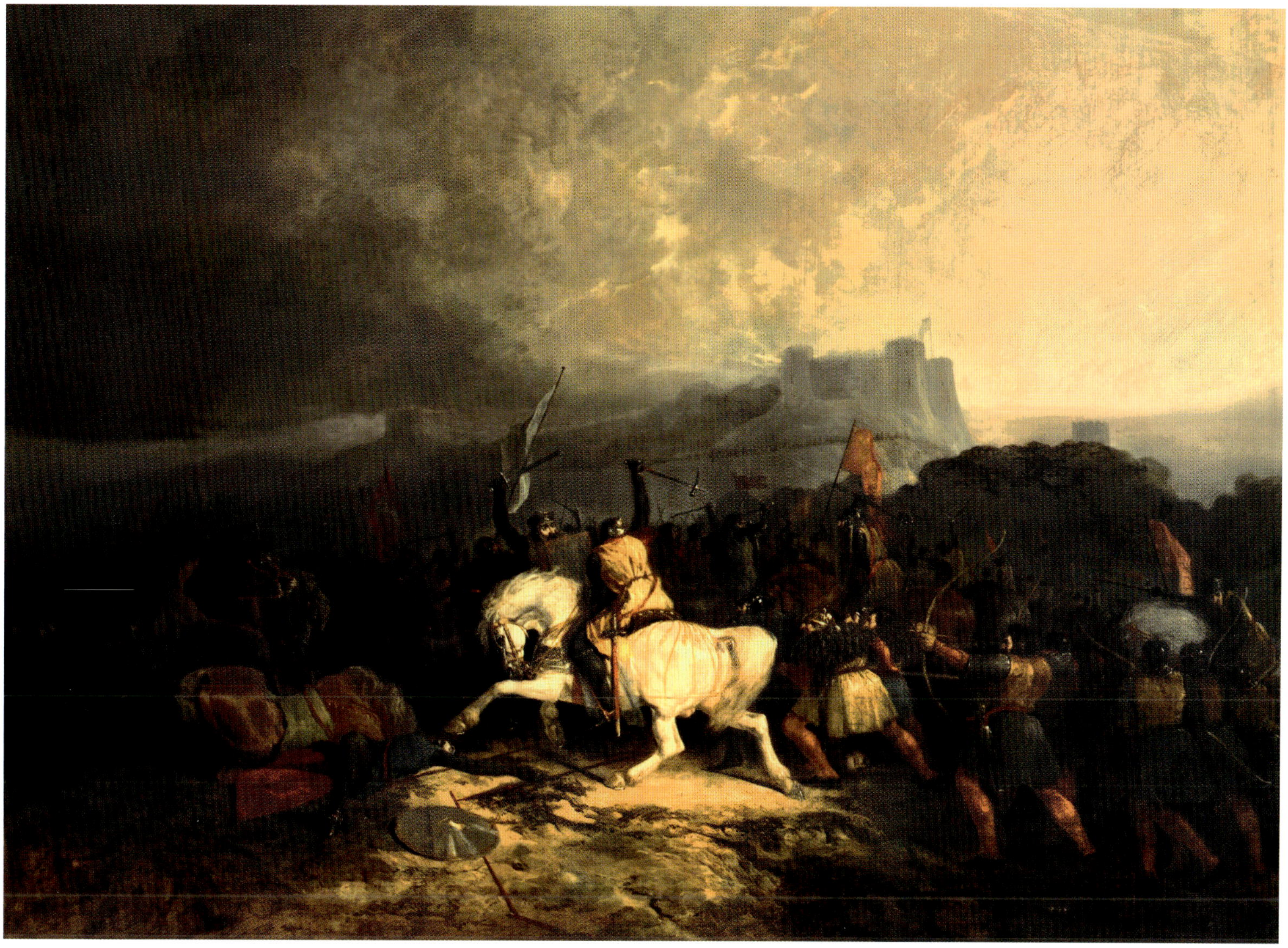

Plate 202: The Battle of Lewes, East Sussex, 14th May 1264, 1835
James Hardy senior. Oil on canvas. 46 x 64cm. Lewes Town Council

requested to meet the Assignee at the Office of Messrs, Benson and Freeman, Solicitors, situated in Bond-Street, in Brighton aforesaid, on the 17th day of December next, at Eleven of the Clock in the Forenoon precisely, when and where the Assignee will declare the amount of the balance in his hands, and proceed to make a Dividend with the same amongst the Creditors whose debts are admitted in the schedule sworn to by the Insolvent, in proportion to the amount thereof, subject to such correction of the rights to receive dividends as may be made according to the Statute.—If any person has a demand which is stated in the schedule, but is disputed therein, either in whole or in part; or if the said Insolvent, the said Assignee, or any Creditor objects to any debt mentioned therein, such claims and objections must be brought forward at the said meeting, in order that proceedings may be had for the examination and decision of the same according to the Statute.[264]

Shortly after this announcement, James and his family (now with four children) moved along the Sussex coast to live at Lewes where his son, Thomas, was baptised. *The Brighton Patriot* of 17 November 1835 described *The Battle of Lewes* (Plate 202), painted by James Hardy senior:

> Mr. Hardy (artist of this town) is engaged in painting a representation of the Battle of Lewes. Many of the gentry have visited his residence since it has been commenced, and have expressed their delight at the wonderful energy thrown into the picture. The figures are beautifully drawn, particularly the young Prince (son of Henry the Third), mounted on a white courser, in the foreground. The Castle (as it then stood) is seen in the distance. The artist has also paid great attention to the costume. It will be finished in a few weeks, and the circumstance (independent of the talent displayed by the artist) of its being the only attempt ever made to delineate the battle fought at Lewes, between Henry the Third and the Barons, will make the painting invaluable to the inhabitants of this town and county.[265]

Today, the painting can be found in Lewes Town Hall.

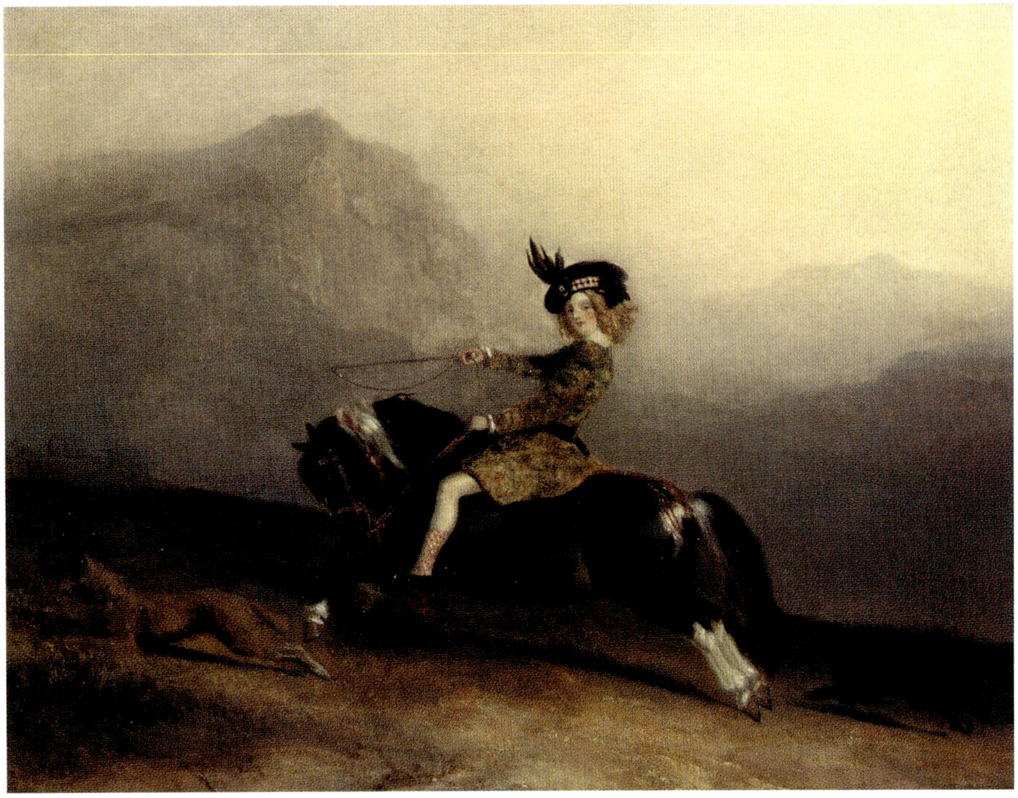

Plate 203: Portrait of Lord George Lennox, Youngest Son of His Grace the Duke of Richmond, on a Favourite Pony, 1839
James Hardy senior. Oil on canvas.
43 x 53.5cm. Private Collection

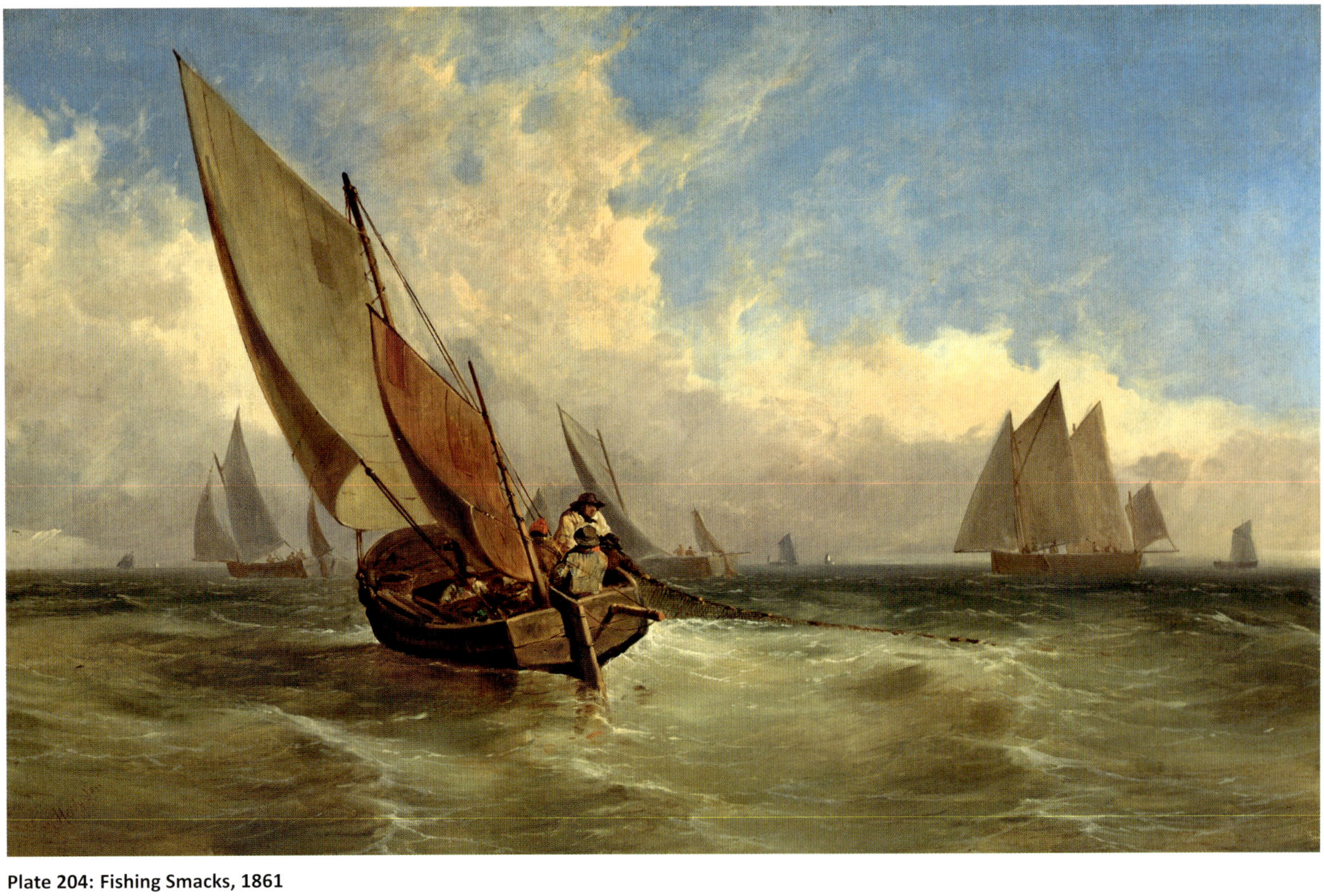

Plate 204: Fishing Smacks, 1861
James Hardy senior. Oil on canvas. 60.7 x 92.1cm. Victoria Art Gallery, Bath

Plate 205: The Monkey's Court, 1863
James Hardy senior. Oil on canvas.
33 x 25.5cm. Wisbech & Fenland Museum[266]

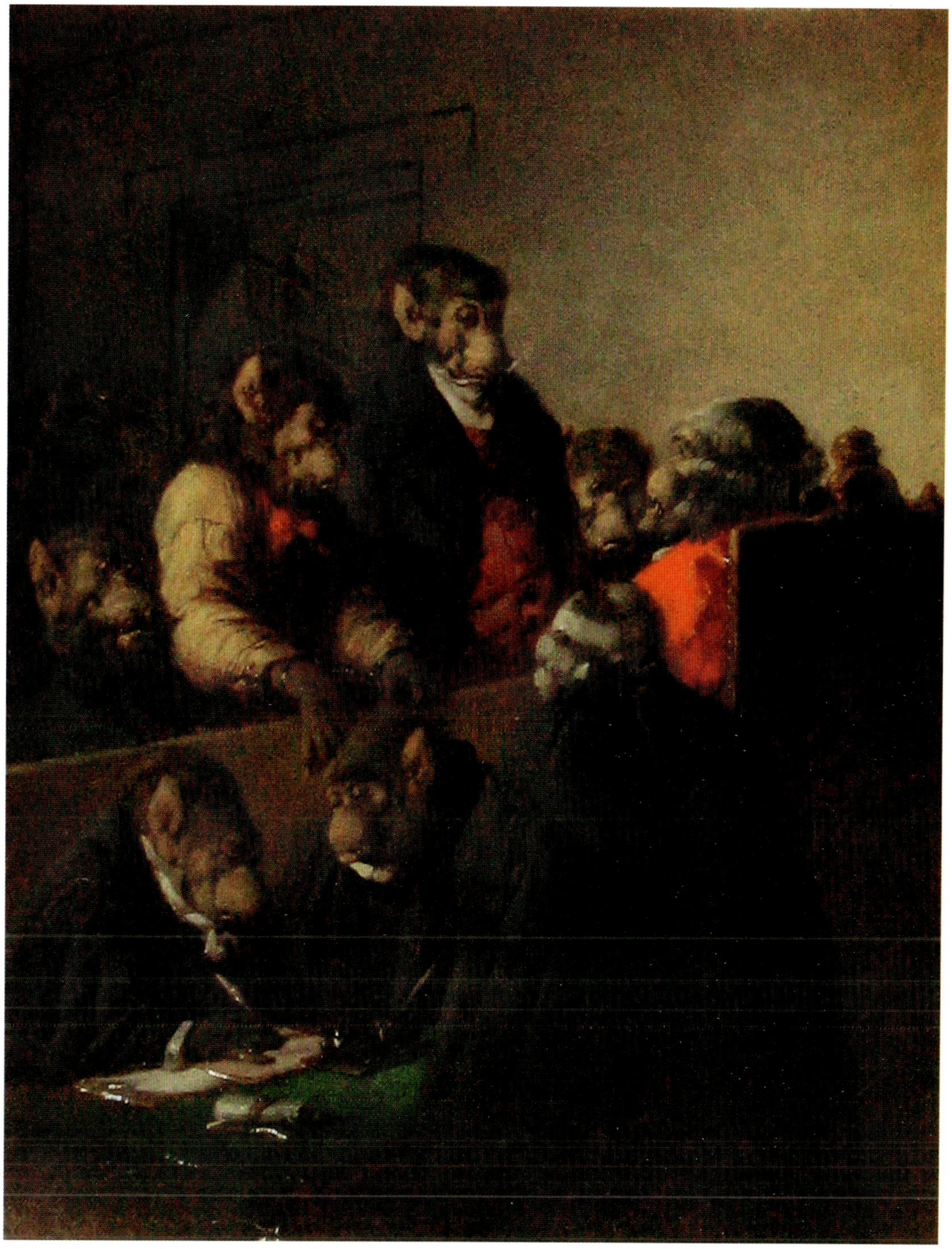

James Hardy and his family moved again in 1837, to Chichester in Sussex. He is described as a "Teacher of Drawing" at West Street, Chichester, in *Pigot's Directory of Sussex (1839)*. James and his family lived at 55 Westgate from 1837 to 1846.

In 1839, he painted *Portrait of Lord George Lennox , Youngest Son of His Grace the Duke of Richmond, on a Favourite Pony* (Plate 203), a picture of the nine-year-old George Gordon-Lennox. This was exhibited at the Royal Academy in 1840; the address he gave when the work was submitted was 21 Gillingham Street, Vauxhall Road, London. This was the address of his eldest brother, William.

In 1846 James and his family continued their move westwards, to Bath. The family lived at 8 Lower East Hayes from 1846 to 1850, next to the London Road, and from 1852 to 1857 close to the centre of Bath at 30 Henrietta Street, a three-storied house. James' studio was the drawing room on the second floor. By 1861, when all his children except Thomas had left home, James Hardy senior moved to smaller houses in Bath, firstly at 2 Cambridge Terrace (from 1858 to 1862), then at 12 Richmond Place (1863 to 1875) and finally to 6 Pulteney Gardens (1876 to 1878). During this period James painted portraits, genre pictures and seascapes. He also submitted a design for municipal buildings in Bath.[267] He exhibited only one more painting at the Royal Academy, a work called *Devotion* (1857).

The Monkey's Court (1863) (Plate 205) might be a comment on his earlier involvement with the insolvency courts and also that of his son, James junior, who appeared at the insolvency court at Bath in 1859. James Hardy senior also painted a picture called *The Monkey Dentist*.[268]

According to his granddaughter, Gertrude Madeline (daughter of James Hardy junior):

> For his new venture in life [giving up his position in the Royal Private Band of music to become an artist] he was lucky in obtaining an extensive and wealthy patronage, chiefly in Bath and for a number of years was in great request. In his later years, however, he gradually lost the patronage he obtained, by developing a religious mania, obtruding his views in an irritating manner upon his patrons in private, and upon the public in general by proclaiming at street corners wherever the opportunity occurred. [269]

James Hardy senior died at Bath in 1879. Six of his children became artists or art teachers: Ada, David, Georgiana, Elizabeth, James and Heywood.

James Hardy Junior (1832-1889)

James Hardy junior (Plate 206), eldest son of James Hardy senior, was born in Brighton in 1832 and baptised at St Nicholas Church, Brighton, on 16 January 1833. When he was a boy his family moved to Lewes, then to Chichester and finally to Bath, where young James had a studio on the first floor of 30 Henrietta Street.

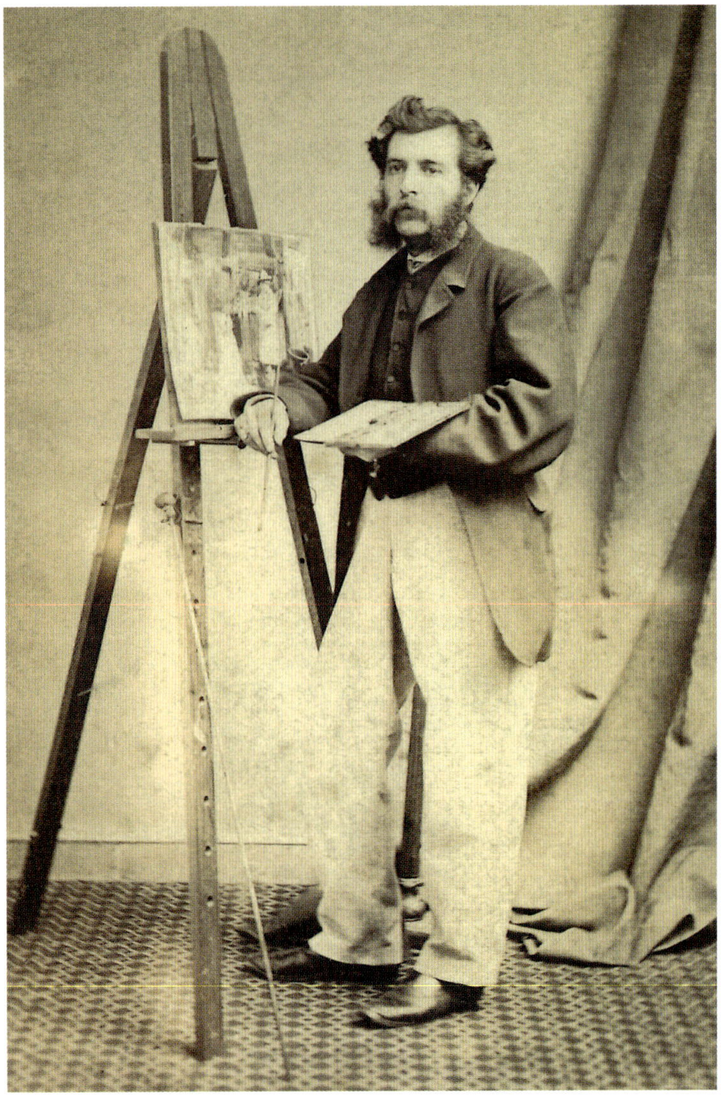

Plate 206: James Hardy junior, 1863

From the photograph album of George and Sarah Hardy. The painting on the easel is a version of *The Rabbit Hutch* (1863) (Plate 214).

James Hardy junior received encouraging comments about his first exhibits,[270] studies of game birds that were shown at the Bath Graphic Society in 1852:

> There is, however, one young artist less known to fame, with whose name we shall close our remarks. For characteristic drawing, dexterous manipulation, and the easy pose of his objects, we scarcely know any one who, at so early an age, has attained equal excellence with Mr. J. Hardy.[271]

His studies of game birds exhibited in Bristol in 1853 were similarly praised:

> Works by a young artist, which would do no dishonour to one of veteran standing. The manipulation of the game is exceedingly minute and careful, the plumage being rendered in the closest imitation of nature. The still-life objects are also painted with a masterly hand, and promise[282] well for the future fame of the limner.[272]

He exhibited in London, at the Society of British Artists (Suffolk Street Gallery), for the first time in 1853: "a picture of dead poultry by J. Hardy jun., which evinces considerable talent in this style of painting".[273] *The Art Journal* commented: "No. 336. 'Dead Poultry', J. Hardy, Jun. The group consists of a peacock, a couple of pigeons, a white cock, and auxiliary items, constituting a very probable association. The birds are well drawn and painted, and worthy of a more careful background."[274] Another reviewer of the exhibition commented:

> Two capital productions of Dead Game, by J. Hardy, Jun. The apparently high finish of these pictures is astonishing when they are narrowly inspected, and the really small amount of labour bestowed on them is discovered. In many places the canvas is barely covered, yet the texture of every object is most effectually rendered. They betoken great power and skill: the grouping in each case is admirable.[275]

However, in 1853, a reviewer was already suggesting he should begin painting subjects other than dead game:

> In Mr. Hardy jun's. "Dead Peacock," we see the same spirited drawing, bold and characteristic execution, and broad effect and shade, which we admired in his work of last year; but why the same only? Has he no judicious friend to point out to him that, however clever his works may be, they want lustre and solidity when placed by the side of those of more advanced artists? As we see no other subjects from his pencil, we presume he only aspires to represent inanimate objects; but why limit the range of these? Is he so enamoured of poulterers' shops that he

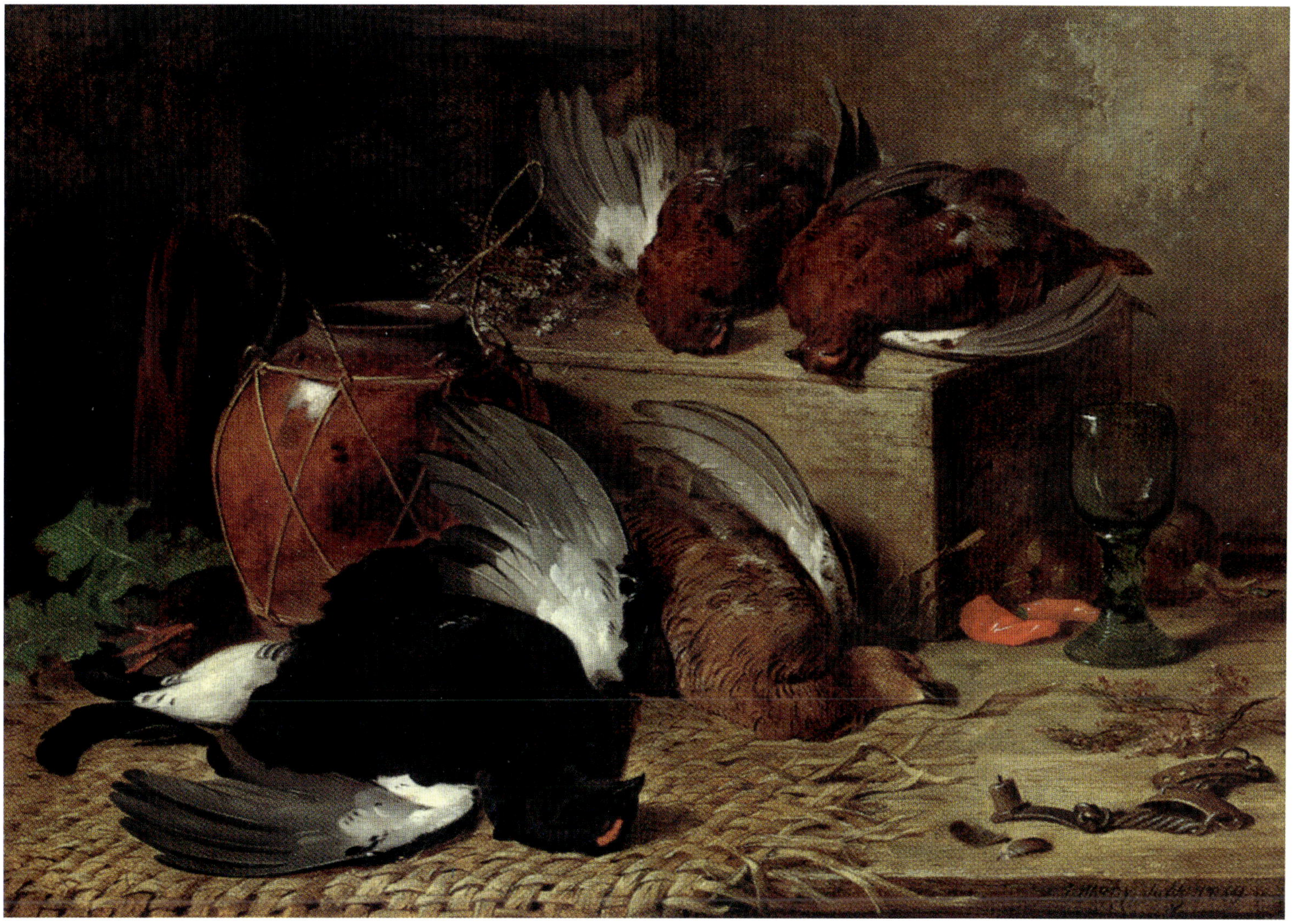

Plate 207: Scotch Game, 1859
James Hardy junior. Oil on canvas. 41.3 x 56.5cm. Private Collection

cannot bestow a thought on Flora and Pomana? Mr. Hardy is still young; and if he will exert himself, we doubt not will rise in his profession; but it is not by repeating indefinitely his own works that this end will be attained.[276]

The following year he seems to have taken the reviewer's advice; his paintings were of a poacher and a dog as well as game birds: "Mr. Hardy, jun. contributed two oil paintings to The Bath Graphic Society exhibition ... they are excellent performances, and promise at a future day a high position for the artist."[277] And from 1854 he spent more time painting figures and cottage interiors, though he continued to include dead game in many of his pictures throughout his career.

It was through his many still-life studies of game birds, in watercolours and later in oils, that he developed his skills. Through his numerous early watercolours painted on tinted paper he gained a good understanding of tonality. Always well painted, game birds were included in all his best sporting paintings made in the 1870s. His study of *Scotch Game* (1859) (Plate 207) and *The Day's Bag* (1862 & 1864) (Plates 208 and 209) are good examples of his early paintings.

Given his expertise in painting dead game, it seems a pity that he did not paint pictures of live birds. Only one such picture has been identified, *Black Game* (Plate 210), a study of a male black grouse with two females.[278] It is surprising that he did not paint more; bird illustrations were popular in the second half of the nineteenth century.

In 1854 James Hardy junior began to paint pictures of sporting dogs. There were few comments about sporting pictures in the art press of the period, but *The Art Journal*'s review of the Society of British Artists exhibition in 1854 recognised his skill in painting sporting dogs:

> No. 368. "Keeping Guard," J. HARDY, Junior. There is in this composition the head of a pointer, which is accurately drawn, skilfully painted, and strikingly characteristic. It is a sporting picture, of which the components are tastefully brought together, and painted with clearness and decision.[279]

The above comment could be made about almost all the pictures of sporting dogs he painted for the next 35 years.

Another reviewer was also impressed by *Keeping Guard*:

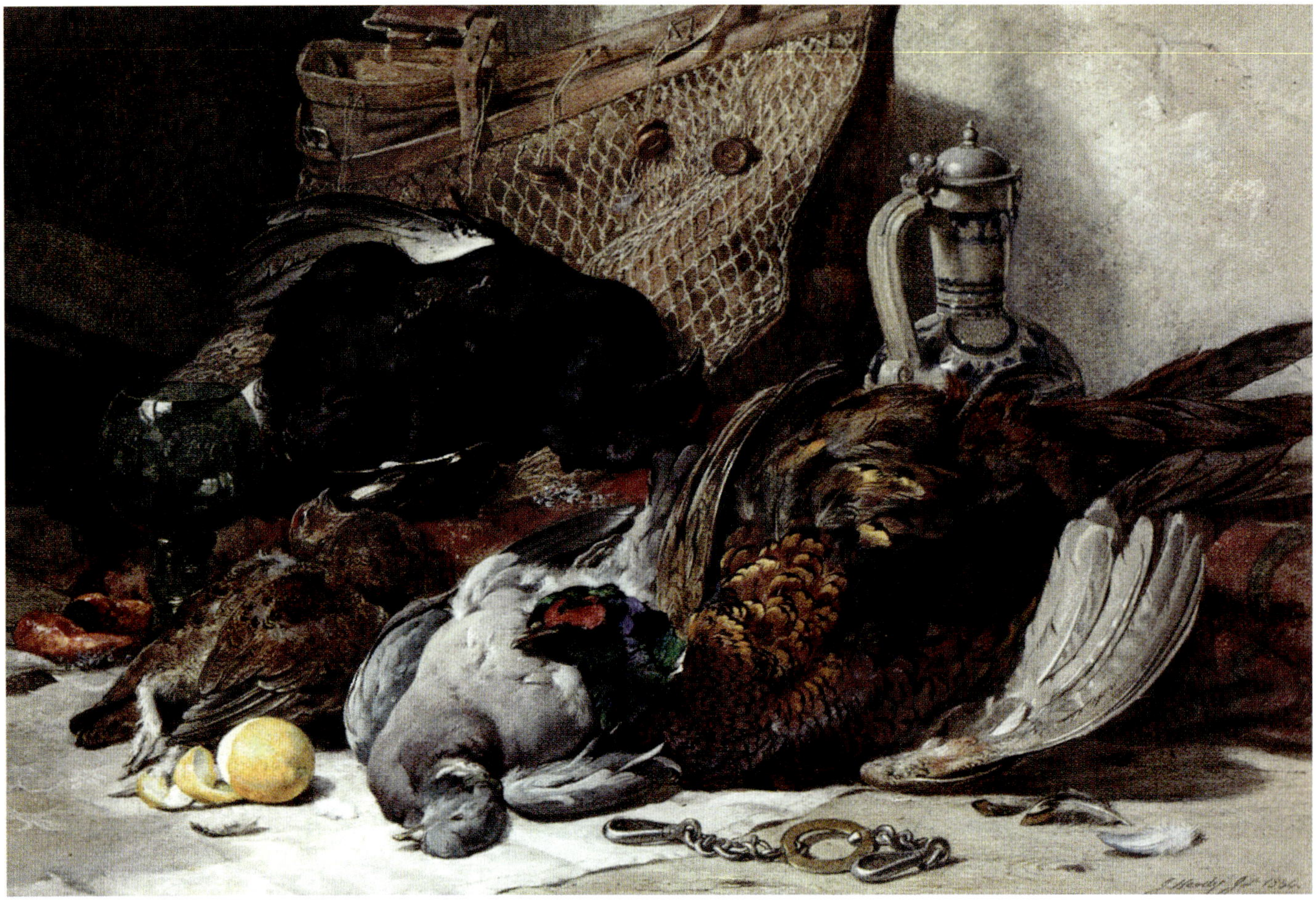

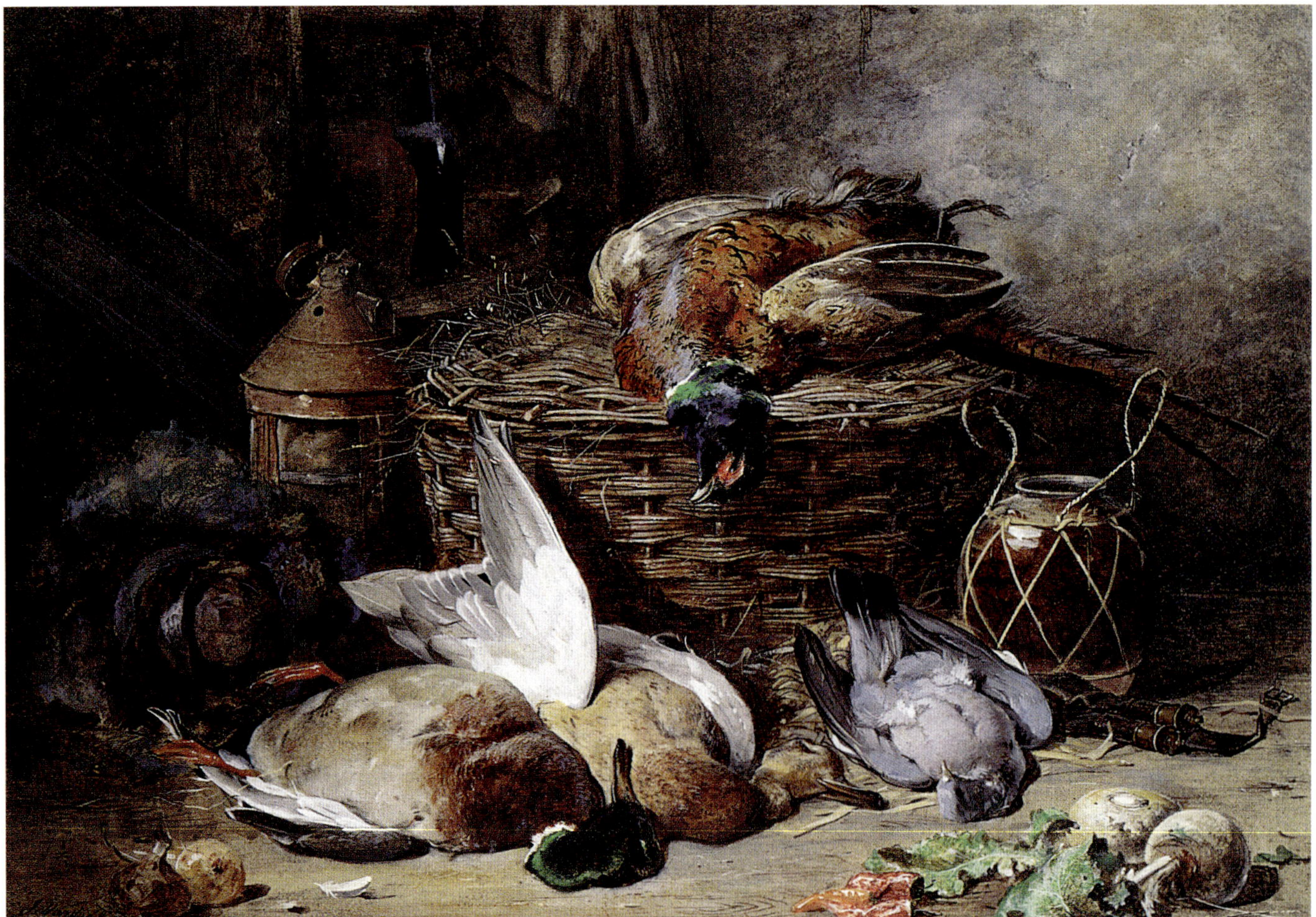

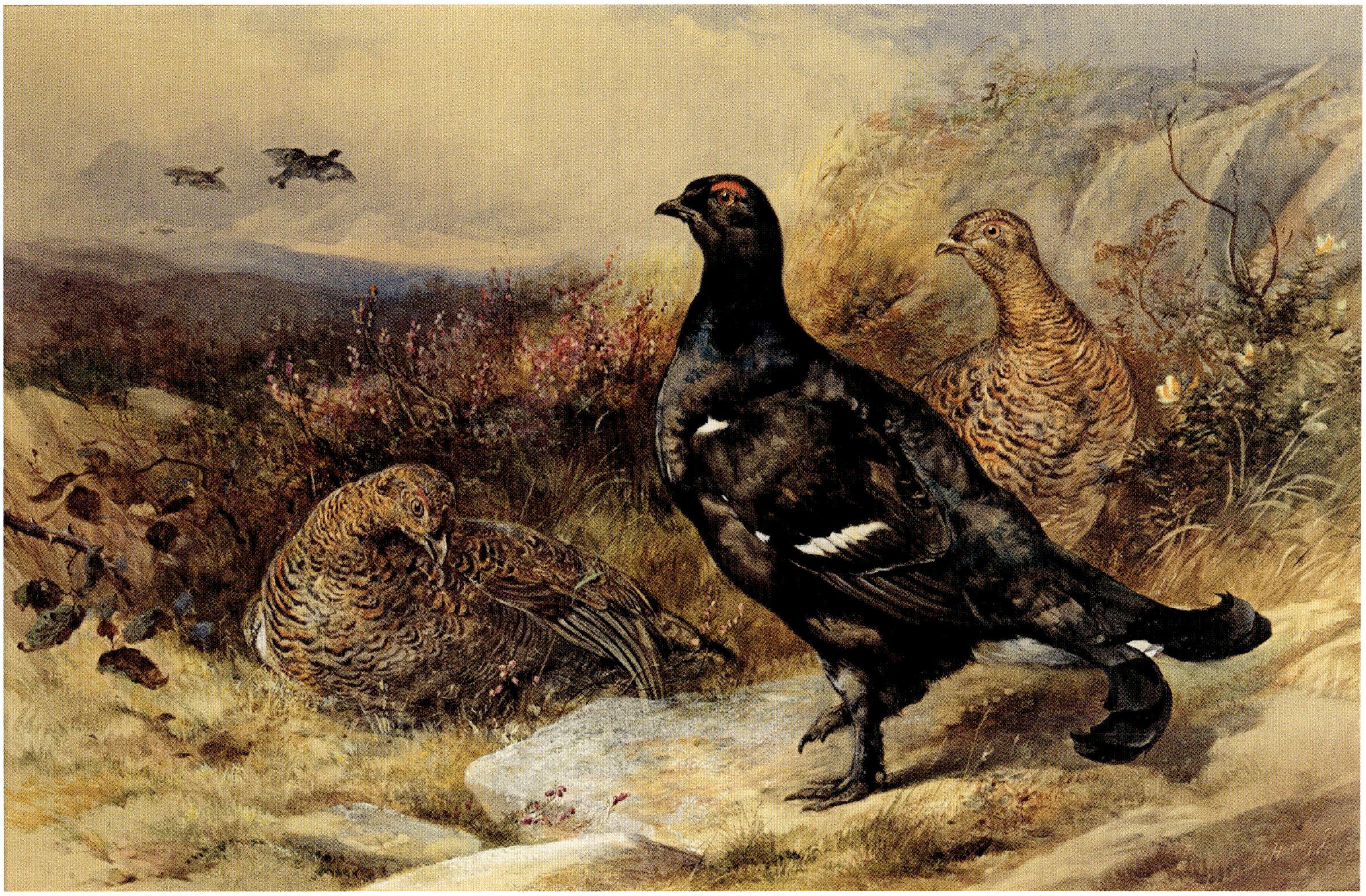

Plate 210: Black Game
James Hardy junior. Watercolour on paper. 53 x 80.5cm. © Bury Art Museum, Greater Manchester

> The attitude of the dog is well studied and true to life. The feathers of the black grouse, which appear to be ruffled by a breeze, are beautifully and faithfully painted; indeed, the whole [is] a masterly composition, and approaches nearer Landseer than any picture we have yet seen.[280]

In 1856 James Hardy junior painted one of his first studies of sporting dogs in a landscape, *Waiting for the Guns*. The figure and landscape are not as well painted as in his later work, but the dogs and game are skilfully drawn.

Though his skills as an artist of sporting pictures were increasingly well recognised, James Hardy junior continued to try to make a living by painting studies of interiors, including a *Berkshire Interior,* which was exhibited by the Royal Society of British Artists in 1854, *A Little Tune* (1856) and *The Itinerant Musician* (1856). His *Berkshire Interior,* showing a mole catcher in a cottage with two children, is well observed and similar in style to paintings made by his cousin, Frederick Hardy, at the same age.

He also painted numerous genre subjects at this time, including *Playing Marbles* (1859) and *The Dancing Lesson* (1859), exhibited at the Exhibition of the Society of Artists. But these paintings went largely unremarked upon in exhibition reviews. However, a reviewer did comment that:

> No. 123, S. [*sic*] Hardy, jun., is deserving notice. It is "The Dancing Lesson," not given to any precocious " Miss" or "Master" in his or her "teens," but to a sweet little girl, by two very dear old people. The expression on the three faces very well worth attention, being true to nature, and of a kind that is worth studying. It is a small work, and the reverse of pretentious, but we dare prophesy good things from it of Mr. Hardy, jun.; and we wish him success and a speedy purchaser.[281]

Plate 208 (opposite page, top): The Day's Bag, 1862
James Hardy junior. Watercolour. 19 x 25cm. Private Collection

Plate 209 (opposite page, bottom): The Day's Bag, 1864
James Hardy junior. Pencil, watercolour and body colour with gum arabic on oatmeal paper. 54.5 x 79.4cm. Private Collection

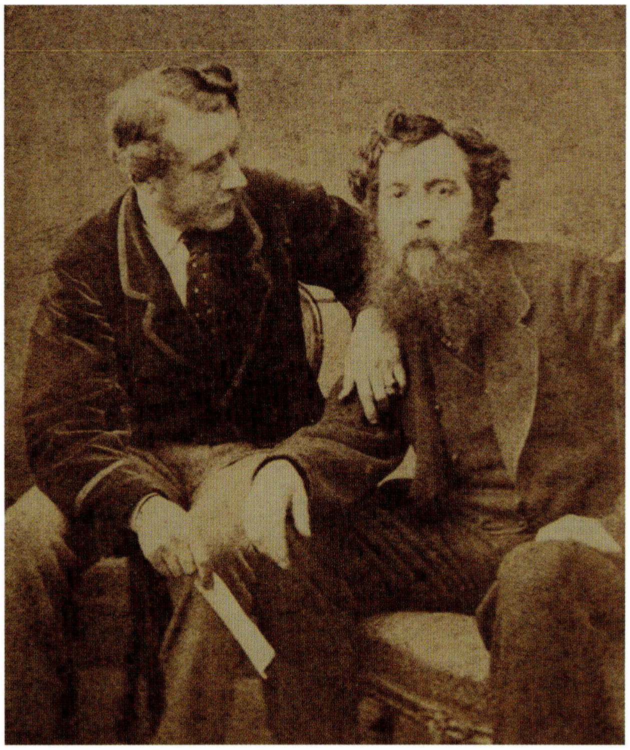

Plate 211: Heywood Hardy and James Hardy jnr.
Photograph courtesy of David Hardy Ivens

Despite early promise, it appears that Hardy found it difficult to make a living as an artist in Bath. In March 1859 "James Hardy, jun., artist, of Henrietta Street, passed his first examination as an insolvent debtor unopposed. The debts amounted to about £240; but there were assets to the amount of £50, available for the creditors."[282] The debt of £240 was a considerable sum; the annual rent of their house at 30 Henrietta Street was £32.[283]

We do not know how James Hardy junior managed to extricate himself from this difficulty or indeed whether the debts were all his own or if he had to take responsibility for the debts of the entire family (his father had already been imprisoned for debt in 1833). Later, in 1859, James Hardy junior left his parents' home in Henrietta Street and moved to Bristol (to 4 Lower Church Lane), some ten minutes walk from where his brother, David, lived in Southwell Street. He gave David's address for most of the paintings he exhibited at this time.

The following year, on 18 October 1860, when he was 27 years old, Hardy married Laura Amelia May. Laura was the daughter of Enoch May, a chemist and druggist for many years at Tewkesbury. They were married by Laura's brother, Rev. Frederick Schiller May, at Trinity Church, Cheltenham. For at least a year after their marriage they lived with her parents at their house in the High Street of Tewkesbury together with her four sisters. Heywood Hardy, then aged 19, also stayed with them for part of 1861. Later in 1861 James and Laura moved to Bristol (to Bedford Villa, Terrell Street)[284 285], about five minutes walk from Southwell Street where his brother David lived with his family. Laura's father Enoch May died in November 1861.

In the early 1860s James continued to paint cottage interiors and genre pictures, including *The Ballad* (1861), *Bob's Cherry* (1862), *Cottage Interior with Family and Pedlar* (1863), *Welcome Visitor* (1863), *The Toy Boat* (1863), *The Stonemason's Dinner* (1863), *Preparing for Dinner* (1863) and *Grandfather's Treat* (1863).

His genre pictures were well painted, demonstrating his improved ability to paint figures. But there were many skilful painters of genre pictures and domestic interiors and it seems that James had no distinctive contribution to make. Eventually, it was in the portrayal of sporting scenes – sporting dogs with their handlers – that James Hardy junior was to excel.

After 1863, he painted few interiors, but focused instead on still-life studies of game and pictures of the countryside with figures, particularly children (Plates 212-214), engaged in country pursuits. During the 1850s and 1860s about two thirds of his paintings were watercolours (heightened with white) and the remainder were oil paintings.

It was not until 1869 that James painted the first of the Scottish landscapes, with ghillies and Gordon and English setters, in which he excelled. Perhaps his younger brother, Heywood, helped James to change direction and become a sporting artist and an expert in painting sporting dogs and ponies in Scottish landscapes. Heywood was an expert animal painter by the end of the 1860s. He and Heywood painted a few pictures together. And a painting by the latter in 1868 foreshadows the Highland sporting scenes of James; *The End of a Day's Hunting* (1868) by Heywood Hardy is a picture of two sporting dogs, a pony and hunter.[286]

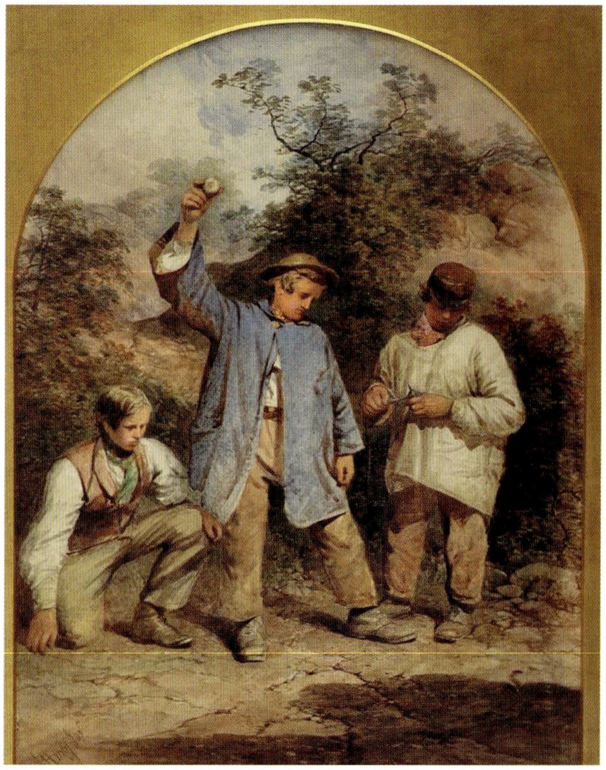

Plate 212 (right): The Top Spinner
James Hardy junior. Watercolour. 68.6 x 48.3cm. Private Collection

Plate 213 (opposite page): The Young Angler, 1865
James Hardy junior. Pencil, watercolour, heightened with white. 31.1 x 30.5cm. Private Collection

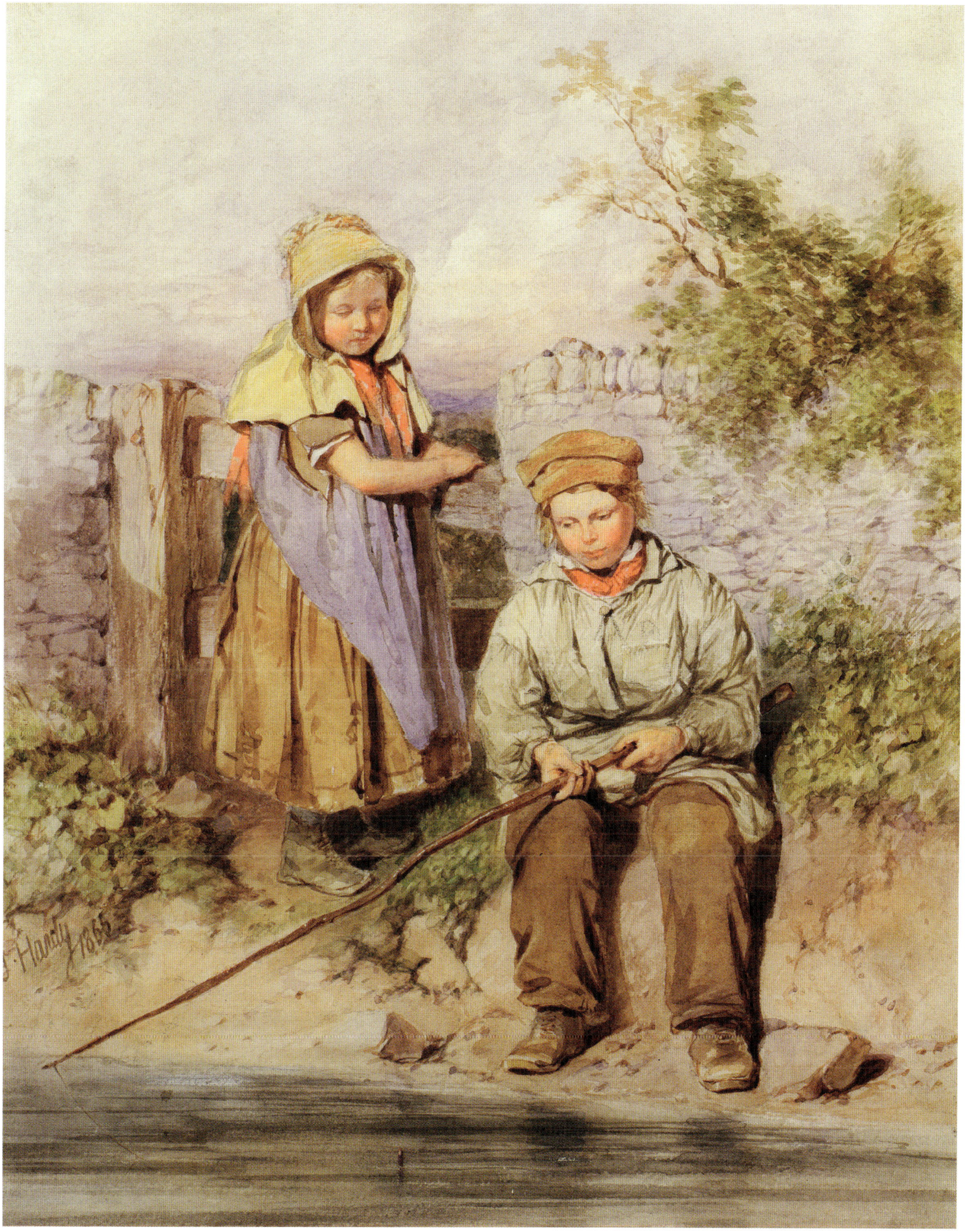

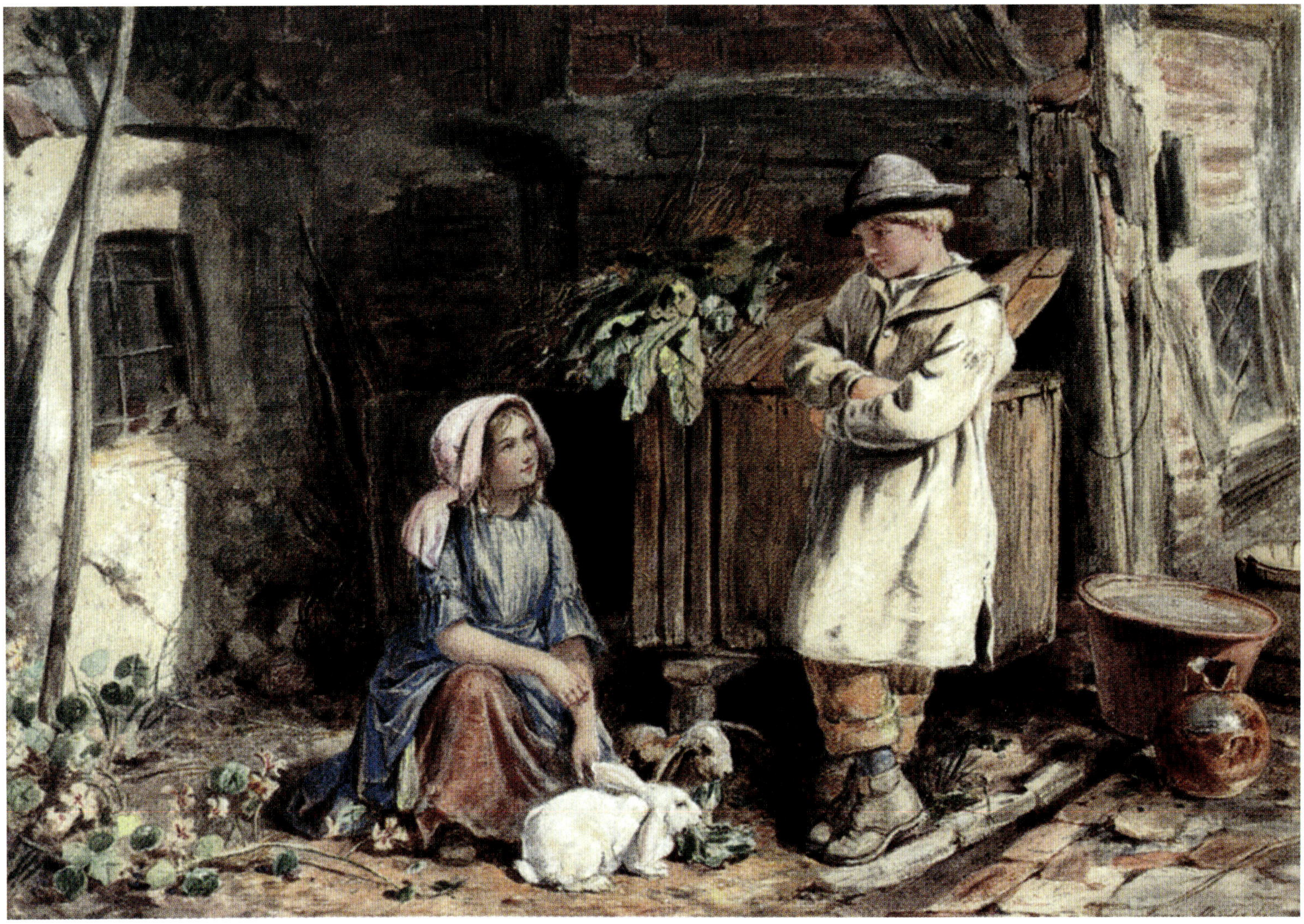

Plate 214 (above): The Rabbit Hutch, 1863
James Hardy junior. Watercolour and body colour. 34.3 x 45.7cm. Private Collection

Plate 215 (right): Waiting for the Shot, 1871
James Hardy junior. Oil on canvas. 39 x 29.5cm. Private Collection

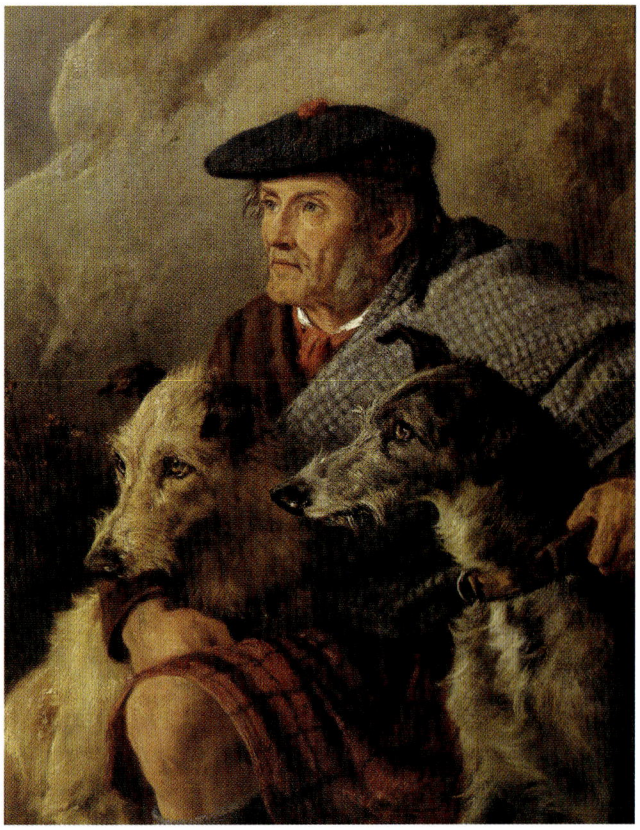

After 1870 James Hardy junior no longer painted genre pictures, but concentrated almost exclusively on Highland scenes. He continued to paint a few still-life studies of game, which presumably appealed to a more limited number of potential buyers, though they were always well painted.

He lived in Bristol until 1870 when his family removed to London. Their two sons and two daughters, James, Laura, Herbert and Gertrude Madeline, were all born in Bristol. By 1871, it seems that his financial problems may have diminished; James and Laura Hardy were living at 61 Gloster Court, St Pancras, with their two sons, two daughters, a nurse and a general servant.[287] In 1881 he was living at Thyra Grove, North Finchley, with his wife, two sons, a daughter and a general domestic servant.[288]

James Hardy junior exhibited nine paintings at the Royal Academy between 1862 and 1886 and 45 paintings at the Society of British Artists between 1853 and 1871. He was elected an associate of the Institute of Painters in Water Colours in 1874 and a member in 1877.

In the year he was elected an associate member it was noted that:

Plate 216 (right): The Gamekeeper's Rest, 1871
James Hardy junior. Watercolour heightened with body colour. 50.8 x 71.1cm. Private Collection

Plate 217 (below): Across the Moors, 1873
James Hardy junior. Watercolour. 54.5 x 75.5cm. Private Collection

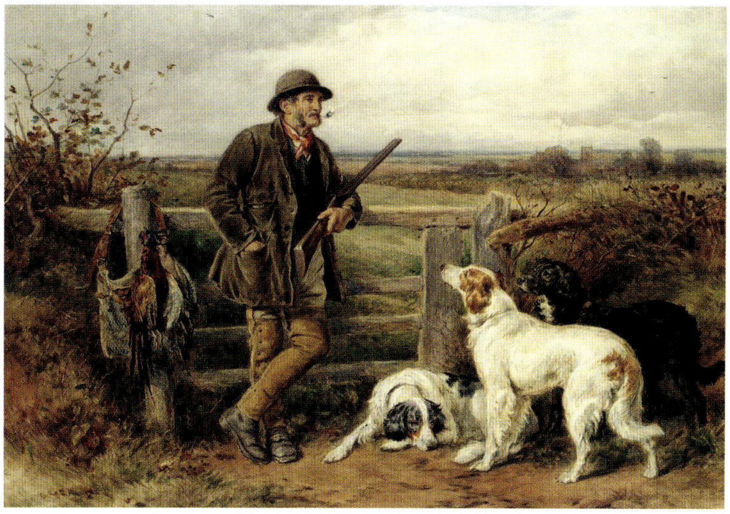

> Mr. J. Hardy, jun., another new member, supplies a class of subject new to this gallery — dogs, game, and figures, reminding us much of Mr. Frederick Tayler, but carried a very great deal further than that painter is wont to go. In "A Scotch Game-keeper" (174) we have a very good specimen of Mr. Hardy's abilities; the dogs are remarkably good, and the colour of the whole composition is agreeable.[289]

He was elected to the Royal Institute of Oil Painters in 1883 and the Royal West of England Academy in 1889.

Waiting for the Shot (1871) (Plate 215) is one of the few pictures by James Hardy that was illustrated as an engraving. The original painting was shown at the Dudley Gallery in 1871 and an engraving was published in *The Illustrated London News,* which described it as "a capital study ... the characteristics, both human and canine, are rendered with very skilful and descriptive handling". Another reviewer thought, "'Waiting for the Shot', by Mr. James Hardy, junior, is a small, clever picture, representing a deerstalker restraining two hounds ... "[291]

Hardy's best pictures were painted in the 1870s. He continued to paint a few watercolours, for example *The Gamekeeper's Rest* (1871) (Plate 216) and *Across the Moors* (1873) (Plate 217), and made sketches such as *Young Ghillie and Spaniels with the Day's Bag* (187?) (Plate 218) and *A Spaniel* (Plate 219), but most of his paintings were in oils.

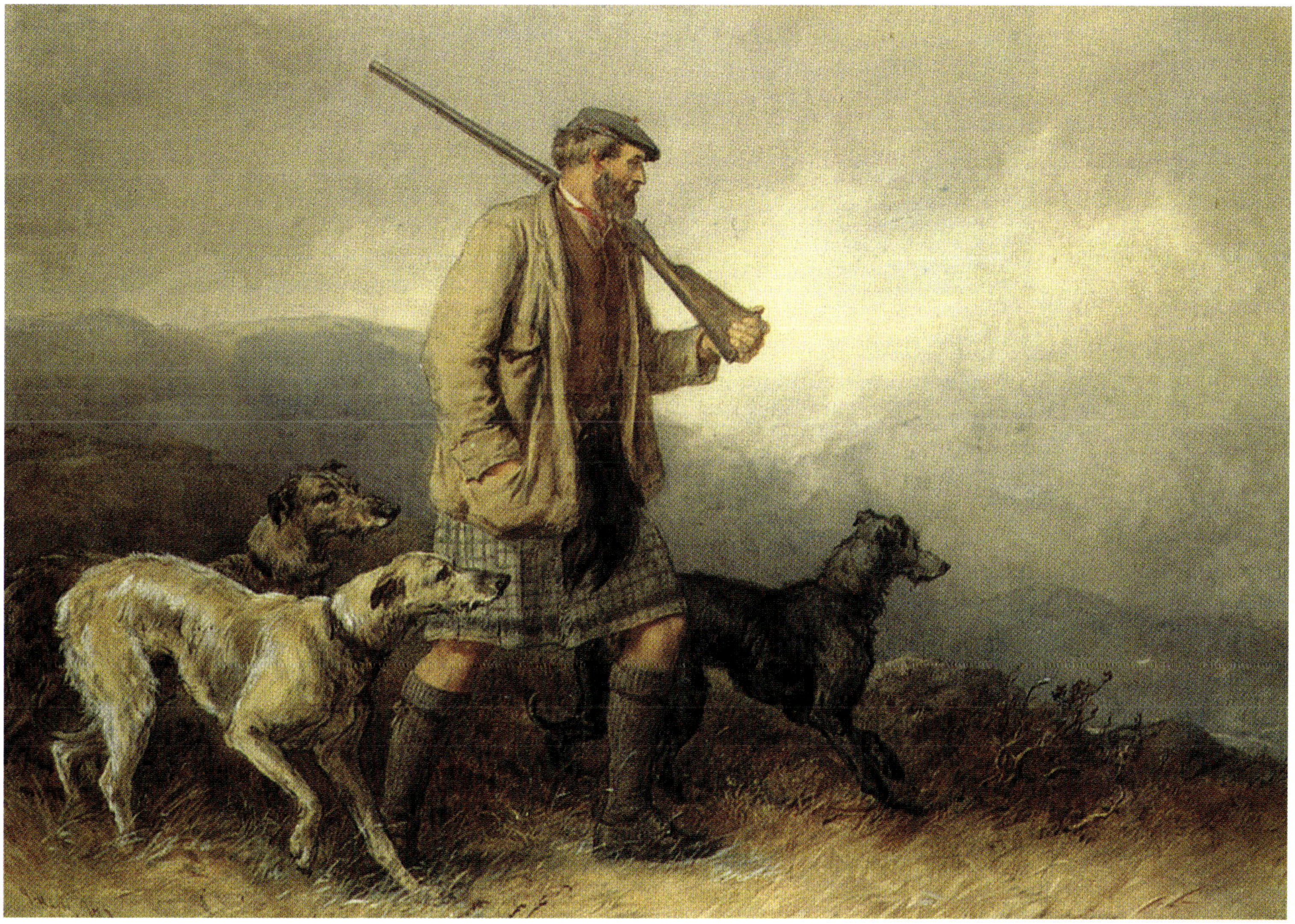

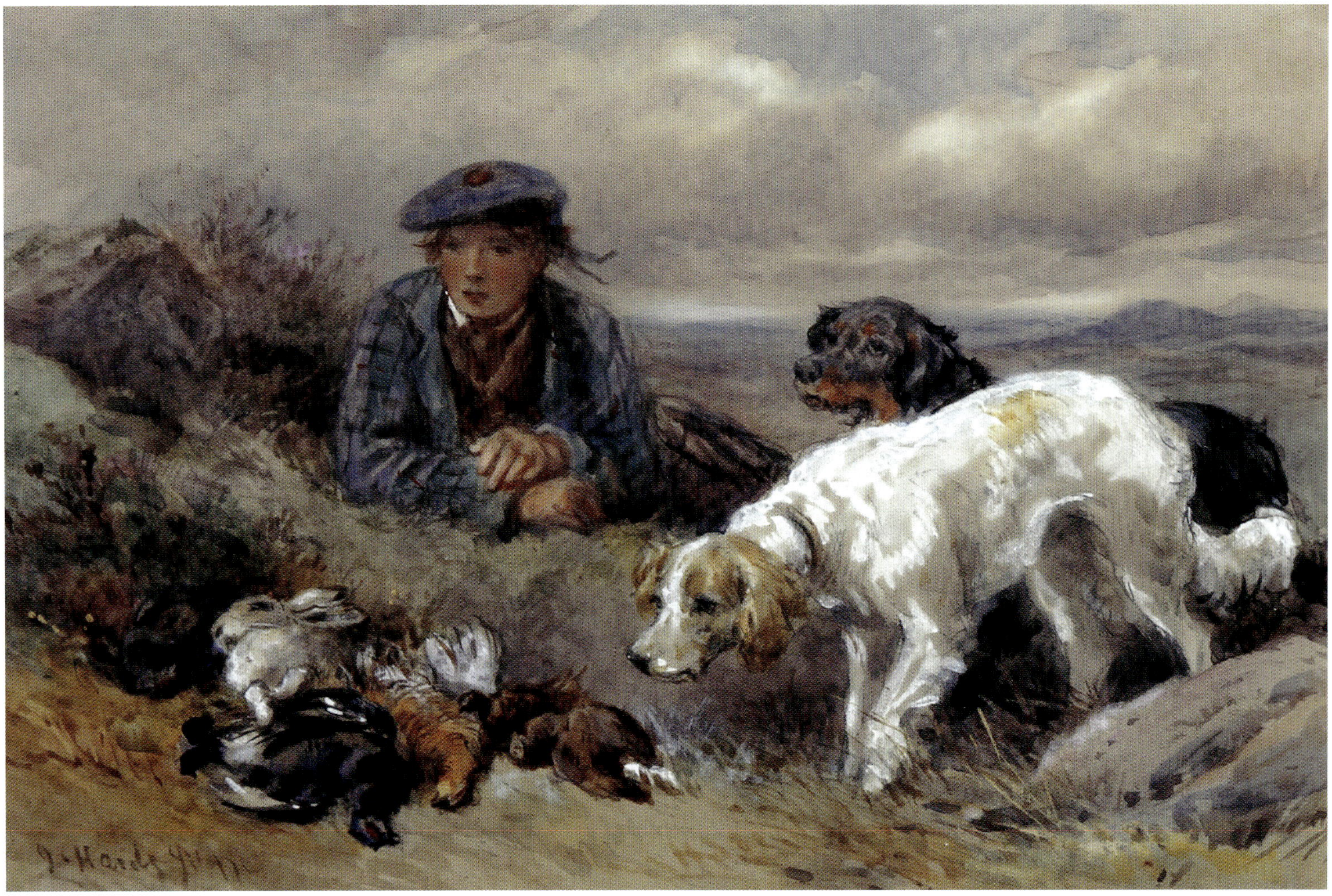

Arguably the best picture he painted was *A Young Gillie, with Setters and Dead Game* (1877) (Plate 228), which is in the Royal Holloway Collection. Typical of his work in the 1870s are *The Young Keeper* (1874) (Plate 220), *The Midday Meal on the Moors* (1875) (Plate 221), *A Good Day's Sport* (1876) (Plate 222), *The Day's Catch* (1877) (Plate 223) and *Loading Up* (1877) (Plate 224).

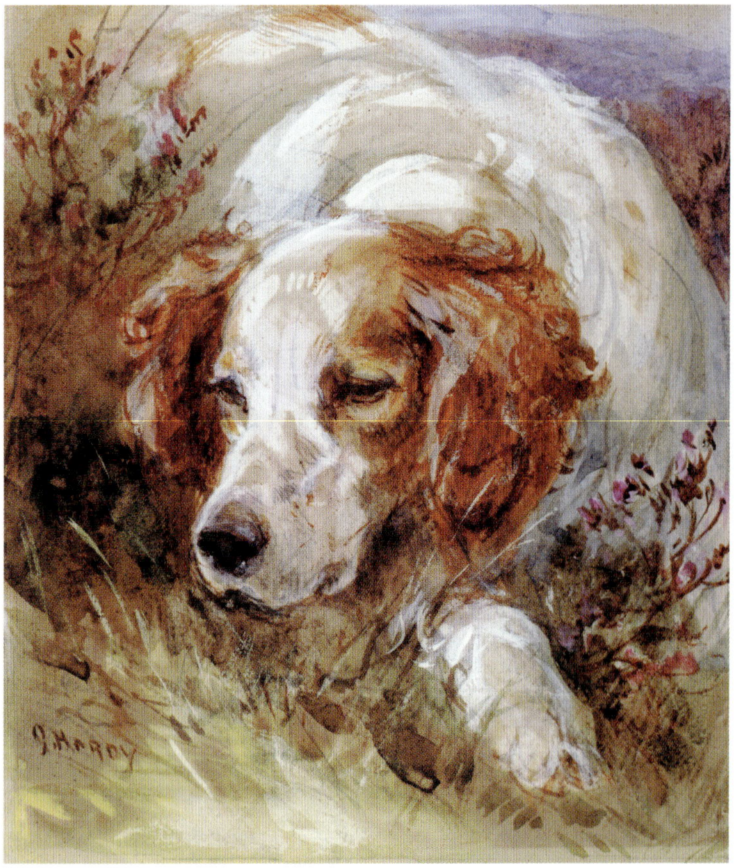

Plate 218 (above): Young Ghillie and Spaniels with the Day's Bag, 187?
James Hardy junior. Watercolour heightened with white. 12 x 17cm.
PRIVATE COLLECTION

Plate 219 (right): A Spaniel
James Hardy junior. Watercolour and body colour on paper. 11.4 x 8.9cm.
PRIVATE COLLECTION

Plate 220 (opposite page): The Young Keeper, 1874
James Hardy junior. Oil on canvas. 85 x 62.5cm.
© BURY ART MUSEUM, GREATER MANCHESTER

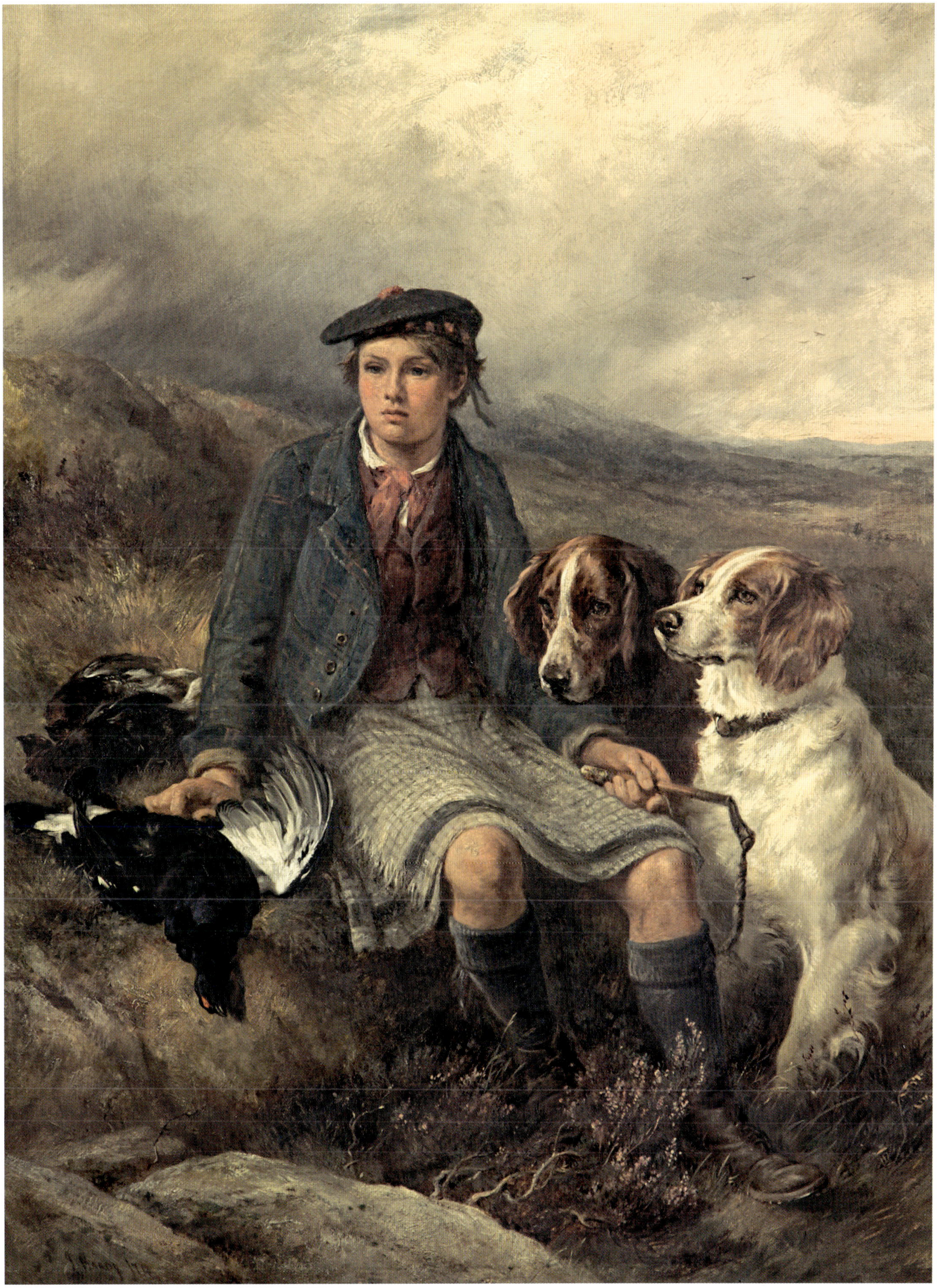

Plate 221 (left, top): The Midday Meal on the Moors, 1875
James Hardy junior. Oil on panel. 71.2 x 91.4cm. PRIVATE COLLECTION

Plate 222 (left, centre): A Good Day's Sport, 1876
James Hardy junior. Oil on canvas. 67.9 x 88.9cm. PRIVATE COLLECTION

Plate 223 (left, bottom): The Day's Catch, 1877
James Hardy junior. Oil on canvas. 61 x 50cm. PRIVATE COLLECTION.[292]

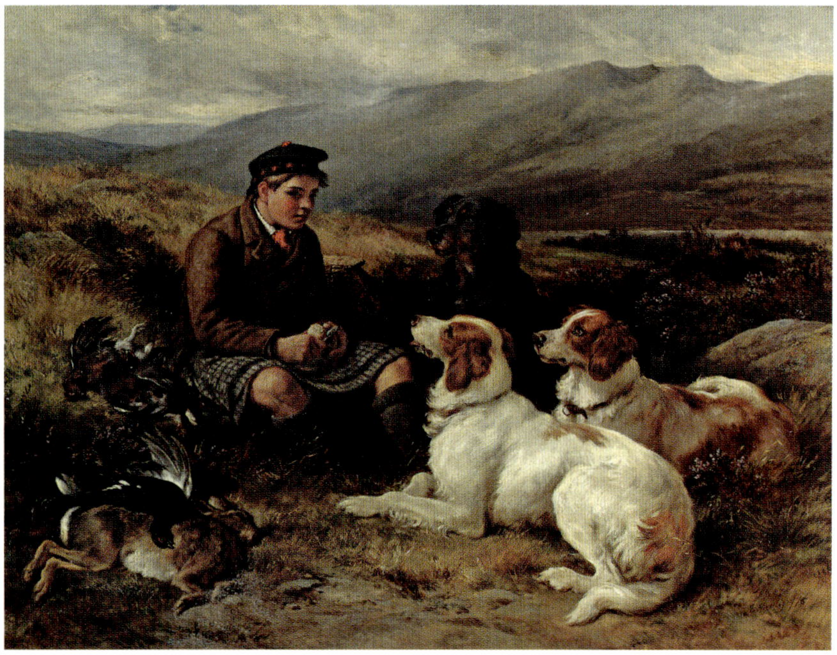

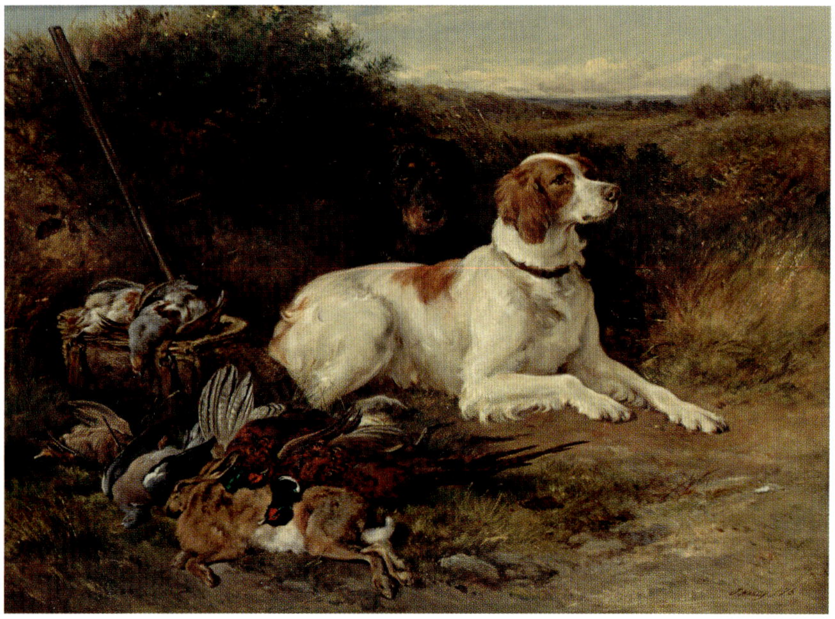

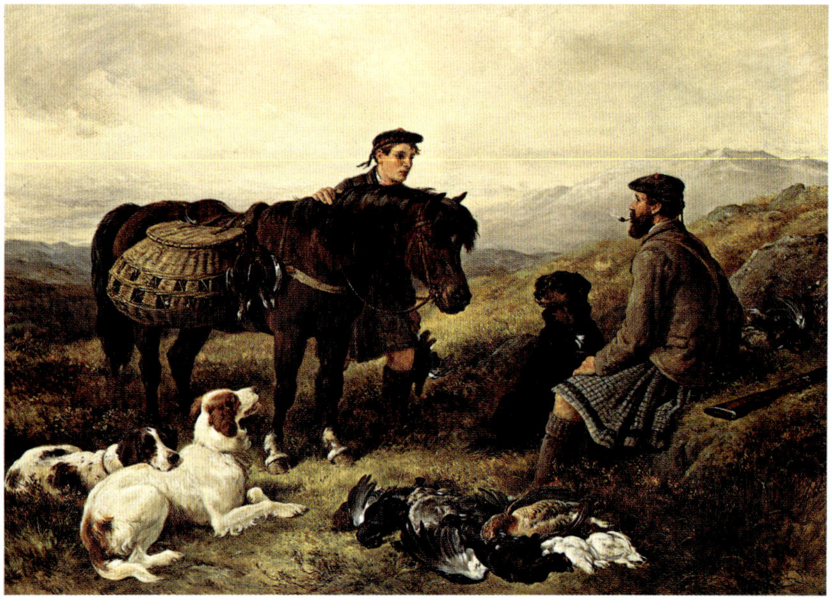

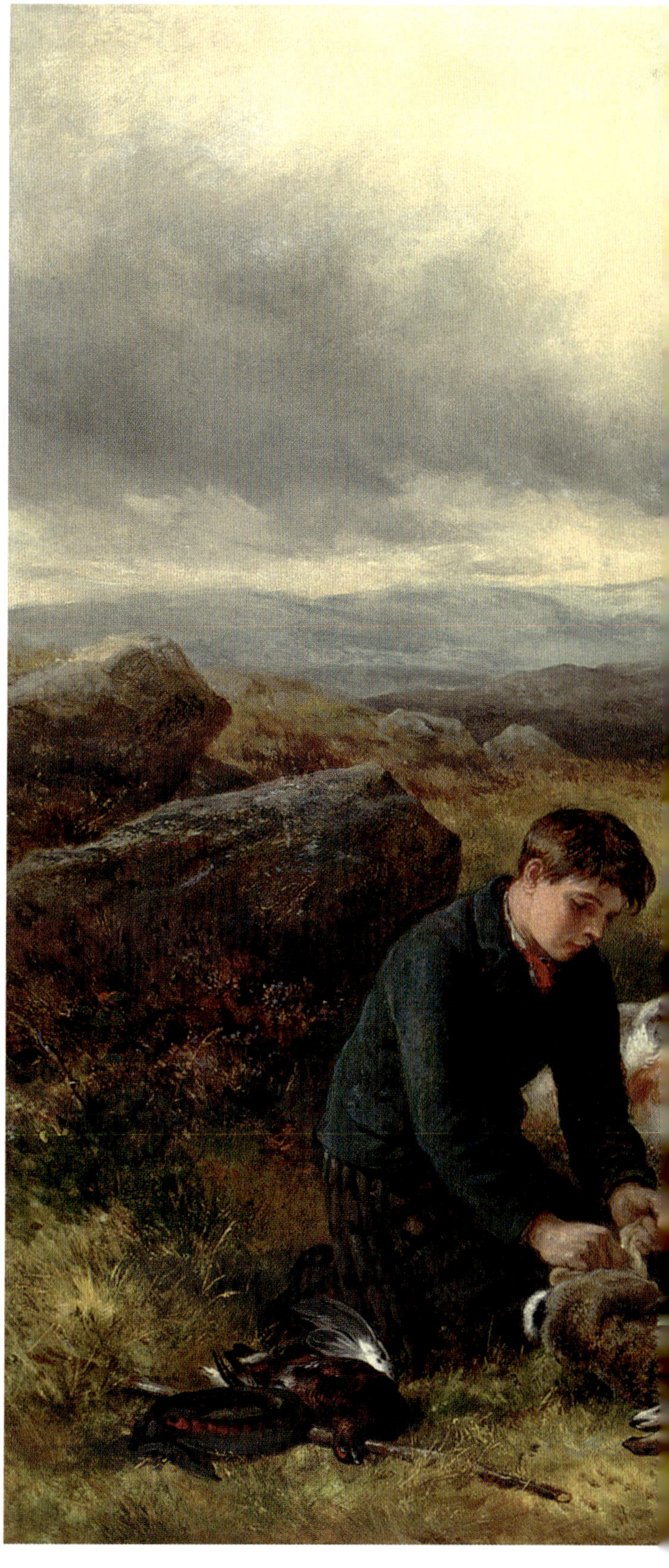

Plate 224: Loading Up, 1877
James Hardy junior. Oil on canvas. 74.3 x 112.4cm. Private Collection

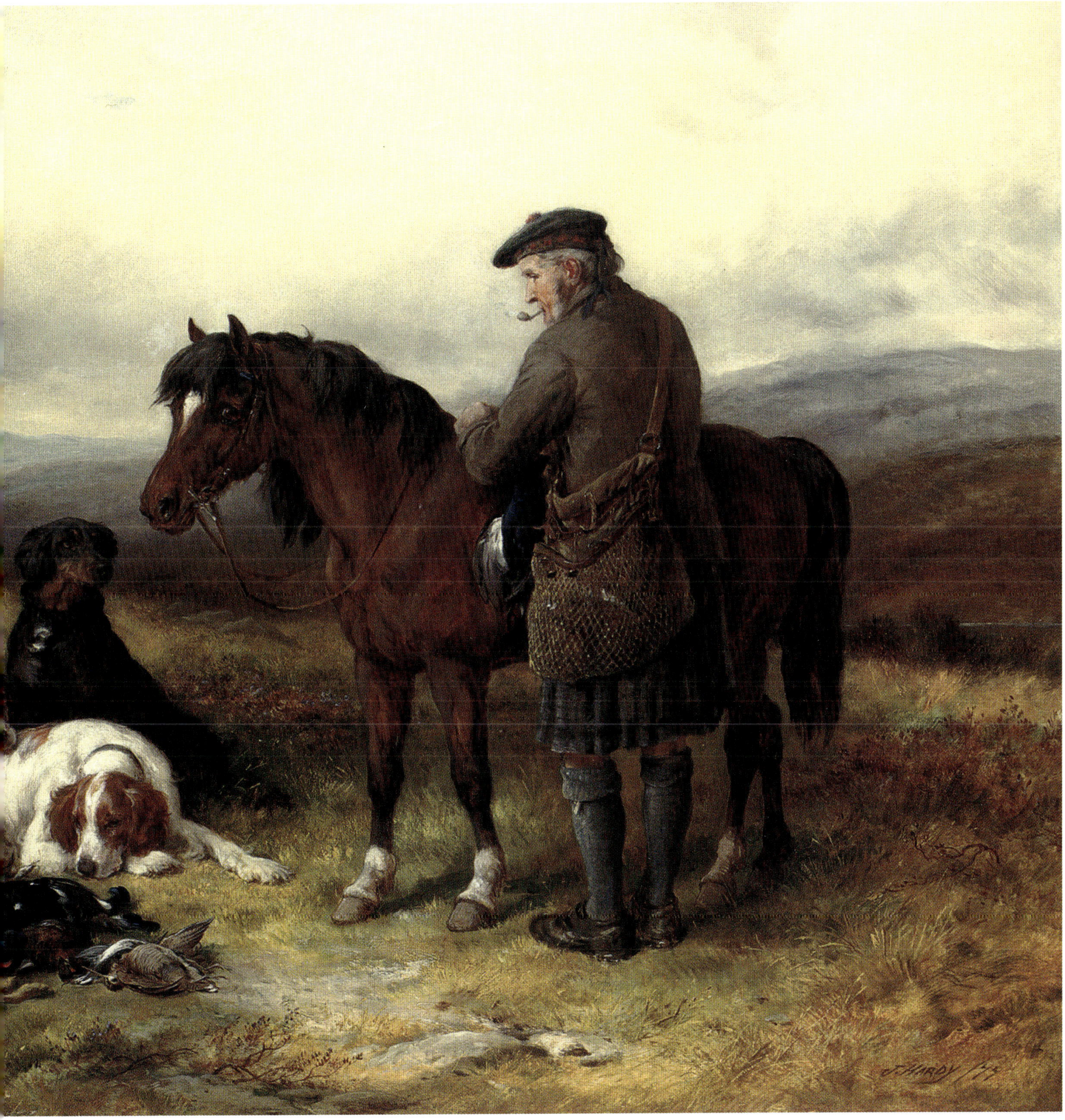

Plate 225 (below): In the Field – Spaniel, 1883
James Hardy junior. Oil on canvas. 20.3 x 31.7cm. Private Collection

Plate 226 (right): The First of October, 1884
James Hardy junior. Oil on canvas. 63 x 87cm. Private Collection

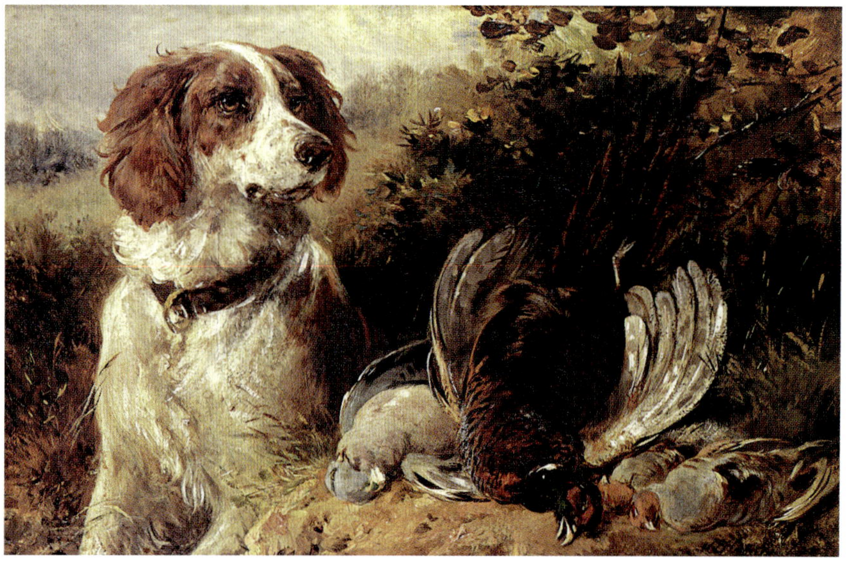

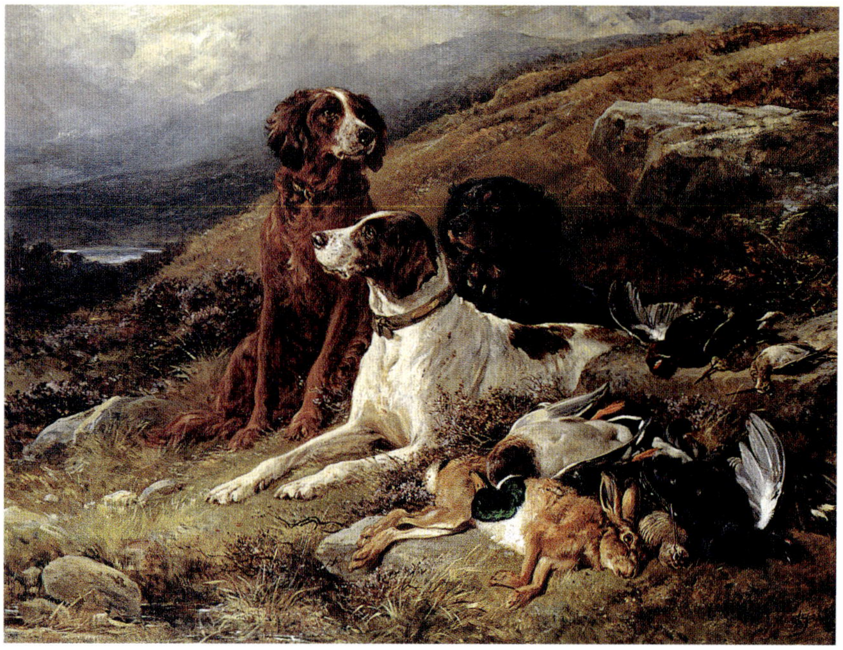

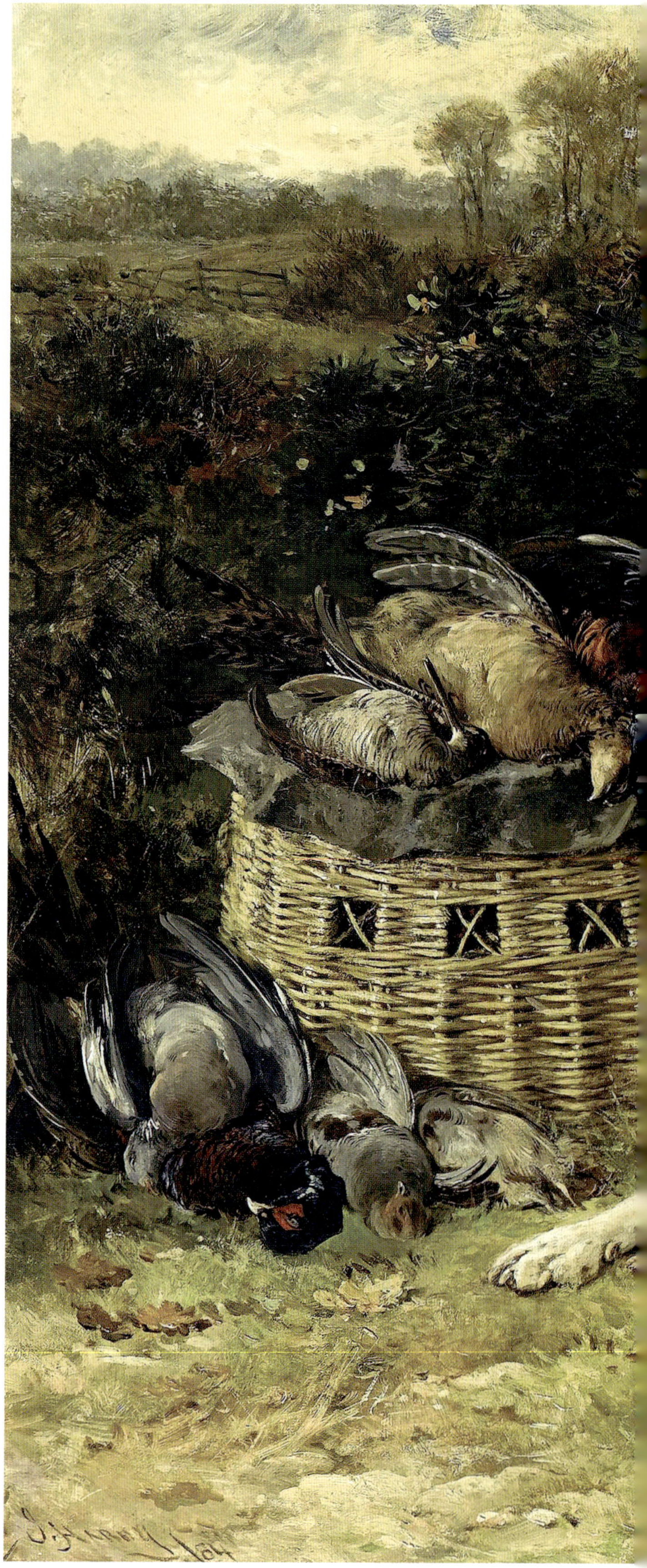

Plate 227 (left): Pointer and Setters with the Day's Bag, 1885
James Hardy junior. Oil on canvas. 71 x 91.5cm. Private Collection

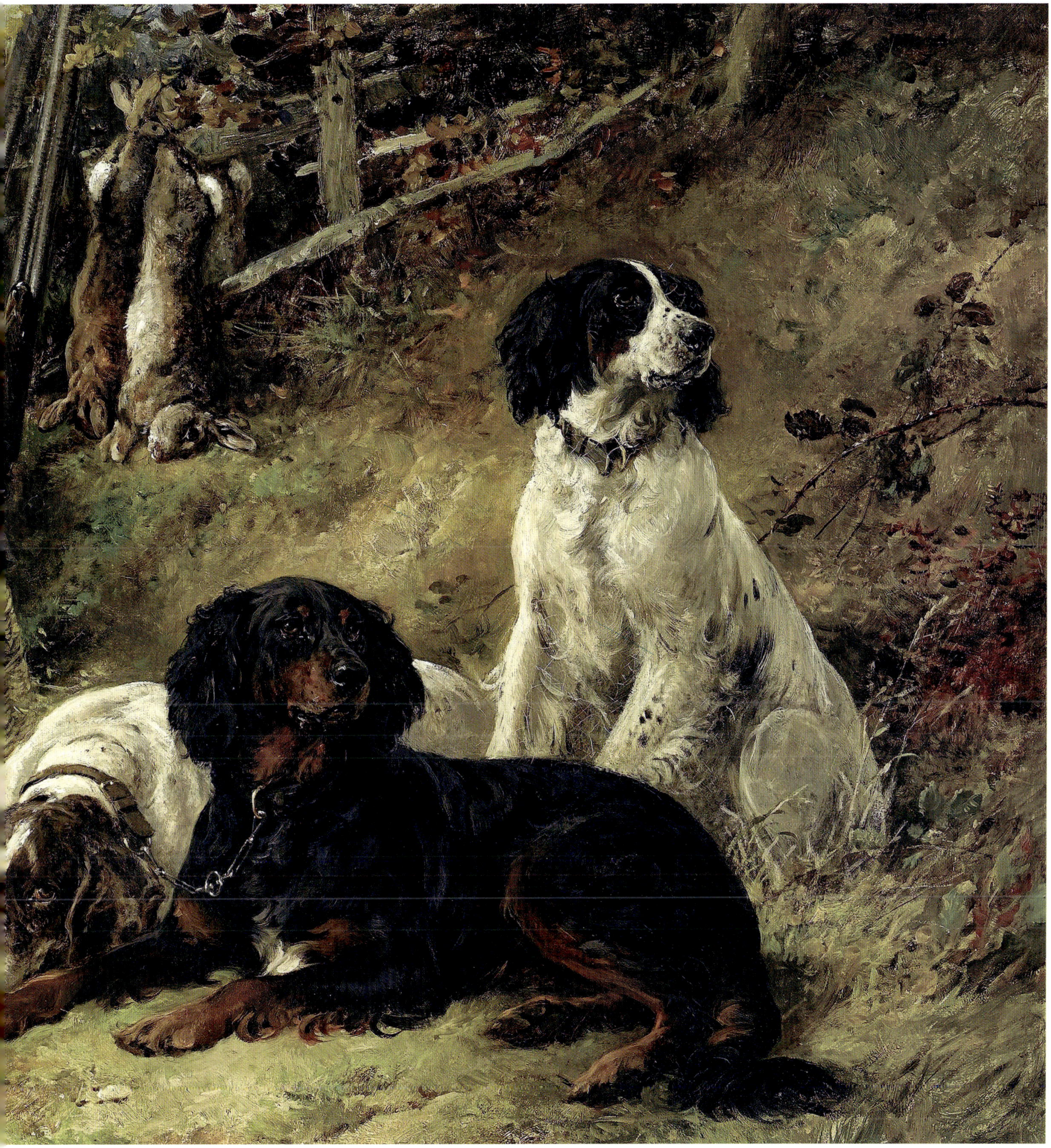

In the 1880s almost all of James Hardy junior's paintings were of sporting dogs. Paintings such as *In the Field – Spaniel* (1883) (Plate 225), *The First of October* (1884) (Plate 226), *Setters with the Day's Bag* (1885) and *Pointer and Setters with the Day's Bag* (1885) (Plate 227) are fine examples of his later work.

On 4 April 1889 there was auction at Christie's in London of more than 250 pictures, drawings and sketches by James Hardy junior "who, after a lengthened period of failing health, has deemed it expedient to part with his property". [293] [294] James Hardy junior died in Holloway Sanatorium on 24 July 1889. His

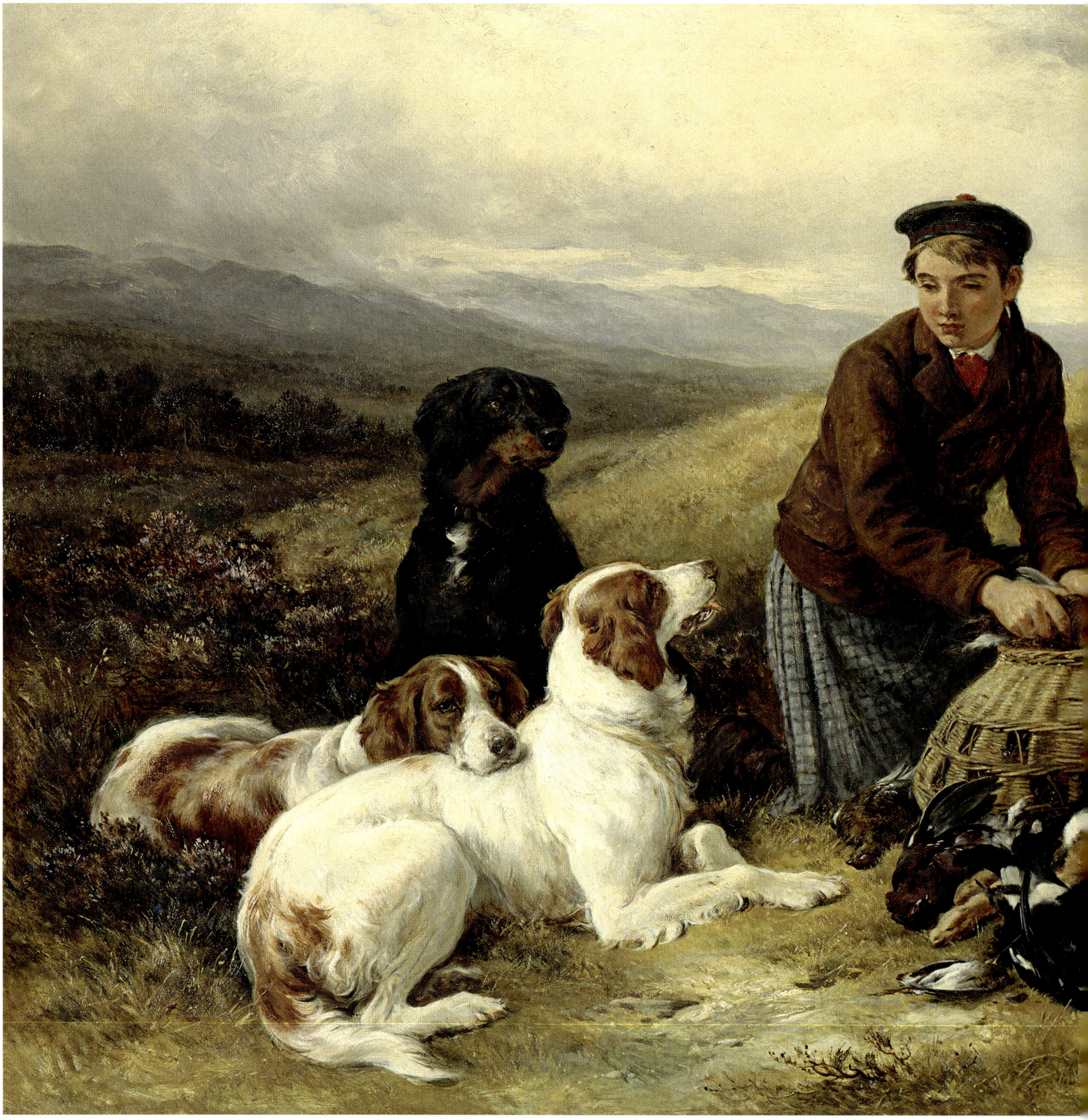

Plate 228: A Young Gillie, with Setters and Dead Game, 1877
James Hardy junior. Oil on canvas. 71 x 99cm. Royal Holloway, University of London

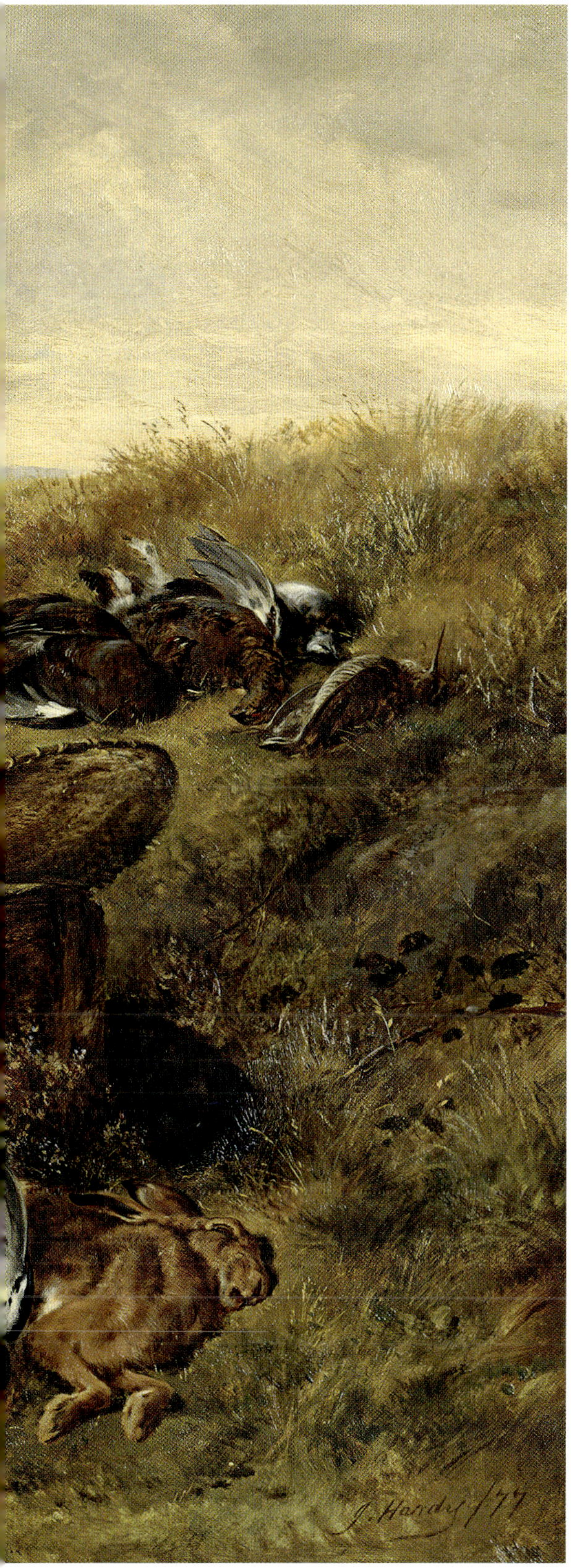

wife, Laura Amelia, had died in 1887. The cause of his death was described by the medical superintendent of the sanatorium, Sutherland Rees Philipps MD, as "Exhaustion from Melancholia. 1 year."[295] The Holloway Sanatorium "for Curable Cases of Mental Disease" was named after its benefactor, Thomas Holloway. The institution, which had an enlightened approach to mental illness, catered for middle-class patients who contributed to their support.

Perhaps James Hardy junior's best painting, *A Young Ghillie, with Setters and Dead Game* (1877) (Plate 228), had been bought by Thomas Holloway at Christie's (William Lee's sale) in 1883. A reviewer of the Royal Holloway Collection thought that the dogs in this painting were "beautifully painted, and the sincere friendship between [the ghillie] and his beautiful dogs, which it is almost an insult to call 'dumb animals', makes the painting doubly interesting".[296]

In his final pictures, such as *Three Setters in a Landscape* (1887) (Plate 229), the dogs do seem to have a particularly sad expression.

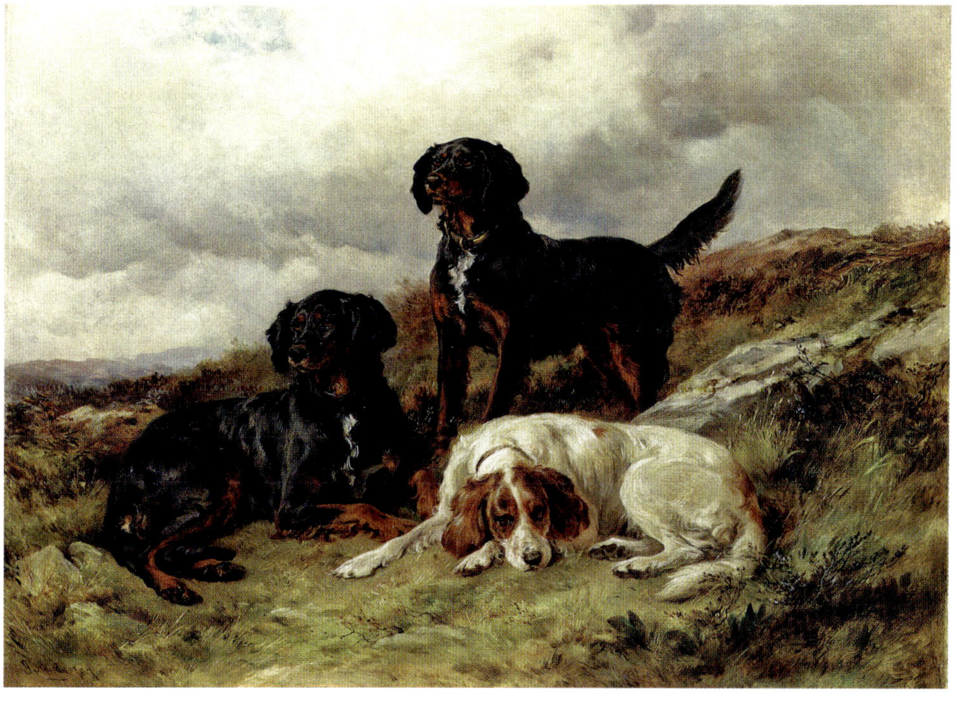

Plate 229: Three Setters in a Landscape, 1887
James Hardy junior. Oil on canvas. 48.3 x 64.8cm.
Private Collection

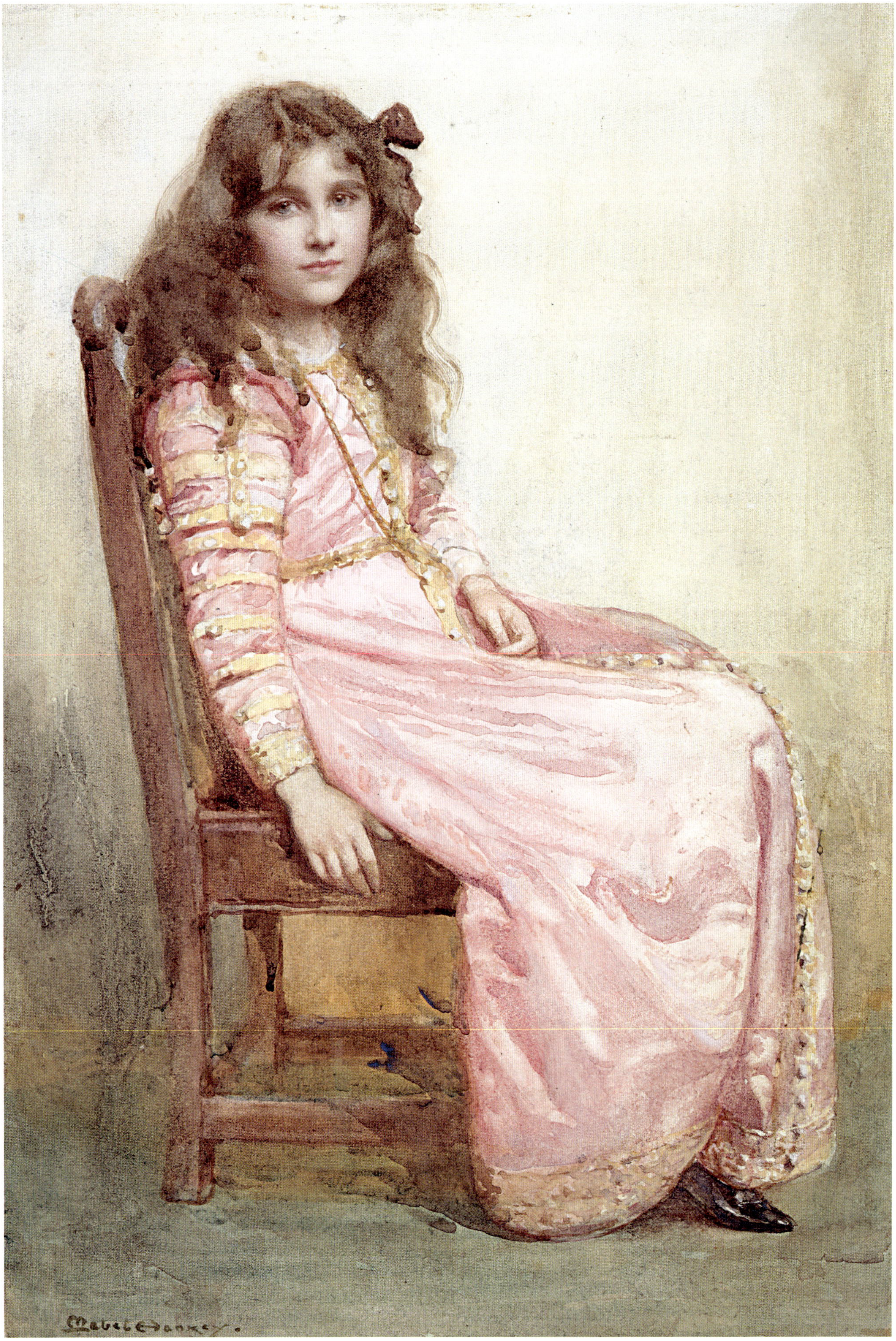
Mabel Dearmer.

CHAPTER EIGHT

Mabel Emily Lee-Hankey

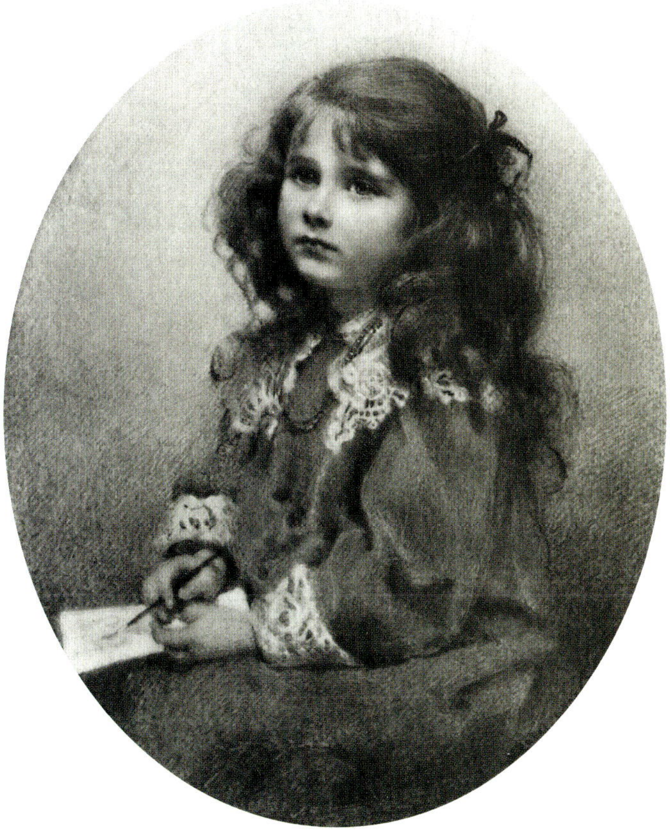

Two of James Hardy senior's daughters became artists, Ada and Elizabeth.[297] Ada Vinson Hardy (1829-1911) learned the art of miniature painting from her father, who began his career painting miniature portraits in Brighton in the 1820s. Ada's studio was in the garret of their house at 30 Henrietta Street in Bath. In 1860 she married the artist Henry E. Hobson, whose father, Henry Hobson, was also an artist in Bath. Their daughter, Mabel Emily Hobson (1868-1943), and their son, Cecil James Hobson (1874-1918), both became artists.

Mabel Emily married the artist William Lee-Hankey in 1896[298] and usually signed her paintings "Mabel Hankey". She exhibited over 70 portraits, mainly of women or children, at the Royal Academy and also showed her work at the Royal Miniature Society, the Royal Society of British Artists and the Society of Women Artists.

Mabel Emily Lee-Hankey painted five portraits of Lady Elizabeth Bowes-Lyon (Plates 230-234) (who would later become Her Majesty Queen Elizabeth the Queen Mother) and there are also several preliminary sketches for the portraits in the Royal Collection. The first portrait (Plate 230) was painted in 1905 at St Paul's, Walden Bury, when Lady Elizabeth was five years old; she is portrayed wearing a dress trimmed with crocheted collar and cuffs, holding pen and paper. In a portrait of Lady Elizabeth painted in 1909 (Plate 231), she wears a dress made by her mother, Lady Strathmore, apparently based on a gown in a painting by Velázquez. Later, Mabel was the guest of Lady Strathmore at Glamis Castle when she painted Lady Elizabeth in a white dress at the age of 15 (Plate 232). The picture painted at the age of 19 (Plate 233) eventually became part of the collection of Her Majesty Queen Elizabeth the Queen Mother.

Mabel Hankey painted portraits of several other members of the Royal Family, including Princesses Elizabeth and Margaret as children.

As a wedding gift for the Duke of York (later King George VI),

Plate 230 (above): Lady Elizabeth Bowes-Lyon, aged five, 1905
Mabel Emily Lee-Hankey. Watercolour. Private Collection

Plate 231 (opposite page): Lady Elizabeth Bowes-Lyon, aged nine, 1909
Mabel Emily Lee-Hankey. Watercolour. 37.8 x 27.2cm.[299]. Royal Collection Trust/© Her Majesty Queen Elizabeth II 2015

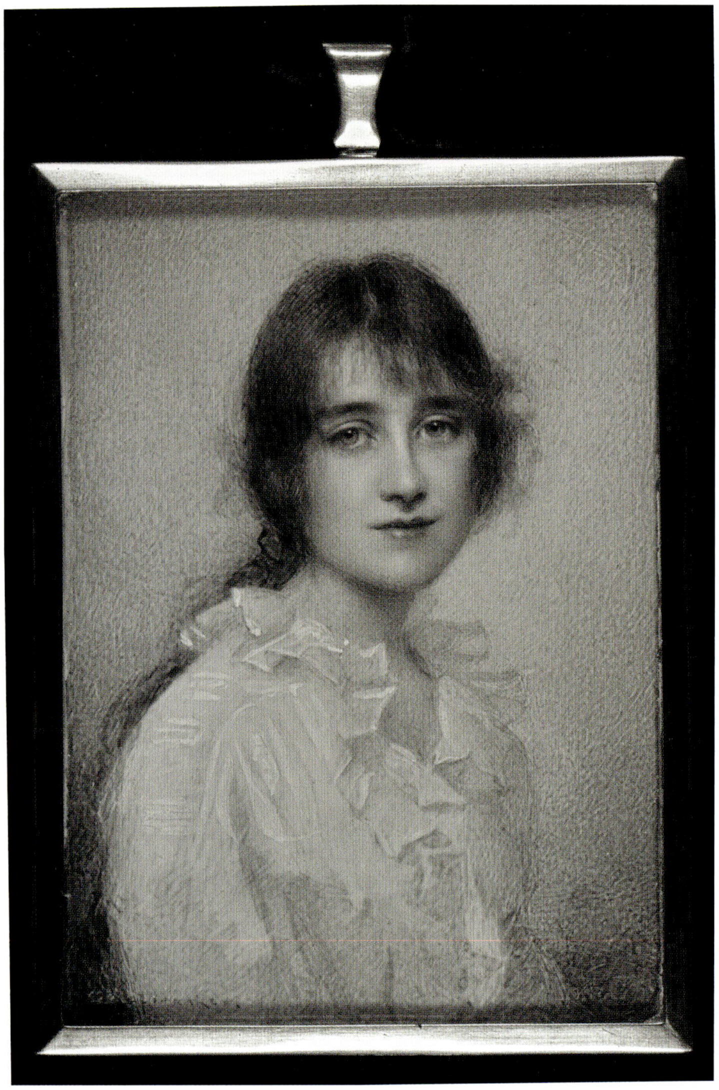

Plate 232: **Lady Elizabeth Bowes-Lyon, aged fifteen, 1915**
Mabel Emily Lee-Hankey. Watercolour.

Plate 233 (opposite page): Lady Elizabeth Bowes-Lyon, aged nineteen, 1919
Mabel Emily Lee-Hankey. Watercolour.

Lady Strathmore commissioned a miniature portrait of Lady Elizabeth in evening dress (Plate 234). (On 23 February 1923 Lady Elizabeth wrote in her diary that a "horrible photographer" had been lying in wait for her when she went for a sitting to Mabel Hankey.) [300] The painting is kept on the writing desk of Queen Elizabeth II in her private sitting room at Windsor Castle.

Towards the end of 1939, Queen Elizabeth commissioned Mabel Hankey to paint her portrait in watercolour, possibly as a means of providing some financial support to her; a memorandum written by the Queen stipulated that Mabel should be paid in advance for the portrait.[301] At the beginning of the Second World War Mabel Hankey moved from London to Storrington ("Fleurbaix" in North Lane), Sussex, where her cousin, the artist and illustrator, David Paul Hardy, lived. In 1942 Queen Elizabeth commissioned portraits of the Princesses Elizabeth and Margaret, and another portrait of herself. The paintings were completed by Mabel Lee-Hankey shortly before she died, aged 75, on 5 January 1943, and were probably the last portraits she painted.[302]

Sir Roy Strong wrote about the portrait of *Lady Elizabeth Bowes-Lyon, aged nine* (Plate 231): "No one was to know in 1900, the year of her birth, nor in 1923, the year of her marriage to Albert, Duke of York, that she was destined to be Queen. But from the earliest little watercolour of her ... by Mabel E. Hankey, there is never any doubt that the sitter has no element of hesitation or shyness in her relationship with portrait painters. The lustrous blue-grey eyes entrance the onlooker, the winsome tilt of the head already exudes that famous abundant charm, an attribute which is mentioned by every artist who has written any account of a sitting." [303]

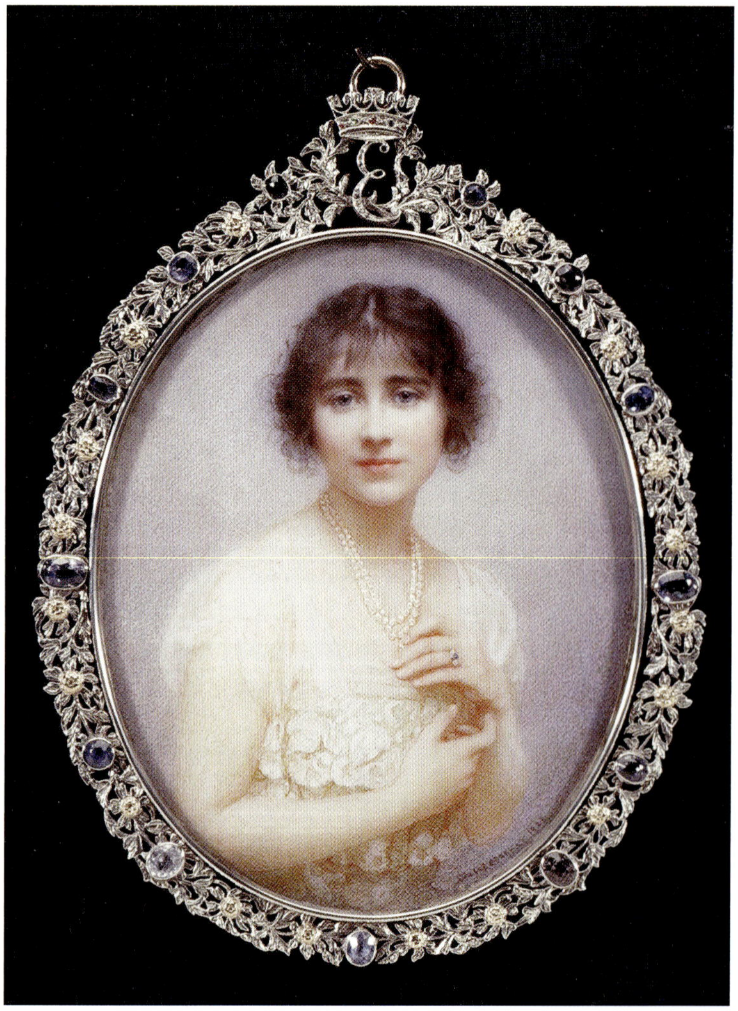

Plate 234: Lady Elizabeth Bowes-Lyon, 1923
Mabel Emily Lee-Hankey. Watercolour.

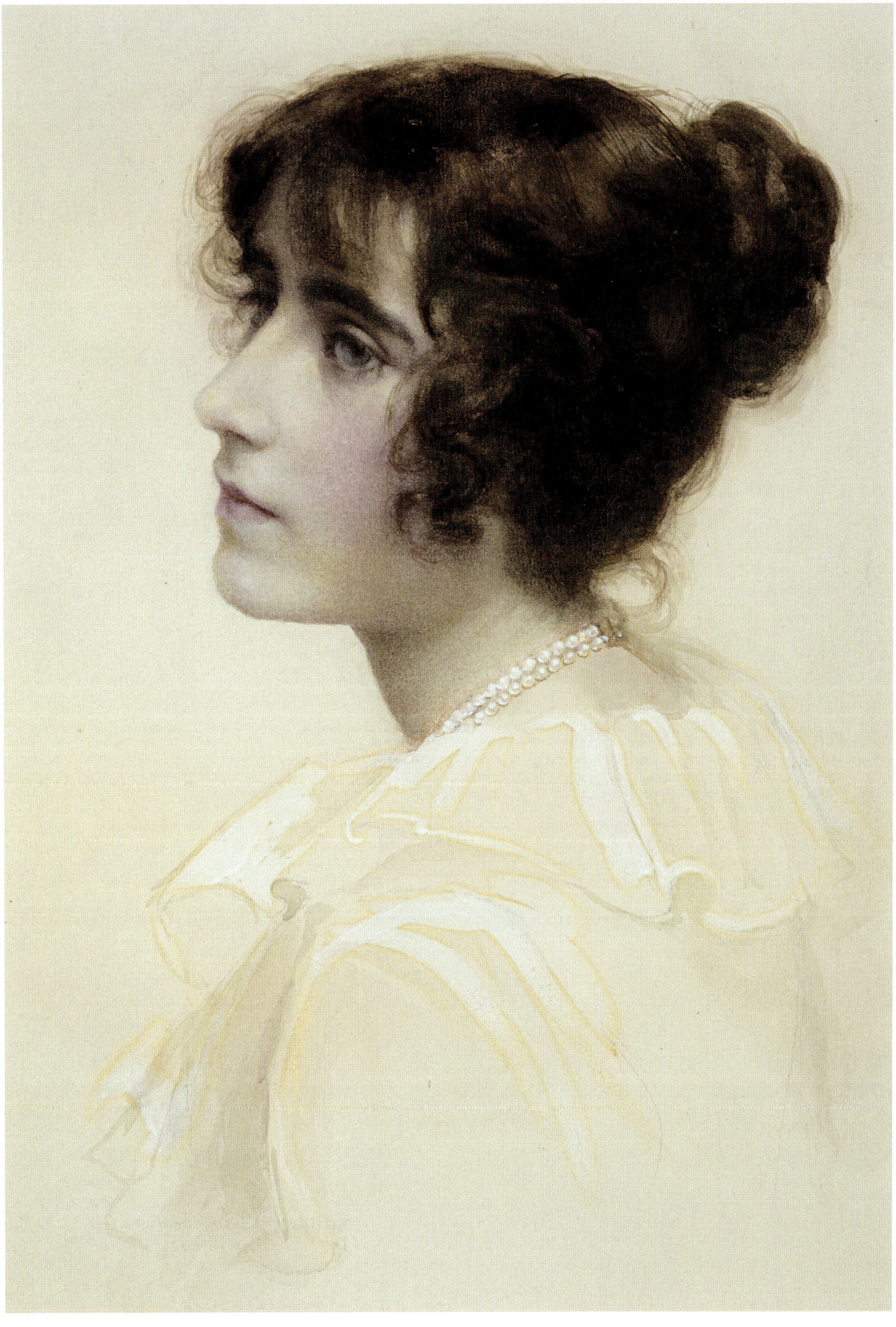

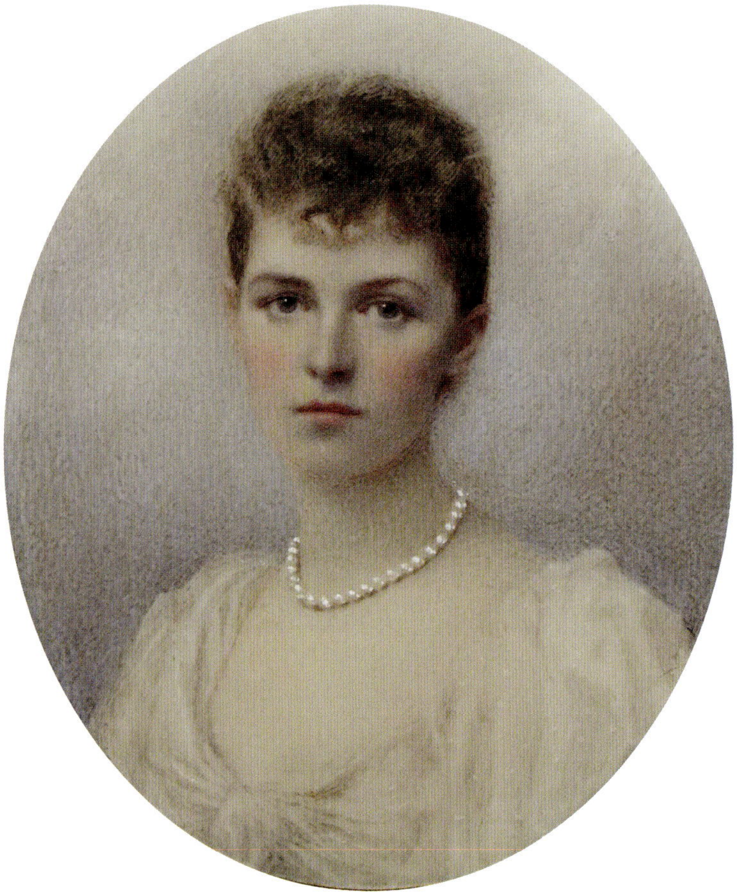

Plate 235 (left): Lady Violet Ida Evelyn Lane-Fox, 16th Baroness Darcy of Nayth, Countess of Powis (1865-1929), ca. 1885
Mabel Emily Lee-Hankey. Watercolour. Oval. Height 6.4cm.

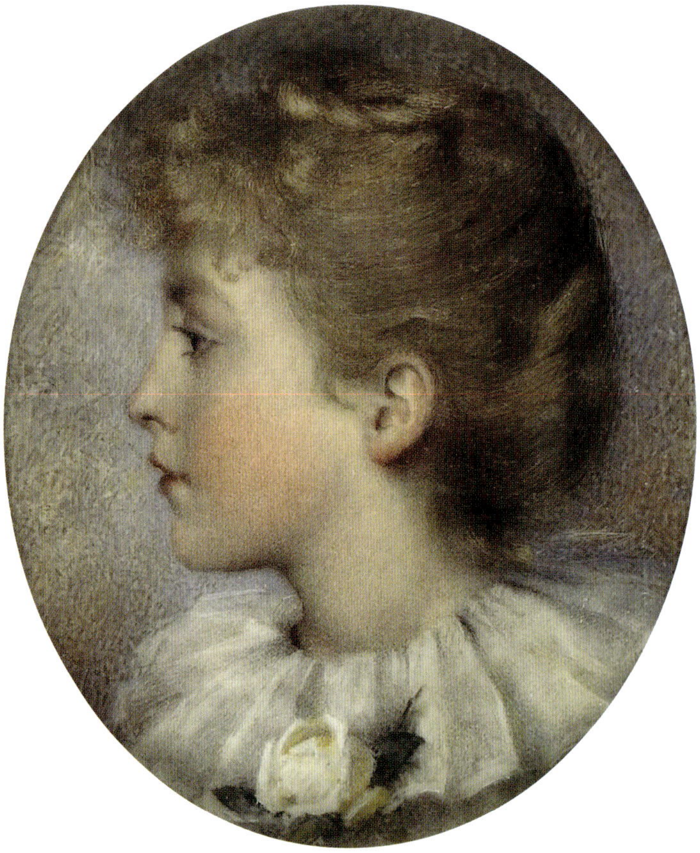

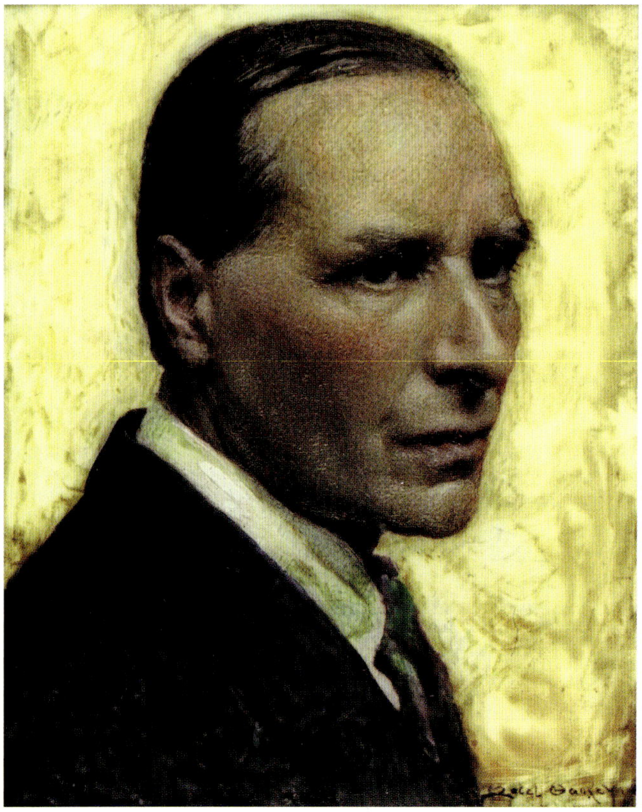

Plate 236 (above): A young girl, profile to the left, wearing a wide-collared white chemise with a pale yellow rose corsage, her blonde hair upswept
Mabel Emily Lee-Hankey. Watercolour. Oval, Height 6.3cm. PRIVATE COLLECTION

Plate 237 (left): Edwin Fagg Esq. FRSL, 1929
Mabel Emily Lee-Hankey. Watercolour. 8.9 x 7cm.
DIPLOMA COLLECTION OF THE ROYAL SOCIETY OF MINIATURE PAINTERS, SCULPTORS & GRAVERS

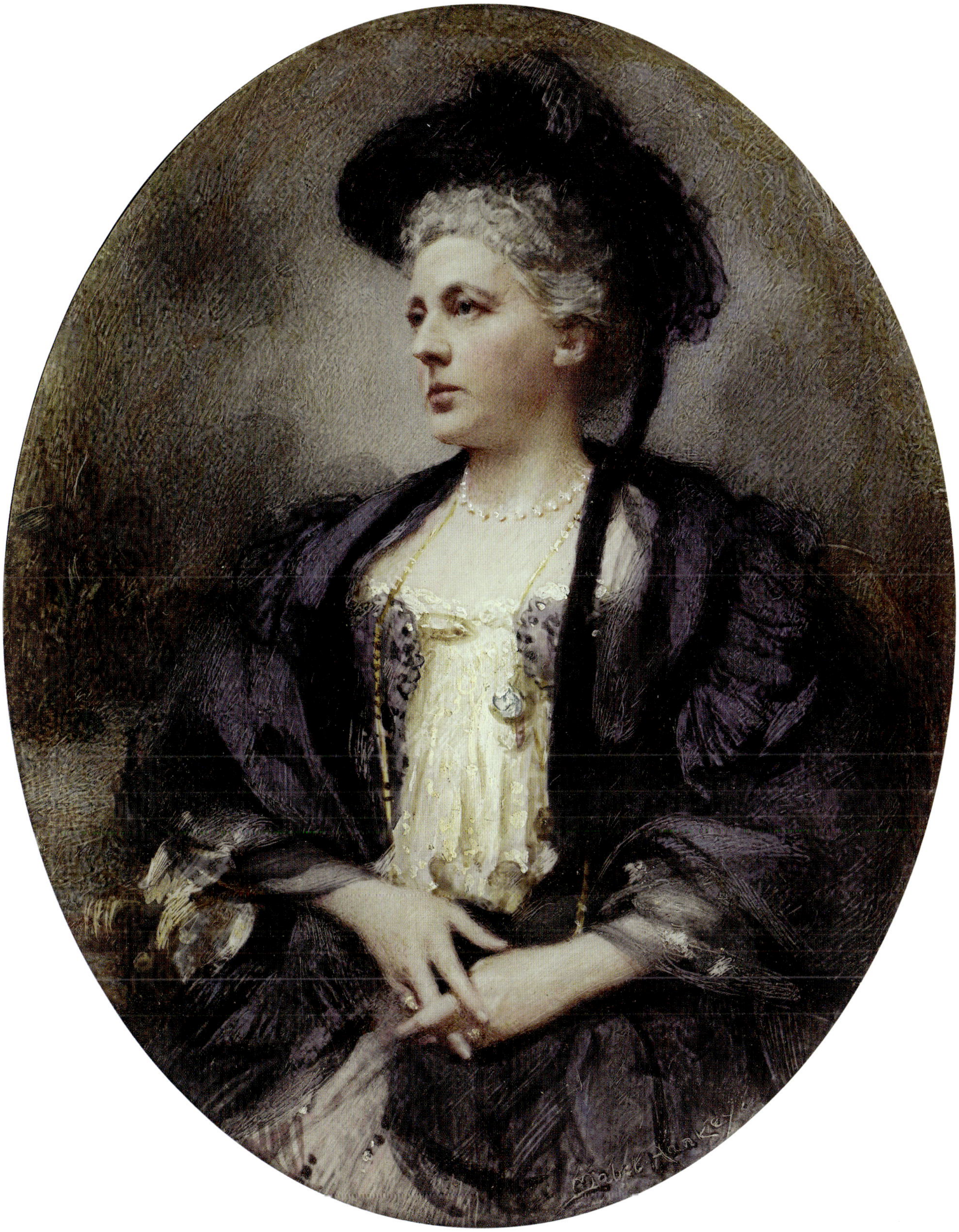

Plate 238: Lady Wimborne, née Cornelia Henrietta Maria Spencer-Churchill, OBE (1847-1927), 1905
Mabel Emily Lee-Hankey. Watercolour. Oval, Height 13.7cm. Private Collection

Especially remembered for her charitable work, an obituary of Lady Wimborne written in 1927 noted that, "Her Ladyship was possessed of great force of character. Had she been of the opposite sex or had she been born 20 years later, she would probably have figured as prominently in politics as her brother, Lord Randolph Churchill, or her nephew, Mr Winston Churchill."

CHAPTER NINE

David Hardy and his Family: Paul, Norman, Evelyn and Dorothy

David Hardy (1837-1870)

David Hardy, the third son of James Hardy senior, was born in Chichester, Sussex, in 1837. His early studies of cottage interiors showed promise, but he had only a few productive years before he became ill, probably with tuberculosis. When he was 19 he was already so ill that he was unable to paint for several months.[304]

David Hardy married Emily Collins, only daughter of the artist John M. Collins of Bath, at Cornworthy in Devon on 28 May 1860.[305] After their marriage they lived in Southwell Street, Bristol, and in 1861 were living there with Emily's mother, Caroline Masters Collins, a governess and schoolmistress, and Emily's elder brother, 23-year-old Frederick Collins, who was an "Artist, Figure Painter". A good example of David Hardy's early painting, *Boys Playing Marbles* (1855) (Plate 239), was first exhibited at the Bath Society of Fine Arts, where it was described as, "a little picture of great promise"[306]. David was 18 years old when he painted the picture. It is similar in style to paintings made by his brother, James Hardy junior, at about the same time, such as *The Itinerant Musician* (1856) and *The Bird Catchers* (1858).

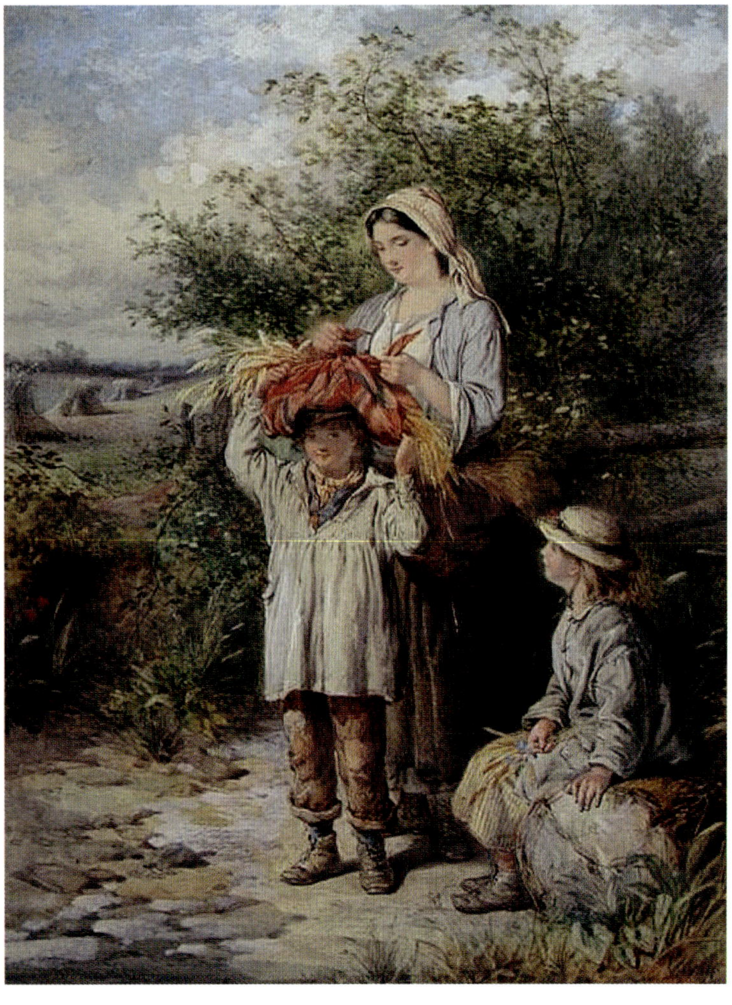

Most of David Hardy's early paintings were of cottage interiors.[307] Later, in the 1860s, he painted figures in the countryside. He painted watercolours mainly, especially during the last years of his life; for example, *A Lady with Two Children at Harvest Time* (1868) (Plate 240).

David Hardy exhibited 20 pictures at the Royal Society of British Artists between 1862 and 1870, the year of his death, and six at the British Institution between 1855 and 1865. He might have exhibited one painting at the Royal Academy exhibition, in 1855, but there are conflicting attributions for the work.[308]

Hardy spent much of his time teaching students in Bristol and sold many of his paintings in Bath. A contemporary report of "The Graphic Conversazione" at Bath that David Hardy frequently attended to meet his patrons, read:

> THE GRAPHIC CONVERSAZIONE. The exhibition was inaugurated last night by the usual conversazione of the Graphic Society. The arrangements for the accommodation and comfort of visitors were much as usual. The vestibule at the top of the staircase leading from the exhibition rooms to the Graphic Society's suite of apartments below was profusely decorated with statuary, and tastefully arranged hothouse plants, emitting a delicious perfume, which were sent by Mr G.H. Ames, of Cote House, and Messrs Garaway & Co. of Durham Down Nurseries. The "Graphic room" and vicinity was neatly adorned with evergreens. In this room was a beautiful collection of watercolour drawings. ... Mr. David Hardy ... sent a number of very superior indoor cottage scenes.[309]

From the mid 1860s, his health and financial circumstances began to deteriorate. His friend, Mr J.W. Miles, wrote that at the end of 1869 "his frame became so enfeebled that Mr Hardy was only able to visit his pupils in a hired vehicle, thus diminishing his income one half. And for several months previous to last week his strength, and consequently his earnings, failed completely".[310] David and his family lived for a few months at 15 Belle Vue Crescent, Clifton, in 1870, perhaps to be closer to his students who were in the Clifton area.

His illness progressed and he died on 5 May 1870 at the house in Belle Vue Crescent. Emily and her four children were left with very little money. Her brother, Frederick John Collins, had died (also probably from tuberculosis) a year earlier in June 1869, at the age of 32; Frederick, also an artist, had lived with the family throughout the 1860s.

Plate 239 (opposite page): Boys Playing Marbles, 1855
David Hardy. Oil on board. 28 x 21.8cm. Victoria Art Gallery, Bath

Plate 240 (left): A Lady with Two Children at Harvest Time, 1868
David Hardy. Watercolour and body colour. 54 x 38cm.[311] Private Collection

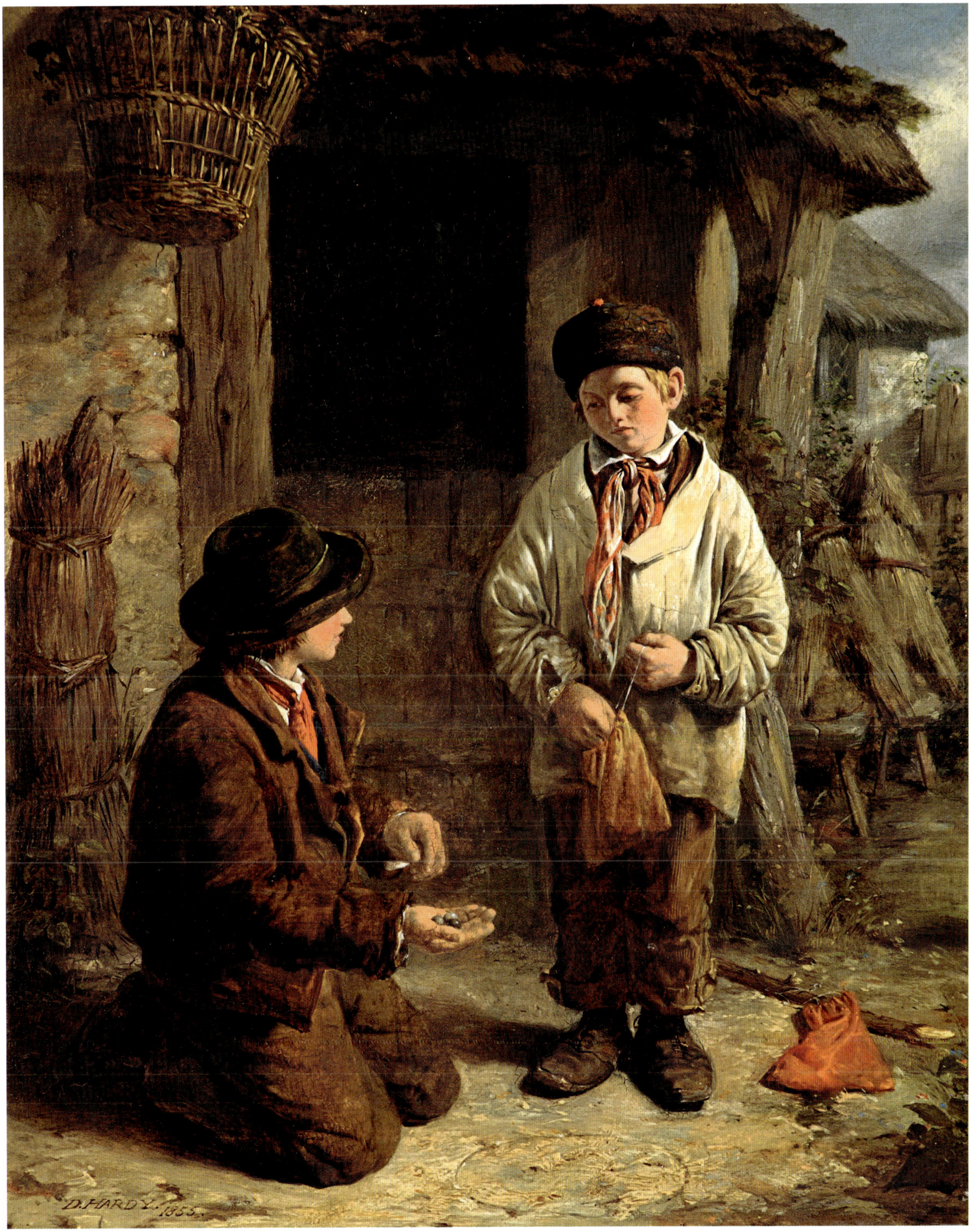
D.HARDY.
1855.

The Bath Chronicle noted David's passing:

> Mr. David Hardy, the artist whose works are familiar to the patrons of art in Bath, more especially in connection with the conversazioni of the Graphic Society, died last week, in Bristol, at the early age of 33, leaving quite penniless a widow and four young children, the eldest but seven years old.[312]

Mr J.W. Miles organised a subscription for Emily and her children. This helped to raise the sum of £286 from donations in May and June [313, 314, 315], a considerable amount bearing in mind that the annual salary of a clerk in London at the time was about £100. Around 230 donations were received: donations from the families of students David had taught in Bristol and Bath, fellow artists such as John Syer; and donations handed in to the local newspaper by people who described themselves variously as "skinflint" and "a poor student". J.W. Miles' appeal in the *Western Daily Press*, on 11 May 1870, remarked on Emily's predicament:

> *Gentlemen, —Will you kindly allow me, through your columns, to endeavour to arouse public attention and sympathy on behalf of the following distressing case.*
>
> *Mr. David Hardy, the clever artist, so well known to many inhabitants of Clifton and Bristol, died last Thursday, at the premature age of 33 years, leaving quite penniless a widow and four young children, the eldest but seven years old. I have had the pleasure of intimate acquaintance with the deceased, and can conscientiously affirm that a harder-working or more worthy man cannot readily be found. A few years ago, however, owing to the pressure of domestic afflictions, personal ill health, and other unavoidable calamities, Hardy's circumstances grew somewhat embarrassed. He thereupon proceeded to fearfully overtax his physical energies in strenuous, ceaseless effort to recover himself, and in that way sowed the seeds of pulmonary affection which has just destroyed his existence. The unfortunate circumstances in which he found himself placed entirely precluded any possibility of his making provision for his hapless wife and children, and this fact I would beg to commend especially to the notice of those who very properly censure and condemn imprudence and wilful recklessness in the head of a household.*
>
> *... A few kind individuals, to whom all the sad details of the case are known, are now striving to organise a public subscription, in order to enable the poor man's widow to secure such occupation as will best enable her to maintain decently herself and her little darling orphans.*
>
> *... We live in an age of great wealth, luxury, and refinement. Aesthetical feelings are permeating English society. The worshippers of Art are multiplying; she is growing more and more the handmaid of Christianity. We love to restore and beautify our sanctuaries. Shall a sceptic be allowed to say that whilst we give cheerfully £1,000 for a stained window, we grudge a half-crown to an unhappy artist's widow and children, and allow them to starve, or sink to the degradation of workhouse?*
>
> *Let us by all means seek unity of worship and catholicity of worship; but let us remember that "Pure religion and undefiled before God and the Father is this—to visit the widows and orphans in their affliction."*
>
> *J. W. MILES, B.A.*
>
> *Grosvenor Villa, Clifton. May 10, 1870.*

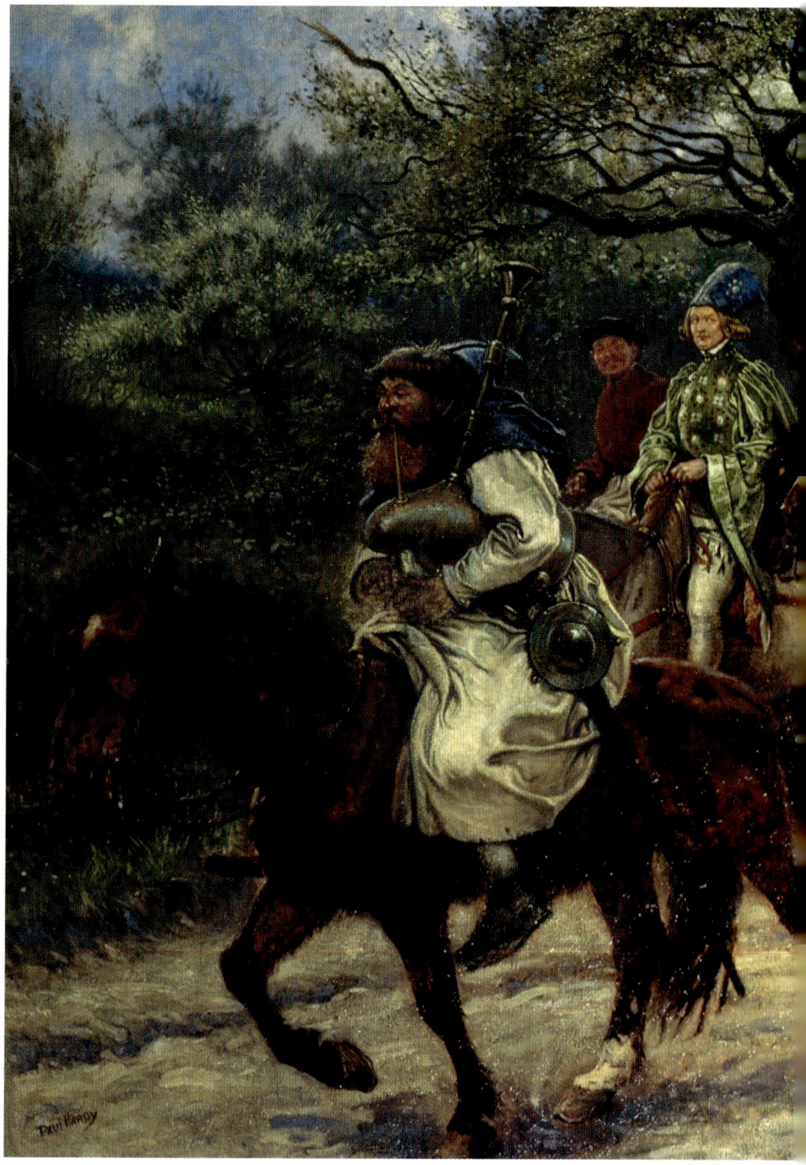

Plate 241: Pilgrims from Chaucer's Canterbury Tales, ca. 1903
Paul Hardy. Oil on canvas. 96.4 x 194.8cm.
Canterbury City Council Museums and Galleries
The pilgrims' costumes are based on the earliest surviving illuminated manuscript of The Canterbury Tales, The Ellesmere Chaucer.

Following the death of her husband, Emily Hardy removed to 5 Meridian Place, Clifton, Bristol, in June 1870, [316] and in 1871 was living there with her four children, her mother, a servant and a lodger, a former governess like her mother. Emily, whose father had been an artist in Bath, gave art lessons and described herself in the 1871 census as an "Artist, Landscape and Figure [painter]". Her own children numbered among her students; all four became artists and illustrators.

By 1881, Emily was living at 18 Meridian Place; Emily and her sons David and Norman were all described as "Landscape Artists". And there was a lodger, Charles Paliner, aged 31, a landscape painter.

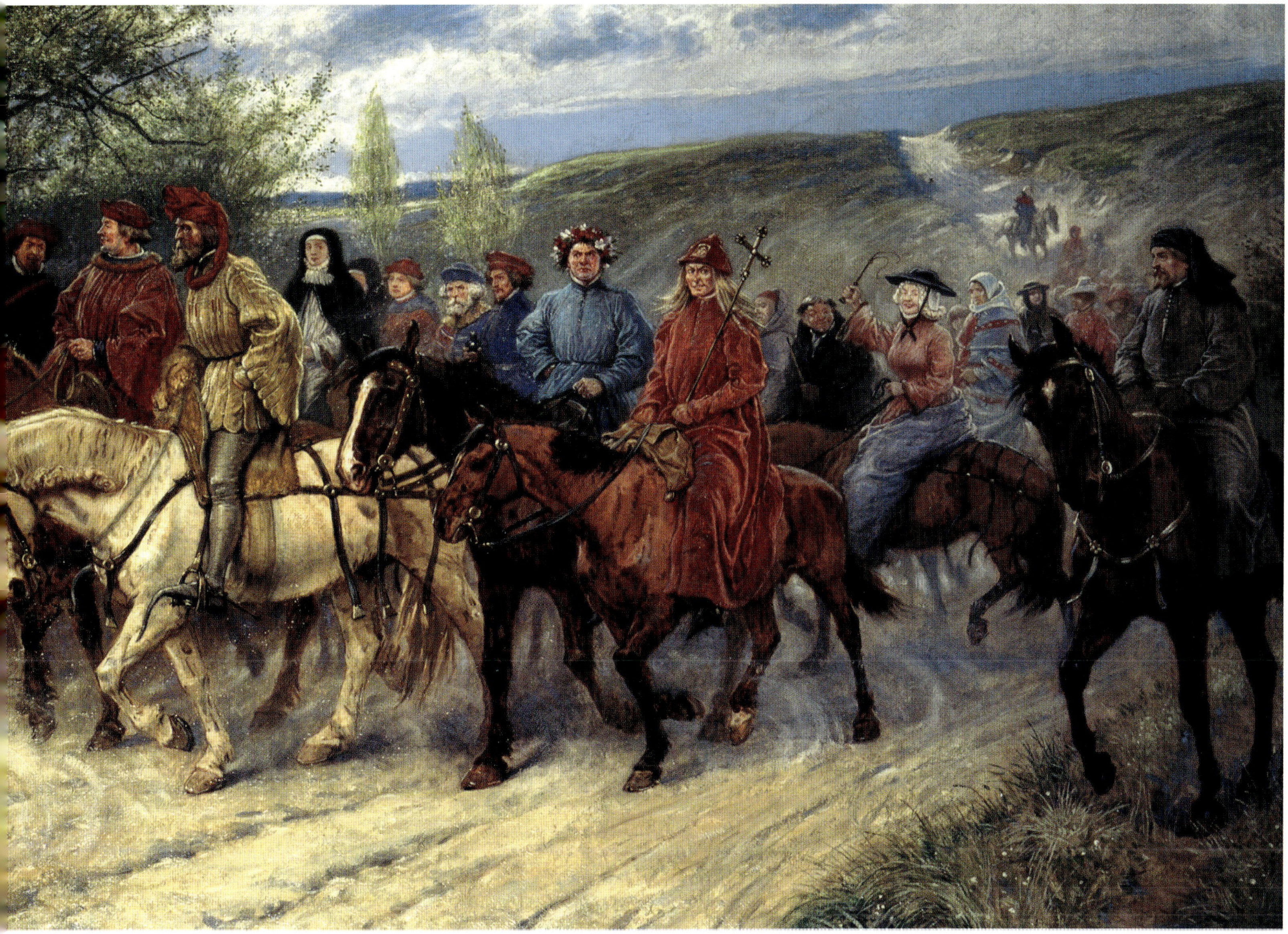

David Paul Frederick Hardy (1862-1942)

Paul Hardy, eldest son of David and Emily, was born on 2 August 1862[317] at Clifton, Bristol, and baptised "David Paul Frederick", although he generally used the name "Paul Hardy". His widowed mother became an invalid when he was 15 years old and Paul had to help provide for the family.[318] Until 1886 he remained at Bristol. He taught drawing and painting, exhibited his paintings at The Bath and West of England Society[319] and illustrated magazine articles, for example "A Glimpse at Bristol and Clifton" by John Taylor, city librarian of Bristol.[320]

In 1886 Paul moved to Chelsea and by 1887 was becoming well established as an illustrator. He illustrated new editions of *The Children of the New Forest* by Captain Marryat and other books published by George Routledge and Sons. And his work was recognised by reviewers: illustrations for *Little Peter* by Lucas Mallet were described in *The Academy* as "as truly sympathetic illustrations as we have seen for many a long day", and in 1890 *The Graphic* thought that "Paul Hardy's pictures are capital."[321]. By 1888 he had begun his long association with Cassell & Co. and contributed numerous illustration to their Christmas Annual *Yuletide*. He would go on to produce illustrations for Cassell's for over 50 years.[322]

Paul married the sculptress Ida Mary Wilton Clarke on 28 July 1888 at St Matthias Church, Earls Court. (Ida's sister, Maud Umfreville Clarke, was also an artist; many of her paintings of horses were published in *The Badminton Magazine.*) Their friend and neighbour, Sir John Everett Millais, painted a picture of Mrs Paul Hardy the following year, a portrait described as "very handsome indeed, with somewhat of a Spanish mien, in a black dress, with jet ornaments."[323] After their marriage, Paul and Ida moved to Bexleyheath in Kent. By 1901 they had moved again and were living at Chobham in Surrey with their son, Gordon, aged six. By this time Ida was breeding prize-winning Persian Blue cats, which must have led to occasional difficulties in the Hardy household.[324] She wrote that her prize-winning stud cat, "Wooshoo", was once so ill "that the vet. had given up on him", but she "kept him going with doses of pure alcohol every two hours day and night until he recovered".

A few years later, Paul Hardy moved to Queen's Road, Cheltenham, where he was given a prominent role, as the judge, in the town's summer pageant in 1908, perhaps because of his interests in medieval armour and costumes, evident in paintings such as *Pilgrims from Chaucer's Canterbury Tales* (ca.1903) (Plate 241).[325] The climax of the week's celebrations was the Fancy Dress Ball, in which more than 700 took part; "an extremely picturesque

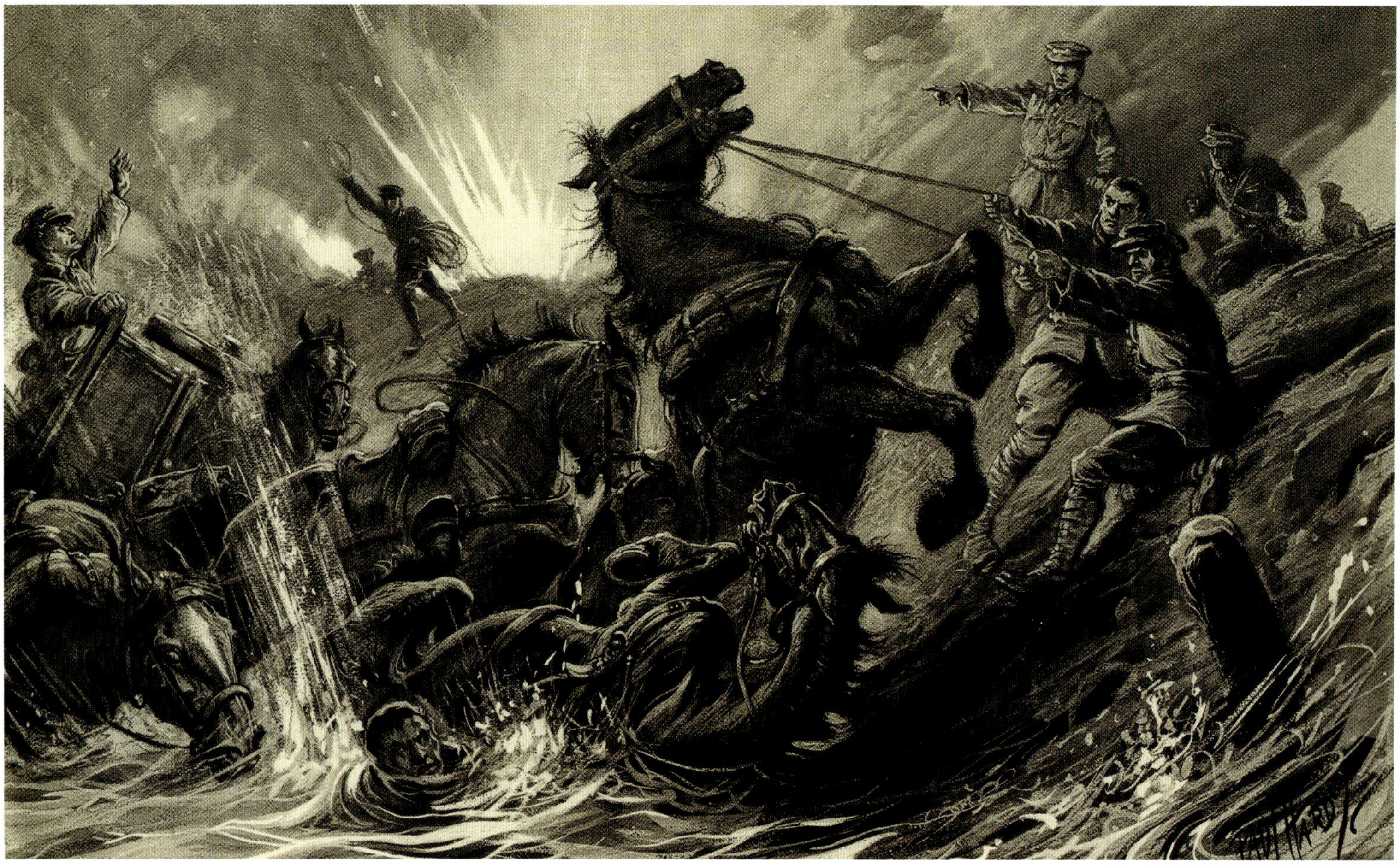

Plate 242: Stampeded by Shell-Fire: A Team with Ammunition Waggon
After Paul Hardy. "Floundering in a Canal. Drawn by Paul Hardy from a sketch by his son[326] at the front." Supplement in *The Graphic*, 1916.

incident in the course of the proceedings was the passing of the whole of the characters around the Town Hall in review order, under the eye of Mr. Paul Hardy, the well-known black and white artist, for the award of the prizes offered for striking costumes in their order of merit." It appears that, "despite differences of opinion" the decisions of the judge (Mr. Paul Hardy), who was dressed as "Sir John Grey (Battle of Tewkesbury)", gave general satisfaction. (It was reported that "there was a little misunderstanding over the award of the third prize, but eventually "Pagent" and "Cheltenham" (Mrs. Boyd Cardew and Mrs. R. L. Webb) were bracketed together.") [327]

Paul Hardy was a prolific illustrator; his illustrations appeared in more than 26 periodical titles and he illustrated many books, specialising in adventure stories, historical novels and military subjects. One of the last books he seems to have illustrated was *The Smugglers,* published by Cecil Palmer in 1923. His paintings were exhibited at the Royal Academy in 1890 and 1899.

Paul Hardy's picture *Stampeded by Shell-Fire* (published in *The Graphic* in 1916) (Plate 242) was based on a sketch made by his son at the front during the First World War.

He contributed to *The Strand* magazine from 1891 to 1907; his first illustrations were for a translation of Alexander Pushkin's "The Queen of Spades" in January 1891. Together with Sidney Paget, the illustrator of *Sherlock Holmes* stories, he illustrated

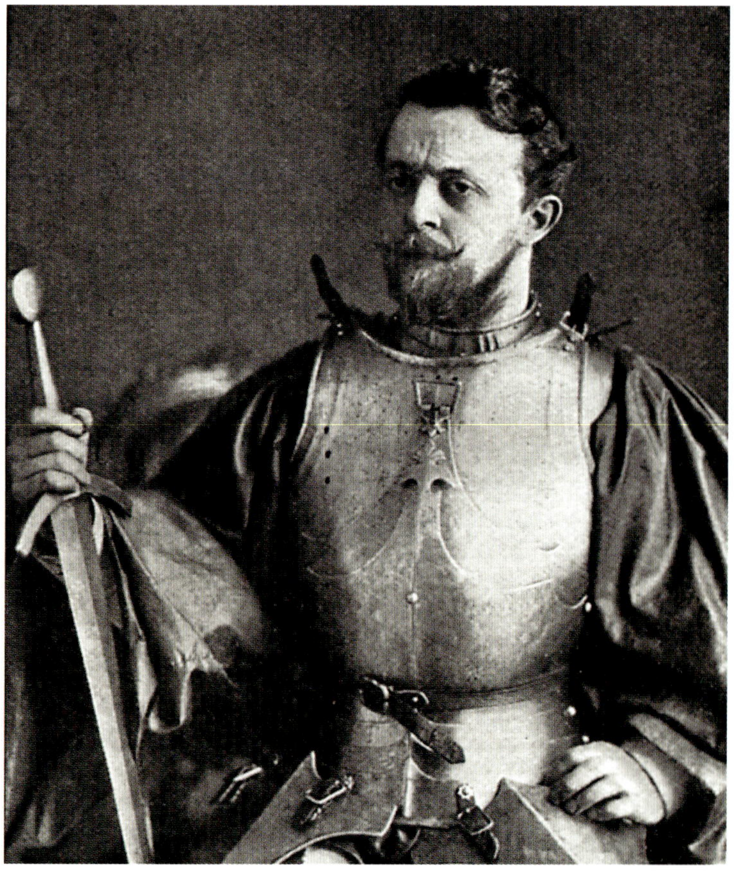

Plate 243: Paul Hardy in 1895.[328]

many popular stories in *The Strand* about the Glasgow detective Dick Donovan. During the 1890s, Paget and Hardy were the magazine's lead artists. *The Strand* wrote of Paul in 1895: "He has worked for a great number of publishers. No artist of The Strand is better known to our readers, as his bold and striking work has appeared in almost every number since the Magazine was started."[329]

Hardy also illustrated several books written by Sir Arthur Conan Doyle, including *The Refugees*, *Round the Red Lamp*, *The Great Shadow* and *Beyond the City,* and he illustrated stories by H.G. Wells published in *The Strand*.

After living in Cheltenham for several years, Paul and Ida moved to Arundel House, Tisbury, Wiltshire. Around 1912 Paul moved to Storrington in Sussex where he lived for the rest of his life.

He illustrated *Canterbury Puzzles, and Other Curious Problems* (1907), written by the mathematician Henry Ernest Dudeney. Hardy also illustrated several novels written by Henry Dudeney's wife, Alice, whose work was much praised at the time. Paul Hardy had met Alice at Cassell's when he illustrated her novel *Gossip's Green*, published in 1906. She described in her diaries her relationship with Paul; their affair had ceased in 1905, began again in 1910 and continued for many years.[330, 331]

Paul Hardy was also an accomplished metalworker and was an advisor to the armoury department at the British Museum.[332] A visitor to his workshop and cottage in 1917 remarked on the suits of armour: " ... A friend was telling me yesterday he had just been visiting Mr. Paul Hardy, the black and white artist, at his home in Sussex and seen him at work in his armoury. Mr. Hardy's hobby is the making of replicas of old armour, and some fine examples of his work adorn the old-world house in which he lives."[333] Hardy's spirited illustrations for *The Adventures of Don Quixote,* published by Bell in 1911, were well received; given his great interest in medieval armour he may have felt a certain empathy with Cervantes' knight-errant (Plate 244).

In 1932 Paul Hardy was awarded a Civil List pension of £80 "in recognition of his work as a black and white artist and his contributions to the study of mediaeval arms and armour". Alice Dudeney helped to get him this pension. In 1939 he also received a Royal Academy pension of £50. The pensions helped resolve some of Paul and Ida's financial problems, although it is clear from Alice Dudeney's diaries that Paul Hardy had little interest in managing his financial affairs. Paul Hardy died at his home, The Cottage, Storrington, in Sussex, on 2 January 1942 at the age of 79.

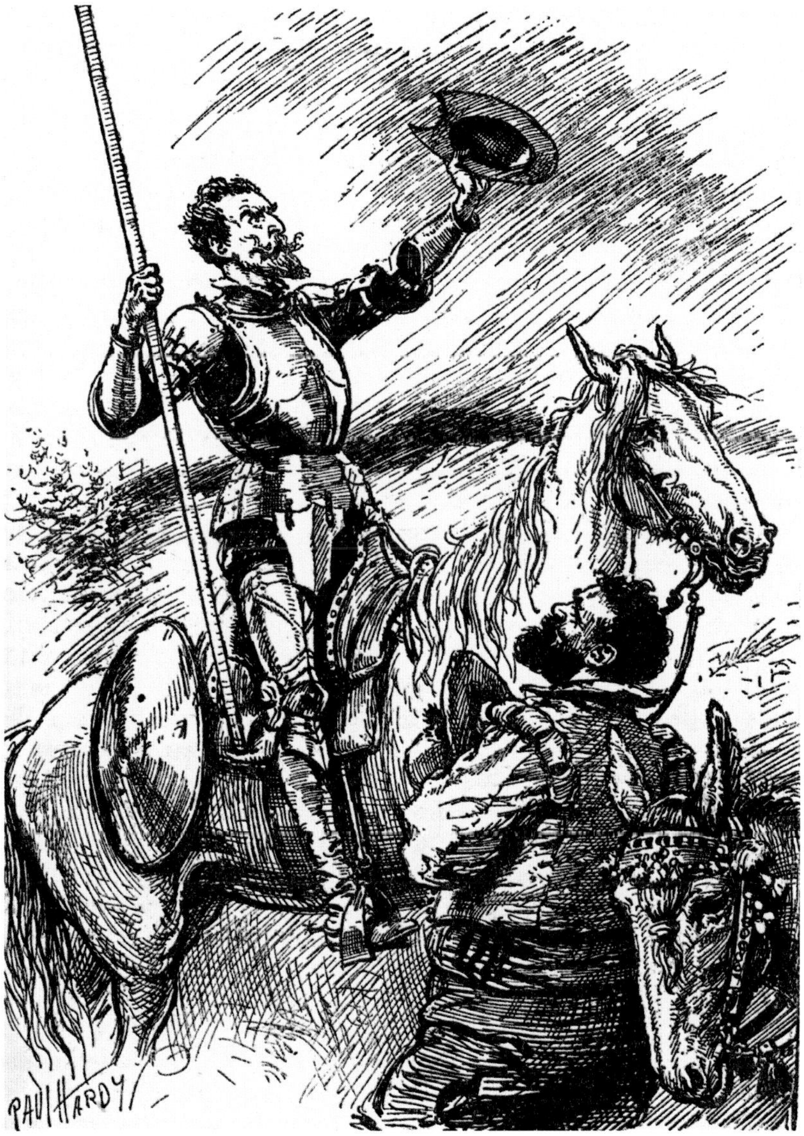

Plate 244: Mambrino's Helmet
Paul Hardy. From *The Adventures of Don Quixote*.[334]

Norman Heywood Hardy (1863-1914)

Norman Heywood Hardy was born in Bristol on 15 November 1863[335] and baptised almost nine years later on 9 August 1872.

He became interested in anthropology through his work for Dr John Beddoe.[336] Dr Beddoe was a physician at the Bristol Royal Infirmary for many years before becoming a full-time anthropologist. Norman Hardy drew most of the illustrations for a new edition of Beddoe's *The Races of Britain; a Contribution to the Anthropology of Western Europe* published in 1885.

After he moved to London in the late 1880s,[337] Norman Hardy worked for the pioneering egyptologist Flinders Petrie. His illustrations of *Recent Antiquarian Discoveries in Egypt, Mr Flinders Petrie's Exhibition at Oxford Mansion, Oxford Street* and *Mr Flinders Petrie's Exhibition of Egyptian Antiquities* were published in *The Illustrated London News*.[338] In 1890 Hardy was elected a Fellow of the Royal Anthropological Institute.

Norman Hardy exhibited at several galleries in London, including Isaac Mendoza's St James's Street Gallery; a reviewer wrote, "The black and white drawings are of very unequal merit, but some are excellent, as Mr. Norman Hardy's admirable study of an Oriental girl's head."[339] By this time he was becoming well known as an illustrator for periodicals and magazines.

Shortly before he left for Australia to work as an artist on *The Sydney Mail* Norman gave a lecture at the Artists Guild, demonstrating how to paint portraits using watercolour washes rather than pen and ink:

> The Artists' Guild is always well to the front in perceiving new fields of employment for women. Now that newspapers and periodicals are so profusely illustrated, clever black and white work is in great and constant demand, and several ladies have already found remunerative employment in connection with illustrated dailies and weeklies, a lady having recently been appointed to a post on the pictorial staff of the Daily Graphic. For such work special technical as well as artistic qualities are needed, and to afford ladies the opportunity of learning the technique of black and white work, the Misses Palmer have organised a series of black and white classes at the Artists' Guild, Berkeley Gardens, Campden Hill, Kensington. The classes will not begin until January, but yesterday a demonstration lesson was given by Mr. Norman Hardy, brother [*sic*] of Mr. Heywood Hardy, the well-known artist. Mr. Hardy, whose admirable black and white work is familiar in reproductions in leading periodicals, illustrated his methods by a clever portrait of Mr. Walter Severn, handing the portrait round at different stages of its progress for inspection by the ladies present. Only brushes and water colour were used, not pencil or pen. The likeness was excellent.[340, 341]

Norman Hardy arrived in Australia early in 1892 to take up his position as artist on *The Sydney Mail*, the weekly illustrated newspaper of *The Sydney Morning Herald*.[342] He spent almost seven years as "Special Artist of the Sydney Mail"; in 1894 he became Principal of the Art Staff of the newspaper. He produced sketches to illustrate the important stories of the day and political, sporting and military events, and drew many portraits of people in the news. Each weekend the front cover of "The Illustrated Supplement" featured a full-page illustration, usually made by Norman Hardy.

Hardy travelled extensively in Australia to produce illustrations for the newspaper. *Coaching in the Araluen Valley, N.S.W., Australia* (1893) (Plate 245) shows the rough gravel track, made in the mid-nineteenth century, that was used during the gold rush by the Araluen Gold Coach. The coach had a police escort to carry the gold from the goldfields during the 1860s. A lithograph of the painting was included as a supplement in the 1893 Christmas edition of *The Sydney Mail*.

Hardy lived with several artists at Curlew Camp, which consisted of a few tents (including a dining tent), a dance floor and a piano, at Sirius Cove on the shores of Sydney Harbour, as described by Sir Arthur Streeton:

> He had evidently travelled very little beyond London before this time. He obtained his first knowledge of the bush during expeditions on behalf of the paper. He arrived with a vivid memory of the London museums, and soon began to collect aboriginal weapons, utensils, &c. He spent his spare time in some caves along the south coast of New South Wales. ... All this time he was in touch with the artists in Sydney, and came to live with five or six other men and myself in a permanent camp of tents at Sirius Cove, Sydney Harbour. There a deal of his London experience was chaffed out of him, and he was held in affection by all the camp.[343]

Between 1895 and 1897 Norman Hardy made three voyages to islands in the South Pacific, Papua New Guinea, the Solomon Islands and Vanuatu (New Hebrides). He produced numerous illustrations for *The Sydney Mail* based on his voyages. And he painted 68 watercolours for a book that recorded his travels, *The Savage South Seas. Painted by Norman H. Hardy. Described by E. Way Elkington*. Despite the attribution, Ernest Elkington had not visited the islands described in *The Savage South Seas*; the text is based on Hardy's experiences.

Hardy's illustrations are an important record of life in Melanesia in the later nineteenth century, particularly in the Solomon Islands and New Hebrides, as discussed by Dr Max Quanchi of the University of the South Pacific.[344]

Several of the descriptions Hardy gave are also of interest. He provided the first accurate description of kite-fishing in the South Seas; a long fishing line is attached to a kite that is flown from a canoe.[345]

Plate 245: Coaching in the Araluen Valley, N.S.W., Australia. 1893
Norman Hardy. Oil on canvas. 55.8 x 43cm. NATIONAL LIBRARY OF AUSTRALIA

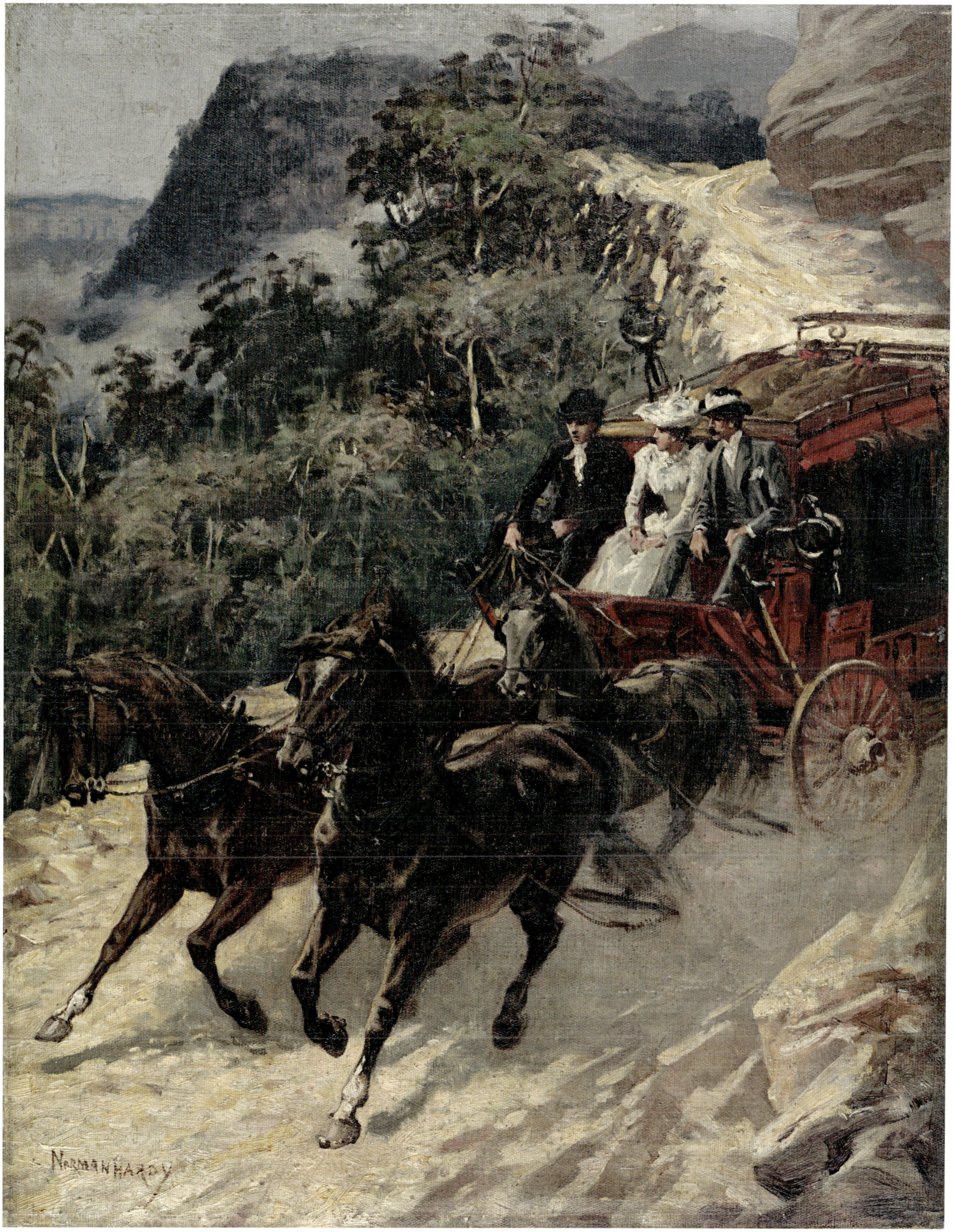
NORMAN HARDY

Hardy was familiar with making sketches and watercolours based on photographs; a few of his illustrations in *The Sydney Mail* refer to their photographic origins. But these are rare and the great majority were original sketches made by Hardy. A few of his paintings, particularly those of Papua, for *The Savage South Seas,* were also based on photographs, but again most were taken from original drawings.

Norman Hardy had six pictures exhibited at the Royal Academy between 1891 and 1909, the majority based on his travels in Australasia. His pictures for 1896 and 1897, *Solomon Island Head-hunter* and *For the Term of their Natural Lives,* were sent from the offices of *The Sydney Herald*. His 1898 exhibit, *Robbery Under Arms,* is the title of a well-known Australian novel about gold mining in the bush. His 1900 picture, *Off to the Shore,* may have been based on *Copra Boys off to the Shore, New Hebrides* that was published in *The Savage South Seas*, showing the islanders taking their boat back to shore after unloading their copra (dried coconut kernels) cargo onto a larger vessel.

While he was in Australia, Norman Hardy also made contributions to the Linnean Society of New South Wales, exhibiting feathered arrows from the island of Espiritu Santo (Vanuatu/New Hebrides), Papuan throwing sticks, boomerangs, a wooden club that belonged to Bungaree, 'chief of the Broken Bay tribe' and rare aboriginal shoes made of emu feathers [346] He gave his collection of arrows, boomerangs, aboriginal strangling cords etc. to the Pitt Rivers Museum in Oxford.[347]

Halftone printing of photographs became more prominent during the 1890s, reducing the need for newspaper illustrators. After spending almost seven years in Australia and the Pacific Islands, Hardy departed Australia on 1 January 1898 on the Japanese Cargo Passenger ship the *Omi Maru* and visited China, Singapore and Ceylon.[348]

The Sydney Mail noted that:

> Mr. Hardy has seen more of Australasia and the islands than any other artist. Not only has he been to nearly every part of this continent for the 'Mail, but he has also been to New Guinea, the New Hebrides, Solomons, various Pacific Islands,

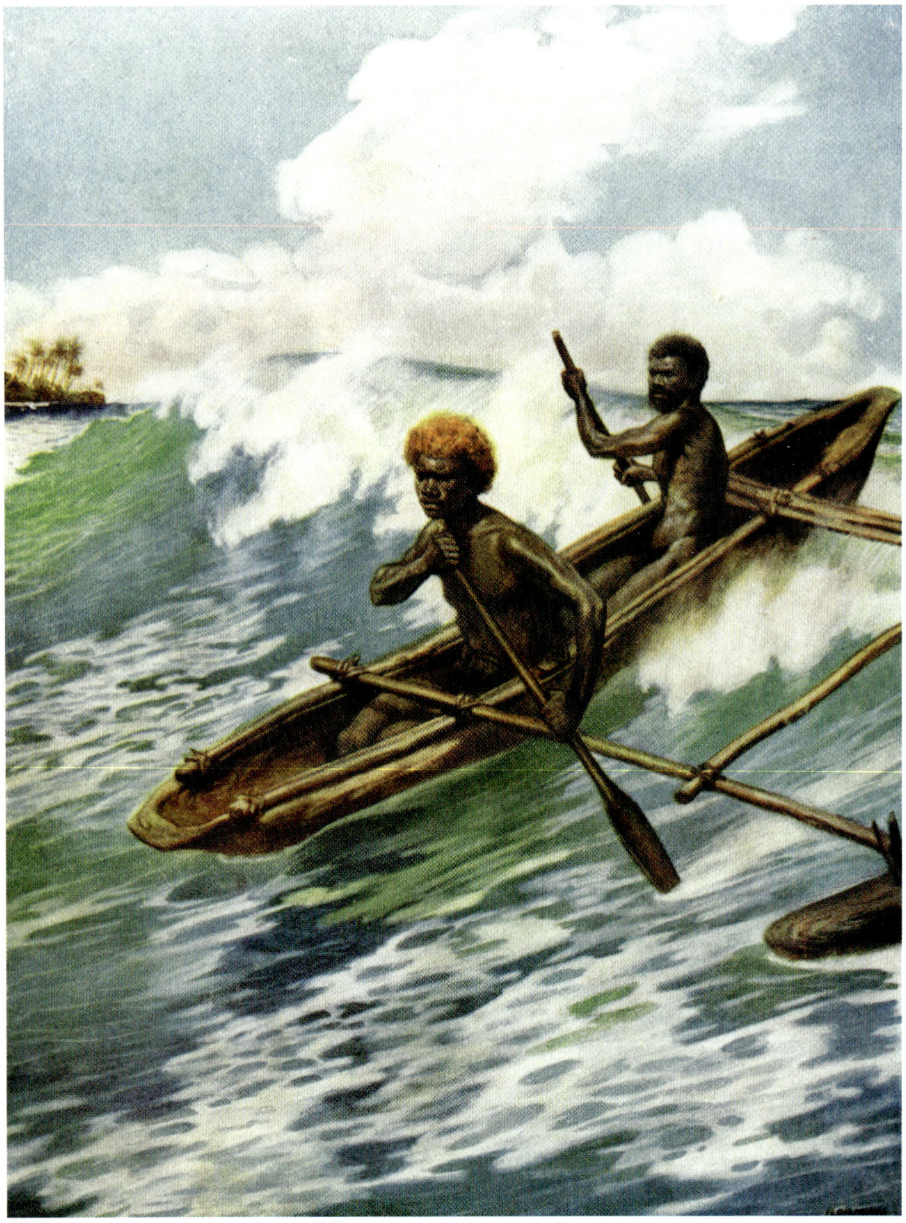

Plate 246 (left): Passing the Reef, Aoba, New Hebrides
After Norman Hardy. From *The Savage South Seas. Painted by Norman H. Hardy. Described by E. Way Elkington*. A&C. Black, London, 1907.

Plate 247 (opposite page): Masolo, a Young Bangongo, in Dance Costume
After Norman Hardy. From *Notes ethnographiques sur les peuples communément appelés Bakuba, ainsi que sur les peuplades apparentées, Les Bushongo.*
Falk Fils. Brussels, 1910.

New Zealand etc. During these tours he has made an anthropological collection of great value. Before his departure Mr. Hardy was presented by the literary staff of the "Mail" with a valuable pair of binoculars as a token of esteem, and was entertained at supper by the artists of Sydney.[349]

Following his visit to China, Hardy joined the group making excavations at Abydos in Egypt that were being carried out under the direction of his old employer, Sir Flinders Petrie.

Hardy lived in London after his work with Petrie. He was a member of the Chelsea Arts Club in the early 1900s[350]; several Australian artists in London were members, including friends from his years in the Antipodes.

In 1907 Norman Hardy joined an expedition to the Upper Congo that was led by Emil Torday and sponsored by the British Museum and the Royal Anthropological Institute. Hardy was the expedition's artist. The explorer M.W. Hilton-Simpson also took part. They arrived in the Congo State by ship in September 1907 and by December were ready to begin their travels up the Kasai River.

In addition to the numerous paintings and drawings made by Norman Hardy to illustrate accounts of the expedition, he also collected many artefacts that were subsequently acquired by the British Museum. Of the 678 items in the British Museum's collection that were sold, donated or painted by Norman Hardy, the vast majority are from the expedition to the Congo. In addition, there are items from his travels to Australia, the Solomon Islands, and Crete.

In his summary of the expedition, John Mack of the British Museum wrote: " ... the collection of objects formed is arguably unequalled amongst those from Central Africa in the coverage it provides of the art and material culture of the whole region lying along the southern fringe of the Equatorial Forest."[351]

The scientific journal *Nature* reviewed Hilton-Simpson's account of the expedition:[352, 353, 354]

> It contains many valuable illustrations, "prises sur le vif," the untouched photographs of the author, besides the beautiful and accurate drawings in colour by Mr. Norman Hardy, who accompanied the expedition during the first half of its stay in Congoland. Amongst these last must be mentioned with special praise for their artistic charm as well as their absolute accuracy, "Wissmann Pool" and "An Incident at Pana" (a charging buffalo).[355]

Hardy remained with the expedition for six months. Hilton-Simpson wrote that Hardy,

> ... much regretted, I think, that circumstances would not permit him to stay on and undertake with us a journey in the equatorial forest; but he had not been in particularly good health, and, on the whole, perhaps it is a good thing for him that he was unable to remain and have to endure the effects of bad climate and shortage of food which we were to go through before the end of the year.

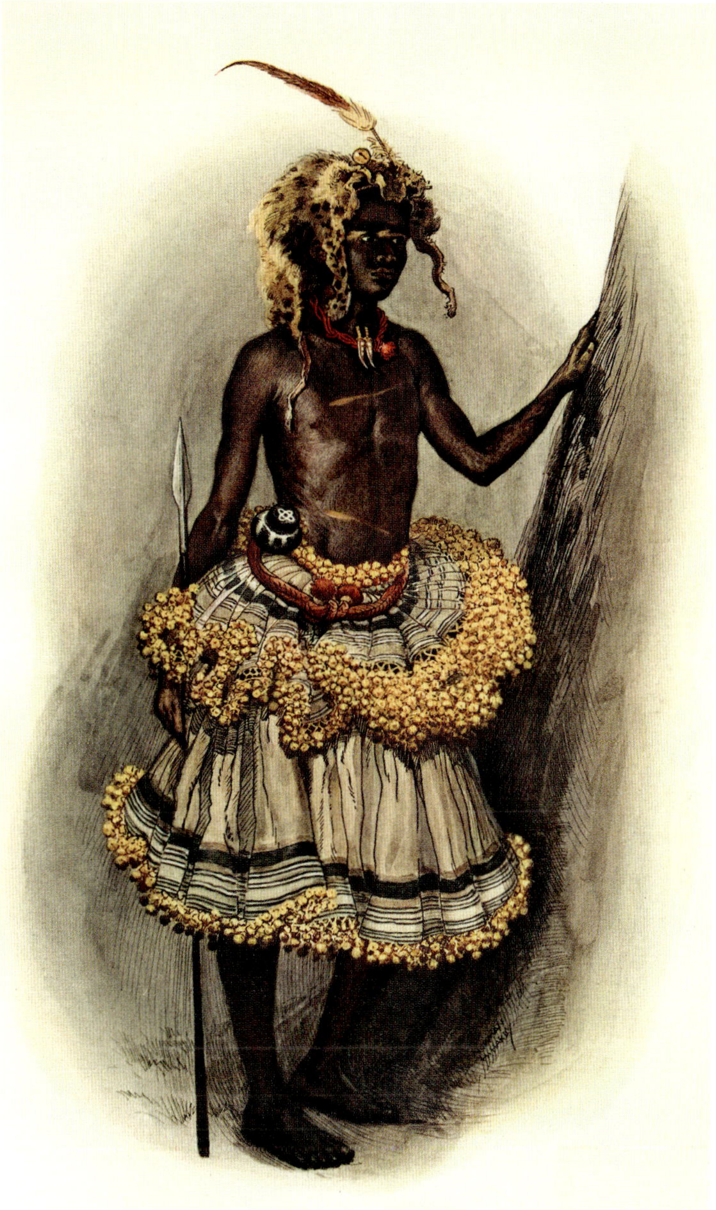

Conditions became much worse for Torday and Hilton-Simpson after Hardy had left the expedition. They both became seriously ill and had to stop for a month to recover. Torday had a reputation of being a somewhat difficult person to be with, becoming rather easily irritated by people.

An example of Norman Hardy's many drawings and paintings made during and after the expedition is *Masolo, a Young Bangongo, in Dance Costume* (Plate 247).

Following his expedition to the Congo, Hardy worked as an artist for the Metropolitan Museum in New York, recording their archaeological work in Egypt. He made facsimiles of wall paintings of tombs at Thebes – exacting work in the early years of the twentieth century; light was brought into the chambers by a series of mirrors. The team of artists developed techniques for making facsimiles that almost exactly corresponded to the colours and brushstrokes on the tomb walls. The facsimiles are an important record of the condition of paintings in Egyptian tombs in the early twentieth century.[356] Hardy's work at Thebes was his last expedition. He died of influenza in New York in 1914.

Evelyn Stuart Hardy (1865-1935)

Evelyn Stuart Hardy (as she became known in the 1880s) (Plate 248) was the third child of David and Emily, born on 10 October 1865.[357] She was baptised Beatrice Evelyn Elizabeth Hardy on 9 August 1872 at St Paul's Church, Clifton, Bristol. All four children of David and Emily Hardy were baptised on the same day.

In census returns from 1881 to 1911, Evelyn's first name varied. Initially recorded as "Beatrice", she then became "Elizabeth", "Evelyn" and finally "E. Stuart Hardy". In addition, though she was correctly recorded as being five years old in 1871, in subsequent census returns her reported age was less than her actual age; by the time she was 45 the census reports her as being only 30 years old.[358]

In fact, Evelyn did appear much younger than she was. There are two reports of her attending the "Salon de Réunion", a musical soirée, in January 1890, when she was 24 years old. The soirée was held at the galleries of the British Artists in Suffolk Street, London. A London Correspondent wrote: "There were a good many well-known people amongst the audience. ... The person who attracted most attention in the gallery was Miss Evelyn Stuart Hardy, the artist. Miss Hardy looks little more than a mere child and always wears a kind of Scottish dress, with a plaid passing across the figure from right to left." [359] Another attendee at the soirée noted the presence of Evelyn, "the young girl whose clever war pictures, contributed to *The Illustrated London News,* attracted so much attention at the time of their appearance". [360]

Perhaps her liking for all things Scottish led Evelyn to add the name of the Royal House of Scotland to her name in the 1880s; there were no "Stuarts" in her own family. Evelyn even played the bagpipes; *The Musical News* reported on a soirée in London: "There was ... a Scotch sword dance, given in quite delightful style by Miss Dorothy Hardy [Evelyn's sister] ..., Miss Evelyn Stuart Hardy supplying the orthodox bagpipe accompaniment."[361]

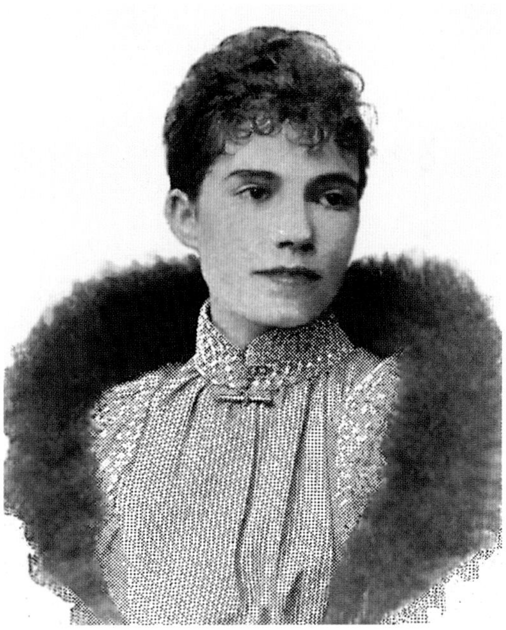

Plate 248: Evelyn Stuart Hardy, ca. 1890
FROM A PHOTOGRAPH BY ALFRED ELLIS, LONDON

Evelyn was taught drawing by her mother and began making illustrations at a young age. According to a review of her work in 1896, she received her first commission at the age of nine,[362] but this might not be a reliable figure given the discrepancy between her actual age and the ages given in census returns.

Evelyn was a prolific illustrator of magazines and books. Her illustrations appeared in numerous magazines including *The Illustrated London News, The Sporting and Dramatic News, St. James's Budget, The Gentlewoman* and *The Jabberwock* (along with illustrations drawn by her brother, Paul).

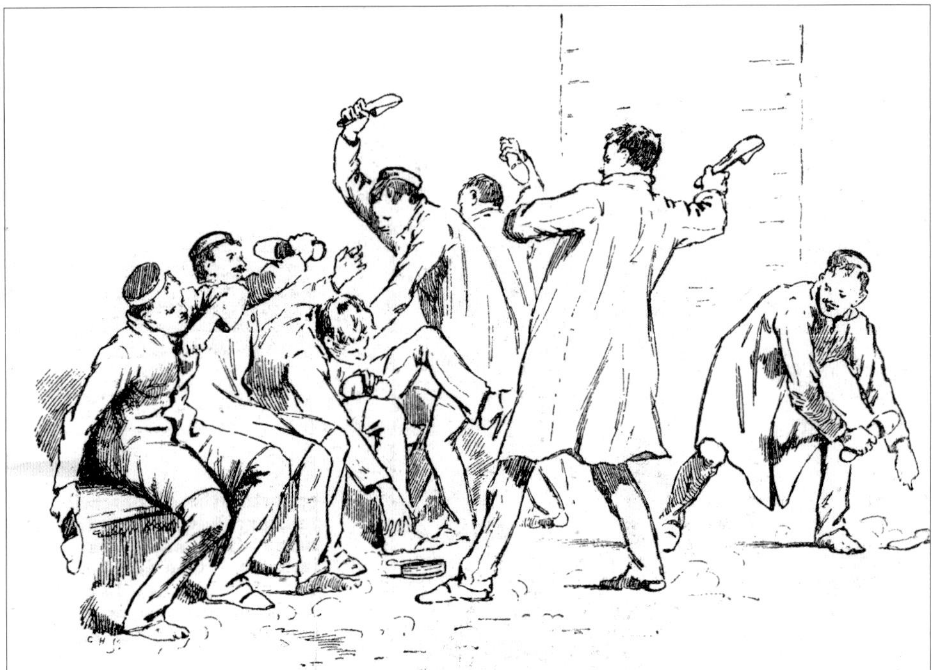

A SHOE FIGHT.

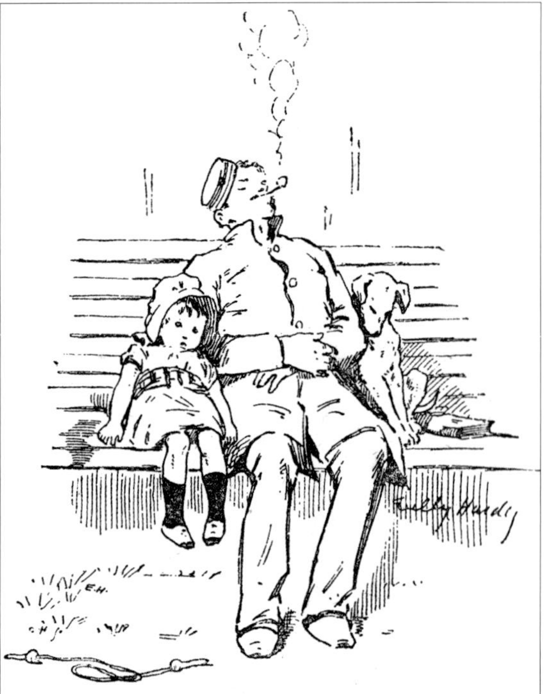

FAMILY PARTY AFTER DINNER.

Plates 249 and 250: Illustrations for *"Tommy Atkins" in Hospital*. Evelyn Stuart Hardy. THE ILLUSTRATED LONDON NEWS (1889)

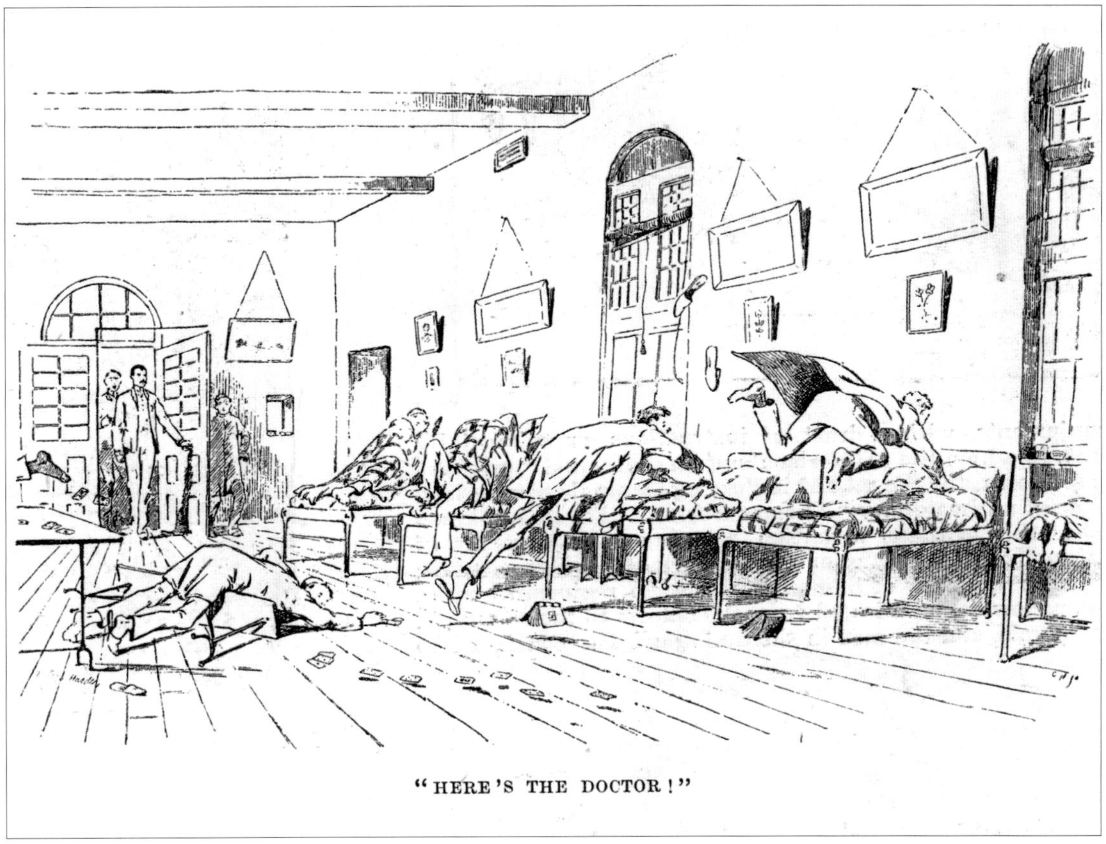

Plates 251 and 252: Illustrations for *"Tommy Atkins" in Hospital*. Evelyn Stuart Hardy. The Illustrated London News (1889)

Her magazine illustrations often had military and humorous themes. For *The Illustrated London News* she produced *Sketches at the Royal Military Tournament, Agricultural Hall, Islington,*[363] *Three Fishers in the Highlands,*[364] *Amateurs with the Highland Bagpipes*[365] and *Two Fools and Their Folly.*[366]

She also spent some time sketching in a military hospital; the drawings were published in *The Illustrated London News* as *"Tommy Atkins" in Hospital*[367] (Plates 249-252).

An article about "Leading Lady Journalists" in 1896 commented on Evelyn Stuart Hardy's illustrations of military life:

> It is perhaps permissible to call her a kind of "John Strange Winter" in black and white, as her inclinations have always been towards military subjects, and the late Captain Drake,[368] of the Royal Horse Guards, seeing her bent, gave her much technical instruction in the correctness of detail. With officers and troopers of the "Blues" she is an especial favourite, and has found many models from life among them. At Aldershot on one occasion she was suspected of being a Nihilist, and another time was taken for a French spy when making some sketches of a fort, but in each dilemma her soldier friends were quickly able to show that she was not a dangerous character, and to restore her confiscated studies.[369]

Evelyn Hardy illustrated several books written by John Strange Winter, including *Bootles' Children,* published 1888, and *A Soldier's Children,* published in 1892. John Strange Winter was the nom de plume of Henrietta Palmer (Henrietta Stannard after her marriage). Henrietta Palmer originally wrote novels under the pseudonym "Violet Whyte", changing to "John Strange Winter" in 1881; she had written several articles for *Cavalry Life*, but the publisher refused to let her use a feminine pseudonym. Perhaps for similar reasons, Evelyn Hardy found it convenient to use "Evelyn" as her first name as it could also be the name of a man. Given her fascination with military life it is not surprising

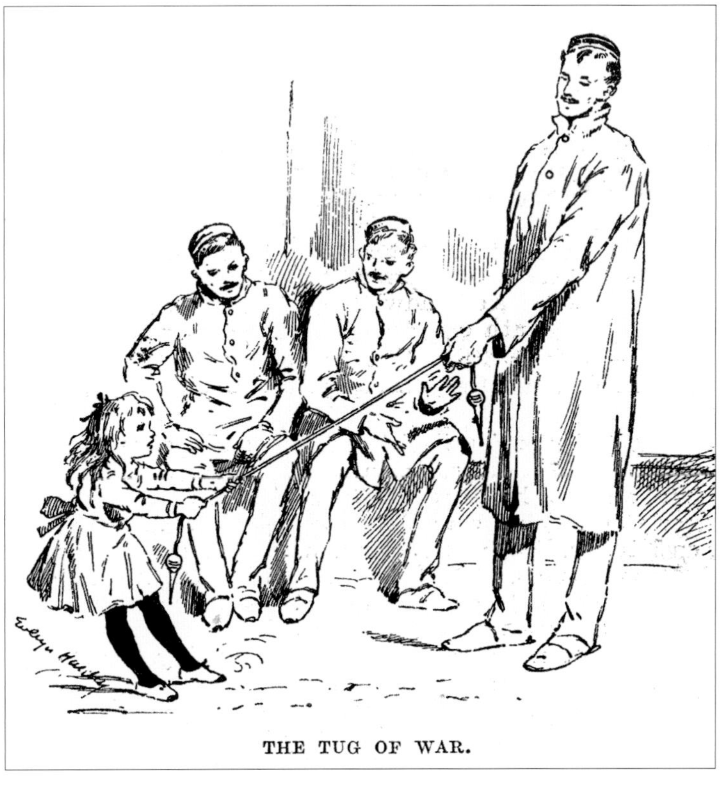

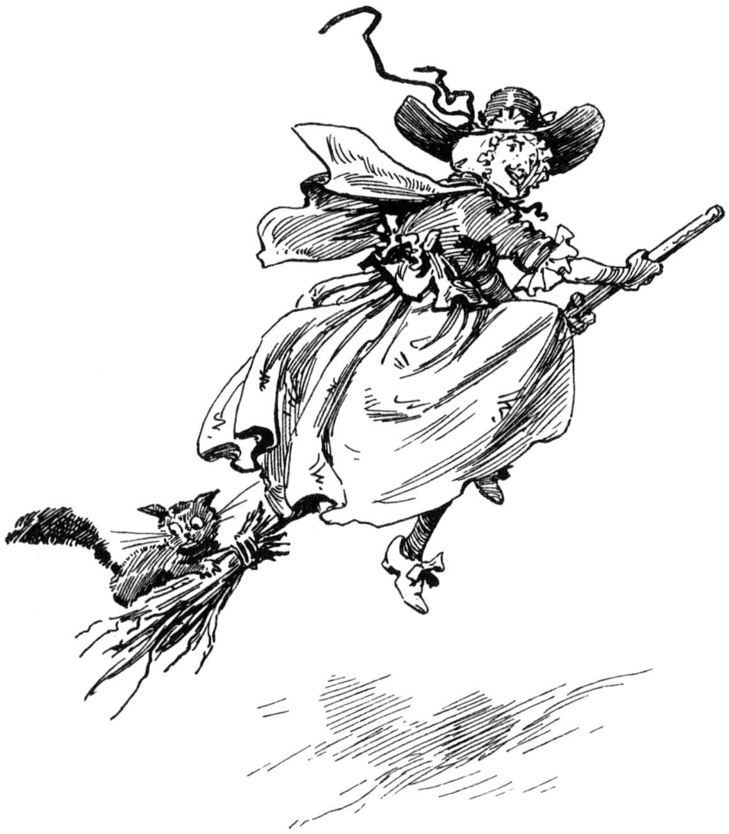

Plates 253 and 254
"There was an Old Woman who rode on a Broom" and "Pat-a-cake, pat-a-cake". Evelyn Stuart Hardy. Illustrations in *Mother Goose's Nursery Rhymes*. 1899. London: Ernest Nister

that she became associated with Henrietta Stannard; John Ruskin thought Stannard was "the author to whom we owe the most finished and faithful rendering ever yet given of the character of the British soldier".

Reviewers and readers sometimes assumed that Evelyn Stuart Hardy was a man; in its review of children's books, *The Spectator* wrote: "Another very attractive fairy-book is the minute volume of Fairy Tales from Hans Andersen, published by Mr. Ernest Nister, and delicately illustrated by Mr. E. Stuart Hardy."

Evelyn Hardy illustrated more than one hundred books, many annuals and hundreds of postcards. And she produced over a thousand watercolour illustrations for editions of the Bible and biblical stories.

She illustrated several books for Ernest Nister (Plates 253 and 254) between 1890 and 1913. Nister was a printer from Nuremberg, the world's centre of expertise in colour printing at that time, who became a publisher in London in 1888 and was one of the most inventive and creative publishers of children's books in the nineteenth century. Evelyn became associated with his company soon after Nister established a London office. The office was directed by the writer Robert Mack from 1888 until 1914, when many activities of Nister's publishing company ceased. Nister himself had died in 1909 and his company eventually closed in London in 1917.

Nister's books were sold in Britain and Germany, many carrying Evelyn's illustrations, and in the United Stated through the publisher E.P. Dutton. Nister was a pioneer in the publication of movable, "pop-up" books – books with movable elements, operated by tabs, with scenes that stood-up when the book was opened. The high quality chromolithography for the books was done in Nuremberg. Evelyn Stuart helped to design and illustrate several movable books, such as *Peeps into Fairyland,* as well as annuals.[370]

Evelyn Hardy began to work for the John F. Shaw publishing firm in about 1914, when it was no longer possible to access the German colour printing used by Nister and others. For Shaw she illustrated numerous books, including *Alice in Wonderland*. Other versions of the classics she illustrated for various publishers included *Aesop's Fables*, *Jane Eyre* and *The Rubáiyát of Omar Khayyám*. She also illustrated the first translations into English of the Indian classics *The Ramayana* and *The Mahabharata*.[371] She had a particular interest in Indian art and illustrated *The Arts of India* by Edmund Russell (1901) and numerous Indian stories by Sarath Kumar Ghosh, published by Pearson's Magazine in the United States. Her uncle, Heywood Hardy, noted that she was a particular expert on Asian dress (Appendix C); like her brother, Norman, she painted many Asian scenes.

Evelyn also produced many illustrated postcards for various publishers. And she wrote several children's books, including *At the Farm* (1920) for which she was paid £20.

Evelyn and her sister, Dorothy, became friends with Annie Oakley when the Wild West Show toured England at the end of the nineteenth century, as recounted on pages 196-197. Evelyn and Dorothy made many sketches of the performances.

After her mother died, Evelyn moved from Greenwich to live with her brother Paul at The Cottage in Church Street, Storrington, in Sussex. She died in Sussex at the age of 70 in 1935.[372]

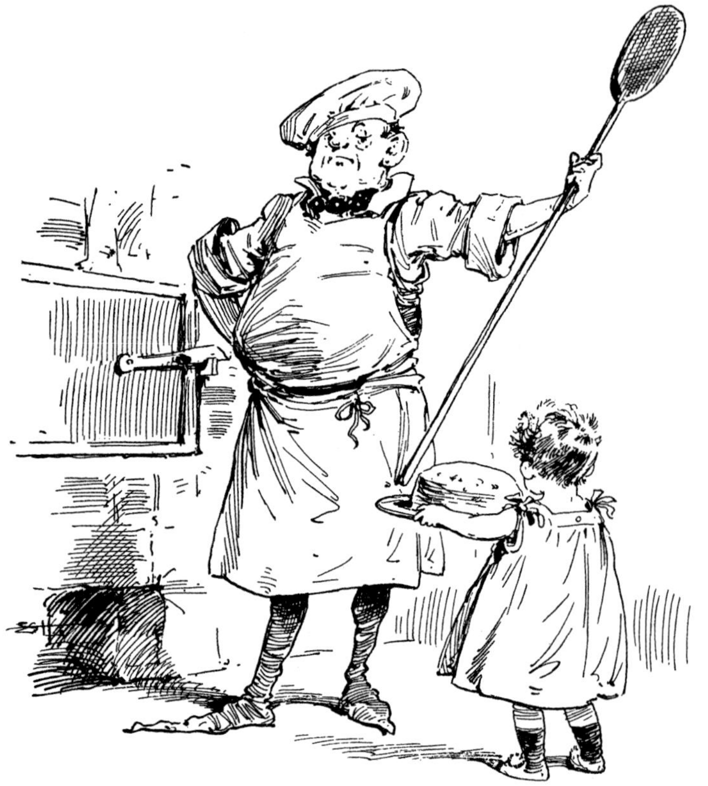

Dorothy Hardy (1868-1937)

Dorothy Hardy, fourth and final child of David and Emily, was born 2 March 1868 at 15 Belle Vue Crescent in Clifton, Bristol,[373] and more than four years later was baptised Mabel Dora Hardy on 9 August 1872 at St Paul's Church, Clifton. The ages that were given in census records from 1881 onwards were less than her actual age; in the 1901 census her age is recorded as 20, when she was 33 years old.[374] In 1906 and 1907 Dorothy Hardy lived in her studio at 1 Upper Cheyne Row "The Cottage", Chelsea. [375] Then she moved to live with her mother and sister at "Arnocot" (an anagram of cartoon) in Georgette Place, Greenwich.

Dorothy Hardy married Kenneth Elwyn Roberts, who worked in advertising and journalism, on 30 July 1908, at Greenwich.[376] After the death of her husband in 1916,[377] she moved to 28 Gordon Place, Kensington, where she lived for the rest of her life.[378]

Dorothy illustrated many children's books, such as Nister's *Holiday Annuals* and Bell's *Arabian Nights* and numerous books on other subjects, including Nordic mythology.[379] She jointly illustrated several books with her brother, Paul, and her sister, Evelyn Stuart. In particular, she was associated with publisher George Harrap for many years.

Dorothy Hardy contributed illustrations to many magazines including *The Bystander, The Badminton Magazine, Sporting and Dramatic, The Windsor Magazine* and *Thomas' Hunting Diary* (Plate 255). Her illustrations for articles on "The Metropolitan Fire Brigade" and "The Royal Veterinary Hospital" were published in the first edition of *The Strand*, in January 1891.

Her best paintings were of horses – pictures of steeple-chasing, polo, hunting and cowboys. She illustrated several articles in *The Badminton Magazine*.[380] And she produced many paintings in watercolours and gouache for prints of horse racing

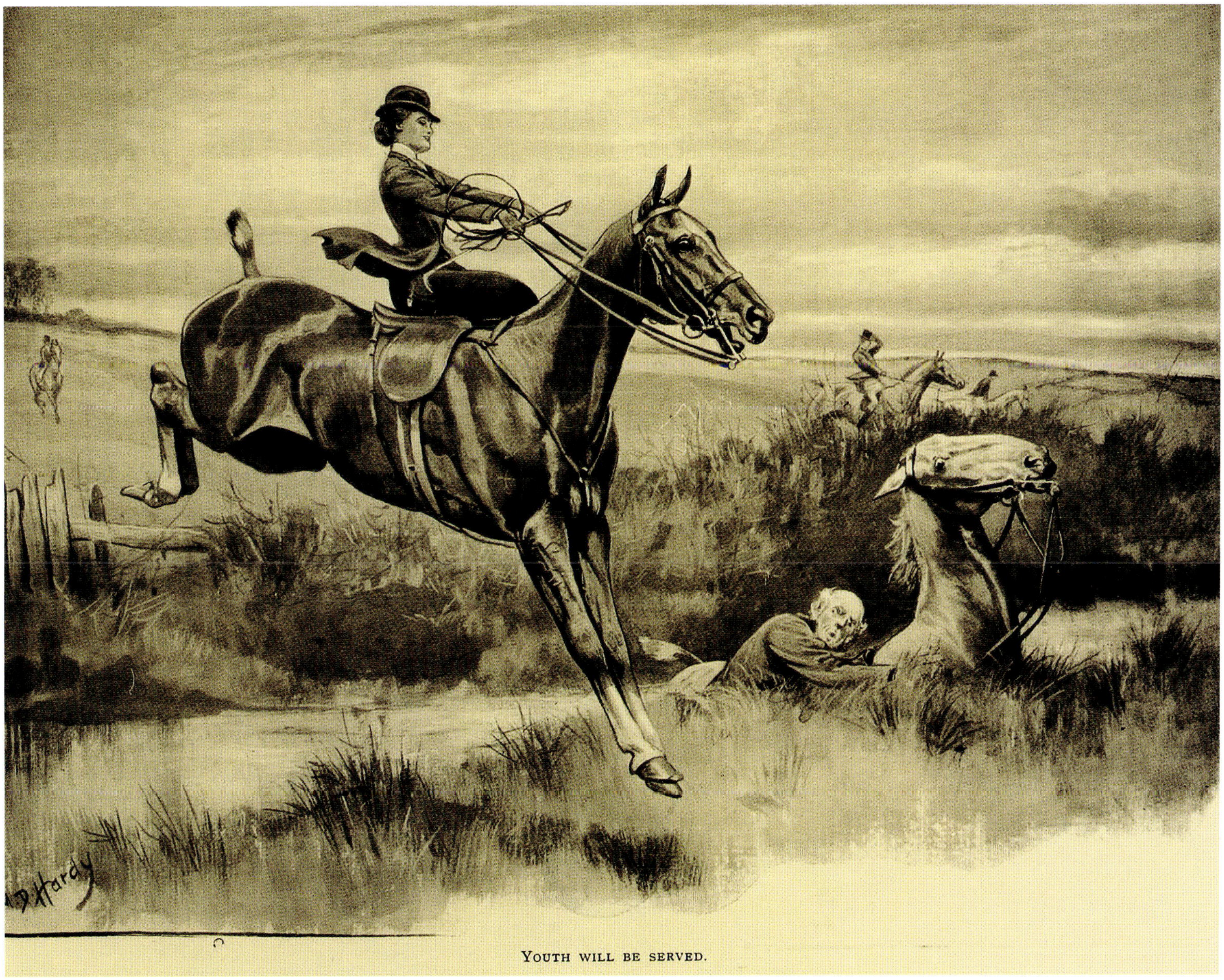

Plate 255: "Youth will be Served." [381]
After Dorothy Hardy. *Thomas' Hunting Diary*. 6 May 1905

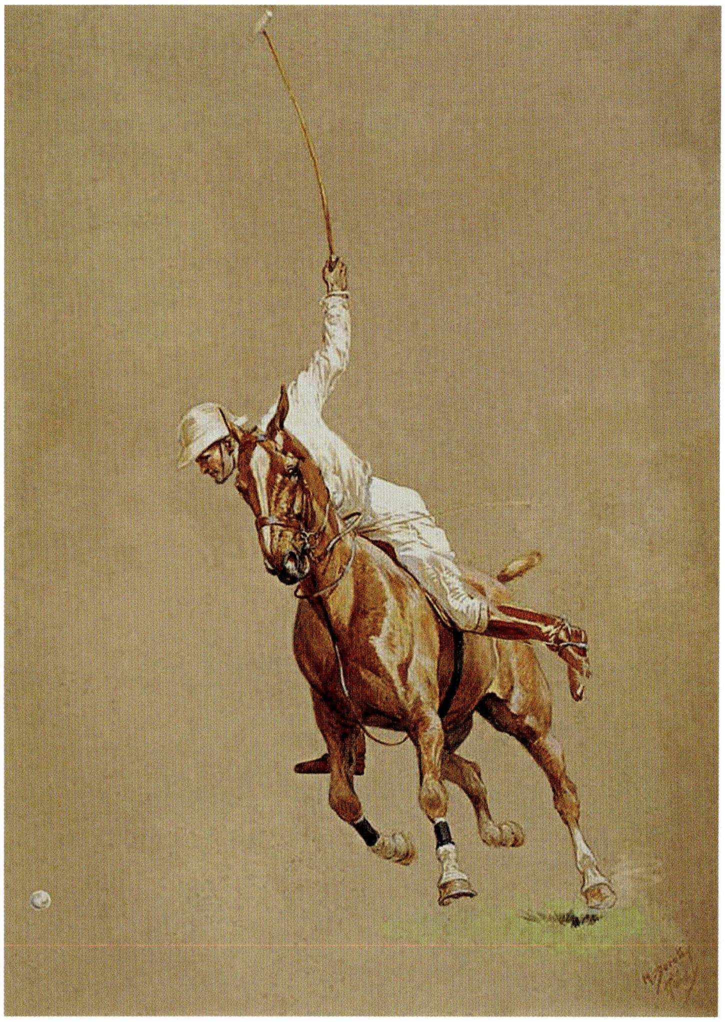

Plate 256 (above): Polo Player
Dorothy Hardy. Watercolour and body colour on paper. 58.4 x 44.5cm.
Private Collection

Plate 257 (below): Hunting Scene, 1908
After Dorothy Hardy. Chromolithograph. 27 x 70cm. Published by Lawrence and Jellicoe, Ltd., London

and hunting scenes, such as *Hunting Scene* (1908) (Plate 257), that resemble paintings by Cecil Aldin.

Dorothy Hardy was an enthusiastic supporter of the Home of Rest for Horses, a charity that was established by Miss Ann Lindo in 1886 and which is now called "The Horse Trust". Dorothy Hardy owned the most famous horse at the Home, "Bones", an old charger of the Horse Guards (The Blues), who had carried his trooper safely through the battle of Tel-el-Kebir in Egypt in 1882. Dorothy Hardy bought "Bones" from the regiment in 1893 and used him as a model.[382]

Dorothy and her sister, Evelyn, were fascinated by Buffalo Bill Cody's Wild West Show, and made many drawings of the performers and their equipment. Several sketchbooks have been discovered with illustrations of the show, marked with Dorothy's name and address (8 Blomfield Rd., London).[383]

The show first came to London in 1887 as part of the American Exhibition at Earl's Court, for the Jubilee celebration of Queen Victoria's 50th year on the throne. After touring Great Britain and various European cities, the show came back to London in 1892. Dorothy and Evelyn attended several performances to make sketches. As there was so much more that they would like to draw, they asked Buffalo Bill Cody if they could make more sketches of the performers; he gave them a pass so they could attend performances and rehearsals whenever they liked.[384, 385] Dorothy met Buffalo Bill and members of the Wild West Show again in 1904, during their final visit to London. [386]

In the 1930s, a visitor to Dorothy's studio found it to be full of mementos of the Wild West Show. There were numerous sketches and paintings of cowboys and Indians on the walls, signed photographs of members of the show, photographs and letters from Annie Oakley, the star of the show, and the free pass given to Dorothy by Buffalo Bill Cody. On the wall was a rifle that she said had been presented to her sister by Annie Oakley at the end of the 1892-1893 tour. She also had a life-sized lay figure dressed as a cowboy sitting on a Western saddle that was on a

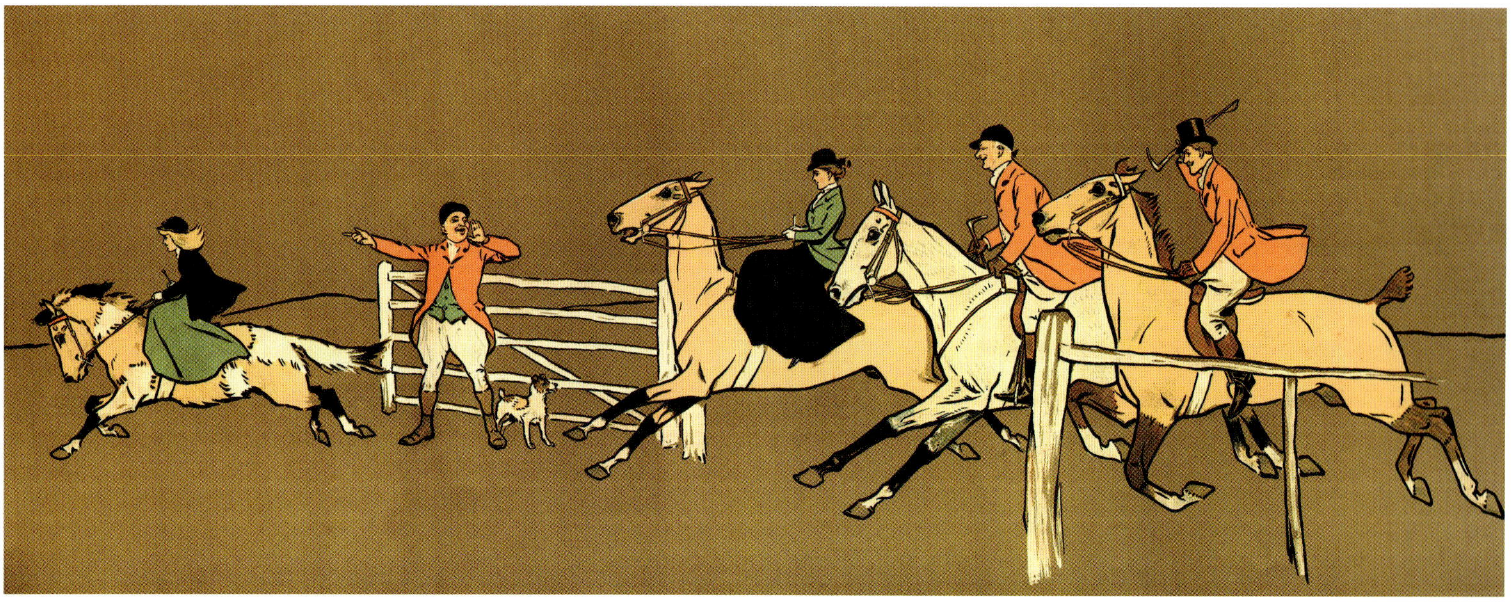

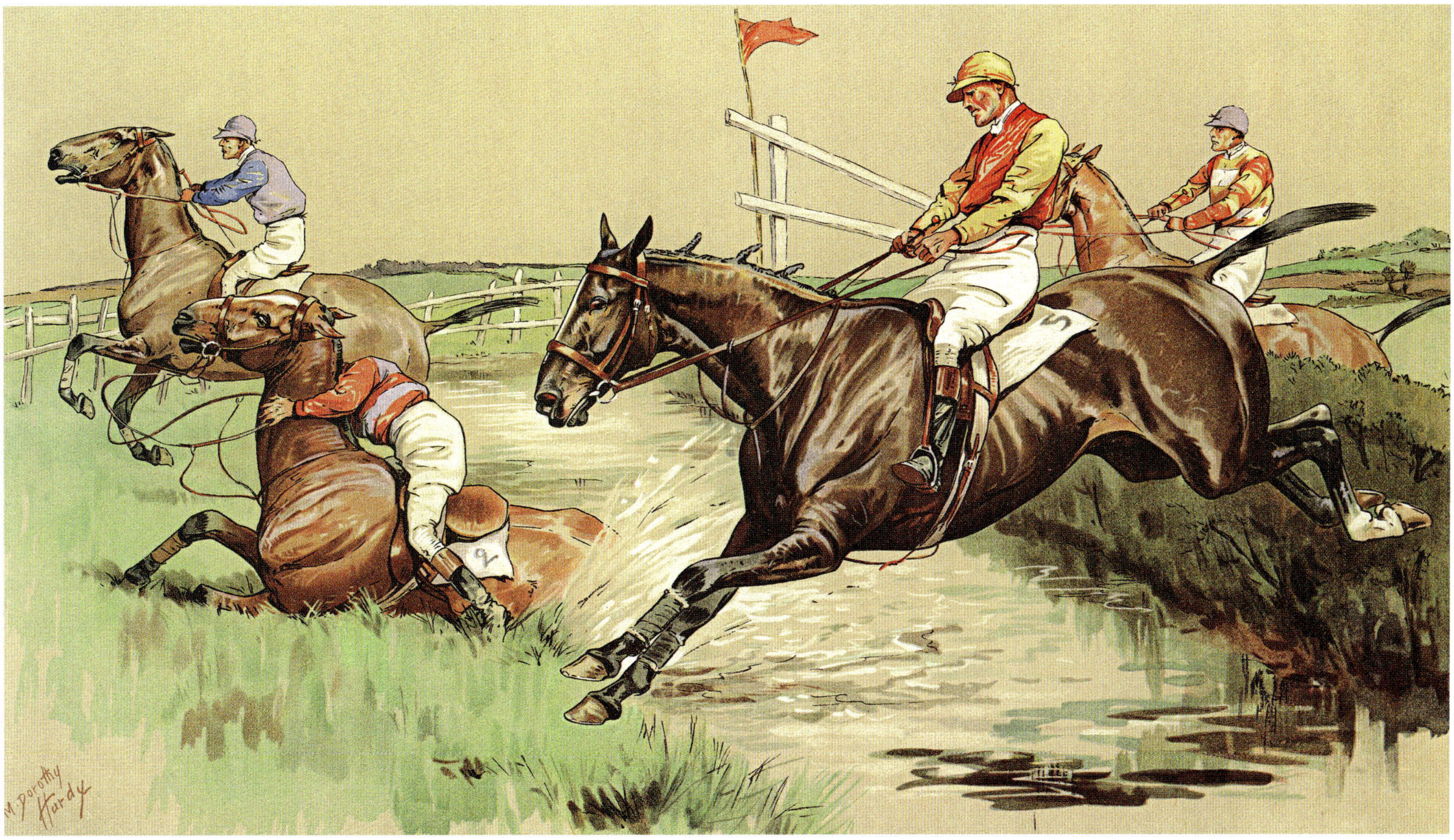

Plate 258: A Spill at the Water Jump, ca. 1910
After Dorothy Hardy. Chromolithograph. 30.5 x 53.1cm.

trestle. She bought the saddle from a cowboy who was in the show at Earl's Court.[387]

The Hardy sisters became close friends with Annie Oakley. She was a superb horsewoman and treasured the sketches that Dorothy and Evelyn made of her on horseback. These showed her shooting as her horse jumped a hurdle, shooting at targets thrown in the air as her horse galloped though a field and leaning from her saddle to pick up a handkerchief from the ground. Photographs show that her portrait by Dorothy Hardy was in a prominent position in the tent that she used when on tour with the Wild West Show. Of all her possessions, the three drawings of Annie Oakley on horseback were the only items specifically mentioned in her will, made in 1925. She bequeathed these to her husband, Frank.[388] American magazines published pictures of Annie Oakley on horseback based on these sketches.[389]

During the 1930s Dorothy Hardy was often visited by Edward H. Blackmore, who had a life-long interest in American Indians. He introduced her to his friend, the Canadian Mohawk Indian Chief Os-ke-non-ton. They met her several times when she became ill in the 1930s and talked about her stories of the Wild West Show.[390, 391]

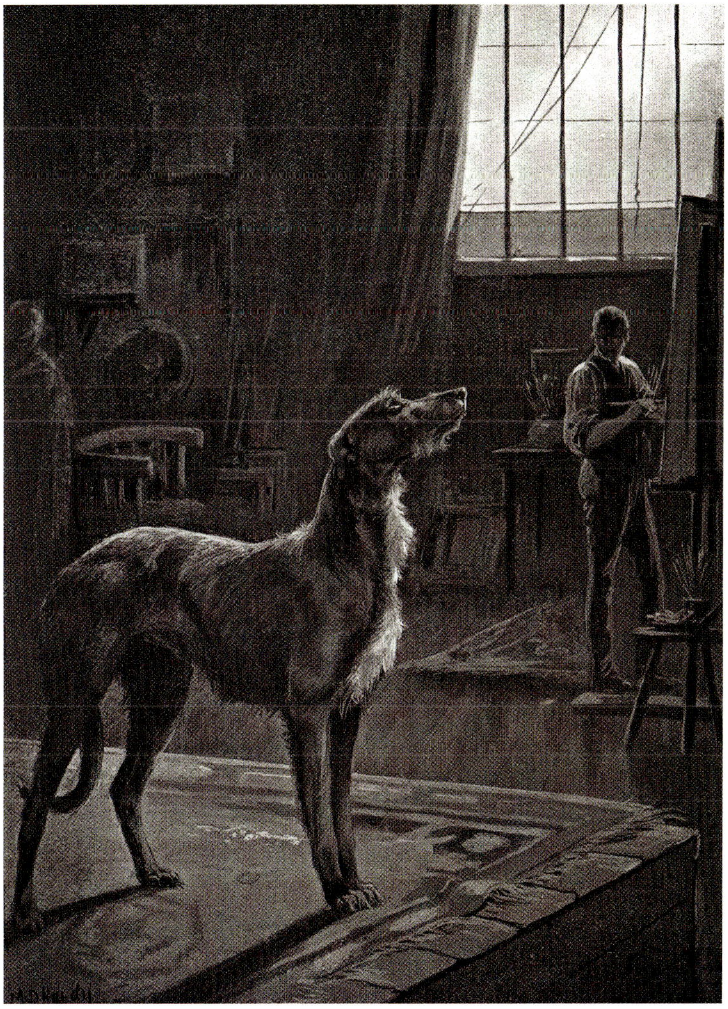

Plate 259: Stay as you are – don't stir! 1910
After Dorothy Hardy.[392]

APPENDIX A

The Hardy Family of Artists: Genealogy

The descent of the Hardy family of artists can be traced from John Hardy of Horsforth in Yorkshire.[393] John Hardy (ca. 1675-1740) is described as a "Justice Clerk" in 1713 in the Horsforth and Guiseley parish registers where the baptisms of his six children are recorded, from 1702 to 1715.[394] John Hardy was Clerk to John Stanhope (1678-1736) of New Hall, Horsforth. John Stanhope, Lord of the Manor of Horsforth, was the Justice of the Peace at Horsforth in the early eighteenth century; he is described as such in the parish register recording the baptism of his twin daughters in 1708.

William Hardy (1715-1762) followed in his father's profession and was Clerk and Steward to John Stanhope (1702-1769), a barrister of New Hall, Horsforth. William Hardy was also a yeoman farmer at his farm, Low Fold Farm in Horsforth.[395]

William Hardy married twice.[396] With his first wife, Elizabeth, he had a daughter, also called Elizabeth (1743-1747), and a son, John (1745-1806). William and his second wife, Mary, had three children: William (1748-1824), James (1752-1827) and Mary (1760-after 1804).[397] William Hardy died in September 1762 at the age of 47.[398]

John Hardy succeeded his father as Clerk to John Stanhope of Horsforth Hall and studied law under Stanhope's supervision. There are reports that Walter Stanhope, heir to the Stanhope estate, was in awe of young John's abilities. John became a successful attorney at Horsforth and Bradford and in 1782 he was appointed a Master Extraordinary in the High Court of Chancery by the Lord Chancellor.[399]

John Hardy became Steward to the Spencer-Stanhope family of Cannon Hall. Through his investments in the Low Moor Iron Works, John Hardy became a wealthy man and founded the fortunes of his branch of the Hardy family. His son, John Hardy (1773-1855), was an eminent barrister and Member of Parliament whose youngest son, Gathorne Gathorne-Hardy (1814-1906) (Plate 260), held Cabinet positions in all Conservative governments from 1858 to 1892, serving under three Prime Ministers. He served as Home Secretary in 1867-1868.

Gathorne Gathorne-Hardy became the Earl of Cranbrook; by coincidence he lived close to his second cousins, Frederick Daniel and George Hardy, who were members of the Cranbrook Colony of artists. Gathorne Gathorne-Hardy acquired the Hemsted House property in Kent in 1857 (it is now Benenden School). Gathorne Gathorne-Hardy's brother, Charles Hardy (1813-1867) (Plate 261), and his descendants also lived in Kent; Charles removed from Odsal House in Yorkshire to Chilham Castle in Kent in 1861. Charles Hardy's son, Charles Stewart Hardy, was a Justice of the Peace and often heard criminal cases at the Magistrates' Office and Police Court at Cranbrook in the second half of the nineteenth century.

The youngest son of William Hardy (1715-1762), namely James Hardy, succeeded his brother as Steward to the Spencer-Stanhope family of Cannon Hall and also continued to maintain the family farm at Low Fold in Horsforth. His son, John Hardy (1778-1849), established a successful watch- and clock-making business in Preston and York.

The artists described in this book are descended from William Hardy (1748-1824), the second son of William Hardy. He left Yorkshire after quarrelling with another young man. In a fight in a meadow next to the Hardy family's farm, William Hardy "dealt his antagonist a blow which caused the latter to fall into one of

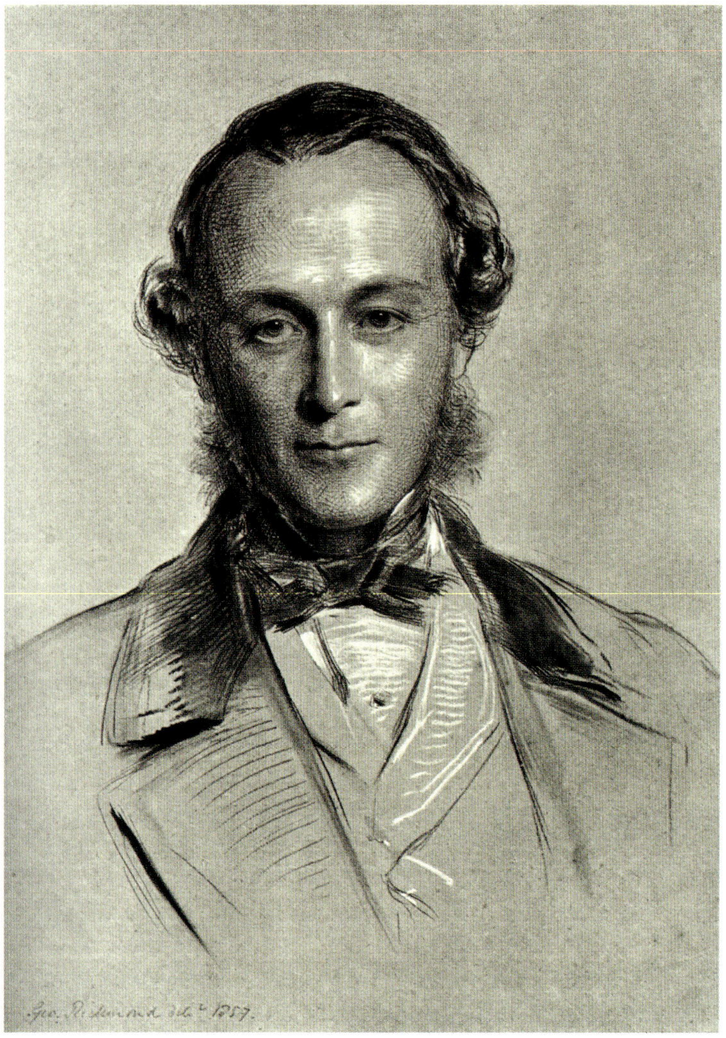

Plate 260: Gathorne Gathorne-Hardy, 1st Earl of Cranbrook, 1857
George Richmond. Pencil and chalk. 78.7 x 63.5cm.
National Portrait Gallery, London [400]

the tan-pits there; and, fearing that he had killed him, and being of a hasty and impulsive temperament, fled without even waiting to ascertain whether he had actually done so, or not".[401]

It is believed that William Hardy went abroad for a time after he left Yorkshire. He then went to London where he worked in a wool warehouse in Glasshouse Street (near Regent Street). Long afterwards he learned that the other combatant had not been killed or drowned in the tan-pit, and had recovered from the effects of the blow. But William never returned to Horsforth.

William appears to have had no further contact with his family in Horsforth and he did not receive a share of the family farm and land that would have been due to him. His family appear to have assumed that he was dead when his father's will was finally proved in 1804, 42 years after his father died; the will was proved by two sons, John Hardy (1745-1806) and James Hardy (1752-1827), and their sister, Mary (Mrs John Field), who were noted in the probate as "the sons and daughter and only next of kin of the said William Hardy, deceased".

On 19 July 1789, at the age of 41, William Hardy married Jane Chapman of West Drayton, Middlesex, at St James's Church, Piccadilly. Around the date of his marriage, he succeeded in obtaining an appointment as Master of the Officers' Mess of the 10th Hussars, a position he held for about 35 years, until his death in 1824. He was stationed with the regiment, successively, at the Cavalry Barracks at Guildford, Knightsbridge, Hounslow, Romford and Brighton. In 1815 he was with the troops when they entered Paris after the fall of Napoleon Bonaparte. When he was stationed with the regiment at the Cavalry Barracks at Brighton, William was sent on regimental business to the barracks at Norwich in wet and stormy weather. He became ill on the journey and died, at the age of 75, in May 1824.[402]

William Hardy, who fled from Yorkshire after a fight as noted above, and his wife, Jane, had two daughters, Elizabeth (1799-1877) and Hannah (1805-1888), who both married. They also had five sons who survived them, namely William (1791-1861), Richard (1793-1828), George (1795-1877), Henry Pope (1796-1864) and James (1801-1879), besides two other sons who died at a young age.

Four of their sons, William, George, Henry Pope and James, joined the boys' band of music that was associated with the 10th Hussars. All four were subsequently appointed members of the King's Private Band of Music (the Prince Regent, later King George IV, was Colonel of the 10th Hussars;[403] the King's Private Band was formed largely from the Band of the 10th Hussars). James Hardy, who was Principal Trumpet in the Band, decided to become an artist circa 1823 and is referred to in this book as James Hardy senior. His three brothers served in the King's Private Band for many years, during the Regency and in the reigns of George IV, William IV and Queen Victoria at the Royal Households in London, Windsor and Brighton.

James' brother, William, played the French horn and the cornopean (an early cornet that had recently been invented) in the Royal Private Band and also wrote musical arrangements that were often performed for Queen Victoria and her guests (his *Fantasia on Russian Melodies* seems to have been one his most popular arrangements; it was played numerous times at

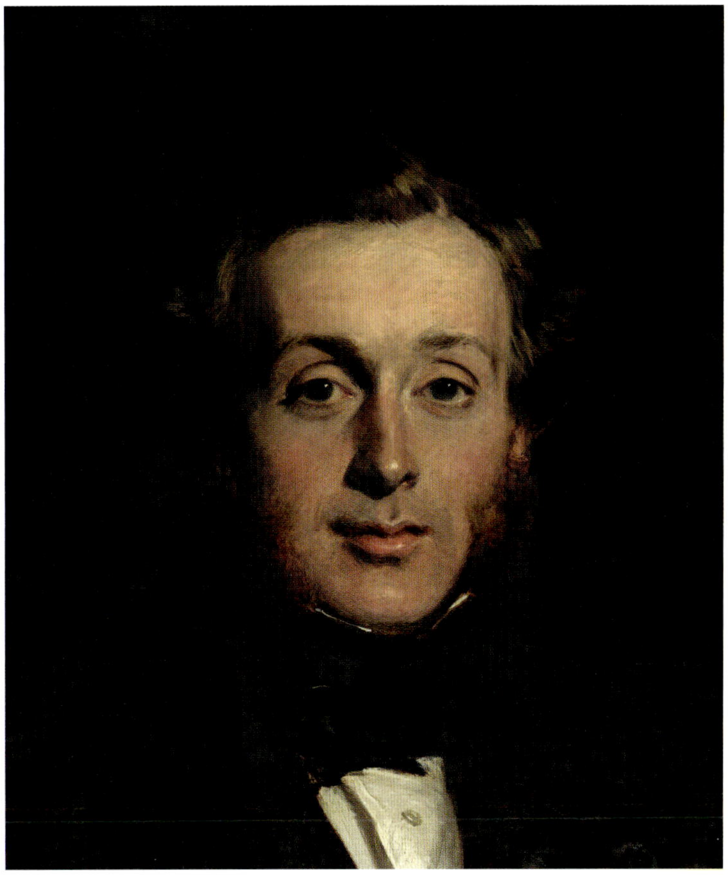

Plate 261: Portrait of Charles Hardy, Esq., 1838
John Prescott Knight RA. Oil on canvas. 91.4 x 71.1cm. Detail.
AUTHOR'S COLLECTION [404]

court during the 1850s). Many scores for William Hardy's arrangements are in the Royal Archives at Windsor. In 1830, William became Leader of the Grenadier Guards Band and at the same time became Conductor of Her Majesty's (Queen Adelaide's) Private Band.[405, 406]

Henry Pope Nye Hardy played the violin, cello and French horn. He was a member of the Private Band of George IV for 23 years and of Queen Adelaide's Band for seven years. He then became Bandmaster of the Scots Fusilier Guards.[407]

The fourth brother, George Hardy, an amateur landscape artist and father of the artists Frederick Daniel and George Hardy, was a member of HM Band of Music (he played the French horn) for 57 years from 1811 to 1868.[408] He was born in London on 17 June 1795 and baptised at Heston near Hounslow on 27 March 1796. He married Sarah Lloyd at St Nicholas's Church, Brighton, on 19 February 1822 and lived at Brighton and afterwards at Windsor (1837-1867), Forest Hill (1867-8), Croydon (1868-1871), New Hampton, Middlesex (1871-3) and Cranbrook (1873-1877), where he lived with his son's family, Sarah and Frederick Daniel Hardy. He died at Cranbrook on 6 October 1877, aged 82. He was buried at Hampton-on-Thames where his wife Sarah was also interred; Sarah Hardy died on 26 December 1872.

George Hardy played at many concerts for Queen Victoria and her guests. His second cousin, Gathorne Gathorne-Hardy (see page 198), was occasionally among the guests.

As well as being a member of HM Private Band of Music, George Hardy was the only musician who was also a member of the State Band of Music. Members of the State Band, called "Musicians in Ordinary", played at Coronations and were entitled to a salary of £45 a year "despite often not playing a note together for decades". George Hardy was the only musician to hold both offices. It seems that one of his fellow musicians, who signed himself "An English Musician", might have been envious of Hardy's position; he wrote to the *Musical Times*, noting that Mr. George Hardy (horn) received £130 a year as a member of H.M. Private Band and in addition £45 a year from the Privy Purse as a member of the State Band, which he described as "a band of wind-instruments ... that should perform at coronations and, I believe, but am not sure, at other grand national solemnities."[409]

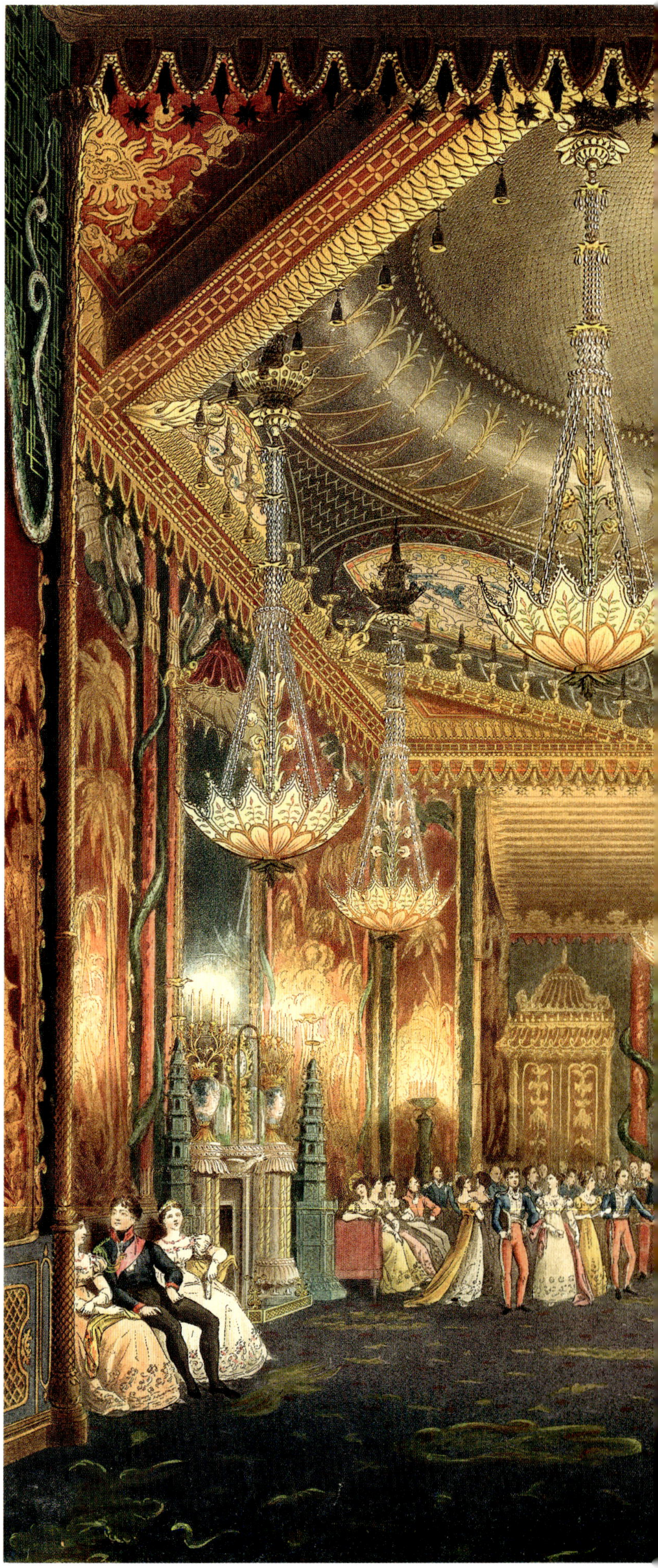

Plate 262: Brighton Pavilion: The Music Room, after Augustus Charles Pugin and James Stephanoff, 1824
John Samuel Agar. Used to illustrate the book *The Royal Pavilion at Brighton* by John Nash (1826). Engraving with aquatint. 26.5 x 34.8cm.

Four members of the Hardy family were musicians in The Royal Band of Music, (shown here playing in the Music Room of the Brighton Pavilion), including George Hardy (an amateur painter and father of the artists George and Frederick Daniel Hardy), William Hardy, Henry Pope Hardy and James Hardy senior (who resigned from the Royal Band in 1823 to become an artist; he was the father of the artists James Hardy junior, Ada, David and Heywood Hardy).

In the picture, the Prince Regent is on the left with his mistress, Lady Conyngham, and her daughter. The Duke and Duchess of Wellington are at the front on the right. The conductor is thought to be Gioachino Rossini who conducted the band on 20 December 1823, playing selections from his operas.

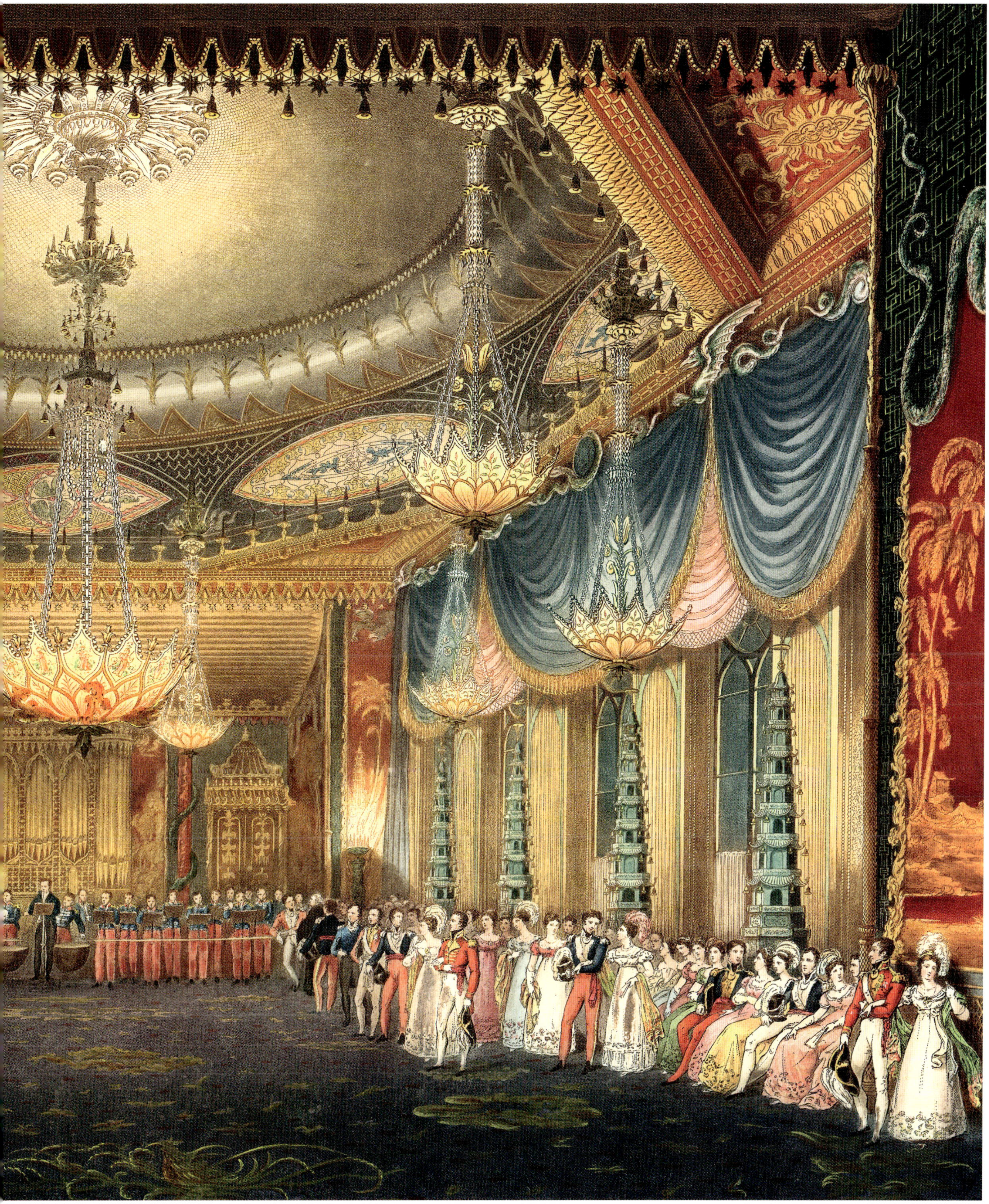

Appendix B:
The Hardy Family of Horsforth, Yorkshire: Genealogy

The principal artists in this book are in blue type

John Hardy
(ca. 1675 -1740)
Clerk to the Justice of the Peace,
John Stanhope (1678-1736) of New Hall, Horsforth

=

Jane
bur. Horsforth 2 Feb. 1754

Jane Hardy
Died in infancy
bur. Horsforth
22 June 1702

Mary Hardy
bapt. Horsforth
3 June 1703

John Hardy
bapt. Horsforth
23 June 1706
bur. there
10 Feb. 1725

Rose Hardy
bapt. Horsforth
2 Sept. 1711
bur. there 23 March 1712

James Hardy
bapt. Horsforth
16 Jan. 1713
bur. there 19 Nov.
1713

(1)
Elizabeth
d. Horsforth
10 Apr. 1747

=

William Hardy (1715-1762)
bapt. Horsforth 13 Mar. 1715
d. there 12 Sept. 1762
Yeoman Farmer of Low Fold Farm, Horsforth, and Clerk and Steward to John Stanhope (1702-1769), barrister of New Hall, Horsforth

=

(2)
Mary
d. Horsforth
27 Nov. 1795

Children of William Hardy and (1) Elizabeth:

Elizabeth Hardy
bapt. Horsforth
3 July 1743
bur. there
21 Apr. 1747

(1)
Annis Atkinson
(1745-1774)
m. 19 Nov. 1770
d. 10 Dec 1774
bur. Horsforth

=

John Hardy
(1745-1806)
bapt. Horsforth
15 Jan. 1745
d. 25 June 1806
Clerk and Steward to John Stanhope, barrister (1762-1769), and to the Spencer-Stanhope family.
Attorney at Bradford.
A founder of the Low Moor Iron Works. Co.

=

(2)
Mary Cockshott
(1758-1804)
d. 12 Jan. 1804
bur. St. James's Church, Bradford

Children of William Hardy and (2) Mary:

William Hardy
(1748-1824)
bapt. Horsforth
15 Sept. 1748
m. 19 July 1789
bur. St. James's Church, Norwich,
14 May 1824.
Master of the Officers' Mess of the 10th Hussars

=

Jane Chapman
(1767-1838)
bapt. West Drayton, Middsx
28 March 1767
bur. 12 March 1838 St. Nicholas, Brighton

James Hardy
(1752-1827)
bapt. Horsforth
18 Feb. 1753
d. there 11 Mar. 1827
Yeoman Farmer at Low Fold Farm, Clerk and Steward to the Spencer-Stanhope family of Cannon Hall
(1803-1827)

=

Margaret
(1753-1801)
bur. 2 Apr. 1801
Horsforth

Mary Hardy
(1760-after 180
m. John Field
Attorney-at-Law
12 Oct. 1782

Son of John Hardy and (1) Annis Atkinson:

Isabel Gathorne

=

John Hardy (1773-1855)
Barrister, Recorder of Leeds, MP for Bradford & amateur artist

Son of Isabel Gathorne and John Hardy:

Gathorne Gathorne-Hardy (1814-1906): First Earl of Cranbrook. Barrister, MP, Home Secretary 1867-68; Secretary of State for War 1874-78 and 1886; Secretary of State for India 1878-80.

Son of James Hardy and Margaret:

John Hardy
(1778-1849)
Watch and clockmaker of Preston and York*

Children of William Hardy and Jane Chapman:

William Hardy
(1791-1861)
b. Guildford 4 Mar. 1791
bapt. West Drayton 3 Apr. 1791
m. St George's, Hannover Square, London, 17 Oct. 1821 to Sarah Crockett of Little Hillingdon
d. 8 Jan. 1861
bur. Brompton Cem.
Conductor, HM Private Band of Music

Richard Hardy
(1793-1828)
bapt. West Drayton
26 May 1793
d. June 1828

George Hardy
(1795-1877)
b. London
17 June 1795
bapt. Heston
27 Mar. 1796
m. St Nicholas's, Brighton,
19 Feb. 1822 to Sarah Lloyd
d. 6 Oct. 1877
bur. Hampton-on-Thames.
HM Private Band of Music (1811-69) and amateur artist

=

Sarah Lloyd
(1803-1872)
b. 10 Apr. 1803
d. Hampton Hill
26 Dec. 1872
bur. Hampton-on-Thames.
Daughter of Francis and Mary Lloyd of Westminster

Henry Pope Nye Hardy (1796-1864)
b. 23 Dec. 1796
m. Mary Ann Campion (1st wife)
5 Jan. 1820 at St Nicholas's, Brighton
m. Lydia Crockett
1833 (2nd wife)
d. Clewer nr. Windsor 7 Apr. 1864
bur. there.
HM Private Band of Music

Elizabeth Hardy
(1799-1840)
b. Sept. 1799
m. Thomas Hogg

James Hardy senior
(1801-1879)
b. Hounslow
23 Aug. 1801
m. 31 Aug. 1825 at St Nicholas's, Brighton
d. 7 Jan. 1879
bur. Locksbrook Cem. Bath.
HM Private Band of Music to ca. 1824, then became an artist

=

Elizabeth Vinson
(1802-1878)
b. Crocker Hill, Boxgrove, nr. Chichester
29 Aug. 1802
bapt. 19 Oct. 1803
d. Bath 15 Feb. 1878
bur. in Locksbrook Cem., Bath.
Daughter of George and Elizabeth Vinson

Charles and John Hardy
died in infancy

Hannah Hardy
(1806-1888)
b. 6 May 1806
m. James Lippscombe
d. Shoreham, Sussex 23 Dec. 1888

SEE PAGE 203
for George and Sarah's descendants

SEE PAGE 204
for James and Elizabeth's descendants

* Watches made by John Hardy are in the British Museum (Courtenay Adrian Ilbert Collection) and the Museum of the History of Science (Barnett Collection, Old Ashmolean Museum, Oxford)

Descendants of George and Sarah Hardy

SEE PAGE 202

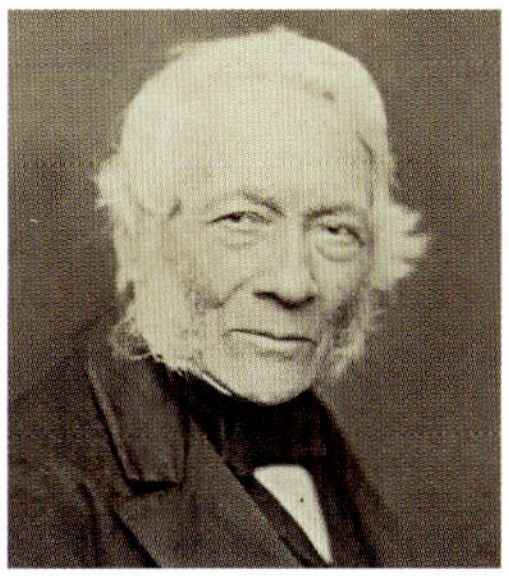

George Hardy (1795-1877)
b. London 17 June 1795
bapt. Heston 27 Mar. 1796
m. St Nicholas's, Brighton, 19 Feb. 1822 to Sarah Lloyd
d. 6 Oct. 1877, at Cranbrook, Kent
bur. Hampton-on-Thames
HM Private Band of Music (1811-69) and amateur artist

= Sarah Lloyd (1803-1872)
b. 10 Apr. 1803
d. Hampton Hill 26 Dec. 1872
bur. Hampton-on-Thames
Daughter of Francis and Mary Lloyd of Westminster

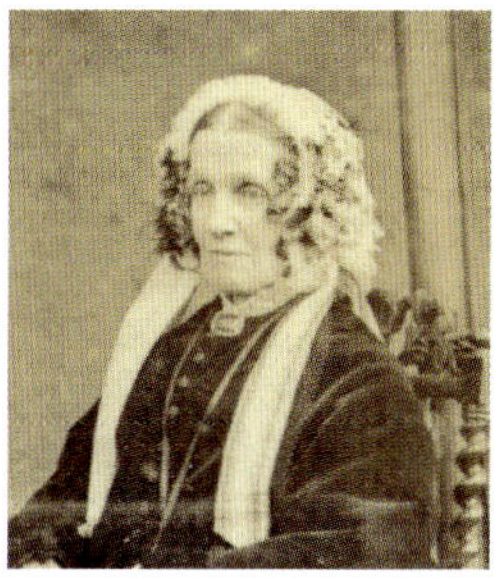

Children

George Hardy (1822-1909)
b. Brighton 21 Nov. 1822
m. St Mary's Church, Stoke Newington 8 May 1862
Lived at Cranbrook, and Staplehurst in Kent and at the Rectory, Warbleton, Sussex
d. 20 Nov. 1909
bur. Warbleton.
Artist

= Ellen Hutton (1833-1894)
b. 15 Apr. 1833
d. 25 Nov. 1894
bur. Cranbrook.
Daughter of Andrew and Jane Hutton of Stoke Newington

Mary Hardy (1824-1873)
b. Brighton 12 Nov. 1824
m. St George's Hannover Square 19 June 1870 to George Budey
d. Canterbury 16 June 1873

Frederick Daniel Hardy (1827-1911)
b. Windsor 13 Feb. 1827
m. Chorleywood, Herts. 11 Mar. 1852
Lived at Cranbrook, Kent, and part of the time in London
d. Cranbrook 1 Apr. 1911
bur. there.
Artist

= Rebecca Sophia Dorofield (1827-1906)
b. 16 July 1827
d. Cranbrook 25 Dec. 1906
bur. there.
Daughter of William and Mary Ann Dorofield of Chorleywood

Eliza Hardy (1829-1910)
b. Windsor 5 Apr. 1829
m. Windsor 29 Dec. 1856 to Edward Tatner of South Darenth, nr. Dartford, Kent
d. Dartford 30 Jan. 1910
bur. there

Rev. Arthur Hardy (1837-1911)
b. Windsor 19 July 1837
Vicar of Old Brampton, Derbys. 1893-1910
m. Elizabeth Knight Hose in 1866 (1st wife)
m. Laura Birtill 1899 (2nd wife)
d. 6 Jan. 1911 at Lytham, Lancs.
bur. there

Emily Hardy (1840-1925)
b. Windsor 24 July 1840
Lived in London, then at Hawkhurst, Kent

Sarah Hardy (1843-1911)
b. Windsor 1 May 1843
Lived with her sister Emily in London and at Hawkhurst
d. 22 May, 1911
bur. Hampton-on-Thames

Alfred Lloyd Hardy (1847-1929)
b. Windsor 30 July 1847
m. Frances Munn of Wilmington, Kent
d. 7 Dec. 1929

Children of George Hardy and Ellen Hutton

Madeline Ellen Hardy (1863-1870)

George Sydney Hardy (1864-1943)

Louisa Hardy (1867-1948)

Marguerite Ellen Hardy (1873-1948) Artist

Children of Frederick Daniel Hardy and Rebecca Sophia Dorofield

Frederick Rembrandt "Dorofield" Hardy (1853-1937)
Artist
Attended RA Schools

Lewis Hardy (1855-1927)

Arthur William Hardy (1857-1942)

Edwin George Hardy (1859-1896)
Architect
Attended RA Schools

Herbert Charles Hardy (1863-1945)

Amelia Gertrude Hardy (1865-1952)

Descendants of James and Elizabeth Hardy

SEE PAGE 202

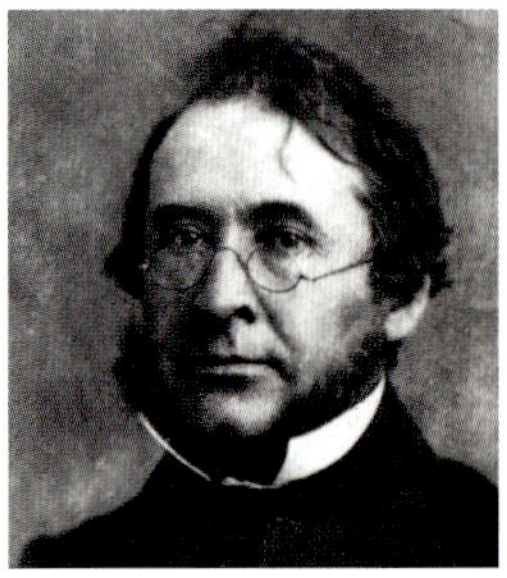

James Hardy senior (1801-1879) HM Private Band of Music to ca. 1824, then became an artist

= Elizabeth Vinson (1802-1878)

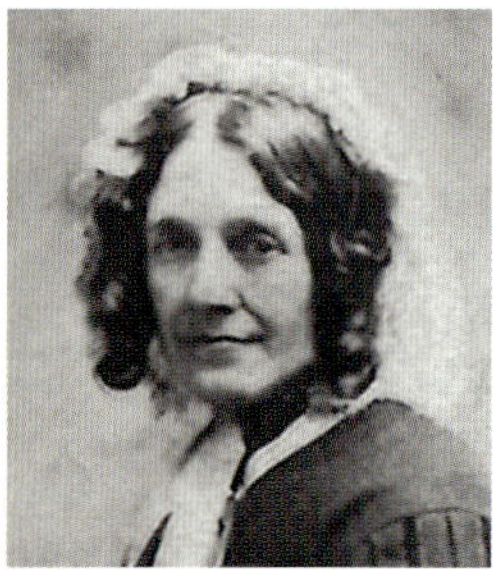

Emma Julia Hardy (1827-1901) bapt. Old Windsor 15 July 1827 m. Bath 1853

Ada Vinson Hardy (1829-1911) bapt. Old Windsor 21 June 1829 m. Henry Edrington Hobson (artist) in 1860 at Keynsham. Miniature portrait painter

Henry Hine Hardy (1831-1832) bapt. St Nicholas's, Brighton 20 July 1831

James Hardy jnr. (1832-1889) b. Brighton 1832 and bapt. 16 Jan. 1833 m. Laura Amelia May (b. 3 Jan. 1834), daughter of Enoch May (chemist) of Cheltenham, 18 Oct. 1860 at Trinity Church, Cheltenham d. 24 July 1889 at Holloway Sanatorium. Artist

Georgiana Hardy (1834-1867) bapt. St Nicholas's, Brighton 4 Apr. 1834. Artist and teacher of drawing and painting; lived with her sister, Elizabeth, at Bath

Thomas Hardy (1835-1905) b. 14 Sept. 1835 bapt. St Michael's, Lewes, Sussex 26 Apr. 1836. Painting assistant to his father, James Hardy junior

David Hardy (1837-1870) b. 1837 Chichester, Sussex m. Emily Collins (Art Teacher) 28 May 1860 d. 5 May 1870 Bristol. Artist

Fanny Hardy (1839-1854) b. Chichester, Sussex

Elizabeth Ann Hardy (1840-1918) b. Chichester 1840 m. John Drummond (artist) 30 June 1868 St Stephen's Paddington Artist and art teacher

Heywood Hardy (1842-1933) b. Chichester 25 Nov. 1842 m. Mary Beechey, daughter of Rear Admiral F.W. Beechey, 30 June 1868 d. 20 Jan. 1933 Epsom, Surrey

Children of Ada Vinson Hardy and Henry Edrington Hobson:

Mabel Emily Hobson (1868-1943) m. William Lee-Hankey (artist) 1896 d. Storrington, Sussex, 1943 Miniature portrait painter

Cecil James Hobson (1874-1911) Artist

Children of David Hardy and Emily Collins:

David Paul Frederick Hardy (1862-1942) Artist and illustrator
(Note: first born of David and Emily Hardy was a daughter, born 21 April 1861, who died in infancy)

Norman Heywood Hardy (1863-1914) Artist and illustrator

Beatrice Evelyn Elizabeth Hardy "Evelyn Stuart Hardy" (1865-1935) Artist and illustrator

Mabel Dora Hardy "Dorothy Hardy" (1868-1937) Artist and illustrator

Child of Elizabeth Ann Hardy and John Drummond:

Nora Drummond (1862-1949) Artist and illustrator

Children of Heywood Hardy and Mary Beechey:

Nina Charlotte Hardy (1869-1949) b. Goring, Oxford m. Edward John Howard Rice 12 May 1891 Holy Trinity Church, Paddington. Artist (portrait painter)

Mary Ruth Hardy (1871 - after 1933) b. Marylebone m. Walter John Curtis

Mabel Francis Hardy "Beldy" (1874-1971) = Charles O. Maugham

- **Daphne Maugham (1897-1982) m. 1931 Artist** = Felice Casorati
  - Francesco Casorati (1934-2013) Artist. Lived in Turin

Sylvia May Hardy (1884-1967) m. Charles W.M. Ivens

APPENDIX C

Letters written by Heywood Hardy to the Curator of the Russell-Cotes Museum

The Rosery
East Preston
Nr Littlehampton
Sussex

September 1st 1927

Dear Sir

In answer to your letter regarding the black and white drawings, I am glad to send you the following details respecting the work. The picture you allude to of the Elephant at the Turnpike, for which I took a medal at the International Exhibition at Philadelphia, and which was exhibited at the Royal Academy, was published as a full-page wood cut in the Illustrated London News the year it was painted, and that is unfortunately the only record I know of it. I will endeavour to get the back number and send it to you if you wish.

As regards my artistic career, which began from childhood, my father and brothers being painters, I find it difficult to say which is my best picture as I have painted so many during my long life, and of such a variety of varied subjects.

After studying in Paris and Antwerp, I settled at St. John's Wood in London and worked a great deal at the Zoo in the old days when I studied comparative anatomy under Garrod who was head of the Scientific Department connected with the Gardens. Mr Bartlett was a great friend of mine in those days, and was told to allow me to go in and set up an easel in the early mornings long before the Public were admitted, and work as long as I liked.

I have had three of four life-sized pictures of lions in the Royal Academy in those days, notably one of the Arab and the Lion. It was called "The Sacred Lion of Algiers".

The subjects I have painted have been Figures, Animals and Landscapes combined, besides portrait painting – equestrian portraits in particular, and presentation Hunt pictures, one particularly of the Zetland Hunt which was 10 ft. long, and contained 26 portraits, representing a Hunt at Aske Hall. It was exhibited at the New Gallery, and was published as an engraving by Goupil of Paris.

Respecting other work, I painted for a time in water-colours and was elected an associate of the Old Water-Colour Society, but gave up water colour painting entirely. I was also a member of the Society of Painter Etchers and the Royal Society of Portrait Painters.

Painting so many horses and hounds naturally led me to paint a great number of Hunting and Coaching pictures for which I am perhaps better known in America.

As I mentioned before, my subjects have been very varied, and I am now engaged in painting a series of pictures in fresco for Clymping Church near Littlehampton representing the Life of Christ.

I am sorry I have no photographs to send you as requested as I have never troubled to keep any record of my work.

Hoping that this letter gives you the details you require

I am
Yours very truly

Heywood Hardy

The Rosery
East Preston
Nr Littlehampton
Sussex

October 30th 1927

Dear Mr Quick

You were quite correct in your surmise that there were many artists in my family.

My father James Hardy Senr, although he began life as a musician, gave it up to follow painting as a profession. He started as an artist in Chichester, where I was born, and where he became known as a miniature painter and afterwards removed to Bath where he settled for the rest of his life.

My eldest brother James Hardy jnr. excelled in painting still-life and game. My brother David died rather young, after having become a most excellent painter of interiors and peasant life, leaving two sons, both clever in art. The elder one, now living at Storrington, produces beautiful metal work and armour, and is also an illustrator of books. His brother Norman who died a short time ago became known as an illustrator, notably of such works as "Customs of the World", "Women of the World" etc., for which purpose he travelled extensively. His sister Beatrice who has illustrated the Bible more than once is a great authority on costume of the East.

F.D. Hardy and his brother George were my first cousins. They were both known as interior painters, especially F.D. who was a regular exhibitor at the Royal Academy.

As regards myself, I have already answered the questions you so kindly asked, but it may interest you to know that my latest work, on which I am engaged at the present time, consists of a lot of seven fresco pictures for the beautiful old Norman Church at Clymping near Littlehampton. I enclose photographic scraps of some of them.

I often look back to the early days of my boyhood to when I began studying animal painting in the old house, 30 Henrietta St. Bath. There were studios from basement to garret. My studio was on the ground-floor, where I could bring in donkeys, goats, dogs etc. On the next floor my brother James had his studio. The drawing room was occupied by my father for painting portraits and miniatures – over that was my brother David's studio, and again above that my sister Ada was painting water-colour heads etc.

Thanking you for your kind letter

I am
Yours sincerely

Heywood Hardy

P.S. You can use the enclosed photographs in any way you like.

ENDNOTES

[1] Wood, Christopher. *Victorian Painting in Oils and Watercolour*. Woodbridge, Suffolk: Antique Collectors' Club, 1996, p. 84. Reynolds, Graham. *Victorian Painting*. London: The Herbert Press, 1987, p. 36.

[2] http://vangoghletters.org/vg/letters/let275/letter.html

[3] Hardy, Alfred Lloyd. Research and correspondence with Capt. A. Hardy. A part of A.L. Hardy's research is summarised in: Notes made by Basil Long, Keeper of the Department of Paintings at the Victoria and Albert Museum, from his discussions with Alfred Lloyd Hardy (Victoria and Albert Museum archives).

[4] Hardy, Alfred Lloyd. *Ibid.*

[5] Hardy, Alfred Lloyd. *Ibid.*

[6] Redgrave, Richard & Samuel. *A Century of British Painters.* Two vols. London: Smith & Elder, 1866.

[7] Incorrectly described as being by George Hardy junior (1822-1909) when sold at auction (Sotheby's 3rd October, 2007).

[8] The picture was presented to Queen Mary on 3 May, 1935, by the artist's granddaughter, Marguerite Tipping of Sherards, Godalming. Millar, D. *The Victorian Watercolours in the Collection of Her Majesty The Queen*. London: Philip Wilson, 1995. Mrs Tipping (née Marguerite Hardy) was the daughter of George Hardy (1822-1909), a member of the Cranbrook Colony of artists.

[9] The picture is signed and dated 'F D Hardy 1849'. On a fragment of an old label attached to the back of the painting it is indistinctly signed and inscribed 'This is my first Interior/ painted in 1849 at ******* / **** *(illegible),* the figures in 1882. F.D. Hardy'.

[10] Wood, Christopher. *Op.cit.,* p.84.

[11] Wood, Christopher. *Paradise Lost.* London: Barrie and Jenkins, 1988, p.131.

[12] *The Art Journal* Vol. 4 1852, p.167.

[13] Rebecca Sophia Dorofield was born on 16th July 1827. The family name was sometimes spelled "Dorrofield".

[14] F.D. Hardy wrote a letter to Thomas Miller (the richest cotton manufacturer in Preston) from Snell's Wood on 31st March 1853 confirming the safe arrival of a picture that was owned by Thomas Miller. He added that he would personally take it to the Academy with high hopes for its placing. On 28th July 1853 he wrote to Miller from 2 Waterloo Place, Cranbrook sending thanks for the loan of the picture. Thomas Miller papers 1847-1865. Royal Academy of Arts Archive.

[15] The photograph album of Frederick Daniel Hardy was sold at auction in San Francisco on 10th June 2011.

[16] Cottage Interior (illustrated below) may be the same as *An Interior* exhibited at the Royal Academy in 1853 and that was commented upon by *The Illustrated London News* 14 May 1853, p.379.

[17] *Sussex Advertiser* 7 March 1865 p.6. "Valuable Pictures.— (at) a sale of valuable English pictures, the property of the late Mr. Samuel Cartwright, which took place at the rooms of Messrs. Christie, Manson, and Woods, King-street, St. James's-square, London, on Saturday, three pictures, respectively entitled "Interior of a Kitchen, with Woman and Child," another "Interior, with Peasant and an Old Woman" seated by the fire (very highly finished), and "Richard and Kate," realized in the aggregate 240 guineas; the three were painted expressly for Mr. Cartwright, by Mr. F. D. Hardy, of Waterloo Place, in this town".

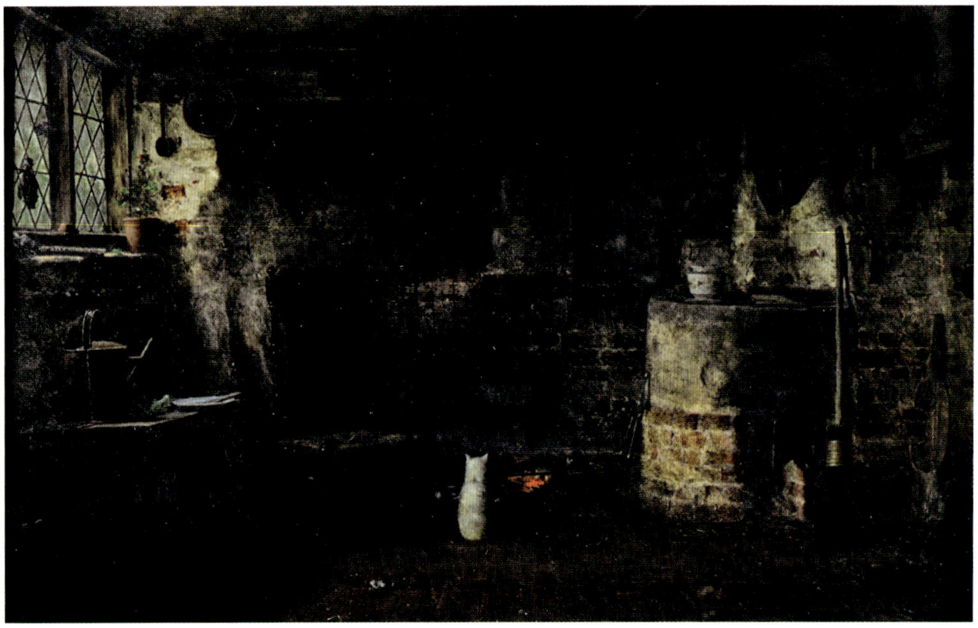

Endnote 16: Frederick Daniel Hardy. Cottage Interior. 1852. Oil on millboard. 19.7 x 29.8cm.
VICTORIA AND ALBERT MUSEUM

[18] *The Art Journal* Vol. 13. 1851, p.154.

[19] This is presumably the painting that was commissioned by John Forster from F.D. Hardy in July 1852; Hardy wrote to Forster, "it shall be as you desire, a cottage interior with a figure" (Victoria and Albert Museum archives). It was painted near Snell's Wood, Chenies, Buckinghamshire and might be the painting *The Day of Rest* that was exhibited at the Royal Academy in 1853. Snell's Wood was close to the Snell's Farm brick works, established by Nathaniel Snell in the late 17th or early 18th century. The cottages at Snell's Wood that Hardy painted were probably made from local bricks (made from a clay rich in iron to judge from the dark red colour of buildings remaining in the area). Perhaps the cottages he painted at Snell's Wood were the homes of brick makers.

[20] *The Examiner* 8 May 1852, p.6.

[21] *The Illustrated London News* 14 May 1853, p.382.

[22] *The Art Journal* Vol 4. 1 June 1852, p.167.

[23] *The Art Journal* Vol. 1 (New Series). 1 July 1862, p.150.

[24] *The Art Journal* Vol. 6. 1 June 1854, p.169. The Royal Academy Exhibition, 1854.

[25] Ruskin, John. Ed. by Cook, E.T. & Wedderburn, A. *Works,* 1904. Vol. XIV. *Academy Notes*, p.59.

[26] Ruskin, John. *Modern Painters.* Vol. I. London: Smith Elder & Co., 1843.

[27] The painting is possibly the same as *The Labourer's Home,* which was exhibited at the Royal Academy Exhibition in 1853, or *Whiff after Dinner,* which was exhibited at The Royal Academy Exhibition in 1855 and that was described in some reports as by David Hardy and in others by F.D. Hardy. See endnote 308.

[28] Greg, Andrew. *The Cranbrook Colony*. Exhibition Catalogue. Wolverhampton: Wolverhampton Art Gallery, 1977.

[29] Thompson, Carol (ed.) *The Cranbrook Colony: Fresh Perspectives*. Wolverhampton, UK: Wolverhampton Art Gallery, 2010.

[30] Frederick Daniel Hardy and Thomas Webster in front of The Studios at Cranbrook. 1896. Photograph by E.J. Holmes, Cranbrook.

[31] Horsley, John Callcott. *Recollections of a Royal Academician*. London: John Murray, 1903, pp.338, 339.

[32] Greg, Andrew *Op. cit*. The girl wearing a white dress appears in other paintings by G.B. O'Neill such as *Mother's Help.*The man on the left seems to be same person who is in F.D. Hardy's *Reading a Will* and *The Wedding Breakfast*.

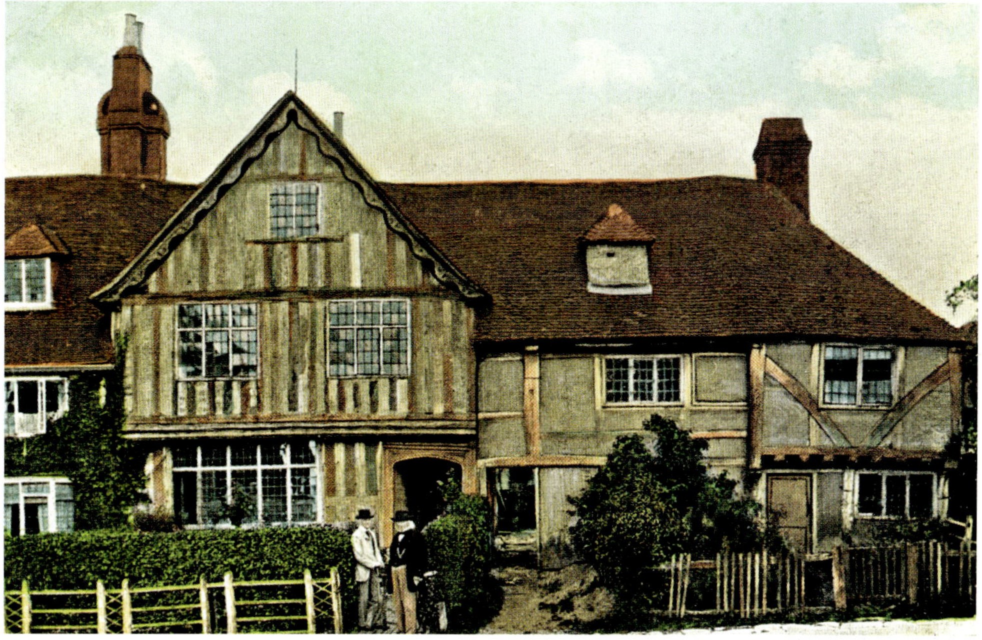

Endnote 30: Frederick Daniel Hardy and Thomas Webster in front of The Studios at Cranbrook. 1896. Photograph by E.J. Holmes, Cranbrook

[33] The print on the wall is *The Infant Samuel* after Sir Joshua Reynolds

[34] Horsley Family papers. University of Oxford, Bodleian Library.

[35] *Journal of the Photographic Society*. 15 January 1863.

[36] Catalogued as "signed with initials and dated 1853 (upper left)" Christie's 23 November 2004. Lot 79.

[37] Greg, Andrew. *Op.cit.*

[38] *The Art Journal* Vol. 5. 1 June 1859, p.163.

[39] Andrew Greg commented on the influence of F.D. Hardy on Thomas Webster's later works (Greg, Andrew. *Op.cit*.)

[40] *The Examiner* 4 May 1861, p.280.

[41] Image courtesy of Tunbridge Wells Museum & Art Gallery.

[42] *The Examiner* 24 May 1862, p.326.

[43] Wood, Christopher. *Victorian Panorama. Paintings of Victorian Life*. London: Faber and Faber, 1976, p.66.

[44] Lambourne, Lionel. *Victorian Painting*. London: Phaidon Press, 1999, p.177.

[45] Versions of *The Sweep* painted in oils are listed in the Table below.

[46] For example: Paxman, J. *The Victorians.* London: BBC & Ebury Publishing, 2009.

[47] Daforne, James. The works of Frederick Daniel Hardy. *The Art Journal* 1875, pp.73–76.

[48] *The Art Journal* Vol. 1. 1 June 1862, p.134.

[49] *The Illustrated London News* 17 May 1862.

[50] *The Spectator* 10 May 1862, p.17.

[51] *The Morning Post* 6 October 1868, p.3.

[52] *The Times* 3 May 1862, p.14.

[53] Lambourne, Lionel. *An introduction to "Victorian" Genre Painting*. Owing Mills, Maryland: Stemmer House, 1982, p.25.

[54] *The Morning Post* 14 May 1863, p.3. Royal Academy. Third Notice.

[55] Sold at Christies's (Flatou sale) for 392 guineas in 1866, one of the highest prices paid for his paintings in the1860s. *The Morning Post* 26 March 1866, p.3.

[56] The Art Journal Vol. 2. 1 June 1863, p.112.

[57] *The Spectator* 24 June 1865, p.13.

[58] *The Art Journal* Vol. 4. 1 June 1865, p.170.

[59] *The Art Journal* Vol. 9. 1 December 1870. p.368.

[60] *The Art Journal* Vol 11. 1 June 1849, p.166.

[61] *The Times* 11 June, 1869, p.12.

[62] *The Art Journal* Vol.9. 1 June 1870, p.170.

[63] *The Times* 6 May 1870, p.4.

[64] *Illustrated Times* 14 May 1870, p.345. Exhibition of the Royal Academy. Second notice.

[65] *The Art Journal* Vol. 9. 1 June 1870, p.162.

[66] *The Graphic* 17 June 1871, p.7.

[67] *The Times* 3 May 1873, p.12.

[68] *The Athenaeum* 1873, p.635.

[69] Hall, S.C., George Cruikshank, George Dalzeil & Edward Dalzeil. *The trial of Sir Jasper: a temperance tale in verse.* London: Virtue, Spalding and Dalby, 1873.

[70] *The Spectator* 30 August 1873, p.19.

[71] Sambrook, Pamela, A. *The Country House Servant*. Sutton Publishing in association with the National Trust, 1999.

[72] *Manchester Times* 4 March 1876, p.7.

[73] *The Art Journal*. New York: D. Appleton & Co. New Series Vol. 1. 1875, p.221.

[74] *The Times* 24 May 1875, p.5.

[75] The painting resembles Thomas Webster's undated picture of a woman and child, *The Post Office (Hope Deferred Makes the Heart Sick)* at the Haworth Art Gallery. Hardy's painting is of a coastal town (the man in the background carries a shrimping net and there is a ship on the horizon). The announcement in the window appeared in newspapers in November 1878:

Version	Date	Size (inches)	Medium	Reference
1	1861	17.8 x 26	Oil on canvas	Royal Academy exhibit 1861. Eden sale, Christie's 1874
2	1862	15 x 19.5	Oil on panel	Flatow sale 1868. Sotheby's June 9, 1999. Christie's November 28, 2000
3	1864	14.8 x 20	Oil on panel	Sotheby's December 11, 1979. Christie's June 11, 1993
4	1866	14 x 20.25	Oil on panel	Wolverhampton Art Gallery. Cartwright collection
5	1885	9 x 12	Oil on panel	Signed and dated 1885. Clevedon Salerooms, November 23, 2003
6	1890	6 x 7	Oil on panel	Signed and dated 1890. Sotheby's, July 13, 2005
7	undated	11.8 x 15.9	Oil on panel	Signed. Sotheby's October 3, 2007
8	undated	21 x 29	Oil on canvas	Indistinct signature. Christie's February 29, 1980
9	unknown	11 x 19	Oil on ??	J. Knowles sale, Christie's April 7, 1865
10	undated	16 x 20.5	Oil on canvas	Acquired by Cranbrook Museum 2015

Endnote 45: Versions of *The Sweep* painted in oils.

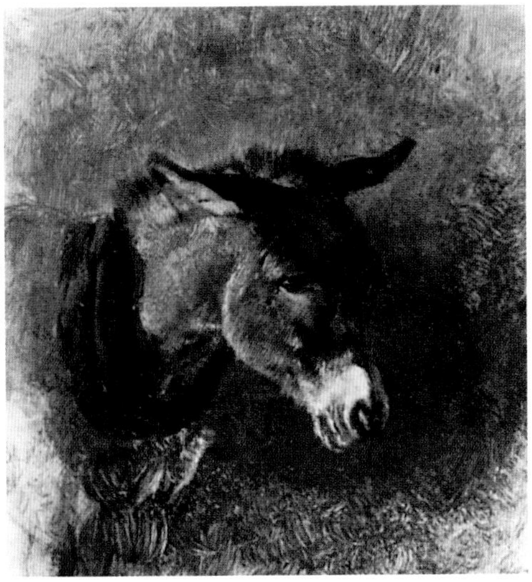

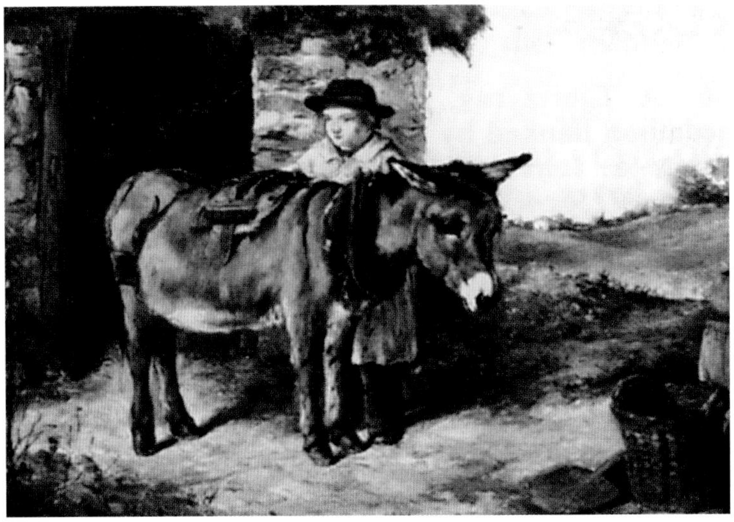

Endnote 115 (far left): Heywood Hardy *Study of a Donkey's Head*. Oil on panel. 24 x 21.5cm.
Private Collection

Endnote 115 (left):
Heywood Hardy. *A Boy and a Donkey Outside a Stable*. 1858. Oil on panel. 15 x 20.5 cm.
Private Collection

Painted when the artist was 15 or 16 years old.

"MAILS FOR BRAZIL BY FRENCH PACKET. Information has been received from the French Post Office that the French packets leaving Bordeaux on the 5th of each month will, for the present, cease to call at Rio de Janeiro on the outward voyage. Under these circumstances, no mails for Brazil will be made up in London for conveyance by these packets until further notice." *The Teesdale Mercury* November 13 1878, p.6.

76 Reynolds, Graham. *Victorian Painting. Op.cit.*

77 *The Illustrated London News* 17 May 1862, p.517.

78 Horsley, John Callcott. *Op.cit.*, pp.338, 339.

79 Ruskin, John. *Modern Painters.* Vol. I. London: Smith Elder & Co.,1843.

80 *The Art Journal* New Series Vol. 1. 1 November 1855, p.293.

81 Rivett-Carnac, Mary Rose. "Frederick Daniel Hardy: English Art's Special Correspondent. " In: Thompson, Carol (ed.) *The Cranbrook Colony : Fresh Perspectives*. Wolverhampton, UK: Wolverhampton Art Gallery.

82 *Blackwood's Edinburgh Magazine.* July 1860, p.70. 'The Royal Academy and Other Exhibitions'.

83 Redgrave, Richard, A Catalogue of the Pictures, Drawings, Etchings, etc. In the British Fine Art Collections Deposited in the New Gallery at South Kensington, Being for the Most Part the Gift of John Sheepshanks, Esq., London; Eyre & Spottiswoode, 1859, p.9.

84 *The Art Journal* Vol. 11. 1 March 1863, p.49.

85 *The Art Journal* Vol. 5. 1 June, 1866, p.166.

86 *The Illustrated London News* 10 October 1868 Supplement.

87 *Westminster Review* July 1856, p.51.

88 *The Graphic* 17 June 1871, p.7.

89 *Sussex Agricultural Express* 3 October 1899, p.3. "On Thursday last, Miss Gertrude Hardy was presented, on behalf of the Cranbrook Croquet Club, with a massive silver waist clasp and illuminated address, in recognition of her valued services."

90 The diaries of Rosamund Horsley (wife of John Callcott Horsley) from 1858 to 1872 are full of engagements with members of the Cranbrook colony. Most frequently mentioned are teas and suppers with Mr and Mrs F. D. Hardy. Children's dancing parties, croquet parties and Balls at Cranbrook and Hemsted House (home of Gathorne Gathorne-Hardy) are recorded. She described the Cranbrook Ball of 1861 as "very successful indeed" and the 1863 Ball as "very brilliant". At the Hemsted Ball of 1865, "All ladies in black and white for King of P**** (illegible)". Diaries of Rosamund Horsley. Horsley Family Papers, Bodleian Library, University of Oxford.

91 *Maidstone Telegraph* 6 January 1864, p.2.

92 *Sussex Agricultural Express* 13 February 1891, p.6.

93 *Sussex Advertiser* 6 January 1864, p.2.

94 Paget, Stephen. *Sir Victor Horsley.* New York: Harcourt Brace and Howe, 1920, p.23.

95 Reynolds, Graham. *Victorian Painters.* London: Studio Vista. 1966, p.36.

96 *Maidstone Telegraph* 24 September 1870, p.6.

"Cranbrook Cricket Club.—The annual dinner of this club was held at the Bull, Cranbrook, on Thursday, September 8th, when a party of nearly thirty sat down to an excellent spread, provided by Mrs Taylor. ... the Chairman proposed the toast of the evening, viz., " Prosperity and Success to the Cranbrook Cricket Club." He was happy, he said, to be able to congratulate the members on the very successful season just over, the club having played seven matches and won five, losing two only. He thought that the club could turn out a decidedly strong eleven, being well represented in batting, bowling, and fielding, though he was rather severe on the too common fault of the " blind swipe" at straight balls, and thought the fielding could be improved by more practice in that department of the game. ... The next toast was the health of the President and Chairman, which was proposed in an eloquent and admirable speech by the Rev. T. A. Carr, vicar of Cranbrook, who particularly dwelt on the good done by cricket in a parish, and the benefits of bringing all classes together in a friendly manner. ... The toast having been received with vociferous cheering, Kentish fire, and other demonstrations of applause, Sir C. Oakeley returned thanks and said that he cordially reciprocated Mr Carr's remarks on the beneficial effects of the game cricket in cultivating a healthy tone both of body and mind. He thought that if our neighbours the French had had a national sport like cricket to develop their superbundant energies upon, and to give them healthy occupation, that the mad passion of desiring to slay their fellow men would not have come upon them, and that this horrible war would never have taken place ... The last toast was that of "The Ladies," proposed by R. B. Masefield, Esq., and returned thanks for by F. D. Hardy, Esq. Altogether the evening passed off in a very satisfactory manner ... "

97 *Sussex Agricultural Express* 3 February 1891, p.2.

98 *The Edinburgh Gazette* 30 November 1860, p.1554.

99 *The Edinburgh Gazette* 19 April 1867, p.453.

100 *Maidstone Telegraph* 7 February 1863, p.5.

"On Tuesday evening the members of the Cranbrook and Tenterden Rifle Corps took part together in a sham fight, by moonlight, at Forstern Green, about midway between the two towns. Each corps mustered about 50 strong, the Cranbrook under the command of Captain Farrar and Ensign Hardy, and the Tenterden under Captain Saunders, with Lieutenant Havers and Ensign Scratton. It was previously arranged that the Tenterden corps (or 3rd Cinque Ports) were to be the enemy, and take up a position near Forstern Green, while the Cranbrook corps (or 37th Kent), were to discover, attack, and defeat them. After a good deal of manoeuvring and harmless shooting, the members of both corps mingled together in good fellowship, and then made a successful attack on a bountiful supply of refreshment."

101 *Sussex Advertiser* 17 September 1864, p.3.

102 *Maidstone Telegraph* 6 June 1863, p.5.

103 *Sussex Advertiser* 3 November 1866, p.2.

"The Members of The 37th Cranbrook Rifle Volunteers were inspected on Saturday afternoon, by Lieut.-Col. Colville in the Bail Field. The men went through a course of preliminary drill in an able manner, under the supervision of Captain Ruxton, the Adjutant, whose knowledge of drill, combined with his gentlemanly courtesy, has done so much for the esprit of the whole battalion.

When the inspector arrived on the ground the men performed their duties with a steady and soldier-like bearing, which elicited that gentleman's approbation. At seven o'clock the corps supped at the Bull Inn, Mr and Mrs B. Taylor catering with their accustomed ability. The band of the corps played some inspiriting music at intervals, and a pleasant evening was spent. "

[104] Lewis Hardy became a Chartered Accountant, Arthur William was a Jeweller, Pearl, Diamond and Precious Stone Merchant (a partner in R.G. Hennell & Sons of Bloomsbury), and Herbert became a solicitor. Herbert Hardy's son Philip Hardy became an architetct; Seal and Hardy designed several Art Deco buildings in the 1920s and 1930s in Bournemouth and the surrounding area.

[105] In the 1901 census his address was 48 Tavistock Court in Kensington where he lived with his wife, daughter Beatrice Mabel and his father F.D. Hardy (then aged 74) who was visiting at the time.

[106] Sketches of Florence were published from 1887 to 1889; for example "Campanile Florence" in *Architectural Association Sketchbook,* Series, Vol. 17. London: Sprague & Co., 1887.

[107] *The Illustrated London News* 5 January 1884.

[108] Bingham, Neil. Two letters from Percy E. Newton to John Summerson. *Architectural History* 36: 159-167. 1993.

[109] Saint, Andrew. *Richard Norman Shaw*. Yale University Press for The Paul Mellon Center for Studies in British Art, 2010.

[110] His death was recorded as suicide: 17th December 1896 at 32 Charlotte Street, London.

[111] *The Art Journal* Vol. 11. 1 June 1849, p.166.

[112] *The Art Journal* Vol. 5. 1 June 1866. pp.167-8.

[113] Hardy, Heywood. Letters written in 1927 to Richard Quick, Curator of the Russell-Cotes Art Gallery and Museum, Bournemouth (Appendix C).

[114] James Hardy junior's studies of dead game were described as "Works by a young artist, which would do no dishonour to one of veteran standing. The manipulation of the game is exceedingly minute and careful, the plumage being rendered in the closest imitation of nature. The still-life objects are also painted with a masterly hand, and promise well for the future fame of the young limner. ... *Preparing for Dinner* ... is likewise a clever interior, with figures, from the same hand." *Bristol Mercury* 3 December 1853, p.6.

[115] The earliest work by Heywood Hardy that has been identified is a small painting, *A Boy and a Donkey outside a Stable* that was painted when he was 15 or 16; it is signed and dated 1858. *Study of a Donkey's Head* has the same provenance; it is undated, but might have been painted at about the same time.

[116] Exhibited as *"Fetch-' em in"* £10.10s at The Society of British Artists in 1863.

[117] *The Bristol Mercury* 6 May 1898, p.5.

[118] His daughter Sylvia May Hardy wrote about his visit to Ireland: "He visited Blarney Castle whilst on a walking tour in Ireland, and actually kissed the Blarney Stone unassisted. The Blarney Stone is the top stone of a window near the top of the high Square Tower of Blarney Castle, and being cracked across the middle, it is held up by two iron bands. He was on the top of the Tower and jumping across the broken parapet he caught the battlements and then let himself down by the two bands till his face was level with the stone, kissed it, and pulling himself up in the same manner he sprang onto the platform. The people below were waving and calling to him, not knowing he was an extremely good performer on the horizontal bars, and at climbing a rope. The Blarney Stone is now railed off to prevent such attempts being made".

[119] *The London Gazette* 26 February 1864, p.888.

[120] *The Bristol Mercury* 11 March 1865, p.8.

[121] *The Bath Chronicle*. 31 March 1859, p.10.

[122] *The Bath Chronicle*, 12 March 1857, p.5.

[123] These were mostly based on weeks of sketching and painting the manoeuvres of soldiers and horses training in camps near Paris.

[124] *The Art Journal* Vol. 6. 1 March 1867. p.863

[125] Marks, John George. *Life and Letters of Frederick Walker A.R.A.* London: Macmillan & Co. Ltd. 1896, p.145.

[126] Written on the back of the painting : "No. 1 Backwater Goring/August 1869/H. Hardy ".

[127] *The Illustrated London News* 8 May 1875. Engraving based on the painting of the same name by Heywood Hardy exhibited at the Dudley Gallery in November 1874.

[128] *Manchester Times* 24 February 1877, p.7. A review of Messrs Agnews' exhibition at the Exchange-street Galleries.

[129] *The Era* 2 November 1873, p.4.

[130] *The Graphic* 31 October 1874, p.14.

[131] Briton Rivière painted several versions of this popular painting. The painting now in the Royal Holloway Collection was exhibited at the Royal Academy in 1878. The engraving of "Sympathy" made by Frederick Stackpoole was very popular.

[132] *The Tablet* 7 November 1874, p.11.

[133] *The Spectator* 21 November 1874, p.15.

[134] *Pall Mall Gazette* 9 November 1871, p.11.

[135] *The Graphic* 18 May 1878, p.498.

[136] *The Art Journal* Vol. 10. 1 June 1871, p.150.

[137] *The Era* 21 May 1871, p.12.

[138] *The Graphic* 30 October 1875, p.10. Review of the Exhibition at the Dudley Gallery.

[139] *The Illustrated London News* 30 October 1875, p.446.

[140] *The Illustrated London News* 29 November 1884.

[141] Supplement to *The Illustrated London News*, 2 August 1873.

[142] The title is from Alexander Pope's translation of *The Iliad*.

"Greece, in close order, and collected might,
Yet suffers least, and sways the wavering fight;
Fierce as conflicting fires, the combat burns,
And now it rises, now it sinks, by turns."

Challenge to the King is a painting by Heywood Hardy that was sold at auction in 1989 and appears to have suffered significant damage. It resembles the engraving by J. Greenaway. However, it is smaller than the Royal Academy painting which had life-size lions. The wood engraving by John Greenaway published in *The Illustrated London News* probably gives the best representation of the original work.

[143] *Lion and Lioness* (1877) resembles a drawing and engraving made by John Frederick Lewis, *Lion and Lioness Prowling.* 1825. London: J & F. Harwood, 26 Fenchurch Street. J.F. Lewis lived almost next door to Heywood Hardy; in 1873 Hardy lived at 19 St John's Wood Road and John Frederick Lewis lived at 22 St John's Wood Road.

[144] *The Times* 3 May 1873, p.12.

[145] *The Morning Post* 3 May 1873, p.6.

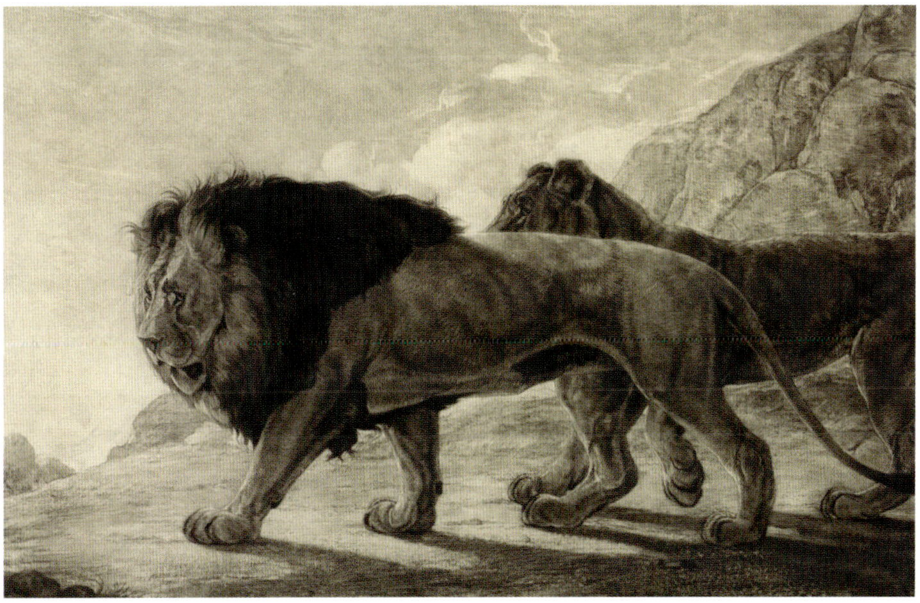

Endnote 143: *Lion and Lioness Prowling*. 1825. After John Frederick Lewis.

[146] *The Illustrated London News* 2 August 1873, p.95.

[147] *Western Times* 7 March 1889, p.2.

[148] *The Chelmsford Chronicle* 1 January 1873, p.7.

[149] *The Morning Post* 15 December 1884, p.2. A comment on *Head of Lion* by Heywood Hardy in a review of pictures at Mr. Mendoza's St. James's Gallery.

[150] Supplement to *The Illustrated London News*, 26 September 1875.

[151] *The Art Journal* Vol. 1 (New Series) 1875, p.187.

[152] *Academy* Vol. 7. February 1875, p.146.

[153] *Portfolio* 1882, p.83

[154] *The Manchester Evening News* [29 November, 1873] noted that, "It would be premature to say yet whether Mr. Heywood Hardy, who is now in Egypt, will finish his important work, "Ulysses Ploughing" [in time for the 1874 Royal Academy Exhibition].

[155] Leadbetter, C.W. *The Soul's Growth through Reincarnation*. Madras, India: The Theosophical Publishing House, 1946.

[156] *The Times* 2 February 1876 p.4.

[157] *The Art Journal* 1 January 1876, p. 296.

[158] *The Illustrated London News* May 16 1874, p.470.

[159] *The Graphic* 10 June 1876, p.571.

[160] *The Spectator* 20 May 1876, p.655.

[161] *The Times* 22 May 1876, p.6.

[162] A letter from Heywood Hardy to William Agnew about Hardy's picture for the 1876 Royal Academy exhibition, God's Covenant with Noah.

19 St. Johns Wood
March 12, 1876
My dear Agnew,

As my academy picture is now finished I shall be very glad to know when I may hope to have the pleasure of seeing you. I am very anxious that you should see it as the time is getting short and you have never seen it since you commissioned me to paint it from the cartoon. I expect some big swells to call next week and if they inquire, what am I to say? Your large lion is finished and much improved by carrying out the suggestions you made about the background. Will you kindly let me know what you would like me to do about sending it to you as it is rather in my way just now.

Hoping for a reply soon.

I am

Sincerely yours

Heywood Hardy

A copy of the letter is on the Art Renewal website, www.artrenewal.org

[163] *The Graphic* 5 February 1876, p.14.

[164] *The Illustrated London News* 2 December 1871.

[165] *Pall Mall Gazette* 9 November 1871, p.11.

[166] *The Times* 14 November 187, p.4.

[167] *The Illustrated London News* 2 December 1871.

[168] *The Illustrated London News* 28 October 1871.

[169] *The Illustrated London News* 22 April 1871, p.391.

[170] *The Times* 11 November 1872, p.4

[171] *The Morning Post* 18 November 1872, p.3.

[172] *The London Evening Standard* 4 March 1872, p.3.

[173] http://vangoghletters.org/vg/letters/let275/letter.html

[174] *The London Evening Standard* 25 May 1880, p.2.

[175] Huskie, D. Impressions and Experiences of a Country Doctor in the Nineties and After. *Transactions of the Medico-Chirurgical Society of Edinburgh.* Vol. 118. p.10. 1938.

[176] From: *The Task*, Book IV: "The Winter Evening", by William Cowper.

"Hark! 'tis the twanging horn! o'er yonder bridge,
That with its wearisome but needful length
Bestrides the wintry flood, in which the moon
Sees her unwrinkled face reflected bright;
He comes, the herald of a noisy world,
With spatter'd boots, strapp'd waist, and frozen locks,
News from all nations lumb'ring at his back.
True to his charge, the close-pack'd load behind,
Yet careless what he brings, his one concern
Is to conduct it to the destin'd inn:
And having dropp'd th' expected bag—pass on."

[177] *The Times* 12 May 1877, p.6.

[178] *The Spectator* 23 June 1877, p.16.

[179] *Derby Mercury* 21 June 1893, p.2.

[180] Blackburn, Henry. *Academy Notes.* London: Chatto & Windus 1878, p.35.

[181] *The Art Journal* Vol. 17. 1878, p.167.

[182] *The Times* 31 May 1878, p.4.

[183] *The Illustrated London News* 6 March 1875, p.230.

"Professor Garrod's second lecture on Animal Locomotion, given on Tuesday last, was devoted to the horse ... he alluded to the disagreement of various writers in their definitions of the paces of the animal ... Having pointed out also the inadequacy of various methods of investigation – whether by inspection, by sound, or by footprints – he described Marey's apparatus for the purpose, which consists of a ball of indiarubber filled with horsehair and attached to the horse's hoof by a contrivance which adapts it to the shoe. When the foot strikes the ground the ball is compressed and drives a part of the confined air through a tube into the registering instrument, held in the hand of the rider. By suitable arrangements, all the movements of the horse's foot may be thus recorded on paper or smoked glass. ... The notations of all these movements and their varieties, the results of numerous elaborate experiments with Marey's apparatus, were exhibited in fine colour diagrams. The lecture-illustrations included several spirited drawings of the horse and his various paces, kindly supplied by Mr. Heywood Hardy."

[184] *Leamington Spa Courier* 24 February 1877, p.4.

[185] In her biography Lady Butler referred to "the long and, on the whole, silly controversy which was appearing in "The Times" regarding the sequence of the horse's steps as he walks. It began by my horse's walk in "The Roll Call" having been criticised ... How many hours I had moved alongside horses to see for myself exactly how a horse puts his feet down in the walk! I had told many people to go down on all fours themselves and walk, noting the sequence with their own hands and knees, which was sure to be correct instinctively. At this same dinner Lady Lothian told me she had followed my advice, and the idea of that sedate "grande dame", with grey hair combed under a white lace cap, pacing round her room on all fours I thought delightful. Since those days I have been vindicated by the snap-shot." Butler, Elizabeth. *An Autobiography*. 1922. London: Constable.

[186] Stewart, Brian and Cutten, Mervyn. Chichester Artists. Canterbury, U.K.: Bladon Press, 1987.

[187] The pile of cowboy magazines was, possibly, more for use by his grandchildren than Heywood Hardy. His daughter Sylvia May Hardy wrote that Heywood Hardy " ... became a great reader and there was hardly a subject he did not dip into. "

[188] *The Morning Post* 29 November 1877, p.6.

[189] *The Graphic* 30 November 1878, p.12.

[190] *Pall Mall Gazette* 5 December 1878, p.11.

[191] *The Art Journal* Vol 18. 1879 p.174.

[192] Blackburn, Henry. *Academy Notes.* London: Chatto and Windus, 1884, pp.85-88.

[193] *The Times* 19 May 1884, p.4.

[194] Blackburn, Henry. *Randolph Caldecott : a personal memoir of his early art career*. London: Sampson Low, Marson, Searle and Rivington, 1890.

[195] Léon Lhermitte and Jules Bastien-Lepage were artists of the French Naturalist School who painted in the Barbizon tradition and were also influenced by the Impressionists. Vincent Van Gogh wrote to his brother Theo about Lhermitte: "He is the absolute master of the figure, he does what he likes with it - proceeding neither from the colour nor the local tone, but rather from the light - as Rembrandt did - there is an astonishing mastery in everything he does, above all excelling in modeling, he perfectly satisfies all that honesty demands. ... But tonight I am too much occupied with Lhermitte's drawings to go on writing about other things. " Letter from Vincent Van Gogh to Theo. 1 September 1885. In, *Van Gogh, A Self-Portrait. Letters revealing his life as a painter, selected by W.H. Auden*. New York Graphic Society, Greenwich, Connecticut. USA. p.247.

[196] *The Era* 7 November 1885, p.13.

[197] Mary Hardy (née Beechey) lived at 43 Biddulph Mansions, Elgin Square, and then from 1870 at 13 Biddulph Mansions where she died on 30th March 1925.

[198] Shaw, George Bernard. *The World.* 22 May 1889. Reprinted in: Weintraub, S. *Bernard Shaw on the London Art Scene, 1885-1950.* Pennsylvania and London: The Pennsylvania State University Press, 1989.

[199] *The Times* 21 March 1889, p.4.

[200] Marcus Stone RA became wealthy mainly by licensing prints of his paintings. The prints were usually made by Boussod, Valadon & Co., successors of Goupil & Cie of Paris and the Berlin Photographic Company. Many were sold by I.P. Mendoza and Arthur Lucas.

[201] *Pall Mall Gazette* 5 July 1890, p.5.

[202] Pirated copies of Heywood Hardy's picture *Too Late* were offered for sale by an art dealer in Croydon. Isaac Mendoza owned the copyright and the dealer was fined 20 shillings and 13 shillings costs for selling the copies. *Lloyds Weekly London Newspaper* 24 March 1889, p.7.

[203] Routh, John Martin. *The law of artistic copyright. A handy book for the use of artists, publishers, and photographers. With explanatory dialogues*. London: Remington and Co., 1881.

[204] Major George Whyte-Melville was a poet and writer of popular Victorian novels about hunting and historical romances. His description of a fox-hound, the first verse of *King of the Kennel,* could apply to many of the foxhounds painted by Hardy:

"On the straightest of legs and the roundest of feet,
With ribs like a frigate his timbers to meet,
With a fashion and fling and a form so complete,
That to see him dance over the flags is a treat !"

Whyte-Melville's popular hunting/drinking song "Drink Puppy Drink" was sung ("amid cheers") at the dinner when Heywood Hardy's painting of Mr George Brendon (MFH) (Plate 143) was presented to him. *The Stratton and Bude Post* July 9, 1904.

[205] Shaw, George Bernard. *The World*. 22 May 1889. Reprinted in: Wentraub, S. *Bernard Shaw on the London Art Scene. 1885-1950.* Pennsylvania and London: The Pennsylvania State University Press, 1989.

[206] *The Morning Post* 18 December 1891, p.3.

[207] *The Graphic* 31 May 1890, p.7.

[208] *The Morning Post* 3 January 1890, p.2.

[209] *The Era* May 7 1887, p.15.

[210] *The Sheffield Daily Telegraph* 6 February 1903, p.5.

[211] The pictures have remained popular with collectors; *Outside the Swan Inn* was sold for £55,000 (including premium) in 2008.

[212] *The Illustrated London News* Vol 62. 1873. Also published in *The Daily Graphic*, New York, 3 May 1873, p.4.

[213] *The Match* was exhibited at the Dudley Gallery in 1873. *The Morning Post* (6th February 1873) commented : "A Match" (310), by Mr. Heywood Hardy. A lady and a gentleman, the former mounted on a grey roadster, the latter on a chestnut, are galloping over the seaside sands in bright, breezy weather. They are racing at emulous speed, and, being lovers, the phrase, "a match," is true in more senses than one. It is more than probable that the grey mare will prove the better horse."

[214] *The Illustrated London News* 8 February 1873, p.138.

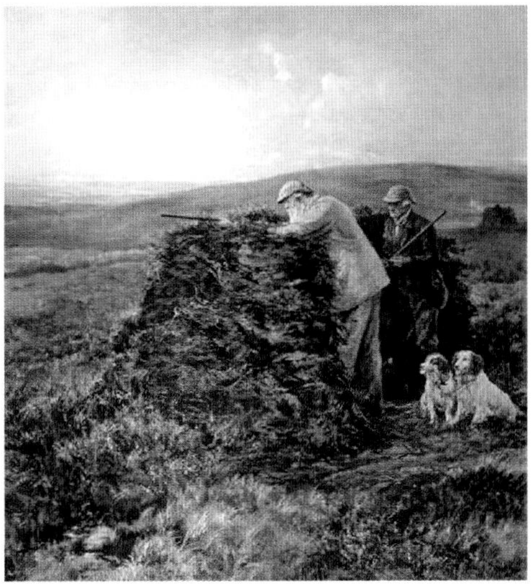

Endnote 234: Heywood Hardy. Sir Frederick Milbank, Bart., Grouse-shooting, 1892. Illustrated in *The Graphic* Supplement, "Pictures of the Year-II" 7 May 1892 and in *The Illustrated London News* 7 May 1892, p.7.

[215] *The Times* 18 March 1873, p.4.

[216] *Sheffield Independent* 11 January. 1889, p.3.

[217] *Northern Echo* 28 March 1888, p.3.

[218] *The Northern Echo* 6 November 1889, p.4.

[219] Pease, Alfred E. *Hunting Reminiscences*. London: W. Thacker & Co., 1898.

[220] *The Morning Post* 6 November 1889, p.5.

[221] Shaw, George Bernard *op.cit.,* p.283.

[222] *The Spectator* 1 June 1889, p.16.

[223] When sold at auction in 2002 the painting was entitled *Master of the Atherstone Hunt - a portrait of W.E. Oakley*, but the painting is of the rider labelled as *Mr Sewell* in the picture of the Zetland Hunt (1890).

[224] *York Herald* 13 November 1891, p.5.

[225] *The Northern Echo* 23 November 1889, p.3.

[226] The painting, owned by a descendant of Mr Brendon, is still in Bude, at the Falcon Hotel.

[227] *The Illustrated London News* 7 June 1890, p.727.

[228] Heywood Hardy's pictures of hunting are popular with collectors of Sporting Art in Britain and the United States; "The Presentation" was sold for $123,500 (including premium) in 1998.

[229] "The meet at the Manor" was sold for £74,100 (inc. premium) in 1996.

[230] *Western Daily Press*. 4 April 1870, p.2.

[231] North Shropshire Nigel (1904) was by Belvoir Viscount (1897) out of South Cheshire Novice (1901); North Shropshire Dandy (1906) was by Atherstone Document (1902) out of Damsel (1900); and North Shropshire Sapphire (1906) was by Atherstone Streamer (1901) out of Gaudy (1903). "In recent years Mr Frank Bibby will be remembered as the breeder of a beautiful pack of hounds *(The North Shropshire)* which were sold for a large sum of money on his retirement in 1909 after ten years' mastership": Bradley, Cuthbert. *The fox-hound of the twentieth century: the breeding and work of the kennels of England.* London: George Routledge and Sons Ltd., 1914.

[232] *Northern Echo* 3 September 1897, p.3.

[233] *The Shooting Party* was sold at auction for £95,000 (including premium) in 2002.

[234] Hardy painted a similar picture of Sir Frederick Milbank in a grouse butt. Sir Frederick Milbank was one of the best shots of his day; he once shot 190 grouse in 25 minutes (*The Field* 28 January 2008).

[235] *Northern Echo* 17 August 1895, p.3.

[236] Stewart, Brian and Cullen, *op. cit.*

[237] The landscape depicts the "Twelve Bens" mountain range in Connemara, Ireland, as shown in the photograph.

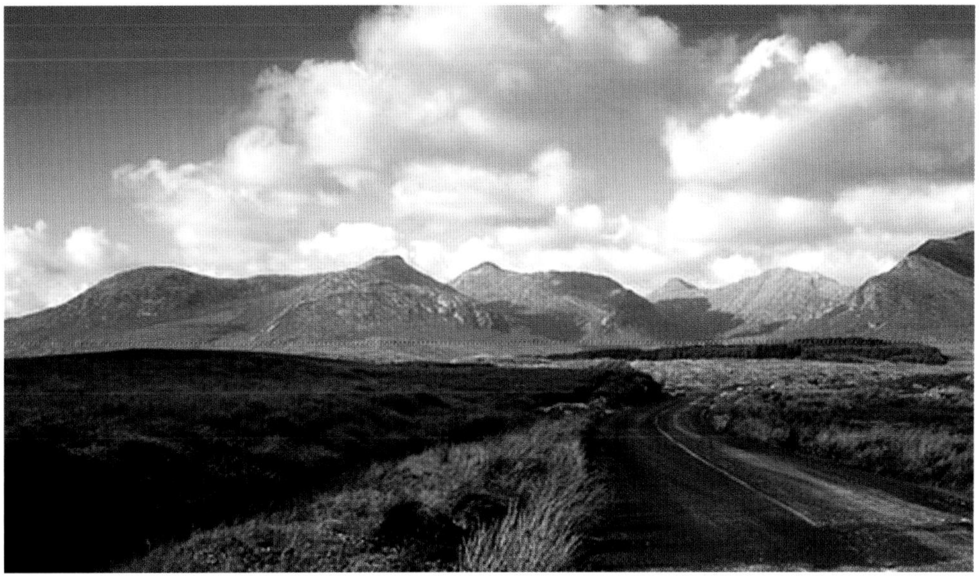

Endnote 237: Photograph of The Twelve Bens in Connemara, the mountains painted by Heywood Hardy in *An extensive landscape with a view towards mountains.*

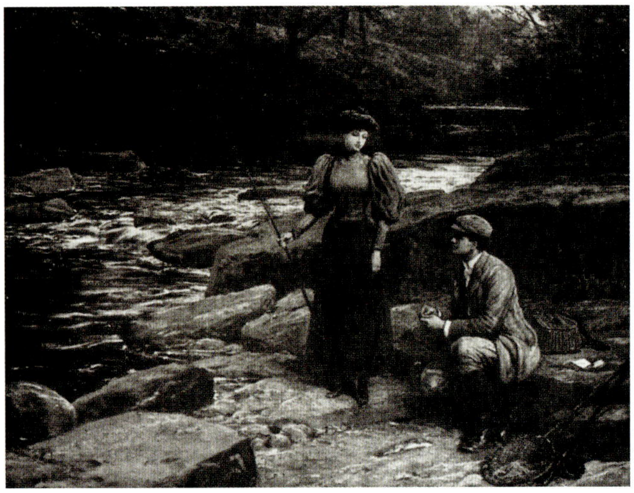

Endnote 238: After Heywood Hardy. *The Gentle Art. Illustrated London News* July 1896, p.24.

[238] After Heywood Hardy. *The Gentle Art. Illustrated London News* July 1896, p.24.

[239] Hardy wrote to Sir George Sitwell on 18th August 1887 (from 10 Abbey Road, St Johns Wood) about arranging for Sir George to visit his friend, the artist Hubert von Herkomer. Hardy also mentioned that he was making arrangements to come to Renishaw Hall in the Autumn. He signed off the letter asking to be remembered to Lady Louisa Sitwell (Sir George's mother) "whose kindness to me I shall always remember". From the Renishaw Hall archives.

[240] Bradford, Sarah. *Splendours and Miseries : A life of Sacheverell Sitwell.* New York: Farrar, Strauss and Giroux, 1993.

[241] Sitwell, Osbert. *Left, Right Hand !: an autobiography.* London: Macmillan & Co. Ltd., 1945.

[242] Sitwell, Osbert. *Ibid.*

[243] His house was opposite the Three Crowns Inn and Mr Boswall's grocer's shop. Mrs Boswall was a maid at Hardy's house before she married Mr Boswall. Hardy's grandson Alastair Hardy Ivens remembered often playing with other grandchildren in the garden at The Rosery while Heywood Hardy was painting (presumably his pictures for Clymping Church).

[244] Heywood Hardy could still paint a good portrait when he was 86 years old; a detail of the *The Healing of Blind Bartimaeus* in St Luke's Church at Haslar shows a figure on the left of the picture squinting in the bright sunlight.

[245] *Pall Mall Gazette* 1 September 1886, p.6.

[246] *Birmingham Daily Post* 5 May 1893, p.5.

[247] William Powell Frith wrote in his autobiography: "Beyond the desire of recording for posterity the aesthetic craze as regards dress, I wished to hit the folly of listening to self-elected critics in matters of taste, whether in dress or art. I therefore planned a group, consisting of a well-known apostle of the beautiful, with a herd of eager worshippers surrounding him." William Powell Frith, *My Autobiography and Reminiscences.* London: Richard Bentley & Son, 1888, p.441.

[248] *The Western Times* 22 January 1881, p.4.

[249] *The Morpeth Herald* 29 January 1881, p.4.

[250] *The Examiner* 19 June 1880, p.746.

[251] *The Times* 28 June 1880, p.5.

James Whistler, who had made many fine etchings early in his career, was not a founder member; he had argued with Haden, his brother-in-law, who had introduced him to etching. The relationship between Haden and Whistler had deteriorated to such an extent that in 1867 they had an argument in a Paris café and Whistler allegedly pushed Haden through a plate-glass window. Haden and Whistler never spoke to each other again.

[252] Stewart, Brian and Cutten, Mervyn. *Op.cit.*

[253] Charles Keene, like Heywood Hardy, was a good singer and sang for many years with the Jermyn Band, which became the Moray Minstrels, an amateur group of musicians and singers formed mainly by artists and writers.

[254] Layard, George Somes. *The Life and Letters of Charles Samuel Keene.* London: Sampson Low, Marston & Company Ltd., 1892.

[255] *The York Herald* 22 November 1889, p.3.

[256] *The Morpeth Herald and Reporter* 1 January 1898, p.5.

[257] *Northern Echo* 23 November 1889, p.4.

[258] Nina Hardy married Mr Edward John Howard Rice on May 12th 1891 at Holy Trinity Church, Paddington. They lived at 55 High Street, Windsor.

[259] *La Presse* (Paris) 13 March 1891, p.5.

[260] Hastings, Selena. *The Secret Lives of Somerset Maugham.* New York: Random House, 2010.

[261] *The Montreal Gazette* 26 December 1936, p.4.

[262] Note in the Bath Reference Library written by: "Mr P.S.V. Brewer (of the Bath Royal Literary and Scientific Institution) and Mme Madeline Hardy Mrs Sidney E. Sargant, 6 Russell St., Bath [James Hardy senior's granddaughter]."

[263] Probably Henry Eddington Hobson, artist and photographer. He married Ada Hardy, daughter of James Hardy senior and Elizabeth Hardy.

[264] *The London Gazette* 12 November 1833, p.2097.

[265] *The Brighton Patriot* 17 November 1835, p.4. Until the present research on the history of the picture, it was incorrectly described as being painted by "Hardy, active early 20th century."

[266] I am grateful to David Wright, Curator of the Wisbech & Fenland Museum for checking the records and signature of the painting which confirm that the picture was painted by James Hardy senior, not James Hardy junior as previously catalogued. The picture was acquired in 1938 as part of the Kirk Collection.

[267] James Hardy senior. *Design for Municpal Buildings, Bath*. Watercolour. 23.2 x 32.2cm. Victoria Art Gallery, Bath.

[268] *A Monkey Dentist* by James Hardy senior was sold at Christie, Manson & Woods London December 17, 1892. (Sale of the property of H.W. Sanders, lot 99). Monkeys wearing human costumes have been depicted in satirical paintings since the middle ages (Tomkins, Ptolomey. *The Monkey in Art.* New York: Scala, 1994). Edmund Bristow, friend of James Hardy's brother George at Windsor painted *A Monkey Alchemist* (Wellcome Library) at about the same date.

[269] Note in the Bath Reference Library written by "Mr P.S.V. Brewer (of the Bath Royal Literary and Scientific Institution) and Mme Madeline Hardy (Mrs Sydney E. Sargant), 6 Russell St., Bath (Hardy's granddaughter)." Mrs Sargant owned a hotel at 5, 6 and 7 Russell Street in 1920.

[270] In the 1851 census, when he was 18 years old, he was described as "Artist. Animal Painter". The first dated picture of James Hardy junior that has been found is a still life of a brace of duck, painted in 1851.

[271] *Bath Chronicle and Weekly Gazette,* 11 March 1852, p.3.

[272] *Bristol Mercury* 3 December 1853, p.6.

[273] *The London Standard* 28 March 1853, p.3.

[274] *The Art Journal* Vol. 5. 1 May 1853, p.136.

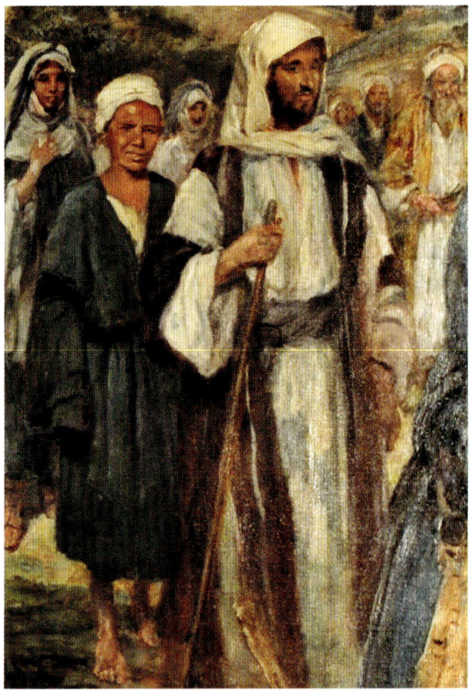

Endnote 244: A detail of *The Healing of Blind Bartimaeus* painted by Heywood Hardy in 1928 for St Luke's Church at the Royal Naval Hospital Haslar, Gosport.

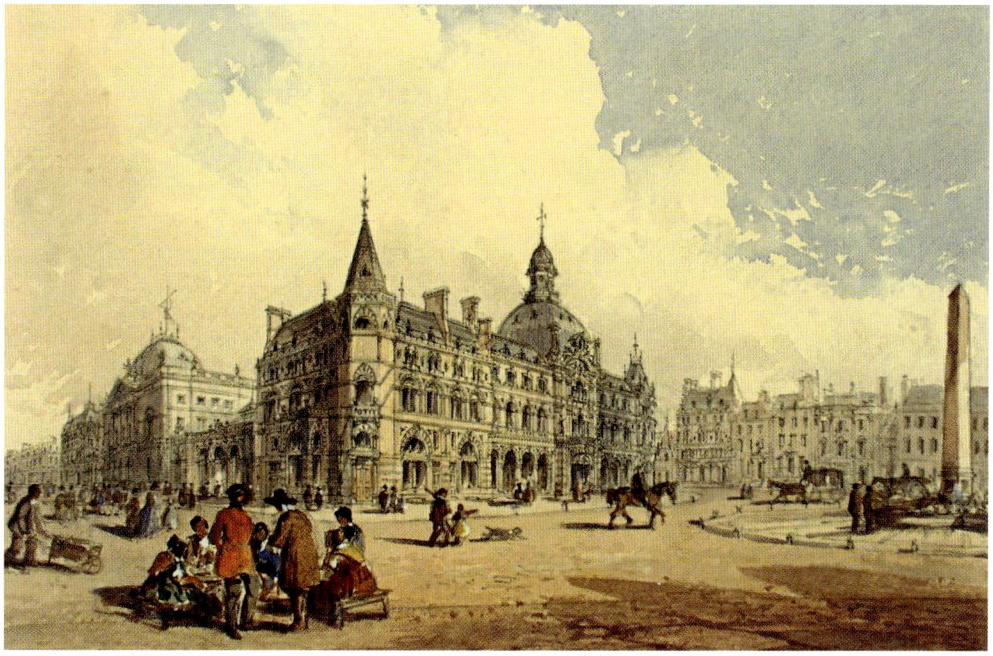

Endnote 267: James Hardy senior. *Design for Municpal Buildings, Bath*. Watercolour. 23.2 x 32.2cm. Victoria Art Gallery, Bath

[275] *The Ipswich Journal* 17 September 1853, p.4.

[276] *Bath Chronicle and Weekly Gazette* 13 January 1853. p.3. Four years later, possibly the same reviewer noted that: "James Hardy jnr. has not made any very serious attempts [to paint pictures other than dead game] but so far as he has gone his success has been unequivocal; his figures are drawn with natural ease of action, and truthful simplicity of expression; his backgrounds and accessories are decided but unobtrusive, and his execution, as in his still-life subjects is a happy union of lightness and firmness." (*Bath Chronicle and Weekly Gazette* 19 March 1857 p.5.)

[277] *Bath Chronicle and Weekly Gazette* 23 February 1854, p.3.

[278] I am grateful to Richard Burns of the Bury Art Museum for identifying this picture.

[279] *The Art Journal* Vol. 6. 1 May 1854, p.127.

[280] *Leeds Intelligencer* 30 September 1854, p.6.

[281] *Birmingham Journal* 1 October 1859, p.2.

[282] *Bath Chronicle and Weekly Gazette* 31 March 1859, p.10.

[283] *The Bath Chronicle and Weekly Gazette* March 12 1857, p.5.

[284] Johnson, Jane. *Works exhibited at The Royal Society of British Artists 1824-1893.* Woodbridge, Suffolk: Antique Collectors' Club Ltd., 1975.

[285] *Bristol Times* 18 June 1864, p.10.

[286] Heywood Hardy. *The End of a Day's Hunting.* 1868. Oil on canvas. 24 x 34cm.

[287] 1871 Census. Incorrectly listed as "61 Gloucester Crescent, Regent's Park" in *Works exhibited at The Royal Society of British Artists,* cited above.

[288] James Hardy junior might have encouraged his two sons not to follow his precarious profession; both became accountants. His daughter Gertrude Madeline attended the Royal Academy of Music and was a soprano who sang (as Mme. Madeline Hardy) at the Royal Albert Hall etc. Madeline was also an amateur painter who occasionally exhibited her work. She owned a hotel (now called the Queensberry Hotel) at 5, 6 & 7 Russell Street, near the Assembly Rooms at Bath. Her first marriage was with Mr Walter Hull MD; and her second marriage was with Mr Sidney E. Sargant.

[289] The *Morning Post* 1 June 1874, p.5.

[290] The *Illustrated London News* 30 December 1871, p.636.

[291] *The London Standard* 26 October 1871, p.6.

[292] *The End of the Day with English and Gordon Setters* (1881) is similar to *The Day's Catch* (1877).

[293] *Morning Post* 11 March 1878, p.6.

[294] *Pall Mall Gazette* 3 April 1889, p.1. And *Western Daily Press* 6 April 1889, p.5.

[295] The date of James Hardy junior's admission to The Holloway Sanatorium has not been found in records from the Sanatorium. The length of stay was normally limited to one year, though some remained for several years.

[296] Cooper, A.B. "Famous Pictures in the Royal Holloway College, Egham". *Sunday Strand* February 1904, p.109.

[297] James Hardy senior's daughter Elizabeth Hardy, an artist and art teacher, married the artist John Joseph Drummond, who was Head Master of the Bath School of Art and an art tutor to the children of the Royal family. Two of their children, Nora and Eileen, became artists. Nora Drummond (1862-1949) lived for a while in Bath with her aunt Georgiana Hardy (an art teacher) before she married Daniel Davies in 1893; and shortly thereafter they emigrated to Alberta, Canada where Nora Drummond-Davies painted scenes of Canadian wildlife, dogs and sporting pictures.

[298] They were divorced in 1917.

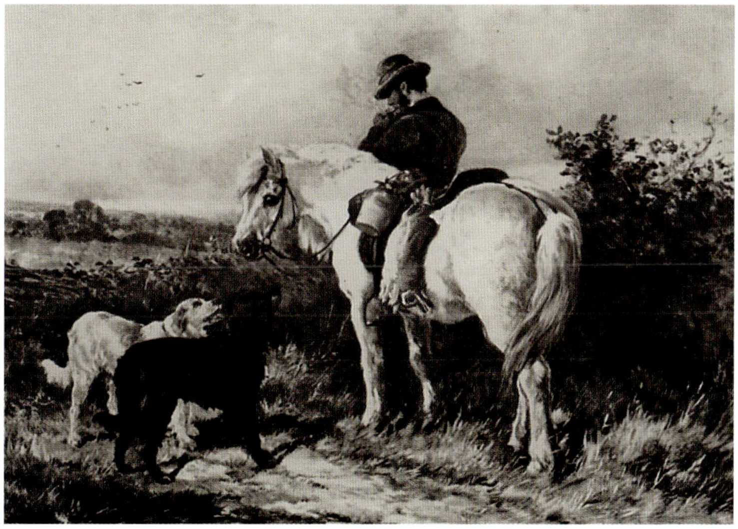

Endnote 286: Heywood Hardy. *The End of a Day's Hunting*. 1868. Oil on canvas. 24 x 34cm.

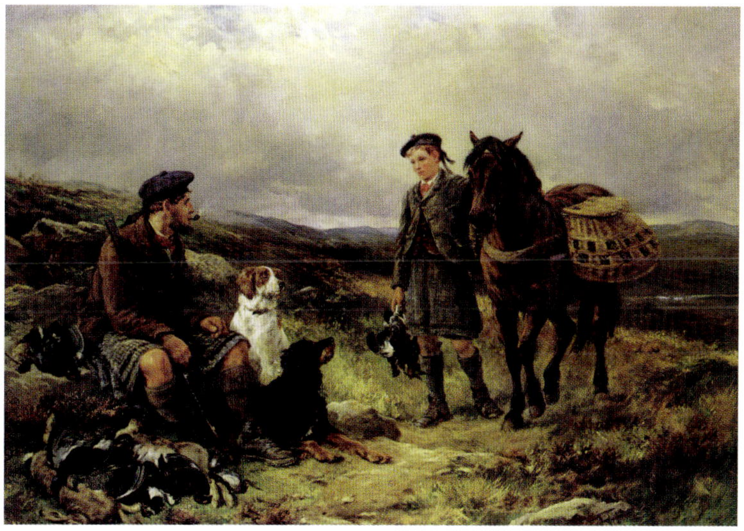

Endnote 292: James Hardy junior. *The End of the Day with English and Gordon setters.* 1881. Oil on canvas. 86.4 x 119.4cm. Private collection

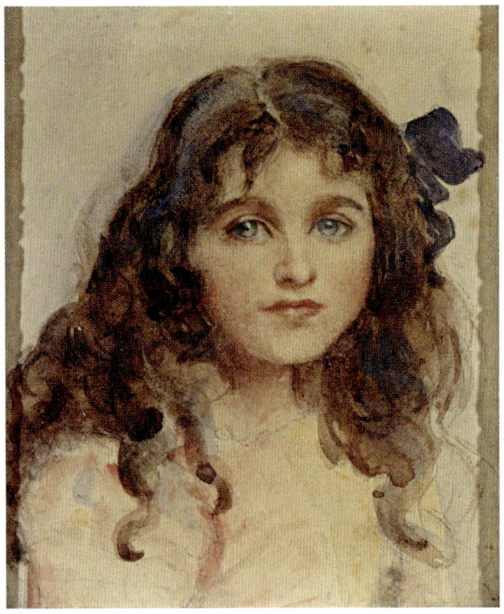

Endnote 299: Lady Elizabeth Bowes-Lyon. Aged 9. 1909. Royal Collection Trust/© Her Majesty Queen Elizabeth II 2015

299 In the Royal Collection there are preparatory watercolour sketches for the painting, Lady Elizabeth Bowes-Lyon, aged 9. 1909.

300 William Shawcross. *Queen Elizabeth the Queen Mother: the Official Biography.* London: Macmillan, 2009.

301 Owens, Susan. *Watercolours and Drawings from the Collection of Queen Elizabeth The Queen Mother,* London: Royal Collection Enterprises Ltd., 2005.

302 Correspondence relating to the commissioning of portraits and arrangements for sittings in 1939 and 1940 and three further letters from Buckingham Palace addressed to Miss Una Hobson (Mabel Hankey's niece) after the death of Mabel Hankey in 1943 were sold at Mallams, Oxford on 7 May, 2004.

303 *Sunday Times* 4 August 1990.

304 *The Bath Chronicle and Weekly Gazette* 19 March 1857, p.5 noted that "Illness obliged him to lay by for a season".

305 *Sherborne Mercury* 5 June 1860, p.5.

306 *Bath Chronicle and Weekly Gazette* 10 January 1856, p.3.

307 For example *News from Afar* (1857). The letter begins with the words "My dear father". On the mantelpiece there is a model ship above a portrait, presumably of the writer of the letter. A colour lithograph of the painting in *The Illustrated London News* (10 October, 1868) seems to be his only published illustration.

308 According to Graves (Graves, A. *The Royal Academy of Arts; a complete dictionary of contributors and their work from its foundation in 1769 to 1904*), David Hardy had one exhibit at the Royal Academy exhibition, *Whiff after Dinner,* exhibited in 1855. The address associated with the painting was 30 Henrietta Street, which was indeed David Hardy's address at the time. However, there is some uncertainty about this report since *The Art Journal* (1869, p.313) refers to "The perfect tranquillity of "The whiff after dinner" by "F.D. Hardy". To confuse matters more *The Bath Chronicle* (10 May 1855, p.3) referred to the painting by "David Hardy jun." being sold for 40 guineas at a Private View of the exhibition. According to *The Morning Post* (4 June 1855, p.3) it was " ... a good piece of rustic life in the Dutch School." Graves does not list any paintings by F.D. Hardy for the year 1855, which is unusual as he had at least one exhibit every year during the 1850s and 1860s. *Whiff after Dinner* might correspond to *A Quiet Evening by the Fire* by F.D. Hardy (Plate 12).

309 *Western Daily Press* 16 March 1864, p.2.

310 *Western Daily Press* 11 May 1870, p.3.

311 Possibly the same painting as *Happy Summer Time* or *The Gleaners* that were exhibited at the Society of British Artists in 1868 and 1870, respectively.

312 *The Bath Chronicle* 12 May 1870, p.5.

313 *Bristol Times* 18 May 1870, p.1.

314 *Bristol Times* 15 June 1870, p.1.

315 *Bristol Times* 25 May 1870, p.1.

316 *Bristol Times* 23 June 1870, p.4.

317 David Hardy was the second child of David and Emily Hardy; a daughter born on 21 April 1861 died in infancy (*Western Daily Press* 30 April 1861, p.3).

318 Harris, Emily in: *The Sussex County Magazine*. Vol. 16 no. 3 1942, p.74. "Paul Hardy, Artist and Craftsman". In the 1881 census he is described as "David", aged 18, a Landscape Painter living with his mother, brother and sisters at 18 Meridian Place, Clifton, Bristol.

319 *Western Daily Press* 5 June 1884, p.3. He gave his address as Royal Park, Clifton.

320 *English Illustrated Magazine*, November 1886. "A Glimpse at Bristol and Clifton" by John Taylor. *Bath Chronicle and Weekly Gazette* 11 November 1886, p.6.

321 *The Graphic* 20 December 1890, p.18.

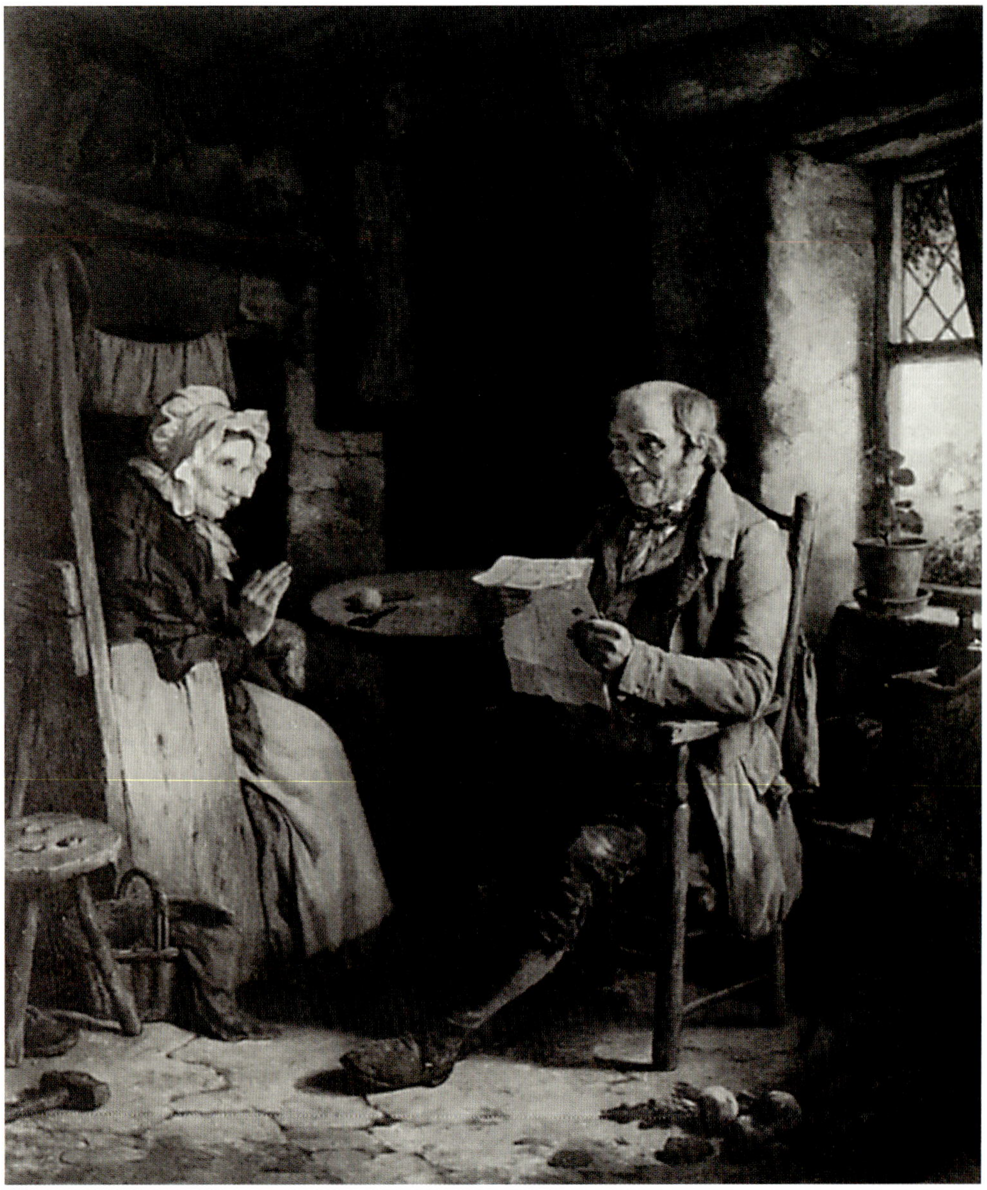

Endnote 307: David Hardy. *News from Afar*. 1857. Oil on panel. 61 x 48.3cm. Private Collection

[322] One of Cassell's long-running publications was the boy's magazine "Chums" with stories often written by David Parry and illustrated by Paul Hardy.

[323] *Reynolds's Newspaper* 5 May 1889, p.8.

[324] Simpson, Frances. *The Book of the Cat*. London: Cassell & Co.,1903. Mrs Hardy was also the designer of a most useful cat basket – "the basket is absolutely secure - not a paw can get out" wrote Frances Simpson.

[325] Paul Hardy's suggestions for the Pageant were welcomed by the mayor of Cheltenham: "If the inhabitants would only display many flowers, some flags, and, as suggested by Mr.Paul Hardy in the "Echo" persian rugs and things of that sort, he would be much obliged. " *Cheltenham Chronicle* 4 July 1908, p.2.

[326] Gordon Paul Umfreville Hardy served in the Royal Flying Corps in the First World War and was a Brigadier, Royal Army Ordnance Corps in the Second World War.

[327] *Gloucestershire Echo* 9 July 1908, p.1. *The Cheltenham Looker-on* 11 July, 1908, p.9.

[328] *The Strand Magazine* no. 6. December 1895, p.786.

[329] *Ibid*.

[330] Dudeney, Mrs Henry & Diana Crook (Editor). *A Lewes Diary, 1916-1944.* Dale House Press, 2013. Alice Dudeney left instructions that no access should be granted to her diaries for 25 years after her death. The owners of the diaries decided to keep the diaries closed until 1988.

[331] Newing, Angela. *Henry Ernest Dudeney : Britain's Greatest Puzzlist*. In Guy, Richard K. *The Lighter Side of Mathematics*. Cambridge University Press, 1994.

[332] Knight seated on a war horse, dressed in removable full armour and mounted on a wooden plinth. The armour consists of interlocking steel plates held together by a series of brass and steel rivets and hinges. The knight figure is adjustable to sit or stand. The miniature is a replica of a 15th century German knight and war horse. The model was donated to the Museum of Applied Arts and Sciences, Sydney, Australia by Mrs Cippico of Hertfordshire in 1965. The armour was made for her by Paul Hardy when she was a girl.

[333] *Daily Mirror* 6 Sept 1917, p.10.

[334] *The Adventures of Don Quixote. Adapted from Motteux's translation with Illustrations by Paul Hardy*. London: G. Bell & Sons Ltd., 1911.

[335] *Western Daily Press* 18 November 1863, p.3.

[336] Dr John Beddoe was a subscriber to a fund established in May 1870 by a friend of David Hardy to help Emily Hardy, Norman's mother, following the death of Norman's father, the artist David Hardy.

[337] In the 1881 census Norman Hardy, aged 17, was described as a "Landscape Painter", living with his family at 18 Meridian Place, Clifton, Bristol. In the 1891 census he was described as aged 24 (his actual age was 27), a "figure painter" living with his brother and sisters at 8 Blomfield Road, Hammersmith, London.

[338] The *Illustrated London News* 21 September 1889 and *Illustrated London News* 20 September 1890

[339] *Glasgow Herald* 16 November 1891, p.7.

[340] *Sheffield Daily Telegraph* 21 December 1891, p.5.

[341] *Glasgow Herald* 21 December 1891, p.7.

[342] His first illustrations for the paper were published on March 19th 1892.

[343] *Man* No. 3 1915. p.10. "Norman H. Hardy. Obituary written by J. Edge-Partington.

By the death of Norman H. Hardy this country loses perhaps the best of its anthropological artists. From his earliest years Hardy had shown a decided taste for natural history and the study of early civilisations, and this was crystallised by his making the acquaintance of Dr. Beddoe in 1883, for whose Races of Mankind he provided a number of illustrations shortly after he left school. Other work for Dr. Beddoe succeeded, and then in 1891 he left England for Australia as a special artist to The Sydney Morning Herald."

A colourful account of Australian artists in Sydney during the time Hardy lived there was written by George A. Taylor : *Those were the Days. Being the Reminiscences of Australian Artists and Writers.* Tyrrell's Ltd., Sydney 1918; the book includes a sketch of Norman Hardy with his friend Frank Mahony.

[344] Quanchi, M., "Norman H. Hardy: Book Illustrator and Artist. " *The Journal of Pacific History* 49 (2): 214-233, 2014.

[345] Barton, G. & Stefan Dietrich. *This Ingenious and Singular Apparatus : Fishing Kites of the Indo-Pacific.* Heidelberg. Völkerkundemuseum. 2009.

[346] *Man* 1901 p.41.

[347] *Man* 1901 p.117.

[348] His illustrations of China appeared in *China* by Lena E. Johnston and Norman H. Hardy, London: A C Black, 1909, and in *Women of All Nations*. 1908. Ed. T Athol Joyce and N.W. Thomas. London: Cassell.

[349] *Sydney Mail* 8 January 1898, p.18.

[350] He lived at 29A Oxford Road, Putney and then at 294 King's Road, Chelsea. His studio address when he exhibited *Allhallow's Eve* at the Royal Academy in 1909 was 2 Margravine Studios, artists' studios in Baron's Court that had just opened in 1909.

[351] Mack, John. *Emil Torday and the Art of the Congo 1900 – 1909.* London: Britsh Museum Publications Ltd., 1991.

[352] Hilton-Simpson wrote about a meeting of Norman Hardy with the Chief of Kasongo and one of his wives:

"Kasongo was accompanied by his wives, the chief of whom was attired in a great deal of white and blue cloth and carried a bead-covered wand. This lady began to make obvious advances to Hardy; she insisted in sitting as near to him as she could get, and favouring him with glances of the tenderest description. Poor Hardy's discomfiture was great, for he could not speak a word of the woman's language, and was at loss to know how to snub her effectually without giving offence; her lord and master, however, did not honour us with his company very long, but soon left us to our dinner, taking his noisy musicians and forward spouse with him".

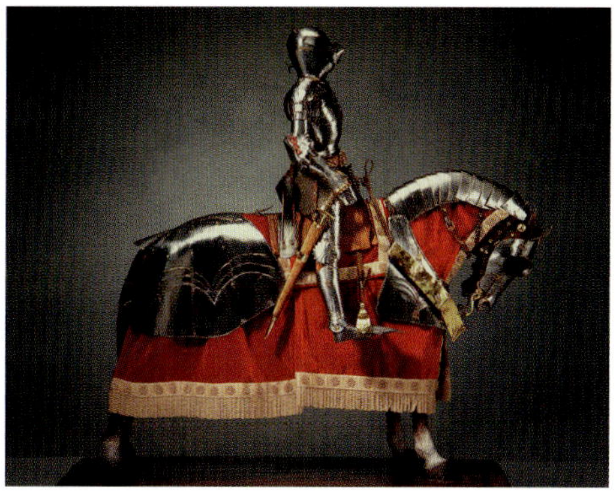

Endnote 332: Paul Hardy. Knight seated on a horse, both in full armour. Replica of German 15th century armour. Ca. 1890. 9. 4 x 9.1 x 2.85cm.
Museum of Applied Arts and Sciences, Sydney Australia

[353] Hilton-Simpson, Melville William. *Land and peoples of the Kasai; being a narrative of a two years' journey among the cannibals of the equatorial forest and other savage tribes of the south-western Congo.* London: Constable & Co. Ltd., 1911.

[354] Today's account of the expedition contains several anecdotes about Hardy who he described as having an "exceptionally generous disposition", happily giving away his possessions as presents during their travels in the Congo. Torday, E. *On the Trail of the Bushongo*. Philadelphia, USA: J.B. Lipincott, 1925.

[355] *Nature* 88, 485-486. 1912.

[356] Norman Hardy's facsimiles of paintings in the tomb of Userhat at Thebes are on view at the Metropolitan Museum, New York.

[357] *Bristol Mercury* 14 October 1865, p.8.

[358] Census returns for Evelyn Stuart Hardy:

1871 "Beatrice" age 5 [actual age 5]. Scholar. 5 Meridian place, Clifton, Bristol

1881 "Beatrice" age 14 [actual age 15]. Scholar. 18 Meridian Place, Clifton, Bristol

1891 "Elizabeth" age 17 [actual age 25]. Student of Art. 8 Blomfield Road. Hammersmith, London

1901 "Evelyn" age 21 [actual age 35]. Art Student. Elouera House, Linacre Road, Willesden Green, Harrow, Mlddlesex. [They called their house "Elouera", an aboriginal word meaning "Pleasant Place", to remember their brother Norman Hardy who went to Australia in 1892.]

1911 "E. Stuart Hardy" age 30 [actual age 45]. Painter (artist) "own account" living with her mother described as a widow aged 60 years. They called their house in Georgette Place, Greenwich "Arnocot" (an anagram of cartoon). This was a few minutes walk from Greenwich Park and the Royal Observatory on the hill that overlooks the Thames.

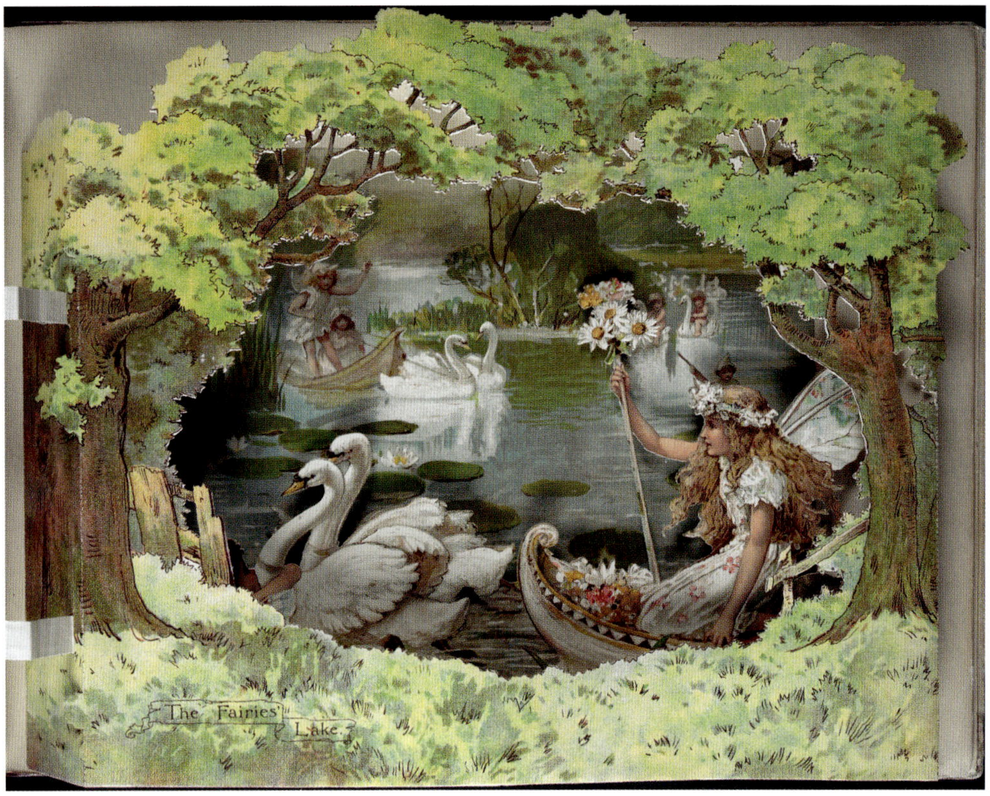

Endnote 370: Evelyn Stuart Hardy. The Fairies' Lake. In *Peeps into Fairyland*. London: Ernest Nister, 1896.

[359] *Manchester Courier* 17 January 1890, p.5.

[360] *The Ipswich Journal* 18 January 1890, p.5.

[361] *Musical News*. Vol. 14. 19 February 1898, p.191.

[362] Pearson's Magazine Vol. II. p.110. 1896. Cope, D & P. *Postcards from the Nursery*. London: New Cavendish Books, 2000.

[363] *The Illustrated London News* 28 June, 1890.

[364] *The Illustrated London News* 20 April, 1889.

[365] *The Illustrated London News* 28 September, 1889.

[366] *The Illustrated London News* 2 February, 1889.

[367] *The Illustrated London News* 19 January, 1889.

[368] Her friend Captain J. B. Wyndham Drake of the Royal Horseguards (Blues) who died in 1895.

[369] Pearson's Magazine Volume II 1896, p.110. Cope, D & P. *Op. cit.*

[370] An example, above, of an illustration by E.S. Hardy for an Ernest Nister pop-up book.

[371] Evelyn Stuart Hardy. "The Fall of Karma". Illustration in Dutt, R.C. *Mahabharata: the epic of India rendered into English verse*. London: J. M. Dent and Co., 1898.

[372] Evelyn Stuart Hardy died on 12th October 1935 at St George's Private Nursing Home, Hurstpierpoint, Sussex.

[373] *Western Daily Press* 4 March 1868, p.4.

[374] Census records for Dorothy Hardy:

1871 "Mabel" age 3 [actual age 3]. Scholar. 5 Meridian place, Clifton, Bristol.

1881 "Mabel" age 12 [actual age 13]. Scholar. 18 Meridian Place, Clifton, Bristol.

1891 "Dora" age 16 [actual age 23]. Student of Art. 8 Blomfield Road. Hammersmith, London.

1901 "Mabel" age 20 [actual age 33]. Art Student. Elouera House, Linacre Road, Willesden Green, Harrow, Middlesex.

[375] "The Cottage" built ca. 1715 is a house that has survived in the middle of Chelsea. Several artists and sculptors had lived there and it was the home of Patrick O'Brian, novelist, during the Second World War.

[376] Dorothy Hardy was married at St Alfege Church, Greenwich in the presence of her mother Emily Hardy, her brothers Norman H. Hardy, David Paul Hardy and her sister Evelyn S. Hardy. Kenneth and Dorothy Roberts lived at Emberfied, Ember Lane, Thames Ditton, Esher.

[377] Her husband died on December 22nd 1916.

[378] Dorothy Hardy is incorrectly described as working at Long Eaton in Derbyshire in Houfe, S. *Dictionary of 19th Century British Book Illustrators and Caricaturists*. Woodbridge, Suffolk: Antique Collector' Club, 1996. The error has been repeated by several authors. The Dorothy Hardy who was born and lived at Long Eaton worked in a lace-making factory.

[279] Illustrations by Dorothy Hardy for Guerber, H.A. *Myths of the Norsemen from the Eddas and Sagas.* London: Harrap, 1909.

[380] A typical article that she illustrated for *The Badminton Magazine* was "Sport with the Imperial Yeomanry" by Geoffrey Gathorne-Hardy. *The Badminton Magazine* January 1901, p.50.

[381] The illustration suggests George Borrow's quote based on the old proverb: "Youth will be served, every dog has his day, and I've had a fine one".

[382] *The London Standard* 2 January 1900, p.7. "New Year's Dinner to Horses": Thirteen years ago the Home of Rest for Horses was founded with the primary object ... to procure rest and good treatment for animals that are failing, not from age, but from continuous work, sickness, or accidental causes, and are likely to be benefited by a few weeks' rest and care. The Society has also instituted a suitable asylum for "old favourites" whose owners, instead of destroying or selling them for further labour, desire that they should be treated humanely for the rest of their days. ... Despite the depressing atmospheric conditions, a fairly large number of ladies and gentlemen, supporters of the Institution, journeyed yesterday from Paddington to Friars-place Farm, Acton, to witness the distribution of the New Year's dinner, the cost of which was defrayed by Mrs. Gore. The extra "feed" for the horses consisted of chopped carrots and apples, and sliced white and brown bread, mixed with a few handfuls of loaf sugar. The meal was served to the animals in their loose boxes, and the avidity with which they dug their noses into the luxuries indicated their eagerness for the repast. There are 43 horses now at the farm, of which 23 are "old favourites," or "pensioners" as they are not infrequently designated. ... Among the "old favourites," the most celebrated, perhaps, is " Bones," the famous charger which originally belonged to a trooper in the Royal Horse Guards (Blues), whom he safely carried through the exciting incidents in connection with the battle of Tel-el-Kebir. Miss Dorothy Hardy, an artist, purchased the animal when it was sold out of the regiment, and used it

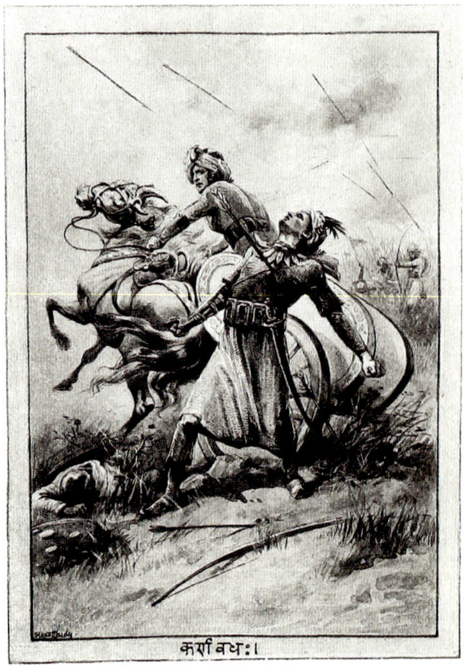

Endnote 371: Evelyn Stuart Hardy. "The Fall of Karma".

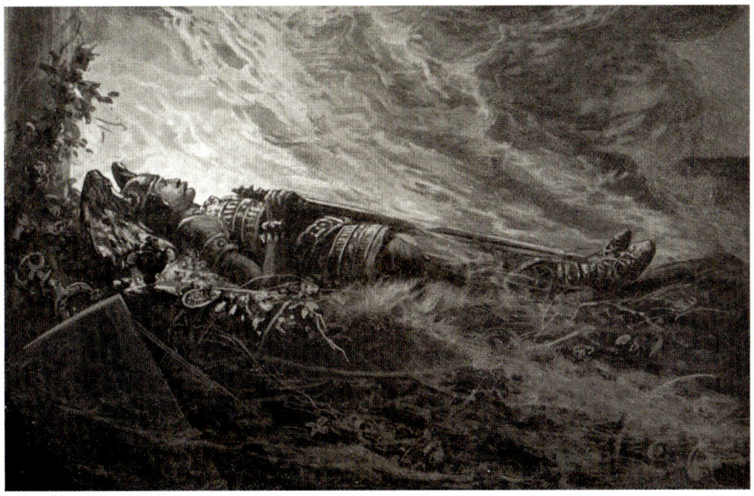

Endnote 279: After Dorothy Hardy. Baldur on the Pyre. 1909. Illustration in *Myths of the Norsemen* by H.A. Guerber.

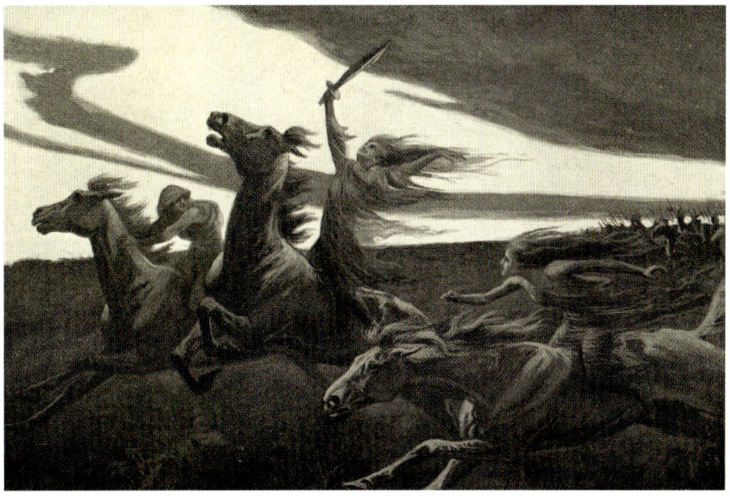

Endnote 279: After Dorothy Hardy. The Dises. 1909. Illustration in *Myths of the Norsemen* by H.A. Guerber.

as a model. "Bones" is now 22 years old, and has been at the Farm since 1893. In an adjoining stall is a brown gelding, the owner of which— a lady— not only provides him with warm coverings, but also air-pillows upon which to rest. The lady has further evinced her attachment to the animal by taking up her residence in the neighbourhood, so as to be in constant attendance upon it."

383 Johnson, B. Correspondence in: *Studies in Illustration*. Imaginative Book Illustration Society no. 37. Winter 2007, p.9.

384 During rehearsals Evelyn and Dorothy Hardy sometimes rode in the legendary Deadwood Stagecoach, now in the Smithsonian Museum. Kicking Bear, the Sioux chief, once rode beside them. He was sharpening his knife on the sole of his moccasin and pointing at their hair with a grin on his face. Rosa, Joseph G. *Relics* Vol. 3. No. 1 Summer 1969.

385 Rosa, Joseph G. *Ibid*.

386 Sketch made by Dorothy Hardy during the visit of Buffalo Bill Cody and the Wild West Show to London in 1904: *Buffalo Bill's Saddle*.

387 Rosa, Joseph G., and Robin May. *Buffalo Bill and his Wild West.* Lawrence, Kansas, USA: University Press of Kansas, 1989.

388 Kasper, S. *Annie Oakley.* London and Norman, USA: University of Oklahoma Press, 1992.

389 *The Illustrated American* Vol. 15 No. 13. 1894, p.343.

390 Rosa, Joseph G. *Relics* Vol. 3. No. 1. Summer 1969, p.8. The Saga of a Saddle. Dorothy asked that all her books should go to Chief Os-ke-non-ton and that Edward H. Blackmore should have her paintings, sketches and saddle. Edward Blackmore also received the clothing and gun holster that was on the lay model (he later gave them to a member of the US Air Force who was serving in England). The saddle was given by Edward Blackmore to the writer Joseph G. Rosa who researched its history and the links between Dorothy and Evelyn Hardy and the Wild West Show.

391 Mabel Dorothy Roberts (née Hardy) died on 25th December 1937 at St Mary Abbot's Hospital, Kensington at the age of 69.

392 In Gask, L. *True Dog Stories*. Illustrated by E.S. & Dorothy Hardy. London: George Harrap & Co. Ltd., 1910.

393 Members of the Hardy family might have been in the service of the Stanhopes before John Hardy who was a "Justice Clerk" in 1713. According to Mrs A.M.W. Stirling (*Annals of a Yorkshire House.* London: John Lane The Bodley Head, 1911), a Thomas Hardy returned from Ireland with John Stanhope (1608-1675) when Stanhope had to escape from the uprising of the Roman Catholics against the Protestants.

Unfortunately, Mrs A.M.W Stirling's writing is not always reliable. Hugh Owen in his book *Stanhope, Atkinson, Haddon and Shaw: Four North Country Families* (Chichester: St Richard's Press, 1985) noted a number of errors in her account of the Stanhope family. For example, Mrs Stirling said that she had transcribed two letters written by Barbara Stanhope and dated them 1769. But in fact she had amalgamated four letters that had been written in 1732. And in his biography of the artist John Herring (*J.F. Herring & Sons*. 1981. London: J.A. Allen) Oliver Beckett noted that " ... from her pages one gleans some homely touches that have an air of authenticity. But Mrs Stirling has a lively imagination, and one feels that some gaps in the story have been coloured with some graphic prose that pays scant regard to chronology." The origins of the Hardy family in the *Memoirs of Anna Maria Wilhemina Pickering.* London: Hodder and Stoughton, 1903 are incorrect as noted by A.E. Gathorne-Hardy in his biography of his father (A.E. Gathorne-Hardy ed. *Gathorne-Hardy. First Earl of Cranbrook.* London: Longmans & Co., 1910.)

There is a record in the Guiseley parish register of the burial of "Thomas Hardie" at Horsforth on 6th March 1683, but there is no evidence to link this Thomas Hardie with the person who might have returned from Ireland with Stanhope. There is no mention of Thomas Hardy in the extensive Stanhope papers that are kept in the West Yorkshire Archives. And there is no record of another Hardy (however the name is spelled) in the 17th century parish registers of Horsforth or in the neighbouring parish of Guiseley, of which Horsforth was a chapelry. Neither a will nor administration of the property of Thomas Hardy or Hardie could be found in the probate registries of York or London. So there is no documented link between Thomas Hardie who was buried at Horsforth in 1683 and John Hardy described as a Justice Clerk in 1713. However, Walter Spencer Stanhope, MP of Cannon Hall gave a speech at Cawthorne (the village adjacent to Cannon Hall) and reportedly said that "the Hardy's had been

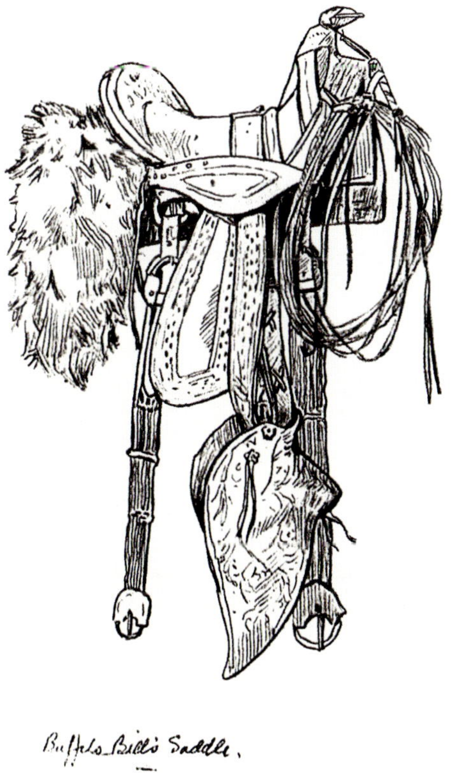

Endnote 386: Dorothy Hardy. Pencil drawing of Buffalo Bill's Saddle.

connected with the Stanhope branch of the family ever since they came to Horsforth between 400 and 500 years ago ... " (*Sheffield and Rotherham Independent* 16 December 1876, p.7). The Stanhopes had lived at Horsforth since about 1553 (Owen, Hugh *op. cit*., p. 5)

[394] Some confusion about John Hardy's occupation has resulted from an entry in the Parish Register for 1715. In the registration of the burial of his son James on 19 November 1713 John Hardy is described as a "Justice (sic) Clerk" in the Guiseley and Horsforth parish Registers. But at the baptism of his son William in March 1715 John Hardy is described as a "labourer". However, the "occupations" described in the Guiseley Parish Registers for the years 1712 to 1715 must be interpreted with some care. Fathers' occupations were not listed for the baptisms at Horsforth Chapel in 1712. In 1713 occupations were described in detail; there were 12 occupations listed such as blacksmith, justice clerk etc. However, in 1714 and 1715 the parish clerk described fathers as either "yeomen" i.e. landowners (there were 5) or "labourers" (there were 12). No details of the occupations were described. The term "labourer" was used in 1714 and 1715 to describe anyone who was not a yeoman (landowner) irrespective of whether they were a blacksmith or Justice's Clerk etc. In the register of the burial of his son John Hardy (10th February 1725), John Hardy is described as a "yeoman", indicating that he had become a landowner by that date.

[395] A small barn that was part of Low Fold Farm remains at Horsforth. It is close to the remains of Horsforth Hall where the Stanhopes lived before the New Hall was built.

[396] His gravestone is inscribed "Here lieth the body of Elizabeth the dear wife of William Hardy of Horsforth, who departed this life the 10th day of April in the 50th of her age 1747. Also here lieth interred the body of the above said William Hardy who departed this life ye 12th of Sept. 1762 aged 48 years. Also here lieth the body of Mary widow of the above said William Hardy who died 27th November 1795 aged 78 years". Northrop, J. Horsforth Garden of Rest 1565-1972. 1972. Horsforth Civic Society. Horsforth Reference Library.

[397] A few errors in Mrs Stirling's book *Annals of a Yorkshire House* have been the source of some confusion. On p.166 it is stated that William Hardy (1715-1762) "had four children" namely Elizabeth (1743-1747), John (1745-1806), William (1748-1808) who was described as a butcher, and James, born 1753. This list is incomplete as William Hardy (1715-1762) had six children. In addition, although the date of birth is correctly given as 1748, William Hardy was not a butcher and did not die in 1808. It happens that there was a family of butchers called Hardy in Horsforth, but they were not descendants of William Hardy (1715-1762). Another William Hardy married Mary Waddington in Armley (a village close to Horsforth) on 20th October 1742. This William Hardy had a son also called William who married Elizabeth Frith. William and Elizabeth were "butchers of this town" as inscribed on their gravestone (No. 87 Northrop (1972) *op. cit.*). William the butcher died on 18th February 1795 aged 48 years. One of their children was named Nathaniel Waddington Hardy and another was named William; he was also a butcher and died on May 10th 1808 "aged 32 years", as inscribed on his tombstone (No. 109) and in parish records.

[398] Remarkably, William Hardy's will was not proved until 1804, about 42 years after he died. It was proved by two of his three sons, John, the eldest and James the third and youngest and by a daughter, Mary. William Hardy's widow, Mary, had died in 1795 without having proved it, as is recorded in the probate. Perhaps the will was mislaid and not found until 1804. A subsequent administration of William Hardy's estate was similarly delayed until 4th February 1826.

[399] *Leeds Intelligencer* 5 February 1782, p.3.

[400] From: Gathorne-Hardy, Alfred E. (ed.) *Gathorne Hardy First Earl of Cranbrook.* London: Longmans, Green & Co., 1910, p.75. Photograph by Emery Walker.

[401] As recounted by William Hardy's grandson Alfred Lloyd Hardy (F.D. Hardy's brother) in letters and documents sent to Capt. A. Hardy (in the author's possession). Other branches of the Hardy family (decended from the Horsforth Hardys) in England and the Spence-Hardy family in Canada also corresponded with A. L. Hardy. Alfred Lloyd Hardy did not write the name of William Hardy's antagonist in the fight near Low Fold Farm. A version of the event passed down amongst descendants of James Hardy (1753-1827) is that the fight was between John (William's elder brother) and William; John had the ability and the opportunity to become a successful attorney, whereas William was expected to do the menial work to maintain Low Fold Farm, and perhaps this may have led to a fight between William and John. But there is no documentary evidence to support this account.

The Hardy family of artists were aware of their family history and their Yorkshire roots. Alfred Lloyd Hardy, who met Basil Long, Keeper of the Dept. of Pictures at the Victoria and Albert Museum to give him details of the family history, had been in correspondence with his brother Frederick Daniel and his cousin Heywood Hardy about the family history. And Paul Hardy mentioned that his father was descended from "an old Yorkshire family" (*The Strand Magazine* December 1895, p.786).

[402] He was buried in the churchyard of St. James's, the garrison church, at Norwich on 14th May 1824. His age is incorrectly recorded in the burial register.

[403] "No musician of any importance came to this country without visiting Brighton to hear the Prince's band. French prisoners from Spain were examined for the purpose of finding any musical talent that might be in them; and Eisert, a German, was transposed from a prison to a palace to become the most excellent player of the clarionet. Kramer (a Hanoverian and Head of the Band) periodically visited Germany and engaged the best talent he could find. The horns, Mssrs Hardy, were very clever performers, whether as regards taste, tone, or execution." The King sometimes conducted the orchestra (he was sometimes a hard conductor to please); when Rossini visited the King at Brighton for three days the music began with a Rossini overture conducted by the King. *Musical World* 29 September 1855.

[404] Exhibited at The Royal Academy Exhibition in 1838, (no. 192, East Room).

[405] *Windsor and Eton Express* – Court Circular. 18 September 1830, p.2.

[407] An example of William Hardy's duties: "Yesterday was the day appointed for the celebration of the King's birthday. It was observed with the usual demonstrations of rejoicing; the King's Guard mounted with the bands of the three regiments in the Standard Courtyard of the Palace. The bands played "God Save the King," the overture to William Tell, a chorus from Proserpine, and Buonaparte's grand march. The performances were under the direction of Mr. Hardy, of the First Regiment." *The Times* 29 May 1833, p.2.

[407] Gleeson, John. *Pomp and Circumstance: A History of the Band of H.M. Coldstream Guards 1685 – 2015.* Manchester: Walker & Co., 2015.

[408] Following the death of King George IV, the Royal Band was disbanded by William IV, but George and Henry Pope Hardy retained their positions, as reported in *The Times* 27 August 1830: "The King has retained four of His Late Majesty's Private Band, two horn-players, Englishmen - George Hardy and Pope Hardy, brothers, and two Germans - Wessex, a bassoon player, and Schenasted, who plays the flute. They were re-engaged by Sir Andrew Barnard. We are informed that His Majesty intends to have a band for the Queen, composed, with the above exceptions, of stringed instruments. It is understood that their services will commence next month."

[409] *Musical Times* 5 April 1855.

PLATE INDEX

INDEX